Kit Carson Days, 1809-1868

Edwin Legrand Sabin

KIT CARSON DAYS
(1809-1868)

BY

EDWIN L. SABIN

Illustrated by more than one hundred half-tones,
mostly from old and rare sources

CHICAGO
A. C. McCLURG & CO.
1914

A. C. McCLURG & CO.

1914

Published June, 1914

W. F. Hall Printing Co., Chicago

COLONEL (BREVET BRIGADIER GENERAL)
CHRISTOPHER CARSON, U. S. V.
COPY OF CRAYON PORTRAIT IN THE HOME OF MRS. WILLIAM CARSON,
WIDOW OF CARSON'S ELDEST SON, ALAMOSA, COLO.

(Photograph by O. T. Davis)

To My Father

HENRY SABIN OF IOWA

A Lover of History

PREFACE

For text and picture in *Kit Carson Days* I have drawn liberally upon chronicles long out of date, thus essaying to get back close to the sources of our knowledge. Perhaps occasional excerpts may strike the modern reader, and particularly the historian, as exaggerated; but it seems to me that the men who participated in the times herein treated, who wrote while yet the events were fresh, must furnish us with a perspective not only interesting, but valuable. If I have erred upon the side of local color, if the viewpoint of romance may be charged to have distorted in places the viewpoint of accuracy, if fancy may have intruded upon sober fact and figure, I make only the defense that I have written *con amore,* and have emphasized also the side of sympathy.

So, in making mention of the numerous excerpts, I would suggest that the notes to the chapters be not neglected. These notes are not always essential to the text. Indeed, frequently they may lead from the text, inciting to a wide reading which may prove delightful and profitable.

For modern authorities I am chiefly obliged to General H. M. Chittenden's *The History of the American Fur Trade of the Far West,* an exhaustive, fascinating compilation, upon which must be based all succeeding histories of beaver days. At the head of the long line of individuals who are co-authors with me would I place Walter B. Douglas of St. Louis, to whose generosity every writer upon western history is, I imagine, deeply indebted. Kenneth M. Chapman, of the Museum of American Archaeology at Santa Fe, stepped aside from his special duties to assist in this, the work of a stranger. J. M. Guinn of Los

vii

Angeles is another kindly partner. Mrs. Teresina Bent
Scheurich, who was born into the very thick of American-
Mexican events, has been most patient with my queries
upon those persons and times still near and dear to her.
Charles C. Harvey, journalist, of St. Louis, has been a
constant encourager. Captain Smith H. Simpson of Taos,
and Major Rafael Chacon of Trinidad, Colorado, comrade
veterans of the same glowing days in southwest history,
have given me facts which only a very few persons now
alive can recall. To the great assistance of Major Oliver
P. Wiggins I have paid especial tribute elsewhere in this
narrative. In Valentine Mott Porter of Santa Barbara,
California, I found a ready advisor. The Señora Petra
Beaubien Abrëu, through her son, Don Jesus L. Abrëu, of
Rayado, New Mexico; Mrs. A. L. Slaughter of Kansas
City; Mrs. Mary St. Vrain Sopris of Denver; General Asa
B. Carey of Orlando, Florida; Colonel John A. Hannay of
La Jolla, California; Aloys Scheurich, now with Kit Carson,
but late of Taos; Captain George H. Pettis, who also has
crossed the Divide, but late of Providence, Rhode Island;
Mayor Daniel L. Taylor of Trinidad, Colorado; Sergeant
Luke Cahill of Las Animas, Colorado; Ferd Meyer of
Costilla, New Mexico; Robert C. Lowry of New York City;
George H. Carson of Fayette, Missouri; Albert H. Pfeiffer,
Jr., of Del Norte, Colorado; Judge John S. Hough of Lake
City, Colorado; Judge Hiram D. Bennet of Denver:
pioneers, soldiers, scouts, and traders of brave days, they
have willingly enriched with the gold of their memories
these printed pages which otherwise would have been poor
indeed. To many readers their names may mean little,
but they will at least indicate how far and wide the lines
of research have led.

   To F. J. Francis of Denver and O. T. Davis of Alamosa,
Colorado, for photographs, and to Messrs. Tishler &
Langer, who copied with much skill and care the yellowed,

difficult lithographs and engravings from the brittle pages, I am deeply grateful. The Missouri Historical Society, the Colorado Historical Society, the Historical Society of Southern California and the Iredell County (North Carolina) Historical Society have rendered me much aid; and I have applied with satisfaction to the historical societies of Oregon, Nebraska, Montana, and New Mexico. It is unnecessary, but none the less pleasant, to state that every communication addressed to the Bureau of American Ethnology at Washington received full attention. Through Senator George C. Perkins of California, the Smithsonian Institution provided me with data of value. The Adjutant General's office and the Bureau of Engineering, of the War Department, have answered my queries with military completeness. The splendid shelves of the Iowa State Library and the Iowa State Historical Library at Des Moines proved a treasure-trove of enlightenment.

Amidst the mass of dates and incidents will be found errors, for the writer is but human. Of these errors he doubtless will soon be made aware. In his narrative he has aimed to transcribe boldly, preferring to err rather than to slight.

And now, out of data confused and tenuous, and heretofore based mainly upon one biography written before the Civil War, and that so frail that the Carson family, even to the hero's father and mother, have been suffered to remain in darkness; out of some six years' work covering by correspondence and interview the country from Los Angeles to New York, from Oregon to Florida, behold *Kit Carson Days* as it has been evolved.

EDWIN L. SABIN.

San Diego, California.

CONTENTS

xi

ILLUSTRATIONS

KIT CARSON DAYS

CHAPTER I

THE CARSON FAMILY

THAT "blood will tell" never has been better exemplified than in the case of the Carson family in America; and when he took the danger-trail, youthful Kit Carson swung as true to his instincts as swings the needle to the pole.

The head of the house of Carson in America seems to have been William Carson, of Scotch-Irish strain, who emigrated from England, possibly Scotland, in the first half of the eighteenth century, to Pennsylvania. Thence moving southward, joining in that impulse which transfused into the Carolinas and Tennessee so much of Scotch-Irish Protestant blood, he laid claim to 692 acres on both sides of Third Creek, in the Loray District of Iredell County, North Carolina. The Carson grant to this tract, from Lord Granville, bears date of December 1, 1761.

Of this William Carson the First the records run in brief that he was a farmer; that he married Miss Eleanor McDuff (McDorf?), and that imprudently drinking from a cold spring on a hot day, before the Revolution, he died, leaving a wife and five children — Robert, Lindsay (head of the Carson family in Missouri), Andrew, possibly an Alexander, Eleanor, and Sarah.

The Carson family, now established in America, proceeded to scatter like quail. An Alexander Carson migrated

1

to Mississippi; Robert Carson to Kentucky, where he lived
until he died; Lindsay and Andrew to the Hunting Creek
settlement in the north of Iredell County. Here Andrew,
at twenty, and Lindsay, at twenty-two, proved the Carson
metal in the fire of the Revolution.

Andrew became a captain in the command of Marion the
Swampfox; and while Lord Cornwallis was harrying South
Carolina he carried dispatches between Marion and Greene.
He was in the battle of Camden, and tradition states that
he bore out in his arms, from under fire, the fatally wounded
Baron DeKalb, stricken while crossing a creek, October 16,
1780.

Of Lindsay Carson's exploits in the Revolution less comes
down to us; but so sturdy an Indian fighter must have
graven deep his signature. After the war he removed to
South Carolina, and married Miss Bradley, to raise another
wilderness brood, the flight of which was to reach from
Kentucky to the Pacific.

This, the first of his two marriages, added to his race
William, b. 1786, who by union with Millie Boone of the
Kentucky Boones, perpetuated around Fayette, Missouri,
the Carson name; Sarah, b. 1788, m. Peyton and lived to
an advanced age; Andrew, b. 1790; Moses Bradley, b.
1792. The mother did not long survive this last child, but
died soon after reaching the new home in Madison County,
Kentucky, whither, 1792, the restless Lindsay moved on.

Here, in Madison County, Kentucky, in 1797, he took
unto himself a second wife, Rebecca Robinson, of Green-
briar County, Virginia, and so resumed the interrupted
sequence; for those were wholesome days of large families. Six more boys and four more girls arrived, with
regularity: 1, Elizabeth, m. Robert Cooper of the Missouri
(and Kentucky) Coopers; 2, Nancy, m. Briggs; 3, Robert;
4, Hamilton; 5, Christopher; 6, Hampton; 7, Mathilda,
m. Adams; 8, Mary, m. Ruby; 9, Sarshel; 10, Lindsay

Second. But this, his namesake, the father never saw, for the birth occurred after the fatality of September, 1818, when Lindsay First died, aged sixty-four, crushed by a falling limb.

Tradition in the Young family, of the Hunting Creek district, North Carolina, asserts that not in Kentucky but in Iredell County the famous Kit was born, while Lindsay and wife were upon a visit to his brother Andrew. Be that as it may, Iredell County of North Carolina has another claim, in the report, reasonably authentic, that Kit Carson's full given name was Christopher Houston, given out of respect to the Christopher Houston who was prominent in Iredell County during the Revolution.

Of this brave family of fourteen, born to Lindsay Carson by juncture with the Bradley and the Robinson clans, all lived to manhood or womanhood. And this in itself is remarkable, for the wanderlust was in the veins. The girls, of course, married; but of the sons it is written, by a son of William, the eldest: " Every one, without a single exception, went west in search of the Indian and the buffalo; now that the Indian is guarded on the reservations and the buffalo is nearly extinct, I am at a loss to know what their descendants will do for a pastime."

When the first Carson entered the Far West, is not known, but an Alexander Carson (possibly son of that Alexander who was son of the first William) was encountered as a trapper upon the upper Missouri by the Wilson Hunt party of Astorians, in the spring of 1811. And he and his companion turned, with the party of Astorians, for the still farther West. Already he had been two years in the beaver wilderness.

Then with the advent in Missouri of the Lindsay tribe, the Carson family entered into the thick of pioneer affairs. The father and Moses served, with the home guard, against the Indians, in the War of 1812; Moses was in several up-river expeditions of the fur trade; a Carson (very likely Andrew, Moses' senior) was with the Ezekiel Williams adventurers who fared into the Southwest, 1811, and were gone two years; William, the eldest of all, was held back in Kentucky by Indian disturbances, until the war was over.

William, Andrew, Moses, Robert, Hamilton, and Christopher certainly rode the Santa Fe Trail; Lindsay Second is said to have been with Fremont on that heroic but futile fourth expedition to the Rockies in the winter of 1848-49; of Sarshel and Hampton I have no record.

CHAPTER II

IN OLD MISSOURI — 1810-1826

THE story of Kit Carson days is the story of beaver and of Indians; of mountain, cañon, valley, desert, and stream ransacked through and through by the fur hunter; of white blood and red blood meeting, striving, and mingling — mingling sometimes in friendly union but far oftener in the struggle of mutual hate; of lonely camp and of boisterous rendezvous; of thirst, starvation and rude plenty; of the trapper followed close by the trader, of both followed by the explorer, of the explorer followed by the emigrant — colonist, gold seeker, settler; of Santa Fe Trail and Oregon Trail and California Trail; of a Bent's Fort, a Fort Laramie, a Fort Bridger — and of trader and Indian marching out, the army marching in; of Black Robe and of missionary carrying Christianity from St. Louis and Boston overland to the mouth of the Columbia; of Ute, Apache and Navajo in the Southwest subdued by the bullet; of a Great Britain on the north, and a Mexico on the south, once touching beyond the Rockies, then cleaved a thousand miles asunder by a westward pressing flag; of a Texas, a California, a New Mexico, and an Oregon acquired, and of a " Great American Desert " fertilized; of a vast and savage West awakened and with astounding swiftness made amenable to the purposes of civilization; of an unknown country two thousand miles wide becoming known; of the United States expanding in three directions until it had reached from the Atlantic to the Pacific, from the Gulf and the Rio Grande and the mouth of the Colorado to Canada and Puget Sound.

5

Kit Carson traveled from Kentucky to Santa Fe by ox team and wagon. Before he died he had traveled from Washington City to the Wyoming Rockies by rail; another year, and he could have journeyed from coast to coast in similar fashion.

Daniel Boone, in 1797, at the age of sixty-five, had moved across the Missouri. Reports from him and his sons filtered back. Then in the spring of 1811, the head of the Lindsay Carson house emigrated from Madison County of Kentucky to this new Boone's Lick district of the even newer American territory of Louisiana. The youngest child (as yet) was Kit, born December 25, 1809.

The Carsons and their southern party settled in what is now Howard County, along the Missouri River, about 200 miles west of St. Louis. Other men and women of the South were here; more arrived; and soon there arose those doughty stockades celebrated in Mississippi Valley history — Forts Hempstead, Cooper, and Kincaid. The name of Linsey (Lindsay) Carson appears upon the roll of old Fort Hempstead, and he is claimed likewise by the descendants of the old Fort Cooper garrison.

This was the extreme frontier of the United States; beyond was the " Indian Country," so to be designated, with but slight variation, for thirty years. The population of the Territory of Louisiana, which comprised that section of the old province north of the Territory of Orleans, or the present state of Louisiana, dwindled speedily as one proceeded northward from the lower Arkansas and westward from the mouth of the Missouri. St. Louis, with its 1800 people, was the metropolis.

Encouraged by the government which was essaying to absorb a continent, the fur trade (the only trade, to date, of this the new West) had increased rapidly. Through many years St. Louis, under domination of the French, had been the headquarters of a fur trade operated mainly by private individuals, or at most by partners; for St. Louis was French, and from the very outset it was the French who in the new continent sought out the pelt of forest, prairie, and stream. But now, at the time of the Carsons' arrival in the Boone's Lick district, the Missouri Fur Company of St. Louis was organized with good backing, and the energetic John Jacob Astor of New York was pushing his American Fur Company. His ship the *Tonquin* was en route for the mouth of the Columbia, and up the Missouri River trail from St. Louis had hastened the supporting overland party of Hunt.

In this Louisiana, soon to be rechristened Missouri Territory, Lindsay Carson continued his Kentucky and Carolina career. He led in many skirmishes with the savages; he and his third son, Moses, were enrolled in the home guards during the War of 1812. In 1814 some fingers of his left hand were shot off during a scrimmage with Indians. In September, 1818, he died by the fall of a limb from a burned tree while he was cutting timber in the forest near home. He left a thriving family, and a rifle of large bore, with the stock (like the fingers of his hand) smashed by an enemy's bullet.

Kit, no longer the youngest in the family, was now almost nine years of age. Two and one-half of these years had been spent under the stockade protection of Fort Hempstead; all had been spent in the shadow of peril by wilderness. He had run absolutely unrestrained except for the spasmodic efforts of a tired mother with many other nestlings. He was thoroughly a settler's child. When he reached fifteen years his mother apprenticed him to a saddler in Franklin, then the chief Missouri frontier settlement.

During the fourteen years since the Carsons had crossed the Mississippi, government, fur trader, and adventurer had repeatedly assaulted the Indian country. Making a rift in an entirely new spot of the bulwarks of the Northwest, in

1820 Major Stephen Long, of the army, ascended the Missouri, past Franklin, in the first steamboat successfully to plough that stream, and from the present site of Omaha proceeded by horse and mule up along the Platte (name already well-known by mouth of *voyageur* and trapper) to the Rocky Mountains. Then swinging south, he skirted the eastern base of the foothills, passing the present site of the cities of Denver and Colorado Springs, and returned by way of the Arkansas.

. The Missouri Fur Company was constantly establishing more posts in that upper Missouri country, and there were half a dozen other companies in the field. William Ashley of St. Louis, first lieutenant governor of the new state, general in the militia and Missouri's leading citizen, had taken up the fur trade as another vocation, to pursue it so industriously that within six years he made his fortune. In 1822 he had escorted up the river his first party, under Major Andrew Henry, who in service of the Missouri Fur Company, a dozen years back, had built the first American fur-trading post on the Pacific side of the Stony Mountains, by the Henry Fork of the Snake River in extreme eastern Idaho at the Wyoming line. General Ashley followed his 1822 expedition with others, accompanying some of them himself. To young Kit Carson these Ashley expeditions should have been of especial interest, for they at once numbered upon their rolls Henry Vanderburgh, the ill-fated; Thomas Fitzpatrick, Carson's first mountain employer; Jim Bridger, discoverer of the great Salt Lake; Jedediah S. Smith, the "knight in buckskin," whose Bible was as close a companion to him as his rifle, and whose trail across the desert into California, Carson would encounter on his initial trip as a trapper; Jim Beckwourth, the mulatto Crow chief; the Sublettes — of whom William was the best captain of trappers in the West; and others whose names figure largely in plains and mountain history, and with whom, in a few more years, Kit Carson, now a boy, mingled as a man, a fellow trapper and an equal.

Moreover, up the river, in the summer of 1823, had passed a punitive expedition sent by government and fur people combined against the fierce Arikaras, who were forcibly obstructing traffic. In the fighting, this "Missouri Legion," as it was styled, had been moderately successful. The way was opened.

So much, briefly, as regards the Northwest. But the Southwest likewise was being exploited. Objective points in the Northwest were the Three Forks country of the sources of the Missouri River, and the Columbia and Oregon region, on the other side of the mountains. The Southwest spelled Santa Fe — that far Mexican metropolis of the "Spanish Settlements." Pike had reported upon it; in 1806 he had found there one James Purcell (or Pursley), an American from Kentucky already domiciled. At present Santa Fe and the Spanish Settlements were in everybody's mouth, for trade in that direction promised an attractive outlet to those Missourians who were not engaged in the fur business of the North.

In June, 1813, Ezekiel Williams had returned to Boone's Lick of Missouri, after a long experience on the upper Arkansas, and had brought back much word of Santa Fe.[1] The next year he went out again and his adventures were reported widely.

In 1821 John McKnight passed through Franklin upon quest of his brother Robert who for nine years had not been heard from. He found Robert imprisoned in Chihuahua, but he found also that rumors were true, and that Mexico was free from Spanish rule, unfriendly to Americans, so he was enabled to bring Robert back with him. The return in the summer of 1822 was chronicled in the *Missouri Intelligencer* of Franklin.

Meanwhile Captain William Becknell of Franklin advertised in the *Intelligencer* of June 10, 1821, for "seventy men to go westward" on a trading project. He assembled his party at the house of Ezekiel Williams (who doubtless could aid with much information about the country), and succeeded in penetrating safely into Santa Fe and in emerging safely therefrom. The following January he arrived in Franklin again, enthusiastic over his profits.

In the spring of 1822 Captain Becknell led another company, with three wagons, and made a new and shorter trail across the Cimarron desert. The Santa Fe trade was fairly started, and the *Missouri Intelligencer* was constantly printing items upon it.

So when Kit Carson was put out at saddlery service in Franklin in 1825, it was locking the cat in with the cream. Northwest and Southwest were thrilling with deeds and adventures, the accounts of which focused in Franklin — Franklin, still keenly mindful of the great reception tendered to Major James and General Atkinson, when in 1819 they had stopped off from their steamboat, en route to the Yellowstone. Ashley was reaping fame and furs. And Santa Fe had come into being.

Thus Kit Carson found Franklin an eddy where two trails joined. Down the river, and up the river to the uttermost sources in the unknown, passed the men of the fur trade; by steamboat, by keel boat, ashore and even afoot, bringing their pelts, their squaws, their scars, and their tales. And here the Santa Fe Trail met the Missouri River Trail. Out of the south of west they came, into the dim south of west they went, those dusty pack trains laden tight with merchandise and escorting not only trader, but broadcloth merchant and health-seeking adventurer. Theirs were tales of desert rather than of mountains; of Kiowa, Pawnee, Comanche, and Arapaho; of the *cibolero*, or Mexican buffalo hunter; of thirst amidst burning sands; and of a romantic, ancient city, 800 miles away, by horse and mule, across the hazy " Indian Country " — Santa Fe of Neuva Mejico, where American goods and labor sold at great profit, and where American visitors were welcomed by the merry fandango.

As against all this, the saddler's craft must have seemed dull indeed to Kit Carson. In a year he had had enough of it; and the following advertisement, which appeared in the columns of the *Missouri Intelligencer* of Franklin, indicates how he left it:

Notice: To whom it may concern: That Christopher Carson, a boy about sixteen years old, small of his age, but thickset, light hair, ran away from the subscriber, living in Franklin, Howard Co., Mo., to whom he had been bound to learn the saddler's trade, on or about the first day of September last. He is supposed to have made his way toward the upper part of the state. All persons are notified not to harbor, support, or subsist said boy under penalty of the law. One cent reward will be given to any person who will bring back the said boy.
(Signed)   DAVID WORKMAN.
                                           Franklin, Oct. 6, 1826.

Shrewdly enough might it be suspected that he had set face to the north, in the line of the fur trade. This was the easier travel and there were countless invitations for a lad to proceed onward with trader, trapper, or Indian — plenty of whom, we may be certain, Kit Carson knew. Anybody who could handle a rifle was free to join any of a hundred wandering bands, white or red; and .Moses Carson, and no doubt others of Kit's brothers, already had traversed the upper Missouri trail.

But the chances for profit were greater on the Santa Fe Trail, and the romance of it was more appealing. So Kit Carson joined a Santa Fe caravan, and, by the irony of events, at the very first opportunity, the next spring, David Workman, saddler, did the same.

Kit never again saw his home, and according to report, he saw few of his kinsfolk for almost two decades. Not until the spring of 1842 did he return to the Missouri frontier, and the sixteen years of spectacular progress had wiped out, as would a landslide, both places and people.

CHAPTER III

THE ROAD TO SANTA FE — 1826

OUT pulled the caravan, one of several dispatched this
year from Franklin, for the Santa Fe trade was
increasing. It was composed in the main of wagons and
other vehicles; the year 1826 marked the passing, on the
trail, of pack animals, and the employment of wheels
entirely, although individuals with pack animals continued
to attach themselves to caravans.

In this year, 1826, all that vast West of today, from
Missouri and Iowa to the Pacific Ocean, bore scarcely a
name save here and there the title of Indian tribe, of lake,
stream, peak and range, and desert; and, principally along
the Missouri River and upper tributaries, of trading post or
fur company's " fort." One army post had been established, at Council Bluffs — Fort Atkinson. The heart of
this country, comprising what are now fertile Kansas,
Nebraska, and the Colorado plains, was labeled " Great
American Desert." It was presumed to be worthless except
for buffalo and uninhabitable by civilized man. Thus had
Major Long, in 1820, reported it. He had pronounced it
a providential barrier against the westward spread of
humanity, and a bulwark, equally providential, against
aggression by other nations from that direction. The geog-
raphies of a generation ago were still clinging stanchly to
this black-shaded patch — the " Great American Desert."

There was not a settlement between New Mexico and the
mouth of the Columbia in Oregon. Indians, more or less
hostile, buffalo, antelope, wild horses, elk, deer, bear, wolves,
beaver, the eagle, hawk, buzzard, other birds and quadru-

18

peds, and many reptiles, made up the citizenship, aside from the trappers and traders. Fur, feather, buckskin, and painted nakedness was the garb in vogue.

The boundary of that territory acquired as the Louisiana Province, from France, was yet rather obscure to the people at large, and even to the authorities. The United States extended to the indefinite Rocky Mountains, on the west; on the south to the Red River, and at the undefined line of the 100th meridian of longitude, in present Kansas, only to the Arkansas. Below, all was Mexico and uneasy Texas — which also was Mexican territory. Across the Rockies — then known as the " Shining Mountains " and the " Stony Mountains," and toward their southern extremity as the " Anahuac " — all was Mexico, generalized as California, up to the northern line of the present Utah. North of Utah everything was Oregon, shared temporarily by the United States and Great Britain, whose representative was the Hudson Bay Company.

Kit Carson's entrance into this unplotted West which he soon would help map was not, we may be certain, heroic. He arrived, beyond any reasonable doubt, at the tail of the horse herd or " cavvy," as many another character prominent in western history has done. Herding this " cavvy " is the boy's and the new hand's job in the West, and always has been.

Chroniclers have given Kit Carson a place from the outset as official hunter for the caravan — his duty being to supply the camp with meat. But he was just a boy of sixteen, undersized, of the gritty but nondescript Scotch-Irish type — sandy-haired, sandy-complexioned, tanned and freckled, with full forehead and wide-set, blue-gray eyes. He was a good shot, self-reliant, wise in woodcraft and pioneer expedients, but these were not exceptional qualities, and regularly appointed " hunters " were not the rule in these early caravans.

The caravan itself is recorded very clearly by Captain Gregg and by Thomas J. Farnham of the same era. The course to Santa Fe lay not as one traveled road, but as a number of chance selected trails, for the most part only discernible to the keenest eyes. The country was, as a rule, flat and bare, and travelers kept a general direction from water to water, from camping spot to camping spot. Like any other long trail, the Santa Fe was merely a succession of convenient or necessary stages. Vehicles traversing it usually took a formation of four abreast, but sometimes they stretched out in single file for a mile and more. However, the column of fours, and later of twos, was imperative in the Indian country, where compactness was a condition of defense.

The journey out usually occupied fifty or sixty days; the journey back, when the wagons traveled lighter, could be made in forty days. The distance was about 780 miles, and a well-laden wagon traveled on an average fifteen miles a day. But in 1826, the time of Kit Carson's first trip, the travel was less systematized, more haphazard, and therefore less expeditious.

From Franklin the Kit Carson caravan would strike away from the muddy river, and leaving Missouri through the green prairie of the then friendly Osage Indians, now aiming for the Arkansas River would cross into the Kansas of today. In addition to the great, heavy, flaring-topped Conestoga wagons, of Pittsburg pattern, each drawn by eight mules, there were a few stylish Dearborn carriages, the conveyances of city merchants and of invalids; for both wealth and health were to be found upon the old Santa Fe Trail. Outriders were before and upon either flank of the column. In the dust of the rear followed the " cavvy," and on his mule, Kit Carson.

As the caravan proceeded, exchanging the green prairies of western Missouri for the arid plains of Kansas, discipline would become stricter, for the Pawnees frequently raided here, and just ahead were the grounds of the fierce Kiowas and the equally dangerous Comanches. The horsemen would look to their arms and at night the wagons would be parked, or joined into a hollow square, the front wheels of one vehicle lapping the rear wheels of another. An opening was left, through which the animals might be driven in case of alarm.

Early in the morning, after the rude but hearty breakfast, the captain of the caravan would sign to his lieutenant; the lieutenant would call, " Catch up! " Taking up the cry, the wagoners would briskly harness their teams. Presently from first one and then another wagoner would come the announcement: " All 's set." The teamsters were ready. " Stretch out, then."

A noble sight those teams were, forty-odd in number, their immense wagons still unmoved, forming an oval breastwork of wealth, girded by an impatient mass of near 400 mules, harnessed and ready to move again along their solitary way. But the interest of the scene was much increased when, at the call of the commander, the two lines, team after team, straightened themselves into the trail, and rolled majestically away over the undulating plain.[2]

The journey, especially to the greenhorn and the boy, and also to every person who loved nature, could not have been monotonous. There was the constant outlook for suspicious figures which might be Indians. And the plains, today so lifeless except as new life has been introduced, in caravan times teemed with their wild animals. The buffalo led in importance, but was subject to seasonal and hunters' influences. Besides the buffalo there was the antelope.

Of that singular animal — the antelope — we saw great numbers; and in the fall, once or twice, many hundreds in a

gang, which, all of one accord, would dash hither and thither
with wonderful swiftness, looking at a distance, like the shadow
of a moving cloud. There was a remarkable species of hare,
nearly twice the size of the eastern; the fleetest of the prairie animals, though in tall grass they were easily caught. I
had a nearly tame one, which fed on rushes, which would
disappear in its mouth as if pushed through a hole. Badgers
were common; and prairie foxes of light and elegant pro-
portions. We met with many prairie dog " villages" ; whole
acres of their burrows, with entrances in a small mound.
Of wolves, there were thousands, of all kinds and sizes,
except the large black wood wolf; never an hour of a night
passed without the accompaniment of their howls; even by
day they were to be seen around. One dark night, being
officer of the guard, I advanced some two hundred paces to
a spot where there was an excavation and a small mound of
earth, and where garbage had been thrown; from the mound,
I saw perhaps a dozen snarling over their unclean food;
sword in hand, I sprang down among them; they scattered,
but I did not stay long to see how far. Rattlesnakes were
very numerous, and dangerous; we lost several horses by
their bites. Wild horses we saw frequently, but not many.
A horse which we lost August 3, was recovered from a gang
a month or two afterwards. Buffalo, wolves, rattlesnakes,
and grasshoppers, seemed to fill up the country.[8]

Pauses would be made at noon for lunch and respite, and
halts at night for camp. There were perils aside from that of
Indians. Accidents often happened. Rain and hail and sand
storms of terrific violence would sweep athwart the route.
Animals would stampede. They and wagons would be
struck. The attack of the elements was appalling; and the
caravan, out upon the vast pampa, like a ship in the midst of
the ocean, was exposed to the ship's perils without the ship's
mobility.

The Santa Feans, when on the march through these plains,
are in constant expectation of these tornadoes. Accordingly
when the sky at night indicates their approach, they chain
the wheels of adjacent wagons strongly together to prevent

them from being up-set — an accident that had often happened, when this precaution was not taken.[4]

On the other hand, miscalculation as to water would result in dreadful suffering or even death from thirst. The Arkansas River was a great blessing. But away from the Arkansas, bewildered by the sameness of the landscape and by the " deep paths made by the buffalo, as if a thousand generations of them had, in single file, followed their leaders from point to point through the plains," the caravan might easily lose its way.

Of the caravan with which Carson traveled only one mischance is recorded. A teamster accidentally shot himself through the arm shortly before the caravan reached the Arkansas River. He refused to have the arm amputated, but by the time the caravan reached the river — along which it would proceed — the flesh had gangrened and amputation became necessary. There was no surgeon in the camp. Three men volunteered to perform the operation, among them being Kit Carson. It is quite unlikely, however, that, as early biographers have affirmed, he was the operating surgeon. He probably held the improvised instruments for the rought but, as turned out, successful cutting and searing.[5]

About fifteen miles on, or another day's march, the caravan would arrive at Pawnee Rock. This landmark has practically disappeared today, not alone from sight, but even also from memory. However, when Kit Carson went out upon the trail it was a bold sandstone promontory beside the trail, jutting up thirty and forty feet, its face carved with the symbols of travelers both white and red. The Indians long had used the rock as a signboard, and the caravans speedily adopted the scheme. Thus, as in the case of Independence Rock upon the northern Oregon Trail, and of Inscription Rock, westward upon the trail taken by the old Spanish *conquistadors* across the Arizona desert, Pawnee Rock indicated that so and so had passed that way.

Now the caravan was in dangerous country and strict watch and ward would have to be maintained. As suggested by the name, this was hostile Indian territory; the vicinity of the rock was a favorite resort of Pawnee and Kiowa war parties, always alert, upon the slightest provocation, to rob a foreign company. It was also the heart of the southern buffalo range, and Indian hunting parties — Pawnee, Kiowa, Comanche, Sioux, Arapaho, even the far northern Crow and Blackfeet — were liable to be encountered, following the slowly drifting, shaggy herds.

But at this time the Ishmaelite bandits of the plains had not yet fully risen to attacking an organized caravan of eighty or one hundred men, their animals and wagons. According to the table prepared by Captain Josiah Gregg in *Commerce of the Prairies*, not until 1828, or two years later, did a caravan report loss of life to its members. Nevertheless, smaller expeditions were constantly being raided; this very year four overland traders had been deprived by the Arapahos of 500 horses and mules; and the cavvy of a caravan was a prize bound soon or late, and at any moment, to draw down upon camp or march a yelling horde. So it may be seen that even the humble post of wrangler or herder had its spice of peril.

Far western romance tells of Kit's caravan of 1826 having an Indian scare at Pawnee Rock, wherein young Kit shoots his mule instead of a Pawnee. But this incident is claimed by Jim Bridger, at an earlier time, for himself; and, in fact, is a current joke ascribed to various individuals, and was perennial with the early trappers and adventurers. I would agree with Captain Chittenden's footnote in his *History of the American Fur Trade*, that it did not happen to Kit Carson, here and now. Nor is there any reference in Gregg or other contemporary authorities to any bloody battle with the Pawnees when any caravan of 1826 had proceeded a short distance beyond the rock. On the contrary, according to the Peters biography of Carson (which misses no legitimate opportunities) the march of the caravan was uneventful after the Broadus affair. So we must leave Kit his mule, and must defer for a time his taking his first scalp.[6]

Some two hundred miles beyond the rock the caravan of this early date would ford the Arkansas. The 100th meridian had long been passed, and when the river was crossed the advance would all be in Mexican territory. Later caravans forded lower down; but for some years there was no one fording spot.

To ford the Arkansas was somewhat risky on account of the quicksands. Teams were strengthened and the wagons were snaked through in double time. On the farther shore all the water which could be stowed away must be stored up; five gallons to the wagon was none too much; and it was found advisable to cook bread and meat sufficient for a two-days' journey. Immediately ahead was a " water scrape," or a dry march: the arid waste of the Cimarron desert in southwestern Kansas, between the Arkansas and the sources of the Cimarron River. It was the favorite haunt of the bold-riding Comanches. The Cimarron, below its sources, was only a dry, sandy bed. Herbage was scarce. Mirages lured, gigantic hailstones fell, the surface of the ground was so hard that wagons made no tracks, and the way was easily lost. The Cimarron " water scrape " grew to be the most dreaded stage of the overland trail to Santa Fe. It was at its worst in the fall, for water was then most scant.

But when that was over — when, having strained through the heavy sandhills that bordered the Arkansas, and across the firm, bare plain of the interior, the wagons, with teamsters and all peering nervously before out of bloodshot eyes, toiled gladly into the valley of the Cimarron and reached the first spring — then there was comparatively clear sailing.

And hereabouts would first be met, if not met previously, a *cibolero*, or Mexican buffalo hunter. Gregg has described him well. Wild as the Comanche, the *cibolero* ranged through the desert like any Arab, clad in trousers and short jacket of goatskin leather, and wearing a flat straw hat. Slung athwart his shoulder he bore bow and quiver; and he had a long lance, suspended beside him in a gaily tasseled case and waving above his head. His pride would be his fusil, or smoothbore musket of huge caliber, its muzzle carefully stoppered with a great wooden plug, also tasseled. His stirrup hoods, or *tapaderas*, swept the ground, and his enormous saddle covered all his pony.

It was considered a good stroke to encounter a *cibolero;* news of the market in Santa Fe could be obtained, and possibly a supply of dried buffalo flesh from his camp, where he, his companions, and their families, would be congregated, all engaged in securing wild meat.

By the landmark of the Rabbit Ear mounds, about where now the panhandle of Oklahoma joins New Mexico, the caravan would know that it was upon the straight course. The country would wax rougher, mountains would be discernible, as hazy outlines, to the northwest. Beyond them lay that prominent Mexican settlement of Fernandez de Taos, which now was awaiting Kit Carson and was to be his home town for forty years. A trail, branching off, led to it and had been recommended by the United States survey party the year before. Anybody for Taos was at liberty to take it; but traders in a hurry pressed on for Santa Fe. The oldest trail, the " mountain division " of the Santa Fe Trail, did not cross the Arkansas until having followed its north bank clear to the Rockies; thence it turned to the south and headed for Santa Fe city. But it is likely that a fall caravan of 1826 would have sought what it considered the shortest route, and would have cut across the desert of the Cimarron to avoid the mountain snows, the sooner to reach its destination, and to be enabled to start back before midwinter.

When Santa Fe was only some 200 miles away it was the custom of the caravans to dispatch an advance party of couriers, as " runners " to announce the approach and to stir up the market. By this time the caravans would show signs of wear. The exceeding dry atmosphere had shrunk and warped the wheels of the vehicles, the roughness of the road was shaking loose tires and spokes, so at every halt much tinkering must be done. Strips of buffalo hide were tied about, and wedges of thin hoop iron were driven in.

At the Rio de las Gallinas, or Turkey River, the first real token of civilization, or semi-civilization, would be passed: a rude adobe rancho, at the foot of a cliff. It had been established before Gregg's time, 1831, and he says that here he was treated to a refreshing draught of goat's milk and a supply of dirty curd. After a long and unvaried diet of bacon, poor bread, coffee, and buffalo flesh, such an innovation would be welcome. Without doubt the rancho was there when the Kit Carson caravan traveled through. Rural New Mexico was a land of few changes. Twenty more miles and the first settlement, San Miguel del Vado, would be reached: an unprepossessing collection of mud huts squatted upon the bank of the rippling Pecos River.

On would plod the caravan. The region was becoming more settled; and Kit Carson must have kept his eyes anxiously looking for the famous old city to loom into view. Then, finally, on an early November day, as the first wagons mounted a rocky ridge, he heard from the advance a great cheering. The word passed along the column: " Santa Fe! Santy Fee! There she is! " And as he also attained the crest he saw in the distance to the northwest, before and below him, a valley dotted by trees, lined in green by ditches,

SANTA FE CARAVAN ON THE MARCH
(From Gregg's Commerce of the Prairies)

SANTA FE IN SIGHT!
(From Gregg's Commerce of the Prairies)

THE COPPER MINES WHERE KIT CARSON WORKED FOR McKNIGHT

SHOWING KEARNY'S DRAGOONS PASSING BY FOR CALIFORNIA, 1846

(From the Emory Report)

cultivated to patches of corn and grain, and blotched with
a splash of low, dun, sprawling structures that, according
to Gregg, in 1831, resembled brick kilns, and according to
Pike, a quarter-century previous, reminded one of a fleet
of flatboats moored against the hill.

It must be borne in mind that Santa Fe was strictly of
Spanish architecture, as adapted to the country: adobe mud
buildings, as a' rule not even whitewashed; flat-roofed, one-
storied. Like the majority of visitors from the states, Kit
Carson must have been disappointed. He had anticipated
something far grander in a city that was the goal of eight
hundred miles.

However, the aspect appeared to please all of the more
experienced. When within touch with Santa Fe, caravans
usually halted to rub up. Clothing was changed to the best
at hand, faces were washed, hair was slicked; each teamster
removed the old cracker from his whiplash and tied on a
new one. These preparations having been consummated to
the best of the wayfarers' ability, on down the slope, across
the short plain at the foot of the ridge, and in amidst the
squatty buildings would rumble and clatter the train. Gallantly would crack the long-lashed whips, the poor jaded
mules, plucking spirit, would try to gambol, merrily would
shout the men. All the population of Santa Fe seemed to
be gathered there on the outskirts of the town. Loud and
shrill pealed the cries of swarthy men and women:

" *Los Americanos!* "

" *Los carros!* " [The wagons.]

" *La entrada de la caravana!* " [Arrival of the caravan.]

More and more extravagantly, then, the proud wagoners
of this November, 1826, travel-worn caravan swung their
whips, snapping the new crackers and showing off before
the black-eyed señoritas. The merchant proprietors sat
stiffly their horses. Trappers grinned; recovered invalids
stared. While at the very rear, pointed to and smiled upon

as *Muchacho! Muchacho Americano! Mire!* [Boy!
American boy! Behold!], confused by the celebration, but
as much excited as anybody, rode Kit Carson on his dusty
mule, driving his *caballada*.

The arrival of a caravan was a stupendous event for old
Santa Fe. It was a visit from another planet. In 1826
very many Mexicans of even the northern territory had
never seen an American, nor had they any clear conception
of the United States; and for more than twenty years thereafter the Caucasian white skin was a constant marvel.

So that night, and for a succession of nights and days,
the men of the Kit Carson caravan were entertained, like
sailors from a foreign port, with a series of fandangos and
other entertainments. As willing as anyone to be amused
was the tanned boy Kit; paid off with his wage of five dollars a month, accrued from seven or eight weeks of labor,
he probably saw the sights — not omitting the palace with
its rumored festoons of dried Indian ears!

CHAPTER IV

NEW MEXICO AND NEW MEXICANS

A T THIS time Santa Fe and its environs were accredited with a population of about 5,000, in which probably not more than a dozen of the permanent residents were
Americans — traders. There was not an American woman
in the country. By American here is meant a *gringo* or
foreigner, for all aliens of light skin were deemed American. The term "white" has ever been accepted as a
reproach by the native Mexican, who considers himself as
white as the Anglo-Saxon, and thus applies the adjective
to himself in distinction from the Indian. However, "white
blood" in New Mexico long indicated Spanish blood, so
bringing to mind the fact that the early Castilian was light-
haired and blue-eyed.

From the first the American, or *gringo,* was admired by
the women and hated by the men, while both sexes agreed
that he was uncouth and exceedingly impolite. The brusque,
straightforward mien of the backwoodsman and the rather
coarse-fibered trapper shocked the ceremonious, Spanish-
trained populace, the worst of whom would stab the stranger
in the name of God, and would not even light a cigarette
without a polite "*Con su licencia, señor*" — "with your
permission, sir." Of course, as the aggressions between
Mexico and the United States waxed more irritating to
both sides — particularly after the Texas affair — the feeling against the American became excessive. From his disregard for conventionalities (which today, as then, is apt
to seem his characteristic to other peoples), he was viewed
as a monster. So that Lieutenant Ruxton, the English

traveler, relates that one night in 1846, when he would have stopped over with a Pueblo family in Ohuaqui, the *patrona,* or mistress, was cautious until she discovered that he was an Englishman. Then —

"*Gracias a Dios,*" she exclaimed. "A Christian will sleep with us tonight, and not an American." [7]

Santa Fe, at Kit Carson's first visit, was a place of great pretensions, but of little beauty. The houses and business buildings were uniformly of one story; of mud bricks smeared with a thin plaster of more mud, and in rare cases whitewashed with *tierra blanca,* or white earth. The mud roofs were flat, windows were protected by wooden shutters, iron bars, or, here and there, with sheets of thin, laminated gypsum in lieu of glass. Mud front joined with mud front, around the central plaza, in monotonous line, until at irregular intervals a winding lane, for a street, cut through. Dirt and squalor, refuse, dogs, and beggars predominated; nevertheless there was much to interest the visitor from the Missouri frontier.

The blanket-enveloped Mexican, smiling in the American's face and scowling at his back, indolent, graceful, eternally smoking his cornhusk cigarette, and ever a *caballero,* or gentleman; the shawled Mexican woman, her face stained crimson with the juice of the *alegria* plant, or coated with a paste of chalk, to preserve her complexion for the fandango; the burros, piled high with enormous loads of cornshuck for fodder, or with wood from the mountains, or with parcels of melons, or balanced with casks of that whiskey termed "Taos lightning"; supplies of *chili colorado* and *chili verde,* vegetables, baked piñon nuts, peaches from the orchards of the Pueblos and Navajos, native tobacco or *punche,* grapes, bunches of *hoja* or husk for the rolling of cigarettes, and other products strange or appealing — or, to a newly arrived caravan, both; the constant gambling, principally at *el monte,* with Mexican cards, by high and low, rich and poor, alike, in open room and upon the street; the religious processions, at which everybody must uncover; aye, there was much to see. So we may picture the lad Kit Carson, discharged and with money in his pocket, wandering, gazing and spending.

As soon as the customs duties had been paid the caravan would pursue its business of barter and sale. It would split into its component units. Detachments, after refreshment, would push on for the markets of El Paso del Norte, down the river, and for Chihuahua and Sonora, of the Old Mexico of today. The Yankee trader never has been content with the near when there was a far which he might hazard; and the merchants from the States already were penetrating on and on, into the interior of their new connections.

Usually it required three or four weeks to settle caravan business in Santa Fe, when, a return caravan having been loaded with the proceeds of the venture, the start back to Missouri was made, conveying the gold dust and the silver bullion, buffalo robes and furs, wool and coarse blankets, and live stock. Having in mind the return caravan, the favorite season for the outward trip to Santa Fe was the spring, that the reverse trip might be made before winter. Those merchants in the Kit Carson caravan who contemplated return to Missouri with wagons would have hurried their business; already it was November; winter soon would threaten desert and plains.

Intending, as he evidently did, to remain there, Kit Carson had entered the far West at an unfortunate season. If his consequent course demonstrated that he was determined to be a mountain man and trapper, this was natural, for the romance of such a life would appeal to him then, as it has always appealed to a boy. But Santa Fe was not trappers' headquarters. Furthermore, through the winter employment would be slack; not much of a caravan would

be returning to the States, so late as this in the fall, and
the stop-over teamsters, adventurers, and all would glut
the little town with wage seekers. So if Kit Carson had
thought of remaining long in Santa Fe he was rebuffed. If,
his money dwindling, he had tried to proceed still farther
southward, with Chihuahua or El Paso parties, because he
did not speak Spanish he would have been nosed out by
applicants who did. So he turned into the north, for
Fernandez de Taos, New Mexico, and arrived there in
December.

What measures, if any, his brothers attempted for him,
at this end of the trail, I may not allege; but it is probabie
that the runaway had no notion yet of going home. There
was still much to be seen; and Taos, or " Touse," mountain men's resort, traders' resort, already somewhat infused
with American blood, was as famous a name in Missouri
as Santa Fe. For anybody who wanted to be in close
touch, in the far West, with the trappers, this was the spot.
But when anybody engaged himself to a Santa Fe caravan,
he was paid off at the journey's end, in Santa Fe.

Taos lies seventy-five or eighty miles north and slightly
eastward of Santa Fe. The trail between, like Taos itself,
is still without a railroad; but even in Kit Carson's first days
it was well traveled. A goal of the earliest caravans, which
took the mountain route to the " Spanish settlements," and
a point of departure and arrival for miscellaneous traffic,
Taos was a place of rank second only to Santa Fe, the
capital.

The lad Kit found Fernandez, set near the head of the
fertile Taos Valley, *el Valle de Taos,* with the sparkling
Taos creek flowing through and the sacred Taos mountain, now snow-capped, and yellow-plashed with the frosted
aspens, standing sentinel over the terraced twin buildings
of the Taos Pueblos, to be a settlement of some 500 people
and the outpost of northern New Mexico. Being upon the

border — rather, the inhabited border, for the actual border was still two hundred miles northeast, at the Arkansas River — it was a custom-place. And being the northern border town, close to the southern extremity of those Rockies whose eastern base was United States territory, and being also connected by caravans with Santa Fe and St. Louis, from the day of the first *gringo* wanderer to those parts until the Civil War, it was the great trappers' stronghold of the Southwest.

To old Taos journeyed, annually or semiannually, through many years, by their trails from the Platte River of Wyoming and northern Colorado, from the hill depths of the upper Arkansas, from the Green River country across the range, the shaggy mountain men, to dispose of their furs and to indulge in the wild relaxations of that easy semicivilization. To old Taos came by caravan or independent party, English traveler, army officer, adventurer — all the flotsam and jetsam of the broad frontier; came General Kearny, Fremont, the Bents, the St. Vrains, the Vigils, Fitzpatrick, Bridger, Jim Beckwourth, Pegleg Smith. Out of old Taos sallied many and many a punitive expedition of mountain man and dragoon against the Apache, the Navajo and the Ute.

Kit Carson arrived there in December, 1826, little realizing, of course, that he had selected his home for forty years. The principal industry of Taos, above the barter of trapper goods, was the manufacture from wheat of a strong *aguardiente*, or "Taos lightning," together with smuggling, and agriculture enough to tide the indolent *ranchero* through the winter and spring stringencies. The natives were of the regulation rural class, ruled by a priesthood not in advance, but rather behind, the times.

Taos, as seen by Lieutenant Brewerton, of the United States Army, who was a guest of Carson in later years, was then, as earlier, but little different from other New Mexican towns. The houses were of adobe, with walls of great thickness, the living rooms provided along the sides with rolls of *serapes,* or blankets — divans by day, and when unrolled, beds by night. Sacred relics, rosaries, and images and pictures of the Savior or the Virgin Mary were the chief ornaments, with other prints and paintings of religious tone.

Some of these pictures of Scripture scenes strike the *gringo* as singular and impair his sense of reverence. Brewerton was called upon by a *rico,* or wealthy Mexican, to inspect what was considered by the anxious owner as a masterpiece. After the dust had been brushed away, the subject was discovered to be the sacrifice of Isaac. But —

Abraham — who stands upward of six feet — in a yellow uniform coat and blue striped pantaloons, with cavalry boots, spurs, and moustaches to match — is about putting an end to Isaac (whose dress, with the exception of the moustaches, is gotten up in nearly the same military style as that of the patriarch) by blowing out his brains with an old-fashioned blunderbuss, the muzzle of which is close to Isaac's right ear. The Angel, however, has arrived just in the very nick of time; for as Abraham, with averted head, is pulling trigger, the celestial visitor discharges a torrent of water from a huge squirt directly into the priming of the gun, thereby saving the brains of the intended victim.[8]

To the uneducated, practically unenlightened, Mexican of that day, this modern version of the ancient story would be the more realistic and effective.

It was amidst such a people, and their free and easy life in the little town of San Fernandez, that Kit Carson entered now, fresh from Missouri, presently to pass his seventeenth birthday, a boy, ragged and worn, strange to the customs, unable to speak the language, fascinated with frontier life, and as susceptible as any boy of his experience and age.

CHAPTER V

AS FARED THE RUNAWAY — 1826-1829

SO IN old Taos, for that is the name used more generally than the rightful appellation, San Fernandez, Carson found society good, bad, and indifferent. Carlos Beaubien, a French Canadian of cultured blood, destined to be appointed by General Kearny one of the first three circuit judges of New Mexico, already was a resident there; also Antoine Robidoux (Don Antonio, forsooth), who, already contemplating a post or two beyond the mountains, was as energetic in the Indian trade as his brother Joseph, progenitor of St. Joe City, Missouri.[9] There were several families of high Spanish breeding — into one of which Don Carlos was about to marry. The Bents (William, the trader, and Charles, who would be the first governor of the territory, under American rule), and the St. Vrains (Ceran, leader in state and war, and his trader brother, Marcellin) were soon to arrive from St. Louis; and Milton Sublette was to drift in, forming a trapper partnership with Ewing Young. Of forceful breed, he; his brother was that William Sublette who had ascended the Missouri with the first Ashley command, and he himself was equally a rover, serving in the North and in the South, and succeeding to a partnership in the Rocky Mountain Fur Company.

Taos, of course, had its round quota of real mountain men, American and French and nondescript, now settled there for the winter with their Mexican or Indian wives. Among them was Ewing Young, one of the earliest trappers and traders of that country, and Kincaid, another pioneer.

No " white man " of any nationality could come to Taos, where the natives were many and the aliens few, and not be given hospitality by the small contingent there, if only for the honor of his kind. The mountain trapper is nothing if not generous; and the boy Kit was housed with Kincaid. Contemporary with forts Cooper and Hempstead, of the Carsons' first years in Missouri, was Fort Kincaid; so it is fair to presume that this Kincaid was from old Howard County, or at least was of the family for whom the fort had been christened.

With Kincaid, Carson, the newcomer, spent the winter of 1826-27. The time of his arrival was unfortunate. Trappers were leaving, rather than entering, the mountains; for the fall hunt was over and no more fur expeditions would be on the tapis until spring. In Taos, even less than in Santa Fe, was there chance of work. Peon labor was cheap; in winter, only the distilleries would be running, and they were small affairs. However, for Kit the winter was not wasted; he was enabled to pick up a good smattering of colloquial Spanish. He appears to have been a natural linguist, learning by ear entirely (for he could not read). To speak Spanish as used in Mexico was absolutely necessary, if he stayed, and he probably had realized this. It was the language universally employed, and was a medium even among the Indian tribes of the north.

The lad's career through the two years following is somewhat hard to understand, when one thinks of his career thereafter, and considered also that his brothers were in and out of Taos and Santa Fe. Although he was now at American headquarters, and under the tutelage of Kincaid, he was not immediately enlisted with trappers or traders, but served as teamster, interpreter, or cook — pursuing the unattractive fortunes of the usual runaway.

One explanation of this is, that by size and means he had nothing to recommend him. He himself told General

Rusling, many years later, that when he first entered the mountain West he "was too small to set a trap." [10] In type he was ordinary; in appearance he was undistinguished all his life. Few persons, not knowing Kit Carson by reputation, would have picked him out for what he really was. Certainly, the mountain men in old Taos would have hesitated about burdening themselves with a slight greenhorn youth who probably did not look even his years.

He would further be deterred from joining any squad because he had no money, supplies, or weapons. A trap cost twelve dollars in St. Louis, and if he had brought a rifle out with him he must have sold it in a pinch. Taos had nobody who would advance an inexperienced small boy an outfit, on speculation, or be responsible for him; for all we know, Kincaid was poor, himself — trapping, perhaps, no longer. His name seems not to appear anywhere among the fur hunts of that period.

In the spring the native population would be dispersing into the fields — but the *rancheros* would tender no living wage to a *gringo*. And what other opportunities would Taos present, with no industries except a distillery or two on the outskirts, with all the winter's money concentrated by spring in the hands of the saloons and gambling houses, and with traders from the States now squeezing the country still drier?

Going down to Santa Fe again, when it was approaching caravan time, having seen the world to the end of his rope, young Kit could do naught but join a caravan leaving on a spring trip to Missouri. Willynilly, he was homeward bound. But at the ford of the Arkansas, a little over half way, they met a Franklin spring caravan, outward headed for Santa Fe. To this caravan Carson transferred his allegiance and turned back with it, to Santa Fe once more.

He was tiding himself along; whatever mirage of romance and golden hope had lured him from home was now vanished, and there remained only the desperate desire to scratch out a living. Back again in Santa Fe, Kit Carson's sole ambition was not scalp nor pelt, but the simple necessity of a woolen shirt. The means for this he earned, at last, by engaging as a teamster with an outfit out of Santa Fe for El Paso del Norte.

Traders from Missouri, as has been said, frequently extended their operations south of Santa Fe, down the Rio Grande and clear to Chihuahua of Old Mexico. Old El Paso, today of Texas, was in 1827 the gateway to the Department of Chihuahua. It was known familiarly among traders as " the Pass " — the name being attributed to the ford here (Ruxton), to the course of the river between two high points (Gregg), or to the retreat of refugees from the north southward, after the Pueblo revolt of 1680 (Gregg). In the boy Carson's time El Paso was noted chiefly for its grape products — " Pass brandy " and " Pass wine." A bottle of either seems to have been a valued concomitant of a Mexican meal. Gregg compares the wine to Malaga, and another traveler compares it to Burgundy.

The caravan trail to El Paso was 320 miles of the trail to Chihuahua, which was still 230 miles onward. It was a trail not without excitement, frequented by bandits and hovered over by the Apaches, for the last two hundred miles of its course totally unsettled, and divided into such delightful stages as the *Jornada del Muerto* (Day's Journey of the Dead), the forbidding *Laguna del Muerto* (Dead Man's Lake), a gloomy cañon wherein the avid Apache loved to lurk, and the *Ojo del Muerto* (Dead Man's Spring) at the farther end of it.

Having made the El Paso trip, in the fall Kit Carson sought Taos again, as the place to spend the winter. But no mention is made of his old friend, the mountain man Kincaid, who may have " gone under," or have changed his location. The haven this second winter, 1827-28, for

the wanderer, was the quarters of Ewing Young, trader
and captain of trappers. Here Carson, eighteen years of
age, cooked for his board.

In the spring of 1828 the luckless Kit was again foot-
loose. It is strange that if his abilities as a hunter and
woodsman were already pronounced, in promise of his
later eminence, he was not enrolled under Captain Young,
who was (as we know) now actively in the trading and fur
business. But instead, deserted, as in the spring before,
by his gods, lad Kit once more turned his face to the east
and to Missouri, with an annual caravan. And as in the
spring before, meeting an opposite caravan at the ford
of the Arkansas, with it he retraced his course to Santa
Fe. By this time he was fluent in Spanish as it was spoken
throughout Mexico. As interpreter for Colonel Tramell,
a trader (whose name I have not again encountered),
he enlisted for the long journey of 550 miles to Chihuahua;
first south to El Paso del Norte, thence inclining into the
west, and occupying forty days.

I can fancy that Kit Carson'was glad of the chance to
visit Chihuahua, the capital of that department, with a
reputation as a city far superior to that of Santa Fe, and
now practically the farthest point to which American traders
as yet penetrated. Here in Chihuahua, so remote from Missouri and yet more closely connected with it through trade
than is the case today, young Carson, the wanderer, encountered an old acquaintance (by hearsay if not by person), that
Robert McKnight whose return to Missouri, by way of
Franklin, in 1822, after nine years' imprisonment in the
Chihuahua *calabozo*, had been chronicled in the *Intelligencer*. His brother John, who had rescued him, had since
been killed, and Robert himself was back in Chihuahua
and vicinity, the first American after Pike to exploit the
region. He was at this time endeavoring to recoup from his
initial hard experience, by trading and by mining in the

ancient copper prospects near the Rio Gila, to the north. The mines being worked by McKnight were in that old *Santa Rita del Cobre* (Saint Rita of the Copper) district in southwestern New Mexico. From them McKnight was planning to make a fortune; the gold in the ore paid the expenses of getting it out, and hauling it and refining it, so that the copper was clear gain. It was mined, with pick and shovel only, in great masses of red oxide. But the country was thoroughly Apache, and before McKnight had made his fortune he was working with as much ease as if he had been in a den of rattlesnakes.

Trading and mining together, McKnight had wagons and pack trains continually shuttling between his outpost and the Chihuahua settlements. Following his incarceration through those nine years, the pendulum must have swung well to the opposite end of the arc; to mine or to trade with the Indians, in Mexico, and particularly in this portion, was, for an American, hedged about with much favor and declaration, and with many open palms.

To Robert McKnight Kit Carson hired out as teamster on the copper mines road; worked thus through the fall of 1828, passed his nineteenth birthday probably in Chihuahua, where Christmas would be celebrated by strange native plays, and spent the main part of the winter 1828-29 at the mines.

McKnight had not been the only American at the copper mines. The Patties, of Kentucky and Missouri, had made the place headquarters between trips farther westward after fur. Other " investors," also, had taken their turn at these mines; so that here had grown up quite a village of low adobe huts for the peons and officials. Later a fort was erected, triangular in shape, with angle bastions. The ruins of fort and huts were noted when in 1846, through this very spot pushed General Kearny's overland column to California.

CHAPTER VI

THE TRAPPER'S TRAIL — 1829

HOWEVER, Kit Carson had nearly reached another crossroads in his career, and the trail was about to broaden. In this interior of Mexico, before foreign blood and foreign methods had invigorated it, the Anglo-Saxon was swallowed; he could only adopt the life as it was; his very name became Spanish; and he became Mexican. In *Don Santiago Querque,* who of the North would recognize Jim Kirker, Scotch trapper? Yet Don Santiago Querque it was, thus incorporated with the citizenship, who led relentless expeditions from Sonora against the savages.

Had Kit Carson stayed among the dons and the peons, as laborer and later as employer of cheap labor, he might eventually have vanished from history, as did Robert McKnight; he could have lived easily, by the customs of the country, and have died rich, but quickly to be forgotten. What impelled him, like a homing bird, toward Taos again, in the early spring of 1829, we may not know. Whether the Apaches temporarily interrupted the mining, whether he had a little money in pocket once more, whether now in the caravan season he preferred the caravan trail to the ore trail, or whether he was just sick for the sight of Americans other than McKnight and his fellows, and for news of his own country, who can say? But leaving McKnight (who in due course made a fortune, and encouraged thereto by the Apaches settled down in Chihuahua to enjoy it), having signed with no caravan in Santa Fe, he arrived in Taos at the end of March, when the trapper parties would be setting out into the beaver country. Here he found Captain

,Ewing Young, and almost immediately was engaged, at last, as a trapper. For Captain Young and Taos were both on the alert, a company which the captain had dispatched for the Rio Gila country, on a spring hunt, having trailed in, driven back by the Apaches.

This was not necessarily unexpected; and very likely it was deserved. Bad as he has since proved, in the beginning of his intercourse with the invading whites the Apache was not as a rule unfriendly or vicious. He soon grew to hate with fierce hatred the Spanish and their descendants, the Mexicans, and met deceit and rapine with rapine and deceit.

You have taken New Mexico, and will soon take California; go, then, and take Chihuahua, Durango and Sonora. We will help you. You fight for land; we care nothing for land; we fight for our rights and for food. The Mexicans are rascals; we hate them and will kill them all.

After such manner spoke the Apache chief to General Kearny, in explaining that Americans were safe; and he fairly well set forth the situation. But it came to be with the Apaches as with the other Indians of the West: they must fight; and once settled down to hostility toward everybody who wore a hat, they accepted their enforced role.

However, it is with this spring of 1829 that our narrative is just now dealing, and with a brigade of forty men, including Kit Carson, about to set forth, under Ewing Young, from old Taos, to punish the Apaches and to trap the Gila and the Colorado.

Immediately upon the report from his defeated detachment, Ewing Young reorganized, reinforced, and led the brigade himself. By virtue of his three winters in the country, the last passed in the exposed districts of the " copper mines," and by virtue also of his previous acquaintance with Captain Young, Kit Carson was, as said, given a berth.

When this expedition had left, Taos must have been pretty well cleaned out of able-bodied mountain men; the time was the first week of April, and the spring hunt had long been summoning into plain and hill.

The roll of this Ewing Young company is still uncalled. The members were Americans, French-Canadians, Germans; no doubt a few Mexicans, and men of mixed blood. Only a few names of the forty have been preserved: Ewing Young's, because he was a leader; Kit Carson's, because he had a Boswell; James Higgins', because he shot "big" James Lawrence — who therefore, also received honorable mention — and Francois Turcôte, Jean Vaillant, Anastase Curier, because they mutinied.

The expedition did not make course at once into the Southwest and for the Rio Gila. It had no trapping or trading license from the Mexican government — nor did Captain Ewing Young intend that it should thus be mulcted.

To understand the license requirement, it must be remembered that the Mexicans themselves would not trap. That was too hard work, and too dangerous. Even as late as 1846 Lieutenant Johnston, of the American column to California, remarking the tameness and prevalence of fur-bearing animals along the Rio Grande del Norte, close to Mexican settlement, adds, "these creatures will not rejoice in the change of Government."

And while the natives would not trap, under Spanish rule foreigners could not trap, except by challenging confiscation for their furs and the *calabozo* for themselves. But after Mexico became an independent republic in 1821, licenses were issued to foreigners for hunting and trapping and trading. As New Mexico was presumed to extend to the Arkansas on the north, and westward indefinitely, it covered the main fur territory of the South, and therefore the great proportion of trapping and hunting licenses were issued from Santa Fe. At first the permissions were granted only with the stipulation that a certain number of the natives should be taken along by the foreigners and "shown how." Later this stipulation was omitted; but at all times the license was a rather spasmodic instrument, with a bad recoil.

Often a license soon after being issued would be declared void because it had been issued under a previous administration. The rise and fall of political parties in New Mexico was so frequent and so sudden that the returning traveler could not foretell what policy he would encounter. It was alleged by Americans that although the license might be pronounced valid, the Mexican officials were not above hiring Indians or other desperadoes to follow the trapper and to rob him of his goods.

However, in many cases the trapper or trader was not an innocent offender. He penetrated into Mexican territory without leave, and took the risk of being unable to evade the authorities or to fight his way out if caught. He was reckless, overbearing, and defiant, treating the Mexicans much as he treated the Indians.

Captain Ewing Young, therefore, took out no license for his party of this April, 1829. He seems to have had some excuse for his course. In the previous year he and Milton Sublette, having trapped under a license from Governor Narbona, were arrested and their furs confiscated by order of his successor, Governor Armijo. A change in the administration had occurred during their absence. The confiscated furs were spread out to dry, before the *guardia*, in Santa Fe; whereupon Sublette boldly seized two packs which belonged to him, carried them off, and secreted them and himself among friends. The whole military force was called against him, and the enraged Armijo even had cannon leveled against a suspected house; but the plucky Sublette finally saved his two packs and himself, reaching the frontier. What Captain Young was doing, Gregg (the chronicler) does not mention. Farnham alludes to the fact that Young " had been plundered by the Mexican authorities of $18,000 or $20,000 worth of fur "; but whether this time or another time, is left in doubt.

As a subterfuge, to cloak overcurious eyes, Young marched his company northward out of Taos, taking possibly the usual trappers' trail, which led over the Raton Pass and down to the Arkansas — a trail which the earliest caravans had used, and which·after the establishment of the historic Bent's Fort was a beaten highway. But long before reaching the Arkansas, beyond which was American territory, the party swung to the southwest, recrossed the ridge, and descended into the latitude which they had just left. There was slight danger that anybody would now ask for a license. Before lay only that wide desert expanse, from the Rio Grande to the Pacific coast, from Chihuahua of Old Mexico to the Salt Lake, totally uninhabited by white people and as yet scarcely trodden by Americans.

Strange to say, although this section of the West was the first to be explored, it was the last to be exploited. The country of the *conquistadors* and the *padres*, penetrated by Cabeza and Estevan in 1531, by Friar Marcos in 1539, traversed by Coronado, Diaz, Alarcon, 1540-1542, and thereafter by Fathers Lopez, Rodriguez, Santa Maria, by Father Baltran and Don Espejo, Oñate, the Jesuit Kino and his companions, establishing missions along the Gila and the lower Colorado, by Garces in 1774, by Escalante in 1776, it remained as in the beginning. The trails of hoof and sandal made so bravely endured not even in memory; for half a century after Escalante's feat, the great, wondrous region between the Rio Grande del Norte and the California coast was all unmolested by any outsider. The missions were deserted, the native ceased to worship his little crosses, the fabulous cities lost their fascination, and the Indian became the *conquistador,* levying upon that civilization which had attempted to levy upon him, the feeble efforts of which had dwindled into but a few shallow indentations along the southern borders. So the Southwest slumbered again.

But the Northwest was awakening everywhere. The contrast was an efficient lesson in the difference between New World and Old World government — between American and Spanish supremacy. Since 1803, the date of the opening of Louisiana Province to the Anglo-Saxon, or during but half of that fifty years while the Southwest slept, under impetus from Saxon and Gaul, Americans together, the Northwest had advanced more than had this same Southwest in its three centuries from 1531 and Cabeza. Trappers, American and French, were exploring the secret places of Wyoming, Montana, Idaho, Oregon, Utah, broadening old trails and making new ones, preparing the way for the hosts of civilization. But western New Mexico, Arizona, Nevada remained uncharted and neglected.

However, the Ewing Young party was not the very first expedition of Saxon proclivities to invade the waiting region. From 1776 — the year of American Independence, which signified naught to this vivid, sunny area, some day, nevertheless, to profit by it — until 1824 there is no record of alien foot set upon sands beyond the Rio Bravo — the Rio Grande del Norte — of New Mexico, save at the copper mines, or as Apache and Navajo returned to their haunts with Spanish-Mexican prisoners, or as occasional punitive columns, in revenge, darted from the white settlements of east and south, and back again. Then, in the spring of 1824, from Missouri boldly struck out the Pattie party of trappers and traders; first determined upon the Northwest, soon, however, to turn and travel down to Santa Fe and on to the Gila of Arizona, which at that time was Nueva Mejico.

Father and son were the Patties — Sylvester and James Ohio, Kentuckians (of course) acclimated to Missouri, the new country. Having thus penetrated to the Southwest, they divided much of their time for two years between the " copper mines," where they preceded Kit Carson, and the " Heelay " to the west; they followed the Gila down to the Colorado; ascended along the Colorado past the Grand Cañon, pushing northward even to the Yellowstone in Wyoming; and ended their wanderings in 1828, in prison at Sta. Catarina of Lower California.[11]

It is claimed that in 1826 Richard Campbell, an early trader of New Mexico, and later a prosperous *ranchero* near Santa Fe, took a pack train across the desert from Santa Fe to San Diego.[12] As has been noted, Ewing Young himself had been trapping, evidently, in southwestern territory, with Milton Sublette, and moreover had just sent out another venture, for the Colorado. So that, having such precedents, the student of early Southwestern history must realize that trapping parties aside from those of the Patties, of Young and Sublette may have been roaming hither and thither, through this region, working, playing, fighting, feasting, suffering, with no pen or pencil to jot down their journeyings.

The Ewing Young party of April, 1829, if not the first expedition since the Spaniards to brave the waiting, inhospitable depths, at least was the first of the kind successfully to cross from the settlements of the Rio Grande to the Pacific coast, and back again. It undoubtedly was encouraged thereto by the reports from the Pattie enterprise; but it seems to have effectually broken the trail through and to have proved what could be done.

CHAPTER VII

TO THE GRAND CANYON, AND ON

SO, AS it happened, Kit Carson, who was to make a name in the Northwest, was to win his spurs in the South-west. A wonderful journey now lay before him. The trail first cut down diagonally through the northwestern corner of the present New Mexico — the realm of the well-formed, light-complexioned, proudly-independent Nav-ajos. Like the Apaches, in the beginning they were friendly to the *Americano* — that is, not openly hostile. But before their men now young had become old, Kit Carson was their conqueror.

After leaving the Navajo country the expedition crossed Zuñi land, the people of which had gained wide, although undeserved, fame as being " white." Thus Father de Nica had defined them in 1539 through seeing, doubtless, one of their albinos.[18] Leaving Zuñi the expedition entered what is today Arizona, and traversing toward the south this home of the Apache, came upon the head of the Rio Salido, or Salt River — on modern maps the Salido. The Salido rises near the New Mexican line, and flowing west through east central Arizona empties into the Gila, of which it is the largest tributary.

Thus far the Ewing Young party had traveled as in a hurry, and by route direct — tracing again, perhaps, the course of that first party which had been turned back. As evidence of all this, it is recorded that upon the sources of the Salido one object was achieved; here were encoun-tered the same Apaches who had been concerned in the previous attack.

But whether the same, or not, it would have made little difference to the trappers. When a Navajo's wife died, he was under obligations to go out and kill somebody. And borrowing from the Indian, the trapper, when an offense had been committed against him or his, took vengeance, if not upon the very offender, then upon the tribe. In this respect savage and frontiersman were much alike.

Seeing the Apaches, the Ewing Young company lured them on with a show of weakness, until they caught them in an ambush and shot down fifteen by crossfire from rifle and pistol. The rest fled.

Having exacted blood atonement, and cleared the way, the Ewing Young trappers might proceed to gather their furs. The valley of the Salt River was and is of exceeding romantic interest; ruins of large towns, *acequias*, or irrigating aqueducts twenty-five feet wide, myriad fragments of pottery, speak of a vanished civilization. While on the road out from Taos the expedition had passed the Chaco Cañon, the pueblo of Zuñi, El Moro or Inscription Rock, and many another witness, mute or speaking, to bygone epochs. But the route, and the Salt River, and what must have been sighted thereafter, have come down to us only in Indians and fur; as unromantic a narration as the *parasangs* of the Anabasis.

The Rio Salido (christened in 1698 by busy Father Kino, who upon one of his pilgrimages surveyed it from a hilltop) is at first a swift, cold mountain stream, until rushing out of the range it enters a series of richly alluvial flats, and swirling on, with rapid, clear current, finally merges with the Gila, in central Arizona. During the lower half of its course it flows over a bed of pure salt, so that its waters are perceptibly brackish. This was another of the wonders which Father Kino met.

The Salido, wherever its banks were wooded, was a beaver resort. The Ewing Young party trapped down it until they reached the mouth of the Verde, or San Francisco — a tributary coming from the north. As was the custom, they turned and trapped up the San Francisco, to its head. " A fine, large stream," has been said of the San Francisco,

in some cases rapid and deep, in others spreading out into wide lagoons. The ascent * * * by gradual steppes, which, stretching into plains, abounded in timber. The river banks were covered with ruins of stone houses and regular fortifications ; which * * * appeared to have been the work of civilized man, but had not been occupied for centuries. They were built upon the most fertile tracts of the valley, where were signs of *acequias* and cultivation.[14]

Indians bothered the trappers almost nightly from the time they reached the San Francisco. Trapped animals were killed and animals and traps stolen. Meanwhile much fur was " caught." Twenty-two of the men were dispatched back to Taos, with the pelts, there to sell them and to buy more traps, for a fall hunt. Retaining seventeen men (among them Kit Carson), and now stocked with the traps of the Taos-bound party, Captain Young decided to strike in the opposite direction, for California.

His retention of Kit Carson is the first definite token that the future celebrity was making good. During the two years and more that Carson had been in the far West his career would not indicate any sudden rise. On the contrary, his offices as wrangler, teamster, and cook, and his failure to be enrolled with the enterprises of these mountain men whom he had met, would relegate him to the ordinary crowd. But when Captain Young divided his company, he would discard the chaff — the weak, the laggard, the inefficient — for return to Taos, and would keep, for the California trail, only the tried and true.

He was now, probably, in the vicinity of Bill Williams Mountain, seventy-five or eighty miles northeast of Prescott, Arizona. Thereabouts the modern traveler disembarks at the station of Williams, en route for the Grand Cañon to the north. And he was, roughly speaking, half way from Taos to the coast. However, California could have been but little known to Ewing Young or his men, as yet, and the distance to be covered must have been only guessed at. Commercial intercourse between New Mexico and California had not yet been established. But lured by some report or by some notion, as if the Golden State were already wielding its magic wand, making his own trail across the grimmest of deserts, Ewing Young led his seventeen men onward to the West.

Warned by friendly Indians (possibly wandering Mohaves, but more likely Tonto Apaches, a degraded tribe frequenting the Bill Williams country) that a dry *entrada* or march, was ahead, the California-bound party remained in camp, around the sources of the San Francisco, for several days, to provision with meat and water. But they killed only three deer.

We are accustomed to look upon the western hills and plains of early days as swarming with game; and so, according to many chronicles, they were. But the game then, as today, was erratic. Here around Bill Williams Mountain were abundant timber, grass, and springs of the great San Francisco forest tract, a favorite resort of deer and antelope; yet the eighteen trappers, good shots all and versed in hunting craft, secured only the three animals.

Making tanks of hides they filled them with water; sufficient, it was hoped, to last the *entrada* through. The flesh was jerked or dry cured. Then, mainly afoot, and driving before them their pack mules, they started upon an unknown way, for the Sacramento Valley, which lay somewhere in Nueva California, far beyond a waterless stretch of one hundred and eighteen miles.

Their course was northwest, and must have been right

across the desolate Colorado Plateau, which borders the Grand Cañon of the Colorado on the south. "A more frightfully arid region probably does not exist upon the face of the earth," says Lieutenant Ives, in his report of the government expedition of 1857-58. His route southward from the Grand Cañon must very nearly coincide with that of the Ewing Young party, northward, thirty years before. The Ives description is vivid: A rolling plateau with occasional thick growths of pines and cedars; with expanses of loose, porous soil wherein the mules sank to their fetlocks; with sharp slopes, forming small, higher plateaus, and unexpected, sheer, impassable *cañoncitos*, or ravines, sometimes so thickly intersecting that the plateau was shattered like a ruin; with an intensely hot sun streaming down through a dry, thin air that sucked moisture from the body; with not an animate thing encountered; and finally, with mules staggering along as if drunken, and men's brains afire with the scorching rays.

Ours has been the first, and will doubtless be the last, party of whites to visit this profitless locality. It seems intended by nature that the Colorado River, along the greater portion of its lonely and majestic way, shall be forever unvisited and undisturbed. The handful of Indians that inhabit the sequestered retreats where we discovered them have probably remained in the same condition, and of the same number, for centuries. The country could not support a large population, and by some provision of nature they have ceased to multiply. The deer, the antelope, the birds, even the smaller reptiles, all of which frequent the adjacent territory, have deserted this uninhabitable district. Excepting when the melting snows send their annual torrents through the avenues to the Colorado, conveying with them sound and motion, these dismal abysses, and the arid table-lands that enclose them, are left, as they have been for ages, in unbroken solitude and silence. The lagoons by the side of which we are encamped furnish, as far as we have been able to discover, the only accessible watering-place west of the mouth of Diamond River. During the summer it is probable they are dry, and that no water exists upon the whole of the Colorado Plateau.[16]

But Lieutenant Ives' party was not the first. The *padres* had preceded him. Cardenas, in 1540, and Garces, in 1776, had penetrated this portion of the great, lonely plateau guarding the south approach to the Grand Cañon. And the party of Ewing Young, containing Kit Carson, were the first Americans, and the first white men after Garces, to cross it.

It was in the middle of April that the Ives expedition traversed the Colorado Plateau; the time of the Young party must have been June or July (they had trapped on the way), so that the region was yet drier. To trace absolutely the trappers' trail is impossible; we can only see them, in our mind's eye, toiling on and on, northwest from the San Francisco country, pigmies amidst the wide desolation of gigantic ruin, *conquistadors* and *padres* again, whose hope was no seven cities nor savage souls, but simply fur. Through four days they had water from the hide tanks doled out to them; each night an armed guard was placed over the scant supply; but when four days had passed they came upon other water, camped beside it for two days, and rested. This may have been the lagoons mentioned by Ives, in the extract just preceding, and located toward the northwestern edge of the plateau, or it may have been a pool or spring (of which there are several) lower down.

From the camp beside the water it was another four days' *entrada*, of hunger and thirst (pleasantly broken, at the close, by purchase from some Mohave Indians of a tidbit in shape of an old mare) to the Colorado, which was struck at the Grand Cañon. I am inclined to think that this point was near the western end of the Grand Cañon proper, or about at the sharp elbow (on the map) where is marked Diamond Creek and the present Walapai reservation.

It " failed not to awaken a thrill of delight in every member of the party," inscribes Peters, Carson's earliest biographer. The rest is left to the imagination of the reader. But this we know: from the time of Cardenas, who, traveling up from the south in 1540, was the first white person to stand upon the cañon brink, until today, none can have gazed into this mighty chasm without an overpowering rush of feeling. This was the point where the Ives expedition, after having experienced a long succession of only slightly lesser cañons below, came upon it.

At the end of ten miles the ridge of the swell was attained, and a splendid panorama burst suddenly into view. In the foreground were low table-lands, intersected by numberless ravines; beyond these a lofty line of bluffs marked the edge of an immense cañon; a wide gap was directly ahead, and through it were beheld, to the extreme limit of vision, vast plateaus, towering one above the other thousands of feet in the air, the long horizontal bands broken at intervals by wide and profound abysses, and extending a hundred miles to the north, till the deep azure blue faded into a light cerulean tint that blended with the dome of the heavens. The famous " Big Cañon " was before us; and for a long time we paused in wondering delight, surveying this stupendous formation through which the Colorado and its tributaries break their way.[16]

As far as is recorded, the Ewing Young party was the second party of Americans to see the Grand Cañon. The Patties, two years before, must have seen it — and their remarks upon the nature of the country are less in admiration than in a great desire to be free of it. Jedediah S. Smith and party (of whom more will be told, presently) did not, probably, see it; they saw only the cañons further down. Before the Patties and Smith, were but the Spanish;

after them, came Ewing Young, Kit Carson, James Lawrence, James Higgins, the three Frenchmen, and their
comrades whose names no man knows.

On the brink of the Grand Cañon the Ewing Young
party now stayed three days, recouping while doubtless
also vainly wondering if it were possible to cross this tremendous gorge. But pass there was none. Mohaves from
the south found the camp, and brought in a small quantity
of corn and black beans. From these Mohaves the trappers
would learn that southward the walls lowered, and a crossing existed. Having rested, the Ewing Young party therefore diverged from the Cañon, and traveling southwest for
three days, by this short cut of the big bend which projects
from northwestern Arizona into Nevada, reached the river
again at the valley home of the Mohaves, where Nevada
tapers to a slender point between Arizona and California.

A people warlike, able to defend themselves, sturdy,
independent, proud, but generally just and friendly to the
whites, have been the Mohaves; devoted less to the chase
than to the raising of corn, squash, and beans, upon the
river bottoms, their land, and to tattooing of their bronze
bodies. The men have been noted for their fine, tall stat-
ures. When aroused they are fierce fighters and as mer-
ciless as other Indians.

The Ewing Young party were not the first trappers who
had visited them. The Patties had passed up the Colorado,
from the mouth of the Gila, two years before; and three
years before Jedediah Smith and party on a beaver hunt
from Utah had passed down, on the same side (the east)
from the mouth of the Virgin River in what is now southeastern Nevada. Bound from the Salt Lake of Utah to the
teeming streams of California was Smith; the first man, he,
to lead across the desert which lies between. At the Virgin
he crossed the Colorado to the east bank; at the Mohave villages he crossed back again by raft, to the west bank, thence

journeying boldly on southwest into the sands, for California. The Mohaves had been friendly; but when he would have repeated the trip, the next year, incited by the Spanish of California to keep the *gringo* out they attacked his raft in midstream and of the eighteen men killed ten. Smith' himself escaped, with his wounded, to reach San Diego by that parching desert trail which he had broken the year before.[17]

Taos being, we may easily believe, the center of mountain gossip in the far West, and Smith and the Sublettes having been associates in the trapping business, the chances are that Captain Young was informed as to Smith's movements — just as he must have been informed, by word from the copper mines and Santa Fe, if not more directly, of the journeyings of the Patties. So he doubtless was upon his guard against the Mohaves. The Colorado was to be crossed by means of the Mohaves' rafts, for although a river people, the Mohaves never have possessed boats or canoes.

The one contemporary biography, upon which all other biographies have been based, states that in the vicinity of the Jedediah Smith " massacre " (when the Indians are the victors in a fight, "massacre" is the proper word), on their route the Ewing Young party met with a dry river, rising in the coast ranges and leading " northeast " into the Great Basin. This they followed for several days before they came to water in it. Making due allowance for errors of geography natural to the first trip in a new country forty years before the same trip was chronicled, we may assume this dry river to have been the Mohave, of the modern map, in San Bernardino County of southern California. There is no other stream with the faculty of flowing " bottom-side up," between the Mohave Valley and Los Angeles, which one might follow for several days' travel, or say one hundred miles.

This is a very singular stream. It may be said to run south-eastwardly about two hundred miles, and empty into the Colorado. But on all its length it does not run two miles without entirely disappearing in the sand. So that it presents to the traveler a long line of little rippling lakes, from two to two and a half feet deep, at one time sunken among hard flinty hills or piles of drifting sands, and at others gurgling through narrow vales covered with grass, and fields and forests in which live the deer, the black bear, the elk, the hare, and many a singing bird.[18]

In four days from the erratic river the trappers arrived at the mission of San Gabriel, near El Pueblo de los Angeles which is today Los Angeles city. This was a welcome station, one goal upon the march of over a thousand miles just for fur. When we read of the distance covered, the perils braved, the discomforts endured, by the western trapper, we can but marvel. It was the prospector's gamble.

CHAPTER VIII

AMERICAN TRAPPERS IN CALIFORNIA

SO HERE was Captain Ewing Young, and here with
him were Kit Carson and the rest, gaunt, burned,
bearded, or bristly, in tattered, patched buckskins, but
steady-eyed, unabashed, handling easily their long rifles,
and, in sooth, a little company compact and formidable.

The missions of California still were prosperous, although
hampered by interference from the new overlord, the republic of Mexico. Materiality was succeeding spirituality, and
the end was near, for secularization loomed upon the horizon and already the priesthood was divided, its powers
upon the wane.

However, they yet were fat, these splendid missions, oozing oil and wine, gathering about them those flocks and
herds and lands coveted by the State which had not earned
them. San Gabriel Arcangel, old (lacking but two years
of being the oldest) and honorable, was proud mistress
over 1,000 Indians, 70,000 neat cattle, 4,200 horses, 400
mules, 54,000 sheep; its vines produced annually 200 barrels of brandy, and twice as much wine; and here were
stationed a priest, and fifteen Mexican soldiers serving as
guard.[19]

The governor of Alta California, in this summer of 1829,
was Colonel Jose Maria Echeandia, " a man of scholastic
bent and training and of Castilian lisp." He it was who
had maintained such close espionage upon Jedediah Smith;
he it was who had retained the Patties: for, first man as he
was to penetrate by land into California, Captain Smith
had been arrested and expelled — pursued by suspicion all

the way from San Gabriel to San Jose of the north; and the Patties, the second Americans to enter by land, likewise were arrested, the father to die. The Hudson Bay Company, entering from the north, knew how to conciliate the authorities; but the American freebooter, as a rule disregarding those niceties of intercourse which marked the *gente de razon* and *gente fina*, was unwelcome.

So Ewing Young did not tarry at San Gabriel; his party, the third one of Americans thus invading from the interior, not only were American trappers, but they had no license — or other conciliations. So Captain Young paused in his course only to trade four butcher knives for a fat ox, and hastened on before the *presidio* of San Diego, under whose protection the mission was, should have been notified. Moreover, the summer was advancing and the valleys of the North waited.

Northward this little party pressed; past the famous olive orchard mission of San Fernando Rey de España, but a short march of thirty miles from San Gabriel, stopping here only an hour or two, and hastening onward. The rounded hills of a landscape already browning in a California summer waxed richer in natural resources; and by reason of streams, herbage, and groves was a pleasing contrast to the desert behind. Such a region, under the soft California sky where never a cloud appeared, roamed over by vast quantities of deer, elk, bear, and wild horses must have appeared as trappers' paradise.

Few civilized beings could have been met. The twenty-one missions, the four *presidios*, San Diego, Santa Barbara, Monterey, and San Francisco; the pueblos, de los Angeles, Monterey, Yerba Buena and San Jose de Guadalupe, all were along the seaboard; the route of the trappers was inland, up the middle of the present state, towards the Sacramento Valley. The settlement by Anglo-Saxons also was entirely by sea and upon the coast — captains of American and English vessels and their supercargoes being the chief *gringo* residents.

Up through the pleasant land pushed the Ewing Young party, until in the Tulare Valley, amidst sign of beaver and otter, they found fresh sign of other trappers. Here had entered the alert, energetic Hudson Bay Company, to glean along the trail of Jedediah Smith.

Perhaps disappointed, and no doubt spurred to renewed endeavor for the purpose of overtaking and passing their rivals, the Ewing Young company made greater haste. They emerged upon the noble San Joaquin (Joachim), where with sweep from the west into the north it continues on through its lush valley for the yet far distant bay.

Trap signs were constant; somebody had been reaping the harvest; and upon the lower San Joaquin the Americans overtook a party in the employ of the Hudson Bay Company of Vancouver, under command of that Peter Skene Ogden for whom Ogden, Utah, is named.

As neither party would let the other go ahead, and as Captain Young must have been too shrewd a trapper and trader to trust much in any professions by that powerful corporation of the Northwest, whose country he really was invading, the two must trap together, more or less amicably. To this, Ogden probably was nothing loath, for he was a jovial, easy-going man, fond of social amenities of the wilderness. And as he had been in the valley since the preceding fall, his packs were heavy with fur.

The two parties trapped down the San Joaquin to its delta, at Suisun Bay, which is the innermost extension of the Bay of San Francisco, and crossed over to the Sacramento. Now was it well into the summer; the fur season was done; the Ogden party, their mules laden high, proceeded up the Sacramento Valley for the Pitt River country beyond, and for Vancouver; the Young party turned back for the lower San Joaquin, and went into camp.

The summer passed with no interference from the jealous Californian government. It is likely that the soldiery of the missions of the few *presidios* cherished a wholesome respect for American trapper rifles. Little was to be gained by armed conflict. And at Monterey Captain Young possessed a friend in residence: Captain Cooper, of famous surname (as witness the Missouri Coopers), but not more definitely designated, and said to be not a woodsman but a seaman, now in business at Monterey.[20]

Fortunately, the Taosans were enabled to be of service to the mission San Jose, situated some twenty or thirty miles westward from the camp, and seventy miles north of the town Monterey. Powerful and rich was San Jose, raising much grain. From eighty bushels of wheat sown were gathered 8,600 bushels. It grazed 60,000 cattle, and in 1825 was suzerain over 3,000 Indians. But it was reputed to be a harsh taskmaster; and in this July, of 1829, the *alcalde* came to the trappers' camp on a hunt for runaway neophytes. He had pursued them to an Indian village, where he had been defeated.[21]

A few years before (in 1826), by the Republic of Mexico a decree had been issued, applying to California, setting free mission Indians. But spiritual power was slow to resign to temporal; and the missions clung to their home-rule policy. The *alcalde* was determined to capture and punish the San Jose refugees.

The camp of the Americans (recognized as invaders, heretics, and ruffians, but great fighters) was appealed to, and twelve men, Kit Carson of course being one, volunteered to help. Thus augmented, the mission force returned to the attack, the village was captured, and " one-third of its inhabitants killed." The demand to deliver over the refugees " was complied with."

Relying now upon the obligations of the mission, Captain Young, a few days after this affair, visited it and engaged

to trade in some furs for horses, of which he was in need.
Tallow, grain, hides, beef, and wine were the California
missions' main support; augmented occasionally by furs
from the stock of foreign trappers (the natives would not
trap), as in this case. Either through the mission, or direct,
Captain Young disposed of his pelts to the skipper of a
schooner, which had put in to Monterey harbor, and took
back to camp with him a fresh outfit of horses. Almost
immediately sixty of the animals were stolen from the camp
cavvy by Indians who sneaked in at night; a revenge, no
doubt, by those savages whom the trappers had needlessly
rendered hostile toward them.

This was serious, as it left only fourteen animals. Evidently Kit Carson, youth though he was, had been demon-
strating that caution and boldness combined, directed by
intuitive right choice, which set him above the majority of
his contemporaries; for Captain Young put him at the
head of ten other trappers, and sent him in pursuit of the
thieves. After a ride of one hundred miles, into the Sierra
Nevada Mountains, the marauders were surprised in the
very act of feasting upon six of the horses; eight were
killed, the rest were routed, and with the regained horses
and three captured Indian children the victorious squad
returned to the waiting camp.

It may here be remarked that whereas the forest and
prairie Indian of the East and the plains and mountain
Indian of the West differed by the use of the horse, the
animal was not at first put to the same purpose by all the
Western tribes. The Eastern Indian traveled either afoot
or by canoe; the plains and the majority of the mountain
Indians traveled horseback, but a portion of the desert
Indians, and of the California Indians, ate the horse rather
than rode him. This was especially the case with those
more or less indolent or impoverished tribes, such as the
Diggers, the Californians, and even the Mohaves.

THE PUEBLO OF LOS ANGELES, CAL.
AT THE TIME OF CARSON'S SECOND VISIT, 1853
(From Vol. V, Pacific Railroad Survey)

OLD FORT UNION, NEW MEXICO, 1853.
SIXTY MILES SOUTHEAST OF TAOS
(Sketch by Lieut. Col. Eaton in Davis' New Mexico and her People)

A CARSON LETTER

DICTATED AND SIGNED BY HIM WHILE COMMANDING OFFICER AT FORT GARLAND, COLO. TERRITORY, ADDRESSED TO MAJOR (BREVET LIEUT. COL.) A. H. PFEIFFER HIS FORMER COMRADE-AT-ARMS, AND IN ITS EXPRESSIONS SHOWING CARSON'S WARM, LOYAL HEART.

(Original letter possessed by A. H. Pfeiffer, Jr.)

Fort Garland, C. T.
October 10th, 1867.

Dear Friend.

It is with extreme regret on my
part that the necessities of the service has at
last separated us, as a brother officer of
six years acquaintance, and an intimate
and esteemed friend of a prior [time I]
have long learned to place in [you my]
confidence as an officer and a man. [It]
is useless for me to make any expressions
of my esteem for you, this is known by
all, and better felt than expressed.

Whilst your knowledge of
frontier and Indian life in this country
is unsurpassed, your courage is too well
known to need any endorsement of mine.
Your loss and sufferings since in the
service are of so peculiarly severe a character as to deserve the thanks of a grateful
country, and receive my hearty sympathy
and commisseration.

Receive with this my brotherly regard and Believe me,

Your true friend,

Bvt. Lt. Col. A. H. Pfeiffer,   C. Carson
    Santa Fe, N. M.   B'v't Brig. Gen'l, U. S. Vols.

At the beginning of fall, or in September, 1829, Captain Young broke camp and with his men started back for New Mexico. However, another episode had occurred. Toward the close of that same July three of his French Canadians — Francois Turcôte, Jean Vaillant, and Anastase Curier, before mentioned — deserted, and announced at Monterey that they were going to stay in California. But the doughty captain apprehended them, and on the charge that they owed him money paid to them in advance forced them to return with the party. He brooked no insurrections.

Having retraced the former route to San Fernando mission, thence the captain made the mistake of paying a visit with his party to the near-by Pueblo de los Angeles. His followers may have importuned him for this dissipation, on the eve of leaving upon their long desert march. The action of the three Canadians has shown that in the ranks were turbulent spirits.

El Pueblo de Nuestra Señora la Reina de los Angeles: the Town of Our Lady the Queen of the Angels, was a place of more pretensions than Monterey, and older. In 1830 it had 1,000 inhabitants; and although the houses were little more than hovels of mud, eight feet high, with roofs of reeds and asphaltum, it was known as a "city of gardens," as today. Amusements were many; the trappers determined to have a final "fling." And Captain Young, unable to produce the proper papers at the demand of the vigilant *alcalde,* saw what an error he had committed.

To arrest eighteen rough-and-ready American trappers and deprive them of their arms and outfits was rather more of a task than the small force at the *alcalde's* immediate service could manage. However, with true natural shrewdness taking advantage of the trappers' bent, he did not press the demand but encouraged his citizenship to show the visitors a good time. Abstinence had been over prolonged; the men were reckless; and Captain Young presently had the chagrin of seeing his charges, plied with free brandy about to be made helpless and easy subjects for the *calaboso*. Moreover, he well knew that when reinforcements arrived (as soon they would) from San Gabriel and from the *presidio* of San Diego or Santa Barbara, he and his party, drunk or sober, would be in serious plight.

The Patties, a year before, had been taken off their guard and arrested without valid reason whatsoever, confined at San Diego, and treated most harshly. Captain Young, trapping without papers, had really broken the law; and this meant confiscation of all property, and imprisonment indefinitely. In the crisis he again put reliance upon youthful Carson, who, as was characteristic of him in after years, evidently had kept his head. Carson was directed to take three of the still somewhat sober men, and the extra horses, and to go on; if the captain and the other men did not catch up, in time, they were to be reported in Taos as having been " massacred " by the Mexicans of California. In that case, Captain Young probably had dreams of being revenged.

Carson succeeded in getting his squad together and heading them into the country. The Californians still hung about, but were hoist with their own petard. The other trappers had meanwhile waxed more turbulent, so that a free-for-all fight occurred among them. This would include knives and bullets; James Higgins shot " Big Jim " Lawrence, and the Californians temporarily withdrew to avoid damage. A trapper at a certain stage in his cups was apt to make less of killing either Indian or " greaser " than of killing a comrade.

The short march to water and the night's sleep restored sense to the hardy mountain men, so that on the next day, under realization of their peril and again united with Carson, they hastened on until out of reach by pursuit. They recrossed the San Bernardino Desert, and after nine days' travel out of Los Angeles stood once more upon the brink of the Colorado.

The homeward course was now pursued leisurely down the Colorado and up the Gila, with many stops to trap likely points. As the lower Colorado and the Gila were in the warm latitudes of Arizona, the party could trap all winter. The Colorado itself never could have been a first-class beaver stream; in those deep, rock-bound cañons, between whose bare walls the waters run turgid and fierce, no beaver would live; only in the more placid spots and wider pockets which intervened now and then would the animal be found. But the progress of the Young party was not monotonous. The lower Colorado and the Gila also had been invaded sufficiently by white people — Spanish, Mexicans, and trappers — to produce the usual friction with the Indians there.

On the Colorado, while Kit Carson and two or three comrades were taking care of camp, the other men being out running traps, a large body of Indians came in: probably Chemehuevi, who occupied a valley down from the mouth of the Bill Williams River, below the Mohaves; or Yumas, who dominated the Rio Colorado from the Chemehuevi country to the gulf. Both are of a cunning, thievish nature. Weapons were concealed beneath the visitors' blankets and shirts, and for a moment the camp must have been in a precarious position. Experience of many years has proven that in a case of this kind there is only the one thing to do. Promptness and boldness are necessary; Carson had both. At a word each trapper selected his man and held cocked rifle against him; addressing one of the Indians who spoke Spanish, Carson ordered him to clear out, with his fellows, at once, or the whites would fire. When it comes to exchanging life for life the Indian balks; and the band sullenly left. They may not have planned any harm at all, but the trappers must be on the safe side.

Having for four hundred miles followed down the Colorado, whose rocky cañons, as they proceeded, became less frequent, and whose welcomed stretches of alluvial beaver ground grew more continuous, the Ewing Young trappers arrived at the flat intake of the Gila, in the southwestern extremity of Arizona. They turned from the Colorado (the prime trapping territory was still below) and entered the Gila. This river, the famous and romantic beaver stream of the Southwest, they ascended three hundred miles to the mouth of the San Pedro, above the present town of Florence in south central Arizona.

A typical stream of the desert country of the Southwest, where sands and trap rock enclose fertile valleys, during the last four hundred miles of its course the Gila, at low water, averages one hundred feet wide and two or three feet deep; now flowing through the green, now through the gray, and now through the whitish yellow. Where was brushy growth, beaver were.

At the mouth of the San Pedro, which enters from the south above Florence, the trappers came upon a camp of those Apaches with whom they had had the brush in the previous spring. They promptly charged the camp, taking it by surprise, driving the Indians out and away, and taking possession of their animals.

Then, that night, while the party were camped, in turn, they were aroused by the trampling of hoofs. More of the tribe were approaching, apparently from a raid into the Mexican borders, driving before them a large bunch of stock. No questions were asked and doubtless there was no time for such preliminaries. As promptly as before, the trappers poured in a volley, shot the Indians down or routed them, and on the theory that thieves have no property appropriated the stock.

This last herd contained two hundred or more horses. " To return the animals to their owners was an impossibility," naively chronicles Peters; and in any case we cannot easily picture Captain Young or other old-time trapper riding very far to restore to Mexicans their Apache-stolen stock. The Young party had thus brusquely accumulated many more horses and mules than they could manage, so they retained only the best, killed two for meat, and let the others go — presumably for the Apaches to round up again!

Having thus effectually reëstablished their claim to the country, the company continued to trap, ascending the Gila until, near its sources, across the line into what is today New Mexico, they were opposite the copper mines. Here they abandoned the river and proceeded south the sixty miles to the mines, where Robert McKnight still was mining and trading.

The bales of pelts were stored in some of the old prospect holes and abandoned workings, McKnight engaged to look after them, and marching on with most of his men for Santa Fe, from the innocent authorities there Mr. Young procured license to trade with the Mimbreños Apaches, who frequented the Mimbres River and the copper mines district. When, having journeyed to the mines, the party quickly returned to Santa Fe with a fine amount of beaver, "everyone considered the trappers had made a very good trade!"

It is stated that the fur aggregated two thousand pounds — which would be some fifteen hundred skins, as a beaver skin weighs about a pound and a quarter — and that twelve dollars a pound was paid. If true, this price was exceptional, six dollars a pound being top price usually in the industry, and the southern skins not being as prime as those of the cold North.

The shares of the venture having been apportioned, every man with a pocketful of money, the expedition, in April, 1830, just a year from departure, rode jubilantly into old " Touse." And right speedily old Touse was feeling the influx of the loose wealth. A trapper home again was like Jack in port. But when the money was gone — there was more beaver.[22]

That the youthful Kit Carson performed his part in contributing to the gaiety of the home-coming we may not doubt. In after years he confessed that in his early days he was rash and quick; and now in token of being a full-fledged mountain man he probably did as his comrades did.

Most readers will be interested to follow the adventures of Ewing Young to the end. California summoned him again. He left Taos in September, 1831, with Moses Carson, Kit's elder brother, in his party, and trapped through to the coast, arriving there in April, 1832. Some time or other he essayed to cross the terrific Great Basin from the Salt Lake region to Upper California, direct. The sequel of this undertaking of the gallant old beaver trader was, that having traveled until his animals had exhausted their supply of fodder, and all had died, he cut food from their carcasses for himself and men and commenced his return to the lake. On the way five of his men perished. The captain and the rest reached the lake in a wretched condition.

After an exhaustive trapping tour up the northern California coast and backward again through California clear to the Gila, the veteran captain of trappers settled at Monterey. In 1834 he joined the company of Hall J. Kelly, bound for Oregon to colonize it for the Americans. In Oregon he located in the Willamette Valley and organized the " Wallamet Cattle Company," from which the Oregon settlers might obtain beef, and returning to California he made a drive of cattle and horses to Oregon. There he erected a whisky still — only to abandon it at the request of the missionaries. " He was one of the three powers of the country — the first being the Hudson Bay Company, the second the Methodist Mission, and the third — Ewing Young." He died February 15, 1841, on his farm near the

Willamette. He was a "man mysterious, a natural leader, a loyal American, courageous, of integrity, and honest," who, in 1829, pioneering across the desert to California, made of Kit Carson a mountain man and trapper, and brought out word of a new market.

CHAPTER IX

THE HEART OF THE ROCKIES — 1830

IN EVERY party of men banded together on a common enterprise, there always are one or two who jump right to the front; who, by common consent, are given leadership. Kit Carson seems to have been such a character. Slight in stature, younger, perhaps, than any of the others, his reputation that of a roving teamster, a hard worker, and a Carson of frontier breed from the Boone's Lick district, he went out with Ewing Young upon the trapper's trail as a promising hand who yet had much to learn; from that trip he came back Ewing Young's lieutenant, and a youth whose cool-headedness and decision already had placed him well above the average mountain man.

So it was with some natural pride that he now might meet, in Taos or in Santa Fe, his elder brother Moses, and trade with him news of the trail for news of home. The brothers would not meet again for twelve, or more likely, fifteen years.

The summer of 1830 would be spent by the majority of the returned trappers in Taos and Santa Fe, for they had plenty of money and the season (this being April) was advanced. By fall the money would be gone, the delights of town life would have palled, the beaver and the trail would call again. When in September word was spread that the Rocky Mountain Fur Company wanted good men, young Kit Carson, among others, enrolled his name. The destination was the Northwest. The ever active Ewing Young already was in fresh enterprises. Whether he and Kit saw one another again is doubtful; but he had served his purpose in Carson's life.

That Northwest country — the upper Missouri and the Platte, and the Rockies of Colorado, Wyoming, Montana, Idaho, Utah and beyond — was then and continued to be for many years the real fur ground of the West. A few trappers, such as Ewing Young, made a specialty of the Southwest, principally because it was on a direct line out of the market, Santa Fe.

Before Kit Carson had swapped the saddler's bench in old Franklin for the back of a mule on the Santa Fe Trail, the Northwest had been well traversed. The impetus given by Lewis and Clark had gained in momentum; and while the steady exodus into New Mexico was mainly along beaten lines staked out by a suspicious Latin government, that to the northwestward was without law and without restriction, diverging, as it traveled, where it pleased, free to seek out whatever spots were to its advantage. The trader established his fort, the trapper on his pony ranged through hill and plain. It was their country: essentially by right of exploration the mountain man's country; he who had succeeded to the *voyageur* and the *coureur des bois* of the eastern rivers and lakes.

In the five years (1825-1830) which Kit Carson had spent as saddler, wrangler, cook, teamster, and finally trapper, the Northwest had advanced rapidly, but its affairs were little changed on the surface. The Missouri Fur Company, in which Moses Carson had served, was defunct; while the great General Ashley, after having achieved a fortune by those splendid expeditions which he had sent out, and having retired from the mountains, was about to enter Congress, there to be stout exponent of the interests of the Far West.

Three of that really brilliant company which enlisted under him — Jedediah S. Smith, David E. Jackson and

William L. Sublette — bought his fur business from him. Smith has been noted as the first American overland into California. The name of Jackson comes down to us in the famous game resort, Jackson Hole, of northwestern Wyoming. Of William Sublette much might be said: a foremost partisan or captain of trappers, he, the best known among five brothers; a fighter and a trader, one of the few recorded, besides Ashley, who "amassed a handsome fortune."

This transfer had been made in July, 1826. To the partnership, which never was known by title save as, occasionally, " Smith, Jackson & Co.," or " Smith, Jackson & Sublette," had succeeded in August, 1830, the Rocky Mountain Fur Company, formed by five other thorough mountain men, of whom two, at least, Thomas Fitzpatrick, and James Bridger, were graduates of the Ashley school. The three others were Milton Sublette, brother of William; Jean Baptiste Gervais, unknown to fame because he has lacked a chronicler; and Henry Fraeb (commonly styled " Frapp "), destined to be slain by the Sioux and Cheyennes.

Thus the Rocky Mountain Fur Company had come into existence, to continue business in the main Rocky Mountains, the Continental Divide being its especial field. Across in the Northwest reigned the Hudson Bay Company of Great Britain; old, powerful, autocratic, its feet upon the ruins of Astoria. But another fur company was already aiming to wrest from Fitzpatrick, Bridger and partners their legacy. This was the American Fur Company, child of John Jacob Astor of New York, whose Astoria had so failed; with a western branch established in St. Louis, during Kit Carson's novitiate of four years in the Southwest it had waxed stronger, and was at last taking decisive steps for advancing from the Missouri River fur trade to the mountain fur trade.

And the fur business was booming. Ashley had given it impetus; Kit Carson entered it in its heyday. Not yet had the western soil been turned by the plough of a settler; the ground of plain and of valley was suffered to lie despised, while north of the Arkansas and west of Missouri the only incentive to the white man was trade and fur. By keelboat and by caravan the bales from post and rendezvous came pouring into St. Louis; by keelboat and by caravan went forth the supplies to rendezvous and to post. Not, as in the North before the West was discovered, was traffic by water alone; now at the opening of this decade of American supremacy in the trans-Mississippi country, the pack train threading lone plan and wooded pass, bearing its cargo, was a recognized institution.

The trading posts were the fur country's principal protection. They were little forts, established in the Indian precincts, and semi-military. They already extended along the Missouri to its headwaters and well up along the Platte. Beyond the Rockies were the posts of the Hudson Bay Company, encouraging a flow of furs westward, not eastward. The only aggressive military occupation of the country had been an expedition (boat and horse) up the Missouri to the mouth of the Yellowstone in Montana, by General Atkinson in 1825, and in 1827 the establishing of Fort Leavenworth on the Missouri in northeastern Kansas.

The Missouri frontier had advanced one hundred and fifty miles, from old Franklin to Independence, toward the mouth of the Kaw or Kansas River where Kansas City now stands. At Independence landing the goods for the Santa Fe trade were unloaded, and from Independence went trailing out into the dusty Southwest the long caravans, as of yore, save that oxen were supplanting mules for teams. Franklin, once "a center of wealth and fashion," was approaching its early decay, and soon was to be abandoned — its graveyard alone remaining as token of the days that were.

The Northwest was still forging ahead of the Southwest,

despite the constantly increasing Santa Fe business. To be sure, beside the mountains south of the Platte, in United States territory, during Kit Carson's novitiate, had been founded, in 1829, Bent's Fort; two hundred miles north of Taos, upon the "mountain" Santa Fe Trail up the Arkansas. But from Bent's Fort northward through Colorado to Wyoming there was not a white man's habitation, other than the rude trapper's lodge, as movable as the tipi of the Indian. As said, up into the Northwest from St. Louis to the mountains, post after post had been established. Such posts had even crossed the mountains, tentatively feeling their way, to meet the Hudson Bay Company posts inward creeping from the Pacific; while the Salt Lake, the Green River, the Henry Fork of the Snake, and the Snake itself in Idaho were becoming to St. Louis, base of supplies, as household words. The Rockies were indeed better known to the East than were the plains.

Such, briefly sketched, is a bird's-eye view of the West when Kit Carson, in this September, 1830, as a seasoned hand, entered in earnest into the trapper calling; from now on he mingled as an equal with the most skilled frontiersmen — hunters, trappers, fighters, and scouts in one — that the world has produced. We know but little of that company with whom he traveled to California and back; it must have contained experts, good men and true; but when he engaged with the Rocky Mountain Fur Company he entered a different atmosphere, where the gay, active *homme du nord — coureur* or *voyageur —* transplanted from Makinaw, vied with the Illinoisan and the Kentuckian; where the mighty pine-clad slopes of the snow-capped mountains invited ever to fresh endeavors; where the air was full of energy, and where the Indian, even, was of type superior to the cowardly Apache and the lethargic, squash-raising Mohave.

Carson served only intermittently with the Rocky Mountain Fur Company. Although it existed, under its title, but four years, yet for its stirring history and for the men connected with it early and late this company should be famous. It had rivals, better known; the American Fur Company, whose boast was to be designated simply as "The Company," and the Hudson Bay Company; but in its search for fur it opened up that wonderful territory now comprising Colorado, Wyoming, Montana, Idaho, and Utah; in the Rocky Mountain center of the United States it reigned, for a time, supreme; and it educated the majority of the scouts and guides who in after day piloted across the wilderness army detachment and colonist column.

From Taos there was a good 300 miles of travel before traps should be set. Four trapper trails were available. They led by the one route (the caravan road) north from the town and over the Raton Range down to the Arkansas, long miles, where Bent's Fort had been located. Thence one trail diverged west, up the Arkansas, into the mountains 100 miles away, and where Cañon City is located at the mouth of the famed Royal Gorge crossed by a Ute and Arapaho trail to the north and into South Park. Another trail branched from this one where Pueblo, Colorado, is located, followed up Fountain Creek, toward Colorado Springs, and turning into the Manitou country crossed by a pass here for South Park and the regions beyond. This also was an Indian-made trail. A third trail, instead of turning into the west at Colorado Springs proceeded on northward, over the little divide between the Arkansas and the Platte, about as the various railroads skirting the foothills from Denver south now run, and at Denver's site, entering the mountains along a trail later widened by the South Park stages, climbed "over the hill," passed the future mining center of Breckinridge, and dipping down, in the north end of Middle Park, joined with the two other trails, before mentioned, at the "junction." The fourth trail, essentially a trappers' and traders' trail (although all these old trails were cut first by the elk, the buffalo, and the red man), from the Arkansas at Bent's Fort or about the mouth of the Purgatoire stretched almost straightaway into the north, traversing the plains well out from the foothills, passing thirty miles east of Colorado Springs and considerably east of Denver, and striking into the South Platte about at the mouth of the Cache la Poudre, or just east of the present town of Greeley. Thence it continued north to the Laramie.

The second trail mentioned — that up the Fountaine qui Bouille Creek, and through Manitou and over — was the favorite. I am inclined to think that the Kit Carson party took this. The routes skirting the foothills or through the plains traversed what was known as the "neutral strip" — a highway, from the Arkansas to the Platte, about thirty miles wide, which was a debatable ground of all the tribes; Crows, Sioux, Blackfeet, Cheyennes, Snakes, Utes, Arapahoes, Kiowas, and even the Comanches and the Apaches. Consequently no traveler here could consider himself safe.

Engaged not as hired trappers but as "skin" trappers, who had contracted only to sell their pelts to the Rocky Mountain Company, the Kit Carson detachment followed into the fur country by the trail up the Fountain. And we can see them, Frenchman, American, Irishman, half-breed Mexican, with long hair, long rifles, fringed buckskins, broad hats, short stirrups, in compact yet mobile squad, at trappers' rack or cow pony trot, pressing on into the hills; around the foot of Pike's Peak, past the boiling soda spring where today the gaiety of a pleasure resort has succeeded the Manitou rites of the Indians, through the strange red-rock region of the Garden of the Gods, over the ridge and on. Behind and about, naught for which they particularly cared; before, beaver, Injun, and maybe death.[23]

Simultaneously with this expedition of the fall of 1830, which took Kit Carson into the mountains, occurred two other events of importance in the opening of the far West. The keel of the steamboat *Yellowstone* was being laid, at Louisville, Kentucky, on commission from the American Fur Company, and thus was born the first steamboat to ascend the upper Missouri. With the next spring it entered the fur trade, thus greatly facilitating the operations of the company which was to crush and absorb the Rocky Mountain Company. And as Kit Carson started for the Northwest, William Wolfskill (Wolfscale), with a party of traders, broke a new trail, soon to be, and long to remain, popular as the " Old Spanish Trail," through to California.

This trail, at best only a saddle and pack trail, from Santa Fe and Abiqui pointed northwest, up the Chama, from the headwaters thereof rounding north of the San Juan River and cutting the southwest corner of Colorado. Passing north of Durango city, and of Cortez town (Colorado) it paralleled for some distance the Dolores River; thence diverged westerly to enter Utah, striking present Moab and crossing the Green about where the railroad crosses now. It passed into the west by Castledale, and bending south, by way of Fillmore (Utah) and the Parowan country, following down the Virgin to the mouth of that river it swerved off for the Smith and Young route across the San Bernardino Desert, the Cajon Pass of the Sierra Madre Mountains, and Los Angeles.

A portion of this trail, or that in southwestern Colorado, had been broken by the Spanish explorer, Juan Maria Rivera, from Santa Fe, in 1761; it was better and further broken by the padre Francisco Silvestre Velez Escalante, in 1776; for that reason it may have been termed the " Old Spanish Trail." The names — such as Dolores, Piedra, Las Animas, Ancapagari (Uncompahgre) — applied by Escalante linger yet.

William Wolfskill, then, enthused by the new report of Ewing Young, in the fall of 1830 revived a portion of the Trail of the Father, and pushed the terminus through to California. It was a longer and more circuitous route than the southern routes; but it afforded, through the first half, grass and water, and it avoided the cañons of the Colorado Plateau, where Ewing Young had struggled. And the Old Spanish Trail, the inception of which was the glory of God and the Catholic Faith, became highway for horse trader and horse thief; and, still later, as between the Utah desert country and New Mexico, known as the "Durango Trail" it became famous for cattle drives and bandit flights.

But to return to Kit Carson. The first traps were set on the North Platte River, probably in what is today North Park, of Colorado; for through Middle Park from South Park trended the trappers' trail from Taos by way of the mountain route. Trapping down the Platte, and across the Wyoming line — while the river ran now pebbly, now smooth, with wide curves washing sage flats and high brushy hills — the fur hunters arrived at the Sweetwater, flowing into the Platte from the west. Up this Sweetwater the Taos squad turned, facing west for the snowy ranges and the country that bided beyond.

Pleasantly falls upon the ear the word "Sweetwater." — word which meant so much to those thirsty emigrants who along this Indian and trapper bridle path, ascending the rapid stream, found a way open to the Salt Lake, Oregon, and California. For the Sweetwater formed a most important link in the trans-continental route of old; at its source was South Pass, over which might pour down, buoyed by the vain trust that at last they were "across the Rockies," colonist, Mormon, and gold seeker. It was Oregon Trail, Mormon Trail, and Trail of the Forty-niner.

What white man first ventured over the original Indian track made by Crow, Blackfeet, Snake, and marauding

Sioux from the Black Hills eastward, we may not know. But it is safe to say that the indefatigable General Ashley was close upon his heels. The French negro, Creole Jim Beckwourth, Crow chief (in time), intimates that in 1823 he and an Ashley party passed this way. In the fall of 1825 another Ashley company adopted the route, and the next spring the doughty general himself, lured from his bride of six months, traveled through by the same course, trundling overland to the rendezvous at Salt Lake a six-pounder cannon — herald, it, of those countless creaking, white-topped vehicles preparing.

In 1827 up the Platte and the Sweetwater trail, from Council Bluffs for the Salt Lake Valley had marched Joshua Pilcher, of the declining Missouri Fur Company, with forty-five men and more than one hundred horses, to emulate the celebrated Ashley's successes. And in the spring of 1830 had passed up also William Sublette, of Smith, Jackson & Co., with eighty-one men upon mules, ten wagons of merchandise, two Dearborn carriages, some cattle, and a milch cow, bound for the last rendezvous of this company, in the Wind River Valley.

Many smaller parties, recorded and unrecorded, had been coming and going, through the dozen years, so that the Sweetwater trail was well defined.

"L' Eau Sucrée" the stream is called in early records — the language another tribute to the French Canadian who through the West as through the North blazed a way for the Anglo-Saxon to follow — "L' Eau Sucrée," or Sweetened Water, a pack mule laden with sugar having, one time, been capsized in the current; or, according to Missionary White, "a company were once passing the stream, and during a drunken carousal, emptied into it a large bag of sugar, thereby, as they said, christening it, and declaring it should hereafter be called Sweetwater Valley, as long as water ran." [24]

Of the two explanations the former is the more credible; for sugar in the mountains was too valuable a commodity to be thrown away by the bag. However, neither need be accepted; the title in English may stand of itself, fully merited by this invigorating, life-saving creek flowing so bravely amidst potash, and salt, alkali, and other bitterness.

Above the mouth of the Sweetwater would be encountered Independence Rock, an isolated, sudden outcrop into the sagy, desolate plain. Like to Pawnee Rock of the Santa Fe Trail, and to El Moro, or Inscription Rock of the Conquistador's trail through Zuñi of Arizona, was this landmark, famed to the Indians, the trappers, and the Oregon Trail: a signboard or bulletin board, so to speak, for all who passed. But the names scratched and painted upon it were as yet comparatively few.

It is the first appearance of a strange ridge of granite masses, near a hundred miles long, which stand in the midst of a great plain, in a direction perpendicular to that of the Rocky Mountains. The Sweet Water for nearly half its course, from the South Pass to the Platte, runs near its southern base. Some of the dome-like elevations are about 1,500 feet high; apparently no tree or shrub — no beast or bird relieves its stern and lifeless gray; its monumental solemnity. For how many ages, since its upheaval by the primitive fires, has it stood — changeless in summer heats and wintry storms — in untrodden solitude; in awful silence.[25]

It is about five miles up stream from Independence Rock that the ridge actually begins; and through a fissure in its lower extremity issues the Sweetwater, boiling out from the hill country. This fissure is Devil's Gate — a spectacular gorge which excited the wonder of the early travelers. And I am dwelling upon these features of the Sweetwater trail, for we must bear in mind that this was Kit Carson's first trip as a trapper into the genuine Rockies. The Sweetwater was an Ashley trail, opened by the men

INDEPENDENCE ROCK

ON THE TRAPPER-MADE OREGON TRAIL

(From Report of the March of the Rifle Regiment to Oregon, 1849)

DEVIL'S GATE

ON THE OREGON TRAIL

(From Report of the March of the Rifle Regiment to Oregon, 1849)

(A) A NINE SHOT PORTER'S PERCUSSION PILL WHEELLOCK, MENTIONED IN TEXT.
(B) A WHITNEY CARBINE, ALSO MENTIONED.
(C) THE FAMOUS HAWKINS RIFLE.
(D) A HUDSON'S BAY FLUKE USED BY INDIANS, AND VOYAGEURS, A TRADER'S STOCK IN TRADE.
(E) A COLT'S REVOLVING RIFLE, SEVEN SHOT.

(From the Collection of Don Maguire)

OLD ARMS OF PLAINS AND MOUNTAINS

whom Kit was at last meeting, and was destined to be the Oregon Trail, peopling with Americans the British Northwest.

The Sweetwater trail of the trappers and those who followed led around the gorge of the Devil's Gate, and over the ridge. But the custom was to ride aside, to the brink of the gorge, and look down in. The depth is some four hundred feet; the width at the bottom estimated as about one hundred; the length, one thousand; and the " deeptoned roar," the " dizzy awe of the downward view," the walls " frowning gloomily above the abyss which had sundered them forever," seem to have impressed all beholders.

Above Devil's Gate extends westward for eighty miles the Valley of the Sweetwater — barren slopes and potash flats on either hand, with the river's course, interrupted frequently by the granite ridge which has been erupted in the middle, wandering between them. The result is a succession of charming verdurous pockets, where in Kit Carson's day were found buffalo, mountain sheep, antelope, deer, grizzly bear, and sage chickens. Short defiles, like miniature Devil's Gates, exist; one gained the name Hell Gate, " so called for being the place where eleven whites were once cut off by the Indians." [26]

Beyond this gap, twenty-five miles above Devil's Gate, is first disclosed, as a rule, the hoary, wild Wind River range far in the northwest, at whose southern base was held the rendezvous of 1830, when the Rocky Mountain Fur Company received new foster parents and new christening. Well might young Kit Carson, with this trapper band now ascending the Sweetwater, gaze, mysteriously moved, at the silently waiting frontage of the grandest realm ever ruled by trappers.

The Kit Carson party continued on, up the length of the Sweetwater and over the great divide by the already famed Southern Pass — the South Pass of the modern map, discovered in the fall of 1822, by Etienne Prévost. Bleak, wide, and open is this South Pass, and of rise so gradual

that but for our geographical knowledge, and the imposing landmarks on our right (the snow-capped peaks of the Wind River Mountains raising their cold, spiral, and barren summits to a great elevation), we should not have been conscious that we had ascended to, and were standing upon the summit of the Rocky Mountains — the backbone, to use a forcible figure, of the North American Continent.[27]

However, it required no guideboards to prove that it was the Continental Divide. The Sweetwater, in dwindling volume, had been hastening eastward; but from Pacific Spring the waters went trickling westward. Furthermore, every trapper knew that when speckled trout were found in the streams, then the Pacific side of the continent had been reached.

So this was Oregon — this farther slope of the smooth swell. Traveling on, the party struck the headwaters of the Green River, in western Wyoming, trapped these to the beginnings, crossed westward into David E. Jackson's favorite quarters of Jackson Hole, continued on into Idaho, clear to the Salmon River, and meeting here other trappers, " a band of their own party, who had left Taos some days in advance of the main body, and for whom they were then hunting," went into winter camp with them upon the Salmon River, among the friendly Nez Percé Indians.

A survey of the map will indicate the distance covered by this one outward trip of the fall of 1830; but it will scarcely indicate the tremendous energy and toil involved. Yet this whole journey, from Taos of New Mexico to the Salmon River of northern Idaho, in the life of Carson presumed to have been dictated by himself, occupies only eleven lines; of such little moment was it considered.

Now about to " winter in," Kit Carson had seen the

nature of this much-reputed beaver country of the Northwest; snow-crowned mountain ranges, crystal, rushing
streams, green valleys flanked by dense pines and firs and
spruces, tremendous cañons of red rock and gray rock,
chasm and crest alike impassable, patches of " bad lands,"
wilderness of park and peak, alive with game and threaded
by the Indian and the pelt hunter.[28]

CHAPTER X

ADVENTURES OF KIT CARSON — 1831-1832

IT IS the way of the West to receive the newcomer with a certain proper reservation, and to take little on hearsay. When Kit Carson entered the mountains he found there men who had been in service longer than himself, and who had already shown the stuff that was in them. Jim Bridger, the Sublettes, Fitzpatrick, old Hugh Glass, Black Harris, and a score and more of others educated in the Missouri Fur Company, the Ashley, the Smith, and even the Astoria school, were ahead of him, comprising a company of the Old Guard. Not until the spring of 1833 do we find even a mention of Carson; but then, as " among the gamest of the trappers," at last he is credited to the ranks of the Rocky Mountain Fur Company. It must be remembered that in 1830 he was yet only a youth.

Now to guarantee a chronological account of Carson's career for the succeeding dozen years, until in 1842 he joins with Fremont, involves the ambitious biographer in a maze worse than the cañoned labyrinths of the Snake itself. The times were distinguished by deeds, not days; and the movement of events was so rapid, so reiterative, that year blended with year in a vaguely defined procession. The beaver hunter thought more in the present and the future than upon the past; and yesterday was always dead and cast aside.

So in reading the narrative of W. A. Ferris, of Zenas Leonard, of Jim Beckwourth, of Captain James Hobbs, the historian with dates at his command is hopelessly bewildered.

The adventures of Kit Carson, while probably not more
varied nor more perilous than those of other mountain
men such as Jim Bridger, Joe Meek and their companions,
are fully indicative of the life upon the beaver trail, and
well bear out the assertion that " wherever railroads now
run, and trails are followed, Kit Carson led the way; and
his footprints are all along the route."

From the commencement of his mountain career he was
a wandering trapper, always with a tendency to hunt for
himself — a tendency which his marked ability in the most
trying situations made most practicable. He must speedily
have became a welcome addition to any squad, as well as
a personage amply sufficient to himself, did he choose to
hunt upon his own account.

In their winter quarters (1830-1831) upon the Salmon,
the men repaired their outfits, killed game for food, and
loafed. But they were not safe from the dreaded Blackfeet; four of their number, while hunting buffalo, were surrounded and slain. Barring this bad luck, in the spring the
party emerged in good condition. Young Kit Carson was
a *hivernan* or winterer; and he had celebrated his twenty-
first birthday.[29]

In April the spring trapping was begun. A course was
laid across country to reach the Snake River, southward.
This took the party through a grim, jagged country, dark
and forbidding; and when the Snake was attained it must
have proved, after all, poor trapping ground. A fierce,
hostile river is the great Snake. It rushes, along its upper
course, through stretches of gloomy lava, the outpouring
of ancient volcanic action. In places its bed is a thousand
and more feet down, its water inaccessible. Three massy
falls are to be found, between the Henry Fork at the
Snake's sources and the mouth of the Salmon, whereon Kit
Carson spent his winter; they rival Niagara, and rapids
are many.

However, occasionally the Snake pours out of its gorges into meadow lands, and coming with much labor to such spots, the trappers found beaver.

From the upper Snake the party crossed over, southward a few miles, to the Bear, which flows south into the Great Salt Lake. From the Bear they turned north, to the Green River, and reached the place of summer rendezvous; the lovely Green River Valley.

Here they found, under William Sinclair of Arkansas, fifteen men of a company which had left New Mexico, via Taos, that spring of 1831. Some of these men were destined to travel on even to California, and there to be prominent settlers; but for Sinclair this was the last rendezvous save one. At the close of the next summer's gathering, in Pierre's Hole, of northeastern Idaho, he was killed during a great battle between the assembled trappers and some Blackfeet.

This annual market, or rendezvous, of 1831 did not prove very successful, for Thomas Fitzpatrick, who in the spring had left for St. Louis to bring back trading supplies and other necessary goods, did not appear. Either Kit Carson was dissatisfied, or the wandering spirit that marks his trapper years was manifesting itself, for learning from the Sinclair party that a Captain Gant was trapping east of the mountains, and his engagement with the Rocky Mountain Company evidently having expired, he and four associates proceeded to seek the banner of the captain. Possibly, also, Taos was in their minds, and they counted upon trapping their way back to the New Mexico provinces.

They worked under Captain Gant that fall, trapping the Laramie Plains; thence southward across many a ridge, to search other streams. Through wild scenes of snow peaks, dense timber, foaming torrents, sheer cañons, flowery meadows, and aspen dales they traveled ever down the middle of Colorado, and came out into Colorado's South

Park, the headwaters of the South Platte River. Being heavily laden with their fur, they struck east for the plains, and, emerging upon the Arkansas River near the foothills, they halted and established camp.

Captain Gant and a companion or two proceeded southeastward to Taos, to deposit the furs and to get supplies. When they returned winter was setting in. So upon the Arkansas was located the winter camp. And a hard winter it was, with the usual forage deeply covered by snow. Had the party not been enabled to cull cottonwood bark and willow bark and branches, the horses and the mules would surely have perished. For the men themselves there were plenty of buffaloes, collected in the bottoms and in the gulches.

In January a party of fifty Crows, who had wandered this far upon a midwinter excursion from their village on the Big Horn in Wyoming, stole upon the trappers' camp by night and drove off nine horses. In the morning the theft was discovered. Kit Carson, naturally a leader here as he had been when with Ewing Young in California, immediately headed twelve men and followed hard upon the Indians' trail. This trended north, for the country of the Crows.

It was a difficult task, for during the night buffaloes had moved hither and thither, treading upon the tracks. The horses that the pursuers were riding were in poor condition because of the strenuous winter; and after forty miles had been put behind it was thought best to camp and rest in a patch of trees descried just before. But smoke was curling out from the timber; the Crows themselves were there.

The trappers halted quickly, and concealing themselves and their mounts cautiously reconnoitered. The Crows had established a permanent camp in two divisions, protected by brush and logs against the weather and against attack.

They were dancing the theft of the nine horses, picketed just outside one of the breastworks.

The trappers watched and waited for darkness to come. A cold job was this, for they could not make a fire, and they were traveling light. But when finally the Indians had danced enough and eaten enough, and had lain down to sleep, Kit Carson and five comrades, crawling nearer through the snow, cut, with fingers numbed, the nine horses' picket ropes. Then they threw pieces of snow at the horses to drive them off toward the other trappers. This was accomplished so deftly that even the Indians' dogs had not been disturbed.

The majority of the trappers then declared in favor of retiring, with the re-captured stock, to the camp upon the Arkansas; for the weather was bitter and supplies were meager. But the impetuous young Carson and two or three others said that the Indians should be punished; the forty-mile pursuit and the cold wait should exact a penalty. This opinion carried; and leaving three men to care for the horses, the remaining trappers walked boldly upon the camp of the Crows.

Their rapid approach over the creaking snow was heard. A dog barked. The Indians in one of the little fortifications sprang to their feet. At the cracks of the trappers' rifles some of them fell; the others ran for the breastworks of the second division, to unite with their fellows.

And now, in the winter half-light, just before dawn, amidst this snow-bound wilderness, back and forth spat the rifles — the ten trappers behind trees, the two score Indians behind their breastworks.

At break of day the savages charged. They were driven back. Soon, knowing how few the trappers were, they desperately charged again — so desperately that the trappers in turn were forced to retreat. From tree to tree they fought; the three men left to guard the horses came up on the run, as reinforcement. At last, by withdrawing, each side signified that it had had enough; the Crows retired into their camp, the trappers with their horses along the back trail to the camp upon the Arkansas.

The Indians had lost a number of men; the trappers, according to their report as it comes to us today, suffered but a few wounds.

Kit Carson and the whole party might well consider that they had come off fortunately in this little set-to. They had regained their horses and had punished the thieves. However, Indian troubles were thickening around them and even their own men were soon to play them a scurvy trick.

When spring came it was decided by Captain Gant to return to the old beaver ground of the North Platte and the Laramie rivers, in New Park and southern Wyoming adjacent. So the fur accumulated since the captain's trip to Taos was " cached " and the start northward was begun. But they had scarcely reached the South Park when one evening two men were missing.

Supposing that they might have straggled, the party waited twenty-four hours; and then Carson and a companion were dispatched back, by Captain Gant, to the Arkansas. They were sent, because now the suspicion had arisen that those " stragglers " had deserted, and were hurrying to rob the cache of fur. When the two riders arrived, the cache had been torn open, and the 300 pounds of fur, beaver and otter chiefly, were gone. Neither the two missing men nor the furs bearing the Gant & Blackwell private mark ever were heard of again.

Why Carson and his partner remained here instead of returning to Gant in the Bayou Salade we may not understand. To be sure, the aspens and the cottonwoods were unfolding their leaves, as signal for the Indians to mount their ponies and ride upon their annual spring forays; but the trail between the winter camp and the Bayou Salade had been traversed twice, and two skilled mountain men would not have been deterred from attempting it a third time. However, there may have been signs that hostiles — the Crows, the Sioux, the Blackfeet, even the Arapahos — were hovering about; for in the Indian country the spring is the most dangerous season. Therefore perhaps it was by discretion, or perhaps by orders to await Captain Blackwell, that Carson and partner now remained in the old winter camp on the upper Arkansas.

This they strengthened. It is likely that the Indian signs were portentous, for we read that the two hunted only in company, and maintained a constant guard. In about a month Captain Blackwell, Gant's associate in business, with supplies and fifteen new trappers, from St. Louis, appeared, having come out by the Bent's Fort branch of the Santa Fe Trail.

About at the same time there entered four men from the Gant camp, who had back-tracked to meet Captain Blackwell and incidentally to find what had happened to Carson and his partner. The Indians certainly must have been on bad behavior, and the trails must have been encompassed closely by eager savages of many tribes, for as the report goes the Gant camp had given Carson and partner up for lost. But now all rode northward for the Bayou Salade, two hundred miles.

This Bayou Salade, or Salt Marsh, forms the source of the South Fork of the South Platte River, in Colorado's South Park. A famous place it was, in trapper days. The salty waters oozing amidst the bottoms attracted vast quantities of buffalo and other animals; the winters were considered mild; and both the Utes of the mountains, and the Arapahos of the plains claimed it as a special hunting ground. Many battles for it occurred. Everybody, trappers and savages, knew of the Bayou Salade, and all trails converged there.

From the Arkansas a trail led north past the foothills, up the Fountain Creek, and westward, to the Fontaine Qui Bouille or celebrated Boiling Spring. This was the Manitou of the Indians — a sacred spring where members of all tribes pilgrimaged to " make medicine " to the great Manitou, or God, and to deposit offerings. The bottom of the spring was covered with beads and amulets. Today this spot still is Manitou, and, thus known, is a resort annually visited by thousands of sight-seers, who drink the waters, climb Pike's Peak, and explore the Garden of the Gods.

Skirting this fantastic red Garden of the Gods, the trail led from the Boiling Spring, and climbing the mountain divide behind, wound on for the Bayou Salade.

Over such a trail, worn smooth through the centuries by countless Indian moccasins, proceeded the Blackwell party. On the fourth day, while the camp was at its early breakfast in the cool grayness among the fragrant sage and pines, the crack of the sentry's rifle and a loud whoop from him spread sudden alarm. As the men sprang to their guns, down charged a band of Indians for the horses. But these fortunately had been hobbled, as well as picketed. So that at the volley the Indians swerved, and fled, leaving a dead warrior and taking only one animal.

The camp hastily packed, and made a forced march of fifty miles. The Indian signs ceased; it was hoped that there would be no more trouble, and accordingly the tired trappers went into camp upon the bank of a little stream, tributary to the Arkansas.

The barking of one of their faithful mongrel dogs aroused them. They could find no reason for his barking; but to be safer they brought their horses in closer, and posted an extra guard. After that nothing especial happened, and morning broke with the camp and its horses unmolested. It was decided that the dog must have barked at a coyote.

Kit Carson and three others rode to explore for beaver. Returning, trotting along and chatting carelessly, as they rounded a curve in their trail they abruptly met almost face to face four Indians, armed and painted and mounted for war. The trappers hesitated not an instant. They charged at a gallop; and pursuing the Indians closely they found themselves decoyed into the midst of sixty more reds, the main war party.

Now is demonstrated how instantaneously and for the best, like the mind of wild animal or domestic cat, the mind of the mountain man could act. Without slackening pace or firing a shot the party continued headlong on, received at twenty paces a volley of bullet and arrow, and still replying not but reserving the menace of their loaded guns, burst the half circle and actually escaped.

The astonished Indians did not pursue — which was just as well for the trappers, since two of them had been severely wounded. However, as to trappers' eyes it was now evident that the savages were upon the warpath and lately had been in an affray, the four whites rode hard and with no little anxiety for the camp. They found it intact, but with another man wounded in an onslaught by this very band. An attempt had been made upon the camp horses; the loose stock had been run off, and four of the whites, pursuing, had regained it only after an exchange of shots, during which an Indian was killed and a trapper wounded. Naturally this had not sweetened the temper of the reds, and Kit Carson and three companions spoke truly when they claimed that "they had retained their scalps by a very narrow shave."

With one of the wounded men borne in a rude litter, the Blackwell party resumed its march for the Gant camp in the Bayou Salade.

Captain Gant seems to have been one of those whom Fortune does not meet halfway. It was he who commanded the party of seventy men, out of St. Louis in the spring of 1831 (a year back), with whom served that Zenas Leonard whose narrative of mountain life has been previously referred to. In the summer of 1831, having reached the mountain beaver country at the Laramie Plains, the party divided into three detachments, and were never reunited. Mr. Blackwell returned with Fitzpatrick, who passed, to St. Louis for supplies for next year. Captain Gant disappears from knowledge, but he evidently makes his hunt southward, and Carson is of his company in 1831-32. As is seen, Mr. Blackwell comes out on time, with supplies.

Now, with the middle spring of 1832 Captain Gant and Captain Blackwell were in the Bayou Salade, and little had been done except to fight Indians. The agreement with the two other parties provided a meeting this spring, at the mouth of the Laramie. The meeting did not occur.

To be sure, the course was laid north, into Colorado's Old Park, or Middle Park. But the season was well along, and Old Park had been trapped ahead of them. The outlook grew less and less encouraging, and the men grew disheartened. In the dissolution which resulted (and which caused the firm of Gant and Blackwell to be reported through the mountains as insolvent), Carson and two comrades diverged for an expedition upon their own account. They wisely plunged into the timber regions; and while the Indians were hunting buffalo on the plains and in the parks, they trapped unmolested.

Captain Gant, discouraged as a trapper, returned to the Arkansas and entered into trading relations with the Arapahos. Of Captain Blackwell we do not hear again.

On the more sequestered streams of central and western Colorado Carson and his companions finished out the trapping season successfully; and as free trappers, in the summer took their furs to Taos.

By so doing they missed the rendezvous of 1832, in

Pierre's Hole, at the close of which occurred the day-long battle, famed through Irving and many another chronicler, between four hundred and more trappers, Flatheads, and Nez Percés, and fifty Blackfeet warriors entrenched in a swampy copse. William Sinclair was killed, William Sublette was badly wounded, and the honors of the fight remained with the Blackfeet, who silently escaped by night.

At this rendezvous appeared, for a baptism of fire, Nathaniel J. Wyeth, the Cambridge youth, who had been convoyed with the remnants of his Boston company by the supply train of William Sublette, thus far upon his road that he might embark in " some business enterprise," its nature yet undecided, on the Columbia. Wyeth at once showed his spirit, and having placed his greenhorns behind their packs, himself led to the attack a squad of trappers and friendlies. And here likewise were initiated into rendezvous ways Zenas Leonard and some of his fellows, refugees from the disorganized command of Gant and Blackwell. Other notables present were Robert Campbell, William Sublette's friend and partner; two grandsons of Daniel Boone, Jim Bridger, Andrew Drips, Vanderburgh (soon to die), Fitzpatrick — the last named just emerged from a terrific hide-and-seek game with the Blackfeet, his form emaciated and his hair grayed thereby so as to make him almost unrecognizable — all men whom we shall meet later in these pages.

THE WEST IN 1835

(From Thayer's Marvels of the New West)

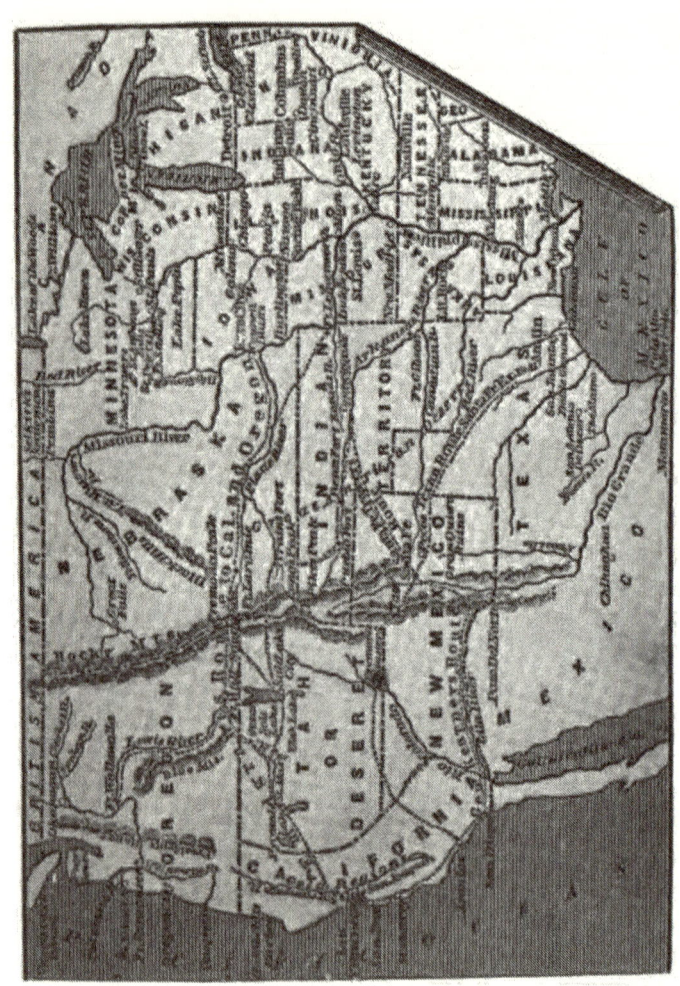

THE WEST IN 1850

(From Howe's Historical Collections of the Great West)

CHAPTER XI

THE FIGHT FOR FUR

WHEN with the spring of 1832 young Kit Carson and his two comrades departed from the sinking Gant and Blackwell ship to make their voyage independently, with Taos as their home port, the fur business of the mountains was at the flood.

As has been said, the country of the far West was becoming a land cris-crossed by the moccasined foot of the American trapper, and in the past decade the restless beaver hunter from the States had penetrated virtually throughout the Northwest and Southwest, between Missouri and the coast. The salient features were accurately mapped by the trapper in trapper mind — a mind tenacious, like that of Jim Bridger, who, in later days, with a piece of charcoal could sketch offhand a range, its passes and valleys, upon a piece of upturned buffalo hide.

It still was a land of romance. Even to the practical mountain men it held many an *ultima Thule*, strangely peopled like the shores of mythology. For among the trappers were Gullivers, Hakluyts, Marco Polos, Munchausens. An island in the Salt Lake was for some years yet to be invested by a race of giants, whose enormous cut timbers from time to time washed ashore. In the depths of the desert of the Colorado and of the Great Basin dwelt other giants armed with clubs. There were cañoned cities, pent from the world, wherein lived as of yore descendants of the Montezuma, fugitives from the rout by Cortez. And there were those bubbling springs, geysers, and oddly tinted or ashy tracts, real but made unreal by imaginary attributes, to which the trapper, like the Indian, threw a sop by " making medicine."

It still was a land misunderstood; a land popularly presumed to be forever condemned, behind its barrier of the chimeric " Great American Desert," and of the beetling ranges which seemed so snowy and austere. In the words of Benton (1825) : " The ridge of the Rocky Mountains may be named without offense as presenting a convenient, natural, and everlasting boundary." And the Robert Greenhow report upon Oregon and the Pacific coast, seven years later than this year of 1832, was to declare that this trappers' battleground from the Rockies to the Blue Mountains of Idaho was either a barren waste or else that the climate was " sufficient to render any attempts at cultivation entirely fruitless."

Hereabout were those favorite rendezvous valleys of the Green, the Bear, and Pierre's Hole; here were the Grand Ronde and Horse Prairie, Brown's Hole, Ogden's Hole, and Cache Valley — all well-beloved of the mountain man for their shelter and their bounty in time of need. Here were the wonders of the Salt Lake, of the Bear Springs, of the Soda Springs, of waters hot and cold, of salt and gypsum and potash. Hereabout were the beautiful Flathead Lake and Pend d'Oreille on the north, lovely Utah Lake on the south, with many a gem of lesser note in between. Here flowed the varied current of the Green, the friendly stream encountered at the very foot of the South Pass, uniting with the equally varied Grand to form the wondrous Colorado; here rushed the fierce Snake, deeply cañoned in stark lava beds, to cross which, as said Jim Bridger, " a bird must carry along its own provisions "; here rippled the Bear; here, coming down from the north to its union with the Snake, rolled to the sea the mighty Columbia; here sparkled the Henry Fork, the Godin, the Uintah, and a hundred other tributaries to the arterial system; here were deer, elk, buffalo, sheep, speckled trout, the friendly Indians. And sentinels facing west, looked over all the snowy tips of the Three Tetons — the trappers' Pilot Buttes.

Hereabout were to appear the two great highways branching from the valley of the Green: the highway north of west, to Oregon; the highway south of west, to Salt Lake and California. Thus already had the fates spun; for in 1831 almost simultaneously had Hall Kelly, the Boston schoolmaster, incorporated " The American Society for Encouraging the Settlement of Oregon Territory," and changing from New York to Ohio the Mormon church had begun its series of heroic moves. And to defy the diagnosis by Robert Greenhow and fellow students, hereabout would blossom and bear the utter desolation of the Salt Lake Valley, and every beaver stream would course by flock and herd and mine and ranch and Alladin-summoned town.

Robert Greenhow, the librarian, in his report to Congress upon Oregon declared — though it was an understatement — that until 1834 there never, at one time, were more than 200 Americans west of the Rockies. But crossing by the South Pass, discovered by Etienne Prévost of the Ashley company in 1824, the Americans, few or many, spread far and wide. Ashley had made known the valleys of the Green or Seeds-skee-dee (Prairie-hen River), and had even tried to descend its cañons by boat (as Major Powell did successfully almost half a century later), and had left his name therein for future explorers to read; he had opened the country of the Bear, north of Salt Lake, the country of Utah Lake and Sevier Lake, southward. With forty-five men and more than one hundred horses Joshua Pilcher had traversed from Council Bluffs west to the Green, north to Flathead Lake and Fort Colville in Washington near the Canadian line, and then by the Athabaska and Red River of Canada back to the Missouri and the States. Jedediah S. Smith had been as far north as the present city of Spokane; he had carried beaver to the British and the Bible to the Flathead, and by his explorations of the country of the Snake and the Columbia, as transmitted to the war department, had supplemented the information previously supplied by the routes of Lewis and Clark and the Astorians; he had been as far south as San Diego, he had thrice crossed the Great Basin, and with Ewing Young had investigated California from the south to the extreme north. Colter, Joe Meek, Jim Bridger, and Robert Meldrum had exploited the Yellowstone Park. There were three trails across the desert of the Colorado — by William Wolfskill in the north, Ewing Young in the middle, and David E. Jackson in the lower part; and there were the trails by the Snake and the Columbia.

Thus the routes to and from the coast had been opened; within another year the Joseph Walker detachment of the Captain Bonneville expedition would open the overland trail from Salt Lake. A trade in horses and mules — a trade legitimate as well as illegitimate — had begun, via Santa Fe and the Santa Fe Trail, between the States and California; Spanish Trail broken by William Wolfskill was being stirred by shuffling hoofs. The Southwest was sufficiently known; the tide of humanity was surely, although still in a manner blindly, setting into the Oregon then present and yet to be. The battle ground of the white race and the red was extending through Wyoming, Colorado, Utah, Idaho, Montana, Washington, Oregon — states yet in embryo, but only waiting.

To be sure, the topography of the West was more hazy than its geography. The Green River — the Seedskeedee, Buenaventura or Spanish River — confused with another mythical Buenaventura, was presumed to empty into the Pacific; and the Great Salt Lake was assigned two outlets

on the west, also draining into the Pacific — a fallacy which
prevailed for yet ten years. The Rocky Mountains were
stated, by competent authority of the day, to present peaks
of 25,000 feet elevation.[30]

But although the main exploring activities were now in
the wide Oregon country which occupied all of the Northwest beyond the Shining Mountains, of American fort or
fur posts there was none — save, perchance, the post of
the enterprising Antoine Robidoux, in the Uintah region
of northeastern Utah. Major Andrew Henry's log fort
upon the Henry Fork of the Lewis or Snake, at the western
base of the Wind River divide, had been abandoned; and
that ambitious structure upon the shore of Utah Lake, to
which the gallant General Ashley, upon his last trip into the
mountains, had hauled his six-pounder cannon had also
been abandoned. Only the Hudson Bay Company posts,
west of the latitude of the Blue Mountains of Idaho — that
long accepted barrier beyond which the Hudson Bay Company was presumed to reign supreme — had persisted as
representatives of white man's enterprise.

The fur trade, if prosperous, was waxing complicated,
also, as cutthroat methods of an avaricious civilization
intruded more and more. Firmly entrenched upon the
western coast, with headquarters at Vancouver, and dominating the blackened remnants of that Astoria which twice
had changed hands, the Hudson Bay Company, proud,
rich, and powerful, tenaciously gathered to itself the streams
of fur heading in north, south, and east. Doing a fur business in Oregon alone of $140,000 annually; with its bri-
gades and its twenty posts as strictly disciplined as any
military force; with its trained *engagés* and clerks and
bourgeois; with its immense resources and experience; its
employees courteous as man to man, but inflexible as trader
to trader — now dining the stranger at a twenty-foot table
lavish with viands and wines, and now refusing him one

ounce of supplies to further him upon the onward trail
into the fur country — the Hudson Bay Company by every
resource within its means resisted the inroads of the American.   When it must outbid, it outbid; when it must under-
sell, it undersold; when it must deceive, it deceived; when
it must play alcohol against blanket, it played; and when it
must crush, it crushed.

The whole of this Oregon country was considered, in
point of law, debatable ground, and was jointly occupied
(again, in point of law) by Americans and British.   But
the great company, consummate in its machinery, yielded
not an inch in the Oregon of today, and the actual debatable
ground was that section before specifically referred to, lying
from the Rockies west to the Blue Mountains, the southern
portion being technically New Mexico.

Now, when Kit Carson entered the mountains, there had
pushed into this western slope district another rival for the
fur trade which the Rocky Mountain Company of Sublette,
Bridger, Fitzpatrick, and others had hoped to inherit from
the efforts of Ashley and Jedediah Smith.   With Henry
Vanderburgh, Lucien Fontenelle, and Andrew Drips as its
mountain partisans, the American Fur Company, which
under another name had failed at Astoria, now operating
out of St. Louis a western department, had not only
ascended the Missouri but had veered into the Northwest.

The fall of 1831 marked its first definite invasion of the
new territory, and fleeing the advance of the prying brigade
under the West Pointer Vanderburgh and the trader Drips,
the Rocky Mountain Fur Company had driven its own men
to the upper Snake and the Salmon River country, in the
Nez Percé fastness.

In addition to this rivalry, and as if further to complicate
matters, now in the spring of 1832 there were leaving
Boston, for Oregon, as " salmon fishers," but destined to
become castaways and beaver-hunters, a detachment of

twenty-one tenderfoot New Englanders under young Nathaniel Jarvis Wyeth of Cambridge, whose building of Fort Hall on the upper Snake was to supply the Hudson Bay Company with an easternmost post. And starting westward from Independence there was wending by horse, foot, and wagon, with his company of one hundred and ten, Irving's hero-to-be, Captain Benjamin Eulalie de Bonneville, of the army — a fur hunter of the Ashley stamp, but not of the Ashley success. Already in the mountains were parties of free trappers — one under bold Sinclair of Arkansas, and another, from Pennsylvania (in the number being the chronicler Zenas Leonard), under Messrs. Gant and Blackwell.

But these detachments, while lending excitement and variety, were only chips in the current. Gant and Blackwell failed, their company dispersed; Sinclair died the trapper's death, and his company dispersed; Bonneville tried hither and thither, opened a new trail to California, reported upon the Great Basin, built Fort Nonsense, had to quit; Wyeth, rebuffed by Americans and British alike, had to quit. The Rocky Mountain Company, the American Company, the Hudson Bay Company, grappled until only the two were left.

Having outlined the country and the combatants, let us consider the methods and then the rank and file.

In this campaign of 1832 and of the half dozen years succeeding, until the last regular rendezvous, at Fort Nonsense, in 1839 — a campaign that decimated the beaver, demoralized the Indian, and killed the goose that laid the golden egg — the Hudson Bay Company, despite its superb organization, in American trans-montane territory was at first under disadvantage; for its organization was met with disorganization under King Alcohol.

A few words are necessary to explain the system of the Hudson Bay Company. Following the splendid example

of that British autocracy the Northwest Company of Can‑
ada, and with true British policy, its principles were high
principles of good business. In this respect it was, and is,
a striking contrast to improvident American methods, which,
under the theory " get while you 're getting," devastate
forests and exterminate fur, fin, and feather.

The Hudson Bay Company never over-trapped, never
over-paid, never connived at offenses in order to receive
favors, never temporized with enmity in order to obtain
a transient friendship, and never willingly debauched busi‑
ness with liquor.

As for over-trapping:

If the annual return from any well-trapped district be less in
any year than formerly, they order a less number still to be
taken, until the beaver and other fur-bearing animals have time
to increase. The income of the Company is thus rendered
uniform, and their business perpetual.[31]

As for prices:

A regular tariff was established on the Company's goods,
comprising all the articles used in their trade with the Indians;
nor was the quality of their goods ever allowed to deteriorate.
A price was also fixed upon furs according to their market
value, and an Indian knowing this, knew exactly what he could
purchase. No bartering was allowed. When skins were
offered for sale at the fort they were handed to the clerk
through a window like a postoffice delivery-window, and their
value in the article desired, returned through the same
aperture.

As for offenses, no Indian culprit, from murderer to
thief, ever was permitted to go unpunished. Even when the
company of the American, Jedediah Smith, entering upon
the Hudson Bay ground in the spring of 1828 was assaulted
by the Shasta Indians on the Umpqua of Oregon, from

Fort George the Hudson Bay Company dispatched instantly a force to punish the Indians and recover the Americans' goods. Such a policy was maintained by the company as a measure of self-defense.

As for temporizing with enmity, as for even suffering friendship to mingle with business interests the Hudson Bay posts would entertain the traveler, but would supply not the trader. It bought the furs of Jedediah Smith the castaway, to prevent other markets from getting them; but when Ewing Young entered Oregon, with some hope of pursuing trade with the Indians, it refused to sell him a single article of clothing.

As for liquor, a modicum was furnished, at stated and well separated intervals, to employees as reward of duty. But until the final fight for furs had to be met with American methods, no alcohol went out in trade. And alcohol was not necessary. The Indians knew, as well as did the company, what furs should bring and what goods should cost, and never found their confidence abused.

On the debit side of the ledger, the Hudson Bay Company existed for its own profit absolutely and only. It was opposed to agriculture — for that invited settlers upon the fur grounds, showed the Indian that hunting was not the only livelihood, and intruded upon the company's business. The company discouraged any competition, healthful or unhealthful, and was entirely a monopoly. Its course in obliterating rivalry was as unscrupulous as the alleged course of Standard Oil, and very similar. In competition it would starve out and drive out with a single-mindedness bent upon the one aim — absolute mastership in the field.

It occupied the beaver grounds west of the Rockies and north of Utah by virtue of that agreement of 1818, extended by the agreement of London, 1827, by which citizens of the United States and of Great Britain should have equal rights of trade and settlement in the Oregon Territory. Its fur business was carried on through the medium of strong posts, of which in 1832 the most eastern in the lower territory was Fort Walla Walla on the Columbia near the mouth of the Snake, in present Washington. But eventually the American rendezvous summoned its traders, and W. A. Slocum, in his report to the government, announced that the Hudson Bay Company especially sent to be present at the American rendezvous of 1836, Chief Trader McLeod.

The " Nor'west " Company, as, by right of succession, the Hudson Bay outfit was known among the trappers generally, was by the Americans feared, hated, combated. In this year 1832 the British influence exerted among the Indians during the War of 1812 was still fresh in the public mind; and it was well understood that the fur traders were the men who exerted the greatest influence of all. They were the go-betweens. With British traders still active in American territory (the Hudson Bay traders west of the Rockies, and traders from Canada coming down upon the upper Missouri), both American lives and property were threatened.

So we see that on February 9, 1829, the indefatigable defender of western interests, Senator Thomas H. Benton, for the Committee on Indian Affairs, makes a strong report to the Senate, embodying memorials and statements from the Assembly of Missouri, from General Ashley, from General William Clark (surviving leader of the Lewis and Clark expedition), Governor Lewis Cass of Michigan, John Jacob Astor, and others. It recites that because of British aggression, aided by the high duties imposed upon scarlet cloth, blankets, and so on, used in the Indian trade, and by the free admission of foreign furs, the fur trade of the United States is seriously ill; and that because of the presence upon American fur grounds of the British traders

500 lives and $500,000 worth of property have been lost, during the past twenty years.

He suggests, as first of the measures to be taken, that " the project of a joint occupancy by the British and Americans, of the country west of the Rocky Mountains, ought to be abandoned; a line of demarkation amicably established, with as little delay as possible; and the citizens and subjects of the two powers, for all the purposes of trade and intercourse with the Indians, confined to their respective sides of it." [32]

Here sounded one of those early calls for the occupancy of Oregon — but not for settlement, only for trade. Pending any such arrangement, General Ashley had in 1823 taken the initiative by sending his men across the divide to the Green, and in 1826 had emphasized his action by hauling that six-pounder cannon over to Utah Lake. Then Smith, Jackson and Sublette, in 1826, had boldly pushed further, until the roving Smith had appeared even upon the Pacific coast — where, with Christian meekness and gentlemanly spirit, he had hobnobbed with Governor McLoughlin himself, chief of the Hudson Bay affairs in America.

But this urbane interview did not represent the American attitude toward the British company, and the American traders and trappers considered the " Nor'westers " fair prey. In 1824 the religious Smith is accused of having, by questionable Yankee methods, gained for himself some packs of furs to which a Hudson Bay factor deemed his own company entitled; and the factor, one Ross, could not but admit that the Americans were " shrewd men," and that Smith was " a very intelligent person." General Ashley is accused of having lifted a Hudson Bay cache, or else of having demoralized with liquor a Hudson Bay party, by which he achieved the turn in his fortunes to wealth; Fitzpatrick rendered an Ogden party foolish with alcohol, and got their furs for a song; and Captain Bonneville descended to honey and alcohol, that hé might befuddle a " Nor'west " guest.

We now come to the American methods of gaining furs for themselves; and the process never was more thoroughly illustrated than when, in 1832, Kit Carson had entered the mountains. The Government, with true but mistaken democracy, recognized no one company, declined to parcel the field among separate companies; such was the dread of a " monopoly," however wisely administered for the public peace.

Instead of blaming upon British aggression the alleged injury to and decline of the fur trade of the West, the trader of the States should have removed the beam from his own eye.

These traders are continually endeavoring to lessen each other in the eyes of the Indians, not only by abusive words, but by all sorts of low tricks and maneuvers. * * * The imposing appearance of the army equipments of the white men and the novelty and convenience of their merchandise had impressed the Indians with a high idea of their power and importance, but the avidity with which beaver skins are sought after, the tricks and wrangling made use of, and the degradations submitted to in obtaining them, have induced a belief that the whites cannot exist without them, and have made a great change in their opinion of our importance, our justice, and our power.[38]

Thus from Council Bluffs wrote Thomas Biddle, in 1819; and herein was shown the folly of the American and the wisdom of the Britisher. Whereas the former, by running after the Indian, would seem to make himself dependent upon Indian favor, the latter by his steady policy, his fixed prices, and the quality of his goods, made the Indian dependent upon him for comforts.

The erratic, scrambling rivalry of the American traders

among themselves continued; so that in 1833 Thomas Fitzpatrick, the trader and trapper of long experience, wrote to
General Ashley, the fur-trade champion at Washington:

If there is not some alteration made in the system of business in this country very soon, it will become a nuisance and a
disgrace to the United States. With so many different companies roving about from one tribe to another, each telling
a different tale, and slandering each other to such a degree
as to disgust the Indians, they will evidently all become hostile
to Americans.[84]

And this, indeed, was the situation now in the spring of
1832, when the two American companies — the Rocky
Mountain Fur Company and the American Fur Company
— and the Hudson Bay Company were locked in a bitter
fight, with Bonneville, Wyeth, Gant and Blackwell, and
the other lesser fry, vainly attempting flank marches.

Of the two principal companies, the American Fur Company (in the West, after its first establishment there, to
be known and referred to simply as " the Company," a title
significant of its masterful character) had possession of
the plains. Operated with John Jacob Astor overseeing
from New York, and Pierre Chouteau, Jr., directing from
St. Louis, with the best organizers and traders in the fur
business upon its list of agents, its posts were located or in
process of location all along the Missouri clear to the Blackfeet country near the river's sources in Montana. Many
of these forts, like many of the highly capable agents, were
inheritance from former companies which " the Company "
absorbed, thus acquiring, all ready to hand, men, territory,
and munitions. It had just installed upon the Missouri the
first traffic steamboat, *The Yellowstone*, for carrying
supplies to the posts and furs to St. Louis. Sternly business-
like, exacting from its employees as much work as possible
with as little risk and expenditure to itself as possible, the

American Fur Company eventually occupied the whole fur field of the West.

The Rocky Mountain Fur Company's stronghold and headquarters were the mountains, where at the outset it held the advantage in that it knew the country. It had no posts, it worked by means of camps and rendezvous, it was versatile, mobile, and lived afield at a minimum of expense. Of its leaders, Fitzpatrick, Milton Sublette, and Bridger had been in the mountains since Ashley's early endeavors of 1823 and 1824; and the chances are that Fraeb and Gervais were almost as experienced. Their men had been taken over from the Smith, Jackson & Sublette outfit — some of them inherited from Ashley; and the names of Fitzpatrick and Jim Bridger and Milton Sublette alone would have induced the pick of mountaineers to join the standard. William Sublette had the contract to bring in the supplies — which insured competent service.

On the other hand, the partisans and many of the file in the American Fur Company, which for the first time was extending its operations to the Rockies and beyond, were strangers in a strange land. The condition was after a manner similar to that at the beginning of the Civil War: the Rocky Mountain Fur Company, like the Confederate forces, fought upon its own soil, and upon ground of· its own choosing; the American Fur Company was the invader. Hither, thither, trapped the Rocky Mountain squads, at first seeking the rich spots known only to them, later conducting feints and retreats, but always pursued by the American detachments, willing to spend to learn. For the campaign of education cost the American Fur Company lives and money; lured into the Blackfeet fastnesses, the gallant Vanderburgh fell, dying like a soldier, and, coming to rendezvous, the supply trains of Fontenelle must witness a camp already supplied by the better endowed Sublette. At last, worn out in the four years like the armies of the South,

the Rocky Mountain Fur Company ceased as an organization. The American Company became supreme in the
mountains as upon the plains.

The fetish of the fur trade, as it was the fetish of the
fur hunt, was alcohol; it was worshiped with the blindness
of the African savage, and it fattened its priests at the
expense of the blood and soul of its devotees.

In the beginning, the Hudson Bay Company, as has been
remarked, forbade the use of alcohol in trading. This was
policy, not principle; and when, in rivalry with the American traders, alcohol was demanded, the company changed
its policy to meet the occasions. Could both nations have
agreed not to use alcohol in the fur country, the result
would have been most beneficial to both. The one side
suspiciously refused so to engage; the other engaged, but
failed to perform.

From the time of Lieutenant Zebulon Pike, who, in
ascending the Mississippi in the summer of 1805, distributed presents of rum to the Sioux, liquor has been a factor
in the Indian country of the West. Up to 1822 it was used
with discretion, for the fur business was then a government
enterprise, conducted from posts or factories — a system
somewhat along the lines of the British companies. But
with the demand that the fur trade be thrown open to the
people (and as usual it was not the people, but the few
personages who benefited), for the next ten years liquor
might be legally taken into the Indian country only for the
use of the white employees en route and at the posts. However, this was a country beyond the law.

What a farce this regulation proved is evidenced by the
padded lists provided by traders even as high in standing as
the Chouteaus of St. Louis, and by the instance of William
Sublette, who obtained a license to carry liquor for his
" boatmen," when his destination was Pierre's Hole, overland across the Rocky Mountains! For in fur days, as in

later days, successfully to defraud the government was held no crime.

Then, in 1832, despite the protests of the fur companies, the government of the Republic — and praise be to its purpose, if not to its execution — by act of Congress, July 9, provided that "no ardent spirits shall be hereafter introduced, under any pretence, into the Indian Country." Upon the government force at Fort Leavenworth devolved the responsibility of confiscating the liquor which might be smuggled that far; but the government search would be limited to the boats ascending; the overland expeditions evaded the regulation. Not until June 30, 1834, was the department of Indian Affairs created, which could oversee or pretend to oversee the wider territory.

Now, after the interdiction of liquor, in 1832, the bitterness of the fight for furs waxed vastly. The Hudson Bay Company quickly took advantage of its rivals' plight, and used liquor more freely than before. And this is a damning blot upon the story of the British success in furs: that when opportunity was presented to eliminate liquor from the fur country, the English did not meet the American spirit halfway. Among themselves the American traders were at odds and ends — and all about who should be supplied with the whiskey. Chiefly the fight waged up and down the Missouri, where the American Fur Company, controlling much of that territory, was in sore straits to compete with the British of the borders and with the small concerns who were not so closely watched. Accusations and counter accusations flew back and forth.

But there was no dearth, in 1832, or for half a century thereafter, of liquor for the Indian trade upon the plains and in the mountains, whither it was transported at first in the flat kegs, on back of mule and horse, and later in wagons.

In 1841 the caravan with which traveled Rufus Sage

conveyed, as a portion of its trading assets, twenty-four barrels of alcohol, moving the truthful chronicler to protest:

This announcement may occasion surprise to many, when aware that the laws of Congress prohibit, under severe penalties, the introduction of liquor among the Indians, as an article of traffic, subjecting the offender to a heavy fine and confiscation of effects. Trading companies, however, find ways and means to smuggle it through, by the wagon load, under the very noses of the government officers, stationed along the frontier to enforce the observance of the laws.

I am irresistibly led to the conclusion that these gentry are wilfully negligent of their duty. * * * It seems almost impossible that a blind man, retaining the senses of smell, taste and hearing could remain ignorant of a thing so palpably plain. The alcohol is put into wagons, at Westport or Independence, *in open day light*, and taken into the territory *in open day light*, where it remains a week or more awaiting the arrival of its owners. * * *

These gentlemen cannot plead ignorance as an excuse. They well know that alcohol is one of the principal articles in the Indian trade — this fact is notorious — no one pretends to deny it; not even the traders themselves. * * * [85]

Smallpox and alcohol were the gifts of the white man to the red; and the latter gift was the worse, for while it scorched the heart of the receiver it withered also the soul of the donor. If the Indian would stop at no sacrifice to obtain his dram, the white would stay at no meanness to supply it. Consequently, by the eagerness on both sides arose those well known practices: the gradual dilution of the keg until the drunken Indian was trading for only water; the false measuring, by inserting thumb or finger into the gill, or covering the bottom of the tin cup with a layer of paraffin; the adulteration by tobacco and pepper, that the dose might poison sooner; all those wretched deceits by which the weak second party should be cheated the more roundly. Truly, the beaver and the buffalo had their revenge.

But what was the coin for which the white trader stooped so far?

Let the reader sit down and figure up the profits on a forty-gallon keg of alcohol, and he will be thunder-struck, or rather whiskey-struck. When disposed of, four gallons of water are added to each gallon of alcohol. In two hundred gallons there are sixteen hundred pints, for each of which the trader gets a buffalo robe worth five dollars. The Indian women toil many long weeks to dress these sixteen hundred robes. The white trader gets them all for worse than nothing, for the poor Indian mother hides herself and her children in the forests until the effect of the poison passes away from husbands, fathers, and brothers, who love them when they have no whiskey, and abuse and kill them when they have. Six thousand dollars for sixty gallons of alcohol. Is it any wonder that, with such profits in prospect, men get rich who are engaged in the fur trade? [86]

Thus writes Jim Beckwourth, Crow chief and likewise Indian trader, after having, himself, turned six kegs of the stuff into eleven hundred robes and eighteen horses, aggregating the six thousand dollars above mentioned, and bringing on the fit of moralizing, which was cheap. Beaver and other furs were gained as improvidently. The Indian was not only befuddled, he was robbed. When he protested, he was cajoled, laughed at behind his back, and befuddled again.

Listen to the Red Man of the West — whose dignity was once portrayed by a Catlin, whose mental and moral status was once extolled by an Irving:

Big man, me. Chief — Black Warrior. Me, American soldier! Love Americans, heap. Big man, me! Love whiskey, heap. White man good. Whiskey good. Love whiskey, me — drink heap whiskey. No give me whiskey drink? Me, Chief. Me, American. Me, Black Warrior. Heap big man, me! Love Americans. Take him hand, shake. White man good. Whiskey good. Me love whiskey! Love him heap! No give Black Warrior Whiskey? No? One leetle drink?

Whiskey good. Me love him. Make Black Warrior strong.
Big man, me — Chief. American soldier. We love American.
Shake him hand. Fight him, bad Indian, no love white man.
Kill him. White man good. Me love white man. Whiskey
good. Me love whiskey. No give Black Warrior whiskey —
one leetle drink? Me, Chief. Big man, me. Etc.[87]

Contrast this with the fancied speech of an Uncas, or
with the real speech of a Keokuk, a chief Joseph, a Sitting
Bull. Truly the beaver and the buffalo did have their
revenge, not only in blood of many a skirmish and horrid
raid, but in the very essence of destruction — the destruction of the spirit.

CHAPTER XII

DRAMATIS PERSONAE

A S THE curtain lifts for this act ushering upon the stage
of the beaver West the year 1832 and the events
which follow it, let us briefly glance at the more important
actors. The popular General William Henry Ashley had
already been elected to Congress. " The most influential
man in Missouri, next to Senator Benton," married three,
perhaps four times, father of the American beaver trade in
the mountains (but with no other child), militia man, trader,
trapper and fur merchant, financier and politician, out of
defeats achieving his success after he was fifty, he died at
sixty (in 1838) to lie in a neglected grave upon a Missouri
farm, beside the waters of the river trail which he had so oft
ascended.

As for Major Andrew Henry, the Ashley partner, already

> He is gone on the mountain,
> He is lost to the forest.

The first American to establish foothold between the Rockies and the coast, he had submitted to his narrow bed
January 10, 1832 — a man of " honesty, intelligence and
enterprise," tall and slender, with dark hair and light eyes,
fond of the violin. His name survives in descendants, and in
the lake and river in the vicinity of his old fort of 1810.

Ewing Young is trapping through the Gila country with
Moses Carson in his company. He will arrive in California
again in April, and will take up residence of two years at
Monterey, thence to sail (1834) with Hall Kelly, the
Oregon colonizer. His Mexican wife and the boy child in

WILLIAM WOLFSKILL

WHO BROKE THE "SPANISH TRAIL" TO
CALIFORNIA, 1830

(Copy of old daguerreotype)

JOSEPH ROBIDOUX

HEAD OF THE FAMOUS FAMILY OF
FUR HUNTERS, AND WHO FOUNDED ST.
JOE, MISSOURI

*(Courtesy of the Missouri Historical
Society)*

JOSEPH L. MEEK

MOUNTAIN MAN, CONTEMPORARY OF KIT
CARSON

(Photograph by Joseph Bucktel.

"OLD" JIM BAKER

TRAPPER, WEARING BEAVER HAT

JIM BECKWOURTH

FRENCH-MULATTO, CROW CHIEF, MOUNTAIN MAN, CONTEMPORARY OF
KIT CARSON

Taos never will see him again, nor does he mention them in his new home.

David E. Jackson ("Davy" to his friends) of "Jackson Hole," on a mule-trading excursion to San Diego, via Santa Rita and Tucson, is taking perhaps the first negro, a slave, into California. Coming back again to the States, he dies a poor man in St. Louis.

Joshua Pilcher, Virginian, hatter, banker of St. Louis, fur trader of long experience dating back to 1819, hero of the "grand tour" swinging around the circle, in 1827, is American Fur agent at Council Bluffs. In six years he will succeed the famous and jovial General William Clark in the Indian affairs superintendency at St. Louis; and in June, 1847, will die, aged only 57.

Etienne Provost (Prévost), first white user of the South Pass, accredited with being the first white visitor to the Salt Lake, is still alive, but his end of worldly wanderings is near.

Jedediah S. Smith is only a memory.[38] For six months his bones have been lying under Southwest soil. Connecticut born, a man of high ideals and of steadfast faith in the Christian religion, a combination of the wilderness hunter and the missionary, he can ill be spared from an area wherein characters like this are sorely needed. His ambition was to present the world with an atlas and history of the western country; but it was never achieved.

Let us call the roll of those, the rank and file, still active in the field:

William Sublette: "Height six feet two inches; forehead straight and open; eyes blue, light; nose Roman; mouth and chin common; hair light or sandy; complexion fair; face long and expressive; scar on left side of chin;" to the Indians, "Cut Face," "Fate," and "Left Hand." Sublette was a Kentuckian, born in 1799, one of five brothers, all of the early trans-Missouri West; a bold, energetic trader, a determined and skillful Indian fighter; known to his associate mountain men as " Billy." He retired wealthy from the mountains in 1842, aspired vainly to Congress from Missouri, would have been satisfied with the superintendency of Indian Affairs at St. Louis, but died young, in 1845, at Pittsburg, Pennsylvania, while on his way to Washington City.

Robert Campbell: An Irishman of County Tyrone, who, in 1825, aged 21, as an Ashley man, sought the mountains for his health, and found there not only health, but wealth. Partner and stanch friend of William Sublette in trading enterprises, later one of St. Louis' most prominent financiers and business heads; banker and owner of the old Southern Hotel; Indian commissioner in 1851 and 1869, and outfitter of government expeditions, he was a man of prized counsel and fine integrity. Outliving most of his contemporary mountain men, he died in October, 1879, aged 75.

Milton Sublette: Brother, and associate in the mountains, of William Sublette, the partner in the Rocky Mountain Fur Company. Second to his brother in prominence,[39] in December, 1836, while still a young man, he died at old Fort William, built by his brother and Robert Campbell and named for his brother, owned by himself in partnership with Fitzpatrick and Jim Bridger, and now in 1836 already being called Fort Laramie.

Baptiste Gervais: Canadian Frenchman; a partner in the Rocky Mountain Fur Company, and a mountaineer without history because he lacked a biographer. After he sold out his interest in the company, 1834, for " twenty head of horse beast, thirty beaver traps and five hundred dollars' worth of merchandise," he disappears.

Henry Fraeb: German; partner in the Rocky Mountain Fur Company. He and Gervais usually hunted together in the mountain region of northwestern Colorado. When in

1834 he sold out his partnership for " forty head of horse beast, forty traps, eight guns and one thousand dollars' worth of merchandise," he continued to hunt for beaver in Colorado. As " Frapp " he lived, and as " Frapp " and " Trapp " he died, being shot while " forted " with his thirty trappers against an attack by three hundred Cheyennes and Sioux, at the confluence of Battle Creek and the Little Snake, in northern Colorado near the Wyoming line, August 21 and 22, 1841. He was buried on the spot with $80 in his pockets; and his grave and the grave of three companions mark the site of the last known " big " trapper and Indian battle in the West.

Thomas Fitzpatrick: " Bad Hand," " Broken Hand," " White Head," trader, partisan and mountain man, fully the equal of William Sublette, and contemporary with Sublette in his beginnings under General Ashley in 1823, but long outliving him; first a partner in the Rocky Mountain Fur Company, and afterward a professional guide for overland parties. He is mentioned with praise by the missionary Elijah White as his guide on the way to Oregon in 1842; praised by Fremont as an efficient guide upon his expeditions across to California, in 1843 and in 1845; by Colonel Philip St. George Cooke as his guide in the dragoon excursion along the Oregon Trail in 1845; by Lieutenant J. W. Abert, as his guide in the government expedition exploring the country from Bent's Fort on the Arkansas to St. Louis; by Lieutenant Johnston and others as guide with the Kearny overland column through the Colorado Desert, 1846, thence turning back with Kit Carson's dispatches to Washington. Called by the Indians " Bad Hand " and " Broken Hand," because of partial crippling through accidental discharge of a rifle, he was named " White Head," later, because of a terrific chase (1832) by Indians, which turned his hair gray. Rather thickset, still young looking when employed first by Fremont, his white hair contrasted strangely with his ruddy complexion. In the fall of 1846 Fitzpatrick was appointed Indian Agent upon the upper Platte and the Arkansas, over Sioux, Cheyennes, Arapahos and "other wandering tribes," with post at Bent's Fort, served thus with notable efficiency, reporting that he "looks out for the old mountain men traders who may not have procured licenses." After the demolition of Bent's Fort, in 1852, he removed his agent's headquarters to the Big Timbers, the site of the new Bent's Fort. He was "greatly esteemed by the Indians, and among white men is reputed to have been the best agent these tribes ever had." Married a half-breed Arapaho girl, daughter of John Poisal, an interpreter known among the Indians as "Old Red Eyes," on account of an inflammation. He died in 1855, while still agent. A man evidently of much energy and judgment, of activities as wide and as useful as those of Carson or Bridger, yet by the singular eccentricity of fate he was to pass away unnoted and with his grave unmarked.

James Bridger: "Old Gabe," "Daniel Boone of the Mountains," the "Old Man of the Mountains," "Casapy" or "Blanket Chief," born in Virginia in 1804, died blind and decrepit on his farm at Santa Fe, Missouri, not far from Kansas City, in 1881, one of the very few mountain men who long survived the beaver days and lived to a ripe age. At nineteen Bridger was an Ashley man; at twenty-two (1826) accredited discoverer (on a wager that he would descend Bear River to its mouth) of the Salt Lake; first exploiter of the wonders in the Yellowstone National Park — and not believed; partner in the Rocky Mountain Fur Company; partner next in the short-lived fur firm of Sublette (Milton), Campbell & Bridger; founder of Fort Bridger, the first trading post for emigrants on the Oregon Trail, erected in 1843 on Black's Fork of the Green River, southwestern Wyoming, "west of the mountains." A blacksmith originally, then beaver trapper, trader, and guide;

guide in 1854-55 for Sir George Gore, the Irish sportsman in the Rockies; for the General Albert Sidney Johnston " Utah column " in the Mormon War of 1857-58; for various army detachments on the plains in the Civil War, and consulted by General Sheridan as late as 1868; for Captain Reynolds of the army in the attempted exploration of Yellowstone Park in 1869; adviser to the survey for the Union Pacific Railroad, 1869, and donator thereto of the cut-off Bridger's Pass. He was a man of spare but powerful Virginian type, gray-eyed, brown-haired, shaven and wrinkled and tanned, with quizzical cast of countenance. A mountain man ranking with Carson and Fitzpatrick, having, according to Father DeSmet, " two quivers full of arrows shot into his body," possessing the qualities of a natural topographer and a born story-teller, he was in his declining years a pathetic figure. The last of the Ashley type of beaver hunters, he died poor, feeling that he had been defrauded by a government which he had well served. But over his body in the Mount Washington cemetery of Kansas City is reared a noble granite monument — token that his deeds and services are not and never will be forgotten.

William Henry Vanderburgh was an American Fur Company man and partisan in the mountain hunts whereby the Rocky Mountain Fur Company was steadily harrassed. An Indianan, a West Pointer (entering 1817), by 1823 a fur trader in the Missouri Fur Company, and in that year a captain under Colonel Leavenworth in the attack upon the Arikara Indians, he was ambushed by the Blackfeet, in October, 1832, while pressing recklessly along a side stream of the Jefferson River in the Three Forks country of southwestern Montana. His horse was disabled, and abandoned by his helplessly stampeded and shattered men, his last words, as bravely he faced the enemy and shot the foremost were: " Boys, do n't run." Thus fell William Henry Vanderburgh, under thirty years of age.

Andrew S. Drips was partisan and agent of the American Fur Company, in the mountain campaigns and on the upper Missouri. A Pennsylvanian, born in 1789, he died in Kansas City, 1860. He entered the fur trade as early as 1820 with the title of "major" — that honorary title applied by government reports to Jim Bridger, Fitzpatrick, and other traders and scouts. In 1842 he was appointed agent for the tribes of the upper Missouri and stationed at Fort Pierre, at the mouth of the Teton River in southeastern North Dakota. He was the first Indian Agent to fight, with genuine zeal, the introduction of liquor into the Indian country.

Lucien Fontenelle: The third in the trio of American Fur Company partisans in the mountain rivalry. A New Orleans Frenchman, of aristocratic blood, a youth born to romance, orphaned by a Louisiana hurricane, made a runaway by a too-strict aunt, exchanging a bank clerkship for the Missouri River frontier, returning to New Orleans, after twenty years, to be identified by and welcomed by an old nurse, but to be repudiated by a sister. Again he became a trader, associated with Andrew Drips at Bellevue, and later led brigades into the Rockies. He was a swart, foreign-appearing man, of a saturnine temperament, which finally brought him to suicide, early in 1836, at that Fort William on the North Platte, where but a few weeks preceding his competitor, Milton Sublette, had died. His children by an Omaha Indian wife were prominent figures in the early history of Nebraska.

Captain Benjamin Louis Eulalie de Bonneville: French born, West Point educated; died June 12, 1878, at Fort Smith, Arkansas. He was "of middle size, well made and well set," his countenance "frank, open and engaging," with a French cast. He had a "pleasant black eye," a high forehead and a bald crown. In the spring of 1832, on leave from the army, he conducted an exploring and fur hunting brigade across South Pass, and along the Salt Lake and Snake and Green Rivers, but was rebuffed by British and American companies, alike. He succeeded in calling more attention to the Great Basin (today bearing his name), and accidentally opening communication with California by the Walker route, sprinkled, as advanced the Star of Empire, with the blood of wretched Diggers.

Captain Gant: An independent trader, of whom we first hear when, in the spring of 1831, he took a party of seventy trappers, many of them greenhorns from Pennsylvania, out of St. Louis across Nebraska and up the Platte to the Laramie Plains. A man well initiated into his western career by bad fortune, he seems to have placed himself in history as the first trader to cultivate a stable outpost among the Arapahos — a people jealous, in their plains ranging along the foothills between the Arkansas and the Platte, of white invasion. He and his partner, Captain Blackwell, had a post upon the upper Arkansas in the early thirties; and the ruins of at least one of their posts, about six miles below the present city of Pueblo, were visible for some years prior to the Mexican War. When Colonel Henry Dodge's First Dragoons in the summer of 1835 swung out from Fort Gibson, on a tour of the Indian country, up the Platte to the mountains and south to return by the Arkansas, " Captain Gant, Indian trader," was the guide. Of his partner, Captain Blackwell, nothing is known.

Nathaniel Jarvis Wyeth: General trader, fur hunter, first enthusiast to put the Oregon question to practical test. Cambridge born and educated in Massachusetts. In 1832, after a preliminary " hardening " by two weeks' camping upon an island in the home river, out of Boston he headed, with his twenty amateur crusaders, to embark in " business " in Oregon! His men were daunted by unexpected hardships and sarcastic over his wagon-boat, dubbed by Harvard students the Nat-Wyethium. Succored by Sublette, he was received by the mountains with the fierce battle of Pierre's Hole. After that his trail was one of constant disappointment and discouragement, and with the title of captain he ultimately returned to New England and an ice business.

Joseph L. Meek: Trapper, first Oregon sheriff, envoy from Oregon " to the Court of Washington." Born in Virginia in 1810, almost at the time of the birth of Kit Carson in Kentucky, he entered the mountains as a runaway in 1828, with William Sublette. A rogue, a wit, a harum-scarum, now here, now there, now prosperous, now poor, the plantation his school and the mountains his college, his adventures upon the beaver trail resulted in one of the best histories of the opening of the Northwest.[40]

William Williams: " Old Bill " Williams, lone trapper, ex-preacher, eccentric. A tall, stooped man of Missouri fever-and-ague type, his thin, leathery face, his nut-cracker jaws, his Punch chin and nose, his small, sharp, twinkling, restless gray eyes, his querulous voice, slovenly habits, elk-hide suit, black with camp-fire smoke and slick with grease, his piebald, hump-nosed Indian pony, were familiar to trappers, traders, and Indians from the Three Forks to the Gila, from the States to California. Aged, infirm, half blind from summer desert and winter hills, in conducting Fremont's fourth expedition around the head of the San Luis Park of Colorado, in the fall of 1848, he failed. With this, an old stamping ground, he seemed utterly unfamiliar. After the rescue of the party, true to his solitary nature and to escape ignominy, he fled from the company of his fellows, and amidst the depth of winter he plunged as of yore back into the snow-bound peaks. In the spring of 1849 his body was found, a bullet wound in its breast, sitting against a tree as if he had been stricken instantly, in a most secret recess of his favorite haunt of Middle Park, Colorado. A medicine man, sacred among the Utes, his friends, he had been convicted by them of betraying a camp to the hostile

Arapahos and a council had decided that he must die.
Thus they had executed him, as, unconscious of danger, he
sat in camp; and as token they had exchanged rifles with
him. He is remembered today as perhaps the most notorious of all the mountain men, and his monuments are the
Williams Fork of the Grand River in Colorado Middle
Park (his burial place), and the Bill Williams Peak and
the station of Williams, Arizona.[41]

Thomas L. Smith: " Peg-leg " Smith, assumed but erro-
neously to be the brother of Jedediah S. Smith; among the
Mexicans " El Cojo Smit " (the Lame Smith); a " stout
built man with black eyes and gray hair "; a " hard drinker,
and, when under the influence of liquor, very liable to get
into a fight "; possessor of a most serviceable wooden leg
(its predecessor having been amputated in the brush after
a scrimmage with the Blackfeet), which, unstrapped, aided
in cleaning out many a barroom and frontier " grocery
store." His mountain-man trapper service dated from
before 1826; and when he died he was almost the last representative of the rough-and-ready, boisterous frontiersmen.

Peter Skene Ogden: Hudson Bay head trader; son of
a chief justice of Montreal; but no match for the American traders in a bargain. " Short, dark and exceedingly
tough, with an inexhaustible fund of humor "; " a fellow
of infinite jest," perhaps o 'er good-natured for business, but
a dweller in the wilds who traveled his trail with a smile
and amidst friends. He died in Oregon, his adopted land,
in 1854.

Captain Joseph Reddiford Walker: Tennessean and Missourian, dark and bearded, six feet tall, weight, two hundred
pounds, thorough frontiersman, mild but resolute, Santa Fe
trapper, Spanish captive, Indian fighter, Missouri sheriff,
Southwest trader, captain under Bonneville into the mountains, breaker of the trail from Salt Lake west across the
Great Basin to Monterey, desert guide for emigrant parties,

California rancher and stock raiser, first of the Arizona prospectors who opened the Prescott region — " one of the bravest and most skillful of mountain men," especially familiar with the desert of the Southwest. He died, famous and respected, on a ranch in Contra Costa County, California, 1876, at the age of 78, his only request being that upon his stone be ascribed to him the discovery of Yosemite Park.

Michel Sylvestre Cerré: Fur trader and captain under Bonneville, St. Louis Frenchman, born April, 1803, and grandson of a pioneer fur hunter of the Mississippi Valley; in the American Fur Company, after the Bonneville expedition; 1848, representative in the Missouri Assembly; 1849, clerk of St. Louis District Court; 1858, sheriff of St. Louis County; died from pneumonia January 5, 1860. The name Cerré still survives, on an equality with the proud name of Chouteau.

———— Markhead: Christian name unknown; " celebrated for his courage and reckless daring," in years as in deeds Kit Carson's contemporary, he was shot in the back by Mexican captors while on the Taos Trail during the Mexican Pueblo insurrection of the winter 1846-1847.[42]

Robert Newell: " Doc " Newell, trapper, Ohioan recruit of 1829 with William Sublette; Meek's comrade, fellow rancher and influential fellow citizen in Oregon, Indian agent and speaker in the Oregon Assembly.

John Hawkins: " Jake Hawkens," trapper, later a rancher and trader, in 1847, at the pueblo on the Arkansas — the settlement where now has arisen Pueblo, Colorado.

Richard Owens: " Dick " Owens, Carson's close comrade and partner in many mountain doings; his partner in ranching it in New Mexico after trapper days; his companion upon the third Fremont expedition, and a captain in California service during the events which followed the Bear Flag. A man " cool, brave and of good judgment."

Jim Beckwourth: Of French-negro blood, trapper with the first Ashley expedition of 1822, and of long, varied service thereafter; Crow chief; alleged army scout in Florida; trader; overlander to California, immigrant trader there and discoverer of Beckwourth's Pass in the Sierras, where, ascending Feather River, today a railroad crosses; a romanticist, whose dictated volume of his life exceeds the best endeavors of a Ned Buntline. In his later years a Denverite; and at the end again a Crow, dying by poisoned soup in a Crow lodge of the North Platte country, Wyoming, 1867, aged seventy. Thus his Crow wife retained his spirit.

Antoine Robidoux:[48] First fur trader out of old Taos, whose post in southwestern Colorado was the pioneer American trading post beyond the Continental Divide of the Rockies; later with a post established at the forks of the Uintah River in northeastern Utah — Fort Uintah, captured and destroyed in 1844 by the Utes. One of New Mexico's earliest gold miners — setting the fashion by " sinking eight thousand dollars." Interpreter and guide with the Kearny overland column of 1846 to California, where his brother, Louis Robidoux, who had preceded him by two years, was *alcalde* and *juez de paz* at San Bernardino; grievously wounded by a lance thrust at the battle of San Pasqual; granted a pension by Congress May 23, 1856; died at St. Joseph, Missouri (former trading post of his second brother, Joseph), in 1860, aged 66. A " thin man," of the French-Canadian type, active member of a family distinguished along the Missouri, in the Southwest and in California. His pass across the rampart Sangre de Cristo range, Colorado, for the inner country, today Mosca Pass, was long a noted wagon trail.

Captain Sir William Drummond Stuart: " Sporting Englishman " with the " two-shoot " gun; seventh Baron of Grandtully; lover of the wild West, and therein beloved; hail comrade with the mountain men, a hunter and a fighter, a thorough Britisher on the big game trail who traveled with courage and with creature comforts which alike astonished camp and rendezvous.

J. M. Stanley: Artist, whose " The Trapper's Last Shot " is among the very few canvases and perhaps is the only one photographic of those numberless events deserving of a Remington, but with, alas, no Remington there; the first artist to attempt this stirring field, and later delineator of the Governor Isaac I. Stevens exploration, and contemporary army explorations, 1853-54-55, for a railroad route to the Pacific.[44]

CHAPTER XIII

ADVENTURES OF KIT CARSON — 1832-1834

WE FIND Kit Carson, in the summer of 1832, as a free trapper back in Taos with his mountain furs. Here he is out of the strife which is embittering the solitudes, and by sale of his beaver he has a competency which would last a youth of his sober instincts some time. But at twenty-two, in the far West of that day, what youth would plan a siesta of long duration? There enters upon the scene " Captain Lee," said to be a minor partner in the active trading firm of Bent, St. Vrain & Co., who recently had established the post of Fort William, or Bent's Fort, northeast of Taos on the Arkansas River in southeastern Colorado, and of whom more will be related presently.

Captain Lee, like Captain Gant and more like Captain Blackwell, seems fated to go down the aisles of history without distinction of name. However, with Captain Lee (previously of the United States Army), in October of 1832, Kit Carson takes a mule pack train of trading supplies from Taos into the Uintah country of northeastern Utah.

The route chosen by Captain Lee and young Carson was that old Spanish Trail, retraced two years previously by William Wolfskill, and since then by various horse and mule expeditions, lawful and unlawful, between New Mexico and Alta California, made well defined.

Not a pleasant trail was this, in its beginnings, through the perilous country of the Apaches — a country heavily timbered in the mountains, but for the most part whitish, gravelly mesas or table-lands, watercourses now dry, sand and cactus, sage and piñon and scrub oak, where lived the coyote and the jack rabbit, the rattlesnake, tarantula and buzzard: yet a country requiring only the irrigating ditch to make it fertile.

In southwestern Colorado the timber became more common, with chaparral or brushy growth and sage covering the mesas, and bare volcanic ridges rising to the north. Ancient stone ruins of forgotten people were passed in the walls of deep, bare cañons, or crowning gravelly hills. At the Dolores the party left the Wolfskill trace and headed more into the north for the Uintah country of northeastern Utah. They may not have known that they were following any but an Indian trail, but this was the course of the original Spanish Trail, as pioneered by good Father Escalante himself.

The country would grow more rugged, filled with spires and peaks, their bases heavily clad with pines and spruces, their crests gaily tinted and specked with patches of snow. Indeed, upon the crests and the passes snow already was falling. It was now Ute country, however, and the Utes were friendly to the trader.

From the White River of northwestern Colorado the Lee-Carson party followed down to the Green, and from the Green a short cut was made northwest to a point where, "at the forks of the Uintah," and "on the right bank, in latitude 40°, 27′, 45″ north, longitude 109°, 56′, 42″ west" was to be located Robidoux Fort, or Fort Uintah, at this time but a rude collection of lodges. Here was established experimentally the veteran Antoine Robidoux, from Taos, and perchance his brother Louis, future *juez de paz* of San Bernardino. The situation was to prove satisfactory, until, in a dozen years, or about 1844, in an attack by the Indians during the absence of the proprietor, the post, of substantial build, was destroyed.

In this fall of 1832 the place was the headquarters of some twenty men, trappers and traders, their squaws and their families.

It would appear scarcely reasonable to presume that Lee and Carson had counted upon this Robidoux camp as their destination and market, for the veteran Antoine would control the territory. However, as winter was setting in, the two companies made winter camp together, further down, at the mouth of the Uintah. Skin lodges were erected, and fuel and meat had to be stored.

In the Robidoux employ was an Indian from California. One night during the winter he disappeared, and with him disappeared six horses, valued at $600; for although horses, in trapper days, were plentiful, yet a good horse was something that could not always be easily replaced. The lowest cash value of a good one was $60. The horse was a common commodity, it was a necessity also, and the pick of necessities is apt to be ranked in value with a luxury. Carson's reputation for skill and reliability was of course known to Robidoux, and he was asked to undertake the pursuit of the thief. Carson probably was nothing loth.

He was warned that the California Indian was very shrewd, and was one of the best rifle shots at the fort. At a Ute village, near by, he picked up a Ute brave, for trailer, and hard and fast, over the winter landscape, they followed the trail of the Californian and his stolen horses.

Down the Green River it sped away, through a grim, bare mesa region fringed with rimrock and cut deep by arroyos. Evidently the Indian fugitive was aiming for California, his home. Then, when by two days of riding the pursuit had covered one hundred miles, the Ute's horse was taken sick and could be used no more.

But the trail was growing warm; the Indian with his six driven horses could not travel as fast as single riders; he could be only a short distance ahead, and Kit Carson continued alone.

After he had proceeded thirty miles more, he sighted ahead of him the thief and the stolen stock. The Indian

well knew that he was being pursued, and he had seen Kit
Carson as quickly as Kit Carson had seen him. Fast and
faster they rode, the Indian to reach cover, just before him,
where he might make a stand, Kit Carson to catch him ere
he did so.

Kit Carson's horse was the swifter, and presently only a
hundred and fifty yards separated pursuer and pursued.
Both men had down their rifles — but the Californian did
not appreciate who was after him. He waited a moment
too long, for it was his purpose to shoot as he reached
cover, and there, under shelter, to reload in readiness to
shoot again, if his first bullet had missed.

Just at the edge of the cover, as he whirled and leveled
his rifle, from the back of the galloping horse behind
cracked the rifle of Carson. The Indian's gun exploded, but
without aim, for he pitched to the ground and instantly
died. Kit Carson had shot first. In due time Carson reached
the Uintah camp with the stolen horses.

As the winter wore away, there arrived at the camp a
small party of men from the upper country to the north,
who reported, among other things, that Fitzpatrick and
Bridger of the Rocky Mountain Fur Company had wintered
in the Snake River Valley and were preparing for the
spring hunt.

Evidently Robidoux had not bought many of the Lee
supplies; and it seemed to the captain and to Kit Carson
that they should start onward, to catch the Fitzpatrick-
Bridger camp before it broke up. Accordingly they packed,
and leaving the isolated camp of Robidoux, headed into
the north.

It was a disagreeable journey of fifteen days, amidst the
snowy, chill weather of late winter and early spring, through
a country very rough, but a region familiar to Carson,
who had been in this vicinity before; and by the end of
the fortnight he and the captain, emerging at the juncture

of the Portneuf and the Snake, in southeastern Idaho, found
there encamped the doughty, winter-bound main force of
the Rocky Mountain Fur Company, under Messrs. Fitzpatrick, Bridger, and Milton Sublette.

Carson, and probably Captain Lee (if associated with
Bent's Fort) therefore met old acquaintances, and around
the lodge fires the news of the mountain world would be
rehearsed. They would hear how the winter here (as like
enough down on the Uintah) was hard, " with skeins of
frost two feet long hanging from the roofs, inside "; they
would learn that William Sinclair, the free trapper from the
Arkansas party, had been killed, that William Sublette had
been wounded, both in a big affray at Pierre's Hole; that
Vanderburgh of the American Company had been " wiped
out " by the Blackfeet in the Three Forks country; and that
Bridger had been shot in the back with two arrows — one
point being there yet.

As Carson's biography states that the Rocky Mountain
Company took over the trading supplies brought in by the
twain, paying therefor in beaver,[45] it is probable that
Captain Lee returned with the pack train to Taos or Bent's
Fort. He then drops from view. Carson stays with the
company for a short time, but long enough to join in a fight.
It may be said of Kit Carson that trouble never dodged
him.

Ere the camp had broken up for the spring hunt the
early Blackfeet, more restless and more vengeful since
that affair of last summer in Pierre's Hole, rushed the
horseherd and ran off most of the saddle stock, including
Jim Bridger's favorite Comanche mount, Grohean. After
a sharp pursuit through the snow by thirty of the trappers,
among them Carson (who here receives his first mention
in trapper chronicle of the day) the Indians were overtaken and a parley resulted. The Blackfeet claimed
that they thought they were robbing their enemies the

Snakes, and not their " friends " the Americans. However, this was but a ruse; and after the savages, in lordly manner, had brought on five of the poorest horses and offered them as full settlement, the council broke up in a general and mutual rush for weapons. The fight was from behind trees and rocks. Trapper Markhead had trouble with the lock of his gun and by quickly changing aim from his own adversary to Markhead's, Carson saved his companion's life but received in the left shoulder the bullet which he might otherwise have avoided.

With shoulder shattered he lay upon the ground until the trappers, badly outnumbered and almost outfought, slowly withdrew, and night put an end to the battle. The night was bitterly cold, but this checked the bleeding of Carson's wound — the only severe wound, so far as recorded, which he ever received at hostile hands.

However, the cold caused much suffering to the trappers, who were in light marching order, and they decided that they were not prepared to pursue the Blackfeet further. So they returned to camp, without the horses; and a supplemental chase by Bridger himself, heading a party, resulted in nothing more.

This spring of 1833 continued fitful and laggard, cold and wet, with much wind and snow. When camp finally broke, for the usual exodus into the hills, Carson again struck out for himself, his reason being

that there were too many congregated together either to accomplish much or to make the general result profitable in the distribution. He accordingly arranged an enterprise upon his own account, and, from his well-established reputation, found more men than he wanted to join him. From those who applied he selected but three.[46]

This argument, whether sound or not, as assigned to Carson, shows him in the light of a shrewd thinker and independent actor. He preferred to make his own trails. And following his biography, we find him this spring trapping, with his little squad, on the Laramie Plains. Before the summer rendezvous he has another of his celebrated adventures.

One late afternoon, while distant from camp, after meat, he shot an elk, and instantly was charged by two grizzly bears. They gave him no time for reloading his rifle. He ran for the nearest tree, and hoisted himself by a limb just as the bears rushed under so close as to brush his dangling legs.

The tree was a young spruce or fir, and low-branching; and now we may understand that Carson had been foolish enough to leave camp without his pistol; for here he must hastily slash off a bough and use it as a club. A bear, when erect, has no mean reach, and these threatened to drag him in shreds from his perch; but he lustily thwacked them upon the nose. After vainly trying him, and being beaten down, having kept him an uneasy prisoner until darkness they retired, and he descended with difficulty, under a cloudy sky, to reach camp again.

While en route to the rendezvous a juncture was made with a Rocky Mountain Company party under Bridger, and the travel was resumed to the Valley of the Green, for the annual market.

The summer rendezvous of 1833, in the well-beloved Valley of the Green, was one of the greatest ever held. The rivalry of the Rocky Mountain Company and the American Company was at its height, and Captain Bonneville likewise was exerting himself to the utmost. No trapper was necessarily out of employment; furs went rapidly.

The rendezvous dissolved, and there was a great parting of the ways. The youth Nathaniel Wyeth, after his winter in Oregon (where, truth to say, he had been more kindly treated by the British company than he had been, or would

be, treated by his American competitors) proceeded on to
Boston, there to close a contract with Milton Sublette for
bringing supplies to the Rocky Mountain Fur Company
rendezvous of the next year; to form the Columbia River
Fishing and Trading Company; and altogether to plan
great things — ignorant, he, as yet (so mysterious are the
works of Providence), that his training had been shaped
to far greater purpose — the escorting across the plains of
the first missionaries, Jason Lee and party, as a wedge
widening the crack made by the fur hunters, so that into
Oregon might enter the creaking canvas-top wagons of the
emigrants from the States.

So from the rendezvous Wyeth, his work cut out for him,
proceeded on courier way home to Boston. In the opposite
direction rode a Bonneville detachment under Joe Walker,
for the west side of the Great Salt Lake, inadvertently or not
to blaze the emigrant Overland Trail across the desert to
golden California.

The various other companies and squads of fur hunters,
for the Rocky Mountain Company, for the American Company, for the Bonneville Company, for the Hudson Bay
Company, for the free companies, separated to trap wherever fortune good or ill indicated.

As for Kit Carson's movements this fall and winter, the
chronicler is confronted by a multiplicity of choices, of
which none are satisfactory. By a few corroborative dates
we may check Carson's adventures: by the founding of
Fort Hall, in 1834; by his alliance with Joseph Gale in
1834; by the date of his duel at the rendezvous of 1835;
by the forting against the Blackfeet, in 1835; by the death
of Fontenelle in 1837; by the rendezvous of 1837. Yet
in any extant biography of him, his wanderings are represented so independently of these dates that time seems to
have been kept by notches on a forked stick.

This fall of 1833 may perhaps have been the one when,

enlisted with a company of fifty men, he traveled to the
Three Forks country of the sources of the Missouri, in
Montana, and there was excessively annoyed by the Blackfeet; but it would be more reasonable to send him southward into western Colorado and the desert of the Southwest,
with the German Fraeb and the French Canadian Gervais,
to hunt and to spend the winter. Meantime the Walker
party, emulating Jedediah Smith, crossed the western desert
in a new place; fully recuperated amidst the hospitality of
Monterey, where bullfights and fandangos and the smiles
of señoritas welcomed them, and in February and spring,
1834, were backward journeying, to report, on the Bear
River, to Captain Bonneville that they had done nothing
with the talents entrusted to them.

A portion of the party, however, swung more to the
south, roistered through the lower country, of the Mohaves
on the Colorado River, and on freebooter course continuing to the Gila, thence turned north and struck the Williams
Fork of the Colorado. This they ascended, and met with
the Rocky Mountain Company division of Fraeb and Gervais, which included Kit Carson, again in his first grounds
of 1829, traversed under Ewing Young.

In this fall of 1833 and spring of 1834 the desert had
suddenly become the fashion — and a strange fashion when
we realize how much more pleasant and profitable were the
mountains.

Two hundred strong, the united parties proceeded eastward to the Colorado Chiquito — the Flax, or the Little
Colorado, River (neither title equaling the Spanish); and
here they lawlessly, in true freebooter style, plundered the
Moqui melon gardens. For resisting, twenty of the Moquis
were shot to death; and the unripe as well as the ripe fruit
was destroyed.

Pointing northwest, having thus sown the seeds of hatred
and death, and leaving the ruined Moquis to curse the

vandal whites, the trappers rode onward across the north-western corner of New Mexico and struck the headwaters of the Rio Grande del Norte, in Colorado's San Luis Park. The objective point was the South Park.

It is likely that some of the party diverged to Taos, now only eighty miles distant, or to Bent's Fort on the Arkansas, for we find Kit Carson, Joe Meek, William Mitchell, and three Delawares, Tom Hill, Jonas, and Manhead (the last-named to be slain in due time by the Blackfeet) on a hunt in southeastern Colorado — " in the country lying between the Arkansas and Cimarron, where numerous small branches of these rivers head together, or within a small extent of country."

Now occurred another Kit Carson adventure — a grim, plains Indian fight, no more, no less than a hundred fights which have by their blood fertilized the Great American Desert, but a fight such as no man wishes to repeat.

On a May morning the six hunters were charged by some two hundred Comanches, those riders of the southern plains equal to their allies, the fierce Kiowas. The whites and Delawares barely had time in which to cut the throats of their saddle mules, and to form a fort of the dead bodies (in trapper style) before the Comanches were upon them, only to recoil before their rifles.

An all-day fight ensued; the trappers strengthened their barricade of mule carcasses by digging pits behind. The Comanches charged again, " the medicine-man in advance shouting, gesticulating, and making a desperate clatter with a rattle which he carried and shook violently. The yelling, the whooping, the rattling, the force of the charge were appalling." Three of the trappers fired, while the other three reloaded; the Comanche horses shrank from the smell of the mule blood; and the warriors could not reach the little fort.

Three medicine men were killed; and each time the

Comanches must retire to choose a new one. During the confabs, the squaws approached to bear off the slain and to revile the defenders. The attacking force was armed principally with the regulation Comanche long lance, attached to hair rope for recovery, and with bows and arrows. The siege and the reiterated assaults lasted until nightfall, so that without shade and water, under the blazing sun, and tortured by dust and heat and powder-reek, the three whites and the three Delawares were desperately put to it.

That the Comanches fought bravely is attested by the record of forty-two killed. Finally, having " lost faith in their medicine," they retired.

When the coast was deemed clear, the six trappers shouldered blanket and gun and maintained a dogtrot all night, making for the mountains and camp, and did not reach water until they had covered seventy-five miles.

The main camp of the party was in Colorado's South Park, where the spring fur hunt was finished out. The summer rendezvous was held as customary in the Valley of the Green.

Here now gathered the various trapping bands of the companies and the free men, save those of Captain Bonneville, which had met in the Valley of the Bear, southward. The Cambridge knight-errant, Nathaniel Wyeth, arrived with supplies and sixty men. He was full of hope, but Milton Sublette proved false to his promise, and the Rocky Mountain Fur Company, favoring William Sublette, the trader, former partisan, and Milton's brother, refused to take the Wyeth goods. So amidst the wassailing and yarning there was bitter feeling; Wyeth protested, Fitzpatrick, " the Bad Hand," railed against the loss of his pack train at the hands of the Crows, instigated, he alleged, by the American Fur Company; Captain Bonneville had been seducing the rank and file by lavish liquor and by proffers of higher pay; the beaver business was demoralized; and early

in the rendezvous the Rocky Mountain Company had issued
the following statement:

Whereas a dissolution of partnership having taken place by
mutual consent between Thos. Fitzpatrick, Milton G. Sublette,
Henry Fraeb, John Baptiste Jervais and James Bridger, members of the Rocky Mountain Fur Company, all persons having
demands against said company are requested to come forward and receive payment, those indebted to said firm are
desired to call and make immediate payment as they are
anxious to close the business of the concern.
Ham's fork June 20, 1834.

THOS. FITZPATRICK
M. G. SUBLETTE
HENRY FRAEB
J. B. GERVAIS
JAMES BRIDGER (his mark)

Wit.:   W. L. Sublette for Bridger & Fitzpatrick.
Wit.:   J. P. Risley for Fraeb & Gervais.
The public are hereby notified that the business will in future
be conducted by Thomas Fitzpatrick, Milton G. Sublette, &
James Bridger, under the style and firm of Fitzpatrick, Sub-
lette & Bridger.
Ham's fork June 20, 1834.

THOS. FITZPATRICK
M. G. SUBLETTE
JAMES BRIDGER (his mark)

Wit.:   W. L. Sublette.

Thus dissolved the Rocky Mountain Fur Company, of
robust lineage. The evil days of bad faith and of con-
cupiscence had fallen upon the beaver trail. At the close
of the rendezvous, Nathaniel Jarvis Wyeth of the Columbia
River Fishing and Trading Company departed, disappointed
but not yet defeated in his endeavor to enter the mountain
trade, hoping to clear himself by ventures at the Pacific end
of the great river of Oregon, and with the threat (well
fulfilled) to " roll into the garden " of Milton Sublette and
associates " a stone which they cannot remove." The bri-

gades and companies departed east, west, north, and south.
For the Columbia was already hastening Captain Bonneville to sweep the country ahead of his fellow struggler
Wyeth. And over the Oregon Trail, yet in its embryo
form, from the rendezvous which they had visited, traveled
the two missionaries, Jason and Daniel Lee, and a company,
bearing the gospel of the white East to the red West.
They, and not the dissolution of the Rocky Mountain
Company, mark the epoch of the summer of 1834. The
beaver hunters were the scouts, the missionaries were the
pioneers, of the westward march of the white civilization.
However, let us not omit Hall J. Kelly and Ewing
Young, who at this moment are out of California and nearing Oregon. Of Ewing Young we know. Of Hall J. Kelly
more should be known. A Boston man, born in 1791;
Harvard graduate, scholar and gentleman; textbook writer,
surveyor, mathematician, through almost thirty years, or
since 1815, inspired by the Lewis and Clark expedition
he has been preaching Oregon, ever Oregon; but for the
most part he has been a prophet dishonored in his own
country. Known to history more or less slightingly as
" the Boston schoolmaster," planning for a great 1832 emigration, in 1827 he issued a circular " To all persons who
wish to migrate to Oregon Territory." He memorialized
Congress upon the subject; in 1829 he asked for a grant,
to American citizenship, of twenty-five miles in the Columbia district. With the traditional schoolman's lack of the
practical he bid without his host, for under joint occupancy with Great Britain such a grant was beyond the scope
of Congress, even should Congress (itself impractical) listen
to his Cassandra voice. Now, in 1834, for four years he
has urged personally in the lobbies at Washington the
American occupancy of Oregon. Heartsick but enthusiastic and determined, all his other schemes for a colonization come to naught, save to interest Nathaniel Wyeth,

in 1833, forty-two years old, by sea and land he headed, via Vera Cruz, for California, thence to make for Oregon, and to send back his reports.

In this summer of 1834 he encounters in Monterey Captain Ewing Young. He has worked in vain to ingratiate himself with Governor Figueroa, a suspicious Mexican. But with Young, nothing loth to embark in a trading venture, and with eight others, with ninety-eight horses and mules, the nucleus of a stock ranch, he continues on for the land of his dreams. Nine " marauders " convoying fifty-six stolen animals join them, and prove their undoing. Young should have known better — but perhaps he was not opposed to despoiling the Latin.

Governor Brigadier General Jose Figueroa, short in reign, " of Aztec blood, and hence swarthy in color," [47] extremely zealous against the foreigner, saw his opportunity, and promptly dispatched word to Governor John McLoughlin of the Hudson Bay Company at Vancouver that a party of American outlaws, with their plunder from California, were upon their way to the British possessions.

Therefore when the Kelly-Young Company arrived at Vancouver — innocent of theft (save by their association with the nine disreputables, who ere this had diverged upon another course) — although upon the trail they had met with succor from Hudson Bay trappers, they were received by Governor McLoughlin with suspicion. Kelly was refused a seat at the " gentleman's mess " of the McLoughlin table; and this cut him to the soul. Young stayed on; he was of fiber innured to rebuff by nature or by man. But remaining scarce a year, a broken crusader, a penniless scholar, a ragged surveyor, a proscribed citizen, ill in mind as in body, Hall J. Kelly sailed again for home — in his pocket to help him on his way thirty-five dollars from the governor, whose right hand was the hand of Company policy while his left hand was so often the hand of human charity.[48]

REV. JASON LEE
LEADER OF THE FIRST MISSIONARIES
ACROSS THE ROCKIES TO OREGON, 1834
*(Courtesy of the Oregon Historical
Society)*

REV. SAMUEL L. PARKER
OF THE SECOND MISSIONARY PARTY
TO OREGON, 1835, WHO PROCEEDED ALONE
FROM THE GREEN, AND WHO WROTE THE
FIRST BOOK ABOUT OREGON
*(Courtesy of the Oregon Historical
Society)*

REV. HENRY H. SPALDING
WHO WITH HIS YOUNG WIFE WAS OF
THE MARCUS WHITMAN MISSIONARY
PARTY TO OREGON, 1836

MYRA FAIRBANKS EELLS
OF THE SECOND PARTY OF MISSIONARY
WOMEN TO CROSS THE MOUNTAINS TO
OREGON, 1838

MARY RICHARDSON WALKER
OF THE SECOND PARTY OF MISSION-
ARY WOMEN TO CROSS THE MOUNTAINS
TO OREGON, 1838
*(Courtesy of the Oregon Historical
Society)*

REV. FRANCIS N. BLANCHET
OF THE FIRST R. C. MISSIONARIES TO
OREGON, 1838
*(Courtesy of the Oregon Historical
Society)*

REV. PETER J. DE SMET
THE BELOVED AND FAMOUS "BLACK
ROBE," MISSIONARY OF 1841, AND
AFTER
*(Courtesy of the Oregon Historical
Society)*

CERAN ST. VRAIN
PARTNER IN BENT, ST. VRAIN & CO.,
SANTA FE AND INDIAN TRADE. DIED,
1870
*(Courtesy of the Missouri Historical
Society)*

CHAPTER XIV

THE AMERICAN WEDGE IN OREGON

IT MAY be said that the first invasion of Oregon Territory by missionaries from the States did not have any conscious purpose of colonizing the Pacific coast. In the spring of 1833, when by the *Christian Advocate and Journal and Zion's Herald*, the " Macedonian cry " was repeated through the Atlantic coast cities, to the people of the East Oregon was an immense, indefinite country, comprising all the fur region beyond the Rocky Mountains, where flowed the rivers discovered by Lewis and Clark and the Astor expeditions. And while the spasmodic irruptions in Congress, the pronunciamentos of the zealous Hall Kelly, and the business endeavors of Nathaniel J. Wyeth, were directing attention afresh to Oregon (even, it is claimed, arousing interest from those who were to be the first of the Protestant missionaries), nevertheless the initial missionary journey of Jason and Daniel Lee, Cyrus Shepard and Philip L. Edwards had in view a gospel establishment among only the Flatheads — whose home was but the nearer edge of Oregon.

Wisely did Representative McCormick of Arizona in an address before the National House of later day call attention to the fact that the western Indians are not cut from the one cloth; but that they " differ as much from each other as Americans do from Japanese or Chinese "; that some incline to barbarism, some to civilization. The American white man has been disposed to regard an Indian as an Indian, and as a bad Indian, and to apply one set of regulations and one standard of measure to them all.

137

From the time of their first contact (so far as recorded) with the whites in the persons of the Lewis and Clark expedition of 1804-1806, the Nez Percé Indians and the Flathead Indians (somewhat confused by early narratives), have been awarded a high plane of intelligence, cleanliness, probity, and morality. A Nez Percé or Flathead wife was the trapper's prize. Through these two tribes ran a strange vein of religious fervor approaching that of the Brahman. Long before the licensed missionary from the East had approached them, the Book in his hand, these Flatheads and Nez Percés appear to have followed a worship akin to the worship of the Christian.

Captain Bonneville, who was among Nez Percés in the fall of 1832, relates the rebuke which he received when he proposed to them a buffalo hunt upon a day set apart by a sacred calendar that they maintained. And the Sabbath was observed regularly by a religious dance and by exhortations from the chiefs as priests.

The Flatheads, also, and the " Skynses " (Skyuses, Cayuses), like their neighbors the Nez Percés, observed the Sabbath with devotional exercises.

In the Southwest, the Roman Catholic priest was the leader in proselyting, but here in the Northwest Protestantism led the way, through a land as dure and as wild as ever confronted the Jesuit and the Franciscan. It seems, however, to have been Romanism that was again first in the field among the so-called infidels; for before ever the famous Flathead delegation in search of the Book of Heaven visited St. Louis, the Roman Catholic religion was well implanted amidst several of the tribes beyond the mountains.

Captain Bonneville found the Nez Percés, the Flatheads and the " Skynses " (Cayuses?) in 1832 already following, after a fashion rude but sincere, the ritual and the calendar of the Roman church, the rites having been propagated among them by two Iroquois Indians from an early Canadian mission.

It must be remembered that throughout the tribes west of the mountains, in the Oregon Territory of the Northwest, there had been circulating for twenty years the employees of the British fur companies, mainly French Canadians and good Catholics. The Indians absorbed much precept and doctrine. And at the posts of the Hudson Bay Company in particular, as at Fort Walla Walla under Chief Trader Pambrun, and at Ft. George (Vancouver) under Governor John McLoughlin, pains were taken to impress the visiting natives with the force of the Roman faith. With Agent Pambrun this was sincere proselyting — but the fact was not forgotten that the Christianized Indian was the better Indian with whom to deal.

John W. York, Methodist minister of St. Louis in 1830, stated to Judge J. Q. Thornton that September 17, five delegates, Nez Percés, Flatheads, or Iroquois from the Columbia, arrived there in quest of religious aid; and that General Clark, who was a Catholic, sent for him and the Reverend Alliston and Edmundson, for inquiry into the possibility of the Methodists replying with missionaries.[49]

But now, in the midseason of 1832 there arrived in New York four Columbia country Indians, seeking General William Clark (whom they remembered from 1805) and inquiring further about the white man's Book of Heaven.

A touch of romance pervades the instigation which urged them to this long trip.

It appeared that some white man had penetrated into their country, and happened to be a spectator at one of their religious ceremonies, which they scrupulously perform at stated periods. He informed them that their mode of worshipping the supreme Being was radically wrong, and instead of being acceptable and pleasing, it was displeasing to him; he also informed them that the white people away toward the rising of the sun had been put in possession of the true mode of worshipping the great Spirit. They had a book containing directions how to conduct themselves in order to enjoy his favor and hold converse with him; and with this guide, no one need go astray; but every one that would follow the directions laid down there could enjoy, in this life, his favor, and after death would be received into the country where the great Spirit resides, and live forever with him.

Thus, in a letter published in the *Christian Advocate and Journal and Zion's Herald,* under date of January 19, 1833, declares William Walker, an educated Wyandotte and missionary among that nation, who was in St. Louis at the time of the Flatheads' visit and who saw them at the house of General Clark. The man who, as a Protestant, instructed the Flatheads in the existence of the Bible, is presumed to have been Jedediah S. Smith; for he spent the winter of 1824-25 among the Flatheads. If indeed his teachings there influenced the deputation of 1832, then, no matter that he died in his prime before his history and atlas were prepared, he did not live in vain.

It is declared by this same William Walker that General Clark did his best to inform the Flatheads upon the Christ and the Bible. However, after having been much fêted (paying the penalty which civilization inflicts upon distinguished guests, and no civilization in a greater degree than the American), in November or December of that year, 1832, they must sadly part, without the Bible or at least without anyone who could translate it to them, and less two of their number, victims of "change of climate and of diet."

The two surviving Indians left; and when, afterward, the famous artist, Catlin, heard of their errand, he declared that they were passengers upon the very steamboat of the American Fur Company by which he himself was taken to the mouth of the Yellowstone, on his initial trip into the

Indian country of the far West. But the religious fervor which the visit of these four strangers aroused must have communicated itself to Catlin, causing him to clutch at straws. As he ascended the Missouri at the opening of navigation in 1832, and the two Indians took the home trail by land, after the close of navigation in 1832, he could not have met them nor immortalized them in his great portfolio.

But let us not probe romance too ruthlessly — although if we strip away banquets and speeches and voyage with Catlin we still have the basic fact that four Indians from the upper Columbia did, in the late summer or early fall of 1832, seek religious instructions at St. Louis. The elder two died, there; the two younger members left, in the late fall or early winter, for their tribe.

Not until spring of 1833 did the news filter through to the East; but then, by publication in the *Christian Advocate,* the Protestant Church from north to south along the Atlantic coast was electrified. In this delegation from a region upon the continent and within the tentative bounds of the United States, but less known than India or the Sandwich Islands, was an appeal which reached every heart.

With a " Hear! Hear! Who will respond to the call from beyond the Rocky Mountains? " Dr. Wilbur Fisk, already at forty a famous divine, and president of Wesleyan College of Middletown, Connecticut, in a ringing editorial summoned Methodism to establish a Flathead mission. " Money shall be forthcoming. I will be bondsman for the church. All we want is men. Who will go? Who? * * * Were I young, healthy, and unencumbered, how joyfully would I go! But this honor is for another. Bright will be his crown, glorious his reward."

At this time, although foreign missions were being zealously prosecuted by all the Protestant churches, the domestic missions among the Indians had not been overlooked.

Instituted first among the tribes of the East and South, and in Canada, as the tribes had been moved westward the missions had accompanied them.

The idea expressed in 1804 by President Jefferson, that the new Louisiana Purchase would afford an asylum for these doubtful wards, the Indians, at last (or in January, 1825,) had been presented in proper shape to Congress by President Monroe as one of the final acts of his administration. The result was the establishment of an " Indian Frontier." By treaty of June, 1825, the Osages and the Kaws or Kansas surrendered their vast hunting range in the Southwest, along the Santa Fe Trail. The government hastened to remove here its Indians from the states of the South; and now the movement of other tribes also was rapidly promoted — the country so exchanged with them " forever secured and guaranteed to them and their heirs or successors," their fate " left to the common God of the white man and the Indian," themselves isolated and independent, left " to the progress of events " — what unconscious irony!

In 1835 the boundaries of the " Indian Territory " were defined by the *Annual Register of Indian Affairs* as " beginning on Red River, east of the Mexican boundary and as far west of Arkansas Territory as the *country is habitable,* thence down Red River eastwardly to Arkansas Territory; thence northwardly along the line of the Arkansas Territory to the State of Missouri; thence up Missouri River to Pimcah (Puncah, *i. e.,* Niobrara) River; thence westwardly *as far as the country is habitable,* and thence southwardly to the beginning."

The italics are the author's. In this Indian country dwelt, according to rough estimate, some 100,000 Indians; and here, beyond the Mississippi, the various churches were represented among the Cherokees, Choctaws, Kansas, Pawnees, Creeks, Omahas, Iowas, Delawares, Otoes, Potawatomi, Shawnees, Kickapoos, and so on, *as far as the country was habitable*. Truly it was a noble work, in which men and women died, and in which the harvest was great, but the laborers were few. Beyond, in that " uninhabitable country," were the Sioux (they, however, being approached by way of Fort Snelling, Minnesota), the Comanches, the Blackfeet, the Snakes, the Arapahos — strange, roving, thoroughly wild people, not yet within the fold.

But the delegation of the Columbia River Indians proffered another foothold. Dr. Fisk had called " for two suitable men, unencumbered with families, possessing the spirit of martyrs," to " throw themselves into the nation — live with them — learn their language — preach Christ to them." He himself had one such man in mind, and that was Reverend Jason Lee, a Canadian but an American, once a pupil of his at Wilbraham Academy of Massachusetts, now stationed at Stanstead, Province of Quebec, and employed in missionary work among the Indians of Canada.[50]

The blood of that great New England preacher, the " Apostle of Methodism," Jesse Lee, must have been strong in this second generation. The summons by Dr. Fisk in the *Christian Advocate* appeared in March, and at the Boston session of the New England Conference in June following, Jason Lee, having resigned his Canadian field, was appointed superintendent of the new Oregon mission! Tall, stooped, awkward and honest, " of good digestion and a sound mind," he was the choice reflecting Dr. Fisk's excellent judgment.

In August his nephew, Reverend Daniel Lee, was appointed as his fellow laborer. He, too, " was not an Adonis "; but like his uncle stood as an example of the plain, orthodox, New England Methodist preacher, and of a youth preordained to the cause of souls.

In the *Christian Advocate* there had been published advice from Robert Campbell, the trader and St. Louis citizen,

upon the prospects of the Columbia country, and upon the
method of getting there, overland: namely, by escort of
fur trader caravan.

And I doubt not but that they would willingly allow a missionary to accompany them; but the privations that a gentleman of that profession would have to encounter would be very
great, as the shortest route that he would have by land would
not be less than one thousand miles, and when he reached his
destination he would have to travel with the Indians, as they
have no permanent villages, nor have the traders any houses,
but, like the Indians, move in their leather lodges from place
to place throughout the season.

Never was a blind cry so blindly answered. But totally
ignorant, as were the great majority of Easterners, of the
far western land, its methods, distances, businesses, phases
of climate, and inhabitants, by naught were the Lees and
Methodism deterred. Transportation was the problem (the
summer being advanced), and a voyage around the Horn
was advocated, until in November "notice appeared in
the public journals that Captain N. J. Wyeth, of Cambridge,
Mass., had recently returned from a tour west of the Rocky
Mountains, and that he contemplated returning to Oregon
in the following spring."

The way seemed opened; and Captain Wyeth, whose
remarkable energy and performances, being directed along
secular lines, had attracted little if any notice from the
spiritual workers of the land, was sought in Boston by
Jason Lee himself. From Captain Wyeth "valuable information was received respecting the state of the country, the
general character and disposition of the Indian tribes inhabiting the Oregon territory; and he likewise manifested a
disposition to give every aid in his power to the mission." [51]

Accordingly, when the Columbia River Fishing and Trading Company ship, *May Dacre*, laden with Wyeth's hopes

and the company supplies, sailed on the last of November, 1833, out of Boston for the port of Vancouver, it bore also the supplies for the prospective missionary station of the Methodist Church in Oregon.

And when, on April 28, 1834, the united caravans of Wyeth and Milton Sublette issued from Independence, they convoyed into the West Reverend Jason Lee, Reverend Daniel Lee, Lay Missionary Cyrus Shepard of Lynn, Mass., and Lay Missionary Philip L. Edwards of Richmond, Mo., crusaders of the church militant.

Besides the four missionaries, so bravely facing two thousand miles of hard travel to which they were wholly unwonted, as guests with the caravan were two other men, scientists who blazed the trail for Audubon. Long before, or in 1811, had John Bradbury, the English naturalist, ascended the Missouri with the Astorian expedition under Wilson Hunt. He was the pioneer, inspired, of course, by the observations of the first-of-all Lewis and Clark. Now in 1834, Thomas Nuttall, Englishman, Harvard professor, and botanist, who had been with John Bradbury in 1811, was about to cross the continent, and had as companion J. K. Townsend, ornithologist, whose name is retained in Townsend's warbler of the Pacific coast.

With seventy men, 250 horses, and the missionaries' cattle, the caravan proceeded, following the regulation trail which led from old Independence across the Kansas River at its mouth, thence to the Platte and through Nebraska up the Platte and the North Platte to the Sweetwater of the Laramie Plains of Wyoming.

Thus the Oregon Trail was for the first time pressed by actual colonizers — the forerunning emigrants of the host already restless behind.

In June the noted spectacles of the trail — Chimney Rock, Independence Rock, Devil's Gate, South Pass, Wind River Mountains — were witnessed, and left; and on the 19th the missionaries pitched their camp amidst the fur rendez-vous upon Ham's Fork in the Valley of the Green. This wild gathering, rife with lawless passion of men red and white, at once fascinating and repellent, must have impressed Messrs. Lee, Shepard, and Edwards with the seriousness of the life before them. And here they might study Indians such as they nor others of their cloth ever had seen; here they might for the first time study the Flatheads, their wards in prospect.

Wyeth must remain two weeks; then, on July 3, with his goods thrown upon his hands by the Rocky Mountain Company, and his first disappointment of 1834 encountered, he pushed on, with him Nuttall and Townsend, and the indefatigable Captain Sir William Stuart, British sportsman.

At the juncture of the Portneuf with the Snake in Idaho, the resourceful Yankee youth, not yet licked, stopped the party (126 horses, forty men) to build his own fort, which should house and distribute his trading goods.

Here arrived Thomas McKay and his company of Hudson Bay employees; half of these were Indians (probably Cayuses, Flatheads, and Nez Percés), and again the white missionaries had the chance to study their future chárges — even having a chance to see them at their devotions, "conducted very seriously, but after a fashion all their own." Jason Lee, who, it is stated, "was a man all liked and respected," and who evidently was making good in trapper opinion if not in trapper souls, preached to the assembled habitants and natives; then, with his associates, with McKay and Captain Stuart, as the fort was not finished, he pressed forward, down the Snake. They left behind Wyeth, with his company, to complete the fort, to name it Fort Hall, to hoist over it an American flag of sheeting, red flannel, and blue patches, and salute this "with damaged powder and to wet it with villainous alcohol." The date was August 5, 1834. Consigning his post to the care and occupancy of eleven men, fourteen horses and mules and three cows, in charge of one Evans, the busy Wyeth hastened onward, on the trail of the preceding McKay and the missionaries, for the coast. There he would meet his vessel, *May Dacre* — and find only more disappointment.

The Lees, Shepard, and Edwards had learned much since they crossed the mountains by South Pass. They could realize how difficult it would be to maintain a mission in the Flathead country, so remote it was, so far from supplies and so sparsely inhabited. And as Protestants they perhaps were indeed received, by Canadians and convert Iroquois alike, with the subtle opposition of a Romanism already established.

Whether rebuffed by the country, or people, or both, the missionary party decided to continue on westward to the lower Columbia and make that their base. So they pressed ahead, through the desolate region along the Snake, to plant the Bible.

At Walla Walla they left their horses and cattle, for later disposal, and embarking upon another wild trip, in Hudson Bay Company log canoes, they descended the Columbia to Vancouver and Fort George of the Hudson Bay Company. Here they arrived on September 15, to sleep again under a roof, for the first time after one hundred and fifty nights in trappers' lodges or under the stars.

Thus may we leave them; the Bible has crossed the continent; the landing of the Pilgrim Fathers scarce was more significant, for the American mission in Oregon meant that the western half, like the eastern half of a continent, was to be settled under a free constitution. From the missionary movement came Whitman, and if we may believe the word of man, Whitman saved Oregon. But even eliminating the human purpose in the ride of Marcus Whitman, a few years of the missionaries of the Protestant Church made the Oregon Territory better known to the eastern people than did all the years of the fur hunters.

Let us pass to the summer of 1835, and to another rendezvous in the Valley of the Green; for inasmuch as the only method of crossing the plains and mountains was under the auspices of the spring trading caravans out of Independence, the annual markets for the next five or six years form paragraphs in the annals of the Protestant missions to Oregon.

At this rendezvous of July and August, 1835, appear Reverend Samuel Parker, A. M., of the Dutch Reformed (Presbyterian) Church, and Dr. Marcus Whitman, missionary physician. Reverend Mr. Parker is from Ithaca, New York; Dr. Whitman is from Wheeler. Since March 14 they have been upon their journey, having left Council Bluffs June 21, with the American Fur Company caravan under Lucien Fontenelle; and from Fort William (predecessor of Fort Laramie) continuing under Thomas Fitzpatrick, who there assumed charge of the march.

These two men, the Reverend Samuel Parker, A. M., and Marcus Whitman, M. D., dispatched by the American Board of Commissioners for Foreign Missions, differed much in character. The Reverend Mr. Parker was typically serious, viewing any levity as verging upon sin, taking life hard, his soul continually "pained." Dr. Whitman, younger, livelier, adaptable, more quickly made friends among the rough trappers and traders.

Down the Ohio and up the Missouri to Liberty and Council Bluffs, Mr. Parker distributed his tracts and held services. The land and people impressed him as heathenish. He and the doctor would not travel on Sunday, at first, and the caravan went on without them — its men offended by the implied rebuke and probably disgruntled over being burdened with finicky tenderfeet. After a scourge of cholera which they lightened, the doctor and the missionary learned that some of the men of the caravan actually had planned to put them out of the way and thus be rid of their wet-blanket presence.

At the rendezvous, Dr. Whitman extracted arrowheads from the back of two trappers — one being Jim Bridger. By conversation, through an interpreter, with the Flatheads, and Nez Percés, Mr. Parker ascertained, to his satisfaction, that the "field was white for the harvest." Dr. Whitman, out of the zeal and energy which characterized him, decided that he ought to return to the East with the caravan, to report in person upon the need of more missionaries, and to bring out a party with the next caravan of 1835, thus saving a year of time. Mr. Parker proceeded alone to the coast.

Joe Meek, the mountain man, in his biography speaks slightingly of Mr. Parker, who did not, it would seem, make the good impression made by Jason Lee. It was difficult for Mr. Parker to temporize with the evils which he met; the wild ways of the mountains visibly shocked him.

He arrived at Vancouver on November 16, 1835. Although his stay in Oregon comprised only about seven months (he sailed thence June 28, 1836, for Connecticut, via the Sandwich Islands) he thoroughly explored the interior of the Columbia basin, the purpose for which he was sent out by the Board. The most notable result of his visit was his book, *Journal of an Exploring Tour Beyond the Rocky Mountains,* which, published with map in 1838, endorsed by Noah Webster, President Humphrey and Professor Hitchcock of Amherst, and written in scholarly manner, is the first account, after that by Lewis and Clark, of the upper Platte and the Columbia country — scenery, inhabitants, geology, zoology, climate and customs — and is the very first book devoted largely to Oregon.[52]

While Reverend Samuel Parker is gathering facts and

spreading the Word up the Columbia of Oregon, further than the Lees and associates had yet penetrated, Dr. Whitman, aflame with great purpose, is hastening hither and thither through New England, not the least of his encouragements his betrothed, the noble Narcissa Prentiss of Angelica, New York. Dr. Whitman had taken back with him, from the Snake River, two Nez Percé boys, that he might present tangible evidence of the work awaiting, beyond the mountains. With these, and through his own efforts, he counted upon forming a party for the caravan trip of 1836.

It is stated that there was some difficulty in obtaining the desired companions; not, let it be understood, that flesh and spirit were wanting, and that the heroic breed of Protestant missionaries had so early been exhausted, but because Marcus Whitman had determined that his young bride should be permitted to make the long journey, and he was looking for another white woman and wife to be her associate.

. . . and then light came from an unexpected quarter. In the early spring of 1836 a sleigh, extemporized from a wagon, was crunching through the deep snows of western New York. It contained the Reverend and Mrs. Spalding, who were on their way, under commission of the American Board, to the Osage Indians. The wife had started from a bed of lingering illness, and was then able to walk less than a quarter of a mile.

Dr. Whitman, having heard of the rare courage of this woman, by permission of the board, started in pursuit.

" We want you for Oregon," was the hail with which he overtook them.

" How long will the journey take? "

" The summers of two years."

" What convoy shall we have? "

" The American Fur Company to the Divide."

" What shall we have to live on? "

" Buffalo meat, till we can raise our own grain."

" How shall we journey? "

" On horseback."
" How cross the rivers? "
" Swim them."

Mr. Spalding decided instantly, as for himself. And after prayer, apart, in the tavern at Howard, New York, Mrs. Spalding appeared with beaming face.

" I have made up my mind to go."
" But your health, my dear."
" I like the command just as it stands. ' Go ye into all the world,' and no exceptions for poor health."
" But the perils, in your weak condition — you do n't begin to think how great they are."
" The dangers of the way and the weakness of my body are His; duty is mine." [58]

The die was cast. They went — the two women, both tender, each a bride and one an invalid. The maxim on the Sweetwater trail long had been: " No white woman can cross the mountains and live."

The little party numbered five: Missionary Physician Dr. Marcus Whitman, aged thirty-three; Narcissa Prentiss Whitman, his bride, aged twenty-eight; Missionary Henry H. Spalding, of Prattsburgh, N. Y., who but three years . before had been graduated from Western Reserve College, and who was about the same age as Dr. Whitman; Eliza Hart Spalding of Trenton, N. Y., his wife; Assistant Missionary William H. Gray, aged twenty-five, of Utica, who would serve also as agent of farming and mechanics.[54]

The start was made in February by the Spaldings and in March by the others. From the very beginning the way was rendered hard. At Pittsburg, Catlin the artist told tales of horrors to them, and would dissuade them. At St. Louis the Fur Company declined to accept them as passengers, and yielded only to the insistence of Whitman, who reminded the men how he had rescued them in the cholera scourge, a year before; how, " from behind the festering spine of a comrade," he had extracted the arrow heads. After the promise, the company's boat passed them, purposely, at Liberty Landing. A mule kicked Spalding; ague attacked him; a cow, plunging overboard from a ferry, dragged him after; a hurricane leveled his tent, and drenched him again; and before the party, hastening after the recreant boat, had reached Council Bluffs, the company caravan had pulled out and was five days in advance.

Mr. Spalding, sick and discouraged, would have turned. But his wife, stronger in spirit than in body, declared: " I have started for the Rocky Mountains and I expect to go there! "

With a cavvy of half-broken Missouri mules, fifteen or twenty horses, cattle, two wagons, and mission goods, the three men and the two women, guided by Dr. Whitman, the only member with any frontier experience whatsoever, set out to overtake the fur traders' caravan. Through a series of accidents which held the caravan back, after a two weeks' chase and after a final desperate spurt (wherein Mrs. Spalding fainted) from daylight until two o'clock the next morning, the race was won at the Loup Fork of the Platte!

But now that the missionary party had carried its point " nothing could exceed the kindness of the men. The choicest buffalo morsels were always kept for our ladies." The party not only had won the race, but they had won the regard of the traders and trappers, who could appreciate pluck. Evidently the two women were not going to be a clog, as had been feared. At any rate, willynilly, the march must continue; and 200 persons, 600 animals, the caravan proceeded with military discipline up the Platte.

Meat was the sole menu, and fresh meat at that. Once or twice this failed, and the camp went hungry. Mrs. Spalding, with whom the diet seemed to disagree, grew weaker; and at Fort William on the Laramie the captain of the caravan, Fitzpatrick, declared that Mrs. Spalding had come far enough; she would die for want of bread.

" No," said she; " I started over the mountains in the name of my Savior, and I must go on." [55]

They went.

By this time she rode a horse only with difficulty, and preferred the lighter of the two mission wagons. The nineteen wagons of the traders were left, as customary, at the fort, and the supplies were transferred to mule back; but Dr. Whitman insisted upon taking his party's two wagons on, for the Columbia. The British big-game hunter, Captain Stuart, who bobs up, as usual, and was with the caravan, not to be outdone took onward a two-mule wagon of his own.

Word had been sent ahead, by means of an express to the rendezvous, that the " Company " annual caravan was approaching, and that with it were two white women. Nothing could have created more excitement in the Valley of the Green. Instantly half a dozen of the trappers, including the ever-ready Joe Meek, had mounted and were speeding away, on a wild race with some of the Nez Percés, to bid the strangers welcome.

So, ascending the Sweetwater for the South Pass, the missionaries witnessed this mad calvacade dashing down upon them, carrying in the muzzle of a rifle the white flag of peace, but by whoop and yelp and headlong charge appearing to give it the lie.

Naturally, all eyes were upon the two women, thus initiated into the wild ways of the wildest West. Some of the trappers had not seen a white woman for ten years; the Indians had never seen a white woman. What they, trappers and Indians, saw now, was a slight, dark-haired, pallid skinned, delicate-featured, demure young woman in a wagon, gazing back studiously but with a quiet reserve. This was Mrs. Spalding. They saw, for the other, a larger, fuller, blue - eyed, sparkling - faced, generous - featured, brightly auburn-haired young woman, in perfect health, upon a horse, returning look for look and smile for smile, as if appreciative of the exhibition. This was Mrs. Whitman.

The caravan and the calvacade mounted South Pass, where, on this the Fourth of July, Mrs. Spalding again fainted. She was permitted to lie upon the ground and rest.

" Leave me and save yourselves," she begged. " Tell mother I am glad I came."

But from the top the caravan sent back for her, and she proceeded. The march of this woman, across the plains and over the pass, and on, while fighting, every step, the pangs of an outraged flesh, her purpose only the good of an unknown and alien people, should rank higher than the march of any Franciscan or Jesuit of the Southwest. The Southwest has its heroes; the Northwest has its heroine.

Presently the Continental Divide of North America had been spanned; before, the waters flowed west; before, opened Oregon, where, crushed by horrors and many fatigues, Mrs. Spalding was later to sleep " under an Oregon clod," and whence, as symbol of martyrdom, returned, after thirty-four years, by the hand of Henry Spalding — an old man broken and bereft — only a lock of Mrs. Whitman's hair, of silky texture and reddish-gold color.[56]

On the Pacific slope of the South Pass the caravan halted, while the little band, at twelve o'clock noon of Independence Day, 1836,

six years before Fremont, following in the footsteps of the women, gained the name of the " Path-finder," alighting from their horses and kneeling on the other half of the continent, with the Bible in one hand and the American flag in the other, took possession of it as the home of American mothers, and of the Church of Christ.[57]

Again are we reminded of Plymouth Rock.

Down from the pass proceeded the caravan and retainers, to be met now by the charging cavalry of the Nez Percés and Flatheads *en masse,* arrayed in their brightest and bravest. With this additional escort the rendezvous was reached. Mrs. Whitman naturally attracted the men, but Mrs. Spalding, ill and delicate and reserved, attracted the women. The Indian squaws took her in charge, administered to her fibrous roots which effectively stopped the exhausting bowel trouble caused by the green buffalo meat, and " from that hour she began to mend, and from that hour her future and theirs were one."

Fortunately this was the summer when the first Hudson Bay trading party, under McLeod, was sent to the American rendezvous; with this party the missionaries traveled westward again. At the rendezvous the heavy four-mule freight wagon was left. At Fort Hall (last American outpost) the light wagon must be transformed into a two-wheeled cart; at Fort Boisé (just erected by the British traders as a counter-post to Fort Hall), even the cart must be abandoned until it could be brought on by some party unencumbered.

But the indomitable Doctor Whitman had demonstrated his theory. In 1826 Messrs. Smith, Jackson and Sublette had taken cattle and wagons to the South Pass; in 1832 Captain Bonneville had taken his wagon train over the South Pass to the Green; now in 1836 women, wagon, and cattle had been taken to the Snake, and the next time they would be taken by Whitman to the coast.

The Columbia at Walla Walla was reached September 1, and the good agent Pambrun received Mrs. Spalding in his arms "as if he had been her father." On November 12 the bateaux bearing the travelers rounded the point where stood Vancouver and Fort George. Flags were waving, songs were resounding, and the Hudson Bay dignitaries, Governor John McLoughlin and Father James Douglass,

" with stately courtesy " escorted into the fort the first white
women over the Oregon Trail. Thus had been performed
" an undertaking pronounced impossible by every mountain
man, by George Catlin and the missonary Lee "; and in
Oregon the Protestant Church had, by importation of the
white American family and of American customs, laid
the foundation of the American commonwealth in the
Northwest.

CHAPTER XV

ADVENTURES OF KIT CARSON — 1834–1835

THE summer market or rendezvous of 1834 is over. The fall beaver ·hunt has succeeded thereto, and a numerous command of trappers under Jim Bridger, of the firm of Fitzpatrick, Sublette & Bridger, are at work in the Black-feet country around the sources of the Missouri in Montana. On a tributary of the Gallatin, one of the Three Forks, signs of trappers above have been discovered by the party with which Kit Carson is working; these signs lead to the company of Joseph Gale — field captain for Nathaniel Wyeth.

This Gale company is but one of the strings to Wyeth's bow. He has also built Fort Hall, an *entrepôt* for supplies and furs; and having followed the missionary party of the Lees, Cyrus Shepard, P. L. Edwards, and proceeded to Vancouver, he has met, just arriving, his ship, the *May Dacre*. The planet Saturn still governs the Wyeth horo-scope, for the *May Dacre* has been struck by lightning, is three months late, and now the salmon shipping season is past! Whereupon, with true Yankee thrift that deserved a better reward, the versatile Wyeth has dispatched from Vancouver to Fort Hall, on a trading trip by land, Skipper Thing, eight mountain men and the crew of thirteen Sandwich Islanders.

The Wyeth luck extends as far as the Wyeth operations; for up among the sources of the Missouri, along the Gal-latin Fork, the Joseph Gale company have been saddled by never-lightened disaster as by the old Man of the Sea. As Joe Meek records: " They had been out a long time. The

Blackfeet had used them badly. Their guns were out of order, their ammunition all but exhausted; they were destitute, or nearly so, of traps, blankets, knives, everything. They were what the Indian and the mountain man called ' very poor.' " Moreover, in the last fracas with the Blackfeet, several of the whites had been shot, and Richard (Dick) Owens had received almost a death wound.

This was Wyeth fortune. In the morning Kit Carson and the other Bridger men left Gale, in order to trap on and join the main camp; but they had ascended along the river only some two miles, when the foremost pair of trappers (claimed by Meek to have been Liggitt and himself) rode into an ambush of Blackfeet. Then ensued a hot race back to the Gale camp, the Blackfeet madly firing and whooping.

From the united camp, of unexpected size, the Indians swerved. They fell back and as they went set on fire the long grass. The camp was located in a bunch of pines and aspens; a strong wind was blowing, and the timber was threatened by flames. The detachment of Gale trappers, being short of ammunition and of serviceable weapons, attended to the horses and the camp equipage, while the Bridger detachment attended to the savages.

Kit Carson says that the fire died out at the edge of the copse. Joe Meek says that the pines caught and that the men were driven into the open, where they used the bodies of dead horses as barricades. At any rate, the battle waged fiercely until mid-afternoon, when, having suffered severely, and having been warned by scouts that a large body of trappers were approaching, the Blackfeet, announcing that they would fight no more, withdrew.

The Bridger main company soon arrived — all unconscious that a battle had been waged, for the strong adverse wind had carried the sounds in the opposite direction. Captain Gale's party, which but for the opportune reinforcement by Meek, Carson, and the others, would surely have been "wiped out" within a day or two, now joined with the Bridger company, for protection, and the Wyeth trapping enterprises in this unfriendly West were practically at an end.

Joseph Gale quit the Wyeth employ this winter, entered the employ of the Hudson Bay Company, eventually migrated westward to settle on the Tualatin Plains of Oregon, and meeting an emergency, became skipper of the first Oregon-built ship — the schooner *Star of Oregon*, which, in September, 1842, with a retired mountain man as captain and green ranchers as crew, sailed from the port of Vancouver for the port of San Francisco — which was safely reached.

Carson's story states that the Bridger command was driven out of the Missouri side of the mountains this fall by the persistent harassing of the Blackfeet, and that all the Bridger men, like the Wyeth men, had to make discretion the better part of valor and cross to the western slope and the Flathead Lake of northwestern Montana, there to meet some Flatheads and to winter with them further south, on the Big Snake.

It well may be this spring of 1835, when, as his biography says, emerging from winter quarters, Carson fell in with Thomas McKay of the Hudson Bay Company, and with five associates joined him in a spring hunt; for the mountain business among the American companies was being badly cut up. The McKay venture proffered success, and it proffered new country: the country of the Great Basin west of Salt Lake.

Consequently Thomas McKay was an agreeable leader for Kit Carson, and association with him was not to be despised. The Snake, between Walla Walla and Fort Hall, evidently was McKay's province, for it was hereabouts, in the summer of 1834, that the overland party of the Lees encamped with the McKay company, and even preached to them.

With five other Americans Kit Carson now joined the McKay command for an expedition down the Mary's River of northwestern Nevada, which was separated from the Snake country on the north by a wide divide of bare, bristling ridges, and by plateaus of sage, sand, and lava falling away into deep dry cañons. It is a region well-nigh impassable by man; and by what trail they traveled we do not know.

Eighteen months previous the detachment under Joe Walker, from the Bonneville brigade, upon their accidental way to California had descended along this river, known as Mary's and as Ogden's, and today as the Humboldt River, to which they applied the name Barren. Since that fall of 1833 no expedition is recorded as having trapped the stream, and McKay evidently expected to reap a harvest, as Peter Ogden had before. But the traps were set in vain.

Down along the Mary's River, which, with its rocky, sterile ridges, its grateful bottoms, its mingling of heat and cold, of springs, alkali ponds, sandy bluffs and grassy camping spots, for two hundred miles was soon to be a feature of the Overland Trail already platted by the stars, traveled the McKay and Carson party, clear to the Sinks of the Humboldt. Here, in the midst of a desert desolation characterized by flats of soda and ash, burnt-rock outcrops, stagnation of earth, air, water, and animate life — a region as appalling as the surface of the moon — the Mary's ceased at a swampy lake with no outlet. The water, scummy and green, and speckled with wild fowl, was sucked up by the dry air faster than it could gather to overflow. This was the Sink of the Humboldt.

According to his biographer, Charles Burdett, Carson here was sent ahead by McKay toward the ranges which showed bluish in the west, to be gone a few days to see if there were not, somewhere, beaver streams.⁵⁸ He found a lake of potash, with pumice stone floating upon it; he found more sinks and deposits of soda — almost underfoot were the gold and silver which since have made western Nevada famous, but he passed careless glances over their resting place; he found dried lakes, like saucers, rimmed with low ridges, pulverized mud and ashes for their bottoms; he found many a wonder — but no beaver. And he returned to McKay.

Then upon this country of ruin they turned their backs and, partially retracing their outward course, they made for the Snake again.

Sage and sand and barrenness encompassed them until, as they threaded among the lonely hills, they occasionally came upon little valleys which flowing water had made green. When they struck the Snake in southern Idaho, midway between its source above Fort Hall and its mouth at the Columbia afar, the party divided. Partisan McKay turned west down the Snake, making for the Hudson Bay Company post of Fort Walla Walla in southeastern Washington; Carson, as captain of the five remaining men, set out in the opposite direction, up the Snake, for Fort Hall.

As McKay was to have the better country, where game and grass were available, he took only a small portion of the provisions and the majority of the horses.

The provisions left were poor enough — roots and a little rabbit meat — and the horses left were poor indeed, sad, hard-worked, famished things which the desert had used cruelly. Kit Carson and men may have had a bad time of it in the Great Basin, but now they were to have a worse. They saw no game, and as their fare grew scantier they saw no Indians from whom they might obtain succor. It was a region deserted, with scenery sublime, but caring naught for man.

When Fort Hall was still four or five days' journey eastward their roots had given out. They had but the one resort left, which trappers had used before; they cut veins in their mules and horses, and, drinking the warm blood, closed the veins again. However, they could not repeat this operation. The mules and horses were too thin and weak.

A debate arose whether or not to kill some of the animals and eat them, bony as they were. But without animals, how could the party proceed, supposing the route continued rough? To kill the animals might put the party in worse plight than ever.

At this crisis they encountered a band of friendly Indians (probably Snakes), and by dint of much dickering and persuasion obtained from them a " fat horse " — which immediately was killed and devoured. This provender lasted during the march on to Fort Hall.

While Carson and his five companions pause to recuperate, let us also pause an instant at old Fort Hall when it was new, for it deserves more than merest mention. Situated " upon the left bank of Snake River, or Lewis' Fork of the Columbia, in a rich bottom near the delta formed by the confluence of the Portneuf with that stream, in lat. 43° 10′ 30″ north, long. 112° 20′ 54″ west," it reflected much credit upon Wyeth's judgment. It was built of the customary palings or palisades, with a sally-port or double gateway facing the Portneuf, the walls " extending back toward the Snake." In 1836 it was transferred by Wyeth to the Hudson Bay Company, and now having become, as the British eastern-most outpost, " the stone in the garden " of the American traders, under agent Captain Grant, it was for more than fourteen years a Hudson Bay Company quarters. The wooden walls were replaced by adobe, which, whitewashed, gleamed as a welcome signal to wayfarers amidst the sagy deserts of the rushing Snake. After the hospitable Mr. Grant retired to settle with his half-Indian family upon a fertile bottom land five miles above his

DR. JOHN McLOUGHLIN

THE FAMOUS HUDSON'S BAY AGENT

(Courtesy of the Oregon Historical Society)

"OLD" JIM BRIDGER

(From a daguerreotype taken about 1846, presented by Bridger's daughter to General Grenville M. Dodge)

CAPT. NATHANIEL J. WYETH

(Courtesy of the Oregon Historical Society)

FORT HALL.
FOUNDED BY NATHANIEL WYETH ON THE SNAKE RIVER IN 1834
(Report of the March of the Rifle Regiment to Oregon, 1849)

FORT LARAMIE, 1842
(From Fremont's report of his first expedition)

former post, the old fort still remained a favorite station
for emigrants over the Oregon Trail, but it was superseded
by the new government post of the same name. Later a
third Fort Hall grew up, dominating the Bannock Indian
reservation.

Here, at the palisaded first Fort Hall, occupied by the
Wyeth garrison hopeful of trade with the Snakes and the
Utes, but bothered much by pilfering bands of invading
Crows, Blackfeet, and Sioux, the Carson party of six rested,
until, making an excursion after buffalo, they invited fur-
ther adventure.

This occurred in the valley of the Little Snake, near to
the dividing line between northwestern Colorado and central Wyoming — and not far southeast from the spot where,
in 1841, the veteran Fraeb forted and was killed. The
locality is definitely fixed by Fremont's journal of his return
from his second tour (1843-44). He says: " We passed
during the day a place where Carson had been fired on so
close that one of the men had five bullets through his body."
But Carson tells his own story:

It was in — let me see — yes, 1835. There were six of us
hunters out after buffalo, up in the Snake country. We had
made a pretty good hunt, and came into camp at night, intending to start in next morning. (Back to Fort Hall, west almost
three hundred miles!) Well, we camped. Had a good many
dogs with us, some of them good dogs. They barked a good
deal, and we heard wolves. As I lay by the fire, I saw one or
two big wolves sneaking about camp — one of them quite in
it. Gordon wanted to fire, but I would not let him, for fear
of hitting some of the dogs. I had just a little suspicion,
that the wolves might be Indians, but when I saw them turn
short about, and heard the snap of their teeth, as the dogs
came too close to one of 'em, I felt easy then, and made sure
it was a wolf. The Indian fooled me that time. Confound
the rascal, — becoming animated — confound the rascal, you
think he had n't two old buffalo bones in his hand that he
cracked together every time he turned to snap at the dogs?

Well, by and by we dozed off asleep, and it was n't long before I was awoke by a crash and blaze. I jumped straight for the mules, and held 'em. If the Indians had been smart, they 'd 'a had us all, but they run as soon as they fired. They killed but one of us — poor Davis. He had five bullets in his body, and eight in his buffalo-robe. The Indians were a band of Sioux, on the war path after the Snakes, and came on us by accident. They tried to waylay us next morning, but we killed three of 'em, including their chief.[59]

Now supplied with meat, the five trappers pitched their lodge just outside the walls of Fort Hall, and waited for McKay to return from Walla Walla. The Wyeth ill luck which attended Fort Hall communicated itself evidently to everyone connected with it under his proprietorship. As a new American post it was treated with small respect by the roving tribes who made their forays into this district. It is safe to say that under the Hudson Bay Company management it commanded a different attitude.

Two or three nights after the Carson squad had come in from the buffalo hunt and had encamped beside the fort, Indians (said to have been Blackfeet, who bore the brunt of general blame) boldly entered the post corral and led away every animal that the trappers had placed therein for security. This was done at daybreak; the sentinel stationed over the cavvy saw two figures approach and let down the bars; and so deliberately was it done that he assumed the customary relief was taking the cavvy out to graze. Whereupon he turned in and went to sleep.

When the horse guard actually did arrive to relieve the sentry, they were amazed to find the corral empty. Investigation showed that the animals had been driven by the two thieves to the main party of Indians, and then trailed across country at a rapid rate. Inasmuch as not a horse or mule was left at the post, pursuit was fruitless.

However, McKay came in, after a month, and brought

with him enough extra saddle animals so that Carson and
his four comrades could ride on to the rendezvous of the
summer of 1835 in the Valley of the Green. Here there
arrived, under escort of Thomas Fitzpatrick, from Fort
John, the two missionaries Samuel Parker and Marcus
Whitman. And at this rendezvous occurred Kit Carson's
celebrated duel with a Canadian mountain man called Captain Shunan, or Shuman, or Shunar, who had thrashed two
men with his fists and was boasting that he would " cut a
stick and switch " any American who interfered. Various
modern accounts of it have appeared — all based upon the
one heroic recital in Peters. But as Reverend Mr. Parker
was present, and is a candid, if not an overglowing narrator
of the wild West as he saw it, we will let him tell, in his
didactic fashion, the incident:

A few days after our arrival at the place of rendezvous, and
when all the mountain-men had assembled, another day of
indulgence was granted to them, in which all restraint was
laid aside. These days are the climax of the hunter's happiness. I will relate an occurrence which took place, near evening, as a specimen of mountain life. A hunter, who goes technically by the name of the great bully of the mountains,
mounted his horse with a loaded rifle, and challenged any
Frenchman, American, Spaniard, or Dutchman, to fight him
in single combat. Kit Carson, an American, told him if he
wished to die, he would accept the challenge. Shunar defied
him. C. mounted his horse, and with a loaded pistol, rushed
into close contact, and both almost at the same instant fired.
C's. ball entered S's. hand, came out at the wrist, and passed
through the arm above the elbow. Shunar's ball passed over
the head of Carson; and while he went for another pistol,
Shunar begged that his life might be spared.[60]

The Peters' biography makes Carson, after a sounding
speech, seek his lodge for a weapon, while Shunan likewise
sought his. Both men appear mounted and armed in the
lists; and when their horses' heads touch, Carson demands:

" Am I the person you are looking for? "

" No," answers Shunan, at the same moment raising his rifle. Carson instantly fires, shattering his opponent's forearm, causing the rifle muzzle to tilt so that the discharge grazes his scalp and powder-burns his face.

Shunan, or Shunar, evidently was one of those large, braggart bravos — the " cock of the woods " when in his cups; a character calculated to overawe a camp and convince it that it were best to let him alone. Kit Carson was exactly the person to undertake him, and in tackling the job acted precisely as would be expected.

However, a motive beyond merely the offensiveness implied by Mr. Parker and by other chroniclers must be assigned to the quarrel; and a well-based story from Carson's own lips — in fact told by him to Captain S. H. Simpson of Taos, declares that the ill feeling culminated over a young squaw, desired by both men. Carson won out, and, to judge from his own story, killed his opponent.[61]

When the rendezvous broke up, August 20, Bridger, with the missionaries and fifty trappers, including Carson, the Flatheads, and Nez Percés, headed north for the upper Snake or the Tetons, from whose base and the western base of the Wind River Range flow the waters of the Henry and the Lewis Forks.

The march was begun on August 21; on the 22d Dr. Whitman turned east to recross South Pass and recruit the missionary ranks for the next year. On the 23d, which was Sunday, in Jackson's Little Hole, the Reverend Mr. Parker's impromptu church services were interrupted by a buffalo hunt. On August 25 Jackson's Big Hole was reached, and Captain Bridger detached a portion of his command to trap the streams.

The trail, ever seeking the beaver, crossed the Teton Pass and descended into Pierre's Hole, westward, where had been fought, three years before, the big trapper-Blackfeet battle. Here the Bridger command diverged for the northeast and the Three Forks country of the Blackfeet, and Mr. Parker proceeded west, with his Nez Percé and Flathead escort, for the lower Columbia.

The Blackfeet were very active this fall and winter. The Bridger camps were constantly harassed, so that " a white man could not leave his camp and go a distance of a single mile without being fired upon." Consequently the company dropped down to the Yellowstone, where they went into the winter quarters of 1835-1836.

CHAPTER XVI

ADVENTURES OF KIT CARSON — 1835–1838

THE winter upon the Yellowstone was to be far from a peaceful one for the Bridger camp, with which was Kit Carson. In this January (1836) a hunting party from the camp crossed a large Blackfeet trail, and as signs of alien Indians in winter could mean only a war party, it was necessary, before the camp could rest easily again, that the country be cleared. Forty trappers, including Carson (who, now at twenty-six, must have been among the best of the mountain men), were dispatched upon the trail.

Trailing hard and fast, through snow and cold, the Kit Carson company — Americans, French Canadians, Mexican Spaniards, Germans, half-breeds, motley in nationality and motley in garb, but one in their hatred of the Blackfeet — overtook the Blackfeet scouts, who fled. As had been expected, the scouts raced for the main body, so that soon the charging whites found themselves stoutly opposed by a fierce array as stubborn as ever.

Joe Meek's account of a similar battle (which may or may not have been the same) says that the trappers discovered the Blackfeet forted upon an island in the Yellowstone, and each man screening himself by a little mesh of twigs and grass, they were enabled to creep up unobserved and deliver a destructive fire from the banks above. But the Carson account says that after a sharp fight the Blackfeet retreated to this island and forted.

Night fell and a truce was necessary. The trappers camped as best they might in the cold and darkness, and waited, to renew at dawn the attack; for in these wildcat fights between Blackfeet and mountain men the cry was, "Give 'em Green River," the cry of extermination and scalps. At dawn the whites charged again, and, hoarsely shouting, crossed upon the ice or even waded when the current intervened. But the fort was deserted. Only "the snow within the fortification was red with fresh blood, and from the place a bloody trail led to a hole in the ice of the stream, where a large number of lifeless bodies had been sunk."[62]

The victorious but disappointed trappers returned to the Bridger camp. A council was held at once. It was folly to presume that the Blackfeet would accept such a drubbing and not retaliate. The location of the camp had been spied upon; the Blackfeet would gather again. Bridger decided not to vacate, but to stick it out and act upon the defensive. Outposts were stationed, and throughout the day a sentinel sat upon a high hill, near by, to watch over the surrounding country. Meanwhile the camp was being fortified as rapidly as possible, but before preparations were completed the sentry on the hill signaled that the Indians were in sight. More packs and logs and rocks were piled to strengthen the barricade, the horse and mule herd was brought in and corralled, arms were grasped and priming freshened.

The advance party of the savages soon appeared in sight, but then they discovered the strength of the trappers, they halted and awaited, distant about half a mile from the breast-work, the arrival of the rest of the band. It was three days before the whole force of the Indians had arrived. They mustered about one thousand warriors. [Joe Meek says eleven hundred.] It was a sight which few white men of the American nation have looked upon. Arrayed in their fantastic war costume and bedaubed with paint, armed with lances, bows and arrows, rifles, tomahawks, knives, etc., some mounted and some on foot, they presented a wild and fearful scene of barbaric strength and fancy.[63]

When the full force had assembled a great war dance was performed, further to intimidate the whites and nerve the warriors. The tumult continued probably through the night (according to Indian custom); and with the morning the Blackfeet, worked up to a high pitch, charged.

But as might have been expected, faced by the breastworks and by the ready rifles, they split. Before they reached the danger zone they wheeled and retired. The Indians of the West never have had the stomach to assault breastworks; each individual Indian thinks of his own scalp.

The trappers jeered and yelled, taunting the Blackfeet to come within range. Carson says that the enemy presently withdrew about a mile and sat in council. This dissolved, the reds divided into two bands, one marching on into the Crow country, the other taking the back trail. Joe Meek says that they, too, forted, throwing up small cottonwood enclosures for ten men each, from which a skirmishing fight was carried on, with small loss to either side, for two days; after which the Blackfeet quit.

The trappers' camp was not molested again during the winter. The spring hunt was pursued in the Crow country of the Yellowstone and the Big Horn, in the Wind River Valley, and thence across to the Lewis Fork and down to the rendezvous near the mouth of Horse Creek in the Valley of the Green.

At the Green River, preceding the rendezvous of 1836, occurred the tragedy whereby Joe Meek's wife, Umentucken, a Snake young woman transferred from Milton Sublette, closed her days. A band of Bannocks, assuming that the whites had stolen their horses, dashed into camp and caught the trappers unprepared.

Bridger stood in front of his lodge, holding his horse by a lasso, and the head chief rode over it, jerking it out of his hand. At this unprecedented insult to his master, a negro named Jim, cook to the Booshway, seized a rifle and shot the chief dead. At the same time, an arrow shot at random struck Umentucken in the breast, and the joys and sorrows of the Mountain Lamb were over forevermore.[64]

The mountain men now rallied, chased the Bannocks, drove them from their village to an island in the Green, and so well avenged Umentucken that finally an old Bannock squaw approached, bearing the pipe of peace.

" You have killed all our warriors," she said; " do you now want to kill the women? If you wish to smoke with women, I have the pipe."

This convinced the trappers that they had done their duty, and they drew off. It also had convinced the Bannocks that the white race were fighters of a new breed; and coming as a first experience, changed a bold nation into a race of bushwhackers as vicious as the Diggers.

Following the fight with the presumptuous Bannocks, the rendezvous time being at hand, Andrew Drips, the American Fur Company partisan, took half a dozen or so of men and rode eastward to meet the caravan from St. Louis. On the Sandy (the Big Sandy and the Little Sandy creeks are two famous streams encountered on the west slope of South Pass, and long famed as the overland traveler's introduction to the Pacific slope) they noted signs of Indians. Meek and Carson, with that habitual caution which twelve years later moved Lieutenant G. D. Brewerton to remark upon it, at the next camp retained the saddles upon their horses and tied the picket rope to themselves. When, just before dawn, the apprehended attack was made, all the horses save those of Meek and Carson were stampeded. But these two wily mountain men were enabled to flee at full speed, not to be rejoined by others of the party until the Sweetwater, across the pass, was reached.

The majority on foot, the party proceeded as far east as Independence Rock, when another attack turned them back.

Strange to relate, the whole party finally rendezvoused again on the Green, not a man having been killed or (which was the same thing) captured.

Into this rendezvous entered, with spectacular escort, the two white women, Mrs. Spalding and Mrs. Whitman, and the other missionaries, Messrs. Spalding, Whitman, and Gray. At this rendezvous also it would be learned that Captain Bonneville, the erstwhile trader and explorer, had been gone a year from the mountains; that Nathaniel Wyeth, the plucky, had failed in every venture, and that he, too, was practically out of the mountain business, his salmon shipments having amounted to naught and his Fort Hall having been opposed by the new Hudson Bay post of Fort Boisé, lower down on the Snake. And doubtless the St. Louis caravan brought out news from Texas, where Americans were fighting for new American territory as important as Oregon.

This fall of 1836 the firm of Fitzpatrick, Sublette & Bridger seems to have ceased entirely, and all the former Rocky Mountain Fur Company personages, save William Sublette, who was still in the field, supported the American Fur Company against the British aggression. Fort Boisé was a menace and Wyeth's Fort Hall was another. From now on for twenty years the only American fur concern of importance in the western trade is that great corporation, " the Company ": the American Fur Company, sometimes referred to as the " Company of North America," as arrogant, east of the mountains, as ever the Hudson Bay Company west of the mountains, and much more despotic over its employees.

From the rendezvous the missionaries departed with the British party of trader McLeod, westward for the Columbia; Bridger and Fontenelle (the Rocky Mountain Company and the American Company united, like the lying down together of the wolf and the lamb) led a large brigade north,

and divided. The Bridger party proceeded to the headwaters of the Snake, and into Pierre's Hole; Fontenelle,
with one hundred men, among them Carson, trapped in the
Yellowstone country. There were rumors among the Crows
that the Blackfeet had been swept by a scourge of smallpox
and were in full retreat from it. The trappers, who had
many old scores to settle with this tribe, accepted the plague
as a gift of providence, and extended their operations the
more freely.

That winter the united bands of Bridger and Fontenelle
went into camp among the Crows of the Yellowstone. The
season was severe.

Fuel, however, was abundant, and excepting the inconvenience of keeping unusually large fires, they suffered but little.
Not so with the animals. It was with the greatest difficulty
that they preserved them from starvation. * * * The
intense cold operated to bring upon them another serious
annoyance, in the shape of immense herds of starving buffalo,
which, goaded on by the pangs of hunger, would watch for an
opportunity to gore the animals and steal their scanty allowance of provender. It was only by building large fires in the
valleys and constantly standing guard that the trappers succeeded in keeping them off.[65]

But if the winter was severe, the mountain men and
Indians alike appear to have made merry, for, according to
Joe Meek " perhaps there never was a winter camp in the
mountains more thoroughly demoralized than this, especially during the months of January and February."

Fontenelle and four men and the party of Captain Stuart
(who was still on deck and in the thick of mountain life) set
off in midwinter for the Laramie (Fort John); and here,
soon after arrival in January, Fontenelle killed himself
while, it is claimed, in his cups.

When spring opened two of the trappers were sent to
the fort on the Laramie for supplies, and never were heard

from at either terminus of the route; and in March the beaver trail was taken for the sources of the Missouri in the presumably desolated country of the Blackfeet.

About this, the most dangerous of regions, the mountain men seem to have hovered with the persistency of a boy haunting a forbidden apple orchard. It was, of course, an excellent beaver district, but there were other beaver districts as prolific, and much less venomous.

The route was northwest from the Powder River headwaters in northern Wyoming, across the Big Horn mountains and the rivers of the Big Horn, Clarke's and the Rosebud (a wild, austere country) to the upper Yellowstone. That not all the Blackfeet were yet dead was proven when near the Yellowstone the Bridger advance struck a Blackfeet village and another brisk fight occurred.

The march continued northwest across Twenty-five Yard River to the Three Forks of the Missouri. The Bridger camp had been three hundred strong and although it must have been lessened during the march, as details dropped off to trap, it proceeded defiantly into the Blackfeet territory. An advance guard of forty or fifty men were sent forward to follow a broad Blackfeet trail; evidently that of a village fleeing from the plague, for the trail was strewn with the disfigured corpses of smallpox victims.

The stricken village noted the pursuit and posted one hundred and fifty warriors to cover its retreat. The point chosen was a narrow valley or bottom, hedged by high, rocky bluffs. But if an ambush had been projected the wily mountain men were too acute; and several of them, leaving their horses, climbed around and above, and surprising the reds, poured in a sudden fire.

For a time it was give and take, with the Blackfeet heroically enduring their losses and acting upon the defensive until the village might escape. After three hours of battle the trappers' ammunition began to run low; and apprised by the slackening fire, the desperate reds suddenly turned like a striking snake, carrying the fight to the trappers.

The voice of Kit Carson and of other recognized leaders rallied the whites, bidding them stand fast. The rifles were emptied and as on the Blackfeet came the pistols were brought into deadly use. Back rolled the feathered, painted tide, only to swell again and again. So hot was the contest among the rocks that sometimes a single boulder separated opponent and opponent, each striving to reach the other.

The reserves from the trapper camp, on the march behind, now arrived with reinforcement of men and ammunition. But the Blackfeet, running amuck and mad with the lust of the fight, declined to loosen their desperate clutch on victory and revenge. The trappers having mounted, the battle was renewed with added fury.

Several of the incidents have been preserved to this day. Doc Newell, dismounting to scalp an Indian presumed to be dead, resuscitated the corpse by the prick of his knife, and, his fingers caught among the gun screws with which the savage's topknot was adorned, he well nigh never got free alive. Joe Meek, unconsciously posing while turned in his saddle, was made by J. M. Stanley, the mountain days artist, who was present at the time, the subject of a celebrated canvas, " The Trapper's Last Shot." A Blackfeet woman's horse was killed, but evading capture she seized the tail of her husband's horse and at full speed was dragged from danger.

Mansfield, trapper, was pinioned under his own horse in the thick of the fray, as he was passing a point of rocks. Six Blackfeet dashed afoot for him, to count a *coup* and take his scalp. But at his despairing cry: " Tell old Gabe [Bridger] that old Cotton [his own sobriquet] is gone," Carson, who had noted, sprang from his saddle and stood

over him. He shot the foremost warrior dead; other mountain men turned their weapons the same way, and only two
of the Blackfeet reached cover. Cotton managed to wriggle
from beneath his horse and make for safety. Kit Carson's
horse, however, during the hurly-burly had bolted, leaving
him exposed in the open. But he vaulted behind a comrade
and was borne away. His mount was caught and restored
to him.

The battle resumed more furiously than ever. Although
confronted by the reinforcements, the Blackfeet yielded not
an inch. The trappers, as usual in such contests, were the
better armed, and at last plied so with rifle ball and pistol
ball that the Blackfeet commenced to waver. By ones and
twos and threes they scurried backward to save their lives,
until, on a sudden, the rout became general; the first trickle
waxed into a torrent, and down the hill slope, through the
valley and away, the defeated Indians fled.

The trappers did not pursue. They let well enough alone;
and camping upon the battle field, buried their three
dead, attended to their several wounded, and rested.

The rendezvous of the summer of 1837 was held in the
Wind River Valley, in present Wyoming, east of the Continental Divide and north of South Pass. Here arrived,
upon his way from Oregon to the Atlantic coast, the missionary William H. Gray, who, the previous year, had
appeared with Reverend and Mrs. Spalding and Doctor and
Mrs. Whitman at the rendezvous in the Valley of the
Green.

Mr. Gray, accompanied by two white men, three Flatheads (one of whom was an educated chief, The Hat), an
Iroquois and a Snake, and nothing daunted by the strenuous journey of the year before, was re-traveling the Oregon
Trail, on mission and personal business. Disregarding
warnings that his escort was insufficient, as a man of God
he proceeded eastward, only upon the plains of the lower

Platte to be spied by the prowling Sioux. To the Sioux
anything from the west of the mountains was fair prey.
The three Flatheads and the Iroquois and Snake fought
bravely, killing fifteen of the Sioux. In the parley promoted
by a French-Canadian trader among the Sioux, Mr. Gray
was promised his life and the life of his two white companions, if the five Indians and their " fine horses " were
delivered over. That this compromise was effected, who
can believe? But the five Indians were slain, the three
whites passed through to the frontier, and ever after the
Flathead tribe accused Mr. Gray of cowardly double-dealing,
and among the mountain men he was a byword. The fact
that he was twice wounded, and while on horseback in the
river was grazed along the top of the head by another ball,
shows how dire were his straits. In this world Mr. Gray
cannot be judged. However, a Protestant mission never
was established amidst the Flatheads, who first had incited
the crusade.[66]

Wyeth's Fort Hall had been sold, this summer of 1837,
to the British. Under the new proprietors it engaged some
of the American trappers, but Fort Davy Crockett, in
Brown's Hole, Colorado, on an elbow of the Green, cour-
teously managed by the mountain men William Craig, Philip
Thompson, and Sinclair (St. Clair), was the fashionable
American gathering place. Thither, after the rendezvous
of this summer, journeyed Kit Carson and seven others.

Thompson and Sinclair were organizing a trading trip
south into the Navajo country of present New Mexico, and
Carson joined them. This was a trip not after furs, but
after horses and mules, and the Navajo merchandise of hair
ropes and blankets. The latter article especially was valued,
as it is valued today. Substantial, warm, waterproof, of
pleasant pattern, the Navajo blanket early appealed to the
Mexican and the traveler over the Santa Fe Trail, was made
popular by the American soldiers of the days of '46 (who

discovered it in Santa Fe), and has maintained itself as a Navajo asset ever since.

Out of the Navajo country, with its peach orchards and ranging flocks, the traders proceeded to Bent's Fort on the Arkansas, where the spoils, principally mules, were sold for the Missouri market.

This winter of 1837-38 Kit Carson spent in Brown's Hole as hunter for Fort Davy Crockett. It is evident that the beaver trail was losing its fascination for him; that the beaver trade was on the wane. Indeed, back as far as the summer of 1832 the astute Astor, while in London, had noted the advent of the silk hat, and in a letter had recorded a fear that beaver fur must soon yield to the cocoon, the trap to the loom.

It is impossible to assert whither Kit Carson made his fur hunt of the spring of 1838. We have choice of the Black Hills (which in those days extended to the Laramie), of the Snake, of the Grand River in Colorado. Operating as an independent trapper, he took his furs to the Robidoux post, Fort Uintah. " But the prices at which he was obliged to sell them did not at all please him." Trapper talk trended to the decision that the beaver business was irrevocably on the decline, and probably with his previous visits to Bent's Fort in mind, Carson, accompanied by his wife and child, by old Bill Williams, William New, William Mitchell and one Fredericks, a Frenchman, all disgusted with the mountain profits, set out for the lower country and Bent's Fort on the plains.

CHAPTER XVII

THE FORKING OF THE TRAIL

FOR several reasons it seems safe to make the summer of 1838 the dividing line between Kit Carson's youth in the mountains and his maturity upon the plains. He leaves the hills to emerge not only into a wider horizon of nature, but into a wider horizon of life, and to take a more active part in general western affairs.

All biographies of Kit Carson assign to him eight consecutive years as resident hunter at Bent's Fort. By sequence of summers and winters these biographies also represent him as occupied in the mountains until the summer of 1840. The problem in addition, to this point, is simple; we have but to add adventure to adventure, rendezvous to rendezvous, winter camp to winter camp; but when to the sum we must add eight years as hunter, and yet send him with Fremont in 1842, and again in 1843-44, and again to California and the conquest, in 1845-6, the task requires more than mathematical ingenuity.

We know that he fought upon the side of Joseph Gale, the Wyeth man, in the fall of 1834 in the Blackfeet country; that in the spring of 1835 he had his adventure with the wolf-imitating Sioux, at the Colorado-Wyoming line; that his duel with Bully Shunan occurred at the rendezvous of 1835; that in the winter of 1836 he was with Bridger, and in the summer of 1836 was at rendezvous; that he spent two winters at Fort Davy Crockett (one winter as hunter), whereas Fort Davy Crockett did not exist until 1836 or 1837; that Captain James Hobbs claims to have met him in the summer of 1837, trading with a small party on the

179

plains of southern Colorado. Meek says Carson was at Crockett in the winter of 1839-40; and he himself says to Colonel Meline, in speaking of Father DeSmet: "I remember he came once among the hunters and trappers up in the mountains, and baptized forty-odd children." But Father DeSmet did not enter the mountain missionary work until 1840.

It is very likely that Kit Carson's adventures were more compressed than he recalls. The accepted chronology is obviously wrong in some of its dates — discrepancies only to be expected, and of course pardonable. But we must accept also that his huntership for Bent's Fort would not deprive him of excursions between seasons into the mountains; and that while hunter he very well could have figured in various mountain incidents, in camp and at rendezvous.

Oliver Wiggins again is authority for the statement that to supply meat for Bent's Fort required only two big buffalo hunts a year; and that to those the Carson company bent all its energies of the moment. And inasmuch as Carson resided at Taos in 1838, I am inclined to the opinion that this huntership at the post comprised four years, 1838-1842, of two seasons each, rather than eight straight years from 1834 on.[67]

Before continuing with Kit Carson in his translation from beaver hunter to accredited guide, before bridging the short interval between the acts, while the scenes are shifted from the beaver trail setting to the setting of the explorer, we may as well say a few last words of the trapper generally. For the withdrawal of Kit Carson from the exclusive pursuit of mountain fur hunting was portentous of a change in epochs.

As has been said, John Jacob Astor in 1832 prophesied that the silk hat spelled the doom of the beaver trade. In 1834 *Silliman's Journal*, without reference to silk, spoke as darkly.

It appears that the fur trade must henceforth decline. The advanced state of geographical science shows that no new countries remain to be explored. In North America, the animals are slowly decreasing, from the persevering efforts and the indiscriminate slaughter practised by hunters, and by the appropriation to the uses of man of those forests and rivers which have afforded them food and protection. They recede with the aborigines, before the tide of civilization; but a diminished supply will remain in the mountains and uncultivated tracts of this and other countries, if the avidity of the hunter can be restrained within proper limitations.

Two hundred thousand skins a year were exported from the western plains and mountains to the markets of Europe; [68] no effort was made at conservation — any more than at conserving the buffalo, later. When the silk hat began to outrival all but the very finest beaver hat, the market for the poorer pelts dropped with a thud, and an ordinary second-grade skin brought only a dollar. When beaver fur was found satisfactory for other uses than in hats, suddenly the animal had become scarce; and although for a squaw-dressed pelt Oliver Wiggins and partners, in 1840 and onward through half a dozen years, obtained eight dollars at St. Joe, except in favored localities trapping was apt to fetch slim bags.

So rapidly did the beaver business in the mountains decline, giving place to the buffalo robe trade of the plains, that at St. Vrain's fort on the South Platte, close to the Colorado foothills, in the summer of 1843, Fremont remarks:

It is singular that, immediately at the foot of the mountains, I could find no one sufficiently acquainted with them to guide us to the plains at their western base; but the race of trappers who formerly lived in their recesses had almost entirely disappeared — dwindled to a few scattered individuals — some one or two of whom are regularly killed in the course of each year by the Indians.[69]

In the combination which produced the decline of the beaver business in the mountains there was another element: the dissolution of the Rocky Mountain Company and the supremacy of the American Company. The American Fur Company was not, to use a cow-puncher expression, " wised " to mountain methods and mountain tribes; the upper Missouri River and the river trails of the plains were its field, posts and not rendezvous were its system for barter; badly organized, the mountain fur business after 1836 rapidly disintegrated.

The rendezvous of the American Fur Company of 1838 was held by Bridger, the partisan, and Drips, the trader, with supplies from St. Louis (or, more likely, from Fort Union) not in the Valley of the Green, but on the head waters of the Yellowstone, within easy reach of pack train from the upper Missouri.

The English captain, Sir William Drummond Stuart, was again at rendezvous; and, more important, there were present new missionaries, coming, apparently, by a more northern route than that of the Snake and the South Pass. And among them were white women, emulating the pioneering two years before by Narcissa Whitman and Eliza Spalding.

Protestant missionary work in Oregon was approaching full tide. Now Reverend Jason Lee and Mr. P. L. Edwards, who had led the march in 1834, with two Chinook boys Christianized under the simple names of William Brooks and Thomas Adams were hastening back to the East, for the purpose of further arousing the Missionary Board to the call of Oregon. This party met at the rendezvous their fellow worker, Reverend William Gray, returning with his bride, Mary Augusta Dix Gray (wooed and won in a courtship of an evening), aged twenty-seven, of Ithaca, New York; Reverend Cushing Eells, aged twenty-eight, of Blandford, Mass., and his bride, Myra Fairbanks Eells, aged thirty-two, of Holden, Mass.; Reverend Asa B. Smith, aged twenty-nine, of Williamstown, Mass., and his bride, Sarah White Smith, aged twenty-four, of West Brookfield, Mass.; Reverend Elkanah Walker, aged thirty-two, of North Yarmouth, Maine, and his bride, Mary Richardson Walker, aged twenty-seven, of Baldwin, Maine; and a lay missionary, Cornelius Rogers, aged twenty-two, of Cincinnati — "a fine young man," who in less than five years was to find a death amidst the swollen winter waters of the Willamette.[70]

But the time had come when the Roman Catholic missionary, so tardy in arrival here, although so early elsewhere, was to bear his banner across from east to west. The accessions to the Protestant missions of 1838 are not the only ones. The Hudson Bay brigade of 1838 brings out to the Columbia Reverend Francis N. Blanchet, newly appointed Vicar General of the Oregon Catholic Missions (and soon to be first Catholic Bishop of Oregon) and his assistant, Reverend Modeste Demers.

On November 24 the two priests arrived at Vancouver, where "the populace rushed to feast their eyes on the first Catholic missionaries, whose presence they had so long expected. In the absence of Dr. McLoughlin, James Douglass received them and saw them well housed and fed."

These two Jesuits, Father Blanchet and Father Demers, had the lower Columbia for their field, with Vancouver as their occasional meeting place. They were reinforced in 1840 by the great and good Father Peter J. DeSmet, also of the Society of Jesus. He was from St. Louis; they were from Montreal. They were French; he was Belgian. They worked among chiefly the Hudson Bay employees and the Cayuses of the Vancouver and Willamette regions; his work was among the Flatheads, who had sent in the call eight years ago. And it is mainly the name DeSmet that spells the best history of Roman Catholicism in pioneer

Oregon, for he was a broad and noble character — a second Marquette.

From St. Louis in the spring of 1840 Father DeSmet traveled to Fort Hall; thence he turned north, over the mountains for the Bitter Root country of the Flatheads, across the present Montana line, whither the Protestant missionaries of 1834 had gazed, but from which they had been deflected. During his first visit of two months, in the spring and summer of 1840, he baptized 600 persons and taught the prayers of the Catholic church to 2,000. The following year he commenced the erection there of a mission establishment, the nucleus of other Catholic missions, first among the Coeur d' Alenes, and later among the Blackfeet themselves.

The rendezvous of 1839 was held near Bonneville's old fort, Fort Nonsense, on the Horse Creek tributary of the Green, in the Valley of the Green. From the rendezvous of 1839 the disgruntled and disheartened mountain men, scattered to the four winds, but not necessarily to the four winds of the beaver trail. " Some went to Santa Fe, some to California, others to the lower Columbia, and a few remained in the mountains, trapping, and selling their furs to the Hudson Bay Company at Fort Hall." The American Fur Company posts drew many; and there was Oregon. Thither, in 1840 and on, trailed squads of the mountain men.

" Come," said Newell to Meek, " we are done with this life in the mountains — done with wading in beaver dams, and freezing or starving alternately — done with Indian trading and Indian fighting. The fur trade is dead in the Rocky Mountains, and it is no place for us now, if ever it was. We are young yet, and have life before us. We cannot waste it here; we cannot or will not return to the States. Let us go down to the Willamet and take farms." [71]

So, one after another, traders, guides, ranchers, Indian

agents, prospectors, squaw-men, nondescripts they became —
some sinking, others rising, and many unable, the rest of
their lives, to adjust themselves to the new conditions of
earning a living.

A surprising proportion of these retired mountain men
were young. Joe Meek was twenty-eight, Jim Bridger was
thirty-eight, Robert Newell was not thirty, Joe Walker was
forty-two, Kit Carson was twenty-eight. And now to
Bent's Fort were his footsteps turned.

CHAPTER XVIII

BENT'S FORT OF THE PLAINS

THE Northwest is assured. But now, while in the East Reverend Jason Lee, assisted by the two Indian boys, is lecturing from Missouri to the Atlantic coast, while reinforcements of artisans, farmers, money, and " young ladies " are being hastened by land and by sea to this farthest frontier where they " have everything to do, and little to do with "; while the first territorial petition is in Congress and Oregon's newest legislative champion, Senator Lewis Fields Linn, of Missouri, is declaiming the cause of secular occupation; while the mountain men, deprived of rendezvous and supply train, are reluctantly wending their way, with squaws and children, to the Willamette; and while at Dubuque, Iowa, inspired by the Welsh civil engineer, John Plumbe, a convention has been held, March 31, 1837, to promote a transcontinental railroad, Kit Carson, at Bent's Fort on the plains and at Taos, New Mexico, is by no means removed from the flutter of the onward reaching flag.

Down here in the Southwest, however, the voice of colonization has not yet been sounded. The Oregon Trail invited the settler; the Santa Fe Trail invited the merchant. Now in 1838 (and for many a year to come) still slowly roll the great Conestogas upon their long way across prairie and desert; wagons are used exclusively and oxen have to a large extent supplanted the mules of the boy Kit Carson days. Old Franklin is old indeed, threatened by the river and abandoned by many inhabitants. Independence, up river toward the mouth of the Kaw, is the terminal point for both caravan and mountain train,

OLD BENT'S FORT
(Sketches by Lieut. J. W. Abert)

WILLIAM BENT

OF BOSTON TEA PARTY DESCENT, HEAD PARTNER IN BENT, ST. VRAIN & CO.
INDIAN TRADER AND FIGHTER.   DIED IN 1869

(Courtesy of the Missouri Historical Society)

but Westport Landing, a few miles above, is the steamboat terminal, and the adjacent Westport town is also bidding for business and inviting a future Kansas City. Civilization is ever edging farther into the Indian country.

The Indian frontier has been definitely established by Congress; and across it, in present Oklahoma, Kansas, and Nebraska, are located the tribes from the east of the Mississippi, to dwell forever and naturally, and guaranteed against invasion by the whites. For this purpose only was the country between the States and the mountains pronounced to be adapted.

In Texas the decisive battle of San Jacinto (April 21, 1836) has been fought, and the paean has welled to the patriotic chorus:

For this we are determined, to die or to be free,
And TEXAS TRIUMPHANT our watchword shall be!

And of the new republic of Texas, extending from the Sabine to the Rio Grande, General Sam Houston is president. Full a year had passed since, August 4, 1837, the new republic had applied for annexation with the larger and older republic and had been refused; but the arguments on both sides bid fair to end in reconsideration.

Near Independence has appeared that new sect, the Church of Jesus Christ of the Latter Day Saints, on that westward movement so fraught with national import. From Independence on to Far West do these strange "Mormons" continue; there to lay, in this summer of 1838, the corner stone of a Zion Temple. But Missouri declines them; from Illinois they will be driven forth, and thus they are led to break the Mormon Trail to Salt Lake, and to California; and Utah is colonized.

In the northwest, Oregon, and in the southwest, Texas, are ready at a touch to burst into full citizenship. Forth-reaching right and left, the United States will harvest them almost simultaneously. And straight in front, beyond the West, California is being prepared as another segment in the mighty circle.

Colonel Jose Maria Echeandia — that "man of scholastic bent and training and Castilian lisp," so suspicious of the *gringo* American — has retired from his governorship; Kit Carson had not yet arrived back in Taos, from that trip under Ewing Young, when to Echeandia had succeeded the mestizo or Indian-Mexican breed, Lieutenant Colonel Manuel Victoria, and to Victoria had succeeded Brigadier General Jose Figueroa, "of Aztec blood, hence swarthy in color." And to Figueroa succeeded others — a long line vexed by revolts in which already the *gringo* American bore customary part.

Isaac Graham, the Tennessean, mountain man with the Captain Sinclair party from Arkansas up the Green in 1831, and at the battle of Pierre's Hole in 1832, has in 1836 supported the native Californian revolt for the cause of Juan Bautista Alvarado, with the result that, following the example of Texas, Alta California, on November 6, proclaimed itself independent of Mexico. Not yet, of course, has the Bear Flag been designed; but the Latin unrest is further agitated by the ferment of the American adventurer, and, a factor of tremendous importance, in 1838 there traversed the Oregon Trail to the Pacific coast Johann August Sutter, to establish himself at New Helvetia on the Sacramento, and by the lodestone of the gold in his mill race to draw from the very ends of the earth a new citizenship.

From the originating point of Missouri, the lines of interest lead to Texas, Oregon, California; and in the midst of the fan-shaped field, caught, as it were, in the web, where the plains are about to meet the foothills of the Rockies, is Kit Carson at Bent's Fort.

Bent's Fort (to which had been vainly assigned the title

Fort William), was built in 1829, and was therefore ten
years old when Kit Carson, out of the mountains, became
its official hunter. Its founders were five St. Louis traders,
Charles Bent, William Bent, George Bent, and Ceran St.
Vrain, whose brother Marcelin also was associated with
him.[72]

The site of Bent's Fort was upon the north bank of
the Arkansas (consequently in American territory) below
the present town of La Junta, Colorado, and about fourteen
miles above the mouth of the Rio Purgatoire, that stream
whose name, anglicized into Purgatory, was further reduced
to the Americanism of " Picketwire." It is also known as
the Rio Las Animas or Rio de las Animas Perdidas (River
of the Lost Souls), but it is thereby confounded with
another Rio Las Animas, in the opposite southwestern corner of Colorado. One hundred and thirty miles west from
the fort were the mountains. Thither, up the Arkansas, ran
a trappers' and traders' trail, for the Fontaine qui Bouille
and the South Park and beyond; north from the fort ran a
trail to the Bent and St. Vrain posts on the Platte, and to
Fort Laramie, 380 miles; south, over the Raton Mountains
ran the trail to Taos, two hundred miles, and to Santa Fe;
while from the east came in the mountain division, the
oldest route, of the Santa Fe Trail, from Missouri, 530
miles. Thus at the crossroads of the plains wilderness was
stationed old Bent's Fort — its dun ramparts a stronghold
and a hospice in one.[73]

It stood alone, with "its high clay walls in the midst
of the scorching plains." A home more isolated did not
exist in North America. The lodge of the mountain man
had the companionship of the mighty hills, but except for
a few low bluffs and a scattering of cottonwoods and willows, the post of Fort William was the sole eminence for
miles about. Fort Laramie was on a trail where passed and
repassed not only the fur trade caravans, and many a trader

and trapper, but also travelers, missionaries, and prospective settlers, a stream constantly increasing and bringing the States to the fortress gate. Bent's was on its own trail, until in 1846 " the wild and lonely banks of the upper Arkansas beheld for the first time the passage of an army "; it was the center of a kingdom of its making, and as a nucleus of white supremacy beyond the frontier can be compared only with Pierre, Union, and early Fort George of Vancouver. But even the upper Missouri was more frequented than the upper Arkansas.

To be sure, in the summer of 1835, swinging out of Fort Leavenworth on a wide circle up the South Platte to the mountains and thence south, the dragoons of Colonel Henry Dodge, guided by Trader Captain Gant, had stopped on their return for a few August days. This was the only exploration of the plains, by the military of the United States, until 1846.[74] To be sure, five miles above the post was the heterogeneous assortment of retired trappers and traders, white and Mexican breeds, and of variously complexioned squaws and children, composing the community of the " puebla " — Fort el Puebla. But Bent's Fort asked neither military aid nor neighbors. With its walls, cannon and employees, it was self-sufficient.

Old Bent's Fort, Fort Bent, or Fort William, was located about sixty yards from the brink of the Arkansas, and amidst a patch of grassy bottom land. The walls, of large adobe bricks after the fashion of the West, were eighteen feet in height, and six or seven feet thick at the base, tapering off to two feet at the top. They formed a rectangle, running north and south, 150 feet by 100 feet. At the northwest and southeast corners they intersected in the axes of twin towers, or bastions, thirty feet high and ten feet in diameter, which, swelling out, permitted the defenders to rake the outside of the walls with gun fire.

The main entrance was a thirty-foot gateway in the east

wall, looking downstream, or along the Missouri Trail, and closed by a pair of immense plank doors. Over the gate was a sentry box, floating the Flag. A six-pounder brass cannon and several smaller ordnance were mounted upon the walls, commanding the court within and the approaches without. The post had a hide press, for pressing robes and furs into bales. This stood in the center of the court. In the cupola of the headquarters building was a " fine spyglass," and a billiard table hauled clear from Independence. Among the clerks and even among the trappers were men who could handle a cue; and when, during the war with Mexico, United States troops occupied the post as a way station. the table was in much demand among the army officers. In the kitchen presided Charlotte, the negress cook, famed for her pumpkin pies!

The situation might seem forlorn and monotonous for the inmates. The rolling, treeless plains of the cattle-range West surrounded them; in summer these lay brown and parched, swept by blasting winds as undiminished in force as if coming across an ocean; and reflected from the white-washed walls and the hard clay of the post's court, the sun fairly blistered all objects exposed. In the winter, the snow, and the bare patches, with the short grass that barely concealed the ground, made the fort a cheerless place.

The post was most advantageously situated for both the Indian and the Mexican trade. The Cheyennes and Arapahos annually held a winter camp in the Big Timbers, a stretch of huge cottonwoods thirty-two miles below and extending twenty-four miles along the river; and in the spring and fall they followed the buffalo back and forth across the Arkansas, with the end in view of marketing their robes at the post. The Red River Comanches, and the Utes likewise, engaged in the summer and winter trading. It is related that in the fall sometimes as high as 20,000 Indians were assembled in the neighborhood of the post. As the post was upon the mountain route between the States and Santa Fe, it was a candidate for the Mexican trade also.

The principal trade with the Indians was in buffalo robes, although of course trappers brought in beaver; and good business was carried on in horses and mules for the Missouri market. The organization of the post was strict, like the organization of the American Fur Company and the Hudson Bay Company posts. Being immune to fire from without, the place, if rightly guarded, need fear no assault.

Bent's Fort was owned and conducted by the St. Louis trading firm, Bent, St. Vrain & Co., whose trade brand was " Quarter-Circle B " [)-B]. They instituted other posts, to make a chain; the principal one being Fort St. Vrain or Fort George, north from Bent's Fort, built for the Arapaho, northern Cheyenne, and Sioux trade, and situated on the plains in north central Colorado where, southwest of the present town of Greeley, the St. Vrain Creek empties into the South Platte. This post was a halfway station between Bent's Fort and Fort Laramie, and was, in its last days, the northern terminal of the first pony express route of the plains, which carried mail and packages from St. Vrain to Taos, and handed down to the emigrant the Cherokee Trail of the fifties.

Fort St. Vrain (whose title of Fort George probably refers to George Bent, brother of William Bent) was established about 1837; and ten years thereafter, or in 1848, on the Canadian River in northwestern Texas the firm established the post of Adobe Walls, for trade with the Kiowas, Comanches, and Prairie Apaches. Here, at Thanksgiving time, 1864, Kit Carson engaged in the greatest Indian fight of his career.

When the pilgrimage of the Forty-niners to California set in, old Bent's Fort was a station on the Arkansas River, Cherokee Trail, and Cherry Creek (the future Denver) route. Colonel Bent, who by this time was the sole proprietor, wanted to sell his post to the government. He asked for the property $16,000; $12,000 was offered; and in the summer of 1852, tired of the dickering, in a fit of wrath he

loaded all the goods he could get on his wagons, sixteen in number, set fire to his premises, and pulled out. A considerable quantity of powder remained in the fort, and, as the train wound its way down the river, the ascending flames accompanied by a succession of loud reports told how effectually the fortress was being converted into a ruin. Thus the Arkansas Valley was again devoid of human habitation.[75]

The rifted battlements of the historic post persisted as landmarks for over a quarter of a century. The next year, or in May, 1853, when Edward F. Beale (late lieutenant, United States Navy, hero with Carson, and now appointed Indian Agent for California) and his companion, Gwinn Harris Heap, passed by, for the coast, they

rode all through the ruins, which present a strange appearance in these solitudes. A few years ago this post was frequented by numerous trappers and Indians, and at times exhibited a scene of wild confusion. It is now roofless; for when the United States refused to purchase it, the proprietor set it on fire to prevent its becoming a harbor for Indians. The adobe walls are still standing, and are in many places of great thickness. They are covered with written messages from parties [i. e., emigrants] who had already passed here, to their friends in the rear.[76]

Colonel Bent journeyed down river thirty miles, and at the Big Timbers erected a few log cabins as a winter trading post for the Indians who were accustomed to gather here. Lieutenant E. J. Beckwith, outward bound in this spring of 1853, for one of the Pacific Railroad surveys, notes them as being then abandoned. But here at the Big Timbers Colonel Bent followed the log cabins with a substantial stone post almost as pretentious as old Fort William above; and this, in 1859, the Government did purchase. Remodeled, it became Fort Wise of the army, old Fort Lyon of the settlers — as differentiated from the new Fort Lyon of later date, twenty-five miles upriver, or back toward the original Bent's Fort. It was at this new Fort Lyon Kit Carson died, in 1868; and near by died, aged sixty, still true to the old trail, William Bent.[77]

CHAPTER XIX

ADVENTURES OF KIT CARSON — 1838-1842

K IT CARSON did not settle down as merely hunter for Bent's Fort. It probably is true that he had the contract to supply the fort with meat. But that he operated from Taos, and not from the post, we know by corroborative testimony of a contemporary, Oliver P. Wiggins.

In the mid-fall of this year 1838, a Santa Fe caravan of fifty-two wagons commanded by Captain Blunt left Independence, Missouri, for the New Mexican market. It happened that after a short period of truce the Kiowas were again about to break forth — as they had the habit of doing every three years — and the Blunt caravan was warned, while on its way, by travelers from the West.

The Kiowas were the fiercest fighters of the southwest plains; not even the Comanches and Apaches were so much dreaded, and even the Pawnees did not outrank those painted horsemen with the truly Indian name.

At the crossing of the Arkansas, in southern Kansas, the much-alarmed train was met by Kit Carson, leading a company of bearded trappers from Taos; and right glad was the caravan to see the reinforcement, for many of the teamsters were greenhorns, and poorly armed. At the rear, driving the cavvy, there jogged along on a humble mule a runaway boy of fifteen, who, accoutered with a stained juvenile dragoon suit of blue, and a pistol "as large as the palm of my hand," was out "to hunt Injuns"! This was Oliver P. Wiggins, for twelve years to be Kit Carson's subaltern and close friend.

The Kiowa territory was beyond. After two days' travel,

when the danger zone was reached, on the third morning the raw teamsters were amazed to witness the vaunted mountain men tie their horses to the rear of the wagons, and pile in, a pair to a wagon, under the canopy tops. This occasioned grumbling and not a few sneers from the Missourians, whose remarks, however, were treated with silent contempt.

But scarcely had the train got under way, when from over the sandhills to the north, down poured the whooping Kiowas; riding hard, brandishing lance and bow and shield, shouting and shooting their fruitless arrows. But if they thought that they had to deal only with the teamsters who foolishly emptied their guns in reply they were much mistaken. Undeterred by the confused parking of the caravan they lunged on — until suddenly from the slightly rolled edges of the wagon tops poked forth the long heavy barrels of the trappers' rifles, and the poised muzzles spat their hot lead. The volley was as deadly as unexpected. Back reeled the remnant of the reds, scurrying, screeching, for those sandhills whence they had so valiantly emerged; and after them raced the trappers, shooting.

The caravan was almost at the Taos Trail — the forking of the Santa Fe Trail, at the Cimarron in New Mexico. That evening, in the twilight, Ike Chamberlain, the Kit Carson lieutenant, approached Oliver, and said:

" Boy, 'stead o' goin' on to Santy Fee, how 'd you like to travel 'long to Touse with us? "

How would he *like* it! The ragged urchin whom everyone had appeared to overlook, Kit Carson, with that kindliness toward youth which was one of his best attributes, had noticed. Before ever he had reached Independence the boy had heard of Kit Carson, and had dreamed of meeting him.

" All right," continued Chamberlain, interpreting his look of joy. " We take the Touse Trail in the mornin.'

There 'll be no more Injuns. I 'll see Kit again, and if he says for you to come we 'll light a fire, after dark where we 're campin'. When it flares up, you 'll know."

Thus Oliver Wiggins accompanied the Carson company to Taos. By this he lost his wages, for the wagon master refused to pay him except at the end of the trail, Santa Fe; but the wages cut little figure compared with the chance offered — and boy Oliver was never sorry. For twelve years he was a " Carson man." [78]

Taos was reached early in December. Here Kit Carson, twenty-nine years old, had home and headquarters, and operated with a company of forty-five trappers. His assistants were Ike Chamberlain and Solomon Silver. Most of the men were Kentuckians. Usually half the company were out at a time, under Chamberlain or Silver, after beaver. Strangely enough, the names of these two lieutenants do not appear in mountain and plains history.[79]

Twice a year, in the spring and fall, the whole party went on a great buffalo hunt, to fulfill Carson's contract with Bent's Fort. Between times there were the beaver, the horse herd, and the Indians.

Carson was the best trapper among all the men, good though they were. The fur trail extended clear to the Wisdom River, north of the Three Forks source of the Missouri. The Blackfeet had quieted, and the Wisdom was found to be virgin ground. At one place the two-foot channel had been dammed and expanded into a shallow pond ten miles wide; from this great collection of lodges the Carson party took 3,000 beaver, which Blackfeet squaws dressed, their payment being the carcasses and an occasional pinch of sugar. Another time, in Colorado's South Park, by cutting a dam the Carson trappers drained a beaver pond and, wading into the muck, at one attack killed eighty beaver with clubs.

The pelts were regularly sent down from the camps, by

the Missouri or the Platte trails, to St. Joe — the former
Blacksnake Hills — where Louis Robidoux, the trader,
handled them. Of the proceeds Carson took ten per cent;
the remainder went to the employees — the year's division
not infrequently amounting to a thousand dollars apiece
for the trappers.

Carson, as may easily be comprehended, even after his
so-termed retirement from the mountains covered a wide
extent of territory, in trapping and hunting trips. Amidst
all he was a captain, operating independently by means
of his employees or by himself. Moreover, working from
Taos, or from Bent's Fort (for Bent, St. Vrain & Co. must
protect their trains) he seems to have been the guardian of
the trail. The incident of the Blunt caravan in the fall
of 1838 has been told. Another similar incident, of 1841,
may be related.

One sunrise that fall there arrived in Taos an excited
group of riders, with the news that about seventy miles
east, on the Santa Fe Trail, a caravan had been held a
day and a night by Indians and was in peril of extermination. At the time Carson was suffering from a pistol wound
in the right leg; his pistol had fallen and had discharged; the
ball passed upward, diagonally, through the calf, and he
was in bad shape for six months. This injury is mentioned
in no biographies, and probably was only a passing incident
of frontier life.

But Ike Chamberlain, now aged twenty-six, was on hand,
and Carson ordered him to get the men out and take the
trail in twenty minutes. However, a slight delay was necessary (at which Carson, with his characteristic impatience of
unreadiness, chafed), to permit some of the men to run
bullets. As quickly as possible twenty-five or thirty men
took the trail.

Oliver Wiggins, eighteen, and the youngest, accompanied
the party, for he had been promoted to man's work, and had

just been rewarded, by Carson's own new percussion-cap rifle, for a recent exploit in which he had summarily disposed of a Kiowa band and recovered stolen stock.

The rescue horsemen from Taos rode all that day, and reached the beleaguered caravan about two in the morning. They managed to pass through the savages, and found the caravan with its oxen almost dead from hunger and thirst. Now followed a stratagem similar to that of November, 1838. The Carson men distributed themselves among the wagons, to await the Indian charge. At daybreak, down swooped the reds — to be lured on by a feeble round of a few muskets and pistols. But when they were well inside point-blank range, the whites delivered the first volley; nevertheless, still the charge continued, for to the Indian mind the defenders now had only empty guns.

Abruptly and disastrously the galloping warriors were made acquainted with an evolution in firearms. The Kit Carson company, according to Oliver Wiggins, was maintained in the highest state of efficiency; the revolving pistol had lately been adopted; and springing from cover to the backs of their animals, the trappers met the Indian charge with a countercharge, shooting right and left *without reloading*. Saddle pads were emptied, the Indians broke and fled, with that accusation which has become historic: " White man shoot one time with rifle and six times with butcher knife!"

These Indians were Kiowas, with a few Comanches, the tribes more or less intermingling. More than a hundred were killed, while the whites lost only one man.

" Ah, what fighters we were, in those days!" sighed old Oliver Wiggins, at eighty-seven, his faded eyes kindling. " Nobody could lick the Carson men! They might kill us, but they could n't whip us!" While the triumphant Taos whites are riding back to report to their disabled captain, let us note what a change had been made in the civilizing weapons of the West. The percussion cap had been invented, cartridges for breech-loading had been experimented with, and the famous Colonel Samuel Colt had brought to comparative perfection his revolver.

The rifle which Oliver Wiggins wielded in this affray was the first percussion-cap rifle owned in Taos, and had been bought of the makers, Golcher & Butler of Philadelphia, by Kit Carson in 1840 for $60 gold. According to Oliver Wiggins, Carson was alert and his men were alert to secure the most advanced ideas in offensive and defensive weapons; and so his party in the fight of 1841, to rescue the wagon train, were armed with the new revolving pistols of Samuel Colt.

Kit Carson is now settled in Taos, and here and at Bent's Fort is sleeping continuously under a roof for the first period in a dozen years. Taos was his home; Bent's Fort but an adjunct. At Taos he had his horses and mule stock; hence, on occasion, he dispatched his punitive expeditions along the Santa Fe Trail; and here he outfitted his men with saddles, when needed — for his short apprenticeship under David Workman stood him in good stead. We may regard him as a rising young citizen, engineering various pursuits engendered by the advantages of his location; a young citizen among other citizens such as Charles Bent, Ceran St. Vrain, Carlos Beaubien, the Padre Martinez, editor and publisher of the first and only newspaper in New Mexico (its life being limited to one month), Lucien Maxwell, Basil Lajeunesse, and others, traders, plainsmen, and mountain men; merchants, traders, trappers; of recognized profession or of less definite status, but forming a select society. For Taos was not without the best blood of the West, and as custom-place of the New Mexican northern border was a settlement second only, if at all, to Santa Fe.

As has been related, in the summer of 1835 Carson fought a duel with Bully Shunan, at the Green River rendezvous,

TAOS IN 1853

*(From a sketch by Lieut. Col. Eaton. From Davis's El Gringo; or
New Mexico and her People)*

CARSON'S OFFICE IN TAOS

HIS HEADQUARTERS AS INDIAN AGENT WERE IN THE ROOM UNDER
THE SIGN

(Photograph by the author)

CARSON'S HOME IN TAOS

THE TWO MEN STANDING ON THE PORCH KNEW HIM AS A FELLOW CITIZEN
HERE. THEY ARE (LEFT), ALOYS SCHEURICH, OLDTIME SANTA FE TRAIL
FREIGHTER, AND CAPTAIN SMITH H. SIMPSON (RIGHT), OF INDIAN AND
CIVIL WAR SERVICE IN THE SOUTHWEST

(Photograph by F. J. Francis)

OLD FORT MASSACHUSETTS, 1853

A CELEBRATED INITIAL ARMY POST IN THE COLORADO ROCKIES, A BASIS FOR
OPERATIONS OUT OF TAOS AGAINST THE INDIANS

(From Vol. II. Pacific Railroad Reports. A Stanley picture)

and the cause of war is said to have been a woman. This girl, an Arapaho, Carson married (with the customary accepted rites of Indian and trapper), and very likely it was she whom, as his " Alice," he brought out with him upon his later trips to Bent's Fort and the plains. At any rate, his only Indian wife of whom we have knowledge died soon after presenting him with a daughter, in 1837 or 1838.

I am unable to find definite record of this Indian wife as resident in Taos. Oliver Wiggins, who was the only person living, so far as I know, with memory going back to Carson days in Taos of 1838, said that he had no clear recollection of the Indian woman; but he recalled well the little girl, and he recalled also her mother's being dead. It may be that in her young wifehood " Alice," the Arapaho girl, was at Bent's Fort and at Taos; but it is assured that before 1840 she had passed away; and that little Adaline was about four years old when, in the spring of 1842, her father decided upon removing her from the uncertain influences to which she was exposed, and taking her to Missouri.

That he was fond of her is very evident. But in all my correspondence with those persons now living who knew Kit Carson, only two or three can recall that he mentioned his wife Alice, and none recall that he mentioned his little daughter. Naturally a reticent man, in his later years, and even after his second marriage, which soon occurred, he would not speak of his Indian marriage, for fear of being misjudged. But at Taos during his widowerhood he declared that he would be glad to have for his second wife " Alice's sister," who, also, " was a good girl." Few traits in Kit Carson so appeal as his honor for the Indian wife who " always had the warm water ready for his feet," and who bore him his first child.

This little girl was named, we may accept, for the Adaline Carson who was born to William Carson, the elder brother, in 1810 and but a few weeks after Kit's own birth in 1809, and was Kit's first niece, and a favorite chum. The second Adaline (Adeline) was, as Oliver Wiggins stated, a dark, elfish child (for the Indian blood always dominates, in mixed offspring, over the white), and it may easily be realized that with the father away much of the time, and the population of Taos and of Bent's Fort so extraordinary in its mingling of races, her bringing up was a problem. And in this episode we see another evidence of Kit Carson's intrinsic sound sense and innate progressive ideas: that for his little daughter, mountain half-breed though she was, he desired a better atmosphere and a better chance.

It was quite practicable to take her to Santa Fe and to put her into convent training; this was done by the majority of the leading families of Taos, Mora, and elsewhere.

However, he seems to have had other views, and in the spring of 1842 she accompanied him from Bent's Fort back to Independence. Report says that he found few persons at Franklin who remembered him, and that the majority of his home people had vanished utterly. But, amidst the changes of sixteen years of a new country, he did find relatives; for if the Carson kin were wanderers, they were also numerous. Among these relatives was a niece, Mrs. Leander Amick, whose mother had been Kit Carson's sister Elizabeth, wife to Robert Cooper of Howard County's first days.

Mrs. L. P. Slaughter of Kansas City, daughter of Mr. and Mrs. Amick, writes:

When I was a child, Kit Carson's daughter Adeline, the daughter by his first wife, lived for several years with my parents on a farm between Fayette and Glasgow, in Howard county, in this State. There and in a St. Louis convent school she received her education. As my mother refused to accept any money for caring for his daughter, he purchased many presents for her, among which was a mahogany rocking-chair which I have still.

In a letter to the author, Mrs. Slaughter writes further (1911):

My sister, if now living, would be 74 years old, and was about the same age of Adeline Carson, Kit's daughter. She stayed with us until about eleven years old. She attended a school named Rock Springs school which was about nine miles from Fayette. When Kit took Adeline away from our home he said he might leave her in St. Louis in school or he might take her with him to California. It is the opinion of most of the Howard County pioneers that Adeline died in California and not in Missouri. She was dark complexioned, black hair and dark eyes. Kit visited her several times while she was with us.

Mr. George H. Carson, of Fayette (Missouri), whose recollections as son of William Carson, Kit Carson's eldest brother, have before been drawn upon, in this narrative, writes to me:

· In 1848, I think, he (Kit Carson) brought his daughter to Fayette and placed her in school. I know she was in school here in 1849, for I spent most of the summer here and often saw her, myself. My remembrance is that he took her west in the early fifties. She married, died, and is buried at Taos, N. M., is family tradition. I know of my own knowledge that he took her west.

This removal to school in Fayette, at the old Howard Female Seminary, occurred during Carson's second trip east from California, bearing dispatches for Washington. Mrs. Slaughter's remembrance, then, that Adaline was eleven years of age when she left the Amick home, in connection with the George Carson recollection of her in 1848 would place her birth in 1837: a date further substantiated by the comparison of Mrs. Slaughter's sister's age, seventy-four, in 1911.

But notwithstanding these various recollections, singularly if not pathetically little Adaline fades from public view. Oliver Wiggins insisted that she died when about ten years old, and died in Missouri; and report does declare that she died while attending school at a St. Louis convent.

Mr. George Carson states that " family tradition " assigns her a grave in Taos, but I failed to find trace of her in the ancient cemetery there, or in the annals of the place.

Mrs. Teresina Scheurich, native of Taos, who, aged six, after the murder of her father, Governor Charles Bent, entered the household of her uncle and aunt, Kit Carson and wife, writes the author that Adaline " married an officer and went to California, 1851 (?), soon after she was married, and died there two years later." This would tend to endorse the report by Captain James Hobbs, in *Wild Life in the Far West*, of a visit by him to Mono Lake, California, in 1869.

I was informed by a gentleman living there by the name of Scott that a daughter of Kit Carson was buried near by. At my request he pointed out her grave to me, when I employed a man to build a fence around it, as a mark of respect to and in memory of her father, with whom I had been pleasantly acquainted. I remembered seeing this girl often, when she was about eight years old. She was a daughter by Kit's first wife, who was called the Pine Leaf and was of the Blackfoot tribe. This girl was called the Prairie Flower, and was born at Bent's Fort on the Arkansas River. Her mother died when she was ten years of age. The girl then lived in Colonel Bent's family till she was sixteen years old, when she married a man by the name of George Stilts of St. Louis, Mo., and went to California with him in 1849. Stilts was a reckless man. * * * After traveling about in California with her husband a while she left him, and went to Mono Lake with a gentleman and his family, and died there. She was a noble looking woman, of mixed complexion, black eyes and long black hair, and could excel most men in the use of the rifle.[80]

But of this Adaline's death as a girl, or of her existence in young wifehood, we have only fragmentary testimony.

She seems never to have been mentioned by Carson in his Memoirs. However, his early efforts in her behalf were rewarded. His trail opened, as he pursued it; for this trip to Missouri resulted in his engagement with Fremont, and thus fate met him half way. We cannot assert that Fremont made Kit Carson. Kit Carson would have made, and did make, himself. But he might have lived at Taos until the Mexican War, at least, without attracting public attention as a valuable man. His name, before 1842, appears in few chronicles and in no official reports.

CHAPTER XX

ON THE TRAIL WITH FREMONT — 1842

WHEN, in June, 1842, on the steamboat ascending the river Missouri from St. Louis, Christopher Carson, the young mountain man out of the West, met Lieutenant John Charles Fremont, the young army engineer out of the East, opportunity joined their hands. Together they entered into fame.

Both were Southerners: Carson of North Carolinan and Kentuckian blood, Fremont born in Georgia but raised in South Carolina. Carson was the elder, being then in his thirty-third year, whereas Fremont was then twenty-nine. Carson was mature beyond his years, and a father; Fremont was youthfully enthusiastic, and a husband of only six months.

The two men were opposites. Carson was Scotch-Irish; gray-blue eyed, sandy complexioned (under his tan), light-haired, rather flat-featured, gritty but so quiet and ordinary both in appearance and manner that few not knowing his name would bestow upon him more than a passing glance. Fremont was French: flashing blue eyes, olive-white complexion, thick brown hair, features regular and oval, disposition sensitive, quick, eager, and indomitable — few would forget him.

Fremont was a scholar, of both American and Continental accomplishments; at this time Carson could not read, nor write even his own name, and his speech, even in 1866, was of *patois* wherein mingled Mexican, Indian, and many a frontier English " thar," " fout," " massacreed," " pore," etc. But he spoke in more languages than did Fremont him-

self; not only being fluent in "English, French, Spanish,
and several Indian tongues, all acquired orally," but also
being well conversant with the sign language of redman
and of trail.[81] Fremont was a student, poet, and adventurer, which combine in the true explorer, and no one can
examine his official reports without being struck by the
painstaking knowledge wrested from an unfamiliar field;
no one can read his *Memoirs* without appreciating the deli-
cacy of expression employed; and no one can ride his trail
without being impressed by his whole-souled methods. It
may be that John Charles Fremont was, as claimed, intolerant, over-ambitious, ill-balanced — and, according to
Oliver Wiggins, headstrong to pursue his own course in
spite of advice. So far as I can find, he was that kind of a
man beloved of Westerners, a man who set out to do his
share of the work, and who, if we except that fourth expedition, made good in what he undertook. He was a hard
man to follow, but those who did follow him were pretty
certain of having their money's worth. He was (as that
disastrous fourth expedition proved), headstrong: the type
of headiness which receives from the western veteran the
growl "fool tenderfoot" — and then impels him, body and
mind, to the rescue, when rescue for such a tenderfoot
is needed.

It seems to me that Fremont, the rash, needed Carson,
the cautious, and that each could estimate and value the
other, for both were brave. In 1842 began a friendship
which was maintained, with many mutual expressions of
goodwill and almost brotherly love, until death. Fremont
constantly refers, with generous praise, to Kit Carson's
qualities of heart and body, and receives him as an equal
into the home. Carson, in his loyal statement for the
Senate, 1848, declares that "he was under more obligations
to Fremont than to any other man alive."

So, in the words of Fremont:

On the boat I met Kit Carson. He was returning from putting his little daughter in a convent school at St. Louis. I was pleased with him and his manner of address at this first meeting. He was a man of medium height, broad-shouldered and deep-chested, with a clear steady blue eye and frank speech and address; quiet and unassuming.

*   *   *   *   *   *   *   *   *   *

I had expected to engage as guide an old mountaineer, Captain Drips, but I was so much pleased with Carson that when he asked to go with me I was glad to take him.

Now, he has become so familiarly known that I will let the narrative tell of the life we had together, out of which grew our enduring friendship.[83]

Carson engaged at $100 a month. Why he engaged, is hard to fathom. He seemed to be doing well at Bent's Fort and at Taos. Possibly a certain melancholy attached to his late visit amidst his boyhood haunts, where few welcomed him; and having safely bestowed his daughter, he was now foot-loose and restless.

At any rate, Kit Carson promptly swung into the trail with which his bridle path had joined; and from the Cyprian Chouteau post whence the start was to be made dispatched two Delaware " runners " to Taos, with a message instructing about fifteen of his own men to meet him at Fort Laramie (Fort John), with equipment.

The Cyprian Chouteau post was on the right bank of the Kansas River, about ten miles above its mouth; and constituted, as says Fremont, " one of the friendly contributions by the St. Louis Chouteaus, which were to come in aid on this and future journeys." The American fur companies realized that the army invasion of plains and mountains would help trade by diverting the warpath, and we find them, large and small, as a rule assisting the government in every way. Colonel Robert Campbell, especially, was a most obliging patron — of course not without profit to himself.

Of the men connected with this, another government scientific and exploring column directed into the western wilds, interest remains longest with the leader; with Carson, the guide; Maxwell, the hunter; Basil Lajeunesse, who became Fremont's favorite, rivaling Carson; bristly-headed and tow-headed Charles Pruess, the plucky German topographer; and the lads, Henry Brant, aged nineteen, son of Senator Benton's niece, Sarah Benton Brant (Mrs. J. B. Brant) of St. Louis, and Randolph Benton, aged twelve, son of Senator Benton himself. The twenty-two or three other members of the party were *voyageurs*, French of Canada and Missouri.

Friday, June 10, witnessed the departure of the column; Monday, October 10, exactly four months later, witnessed its return to the mouth of the Kansas.

Technically, this expedition, known as " Fremont's First Expedition," was " An Exploration of the Country Lying Between the Missouri River and the Rocky Mountains, on the line of the Kansas and Great Platte Rivers." Theoretically, it was an exploration to acquaint the Government with the nature of the "rivers and country between the frontiers of Missouri and the base of the Rocky Mountains; and especially to examine the character, and ascertain the latitude and longitude of the South Pass, the great crossing place to these mountains on the way to Oregon." Officially it was an expedition " ordered by Colonel Abert, chief of the Topographical Bureau, with the sanction of the Secretary of War." But actually, while including the above scope, it was a Benton-Fremont expedition for the political triumph of one, the professional triumph of the other, and the encouragement (involved with both designs) of the emigration to Oregon.

The first Linn bill for Oregon occupation, the bill of 1838, was dead. The Linn bill of the winter of 1842-43 had not yet been announced, and this expedition was a pre-

paratory measure. Thus coming events cast their shadows
before, and deep run the waters of politics. As Fremont
narrates, in his *Memoirs,* the object of his exploration was
" auxiliary and in aid to the emigration to the Lower Columbia "; his real commission was to " indicate and describe
the line of travel, and the best positions for military posts,"
as well as to fix the location of the South Pass.

Senator Benton, than whom a greater statesman and
more astute politician never lived, and Lieutenant Fremont,
than whom a more willing explorer never lived, worked well
together; for they were united by the ties of profession,
family and ambition. Senator Benton worked at home,
Lieutenant Fremont worked in the field, and the results
justified the mutual confidence.

As to this expedition, Senator Linn, able colleague of
the great Benton with the eagle nose, summarized it in his
presentation to the Senate of the official report. His breathless style carries unseen exclamation points — as a press
agent Dr. Linn scores. The report is to be classed as that
species of gratuitous reading matter with which newspapers
and magazines are flooded and which usually have another
than a purely news motive.

In executing his instructions, Mr. Fremont proceeded up the
Kansas River far enough to ascertain its character, and then
crossed over to the Great Platte, and pursued that river to its
source in the mountains, where the Sweet Water (a head
branch of the Platte) issued from the neighborhood of the
South Pass. He reached the Pass on the 8th of August, and
describes it as a wide and low depression of the mountains,
where the ascent is as easy as that of the hill on which this
Capitol stands, and where a plainly beaten wagon road leads
to the Oregon through the valley of Lewis's River, a fork
of the Columbia. He went through the Pass, and saw the
headwaters of the Colorado, of the Gulf of California; and,
leaving the valleys to indulge a laudable curiosity, and to
make some useful observations, and attended by four of his

men, he climbed the loftiest peak of the Rocky Mountains, until then untrodden by any known human being; and, on the 15th of August, looked down upon ice and snow some thousand feet below, and traced in the distance the valleys of the rivers which, taking their rise in the same elevated ridge, flow in opposite directions to the Pacific Ocean and to the Mississippi. From that ultimate point he returned by the valley of the Great Platte, following the stream in its whole course, and solving all questions in relation to its navigability, and the character of the country through which it flows.

However, the first portion of the journey, that from the Missouri to Fort Laramie, is not without interest, just as, in the matter of speaking well of the character of the valleys, it was not without value. With customary Fremont thoroughness the company was divided; the main party, under Clement Lambert as chief and Carson as assistant, proceeding by the Oregon Trail route up the North Platte, while Fremont himself, with four others including Lucien Maxwell, continued on up the South Platte to Fort St. Vrain, thence to march, northward, for the rendezvous at Fort Laramie.

Previous to this separation the rubber boat, a Fremont idea ridiculed later by the Carson men, had capsized in crossing the Kansas, and some provisions, the most important being a sack of coffee, were lost. By their aquatic efforts at rescue Carson and Maxwell both were made ill.

The Fremont trail to Fort St. Vrain was uneventful, save for spring storms and one or two Indian scares. The Lambert-Carson detachment met Jim Bridger convoying down the North Platte trail a company of traders, and by this company were informed that the Sioux, Gros Ventre Blackfeet, and the Cheyennes were combined; that all were out for revenge, after the casualties of the battle with Fraeb, the trapper partisan, in the preceding August; and that the Sweetwater route — the route from Laramie to South Pass — was very hazardous. This spread consternation among the in-going company, who paid serious attention to the opinion of such a seasoned campaigner as old Bridger. So genuine was the gravity of the situation that at Fort Laramie Carson made oral will — an incident not unusual among trappers, but here not calculated to relieve the tenseness of the situation.

At Laramie, and at Fort Platte below, agents and Indians all urged upon the expedition to wait at least until the war parties which were out, upon the trail beyond, should return. However, Fremont was no man to be intimidated. Perhaps this was the rashness of a tenderfoot in the mountains — perhaps it was wisdom, foreseeing that to have yielded now might have established a precedent among the Indians, and have encouraged them to future dictation. For a government officer to back down and let the trail be closed against him, was poor policy. Besides, this was a white trail — and a settler trail; and the lives of countless companies to follow, might hang upon decisive action now.

Anyway, Lieutenant Fremont wavered not an inch, opposed though he was by veterans such as Carson and the traders of both posts. He informed his company that he was going through, and he called the roll, and only one member refused.

As it happened, the trip out to the South Pass and neighborhood, and back to the post, was made with no direct opposition, beyond words, by the Indians; in fact, few Indians were sighted on the Sweetwater trail; and the chief peril was when, during the return, in the Red Narrows of the Platte the rubber boat was wrecked and its crew barely escaped drowning.

To revert to the Linn report, again, in which the scientific aspects of the journey are reviewed, these being the latitudes and longitudes, elevations, character of soils, practicability of routes, geological, botanical and meteorological features:

Eight carts, drawn by two mules each, accompanied the expedition; a fact which attests the facility of traveling in this vast region. Herds of buffaloes furnished subsistence to the men; a short, nutritious grass, sustained the horses and mules. Two boys (one of twelve years of age, the other of eighteen), besides the enlisted men, accompanied the expedition, and took their share of its hardships; which proves that boys, as well as men, are able to traverse the country to the Rocky Mountains.

The result of all his observations Mr. Fremont has condensed into a brief report — enough to make a document of ninety or one hundred pages; and believing that this document would be of general interest to the whole country, and beneficial to science, as well as useful to the government, I move the printing of the extra number which has been named.

" The printing was ordered "; not only accomplishing the purpose of encouraging prospective emigrants by the " apparent interest which the government * * * took in their enterprises," but also (although it does not strike me that the Fremont report supports the Linn contention) spreading the first truth about the Great American Desert: " that the country, for several hundred miles from the frontier of Missouri, is exceedingly beautiful and fertile; alternate woodland and prairie, and certain portions well supplied with water," and that " the valley of the river Platte has a very rich soil." Thus the chimera of the Great American Desert received its initial puncture — albeit persisting as a bugbear until the *ignis fatuus* of the gold beyond had been pursued to the end.

The details of this first expedition of Fremont, by which Kit Carson likewise was " drawn into the current of important events," cannot be better told than by Fremont himself, who, a young lieutenant inspired by freshness of achievement, backed by authority of his first command and by the knowledge that he is making history, produces a narrative that reads like a tale of some knight-errant. He thoroughly enjoys the venture. He enjoys the spectacle of Carson, " without a saddle, and scouring bareheaded over the prairies, * * * one of the finest pictures of a horseman I have ever seen "; he enjoys the alarms — " in an instant, every man's weapon was in his hand, the horses were driven in, hobbled and picketed, and horsemen were galloping at full speed in the direction of the newcomers, screaming and yelling in the wildest excitement." His buffalo hunt is so contagious as to be quoted to this day — " My horse was a trained hunter, famous in the West under the name of Proveau, and, with his eyes flashing, and the foam flying from his mouth, sprang on after the cow like a tiger!" The atmosphere of the wild plains and of the lofty peaks, so vast, so tremendous, so immutable, entered into his blood; as did the deeds which they fostered among their inhabitants. High romance and the spectacular were to John Charles Fremont the wine of life. What army officer of later day, what scientific explorer would think to embody in a formal report a side allusion such as this which follows a description of an Arapaho and Cheyenne village:

I remarked near some of the ledges a kind of tripod frame, formed of three slender poles of birch, scraped very clean, to which were affixed the shield and spear, with some other weapons. All were scrupulously clean, the spear head was burnished bright, and the shield white and stainless. It reminded me of the days of feudal chivalry; and when, as I rode by, I yielded to the passing impulse and touched one of the spotless shields with the muzzle of my gun, I almost expected a grim warrior to start from the lodge and resent my challenge.[88]

That was Fremont — to yield to the impulse, and boyishly playing the knight, touch the transformed shield.

This first expedition of Fremont has been misunderstood — and sneers have been cast upon it because, after all, it traversed only ground already familiar to the public, by years of previous travel. There is no indication that Fremont or the Government ever claimed to have discovered the South Pass; on the contrary, the South Pass is named in advance in the instructions. But since the Major Stephen Long army expedition of 1820, no scientific report by a trained observer, save the report of Reverend Samuel Parker, had been made upon the Platte River route to the mountains; and the Major Long report was of the South Platte and the Arkansas, and not upon the North Platte. The Parker narrative naturally would be considered, if considered at all in army circles, with the interest of suspicion — of toleration indulgent to the cloth .

Aside from the real purpose to which the expedition was fitted by the expansionist senators, Benton and Linn, there was a necessity in the War Department for accurate authorized data upon the North Platte country. Maps must be kept up to date, and memoranda filed away for future reference. With this exploration concluded, the War Department might consider itself fairly well posted upon the features of the trans-Missouri Country, to the mountains. Lieutenant Fremont now reported upon both the North Platte and the South Platte. Major Long had reported upon the South Platte, base of the mountains, the Arkansas, and the Red River. Again, in 1835, Colonel Henry Dodge had repeated the tour via the South Platte and the Arkansas and had supplied additional information, chiefly upon the Indian tribes.

Mention has been made that Carson sent runners from the Missouri to Taos, and summoned a party of his own men. This was natural — and that Fremont does not refer to the accession, in his official reports, proves naught. Oliver Wiggins, who accompanied the squad, and who was on the Fremont second expedition also, declared that names figured very little, in those days, and that the Fremont lists were incomplete and inaccurate. Moreover, the appropriations for the expeditions were small, even inadequate, so that the lieutenant would have risked criticism by extending his roll call unnecessarily. However, the Carson squad was an independent command. Wiggins relates of the trip:

The order from Kit direct was the cause of rejoicing among our crowd, and we started in time to reach the fort ahead of the government party.

We hurried away late in June with laden pack horses, and pushed east and north along the Indian trail, up through Pueblo, then a Mexican village of adobe buildings, up through the old trail fourteen miles east of the present city of Colorado Springs, crossing Cherry Creek at Denver, where at that time there was not even a cabin or permanent tent, and joining the party at the fort. We trappers were not engaged as a part of the Fremont company, but the territory through which we were to travel was wild and the Indians were plentiful, and Kit, with his usual foresight, preferred to have his men within call in case of trouble. It was a continuous hunting trip for us, with plenty of big game along the route. We lived much like Indians as we traveled, and I can not say that we were not much like them except for racial differences.

Fremont went 110 miles west of Laramie to Sweetwater River, then up the Sweetwater. Leaving that stream we journeyed through unbroken mountains and forests to Atlantic and Pacific Springs, on the West Slope. About thirty miles west of the Springs Kit left Fremont, rejoined us, and we returned with our pelts to Taos, where we spent the winter. Fremont had learned many things heretofore unknown to the government, and when we parted company it was with the understanding that Carson was to act as guide for a second expedition the next year.

Back again in Taos, pending the second expedition, Kit Carson again married, just previously being baptized into the Roman faith. The marriage entry in the parish book, which is still maintained by the resident priest at Taos, reads as follows:

Cristover Carson & M*. Josefa Jaramillo married on the 6th day of February, 1843, by the parish priest Antonio Jose Martinez.

C. Carson, son of Linsey Carson and Rebecca Rovenson of the State of Mo.

Maria Josefa Jaramillo, daughter of Francisco Jaramillo and Maria Polonia Vigil.

Witnesses: George Bent and Cruz Padillo, Juan Manual Lucero and Jose Maria Valdez.[84]

The Señora Carson, aged scarce fifteen, and therefore some eighteen years younger than her husband, was of marked brunette type, upon Spanish lines. " A style of beauty," observed the impressionable Lewis Garrard, seeing her at Taos in April, 1847, four years after the wedding, " of the haughty, heart-breaking kind, such as would lead a man, with the glance of the eye, to risk his life for one smile. I could not but desire her acquaintance." [85] Carson had married well. The Jaramillo and Vigil families were highly connected with the best interests of New Mexico. A sister of Carson's bride was the wife of Charles Bent, leading American at Taos, and Donaciano Vigil, of Taos, had been military secretary to Governor Armijo.

To the union of Carson and girlish Señorita Jaramillo of heart-breaking glance were born eight children: Charles (who died at nine months), William, Teresina, Christopher (Kit), Jr., a second Charles, Rebecca, Stella, Josefita. The union endured happily for twenty-five years, and then was only briefly interrupted by death, which removed Mrs. Carson first, for a month's absence from him.

But this is anticipating. For the year is 1843.

CHAPTER XXI

ON THE TRAIL WITH FREMONT — 1843-1844

BETWEEN his scouting duties with the Bent, St. Vrain & Co. caravans, and his other trips, Kit Carson was allowed but scant newly-wedded bliss before, three months later, he was summoned to the second expedition of Lieutenant Fremont.

The effect of the first expedition had been instantaneous. Aroused by Marcus Whitman, waiting upon the frontier of Missouri was gathered the first great influx of American colonists into Oregon. Still the Government hesitated, confronted by the equal claims to Oregon of Great Britain. The expansionist bill of Dr. Linn had survived the Senate, but had been killed in the House. Nevertheless, the expansionist spirit was not dead. Even before the first survey by Lieutenant Fremont had been completed, the second survey must have been projected; inasmuch as parting with Kit Carson in the mountains Lieutenant Fremont had engaged him for the next year. Fremont himself says, in reviewing the report of the expedition, by Senator Linn: " In the meantime the second expedition had been planned." And Senator Benton records: " His first expedition barely finished, Mr. Fremont sought and obtained orders for a second one." The Oregon machine worked smoothly; its product to be, not that fabric of selfishness which so often comes from the loom of politics, but a finished tapestry without the pattern of ignoble private aims. In urging Oregon, Senator Thomas H. Benton, aided by Senator Lewis Linn, seems to have been a true patriot, under no

COLONEL JOHN C. FREMONT

HON. THOMAS HART BENTON

FAR WEST EXPANSIONIST IN CONGRESS. FATHER-IN-LAW CF
FREMONT, AND FRIEND OF CARSON

(From his Thirty Years' View)

THE PASSAGE OF THE SIERRAS

FREMONT AND CARSON PARTY, WINTER OF 1843-44

(From Fremont's Memoirs)

suspicion of the land-grabbing schemes which so attach to the throwing open of new territory today.

This second expedition again was one, states Senator Benton, by which the administration at Washington is entitled only to the credit of compliance, not to any credit of origination. It was authorized by the War Department, to pursue on the west side of the Rockies, in joint territory, the same objects that had been pursued on the east side, in American territory: or technically, "to connect the reconnaissance of 1842 with the surveys of Commander Wilkes on the coast of the Pacific ocean, so as to give a connected survey of the interior of our continent." It is known officially as the "Exploring Expedition to Oregon and North California, in the years 1843-44." Practically, it extended far beyond its scope — farther than even Fremont himself, who, once cut loose from red tape, rambled as the spirit moved him, could foresee. It suggested Utah. Mrs. Fremont declares that it led to the acquisition of California; and it did, in that the leader returned enthusiastic over a country which had been misjudged as badly as the coast to the north. He sowed fresh seed of covetousness in the heart of the American people.

The Fremont second expedition left the village of Kansas (or Westport Landing) on the south bank of the Missouri at the present Kansas-Missouri line, May 29, 1843, and returned thereto July 31, 1844. It left hurriedly, on a message from Mrs. Fremont, who had opened orders from the War Department directing the leader to return to Washington and explain why he was taking along a brass howitzer. And, truth to tell, just at this period of territory agitation and of war talk between the United States and Mexico and England, a brass howitzer imported by a strictly scientific expedition into disputed bounds might fire another shot "heard 'round the world;" especially in the hands of the impulsive Fremont.

Besides this brass howitzer (supplied legitimately by Colonel Stephen W. Kearny, from the arsenal at St. Louis) were taken other anomalies, in shape of Jacob Dodson, young free negro in the service of the Benton family; a Prussian ex-artillerist, for the howitzer; two Delaware Indians for hunters. Thomas Fitzpatrick, " the Bad Hand," " whom many years of hardship and exposure in the Western territories had rendered familiar with a portion of the country it was designed to explore," was the guide. Supernumeraries were Frederick Dwight, a tenderfoot from Springfield, Massachusetts; Theodore Talbot, a young government draughtsman, and William Gilpin, page to Andrew Jackson, West Pointer of one year cadetship, lieutenant in the Seminole War, editor of the *Missouri Argus*, St. Louis (a Senator Benton paper), secretary of the Missouri General Assembly, friend in the Benton family, soon now to be major and lieutenant colonel of Missouri Volunteers in the Mexican War, and later to be first governor of Colorado Territory. Lucien Maxwell accompanied them on his way home to Taos. The force was larger than that of 1842, the men, besides those especially mentioned, listing as thirty-two — the great majority, as before, Creole French or Canadians, but the enrollment naming such as Patrick White, two Campbells, Henry Lee, etc.[86]

From the Missouri at the mouth of the Kansas, the route of the expedition — Fremont and the horsemen preceding, Fitzpatrick and the wagons following — led westward up along the Kansas, thence up the valley of the Republican, and westerly again through the northern border of Kansas, where drain the southern tributaries of the Republican; it struck the South Platte in northeastern Colorado, and followed it up to Fort St. Vrain. This was reached July 4.

From the post a detour was made southward, to obtain mules from Taos. At the mountain-man settlement of the Pueblo (name retained, in the same spot, by the second city of Colorado) it was learned that owing to the fomentation by the Texans against Mexican peace and prosperity the Mexican frontier was being closed to traffic, and that exportation of supplies from Taos was doubtful. But here at the Pueblo they " accidentally " encountered Kit Carson. He readily undertook a mission to procure mules from Charles Bent of Bent's Fort, seventy-five miles down the Arkansas.

From the Pueblo the party returned, with a slight digression on the way to examine the Boiling Springs of the present Manitou, to Fort St. Vrain, which had been appointed as the rendezvous with Fitzpatrick and his carts, and Carson and his mules. Lucien Maxwell had proceeded from the Pueblo south for Taos.

As upon the previous expedition, Carson decided to take along his own retainers — who were not loth to go.

Fort St. Vrain, the meeting-place agreed upon, was a trading post at the mouth of the St. Vrain Creek, forty-two miles from the present city of Denver. Chamberlain, the lieutenant under Carson, started for the fort in time to reach there July 4, and that very day something happened that resulted in a serious breach between the Carson and Fremont parties. St. Vrain's people, assisted by the Fremont men, were having a celebration. It had been a long time between Fourth of July celebrations with us fellows out on the plains, and we wanted to get in on a little of the fun. I was out with the horses some distance from the fort and a sergeant of the Fremont company was in charge. I insisted upon going to the fort, and Pat White, the sergeant, refused permission. He was new to the ways of the plainsmen and forgot that we were not soldiers, hence not under any orders from his commander. Pat thought he was physically capable of making me submit to his orders, but when I went into the fort I asked them to send a wagon out after the sergeant, while I enjoyed the fun. There was a sharp scene between Fremont and Carson over the affair, but Kit was firm and Fremont finally instructed his men to keep out of trouble. Here Carson's character and determination cropped out plainly, and Fremont learned what kind of men had opened the pathways over the plains. Carson's men were out-numbered, but he plainly warned Fremont that although he was not a government officer, his word was supreme with his men, and that a few men armed with repeating rifles were more dangerous than a small army with old-fashioned guns and government authority.[87]

At St. Vrain's fort there joined the party as official hunter, Alexander Godey, " a Creole Frenchman of St. Louis, of medium height with black eyes and silky curling black hair, which was his pride " — and which he permitted no one to disparage. In 1843 he was about twenty-five years of age, a trapper and trader of Indian country experience, and " in courage and professional skill a formidable rival to Carson." Here also joined the company " an Indian woman of the Snake nation, desirous, like Naomi of old, to return to her people." Newly widowed, she took her two children, " pretty little half-breeds, who added much to the liveliness of the camp." So narrates Fremont.

In two divisions again, the expedition left the post. With the heavy baggage Fitzpatrick, " the White Head," proceeded north to strike the Platte at Fort Laramie, and thence crossing by the South Pass, to unite with the first division at Fort Hall on the Snake. With Carson and other tried men Fremont struck up the Cache la Poudre River, and past Fort Collins of today, making northwest, around the north end of the Medicine Bow Mountains in northern Colorado, around North Park above the Wyoming line, and to the Sweetwater, approximating the future Overland Stage route from Denver to Salt Lake, via Bridger's Pass.

At the Sweetwater he found already a " broad, smooth highway, where the numerous heavy wagons of the emigrants had entirely beaten and crushed the artemisia (sage), a happy exchange to our poor animals for the sharp rocks and tough shrubs among which they had been toiling so long."

The emigrant trail was followed into the valley of the Bear, where the various curiosities, known to trappers, were investigated. Fremont could not resist the lure of the lonely Salt Lake; and who may blame him? " Its islands had never been visited; and none were to be found who had entirely made the circuit of its shores. * * * It was generally supposed that it had no visible outlet; but among the trappers, including those in my own camp, were many who believed that somewhere on its surface was a terrible whirlpool, through which its waters found their way to the ocean by some subterranean communication."

Not surfeited by his descent of the Platte Narrows the year before, Fremont, the indefatigable, had brought with him on this trip another rubber boat; and the act would indicate that out of his prosaic instructions by the War Department he had been inspired by thoughts which the department, from its office chairs in the East, little dreamed.

Thus, with the keen enthusiasm of a Balboa (as he says), from a butte at the debouchment of Weber's Fork he gazed, the morning of September 6, upon the white-capped waters of the sluggishly rolling lake. I can fancy that Carson, beside him, surveyed them likewise with a gleam of studious, calculating interest in his usually mild, blue eye. That he had visited the lake before it is reasonable to presume; but only incidentally, with his mind upon beaver.

On the morning of September 9, 1843, the rubber boat, its crew Kit Carson, the mountain man; John C. Fremont, the army man; Preuss, the German topographer; Basil Lajeunesse, the Creole trapper; and Baptiste Bernier, the Canadian *voyageur*, cleared away for a low island; and if white men were not then for the first time upon these mysterious waters this was at least the first " deep sea voyage " recorded. And much like the mariners of the Columbus caravels must the explorers have felt; even the steady Carson, here out of his element, betrayed nervousness:

" Captain," said Carson, who for some time had been looking suspiciously at some whitening appearance outside the nearest islands, " what are those yonder? — won't you just take a look with the glass? " We ceased paddling for a moment, and found them to be the caps of the waves that were beginning to break under the force of a strong breeze that was coming up the lake.

No other portents were encountered. Beyond being more lonely, it was the lake of today.

After a night's stay upon the island, whose haunted solitude undoubtedly was, on this September the 9th, 1843, for the first time broken by · " the cheerful sound of human voices," return was made to the shore. The island, about eight miles out, named " Castle Island " by the first Mormons, was by the government party of Captain Howard Stansbury, in 1849, christened Fremont Island, as was proper.[88]

Having done a little more than the previous explorers, Fremont and Carson might head north, up the Bear, for the rendezvous with Thomas Fitzpatrick at Fort Hall.

At old Fort Hall (which had been drained of provisions by the passing emigrants) the long threatened rupture between the Fremont party and the Carson party occurred; and that such a rupture was inevitable may easily be understood, when we understand also that the Carson men were mountaineers, under no obligations to the leader, and that the Fremont men were French *voyageurs* and American Fur Company *engages*. And without doubt the Taos party were tired of the methodical measures of the army expedition. They foresaw much hard work, and, perhaps, little satisfaction.

It was now late in September and very stormy, with rain and snow. When the Taos men learned that the goal was the coast, they balked. Many of them had been to the westward, and they knew what a tough trail it was, down the

Snake, and that the desolation would be heightened by the bleak season approaching. California was mentioned, and this made matters worse, for the snowy passes of the Sierras had been a spectre ever since the Jedediah Smith and the Joe Walker ventures.

According to Oliver Wiggins, the Carson contingent told Fremont that they would continue if he would winter at Walla Walla and postpone further exploration until spring:

Fremont's men refused to go on the California trip unless driven to it, and the nervy youngster was told by the mountaineers in the party that to be caught in the passes with sixty to seventy feet of snow to block the way would be certain death.

Carson tried to dissuade the impetuous Fremont, but he was not a man to be balked, and retorted:

" I 'll show you fellows who think you know all about mountain exploring that I can go where I please."

" All right, boys," said Kit to us; " I shall go with Fremont; I cannot ask you to go."

Fremont threatened to put us all under arrest for insubordination, or something equally as terrible, but Kit faced him with a calm determination to prevent trouble.

*   *   *   *   *   *   *   *   *   *

However, Fremont placed us under arrest as a matter of form, allowing us to retain our arms. The Irish sergeant with whom I had been unpleasantly mixed up early in the year, was in charge of the party, and we were sent on ahead. A particularly rocky cut caused a hurried order from the explorer to the prisoners to return and assist in clearing a passageway for the wagons, and we sent back a very saucy answer. When the messenger returned, full of wrath, our men were far up the mountains in another trail, going faster all the time, and with the helpless Irishman, whom we all hated, trying to hustle along and keep track of his prisoners.

The sergeant (Patrick White, as would appear) abandoned the long-winded mountain men as impossible charges, and descended to join the main party. As for the Taosans,

" it broke us all up to leave Kit to the whims of Fremont, but we knew our traveling with the Fremont party was all off, and we started back alone."

Blankets and a few supplies were obtained at Fort Hall. Taos was not reached until January.

As for the onward bound expedition, the van, commanded by Fremont and guided by Kit Carson, the rear being in charge of Thomas Fitzpatrick, marched along the Oregon Trail down the Snake, passing many emigrants and noting where, at Fall Creek — a short distance above Raft River of Idaho — a fresh wagon trail branched off, a trail made by the main division of the Chiles California party guided by the veteran Joe Walker of Bonneville fame.

November 8 Fremont called upon Governor McLoughlin, at Vancouver, "who received me with the courtesy and hospitality for which he has been eminently distinguished."

This completed the survey as ordered. Now Lieutenant Fremont was officially expected to seek his station. " He might then have returned upon his tracks, or been brought home by sea, or hunted the most pleasant path for getting back," announces his zealous patron, Senator Benton; " and if he had been a routine officer, satisfied with fulfilling an order, he would have done so." Possibly life would have flowed smoother for Fremont, and he would have escaped humiliation had he been more of a routine officer. As to his returning, in winter, by the trail of the Snake and the South Pass — that would have been a problem. However, with true Fremont audacity and *largesse* of toil — likewise with true Fremont zest for spectacular endeavor — for his return east he headed south.

The Great Basin haunted Fremont. " All that vast region, more than seven hundred miles square, equal to a great kingdom in Europe, was an unknown land, a sealed book, which he longed to open and read." [89] After consultation with McLoughlin, he aimed to strike diagonally south-

east and by cutting from the lower Columbia of Oregon
down to the upper Colorado of Arizona, cleave the heart
of the mystic mid-region of the continent.

The Great Basin had already been traversed from east to.
west: by Jedediah Smith, Joe Walker, the Bartleson-Bidwell
party, and more than halfway by Carson himself. It has
been traversed from east to west many a time since. But
it had not, and has not, been traversed from north to south.
That is a different proposition. However, such a fact
never would deter Fremont.

Although the courtly Captain Bonneville's map and
report, showing the contrary, had now been half a dozen
years in circulation, still it suited the credulous world, persistent in this, as it was for a Northwest Passage, to believe
that from the interior of the Great Basin of Utah and
Nevada there flowed rivers to the western sea. The coast
range was ignored, the distance was ignored, the dry atmosphere which withered streams at their source was ignored,
and ignored were the failures to locate such rivers. Popular superstition, dating back to Father Escalante, named
the principal stream the Buenaventura. And the Buenaventura, as the Green itself, or as a river with its head in the
Salt Lake or some Lake Salado; the River Los Mingos or
Timpanogos; or other river, draining that Great Basin
country, connecting the western slope of the Rockies with
the Pacific Ocean, thus continuing a waterway from the
Rocky Mountains to the coast, was confidently anticipated.

To locate such a stream; to locate the Tlamath (Klamath)
Lake; to locate another lake termed " Mary's " — these
were the three chief objects of the desert trail by Lieutenant
Fremont in the winter of 1843-44; and only one of the
three objects was attained.[90]

With a band " of many nations, American, French, German, Canadian, Indian and colored — and most of them

young, several being under twenty-one years of age;" 104 mules and horses, many of "thin, inferior quality," and the howitzer as the only thing on wheels, at noon of November 25, "weather disagreeably cold, with flurries of snow," they started from the Protestant mission at The Dalles.

On March 8 asylum was gained at Sutter's Fort, in California, near the present site of the city of Sacramento. The party had found the desert stern and implacable, giving naught and requiring all, even to life. They had found it hedged along its border by mountains of snow. And they had found no great river "with rich bottoms covered with wood and grass, where the wild animals would collect and shelter!" When they traveled the sparsely timbered highlands they were frozen and impeded by snow; when they descended to the bare lowlands they were starved; and at last, like a bird beating against the wires of a cage, having clung along the east base of the Sierra to the latitude of San Francisco Bay, they had the alternative of perishing here on the desert or of crossing the snow mountains — there as well, perchance, to perish. The decision was made January 18, and the next day the ascent of the divide was begun. The howitzer soon had to be abandoned. Out of the sixty-seven horses and mules present at the east base, only thirty-three reached the west base of the Sierra; and among the lost was the buffalo horse Proveau. But, leading the other animals — "a woeful procession crawling along one by one, skeleton men leading skeleton horses" — the explorers, after having encountered, as they had been forewarned by Indians, snow deep as a tree and precipices whence the wayfarer would fall half a mile, the travelers appropriated the future trail of the Forty-niners, topped the high Sierra and following a little creek which, ice-covered, waxed to a rushing river, the American, they won out, on the last of February, into the genial, paradise valley of the Sacramento.

Here was Captain Johann August Sutter, Swiss-American, who, in 1839, had wandered down from the Oregon Trail, and with his "eight Kanakas, three white men, an Indian and a bulldog," having out of his awarded inch taken an ell, was now, the self-styled Gobernador de Forteleza de Nueva Helvecia, as secure as any pirate king or baron of rock-eyried castle on the Rhine. Governor John McLoughlin himself of Vancouver, was a *seigneur* scarce more powerful.

"Sutter's Fort" was destined to be the Mecca for the gold pilgrimage of '49, was destined sooner to be the base for the Fremont invasion of the memorable year '46, and was already a harbor for revolutionists and always a haven for the traveler and particularly the *Americano*.

The outer walls, 150 by 500 feet, according to Lieutenant Joseph Warren Revere of the United States sloop of war *Cyane*, were fifteen feet high and two feet thick, flanked by the customary bastions at diagonally opposite corners.[91]

Recuperated by the kindly offices of the sturdy, bald-headed, blue-eyed Captain Sutter (whom men like Carson and Thomas Fitzpatrick, as well as Fremont himself, could appreciate) the expedition proceeded southward up the valley of the San Joaquin, scene of Kit Carson's first excursion through California, as a boy, 1829, with Ewing Young. Ewing Young had been dead three years; and the California as he knew it was soon to be dead, also.

About the northern latitude of southern California, or opposite San Luis Obispo above the Point Conception, the expedition, which had been skirting the inner flanks of the Sierra Nevada range between California and the desert, made obliquely to the east, and led by a native refugee Christian Indian through the Tah-ee-chay-pah Pass (the route today followed by the Santa Fe railroad from the desert to Bakersfield), emerged upon the awaiting arid stretch of the Mohave Desert.

Across this Mohave Desert had Kit Carson toiled westward, on his trapping trip under Ewing Young; and back across it had he and Captain Young fled, evading the outraged authority of the *alcalde* of Los Angeles. But this third trip, of 1844, was in April, when, if ever, the desert had softened and bloomed.

After a continued traverse southward, the Spanish Trail was encountered; and by this, leading northeastward, the Great Basin was skirted — not, as Fremont had planned, cut asunder. The energetic Joseph Walker, again returning to the States, via Santa Fe, with a great caravan of horses and mules, the first of the spring caravans out of Los Angeles, joined the party at the good-water camp of Las Vegas de Santa Clara (the Santa Clara Meadows), and accompanied them from the rim of the desert, past Utah Lake, and over the Wasatch.

Now by the Uintah of northeastern Utah (where Antoine Robidoux was maintaining his fort for the last year), eastward up the Yampah of northwestern Colorado, and along the Wyoming line (where the veteran Fraeb had forted and died) they traveled fast, turning south, descending through the three parks of central Colorado — North or New Park, Middle or Old Park, South Park or the Bayou Salade, familiar and reminiscent ground to all trappers and traders, but yet, as Fremont explains, " unknown to science and history."

From the Bayou Salade crossing to the upper Arkansas, the party descended, having Pike's Peak as a landmark, to the Pueblo, " where we had the pleasure to find a number of our old acquaintances." And now

our cavalcade moved rapidly down the Arkansas, along the broad road which follows the river, and on the 1st of July we arrived at Bent's Fort, about 70 miles below the mouth of the Fontaine-qui-bouit. As we emerged into view from the groves on the river, we were saluted with a display of the national flag and repeated discharges from the guns of the fort, where we were received by Mr. George Bent with a cordial welcome and a friendly hospitality.

As chronicles the Peters biography of Carson: " On the following Fourth of July Mr. Bent gave a dinner in commemoration of the occasion to Fremont and his party. Although hundreds of miles separated from their countrymen, yet they sat down to as sumptuous a repast as could be furnished in many towns of the States." The icehouse and the carefully doled stirrup cups for which the post was famous, doubtless added zest to the banquet.

At the post the expedition practically disbanded; and those who wished to remain did so. Carson, and probably Captain Joe Walker, on his way to Santa Fe, rode for Taos, the former to seek his home and bride, after a year's absence and the completion of his longest continuous trail, roughly 5,500 miles, the trail of the explorer surpassing the trail of the trapper.

With his spoils of the country — with his Indians, his Mexicans, his saddle-horse Sacramento, iron-gray, " of the best California stock," gift from Captain Sutter — Lieutenant Fremont set out for St. Louis. He arrived, " inspired with California," full of facts and theories, convinced that the Buenaventura and other alleged rivers draining the Great Basin into the Pacific were myths, but to write upon his map in a long arc covering that immense vacant area from the Salt Lake to the Sierra, from the Columbia River to the Mohave of southern California:

THE GREAT BASIN: diameter 11° of latitude, 10° of longitude; elevation above the sea between 4 and 5,000 feet; surrounded by lofty mountains; contents almost unknown, but believed to be filled with rivers and lakes which have no communication with the sea, deserts and oases which have never been explored, and savage tribes, which no traveler has seen or described.

But he returned to fame and to the double brevet (well

earned) of first lieutenant and captain, and, if conquered
by the desert, nevertheless to spread word, by authority, of

the Great Salt Lake, the Utah Lake, the Little Salt Lake; at
all which places, then desert, the Mormons now are; the
Sierra Nevada, then solitary in the snow, now crowded with
Americans digging gold from its flanks; the beautiful valleys
of the Sacramento and San Joachin, then alive with wild horses,
elk, deer, and wild fowls, now smiling with American cultivation; the Great Basin itself, and its contents; the Three Parks;
the approximation of the great rivers which, rising together
in the central region of the Rocky Mountains, go off east and
west, toward the rising and the setting sun: — all these, and
other strange features of a new region, more Asiatic than
American.[92]

Where in 1844 only that arc of Fremont's printed words,
in lieu of any trail, traversed Utah and Nevada, condemning
them, today are scattered the homes of enlightened men,
despoiling of fruit and ore the giants' caches in earth and
rock.   But even knowing this, we cannot disparage the
accurate guess of Fremont as to the topography of the vast
country; and it was his report upon the territory along the
east of the Salt Lake (" good soil and good grass adapted
to civilized settlements ") which attracted the eye of Brigham Young.   Or, at least, so rather superciliously states the
Mormon governor himself:

From Fremont's reports, we determined to get our wagons
together, form a grand caravan and travel through the country
to the Salt Lake, 1,000 miles from any civilized settlement.
We started out with 147 people and 73 wagons.   This was
in 1847.   *   *   *   Salt Lake plain is a natural desert.   When
we struck this plain there was nothing on it but sage-bushes.[98]

In this the second of the government explorations engi-
neered by the Oregon expansionists, but which really
exploited California (for Oregon was taking care of itself)
Kit Carson might have just pride.   It was a distinct achievement and he had played a Carson part.   The first expedi-

tion, to the South Pass and back, had required of him little extra ability, and had brought him no added repute. He had proved a safe guide; that was all.

On this second expedition he was given opportunity to demonstrate his high qualities of frontiersman. Moreover, although his status in the expedition is not declared, Fitzpatrick being the guide and Godey being the hunter, he appears to have been an important factor. When messages were to be carried he usually was selected; and when the commander chose a bodyguard he was in the number. It was his descriptions of the vales of the Sacramento which put heart into the company, toiling amidst the snow and ice of the Sierra; and it was his keen eye and his experience, out of all the party, which enabled him to renew hope again languishing.

Far below us, dimmed by the distance, was a large snowless valley, bounded on the western side, at the distance of about a hundred miles, by a low range of mountains which Carson recognized with delight as the mountains bordering the coast. " There," said he, " is the little mountain — it is fifteen years ago since I saw it; but I am just as sure as if I had seen it yesterday." Between us, then, and this low coast range, was the valley of the Sacramento; and no one who had not accompanied us through the incidents of our life for the past few months, could realize the delight with which at last we looked down upon it.

The one incident which stands out above the routine of daily heroism shared by all the company announces Carson, and must have fixed him indelibly in the minds of the Government. And, at the same time, it shows that in the West Kit Carson did not possess the only stock of generous courage. Alexander Godey, younger and less widely known, was a man who, granted the opportunity, was doubtless Kit Carson's equal in dash and bravery. Whether he possessed those intrinsic qualities which elevated Carson above the

majority of the mountaineers and plainsmen, no matter how
daring, we cannot judge. Of course, it takes more than the
deed to make a man; motives are to be considered.

But for the incident: on the homeward way by the Spanish Trail two Mexicans, Andreas Fuentes and an eleven-
year-old boy, Pablo Fernandez, came as refugees into the
Fremont camp, reporting that the remainder of their party
(the wife of Fuentes, the father and mother of Pablo, and
one Santiago Giacome), surprised in camp by the Indians,
had probably been killed or captured. The two refugees,
on horse-guard, had escaped with about thirty horses.

The Fremont camp took the back trail of the two Mexicans, found that the horses, left at a watering place, had
been seized by the savages and driven away; and here
Carson, Godey, and the Mexican Fuentes set off upon the
fresh trail to pursue the marauders.

The Mexican presently was back with Fremont, his horse
having failed. But

in the afternoon of the next day a war-whoop was heard,
such as Indians make when returning from a victorious enterprise; and soon Carson and Godey appeared, driving before
them a band of horses, recognized by Fuentes to be part of
those they had lost. Two bloody scalps, dangling from the
end of Godey's gun, announced that they had overtaken the
Indians as well as the horses.

The entrance was spectacular and truly mountain-man.

The twain, Carson and Godey, had continued the pursuit,
and at nightfall had entered among mountains. They followed the plain trail by moonlight, until the moon was low
and did not penetrate into defiles. The trail was to be distinguished only by feeling, while the two led their horses and
groped for it. They judged that the fugitives were but a
few hours ahead, so they unsaddled and camped, without
fire or food, to rest and wait until daybreak. Early in the

RETURN OF CARSON AND GODEY

AN INCIDENT OF THE SPANISH TRAIL IN THE FREMONT SECOND EXPEDITION,
SPRING OF 1844

(From Fremont's Memoirs)

SUTTER'S FORT

THE BASE FOR THE FREMONT INVESTMENT OF CALIFORNIA AND SUBSEQUENT CONQUEST

(From Revere's A Tour of Duty in California)

CAPT. JOHN AUGUST SUTTER

OF THE FAMOUS " SUTTER'S FORT " OF
CALIFORNIA

*(From Colton's Three Years in
California)*

morning they did make a small fire for warmth, trusting that in the seclusion of the ravine it would be inconspicuous. Then they resumed the trail.

Just at sunrise the Indians were discovered, about two miles in advance, in camp among the bare hills, and breakfasting on horse steaks. The stolen stock was grazing without guard; and Carson and Godey decided to creep down among the horses, possibly to edge the animals away and stampede them. They made a successful stalk; but scarcely had they arrived safely when " one of the young horses of the band became frightened at the grotesque figures cut by the two creeping men, and exhibited his fear by snorting and kicking up his heels."

The Indians sprang for their arms. Instant action was the only salvation for the mountain men. With a loud yell they charged. They shot at the same man, who fell; and Godey, swiftly reloading, struck down another. The Indians replied with their long bows or war bows (desert weapons more formidable than even those of the tribes of the Rockies and the plains), and an arrow passed through Godey's shirt collar, grazing his neck. Astonished and puzzled by the boldness of two men who charged thirty, the savages, suspicious of a trap, fled, leaving the horses, the two fallen comrades, and a boy.

In possession of the camp, Godey proceeded to scalp the victims while Carson stood guard. The Indian shot by Godey was dead; but the other Indian, with two balls through his body, revived during the scalping process, and

sprang to his feet, the blood streaming from his skinned head, and uttered a hideous howl. An old squaw, possibly his mother, stopped and looked back from the mountain side she was climbing, threatening and lamenting. The frightful spectacle appalled the stout hearts of our men; but they did what humanity required, and quickly terminated the agonies of the gory savage.

The abandoned boy, the bulk of the stolen horses, a quantity of horse beef boiling in large clay pots, and several baskets containing fifty or sixty pairs of moccasins were the fruits of the conquest.

CHAPTER XXII

ON THE TRAIL WITH FREMONT — 1845

IN THE spring of 1845 John Charles Fremont, possessed of his double brevet of first lieutenant and captain in the Topographical Engineers of the United States Army, has finished the dictation of his adventures and observations, and upon March 1 the report has been given to Congress. A third expedition is being prepared by a southern route to the Sierra again: scientific exploration of Mexican territory its reason, its object the presence of an American force to take advantage of circumstances. For Texas is about to be annexed, the Oregon boundary is to be settled, and California, too, is to be added to the territory of the Republic. The Oregon and California migrations continue; the Texas migration is under way; and at Nauvoo, Illinois, the Mormon dictator, Brigham Young, is considering the hegira of 1846-1847.

Meantime Kit Carson has gone to farming in New Mexico. About this move upon his part is something typical of his dual nature. A mountain man, a roamer, " who for fifteen years saw not the face of a white woman, or slept under a roof," a terrific Indian fighter, he also was a home man, or lover of fireside and family and of peaceful ways. We find him now in the summer of 1845 settled with his younger mountain-man friend, Dick Owens, upon a tract of land near the Cimarron about fifty miles east of Taos.

Here we may see him supervising tilling, planting, building and gathering about him his herds and implements; a change which does him double credit, for in all the great company of mountain men he was one of the very few who realized that wealth and prosperity lay in the land over which they had ridden, not in the animals and the people who were transient. It took many years more of the West to teach this to the world. The Eldorado of the beaver trap must first be succeeded by the Eldorado of the miner's shovel and pick, and the rodeo of the long-horn cow trample into dust the ground later to be abloom with wheat and corn, apple and potato.

In August, 1845, Kit Carson, settled down to a life which he was but rarely to enjoy, vainly planning to be quiet in the midst of world-changing events, received word by express rider from Bent's Fort that Captain Fremont was there and awaiting him.

Oliver Wiggins claimed that Carson was by this time tired of Fremont; and moreover was cautious of such leadership. But we do not need the Wiggins assertion. Kit Carson had resolved to change his mode of life, to devote himself more to his family, and to make the most of this fertile country. No doubt he did much regret having promised his services again to Fremont. But he had so promised (Wiggins says that he had signed a contract), and " With me," declares Fremont, " Carson and truth are one."

Having probably given up his home in Taos when he removed his family to the rancho, Carson must dispose of his wife as well as of his ranch; and as if apprehending that his absence was to be long, again, and that troublous times were hovering upon the horizon, he placed her with the household of Charles Bent, whose own wife was a Jaramillo, sister to Mrs. Carson. His ranch he sold at a sacrifice price.

The Fremont third expedition, starting from St. Louis but organizing at Bent's Fort, contained many familiar faces. Carson was there; Lucien Maxwell was there; Basil Lajeunesse was there — not to return again; Godey was there, McDowell, the former tenderfoot, and Talbot of

HON. JOHN S. HOUGH OF LAKE CITY, COLO.

WEARING KIT CARSON'S BUCKSKIN HUNTING SHIRT. THE HOUGH AND
CARSON FAMILIES OCCUPIED PARTS OF THE SAME HOUSE AT BOGGSVILLE IN
1867-68, AND CARSON'S DAUGHTER TERESINA WAS REARED BY MR. AND MRS.
HOUGH AFTER HER FATHER'S DEATH

(Photograph by George L. Beam)

KIT CARSON III
GRANDSON OF THE SCOUT, WEARING THE FULL BUCKSKIN SUIT OF HIS
OTHER SCOUT GRANDFATHER, TOM TOBIN

(Photograph by O. T. Davis, Alamosa, Colorado)

Washington, Jacob Dodson, the negro, and Thomas Fitzpatrick, and probably Joe Walker, and the iron-gray horse
El Toro del Sacramento — the Bull of the Sacramento.

Among the new faces were twelve Delawares and an
Iowa half-breed, under the Delaware chiefs, Swanok and
Sagundai; Lieutenant J. W. Abert and Lieutenant G. W.
Peck; Edward Kern of Philadelphia, topographer, succeed-
ing the German Preuss; Archambeau, the Canadian hunter;
Stepp, the gunsmith, who was to spike the cannon at the
Golden Gate; and Richard Owens, " Dick " Owens, within
a year to be Captain of Company A, First California Bat-
talion of Mounted Riflemen, Colonel John C. Fremont com-
manding, but at present characterized only as a friend of
Kit Carson.

Lieutenants Abert and Peck, with Thomas Fitzpatrick as
guide and the trader Hatcher (whom Garrard, in his *Wah-
to-Yah* makes famous) as hunter, and with some thirty
other men, were detached for reconnaissance from Bent's
Fort down the Canadian River country through northern
Texas to the lower Arkansas, thence north to St. Louis.

On August 26 Captain Fremont himself left Bent's Fort
with 200 horses and a " well-appointed, compact party of
sixty, mostly experienced and self-reliant men, equal to any
emergency likely to occur and willing to meet it."

So from Bent's Fort, which was having its last year of
lordly isolation, they set out ostensibly to explore " that
section of the Rocky Mountains which gives rise to the
Arkansas River, the Rio Grande del Norte of the Gulf of
Mexico, and the Rio Colorado of the Gulf of California;
to complete the examination of the Great Salt Lake and its
interesting region; and to extend the survey west and southwest to the examination of the great ranges of the Cascade
Mountains and the Sierra Nevada."

From Bent's Fort they ascended along the Arkansas by
the trappers' trail into the foothills, and to the mouth of

the Grand Cañon of the Arkansas; here, at the site of present Cañon City, Colorado, they camped for a night. Thence diverging northward, to circumvent this Grand Cañon, they traveled through the region of Cripple Creek, and westward, evidently up Four Mile Creek, through the lower end of the South Park or Bayou Salade until they struck the Arkansas again near Buena Vista. Now they ascended along the river, paralleling the later route of the Denver & Rio Grande railroad, camped on the west shore of the upper of the beautiful Twin Lakes; and passing over the continental divide near Leadville (where they noted the lakes of the high country) by the divide between the Eagle and the Blue rivers they reached the Piney River, tributary of the Grand. Crossing, still on a course north by west, to the White River, they descended by Indian and trapper trail to the juncture with the Green of Utah, and probably by that post road which still exists, they pressed west, beyond the Green, through the Uintah country, to Provo near the shore of Utah Lake. From here the southern part of the Great Salt Lake was readily accessible.

So far the route of the Third Expedition had approximated the homeward route of the Second Expedition, 1844. At Great Salt Lake little new was developed; systematic observations were taken, and Antelope Island, familiar today to all visitors to the lake, was investigated. But the trail which awaited was a quantity as yet undeterminable. Fremont proposed to test it out.

At this point we were to leave the lake. From any neighboring mountain height looking westward, the view extended over ranges which occupied apparently the whole visible surface — nothing but mountains, and in winter time a forbidding prospect. Afterwards, as we advanced, we found the lengthening horizon continued the same prospect until it stretched over the waters of the Pacific. Looking across over the crests of these ridges, which nearly all run north and south, was like looking lengthwise along the teeth of a saw. * * * The country looked dry and of my own men none knew anything of it; neither Walker nor Carson. The Indians declared to us that no one had ever been known to cross the plain, which was desert. * * * Men who have traveled over this country in later years are familiar with the stony, black, unfertile mountains, that so often discouraged and brought them disappointment.⁹⁴

Jedediah Smith the omnipresent, had, however, crossed, about here, in 1827, returning from California; and soon the Hastings emigrant trail was to trace lasting furrows for women and children to follow.

On October 28, Carson, Maxwell, Archambeau the hunter, and a camp tender, were sent ahead, supplied with water, to cross the sagy, arid plain which intervened between the Salt Lake and those bare, saw-tooth ranges westward; to ascertain whether there was water beyond, and to signal back by smoke. For Fremont, taught one lesson by that desert which yielded not a whit to any enthusiast, was cautious.

These four, with a pack mule, made a march of sixty miles before, at the foot of the mountains, they found water and grass. They signaled by smoke, and Archambeau rode back to meet Fremont. He found him advanced into the desert, but abandoned by his Indian guide — whom the terrors of the unknown had so affected that "his knees really gave way under him and he wabbled like a drunken man. * * * He was so happy in his release that he bounded off like a hare through the sagebrush, fearful that I might still keep him."

Now, by a succession of little passes connecting short low range with short low range, the expedition proceeded westward, until on November 5, at the eastern side of the Humboldt chain of mountains, the party divided — the major portion, under topographer Kern and Joe Walker, the desert guide, being directed to strike the Mary's or Ogden's River to the northwest, and follow it down. Fremont, with ten selected men, "some of whom were Delawares," the others including Carson, Owens, Maxwell, meanwhile continued across the southern half of the Great Basin.

The meeting place was to be the vicinity of Walker's Lake. The Fremont trail thereto led from Franklin Lake and the south end of the Ruby Range, in eastern Nevada, southward through Eureka County, well into Nye County, thence through Esmeralda County to Walker's Lake. The lake was attained without incident. Another joint (the first being the Mary's River) had been found in the armor of the Great Basin; and although the Fremont route was improved upon by later explorations; although, in consequence of the California troubles, his investigations of 1845 received less notice by the world and were less thoroughly exploited by himself than those of his which preceded, he really pioneered the most feasible trail at that time; and, as he claims in his report, he and his party were the first white men to traverse this, the prospector's end of Nevada, today still a *terra incognita* save to the stage, the pack animal, his companion treasure seeker, and the wandering Indian.

Previous to this exploration in the late fall of 1845, in maps and in public assertion the whole of the Great Basin from the Salt Lake to the Sierras was represented "as a sandy plain, barren, without water, and without grass." But of the southern half,

instead of a plain, I found it, throughout its whole extent, traversed by parallel ranges of mountains, their summits white with snow (October); while below, the valleys had none. Instead of a barren country, the mountains were covered with grasses of the best quality, wooded with several varieties of trees, and containing more deer and mountain sheep than we had seen in any previous part of our voyage.[95]

From Walker's Lake, again in two divisions the party assault the Sierra ramparts of alluring California: the Fremont squad by the north, past Reno, and up the Truckee (Salmon Trout) River and over — the trail of the Forty-niners, and of the later Pony Express; the Kern-Walker company by a route farther southward and already known to Walker.

For winter had arrived (as Fremont knew that winter would arrive); it had caught them upon the desert (as Fremont knew that it would catch them), and for provisions they must digress into California again (as Fremont knew that they would digress). Thus the case stands. With the alleged legitimate excuse of the year before, he entered the fair estate, and on December 9 he was safely at Sutter's Fort. The fascination of that second visit which always tantalizes the trespasser had proved too much.[96]

At Sutter's Fort he was " received with the same friendly hospitality which had been so delightful to us the year before "; and, as he naïvely adds:

I found that our previous visit had created some excitement among the Mexican authorities. But to their inquiries he [Sutter] had explained that I had been engaged in a geographical survey of the interior and had been driven to force my way through the snow of the mountains simply to obtain a refuge and food where I knew it could be had at his place, which was by common report known to me.

So here, within less than a year, were again the same *Americanos;* and in view of the fact that Captain Sutter was under suspicion, that the American explorers were under suspicion, and that the times were under suspicion, who may marvel that the conjunction of the three was a portent of much evil omen in the Mexican horoscope?

Various decrees had been issued forbidding the entrance of strangers without passports — and particularly the entrance of foreign troops or of *gringo* families. Yet what did they amount to, if here was to be admitted not only a fresh party, but a party armed and under a United States army captain?

However, these discussions may be postponed, as postponed they were, while the zealous Fremont, needing, after all, no recuperation at Sutter's Fort (for he had gathered supplies of food, fodder, and strength on the way down) turned to the southward, up the San Joaquin, for the rendezvous near Lake Tulare with the Kern-Walker company. But through an error in mutual understanding the reunion did not occur until the middle of February, about twelve miles south of San Jose, at the Pacific rather than at the Sierra side of the uneasy territory.

Carson and Dick Owens were the twain who, scouting on information from the natives, effected the juncture of the two parties. This was Carson's third exploration of California. Like Fremont he was enamored of the place, and reports secondhand would indicate that he, like Fremont, and in fact like the majority of tourists, had designs of living here. But he never did live here. After the Mexican war he made but one visit to the country, of brief duration.

The third expedition had so far brought few thrills, and Carson had little opportunity to demonstrate his prowess. In the trip up the San Joaquin Valley there had been skirmishes with the " Horse-Thief Indians " — the renegades from the secularization of the missions; skirmishes fatal to the aborigines, but practically harmless to the invaders.

" Wait, you rascals! " these natives threatened, after their first discomfiture. " Wait, till morning! There are two big villages up in the mountains close by; we have sent for the chief; he 'll be down before morning with all the people, and you will all die. None of you shall go back; we will have all your horses."

But they had found in the new race, with buckskins and long rifles, a foe of a new fiber, a foe skilled in brush fighting, apt with the bullet, and undeterred by threats or apparent odds.

Now Fremont is snug in California again. Outside is that Great Basin, branded with the Fremont irons — Humboldt River, Humboldt Mountains, Pilot Knob, Basil Creek, Sagundai Spring, Walker River, Walker's Lake, Owens Lake. Some of the brands have stuck, others have been changed and may scarcely be recognized, as if the desert sands and sage had grown over them.[97]

CHAPTER XXIII

THE YEAR '46

THE grasp of Mexico upon California is the grasp of a palsied old man upon a wayward child; and as such a weakling is Mexico to be treated.

Captain Fremont has been to Monterey, where he has called upon Consul and Confidential Agent Thomas O. Larkin, ex-Governor Colonel Juan Alvarado, Captain Manuel Castro, the prefect, Don Jose Castro, the general commanding, and the *alcalde;* has explained what were the ostensible purposes of the expedition, being " in the interests of science and of commerce," and that the party are citizens, not soldiers; that he wished to obtain supplies and to proceed to Oregon. It is claimed that this permission to recruit was fully given, with the gracious *Bueno, Señor,* of the Mexican high and low. But instead of pursuing a course northeastward, around San Francisco Bay and on to Oregon, the Fremont party, sixty strong, to the discomfiture of the Department of Monterey, resumed their course southward, as for the coast and Monterey itself.[98]

At the Salinas River, March 5, " in the afternoon the quiet of the camp was disturbed by the sudden appearance of a cavalry officer with two men." He was Lieutenant Chaves, with a very natural if unexpected order from headquarters that the Americans leave the boundaries of the department by the quickest route.

Despite the fact that the message was irritating in its brusqueness (military though that was) and in its threat to use force, and was irritatingly delivered by the *caballero* who despised the *gringo,* Fremont's reception of it was wrong. Hot-headed, and supported by followers likewise intolerant of anything Spanish, he reproved the officer and sent by him word that departure from the district would be made as suited convenience. " I desired him to say in reply to General Castro that I peremptorily refused compliance with an order insulting to my government and myself." [99]

As much of a freebooter as any Francis Drake, Captain Fremont, early in the morning of April 6, moved a few miles to the crest of the hill-divide about thirty miles east of Monterey, between the Salinas and the San Benito rivers, and on Gavilan, or Hawk Peak, which overlooked the mission of San Juan and the valley of the Salinas, he built " a rough but strong fort of solid logs," and upon a tall sapling " the American flag was raised amidst the cheers of the men."

Here he had turned at bay, defying the government of California — that feeble arm of old Mexico — to budge him from the field of trespass. He had no shadow of right on his side, save the right of self-defense; whereas General Castro was acting entirely within his rights, having received a fresh order from Mexico that the Fremont company were not upon any account to be admitted into the district.

Thus the American flag by land first broke out belligerently in Alta California; and it practically was not furled.

Meanwhile, on March 11, in the East, General Zachary Taylor had crossed the Rubicon also by marching from the Nueces for the Rio Grande, carrying the flag into the 119 miles of unsurrendered Mexican territory. The word had gone forth: and from this second week of March, 1846, dates 5,000 miles of new American seacoast and 1,000 miles square of new American interior. At the same time President James K. Polk's absolute declaration, in his first message to Congress, December, 1845, that he stood out for " Fifty-four Forty or Fight," had reached the British ministry.

Now from the hilltop the Fremont half-hundred, of one mind against the Spaniard, watched the forces of Don Castro mobilizing at the San Juan Bautista mission below. The raising of the flag was spectacular enough to satisfy even a Fremont, and it was a new sensation to the majority of the men. Fremont himself, suddenly in command in a moment of war, rather courted the experience; and when a body of cavalry approached he went down a short distance to meet and ambush them. Whether he had military ability (appointed from civilian life to a corps which required no training in tactics) we shall never know, for the ascending party turned back and the hill was not stormed.

In truth, a force of 300 soldiers, regular or irregular, might long hesitate ere assaulting a fortified hill patrolled and garrisoned by American sharpshooters, with their keen eyes, steady hands, and long rifles. The battle of New Orleans had proved the breed.

Having three days awaited the enemy, and the flag having fallen with weariness, Captain Fremont concluded to obey, as he ingenuously puts it, the obligations of a scientific party in foreign territory, and go upon his way.

The Americans proceeded inland across to the valley of the San Joaquin; General Castro captured the fortress on Gavilan and munitions of war to the extent of the flagpole, some extemporaneous tent poles, a few old garments, two discarded pack saddles, and some stray native horses. Whereupon might it be reported by proclamation that the band of highwaymen under this Captain Fremont had been driven out and sent into the back country; as a matter of fact, forced into hiding among the bullrushes of the Sacramento!

Leaving behind them a trail of unwholesome excitement, fed by rumors of all kinds, in the fascinating aftermath of the California rainy season, the Americans proceeded, unmolested and unpursued, down the lush, green valley of the San Joaquin, and up the equally pleasing valley, poppy-strewn, of the Sacramento; again past Sutter's Fort, past the site of Marysville where the Yuba empties into the Feather River, and ever toward the Sierra — a northward course which they should have taken at the outset. The ranch of Joseph Neal, mountain man and blacksmith with the second expedition, but now a farmer, was visited on a side stream of the Sacramento above Sutter's; and May 6 the company were at Klamath Lake, southern Oregon — the lake of the winter of December, 1843, when the trail from The Dalles of Oregon southward for the fabled Buena-ventura and Mary's Lake skirted it.

Here Captain Fremont was in his chosen element — and the word is used literally, for his element was the wilds wherein he loved to believe that he was the first white man. From the Klamath Lake west across the Cascade Range to the coast were mountains, streams, and lakes (he pictured) forming a land which " had never been explored or mapped, or in any way brought to common knowledge, or rarely visited except by strong parties of trappers, and by those at remote intervals, doubtless never by trappers singly. It was a true wilderness. * * * All this gave the country a charm for me. It would have been dull work if it had been to plod over a safe country and here and there to correct some old error." [100] Nothing better reveals the Fremont character than this concluding sentence. The conventional did not appeal to him.

To penetrate these tempting recesses, to climb these beck-oning summits, to open mysteries, to emerge perhaps upon a new and valuable harbor, to find perhaps a good untrav-eled trail, to discover perhaps game in new abundance and new variety, to be able to announce new vegetation, new scenery — with such hopes Fremont thrilled, as did Carson,

Maxwell, and all the adventurers, facing, like the Cabots, the Hudsons, the Drakes, upon an enchanted sea.

Man proposes; but a Higher Will disposes. California apparently had been left far behind; and from fighters the company had become once more peaceable explorers. The change back again was even more· dramatic. I cannot improve upon the lines of Fremont himself:

How fate pursues a man! Thinking and ruminating over these things [i. e., the scenes and discoveries anticipated], I was standing alone by my camp fire, enjoying its warmth, for the night air of early spring is chill under the shadows òf the high mountains. Suddenly my ear caught the faint sound of horses' feet, and while I was watching and listening as the sounds, so strange hereabouts, came nearer, there emerged from the darkness — into the circle of the firelight — two horsemen riding slowly as though horse and man were fatigued by long traveling. In the foremost I recognized the familiar face of Neal, with a companion whom I also knew. They had ridden nearly a hundred miles in the last two days, having been sent forward by a United States officer who was on my trail with dispatches for me; but Neal had doubted if he would get through.[101]

The meeting of Livingston and Stanley in the wilds of Africa was not more startling than this meeting, on May 8, 1846, of the Fremont party in camp by the lonely lake and the two messengers from Lieutenant Gillespie.

Neal and his comrade Sigler reported that the officer, left behind, had dispatches from Washington for Fremont, and that he was threatened by Indians; that he had with him only three men, and that rescue might not arrive in time.

The trail by night would be impassable; but early in the morning the Fremont relief squad set out — Fremont, Carson, Owens, Stepp, Godey, Basil Lajeunesse, Denny the Iowa half-breed, and four Delawares. After a hard ride of forty-five miles, on the back trail, at a previous camp by a small stream in a glade the messenger, Lieutenant Archibald Gillespie of the Marine Corps of the Navy, and his three men, were sighted.

The dispatches, which were in the shape of letters, had left Washington, in the hands of Lieutenant Gillespie, the previous October, had traveled with him through "the heart of Mexico, from Vera Cruz to Mazatlan," thence up the coast of California to Monterey and inland to the Klamath Lake of present Oregon. Now, May 9, they were delivered.

The nature of these missives has long been a topic for debate. The Government is silent upon them — as the Government always would be silent upon matters of statecraft. We have the word of Fremont, of Mrs. Fremont, and of Senator Benton, as to their contents, and that should be sufficient. The dispatches consisted of a letter of credentials from the Department of State, a letter from Senator Benton, letters and newspapers from "home" ; and the verbal interpretation of Lieutenant Gillespie. That verbal interpretation is the fraction hardest to estimate.

Many fractions must be added, to make the sum: the fraction of Fremont's conversations, before leaving Washington, with Secretary Bancroft, Senator Benton, and others; the fraction of the dispatches having pursued him with such persistency; the fraction of the tenor of the various missives — a fraction very elusive, this; the fraction (another delicate, almost undeterminable item) of Lieutenant Gillespie's words and accented syllables and emphasized sentences; the fraction of conjectures as to what had occurred in the last six months; and summed to what result? Simply that Fremont was burdened with the responsibility of his own discretion.

The various letters contained, individually, nothing decisive. By veiled allusions they must dovetail according to the intuition of the reader. War with Mexico was at hand; the wheel of the ship California was not to be seized, but she was adroitly to be piloted past English and French signals into American waters.

Was Fremont the man to be entrusted with such discretion? The debate over this also has been long, and never will end. He was young, fond of power, impulsive, imaginative, not bred to the repressive school of the service to which he had been appointed; he was practically alone in authority upon land, the dream of empire loomed large; he passionately loved his country and his share in making it; he knew California better than did those at home — and such a preponderance of knowledge is always dangerous to a subordinate.

It is not probable that he took into council Carson or anyone save Lieutenant Gillespie — and perhaps not fully Gillespie, who (according to the *Memoirs*) " was directed to act in concert with me."

I saw the way opening clear before me. War with Mexico was inevitable; and a grand opportunity now presented itself to realize in their fullest extent the far-sighted views of Senator Benton, and make the Pacific Ocean the western boundary of the United States. I resolved to move forward on the opportunity and return forthwith to the Sacramento valley in order to bring to bear all the influence I could command.

Except myself, then and for nine months afterward, there was no officer of the army in California. The citizen party under my command was made up of picked men, and although small in number, constituted a formidable nucleus for frontier warfare, and many of its members commanded the confidence of the emigration.

This decision was the first step in the conquest of California.[102]

His course he had about thought out when he was interrupted by a movement of alarm among the animals on the shore of the lake, about one hundred yards away. Without notifying his men, who were exhausted and asleep, Fremont, pistol in hand, went down, through moonlight and forest shades, to investigate — and this was a plucky and a reckless act. He returned, having found nothing alarming, to his fire — one of the three around which the party were lying under their blankets. The camp was hedged on three sides by low cedars; and scarcely had the captain turned in last of all, to invite sleep, when the adventure occurred which, for the next day or two, effectually interrupted those thoughts upon future conquest.

Carson may tell the story, for it was Carson's quick ear which comprehended first. Had he been the one to hear the uneasiness of the mules, the succeeding attack might have failed.

Mr. Gillespie had brought the Colonel letters from home — the first he had had since leaving the States the year before — and he was up, and kept a large fire burning until after midnight; the rest of us were tired out, and all went to sleep. This was the only night in all our travels, except the one night on the island in the Salt Lake, that we failed to keep guard; and as the men were so tired, and we expected no attack now that we had fourteen in the party, the Colonel did not like to ask it of them, but sat up late himself. Owens and I were sleeping together, and we were waked at the same time by the licks of the axe that killed our men. At first, I did not know it was that; but I called to Basil, who was that side: "What's the matter there? What's the fuss about?" He never answered, for he was dead then, poor fellow — and he never knew what killed him. His head had been cut in, in his sleep; the other groaned a little as he died. The Delawares (we had four with us) were sleeping at that fire, and they sprang up as the Tlamaths charged them. One of them (named Crane) caught up a gun, which was unloaded; but, although he could do no execution, he kept them at bay, fighting like a soldier, and did not give up until he was shot full of arrows, three entering his heart; he died bravely. As soon as I had called out, I saw it was Indians in the camp, and I and Owens together cried out "Indians." There were no orders given; things went on too fast, and the Colonel had men with him that did not need to be told their duty. The Colonel and I, Maxwell, Owens, Godey and Stepp jumped together, we six, and ran to the assistance of our Delawares. I do n't know who fired and who did n't; but I think it was Stepp's shot that killed the Tlamath chief; for it was at the crack of Stepp's gun that he fell. He had an English half-axe slung to his wrist by a cord, and there were forty arrows left in the quiver, the most beautiful and warlike arrows I ever saw. He must have been the bravest man among them, from the way he was armed, and judging by his cap. When the Tlamaths saw him fall, they ran; but we lay, every man with his rifle cocked, until daylight, expecting another attack.[108]

Basil Lajeunesse had been brained by the chief's axe; the half-breed Denny had been killed with arrows, as he lay; Crane the Delaware, who had snatched up an unloaded rifle (some of the men, having cleaned their guns by discharging them, had carelessly omitted to reload them), with the butt endeavored to defend himself as he jumped from side to side, vainly dodging the arrows. He fell. Carson's own rifle was useless, by reason of a broken cap tube (another piece of criminal negligence); he threw it aside, and with his pistol shot at the bold chief, who was rapidly pouring his arrows into the helpless Delaware. The ball only cut the half-axe from the red wrist. Maxwell fired, as the chief now dodged, and wounded him in the leg. The chief was about to plunge into cover (whence his men were delivering a storm of shafts), but the bullet of Stepp, the gunsmith, caught him, and brought him to earth.

With their dead covered by blankets, with fires extinguished and with blankets hung up to give shelter, the whites lay close and bided the next movement of the enemy.

At daylight the whites might venture out. Carson seized the half-axe of the dead chief and in Indian revenge knocked his head to pieces with it. Sagundai, Delaware

BATTLE AT KLAMATH LAKE

INCIDENT OF THE FREMONT THIRD EXPEDITION, SPRING OF 1846

(From Fremont's Memoirs)

MONTEREY IN 1846

WHEN CAPITAL OF CALIFORNIA SEIZED BY COMMODORE STOCKTON
SUPPORTING FREMONT

(From Revere's A Tour of Duty in California)

SANTA FE IN 1846

AT THE TIME OF OCCUPATION BY THE KEARNY COLUMN

(From the Emory Reports)

chief, wounded slightly, scalped him. The arrows which Carson admired so much "were all headed with a lancet-like piece of iron or steel — probably obtained from the Hudson Bay Company's traders on the Umpqua — and were poisoned for about six inches. They could be driven that depth into a pine tree."

The attack had been a true Indian surprise. Only a few days before, the expedition had divided with these very Klamaths a scanty supply of meat; and the dead chief was recognized, before disfigurement, as the man who had yesterday presented Lieutenant Gillespie with a salmon, and had shown him a ford. Fremont's reinforcement of the Gillespie party undoubtedly saved them from annihilation.

By the tracks examined in the dawn, it was estimated that the attacking savages numbered some fifteen or twenty. As matter of habit, the Americans decided that the animosity should be laid to the influence of the British traders — the Hudson Bay Company in particular.

The three dead — Basil Lajeunesse the Canadian, Crane the Delaware, Denny the breed — were carried upon the pack mules for ten miles; and then, the enemy hovering near and the trail becoming bad by reason of the heavy timber, they were buried in a copse beside the Klamath Lake.

The attack had occurred on the night of May 9. This day General Taylor had fought and won the battle of Resaca de la Palma; two days before, or on May 7, he had fought and won that initial struggle of the war, the battle of Palo Alto. But isolated here by Klamath Lake of the Pacific coast, Fremont knew naught; and anyway, he and his men had plenty to do, fighting their own battles.

The trail of Fremont and Gillespie and company back to the valley of the Sacramento was a succession of skirmishes, and more than skirmishes. The Indians seemed suddenly inflamed. The march of the reunited parties led around the lake. The Klamath village was assaulted, four-teen of the enemy killed at one stand, and the others put to flight so precipitously that they had no time to gather up their arrows, laid in a fan-shape, ready to be picked one by one from the ground, about each warrior. The village was burned.

In the heart of the wood we came suddenly upon an Indian scout. He was drawing his arrow to the head as we came upon him, and Carson attempted to fire, but his rifle snapped; and as he swerved away the Indian was about to let his arrow go into him; I fired, and in my haste to save Carson, failed to kill the Indian, but Sacramento, as I have said, was not afraid of anything, and I jumped him directly upon the Indian and threw him to the ground. His arrow went wild. Sagundai was right behind me, and as I passed over the Indian he threw himself from his horse and killed him with a blow on the head from his war-club. It was the work of a moment, but it was a narrow chance for Carson. The poisoned arrow would have gone through his body.[104]

" I owe my life to them two. The Colonel and Sacra-mento saved me," quoth Carson, afterwards. While: " By heaven, this is rough work!" that night declared Gillespie, teeming with the incidents so foreign to his pre-vious experiences, upon a man-of-war. " I'll take care to let them know in Washington about it."

" Heaven does n't come in for much, about here, just now," answered Fremont, matter-of-fact; " and as for Washington, it will be long enough before we see it again; time enough to forget about this." His second assertion was not without considerable common sense.

The trail was resumed, for the Sacramento. The com-pany kept their advance covered and their flanks protected, and at night " forted " by falling trees. After a day of quiet, Maxwell and Archambeau rode ahead, to hunt, and their companions, following, passed a fresh bloody scalp stuck upon an arrow, in a trail. As it was an Indian scalp, more curiosity than alarm was felt. Curiosity was satisfied by the story when told. The two hunters had been met by a single Indian, coming up the path. Upon seeing them, he had halted, calmly disposed, in the grass, of some young crows which he was carrying in his quiver; and, like a Horatius holding the bridge, had promptly let fly an arrow at Maxwell. Maxwell flung himself from his saddle just in time; the shaft sped across it. After a lively duel, of two men with rifles and pistols against one man with bow and arrow, the audacious native was killed. His scalp was planted in the trail, as notice to friend and foe.

Another adventure remained. By wisely circuiting a, cañon, instead of traversing it, the company escaped an ambush, but not another attack. The Indians boldly rushed out, determined to fight. They recoiled, and Carson, Godey, and a third of the whites charged on. One warrior, in a rock shelter whence he was plying his arrows, kept the whites dodging. Fremont continues to relate:

He had spread his arrows on the ground and held some in his mouth, and drove back the men out of range for some moments, until Carson crept around to where he could get a good view of him and shot him through the heart. Carson gave the bow and arrows to Mr. Gillespie.

The Indians ceased their harrying espionage, and on May 24 the company were encamped in the valley of the lower Sacramento.

Now with the events immediately succeeding, important and stirring as these events were, we may not linger. But it may easily be comprehended that with the return into the valley, of this fiery Fremont, officer of the United States army, and this undaunted Gillespie, officer of the United States navy, and their armed Americans, both turmoil and distrust spread as spread the news.

Alta California, and particularly that California between

Los Angeles and San Francisco, where the chief seditions and the chief immigrations were housed, was divided into two camps: one portion of the resident native people favored American jurisdiction, another portion opposed it, preferring England or France. And there were the Mexican minority and the American settlers, as other ingredients of the boiling pot.

The anti-American sentiment seemed to be gaining ground. Signed with the popular Mexican watchword, knightly in its ring if not always inspiring to knightly deeds, a *banda* or proclamation, headed " God and Liberty," had on the 30th of April, 1846, been issued from Monterey against the "multitude of foreigners abusing our local circumstances without having come with the requisites provided by law."

Fremont located camp at the Buttes of the Sacramento, near to the juncture of the Bear and the Feather rivers, below the present town of Marysville. Here he awaited developments, but particularly the arrival of supplies from the American squadron, to which, lying in the bay of San Francisco, Lieutenant Gillespie had descended with a message. He must have hesitated, perplexed, and wondering whether war between the United States and Mexico had actually commenced, and to what length he was justified in going.

The Indians of the Sacramento Valley assumed a threatening attitude, incited (the settlers were told) against immigrants by the Mexican authorities. Fremont's camp was being made the rallying place of his fellow countrymen, and in their protection he took it upon himself to teach the still unsophisticated aborigines a wholesome fear of white prowess.

Ere they could burn the wheat, now ripening, he sallied upon them, striking a blow for himself as well as a blow for the ranchers.

I judged it expedient to take such precautionary measures as in my forward movement would leave no enemy behind to destroy the strength of my position by cutting off my supplies in cattle and break communication with the incoming emigrants.

Little loth would be the camp, augmented by the choice spirits who had constantly been joining, to assume the offensive. The Indian *rancherias* up the valley were surprised, one after another, and the inhabitants (many, indeed, it is alleged, already in war paint) with the customary white impetuousness were driven headlong in flight.

Rumors of projects by General Jose Castro, commanding general of the province, for the purpose of expelling, by force of arms, the distrusted *gringos* infesting the valley of the Sacramento, steadily gathered. Captain Fremont on June 8 moved his camp from the Buttes down to the vicinity of Sutter's Fort, which, under the doughty Swiss Bourbon-American Sutter, now in the face of the reports flying hither-thither had assumed a menacing aspect.

June 10 Ezekiel Merritt, issuing forth with a dozen comrades from the Fremont camp if not by the Fremont connivance, deprived Lieutenant Francisco Arce, Castro subaltern, of 170 horses destined for the Castro reinforcement — possibly for a Castro demonstration against the American intruders. This was the first voluntary act of war by the Anglo-Saxons in California. Word was left with Lieutenant Arce that if General Castro wished the horses, he might come and take them.

The California government had proclaimed; the Americans performed. Scarcely had the horses been stowed safely at Sutter's Fort, when Ezekiel Merritt, Dr. Robert Semple, John Grigsby (hard names for the Mexican language to master, as the bearers were hard nuts for the Mexican authorities to crack) with some thirty followers marched across westward, for the old mission of San Francisco Solano, now the *presidio* of Sonora, north of San

Francisco Bay. On the morning of June 14 they appeared before it, easily captured it, accepted the capitulation of the commandant General Mariano Guadalupe Vallejo (previously friendly to the cause of independence), his brother, Don Salvador Vallejo; his secretary, Victor Prudon (a Swiss), and his son-in-law, the American, Jacob P. Leese; and with the munitions, horses, and the stimulation of considerable liquid refreshment, declared themselves in behalf of a revolution " to make California a free and independent government."

On June 15, " they ran up a flag sufficiently significant of their intentions — a white field, red border, with a grizzly bear eyeing a single star, which threw its light on the motto, ' The Republic of California.' To this flag and its fortunes they pledged themselves in mutual confidence." [105]

On this day, June 15, 1846, at Washington was signed by the Secretary of State and the British minister the Oregon treaty, in which the parallel of forty-nine was extended as a national boundary from the Rockies to the Pacific. Three stars at once — Oregon, Washington, Idaho — were added to the flag. At the same time 16,000 Mormons, trekking westward, had crossed the Mississippi River, and the van had reached the Missouri at Council Bluffs, Iowa. In the Southwest 50,000 American volunteers from a populace inflamed for service against Mexico had swarmed to the colors; the American arms under General Taylor had achieved abundant and brilliant successes on the lower Rio Grande; the war was in full blast; and at Fort Leavenworth the celebrated Army of the West had assembled, under General Stephen Watts Kearny, soon to begin its unprecedented march across the plains, thence to seize New Mexico and by desert route from Santa Fe authoritatively to enter California.

So the Bear flag flies over the rude fortress of Sonoma; the new commander, William B. Ide, installed, is preparing

for issuance, on June 18, the proclamation of the revolutionists, bidding the inhabitants of the District of Sonoma
to have no fear, and inviting all citizens "to repair to my
camp at Sonoma, without delay, to assist us in establishing
and perpetuating a republican government." The Sonoma
prisoners — the two Vallejos, Lieutenant Colonel Prudon,
Jacob Leese — have been received by Fremont and turned
over to the custody of Sutter's Fort, where, as Leese records
poignantly, "we pass'd the next day in the most aughful
manner a reflecting on the cituation of our familys and
property in the hands of such a desperate set of men ";
and Fremont himself, taking the decisive step, assumes control of Sutter's Fort by placing over it the topographer,
Edward Kern. At the same time he draws up his resignation from the army, that he may release his Government
from responsibility, and shortly after he starts with his
force for Sonoma, to succor the eighteen men of Ide.

The Fremont resignation, not yet, of course, forwarded
to headquarters or accepted, was but precautionary "hedg-
ing," and would not have saved him from court-martial
or the Government from responsibility. However, he would
rather be sacrificed for doing too much than for doing too
little; and the men under him, Carson, Lucien Maxwell,
Alex Godey, Dick Owens, and the Delawares, had been
free rovers over-long to reflect much upon the consequences
of actions.

The Fremont company, largely augmented since their
return a month previous, were irrevocably embarked upon
the current of conquest; they had cast their fortunes with
the revolution. From Sonoma they marched, 160 strong,
for the San Rafael mission across the Golden Gate and up
the bay from Yerba Buena which is today San Francisco.
Already blood had been shed; for about a week before,
or on June 19, two Americans of the Ide command, Fowler
and Cowie, captured by Californian cavalry of the detach-

ment of Captain Joachin de la Torre were " butchered with knives." The march by Fremont from Sonoma south to San Rafael, about twenty-five miles, was for the purpose of attacking the de la Torre forces — an event strongly desired by the now savage hearts of the backwoodsmen. At the mission was made the one blot upon the Carson escutcheon — a blot extending, it is true, from the Fremont escutcheon. Across the bay from San Rafael was the point of San Pablo. While the Fremont company were at San Rafael waiting upon revenge, on June 28

a boat with four strangers was seen approaching from San Pablo. This boat Kit Carson with a squad was sent to intercept. It landed at Point San Pedro, and three of the strangers having debarked, Carson and his men left their horses, advanced, took careful aim, and shot them down. The victims proved to be Francisco and Ramon de Haro of San Francisco, and José de los Berreyesa, an aged ranchero of Santa Clara. An eye-witness of the affair, Jasper O'Farrell, stated in 1856 that Carson asked Fremont whether he should make prisoners of the strangers, and that the lieutenant, waving his hand, replied, "I have no room for prisoners." [106]

This was not like Carson, trained though he had been in the exigencies of frontier warfare where no quarter was given nor expected. Fremont glosses over the circumstance, laying it at the door of " my scouts, mainly Delawares "; and Senator Benton, reporting in the Senate, merely says: " In return for the murder of Cowie and Fowler, three of de la Torre's men, being taken, were instantly shot." But Fremont's company were supposed to be aiding the cause of civilization, of " liberty, virtue, and literature," under " favor of Heaven " (as appealed the Bear flag proclamation), and this wanton killing, without accusation or any trial, never can be justified. In later years Carson would not have countenanced it.

Now from the settlement of Sausalito below San Rafael,

Captain Fremont with twelve of his best shots, including Carson, by means of a boat of the American trading ship *Moscow* (William D. Phelps, captain) crossed the Golden Gate straits for the Castillo of San Joachim.

Pulling across the strait or avenue of water which leads in from the Gate we reached the Fort Point in the gray dawn of the morning and scrambled up the steep bank just in time to see several horsemen escaping at full speed toward Yerba Buena. We promptly spiked the guns — fourteen — nearly all long brass Spanish pieces. The work of spiking was effectually done by Stepp, who was a gunsmith, and knew as well how to make a rifle as to use one.[107]

Rat tail files, like the boat, had been supplied by the enthusiastic Captain Phelps. Whether Fremont was technically right in his support of the revolution may be debated; but the unanimity in the approval, by all his countrymen, of his acts is remarkable; he had the enthusiastic cooperation of his men, the open assistance of American merchants by land and by sea, and the discreetly covert commendation and good wishes of the naval officers on the coast. That any of the foreigners opposed was due only to their desire to accomplish the same conquest themselves; and even a faction of the Californians favored the American jurisdiction — preferring it, however, imposed in a less " bear-like " manner.

But let us keep pace with events. Another Fourth of July has arrived, and Fremont and Kit Carson are at another banquet. But it is a far cry to Bent's Fort and the banquet of 1844; it is a far cry to the Fourth of 1845 intervening, the peaceful day at Washington for the one, at his New Mexican farm for the other. This Fourth of July, 1846, was spent at Sonoma, where " the day was celebrated by salutes and a ball in the evening." Here on this date and upon the following date, July 5, was organized the California Battalion of Mounted Riflemen, 224 men, Captain John C. Fremont, U. S. A., colonel commanding; Lieutenant Archibald H. Gillespie, U. S. N., major; company captains, Richard Owens, Henry L. Ford, Granville P. Swift, John Grigsby, John Sears; among the privates, William B. Ide, late commander of the Sonoma *presidio,* and so far as we know, Kit Carson himself. The organization was democratic.

In the meantime, over the Oregon Trail has been toiling an increased emigration — part for Oregon, part for California. The California trains include the party of Edwin Bryant, who will be *alcalde* of San Francisco, and who will write an entertaining book; arriving at Sutter's Fort, September 1, he will be astonished to see sitting at the gateway several foreigners,

dressed in buckskin pantaloons and blue sailors' shirts with white stars worked on the collars. I inquired if Captain Sutter was in the fort? A very small man, with a peculiarly sharp red face and a most voluble tongue, gave the response. * * * He said in substance, that perhaps I was not aware of the great changes which had recently taken place in California; that the fort now belonged to the United States, and that Captain Sutter, although he was in the fort, had no control over it.[108]

The California trains include also the company of James T. Reed and the Donners, which after terrible experiences upon an untried road through the Great Basin, caught by the snows of the Sierra lose forty members.

Leaving Fort Leavenworth June 26, in this July, 1846, over the Santa Fe Trail, "tracked with the bones of men and beasts," march in the panoply of war, following the flag, 1658 volunteer infantry and mounted riflemen, bound for Bent's Fort, Santa Fe, and California — a route of more than 2,000 miles, half of which is through a hostile country .

A Colonel's command, called an army, marches eight hundred miles beyond its base, its communication liable to be cut off by the slightest effort of the enemy — mostly through a desert — the whole distance almost totally destitute of resources, to conquer a territory of 250,000 square miles; without a military chest, the people of this territory are declared citizens of the United States, and the invaders are thus debarred the rights of war to seize needful supplies; they arrive without food before the capital — a city two hundred and forty years old, habitually garrisoned by regular troops! I much doubt if any officer of rank, but Stephen W. Kearny, would have undertaken the enterprise; or, if induced to do so, would have accomplished it successfully. This is the art of war as practiced in America.[109]

And in this July has been biding uncertainly, at Monterey, the American flagship *Savannah;* on board, Commodore John D. Sloat, commander of the Pacific squadron, who has hesitated in acting until he is assured of formal declaration of war. If Captain Fremont is precipitate, Commodore Sloat seems over-cautious; nevertheless he is an older man, he understands that princes and republics alike are liable to the imputation of ingratitude, and that to annex California prematurely is a large order. Commodore Jones had made one error at Monterey; that error must not be repeated.

At Mazatlan of the Mexican coast Sloat had learned of the battles by General Taylor, and of the blockade of Vera Cruz; closely observed by the English fleet, also at Mazatlan, he had set sail for Monterey. Arriving there July 2 he learned of the operations of Fremont; and emboldened thereby and by additional news, brought through by Indians, of battles on the Rio Grande, and by evidences of British designs for a protectorate over California, on the morning of July 7 he landed at Monterey 250 men from the various vessels of his squadron; at ten o'clock " the flag, in charge of Lieutenant (Edward) Higgins, was raised on the flagstaff of the Custom-House, and the Proclamation of Occupation was read by Purser (Rodman M.) Price, in Spanish and in English, before our own force and the assembled citizens of the place, from the porch of the Custom-House." [110]

Thus, upon July 7, 1846, was fair California formally and eternally annexed to the republic. On July 16 sailed into the harbor the British flagship *Collingwood*, eighty guns, Rear Admiral Sir George Seymour — sailed in nine days too late, having, it is claimed, been deceived in the course first laid from Mazatlan by Commodore Sloat. The American ships flew the recall for their shore parties and beat to quarters. But the British Admiral is accredited only with saying:

" Sloat, if your flag was not flying on shore I should have hoisted mine there."

Meanwhile, July 9, the same flag had been raised at San Francisco by Lieutenant Revere of the *Portsmouth*, and on the same date had superseded the Bear flag at Sonoma. July 10, at Sutter's Fort Captain (or Colonel) Fremont received word and flag from Captain Montgomery of the *Portsmouth*, and at sunrise of July 11 at Sutter's Fort also breaks out, to the salute of twenty-one guns, the stars and stripes.

The Bear war, merged with a movement much weightier in its momentum, henceforth ceased. General Castro realized that this was war in earnest; and as he fell back before the sudden combination of land and sea forces, Fremont, deeming that under the new authorities and the new accessions the Sacramento Valley could stand alone, led his Rough Riders toward Monterey.

On the tenth of July, the whole northern district, including the Bay of San Francisco, was in possession of the United States, and the principal points garrisoned by our troops. All the Americans, and most of the foreigners, took up arms, and volunteered *en masse* to defend the American flag, which they regarded as the symbol of liberty, emancipation, and regeneration. Proceeding to the principal posts they offered themselves to the American officers as volunteers, without pay or emolument, each man taking with him his trusty rifle and accoutrements. It was a touching evidence of the influence of our free democratic institutions, to see these rough old trappers, whose lives had been passed with the Indians and wild beasts, rally around the flag of their native land, to which they owed nothing but the accident of birth, and that abiding love of liberty and independence which is inherent in our people. Nor was the devotion of the settlers from the old world less worthy of admiration. They had sought in the far-off wilderness a refuge from oppression, and found that they had fallen under a worse despotism than they had left at home. When therefore a fair opportunity occurred for dealing a death-blow to the dominion of the mock republic of Mexico, these sons of Europe flew to arms with an enthusiasm unknown to the reluctant tools of tyrants. We could do no more than to select the most youthful and hardy of these gallant men, who were hastily organized into a battalion under Captain (since Colonel) Fremont, and marched eagerly to meet the enemy in the field. Many of these new recruits had withheld their support from the " Bear Party," which did not seem to them to possess stability.[111]

With Fremont went Kit Carson, soon by fate to be assigned, as customary, an individual part in nation making.

CHAPTER XXIV

THE MEXICAN WAR — CARSON UNDER KEARNY

"CAPTAIN FREMONT and his armed band, with Lieut. Gillespie of the marine corps, arrived last evening from their pursuit of Gen. Castro." So chronicles, July 20, 1846, the Reverend Walter Colton, chaplain of the frigate *Congress*, newly anchored in the bay at Monterey.

They are two hundred strong, all well mounted, and have some three hundred extra head of horses in their train. They defiled, two abreast, through the principal street of the town. The ground seemed to tremble under their heavy tramp. The citizens glanced at them through their grated windows. Their rifles, revolving pistols, and long knives, glittered over the dusky buckskin which enveloped their sinewy limbs, while their untrimmed locks, flowing out from under their foraging caps, and their black beards, with white teeth glittering through, gave them a wild, savage aspect. They encamped in the skirts of the woods which overhang the town. The blaze of their watch-fires, as night came on, threw its quivering light into the forest glades and far out at sea. Their sentinels were posted at every exposed point; they sleep in their blankets under the trees, with their arms at their side, ready for the signal shot or stir of the crackling leaf.[112]

Thus Fremont and his men returned in force to Monterey, whence they had retired, although sullenly, four months previous, before this same Don Jose Castro. He as commanding general, must now himself retire southward, soon to meet, in an alliance of mutual protection, with the Governor, Don Pio Pico. at Los Angeles, where six months later the American leader would appear with his battalion.

The re-entry into Monterey and civilization of the famous explorer and his men attracted the attention that today is attracted by a Wild West parade; for their deeds had preceded them.

The English admiral was still at Monterey * * * and looked on with his officers with much interest. It was, indeed, a novel and interesting sight — the command, numbering two or three hundred men, marching in a square, within which was the cattle which they were driving for their subsistence. They were mostly clothed in buckskin, and armed with Hawkins rifles. The individuality of each man was very remarkable. When they dismounted, their first care was their rifles. Fremont * * * was the conspicuous figure. Kit Carson and the Indians accompanying him were the objects of much attention.[118]

It was a unique experience for many of the Fremont battalion. Few in the original expedition ever had seen the ocean — "a great prairie without a single tree." In the interval while Fremont was explaining to the alarmed Commodore Sloat that he had not been acting under written orders from Washington, and that he had not been notified of the declaration of war, his riflemen more or less cautiously ventured among the ships. Meanwhile the report by Fremont had thrown Commodore Sloat into a wretched state. Now, having climbed so far, he feared a fall. Pending the announcement of formal declaration of war between the United States and Mexico, he declared that he would do nothing more; and finally he cut the Gordian knot by resigning command and responsibility into the hands of Commodore Stockton of the *Congress* and by starting for home on the plea of ill health. Commodore Robert F. Stockton, a Princeton man, with the Princeton spirit, courted the command and the responsibilities, gladly assumed them; immediately, or on July 24, he appointed Fremont a major, Lieutenant Gillespie a captain, and enrolled the woodsmen as that unique organization, the Navy Battalion of Mounted Riflemen!

But they suffered for the distinction. On July 27, in their new service, they sailed on the sloop of war *Cyane*, Commander Dupont, for San Diego, 400 miles by land and more by sea. Amused eyes watched them embark, and the Reverend Mr. Colton took a malicious pleasure in soon making the accurate prophecy: " The wind is fresh, they are by this time cleverly sea-sick, and lying about the deck in a spirit of resignation that would satisfy the non-resistant principles of a Quaker. Two or three resolute old women might tumble the whole lot of them into the sea."

It is safe to say that Kit Carson, for one, would willingly have exchanged his misery in the scuppers for another dead mule rampart, and siege by the Comanches, on the plains.

By a march from San Diego, Los Angeles was taken without bloodshed; the combined forces of Stockton and Fremont entered the pueblo; Governor Don Pio Pico and Commandante-General Jose Castro retired, and Commodore Stockton issued, on August 17, a proclamation, declaring the country a territory of the United States. He appointed himself governor of California, Major Fremont military governor, and Captain Gillespie commandant of the Southern District, with headquarters at Los Angeles; and he sailed away.

Kit Carson set out, with his friend, Lucien Maxwell, overland with the news for Washington; and across the desert from Santa Fe was meanwhile approaching the real governor of California, General Stephen Watts Kearny, leading the remnants of his Army of the West.

This dispatch duty to which Carson was assigned seems to have been a personal tribute to his abilities. It was awarded to him to be an achievement and a privilege in one. He would, if the plan were carried out, have the pleasure and the honor of announcing direct to the President the alleged conquest of California, and en route he would see wife and friends at Taos. " Going off at the head of his own party, with *carte blanche* for expenses and the prospect of novel pleasure and honor at the end, was a culminating point in Carson's life," adds Fremont.

Thus far rank had passed Kit Carson by. Godey was a lieutenant, Talbot was lieutenant and adjutant, Dick Owens was a captain, all in the California Battalion service. Therefore it is with real satisfaction that we witness, on September 15, 1846, Carson, as lieutenant upon special service, starting out with an escort of fifteen men (six being Delawares) and fifty horses, from Los Angeles for Washington, and engaged to make the round trip in 120 days! It is the first of three round trips across the desert, carrying government dispatches. This time he travels from California almost to Santa Fe and back; within a few months he must travel from California to Washington and back to California; and soon thereafter he must travel from California to Washington, and back to New Mexico. The aggregate of the three journeys, each through perilous territory, was 16,000 miles, more than half being by horse or mule back.

This route of 1846 was not unknown to him, for he had traversed the same country, between Los Angeles and Taos, in 1829 and 1830 with Ewing Young; and there now was a traders' trail, slight, to be sure, from Santa Fe to San Diego by the Gila and Yuma. But the Apaches and hostile Mexicans still infested the desert.

Almost upon the same date that Carson set out upon his ride, or upon the 25th of September, from ancient Santa Fe, which now also flew the American flag, General Stephen Watts Kearny set out for the coast. Santa Fe had been captured without a fight; New Mexico had been annexed; Charles Bent was governor of the Territory; and with his 300 men " the Horse-Chief of the Long Knives " (as he was known among the plains Indians) proposed to complete the subjugation of California, a thousand miles away. Moreover, 448 Mormons, intercepted in their pilgrimage from Nauvoo, and enlisted as a separate battalion, infantry, were expected to follow — their services having been promised to the Government — under Lieutenant Colonel Philip St. George Cooke.

Thomas Fitzpatrick guided the Kearny column; Antoine Robidoux was interpreter; and the topographer was J. M. Stanley, the beaver-days artist.

On the Rio Grande del Norte, ten miles below Socorro, New Mexico, the Kit Carson party, hastening east, and the General Kearny column, toiling west, met. The dragoons were eleven days out of Santa Fe and had covered 150 miles. The Carson company were twenty-six days out of Los Angeles and had covered 800 miles. They had worn out thirty-four mules, but they were on schedule time. Carson was not entirely unprepared for the meeting, which we may best describe in the words of Captain Abraham Johnston, who rode to his death at San Pasqual.

October 6 — Marched at 9, after having great trouble in getting some ox carts from the Mexicans; after marching about three miles, we met Kit Carson, direct on express from California, with a mail of public letters for Washington; he informs us that Colonel Fremont is probably civil and military governor of California, and that about forty days since, Commodore Stockton, with the naval force, and Colonel Fremont, acting in concert, commenced to revolutionize that country, and place it under the American flag; that, in about ten days, their work was done, and Carson, having received the rank of lieutenant, was dispatched across the country by the Gila, with a party to carry the mail; the general told him that he had just passed over the country which we were to traverse, and he wanted him to go back with him as a guide; he replied that he had pledged himself to go to Washington, and he could not think of not fulfilling his promise. The general told him he would relieve him of all responsibility, and place the mail

in the hands of a safe person, to carry it on; he finally consented, and turned his face to the west again, just as he was
on the eve of entering the settlements, after his arduous trip,
and when he had set his hopes on seeing his family. It requires
a brave man to give up his private feelings thus for the public
good; but Carson is one such! honor to him for it! Carson
left California with fifteen men ; among them six Delaware
Indians — faithful fellows. They had fifty animals, most of
which they left on the road, or traded with the Apaches, giving
two for one; they were not aware of the presence of
the American troops in New Mexico; they counted upon
feeling their way along, and in case the Mexicans were hostile,
they meant to start a new outfit, and run across the country.
When they came to the Copper-mine Apaches, they first
learned that an American general had possession of the territory of New Mexico. The Apaches were very anxious to be
friendly with the Americans, and received them very cordially,
much to their surprise.[114]

Thomas Fitzpatrick turned east, for Washington, with
the precious mail; Kit Carson turned west, for California
again, with the dragoons. The act brings tribute not only
from Captain Johnston, but from Colonel Cooke. " That
was no common sacrifice to duty."
However, Carson was not persuaded. He testifies that
he was not persuaded, but obeyed orders. " And I guided
him through, but with great hesitation, and had prepared
everything to escape in the night before they started, and
made known my intention to Maxwell, who urged me not
to do so." [115] All in all, the occasion was one of much
perplexity for Lieutenant Kit Carson. The conflict of
authority now, and to come, perplexed men more experienced than he. He was fortunate, in his simplicity and
honesty, to get off as easily as he did; for in Stephen Watts
Kearny he met the superior officer, a soldier from the
ground up, and a man with an eye of blue colder than that
in the eye of the Fremont whom he outranked.
Reduced after hearing that California was pacified, the

column proceeded: 100 enlisted men, six eight-mule wagons, two howitzers, with a flag strange to the desert solitudes. Kit Carson dryly informed them that at the rate they were traveling they would not get to Los Angeles in four months!

Within three days after leaving camp below Socorro, the six wagons had to be dismissed, and packsaddles substituted. To Captain Cooke and his luckless Mormons fell the uncertain privilege of making the first wagon road through the farthest Southwest — Santa Fe to southern California.

For a week the Kearny trail descended along the Rio del Norte; 230 miles below Santa Fe, under Carson's guidance, it diverged to the west and entered the Mimbres country. Thence the dragoon column crossed, October 20, to the head of the Gila, which was to be followed to its mouth at the Colorado, 600 miles away.

Dragging the constantly disabled howitzers, with mules continually failing, the men without shoes, partially naked, and exposed to night temperatures below freezing, and days of thirst, hunger, and burning sun, the First Dragoons, C and K Companies, plodded along the trail first traversed by the beaver-hunting Patties in 1827; afterward in 1830 by the homeward returning Ewing Young and Kit Carson, his assistant, and in 1831 by the trading party of Davy Jackson, the mountain man, and William H. Warner, who became one of the first American ranchers of California.

Lieutenant Carson, the guide, was invaluable; the route was the one by which he had met the column, and so he knew its peculiarities. Every day Lieutenant W. H. Emory, of the topographical corps, recorded his meteorological observations, wrote up his diary; every day the fated Captain Abraham Johnston, Kearny's aide-de-camp, maintained the official journal. If the march was hard, it was not uninteresting, for the many ancient ruins still awaited the depredations of the vandal. The Indians were uniformly friendly, viewing the Americans as allies against the hated Spanish, and as good customers who paid promptly for what they obtained.[116]

November 22 the juncture of the Gila and the Colorado was just ahead.

The day was warm, the dust oppressive, and the march, twenty-two miles, very long for our jaded and ill-fed brutes. The general's horse gave out, and he was obliged to mount his mule. Most of the men were on foot, and a small party, composed chiefly of the general and staff, were a long way ahead of the straggling column, when, as we approached the end of our day's journey, every man was straightened in his saddle by our suddenly falling on a camp, which, from the trail, we estimated at 1,000 men, who must have left that morning. Speculation was rife, but we all soon settled down to the opinion that it was Gentral Castro and his troops; that he had succeeded in recruiting an army in Sonora, and was now on his return to California. Carson expressed the belief that he must be only ten miles below, at the crossing. Our force consisted only of 110 men. The general decided we were too few to be attacked, and must be the aggressive party, and if Castro's camp could be found, that he would attack it the moment night set in, and beat them before it was light enough to discover our force.[117]

Lieutenant Emory and squad reconnoitered; horses were heard neighing, and a fire was seen blazing. But the 110 did not attack the fancied 1,000, for the camp was found to consist of Mexican traders, conveying some 500 horses from California.

The chief of the party, a tall, venerable looking man, represented himself to be a poor employe of several rich men engaged in supplying the Sonora market with horses. We subsequently learned that he was no less a personage than José Maria Leguna, a colonel in the Mexican service.[118]

The next day, however, was marked by a more portentous meeting, which resulted in the capture of a Mexican jogging as upon a journey. Taken to the tent of General Kearny, he was found to be carrying California mail.

Among the letters was one addressed to General José Castro at Altar, one to Antonio Castro, and others to men of note in Sonora. * * * We ascertained from them that a counter revolution had taken place in California, that the Americans were expelled from Santa Barbara, Puebla de los Angeles, and other places, and that Robideaux, the brother of our interpreter, who had been appointed alcalde by the Americans, was a prisoner in jail. They all spoke exultingly of having thrown off "the detestable Anglo-Yankee yoke," and congratulated themselves that the tri-color once more floated in California.[119]

Here was news, indeed, for an invading column of 110 men, without a base, and the desert behind. The date of the letters was October 15. What had been occurring in the meantime? The 110 pushed on to the Colorado, and ten miles below the mouth of the Gila crossed by a ford known to Carson into the sandy, dry-wash Colorado Desert of southern California.

This last of the desert *jornadas* was begun on November 25. The distance was about ninety-one miles. The wild horses seized from the Mexican "traders" were soon tamed, and sank and died. On November 30 the men were inspected. "Poor fellows! They are well nigh naked — some of them barefoot — a sorry looking set. A dandy would think that, in those swarthy, sunburnt faces, a lover of his country will see no signs of quailing. They will be ready for their hour when it comes." And the hour was at hand.

In the face of high, cold winds and hostile surroundings, salty grass and water, deep sand, hot days and numbing nights, the column toiled on to the foothills of the other edge, and with one horse and a few worn mules, on December 2, arrived at the green valley of the Agua Caliente, where was situated the ranch of Warner, the American. San Diego was now but sixty miles southwest; Los Angeles some 100 miles northwest. The trail through Warner's rancho was the Sonora Trail, and General Kearny, thus informed, might congratulate himself that he was blocking Mexican traffic between Sonora and Southern California points. That evening Lieutenant J. W. Davidson, with Kit Carson as guide and with twenty-five men, rode fifteen miles and despoiled a herd of unbroken horses and mules held for the command of General Flores.

By the English rancher, Señor Stokes, a letter was sent on to Commodore Stockton, who was reported as still in possession of San Diego. The commodore was apprised of the arrival of the Kearny dragoons, and asked to open communication " as quickly as possible." On December 4 the march for San Diego was resumed. The weather was murky and cold, with an all-day rain. Little definite information had been gained as to the state of the country ahead, except that everything between San Diego and Santa Barbara was in the hands of the " country people."

What was the situation in California since Kit Carson and his fifteen men had departed, September 15, to carry to Washington the word that Fremont and Stockton had " pacified " the coast? In August, Castro, the inefficient, complaining that he was unable to gather more than " one hundred men, badly armed and worse supplied," and Governor Pico, his colleague, had delivered a farewell proclamation and fled together over the Sonora road, not to return until 1848. But scarcely had the Kit Carson command spurred forth to bear their tidings east, when the chafing Mexican citizenship squirmed into renewed life.

This was due in part to Archibald H. Gillespie, formerly lieutenant in the marines, but at that time captain in the California Battalion, and as commandant of the southern district of California, stationed with a company of forty men at the Pueblo de los Angeles. "A man of Fremont ideas," he was without the Fremont finesse; instead of conciliating the people, he had tactlessly enforced his orders. Consequently, on September 24, he had waked up to find a rebellion in full flower, the head gardeners being General Jose Maria Flores, Colonel Jose Antonio Carrillo and Captain Andres Pico, former Castro officers. The small American garrison of the town yielded perforce, and on October 4 they marched, with the doubtful honors of the defeated, to embark at San Pedro (Los Angeles' port) and sail for Monterey.

From Santa Barbara the hard-fighting young Washingtonian, Theodore Talbot, sergeant major and first lieutenant, had cut his way with his squad to the hills; thence, smoked out by fire in the brush, they had made retreat for Monterey. From San Diego the redoubtable Ezekiel Merritt and his little command of hunters had abruptly sought the incongruous sanctum of a whale ship in the bay. Commodore (who was also Governor) Robert Stockton was at San Francisco; Lieutenant Colonel and Military Governor John C. Fremont had been in the valley of the Sacramento, bear hunting and recruiting, unsuccessfully, for a Stockton descent upon the western coast of Mexico and a conquering march inland to the City of Mexico. A hurried message from the commodore had recalled him to San Francisco, and a boat squadron from the ships had met him at the head of Suisun Bay to hasten him on.

With the California Battalion (428 men, including Indians and servants, says Lieutenant Edwin Bryant, the newly arrived emigrant) now augmented by three companies of emigrants, a party of Walla Walla Indians and two pieces of artillery, on November 30 Major Fremont, soon promoted to a lieutenant-colonelcy, had set out from the neighborhood of his first campaign, the mission of San Juan Bautista, under Gavilan Peak, to retake Los Angeles. Commodore Stockton moved to San Diego, which he found closely beleaguered by California horsemen.

In the midst of such alarms the little battalion of Kearny's First Dragoons, piloted by Kit Carson — himself presumed to be in Washington — arrived from their long desert journey. December 3 Commodore Stockton, seaman turned land commander, and chafing at the mobile enemy, in his headquarters in San Diego received at the hand of the merryfaced Señor Stokes the tidings that a detachment of troops from New Mexico were as far as Warner's rancho; and that "by orders from the President of the United States," a new commander in chief was near.

CHAPTER XXV

THE MEXICAN WAR — CARSON AT SAN PASQUAL

"SO WE slept till morning." In these, the last penned words of Captain Johnston, is something prophetic and comforting. His journal reads:

December 4 — Marched at 9, and took the route for San Diego, to communicate with the naval forces and to establish our depot, not knowing yet in what state we would find the country. Marched 15 miles in a rain, cold and disagreeable, and encamped at St. Isabella, a former ranch of San Diego mission, now, by hook or by crook, in the possession of an Englishman named Stokes; here hospitality was held out to us — Stokes having gone to San Diego. We ate heartily of stewed and roast mutton and tortillas. We heard of a party of Californians, of 80 men, encamped at a distance from this; but the informant varied 16 to 30 miles in his accounts, rendering it too uncertain to make a dash in a dark, stormy night; so we slept till morning.[120]

Lieutenant Emory must continue the journal.

December 5 — A cold rainy day, and the naked Indians of the rancheria gathered about our fires. We marched from the rancheria of San Isabel to that of Santa Maria. [This was another of the Stokes ranches.] On the way we met Capt. Gillespie, Lieutenant Beale, and Midshipman Duncan of the navy, with a party of thirty-five men sent from San Diego with a dispatch for Gen. Kearny. We arrived at the rancheria after dark, where we heard that the enemy was in force nine miles distant, and not finding any grass about the rancheria, we pushed on and encamped in a cañon two miles below.[121]

The day had been so murky that little of the country was visible, and any movements of the reported enemy were concealed. The country hereabouts is rolling, the sparsely timbered but brushy southern California hills undulating monotonously. The Kearny dragoons, worn by their desert march of 900 miles and more, poorly mounted on untrained horses and fagged-out mules, were at great disadvantage as opposed to the native cavalry, superbly mounted and acquainted with all the trails.

But Gillespie was burning for revenge to counterbalance his discomfiture at Los Angeles. He made light of the California valor. So did even Kit Carson, who, in common with other mountain men of the Southwest, thought little of Latin courage. After their easy conquest of New Mexico, when the march from Bent's Fort to Santa Fe, the capital, had been practically undisputed, General Kearny and his officers and men also were inclined to dismiss the Californians curtly.

Influenced by the contempt of Gillespie and Carson, and not realizing that here the fight was with free Californians accustomed to more initiative than the New Mexicans, General Kearny's council decided to push on for San Diego, and to attack the enemy if they were opposed. In this plan was sound military sense. Boldness would win a way, whereas hesitancy might result in the little force being shut off from the sea and all supplies, and, by a constantly increasing foe, confined helplessly inland while their chances grew less.

So, in the night of December 5, through the darkness from the camp

a party under Lieut. Hammond was sent to reconnoiter the enemy, reported to be near at hand. By some accident the party was discovered, and the enemy placed on the *qui vive.* We were now on the main road to San Diego, all the " byways " being in our rear, and it was therefore deemed necessary to attack the enemy, and force a passage. About 2 o'clock, a. m., the call to horse was sounded.[122]

San Diego was forty miles distant; the Californians were between. "I then determined," reports General Kearny, "that I would march for and attack them by break of day."

With the advance guard of twelve under Captain Johnston was Kit Carson, scout; behind this advance guard rode the general himself, with lieutenants Emory and Warner and four enlisted men. Upon this little detachment devolved the brunt of the first onslaught.

The Californians under Captain Andres Pico, brother of Don Pio Pico, the late governor, were encamped comfortably at the small Indian village of San Pasqual (Pascual), seven miles ahead, and thereby about thirty miles from San Diego.[123] At dawn the advance guard of the Americans, with the general and staff close following, from a mile away sighted the fires, which "shone brightly." The general himself now "ordered a trot, then a charge, and soon we found ourselves engaged in a hand to hand conflict with a largely superior force."

Captain Andres Pico, ignorant of the numbers of the invaders, as the invaders likewise had been ignorant of his numbers, upon learning of their approach by way of Warner's ranch, had planned not to oppose at once, but to reconnoiter until he had drawn them to ground of his own choosing. When the advance guard of twenty men (for the general and his escort joined the Johnston command) charged, as the general states, "furiously," downhill upon the pickets, the latter, vaulting to ready horse and clutching bridle, spurred for the main camp. The twenty Americans pursued hard down the hill into the village. Kit Carson's horse stumbled and threw him headlong, shattering his rifle at the grasp. At the same moment the Pico force, astonished by the rash valor of the few, and pausing to see if there was a large support behind, in their saddles received the charging dragoons with a volley from carbine, *escopeta* and pistol, killing Captain Johnston and a dragoon.

Carson, lying still while his comrades rode over him, staggered up unharmed, and, seeing the dead dragoon near, grabbed carbine and cartridge box, caught a horse, remounted and hastened for the fray. In the village and just beyond the Californians were now standing their ground. Cheered on by Captain Ben Moore, down thundered the fifty men of the support, and the Californians gave way. Captain Moore on his white horse led in pursuit; the Californian horses easily distanced the dragoon horses, and the dragoon horses distanced the dragoon mules. Thus the pursuit strung out over half a mile of road, when, quickly grasping the advantage, the Parthian Californians rallied, and turned compact. They were eighty or more (official reports place the number at 160), and they were enabled now to take the dragoons, little squad by squad.

Here the lance, wielded from horses as agile as wasps, proved its worth. Against these nine-foot staves the saber and the clubbed carbine, swung from fagged and stubborn animals (the mule is always badly bitted and badly dispositioned for a cavalry fight), were totally ineffectual.

Conspicuous on his white horse, Captain Moore was lanced to death; Lieutenant Hammond was lanced so that he died soon after; General Kearny was wounded twice and would have been thrust through and through had not Lieutenant Emory stopped his assailant by a lucky pistol ball; Lieutenant Warner was lanced in three places, Captain Gillespie in three places, Captain Gibson, and even the veteran trader, Antoine Robidoux, likewise were wounded. Of enlisted men were killed two sergeants, two corporals, ten privates of the dragoons; a private of the Gibson company of volunteers and an employee in the topographical service; wounded, one sergeant, one " bugleman," nine privates of the dragoons. Total, eighteen killed; fifteen wounded — of the latter " many surviving from two to ten lance wounds, most of them when unhorsed and incapable of resistance."

The howitzers arriving on the gallop, the Californians fled. When the pieces were being unlimbered the span of mules drawing one ran off with it into the midst of the retreating enemy, but fortunately the Pico force did not try to make use of it.

Such was the battle of San Pasqual, thirty miles northeast of San Diego, fought at break of day, December 6, 1846, and resulting in the discomfiture of the American regular dragoons and the vindication of the Californian irregular cavalry.

The killed and wounded (General Kearny reports that six Californians also were left on the field) were being gathered, when, records Emory:

a large body of horsemen were seen in our rear and fears were entertained lest Major Swords and the baggage should fall into their hands. The general directed me to take a party of men and go back for Major Swords and his party. We met at the foot of the first hill, a mile in rear of the enemy's first position. Returning, I scoured the village to look for the dead and wounded. The first object which met my eye was the manly figure of Capt. Johnston. He was perfectly lifeless, a ball having passed directly through the center of his head. The work of plundering the dead had already commenced; his watch was gone, nothing being left of it but a fragment of the gold chain by which it was suspended from his neck. By my directions Sergeant Falls and four men took charge of the body and carried it into camp. Captain Johnston and one dragoon were the only persons either killed or wounded on our side in the fight by firearms.

It was found that the mules were not strong enough to transport the dead to San Diego; and in order to save the bodies from further plundering the American dead were buried at night, to the sound of the howling of coyotes, under a willow at the east of the battle field camp.

Before allowing his injuries to be dressed the general fainted. Captain H. S. Turner, as senior officer left, assumed the command. The surgeon of the column, Dr. J. S. Griffin, was occupied until late afternoon in stanching the many lance wounds of the rank and file. A sorry sight was the bloody camp. " Provisions were exhausted, horses dead, mules on their last legs, men, reduced to one-third of their number, were ragged, worn and emaciated." So records Lieutenant Emory. Ambulances were lacking, and soon after the fight Lieutenant Godey, with three others, was sent to make his way, with best mountain-man skill, through byways to San Diego for wheeled vehicles. Already the English ranchero, Stokes, was nearing there, posthaste, with an excited tale of the fight.

The dragoon camp was unmolested throughout the day; the night settled cold and damp from the previous rains, and " the ground, covered with rocks and cacti, made it difficult to get a smooth place to rest, even for the wounded * * * and notwithstanding our excessive fatigues of the day and night previous, sleep was impossible." December 7, says Emory,

dawned on the most tattered and ill-fed detachment of men that ever the United States mustered under her colors. The enemy's pickets and a portion of his force were seen in front. The sick, by the indefatigable exertions of Dr. Griffin, were doing well, and the general enabled to mount his horse. The order to march was given, and we moved off to offer the enemy battle, accompanied by our wounded, and the whole of our packs. The ambulances grated on the ground, and the sufferings of the wounded were very distressing. We had made for them the most comfortable conveyance we could, and such as it was, we were indebted principally to the ingenuity of the three remaining mountain men of the party, Peterson, Londeau, and Perrot. The fourth, the brave Francois Menard, had lost his life in the fight of the day before.

Kit Carson, with his usual fortune, had come out of the fight practically unscathed.

The slow column moved on — the wounded and the packs in the center. Upon the hills about hovered the lancers of the Californians, constantly threatening, but ever yielding the advance. In about nine miles was attained the rancho San Bernardo. Here the column commandeered water for the animals and chickens for the men; but there was no grass, and the march must turn aside, " driving many cattle before us," for the rich San Bernardo River bottoms, south.

We had scarcely left the house and proceeded more than a mile, when a cloud of cavalry debouched from the hills in our rear, and a portion of them dashed at full speed to occupy a hill which we must pass, while the remainder threatened our rear. Thirty or forty of them got possession of the hill, and it was necessary to drive them from it. This was accomplished by a small party of six or eight, upon whom the Californians discharged their fire; and strange to say, not one of our men fell. The capture of the hill was then but the work of a moment, and when we reached the crest, the Californians had mounted their horses and were in full flight. We did not lose a man in the skirmish, but they had several badly wounded. By this movement we lost our cattle, and were convinced that if we attempted any further progress with the ambulances we must lose our sick and our packs.

The tactics of Captain Pico were apparent: the Americans must permit themselves to be menaced from higher ground, or must take the hill and lose their cattle; they now must occupy the hill and cease their advance, or else be flanked again and again until they lost all their packs and probably their wounded, too. General Kearny decided to occupy the hill until the wounded were so improved as to require less attention from the able-bodied.

The night of December 7 was spent upon the hill. One hundred more Californians were on their way from Los Angeles to reinforce the besiegers, but the Kearny company did not know it, and could only fear as yet that every hour was making their position worse. On the hill there was no forage except the mahogany and manzanita brush. There was no water until, by boring holes, a modicum was obtained, for the men only. The animals must constantly be guarded, lest they break for the grass and the river below. The fattest of the mules was slaughtered for meat.

While the camp was wondering whether Godey and his companions had succeeded in winning through with the message to Commodore Stockton, Captain Andres Pico sent in word under flag of truce that he had four prisoners, just captured, whom he would like to exchange — and the hopes of the camp were dashed. The prisoners could be no others than Godey and his companions. The Americans had only one prisoner, but Lieutenant Beale was delegated to meet the Californian representative and treat for an exchange on that basis. The request for Godey was refused by Pico, he being considered too valuable a man; but one Burgess, the least intelligent of them all, was offered. However, upon Lieutenant Beale reporting to the general, Lieutenant Emory was sent down with the prisoner to make the exchange. He found Captain Pico to be a " gentlemanly looking and rather handsome man," and in demeanor evidently as courteous as the Spanish-Mexican customarily is.

Burgess took " rather a contemptuous leave of his late captors." He related that the Godey party had safely reached San Diego, but that when in sight of the camp, on their return, they had been spied and taken by the Pico videttes. Before capture they had " cached " their dispatches under a tree. He did not know what was in the dispatches; he did not know what Godey had communicated to Commodore Stockton, and therefore the exchange of prisoners resulted in but little satisfaction to the Americans upon the hill. They could not guess that, apprised both by the excited Stokes and by Godey, Commander Stockton was

at this moment assembling all his available sailors and
marines for a forced march to their relief. At this juncture
the young Lieutenant Beale volunteered to take his Indian
servant and try with another message for Stockton; Kit
Carson instantly offered himself as the third.

Of Kit Carson we have heard much; the Indian must pass
on to Valhalla as only one of the earth's heroes unnamed
and unsung; but Lieutenant Edward Fitzgerald Beale on
this December 8, 1846, made himself famous. The grandson of Commodore Thomas Truxtun of the old navy when
it was new, and son of another naval officer, Lieutenant
George Beale, born in 1822 Acting Lieutenant Beale was
now but twenty-four years old and sixteen months commissioned as midshipman. But the American traditions
animating him dated back through seventy years. Now

the brief preparations for the forlorn hope were soon made;
and brief they were. A rifle each, a revolver, a sharp knife,
and no food; there was none in the camp. General Kearny invited Beale to come and sup with him. It was not the supper
of Antony and Cleopatra; for when the 'camp starves, no
general has a larder. It was meager enough. The general
asked Beale what provision he had to travel on; the answer
was, nothing. The general called his servant to inquire what
his tent afforded; a handful of flour, was the answer. The
general ordered it to be baked into a loaf and be given to
Beale. When the loaf was brought the servant said that was
the last, not of bread only, but of everything; that he had
nothing left for the general's breakfast. Beale directed the
servant to carry back the loaf, saying that he would provide
for himself. He did provide for himself; and how? By
going to the smouldering fire where the baggage had been
burnt in the morning, and scraping from the ashes and embers
the half-burnt peas and grains of corn which the conflagration
had spared, filling his pockets with the unwonted food. Carson
and the faithful Indian provided for themselves some mule
beef.[124]

San Diego was still thirty miles southwest. This, it must

be understood, was the old San Diego — later called Old
Town — about two miles north of the present city, or
between it and the mouth of Mission Valley, which opéns
upon the flats of Mission or False Bay. Here, back of the
squalid collection of adobe huts, Stockton was fortifying
his quarters on a hill commanding the *presidio.* The
interior country, to the Kearny position, was composed
of mesas and abrupt hills covered by the chaparral, or brush,
mingled with prickly pear and other cacti, and cut by deep
clay and gravelly ravines or arroyos. It was the rainy
season, although General Kearny, in a letter to his wife,
reports the country to be very dry.

With the fall of dusk the three started. Knowing that
among the *Americanos* pent upon the hill was Kit Carson,
the renowned hunter, and knowing also that every effort
would be made to effect a juncture with Stockton, at night
Captain Pico threw a double and triple cordon of sentries
around the base of the hill and kept a patrol moving. He
warned his men with the significant Spanish: "*Se escapara
el lobo*" — "The wolf will escape!"

To descend the hill slope the three scouts must crawl, in
order not to limn themselves against the sky line. That
the twigs should not crack underfoot, and that stones should
not ring, the two whites removed their shoes and tucked
them in their belts. Speedily their feet were afire with the
stinging spines of the cacti. Presently the canteens were
discarded, lest they, too, give out the alarm.

Slowly, but surely, they evaded the vigilant guard of the
Mexican sentinels, whom they found to be mounted and three
rows deep, * * * So near would they often come to these
Mexican sentinels, that but a few yards would measure the
distance between them and their enemies, yet, with brave
hearts they crept along over the ground foot by foot ; they
were almost safe beyond these barriers, when all their hopes
came near being dashed to pieces. This alarm was caused by

one of the sentinels riding up near to where they were, dismounting from his horse and lighting, by his flint and steel, his cigarette. On seeing this, Kit Carson, who was just ahead of Lieutenant Beale, pushed back his foot and kicked softly his companion, as a signal for him to lie flat on the ground as he (Carson) was doing. The Mexican was some time, being apparently very much at his leisure, in lighting his cigarette ; and during these moments of suspense, so quietly did Kit Carson and his companion lie on the ground, that Carson said and always after affirmed, that he could distinctly hear Lieutenant Beale's heart pulsate.[125]

Presently the unconscious Californian remounted his horse and rode away.

It was during an interval of despair such as this that the lad Beale, his stout spirit worn by the torture, physical and mental, wavered, and reaching for Carson, whispered in his ear: " We are gone. Let 's jump and fight it out ! " But Carson, of longer experience in this work, and of a frame and spirit inured to keen dangers, answered: " No. I 've been in worse places before." And the boy was encouraged.

They passed through the cordon of sentries and videttes; and before them lay two miles of open valley across which, despite the clustering cacti and the sharp stones, they must still crawl. Here beyond was broken ground, with covert of chaparral and of some trees. This slight vantage ground they gained at last.

Now they might stand and don their shoes — but they found that the shoes had been lost from their belts, and that the remainder of the way, like that preceding, must be traveled in tattered stockings or bare soles. Reckless of the cactus, they proceeded, as rapidly as possible, and daylight caught them well on their circuitous trail for San Diego. They left the high ground and took to the cañons. Their feet swollen by bruise, cut, and cactus spine, their throats parched, they were yet elated at the progress they had made. However, the cordon thrown about San Diego awaited to be pierced.

Meanwhile the camp on the hill had passed another wretched night. Among the sufferers who seemed doomed was Don Antoine Robidoux, the trader of Fort Uncompahgre and Fort Uintah. He, "a thin man of fifty-five years," slept next to Lieutenant Emory, who describes his plight:

The loss of blood from his wounds, added to the coldness of the night, 28° Fahrenheit, made me think he would never see daylight, but I was mistaken. He woke me to ask if I did not smell coffee, and expressed the belief that a cup of that beverage would save his life, and that nothing else would. Not knowing there had been any coffee in camp for many days, I supposed a dream had carried him back to the cafes of St. Louis and New Orleans, and it was with some surprise I found my cook heating a cup of coffee over a small fire made of the sage. One of the most agreeable little offices performed in my life, and I believe in the cook's to whom the coffee belonged, was to pour this precious draught into the waning body of our friend Robideaux. His warmth returned, and with it hopes of life. In gratitude he gave me, what was then a great rarity, the half of a cake made of brown flour, almost black with dirt, and which had, for greater security, been hidden in the clothes of his Mexican servant, a man who scorned ablutions. I ate more than half without suspicion, when, on breaking a piece, the bodies of several of the most loathsome insects were exposed to my view. My hunger, however, overcame my fastidiousness, and the morceau did not appear particularly disgusting till after our arrival at San Diego, when several hearty meals had taken off the keenness of my appetite.

This day, December 9, the Kearny camp stayed upon its hill. As for the three scouts, they made what progress they might, unseen, through the *cañoncitos,* and at evening were within twelve miles of San Diego. Now they nerved themselves for another ordeal. At dusk they separated to attempt the settlement by three routes and thus triple the chance of success.

In San Diego Bay, on the frigate *Congress* and the sloop *Portsmouth* and the merchant vessels two bells were striking for the hour of nine, and in the town itself the Stockton relief force were just starting for a night march to rescue Kearny, when an outpost challenged and was answered by an Indian. It was the first of the three scouts — the Indian had won. He was taken to Stockton and scarcely had finished telling his story in Spanish when Lieutenant Beale was carried in, unable to walk. By the time Carson arrived, about three in the morning, last because to assure success he had taken the more roundabout course, the relief force had long been upon their way, and the Indian, exhausted, and Beale, partially out of his head, had been cared for by the surgeon.

Thus terminated what may be regarded as one of Kit Carson's greatest feats — a feat in which he was not alone, but in which he was rivaled by a sailor and an Indian. Although, without doubt, he would have got through by himself, and without doubt Lieutenant Beale, if alone, would have failed, lacking the mature advice and the example of woodcraft supplied by his more skilled companions, to me the chief merit of the feat lies in the fact that its incentives were not escape for themselves, but succor for their comrades. The danger was not so much capture (Pico seems to have been a kindly host, respecting bravery) as failure; and the chief sufferings to be feared were those which they did endure through thirst and cactus, and those which they would have endured had their efforts come to naught. That their tidings had preceded them does not lessen the merit of their performance.

Carson was disabled for several days; Beale was so broken that for more than a year he was not in good health; of the heroic Indian we hear naught. His was the

CARSON-BEALE TABLET
IN THE SMITHSONIAN INSTITUTION
(Courtesy of the Smithsonian Institution)

ROBERT F. STOCKTON

CARSON IN THE MEXICAN WAR

A WOOD CUT, PERHAPS HIS EARLIEST PUBLISHED
PICTURE, DATE, 1847

(From General Scott and his Staff, 1848)

burden of stoicism and anonymity. Back at the beleaguered camp on the hill Sergeant Cox had died from his wounds.

December 10 — The enemy attacked our camp, driving before them a band of wild horses, with which they hoped to produce a stampede. Our men behaved with admirable coolness, turning off the wild animals dexterously. Two or three of the fattest were killed in the charge, and formed, in the shape of a gravy-soup, an agreeable substitute for the poor steaks of our worn down brutes, on which we had been feeding for a number of days.

The surgeon announced that the wounded and ill were about ready for the saddle. Dependence could not be placed upon the scouts, who had not been heard from; and when the cache under the tree, where Burgess said the dispatch from Stockton was placed, was examined, no letter was found. This left the camp apparently without resource; and yielding to the importunities of his officers and men, General Kearny determined to cut his way to the coast, regardless of sacrifice.

By orders, all the baggage, even to the greatcoats, was burned; and on this, the evening of the 10th, the camp sought its hard beds. Again quoting Emory:

We were all reposing quietly, but not sleeping, waiting for the break of day, when we were to go down and give the enemy another defeat. One of the men, in the part of the camp assigned to my defense, reported that he heard a man speaking in English. In a few minutes we heard the tramp of a column, followed by the hail of a sentinel. It was a detachment of 100 tars and 80 marines under Lieutenant Gray, sent to meet us by Commodore Stockton, from whom we learned that Lieutenant Beale, Carson, and the Indian had arrived safely in San Diego. The detachment left San Diego on the night of the 9th, cached themselves during the day of the 10th, and joined us on the night of that day. These gallant fellows busied themselves till day distributing their provisions and clothes to our naked and hungry people.

The union of sailors and dragoons, revealed by morning, was a disagreeable surprise to Captain Pico. He withdrew his forces, the Americans marched down from their hill, and, gathering the abandoned cattle, proceeded on the road now open to San Diego and the sea.[126]

CHAPTER XXVI

THE RE-CONQUEST OF CALIFORNIA

AT THE hamlet of San Diego (" a few adobe houses, two or three of which only have plank floors ") Kit Carson, and presumably the forgotten Indian, speedily recovered, although for a day or so it was feared that Carson might lose his feet. Lieutenant Beale remained in a bad way.

Meanwhile Commodore Stockton carefully conserved his titulary position as commander in chief and governor in the province which he claimed by uncertain conquest, and in the north Lieutenant Colonel Fremont still marched at the rate of three to fifteen miles a day upon Los Angeles. In New Mexico a revolt kindred to one which upset the Stockton-Fremont plans was about to interrupt the Kearny pacification also; and in Old Mexico the Missouri volunteers of the noted Doniphan column, offshoot of the Army of the West, pressed another desert march into populous Chihuahua.

The principal news, of course, was war news; nevertheless amidst the roll of cannon, the clank of saber, and the creak of army wagon and pack mule leather could plainly be heard the crack of the emigrant's lash and the groaning lurch of his white-topped wagon. *A History of Texas; or, the Emigrants' Guide to the New Republic, by a Resident Emigrant* (New York, 1845), was a rival of Scott's *Tactics*, and itself was rivaled by the Oregon books of Robert Greenhow and C. G. Nicolay.[127] Upon the Overland Trail by the South Pass another new *vade mecum* was *The Emigrant's Guide to Oregon and California*, by L. W. Hastings of " Hastings' Cut-Off " — the Fremont-Kern byway of 1845 from Salt Lake to the Humboldt River. The last of two thousand emigrants by land were assailing the Sierra.

As to the mid-West, the Latter Day Saints, pressing forward from the new state of Iowa, were spending a hard winter among the Potawatomi at the edge of that Indian country beyond which lay a promised land; and six months more were to witness the Mormons marching in to accept old Jim Bridger's challenge of $1,000 for a car of corn from the Salt Lake valley.

But we are with Kit Carson at San Diego and our ways are not the ways of peace. He who traveled with Carson rarely lacked for action; and here in California there was still in the field, assisted by the Picos and Manuel Castro, the *ex tempore* governor, Jose Maria Flores, whose dictum read:

1. We, the inhabitants of the Department of California, as members of the great Mexican nation, declare that it is and has been our wish to belong to her alone, free and independent.

2. Consequently the authorities intended and named by the invading forces of the United States are held null and void.

3. All the North Americans being enemies of Mexico, we swear not to lay down our arms till they are expelled from the Mexican territory.[128]

On the morning of December 29, the allied forces of those rivals, the general and the commodore, marched for the north to meet Flores, to support Fremont, or to take Los Angeles, or all three. Carson accompanied as chief of scouts;[129] Beale was still on the disabled list in the sick bay of the *Congress* and a month was to elapse before he would be able even to hold a pen.

Fifty-seven dragoons out of the original 110; sixty riflemen Volunteers, 433 sailors and marines (forty-six of the tars being artillerists), three engineers, three medical officers, twenty-five Indians and Californians as teamsters, etc., made up the force of about 600 men, who were divided into four battalions, commanded by Captain Turner of the Dragoons, Captain Gillespie of the Volunteers and Lieutenants Renshaw and Zielin of the Navy. The battery of six pieces, " got up with great exertion, under the orders of Commodore Stockton," was commanded by Lieutenant Tilghman of the Navy; the wagon train " of one four-wheel carriage and ten ox-carts " was in charge of Lieutenant Minor of the Navy. The wheels of the carts being only two feet in diamater, and (*carreta* fashion) literally rough-hewn from cross sections of trees, the march was somewhat impeded.

Paralleling the romantic highway of the fathers — the *Camino Real*, which connected the missions, but which was not by any means the smoothly traveled highway that the title, " Royal Road " implies — in the form of a square termed by the sailors a " Yankee corral " (baggage in the center, artillery at the four corners), the column marched laboriously, taking ten days to cover 125 miles. Sometimes in sight of the surf, sometimes not within sound of it, up one sandy hill and down another whereon the grass was already sprouting, and amidst occasional ranch patches, past the abandoned missions of San Luis Rey de Francia and San Juan Capistrano, proceeded the toiling *Americanos,* until on the afternoon of January 8 the Californians, under Flores himself, assisted by his colonels, Andres Pico and Jose Antoine Carrillo, gave the battle with artillery and 500 cavalry, at the Rio San Gabriel.

With skirmishers out, in the face of cannon muzzles ranged point blank along the opposite high bank only 100 yards distant, the Americans dragged their pieces across the knee-deep current and through quicksands, into counter battery, and now, " very brisk in firing," protected the crossing of the wagons and cattle. The grape and ball of the enemy, directed from the bank beyond, for the most part sped too high. Californian cavalry, which had been showing their heads on right and left, suddenly charged the American rear (the favorite Mexican lancer practice) but were repulsed. Another furious but ineffectual charge or two, a counter charge (afoot), and the battle of San Gabriel, January 8, 1847, was won.

The Californians then withdrew a short distance, while the Americans camped on the field. But when on the morning of January 9 the Kearny-Stockton forces looked about them, the Californians had vanished from the hill. The Americans marched across the mesa of the angle between the San Gabriel and the Fernando (Los Angeles) rivers. The Californians were awaiting them. Says Emory:

> Here Flores addressed his men, and called on them to make one more charge; expressed his confidence in their ability to break our line; said that yesterday he had been deceived in supposing that he was fighting soldiers.

Flores fired at long range with his nine-pounders on the right. The Americans did not reply, or halt except for a moment. Los Angeles was only a few miles before.

Flores sallied and made a " horseshoe in our front "; his cannon extended on the points of the right and the left. The Americans marched into the horseshoe, silenced the nine-pounders on the right flank, received with deadly carbines and rifles a charge on the left flank, and another charge on the rear; with a round of grape completed the discomforture of the enemy; and while considering that this was but the beginning of a good fight, found that it was the end!

It was now about three o'clock, and the town, known to contain great quantities of wine and aguardiente, was four miles distant. From previous experience of the difficulty of controlling men when entering towns, it was determined to cross the river San Fernando, halt there for the night, and enter the town in the morning, with the whole day before us. The distance today, 6.2 miles.

And so passed the battle of Los Angeles, January 9, 1847, ✓ the final battle in the re-conquest of fair ·California. On the morning of January 10 the capitulation of Los Angeles was accepted, and Captain Gillespie " raised again the banner which four months before he had lowered."

From the north Fremont, having in one black, rainy Christmas lost among the ravines a hundred horses and mules, on January 11 defiled upon the plain of San Fernando, twenty miles north from Los Angeles. To him, the third party, fell the spoils; and if there was anything in " Fremont luck," he here sipped of the last savory cup that fate had in store for him through many a month to come; for to him, at the *rancho* Cahuenga, January 13, Andres Pico and Jose Antonio Carrillo engaged to " deliver up their artillery and public arms " and to " assist and aid in placing the country in a state of peace and tranquillity." In return Fremont guaranteed them " protection of life and property " and permission to leave the country " without let or hindrance."

So much for the Treaty of Couenga, made, as protests that army martinet, Colonel Philip St. George Cooke, by Lieutenant Colonel Fremont " with enemies he had never met, in a camp twelve miles from the capital and headquarters of two superiors in rank and civil authority, who had recently fought and defeated them." And albeit Commodore Stockton was properly annoyed, and General Kearny was properly astonished, the measure was ratified. After all, the Fremont way, if not the orthodox way of negotiating with alleged rebels who had broken their paroles, was the best and shortest way between the two points of war and peace.

On January 14 Lieutenant Colonel Fremont and his hardy battalion marched into the Ciudad de los Angeles; and Kit

Carson had the opportunity of again meeting his old commander.

On January 16 Lieutenant Colonel Fremont became, by virtue of Commander in Chief Stockton's proclamation, Governor and Commander in Chief of the territory of California, Upper and Lower, "until the President of the United States shall otherwise direct." · The California Battalion stuck by their colonel; and on January 18 General Kearny, impotent in his rival governorship, took his few men and his ox carts back to San Diego, whither went, at the same time, the triumphant Commodore Stockton, with his sailors and marines "to sail as soon as possible for the coast of Mexico, where I hope they will give a good account of themselves." At the same time the new Commander in Chief by sea, Commodore W. B. Shubrick, was approaching Monterey with dispatches which would break the deadlock. Meanwhile in Taos and its environs was coming to a head that bloody revolt of January 19 which was to kill Carson's best friend and imperil his wife. But of this impending horror Carson was to be, for at least sixty days, utterly ignorant. He remained at Los Angeles with Fremont, who, *persona grata* to the Californians, whom he well understood, had taken up his governorship of less than two troubled months.

CHAPTER XXVII

CARSON ACROSS THE CONTINENT — 1847

IT MAY have been fortunate for Kit Carson that at this time of conflict of military and civil authorities among the *conquistadors* he was detached again upon express duty with dispatches for Washington. He started February 25, accompanied by Lieutenant Beale, with dispatches from Fremont for Senator Benton at St. Louis, for the President and the Departments at Washington, and for the Fremont family, wherever they chanced to be. Lieutenant Emory was meanwhile hastening by way of Panama with Kearny's dispatches, and Lieutenant Gray of the Navy with Stockton's dispatches. Commodore W. Branford Shubrick had been a month at Monterey, there by Washington authority to assume the chief command — a command only nominal, however, until fresh dispatches confirmed it. In the sarcastic words of Lieutenant Colonel Cooke of the Mormon Battalion (also arrived):

General Kearny is supreme — somewhere up the coast; Colonel Fremont is supreme at Pueblo de Los Angeles; Commodore Stockton is "Commander-in-Chief" at San Diego; Commodore Shubrick, the same at Monterey; and I, at San Luis Rey; and we are all supremely poor; the government having no money and no credit; and we hold the Territory because Mexico is poorest of all.[130]

Kit Carson is well out of this mess; and he will be doubly blessed if he does not, like a vessel in a typhoon, run into the other side of it at Washington.

Lieutenant Beale is still much the worse for wear. He

must have come up on the *Cyane* from San Diego to San Pedro of Los Angeles, thence to be invalided East. Says Carson:

During the first twenty days of our journey, he was so weak that I had to lift him on and off his riding animal. I did not think for some time that he could live; but I bestowed as much care and attention on him as any one could have done under the circumstances. Before the fatiguing and dangerous part of our route was passed over, he had so far recovered as to be able to take care of himself. For my attention (which was only my duty) to my friend, I was doubly repaid by the kindness shown to me by his family while I stayed in Washington, which was more than I had any reason for expecting, and which will never be forgotten by me.[181]

Save for a slight attack by Indians on the Gila, Carson's journey by desert trail was uneventful. A delay of ten days was occasioned at Santa Fe, where, from the new Fort Marcy, " our glorious flag, with its graceful stripes, playing in the wind," kept watch over the old, flat-roofed capital. But here arriving after forty days of travel from the California frontier, Kit Carson must have speedily lost interest in the change which had taken place in local affairs. If he had anticipated meeting Governor Charles Bent and receiving news of wife and children, he was disappointed. Governor Charles Bent was dead — murdered by his own townspeople and neighbors; and the womenfolk of the Taos home had barely escaped. Following the massacre, troops, regular and volunteer, had stormed the Taos pueblo, shattered the ancient church, scattered the defenders, captured both Indian and Mexican alleged ringleaders, and hanged them, as fast as tried and condemned, at the outskirts of the excited town.

The news had in it every element to shock even so hardened a fighter as Carson: it concerned family, friend, and acquaintance, and revealed barbaric depths all unsuspected.

For the Pueblos, particularly the Taos Pueblos, had been inoffensive during more than 100 years.

The tale as it has come down to me through the one eye-witness living,[132] and probably as it was told to Kit Carson, when, impatient of delays, he galloped in (three months late for the revenge which he regretted all his life had been delegated to others), is this:

Even before Charles Bent, governor of less than three months, started, January 14, 1847, from Santa Fe, his official quarters, upon his last ride to visit wife and children at his home in San Fernandez de Taos, one conspiracy by a Mexican clique against all Americans and American sympathizers had been exposed, and the governor had been warned that another was brewing. Nevertheless, fearless and singularly credulous for a man who had lived twenty years among such an unstable people, he went to Taos, and with him went a company of five other Taosans.

Don Carlos, the American governor, and his party arrived at Taos on the second day, which was January 16. Even yet grace of three days remained, for the fateful date was January 19. But Governor Bent had said: " I am not afraid. When they [the Mexicans and Pueblos] have been hungry, I have fed them; when they have been sick, I have attended them. Why should they harm me, their friend? "

Thus his doom was sealed by himself. Just before eight o'clock on the morning of January 19, while yet Taos was scarcely astir (for New Mexican villagers are not early risers), the Bent home was aroused by a tumult in the dusty, crooked street outside. Mexican threats, and wild shouts and chants, and the Bent name sounded above the shuffle of feet. Scarcely had Mrs. Bent called in alarm, and the governor sprung from his couch, when the wooden door of the entrance to the *patio* was burst in, and headed by Tomasito Romero, *alcalde* of the Indians at the pueblo three miles from the village, over the door poured the mob

— Mexicans, Taos Pueblos, with a few Apaches, a Delaware desperado, and other strays.

In the house, a one-story adobe structure continuous with a row of similar dwellings, were the governor, his wife, who had been the Señorita Maria Ignacia Jaramillo, Kit Carson's wife (left in safe keeping), who had been the Señorita Josefa Jaramillo, Mrs. Thomas O. Boggs, who was stepdaughter of the governor and the wife of his nephew (a trader from a famous Missouri frontier family), and the Bent children: a company of one man, three women, and three children, the eldest of whom was ten years.

The clamorous mob beat upon a door of the house, and the governor opened to them. They surged upon the threshold. He faced them boldly, while behind him cowered the women and children. A bullet struck him in the chin.

" What do you want, my friends? " he asked.

" We want your head! We want your *gringo* head! "

Already the *insurrectos* had killed on his own doorstep the sheriff, Stephen Lee, and the prefect (pure-blood Mexican but an American adherent), Cornelio Vigil of the Jaramillo connections. These two men had been of the Bent company which left Santa Fe January 14. Governor Bent may have but dimly realized that murder had been committed. However, he fully realized that murder was inevitable; and he resolved to be the propitiatory sacrifice to the Moloch of savagery.

Mrs. Bent, now at his side, alternately pleaded with him either to fight or to escape by a back way, and with the mob to spare him. In another room Mrs. Carson and Mrs. Boggs were digging frantically with poker and iron spoon to make a hole through the adobe wall into the adjoining house. And little Alfred Bent, aged ten, lugging a shotgun, took his stand by his father's side and said:

" Papa, let us die like men."

The governor now was bleeding from other wounds by

arrows and slings. The mob was pressing close, too close for effective work, but were awed by the steady front of this one man. However, upon the roof of poles and mud, eager hands, coppery and hairy, were chopping with axes.

Escape for Governor Bent was impossible. No Mexican would dare to shelter him who was the chief prospective victim. And knowing this, he refused to flee; knowing more than this, he refused to fight. Too well was he versed in Indian character. His pistols were thrust into his hands, but he declined them.

" They wish my death. That is all. If I resist they will kill every one of us," he explained. " I must not imperil my women and children."

Through the window and from the housetops behind the mob, missiles were showering upon him; at the roof, which was the ceiling, hands were chopping and tearing. But now the hole in the division wall was hacked through. The governor, sorely spent, heard the dear voices calling to him, and left his post. For a brief instant he and his were by themselves in that inner room; but even while the mob raged beyond the thin door separating life and death, he calmly insisted that the women and the children enter first through the hole. They did. They heard the mob crash into the room which the governor was still occupying; and presently he came feebly crawling through, scalped and holding his hand to his gory head.

The house in which refuge had been sought was the dwelling of a Canadian, whose Mexican wife was the only inmate at home. Of course she could do naught to aid the fugitives. By the windows, by the hole in the wall, and by a hole in the ceiling, into the haven rushed the murderers, mad with blood-lust. Amidst the screams of the women and children the governor tried to write a message on a piece of paper; he held up his hands in defense, and they were slashed down; he still survived long enough to pluck two or three arrows from his face; and then shot in the face by a pistol at close range, he died. After that his head was hacked off.[133]

The mob left, parading through the town his gray scalp, stretched with brass tacks on a board. Other victims were Pablo Jaramillo, brother-in-law of Bent and Carson; J. W. Leal, ranger and circuit attorney, and third companion of the governor upon the ride from Santa Fe, now also scalped alive; and even Narcisso Beaubien, son of Judge Charles Beaubien, brother-in-law of Lucien Maxwell, and just home from five years of college at Cape Girardeau below St. Louis. He had hidden himself under a heap of straw, and had evaded the search. But a woman servant in the family, spying him, called to the departing questors: "*Ven'!* Kill the young ones and they will never be men to trouble us!" So back hastened the crowd, slew him and scalped him. His mother was of the country.

All this did Kit learn, spurring in too late even to see the hangings. He learned that his wife, Mrs. Bent, and Mrs. Boggs had escaped so narrowly that they barely saved their lives, and took only the clothing they wore; that General Elliott Lee, of St. Louis, visiting his brother, the murdered sheriff, had been saved only by the firm stand of a priest; that at the Arroyo Hondo settlement, twelve miles northwest, after a brave defense, the hospitable miller and retired mountain man, Simeon Turley, and six mountain men friends, had been killed; that at the Mora (future home of Ceran St. Vrain) had been murdered eight other American "foreigners" including Lawrence Waldo of the Santa Fe trade Waldos; and that on their way to Taos with beaver pelts two other trappers, William Howard and that Markhead for whom Carson had received a Blackfeet bullet in the shoulder, also had been foully slain, by their Mexican companions.

He heard, too, with added items, how Charles Townes of the 1843 Fremont expedition had escaped, the only resident

American to do so — hurrying by night from Taos on the back of a swift mule supplied him by his Mexican father-in-law, to carry the news to Santa Fe; how over the mountains, by forced march in dead of winter, there had pushed to the relief of the place the hastily mustered troops of Colonel Sterling Price — a detachment of sixty-seven men being volunteers under Ceran St. Vrain as captain, lucky Ceran St. Vrain, whom only apparent accident placed in Santa Fe that bloody day, instead of at his customary home in Taos.

He learned how the revolutionary forces, 1,500 strong, were met the next day, January 24, at the pass of La Cañada (Santa Cruz) on the Taos trail, twenty-five miles north of Santa Fe, and were defeated; how, reinforced to 480 men by the gallant Captain Burgwin of the First Dragoons (coming all the way from Albuquerque), the Price column had pressed on, cleared the pass at Embudo, and on February 3; "exhausted and half frozen, reached Fernandez de Taos to find that the insurgents had fortified themselves in the Pueblo de Taos " — the warriors occupying the massy old church.

He heard how the determined little army paused before the stronghold; how for two hours they vainly battered the church; how by morning the canny Colonel Price and his young staff had evolved their plan of battle; how the combat was renewed; how from two sides bellowed the cannon; how by noon no appreciable damage had been wreaked; how the soldiers now charged with ladders and axes; how they hewed and clung, throwing shells by hand, firing the thatched roof, repelled by bullet and arrow and lance, so that the scene was one of the Middle Ages; how the storming column of the First Dragoons recoiled from the church door, their captain, the lamented Burgwin, mortally stricken by a ball from the musket of the renegade Delaware, " Big Nigger "; how now the sun was past the meridian, and while the Pueblos and the few Mexicans still defended desperately, although with waning strength, another storming column, led by Lieutenant Joseph McIlvaine, assailed with axes, chipping at the thick wall itself; how at three o'clock a breach was effected, at which battered from sixty yards the six-pounder howitzer; how all the air was heavy with the reek of the fight, and how, amidst it, run up to within ten yards, the howitzer poured shell and grape through the breach; how "the mingled noise of bursting shells, firearms, the yells of the Americans, and the shrieks of the wounded, was most appalling"; how at last through breaches and door burst the grimy soldiers, to find the church filled with smoke but almost empty of human beings; how the Pueblos, leaping from the gallery, were streaming for their *casas grandes* and for the Sacred Mountain behind; and how, thus in the open, they were savagely picked off, fifty-one out of fifty-four or five, by the mounted riflemen under vengeful St. Vrain and Captain Slack; and how to the rifle of Ceran St. Vrain himself fell the Mexican ringleader, Pablo Chaves, wearing at the time Charles Bent's shirt and coat.[134]

He was told how, with 150 dead and with the living disheartened by the failure of their religion, new or old, to protect them, the Pueblos the next morning, "bearing white flags, crucifixes and images," sued for mercy; how it was granted upon condition that they deliver over the chief Tomasito; how the Mexican conspirator, Pablo Montoya, — self-styled "the Santa Ana of the North" — was captured and hanged three days thereafter, on February 7, in the Fernandez plaza; how, at the civil trial, the Señoras Bent, Carson, and Boggs were the chief witnesses; how the Señora Bent with steady finger pointed to the murderer of her husband, and how a Missourian guard placed over the prisoners at the *calabozo* deliberately shot Tomasito; how six of the prisoners were hanged on April 9, near the jail

TAOS PUEBLO

REMAINS OF THE OLD CHURCH BATTERED BY PRICE'S CANNON

(*Photograph by the author*)

CROSSING THE PLAINS

EMIGRANTS FOR OREGON AND CALIFORNIA

(From Bowles' Our New West)

BRIDGER'S FORT

CELEBRATED EMIGRANT AND TRADER STATION ON THE OVERLAND TRAIL, AND
MANAGED BY JIM BRIDGER

(From Stansbury's Exploration of the Great Salt Lake)

at the edge of town; and how nine more, four Indians and five Mexicans, were to hang April 30.

All this, and more, did Kit Carson hear; for he had been from home a year and nine months. However, little was there for him to do now; and as a soldier he must get his dispatches through. It is evident that he arrived at Taos between the two wholesale hangings; for in the middle of April we find him descending along the Purgatoire of the Taos Trail to Bent's Fort; and on the evening of April 20 (about) he is here encountered by Louis Garrard, who is just from the tragedies at Fernandez.

Carson was now traveling on horses, posthaste after his delays. On May 6, at the mouth of the Purgatoire, fourteen miles below the Bent post, Mr. Ruxton, en route with a government train to the States, records:

> At this camp we were joined by six or seven of Fremont's men, who had accompanied Kit Carson from California; but, their animals "giving out" here, had remained behind to recruit them.

It must have been after leaving Bent's Fort that Carson had a skirmish with the Pawnees, who frequented the plains and not the mountain country; and we know, by the fact of Carson having been met by the Garrard camp on the upper Purgatoire, that he was taking the mountain branch of the Santa Fe Trail, via Taos. As for the skirmish itself, all we know is by the pen of Ruxton — that the Santa Fe Trail down the Arkansas was infested by Pawnees; that in this preceding winter a government train had been attacked; and that the Pawnees " had likewise lately attacked a party under Kit Carson, the celebrated mountaineer, who was carrying dispatches from Colonel Fremont to the government of the United States."

But the Carson chronicles are silent as to the Pawnee " scrimmage "; and within thirty days, or before the end of May, armed with the Fremont encomium — "With me, Carson and truth mean the same thing. He is always the same, gallant and disinterested," — Carson was at St. Louis, where Senator Benton received him hospitably. The senator carefully perused the personal letter from Fremont, (the governor already deposed), obtained from the messenger sundry statements to be used later, and, forwarding to the President both epistle and messenger, instructed the latter to make the Benton home in Washington his quarters.

At St. Louis, also, Carson was in line to receive sincere compliments upon the celerity with which he had traveled — he having made the overland trip from the coast, "notwithstanding the inclemency of the season, and an unavoidable detention at Santa Fe, in a shorter time [so states a personal sketch of him, in 1848] than it was ever before accomplished." He had left on the 25th of February, and had arrived in the middle of May.

The dispatch bearer continued with Lieutenant Beale and probably Lieutenant Talbot. The route from St. Louis doubtless was the route taken next year by that other mountain man and messenger, Joe Meek, envoy from Oregon, bearing another tale of massacre and a call for protection. From St. Louis to Washington City was a ten-days' journey, and inasmuch as (according to the Polk memorandum upon the back of the Benton letter) Carson delivered his dispatches June 8, he must have left St. Louis about the last of May. From St. Louis the popular and doubtless the shortest road to Washington was by boat down the Mississippi, up the Ohio to Pittsburg; thence by stage southeast up the valley of the Youghiogheny and over the Allegheny Mountains, 125 miles to Cumberland, just below the Maryland line; from there by the enterprising Baltimore & Ohio Railroad 170 miles to Relay Station, eight miles below Baltimore, then on by the Washington branch, 31 miles south to the national capital.

Mrs. John C. Fremont, daughter of Colonel Benton, and wife of the distinguished explorer, was in attendance at the railroad depot when the train of cars in which Kit Carson was traveling arrived in Washington. It was quite late in the evening when he reached the terminus of his journey; yet, notwithstanding this, Kit had hardly landed on the platform of the depot before he was addressed by a lady who said that she knew him from her husband's descriptions of him, and that he must accept the hospitalities of her father's house.[185]

This Carson did — glad, naturally, to be afforded a haven amidst surroundings so utterly strange to him. He had none of the Joe Meek bravado and audacity which made that erratic individual glory in his wild-man character and put up at the fashionable Coleman House, where he ordered antelope steak! The Fremont and Benton household was Carson's anchorage; and according to Fremont, his " modesty and gentleness quickly made him a place in the regard of the family, to whom he gave back a lasting attachment."
The partial seclusion afforded by the Benton home must have been doubly appreciated by Carson, because he was doubly embarrassed by the new environment in which he found himself, here in the focus not only of the country's rank and fashion, but also of the country's gaze. His name had preceded him; and the fame thereof abashed him. He encountered himself in the new guise of a mighty hero. The Fremont reports of the first two exploring expeditions had spread Carson's name farther than he had any adequate idea, for he was by nature mild and unimaginative and by training matter-of-fact. The one recital by Fremont of that one deed, when on the journey homeward from California, in the spring of 1844, Carson and Godey made a bold desert ride to avenge the Fuentes camp, would have been sufficient to emblazon upon the mind of the East his alliterative name. This would have given the newspapers their cue; and since those expeditions he had been mentioned in Fremont letters

to Senator Benton and more briefly in dispatches; and frequently, with varying degrees of fact and fiction, in chronicles filling the press. Moreover, the California Battalion in the Bear Flag war and in the conquest immediately succeeding had, by June, 1847, become historic.

But now here he was, himself, Kit Carson, the mountaineer and guide, overland from Los Angeles and able to tell not only of events there, and (if he were not wise) of the controversy impending, but also of the bloody insurrection in New Mexico.

The newspapers of Washington, Boston, New York, and Philadelphia did their best, in their journalistic style so carefully pedantic, so refreshing as compared with the hotly eager style of today, to make of Kit Carson and his arrival a story; but I do not find that he was awarded any scare heads. The East was still conservative toward the West — that West which for the East existed only vaguely.

Thus in June of 1847 Kit Carson, from the far West, first experienced the conventionalities of the far East. He would re-visit the East — Washington, Boston, New York — time and again; and an eastern trip will be made twenty years after this initial venture, almost the last act of his life. But during these twenty years he will have grown accustomed to travel amidst cities, and to being lionized.

Aside from the pleasure in the friendship of the Bentons and Fremonts and Beales, and probably of the Talbots, one other recognition in Washington of his services must have greatly gratified Kit Carson. On June 8 he delivered to the President his dispatches and the Benton letter; on June 9 he was appointed by President Polk second lieutenant in the young regiment of the United States Mounted Riflemen; soon thereafter he was assigned to duty again in California, and was ordered thither with dispatches.

Lieutenant Beale accompanied him westward as far as St. Louis; there he was too ill to continue and had to stop off. Lieutenant Carson improved the opportunity afforded by this return trip, in the summer of 1847, and according to Mr. George H. Carson, his nephew, " visited all his relatives in Howard County. I remember him very well, it being the first time that we had met, he having left Missouri three years before I was born."

From St. Louis and Howard County Lieutenant Carson proceeded up to Fort Leavenworth; reported, and with a company of fifty recruits for the reinforcement of the needy Colonel Sterling Price at Santa Fe, set out along the Santa Fe Trail, into his own country.

He took the desert route, this time, which at the crossing of the Arkansas diverges from that guiding river for the dry march, or drive, over the arid stretch of the plains of the Cimarron in New Mexico. At Point of Rocks, only 160 miles this side of Santa Fe, he caught up with a company of Lieutenant Maloney's, escorting a supply train for Santa Fe. Here occurred a small brush with the Comanches, who attempted to run off the Maloney stock — and partially failed only because they ran *into* the Carson camp. As it was, the Indians, the boldest horsemen of the plains, succeeded in getting away with twenty-seven of the Maloney horses and two of the Carson.

At Santa Fe Carson (so asserts the not altogether reliable Burdett) met his wife; and by this I suspect that, at the forking off of the Taos branch of the trail, he may have detached an express for his home place; or he may have sent on word ahead, from Missouri, recounting his new prospects.

At Santa Fe his volunteers were delivered to their station; and here Carson found awaiting him not only his wife but fifteen mountain men of his celebrated Taos forty-five. Strengthened by these, he pushed ahead for California; but, if we may believe Peters, not by the southern trail of the Gila, where perhaps he feared that Indians, instigated by refugees from Mexico and California, might be awaiting the passage of travelers. Moreover, the Gila Trail had been devastated of grass and wood by the marches of the dragoons and the Mormons.

His course lay northwest by the Spanish Trail, cutting across southwestern Colorado into Utah and down through the Fillmore and Sevier Lake country to the trapper-christened Virgin River.

On the Muddy River, tributary of the Virgin, in southeastern Nevada, his party unexpectedly rode into a camp of 300 Indians, treacherously inclined, who, however, by threats and leveled rifles were made to keep their distance. Carson, knowing Indian character, repeated his success of 1830, when on the Gila, south, he had likewise to clear the camp of undesirable neighbors. Now, as before, he gave the savages a limited time within which to move away; when, after the time had expired, several still lingered as if to test his nerve, he ordered his men to fire. One Indian was killed; three or four wounded. Such prompt action brought success.

When Lieutenant Carson of the United States Mounted Rifles arrived in Los Angeles he found the aspect of affairs changed. A new dynasty reigned; the troubled waters were smooth. Colonel Richard B. Mason, of the famous First Dragoons, was governor of California and commander in chief upon land; upon sea, Commodore James Biddle, the veteran of almost fifty years' naval service, succeeded Commodore Shubrick; " Fighting Bob " Stockton had gone to Washington voluntarily to submit his defense in the Kearny-Stockton-Fremont imbroglio, to repair his political fences, to resign from the navy, and to be United States senator from New Jersey; Lieutenant Colonel John C. Fremont had on June 14, 1847, at Sutter's Fort, or New Helvetia, received from Monterey the following order from Kearny:

CARSON'S COMMISSION

AS SECOND LIEUTENANT, U. S. MOUNTED RIFLES, JUNE, 1847. SIGNED BY
PRESIDENT POLK

*(Courtesy of K. M. Chapman, from original in the New Mexico
Historical Society collection)*

GOVERNOR CHARLES BENT

FIRST TERRITORIAL GOVERNOR OF NEW MEXICO, ASSASSINATED AT
TAOS, JANUARY, 1847

*(From oil painting in possession of his daughter, Mrs. Teresina
Scheurich, of Taos)*

I shall leave here on Wednesday, the 16th instant, and I require of you to be with your topographical party in my camp (which will probably be fifteen miles from here), on the evening of that day, and to continue with me to Missouri.

Fremont suffered the ignominy of being assigned to the rear of the Kearny column, with instructions not to camp at more than a mile interval; and, at Fort Leavenworth, had been relieved of his government property and ordered to report, under arrest, to the adjutant general at Washington.

At Los Angeles Kit Carson, finding no one to whom to report, was directed to the strange governor, already in office three months, and last of the line of four American commander governors of 1847. To Colonel Mason at Monterey he delivered his dispatches, and was assigned for dragoon recruiting service under Lieutenant (Captain?) Andrew Smith Johnson of Colonel Cooke's Mormon Battalion.

Next we find Lieutenant Carson transferred to a command of his own and to a service probably more agreeable: that of guarding Tejon Pass, ninety miles north of Los Angeles. Smuggling and predatory bands of Indians and Mexicans were wont to travel a trail here between the desert on the east and the Los Angeles country on the southwest. Carson's business was to examine manifests and packs, and to curb the illegal traffic. At Tejon Pass, therefore, where for a brief space was the United States post of Fort Tejon, he spent a not unpleasant winter.

CHAPTER XXVIII

"A RIDE WITH KIT CARSON" — 1848

WRITING home from Monterey, young Lieutenant
William Tecumseh Sherman, of the Third United
States Light Artillery, which after a long voyage around
the Horn had finally arrived in port January 28, on the
man-of-war *Lexington*, refers as follows to a Carson trip
eastward:

> Monterey, Calif., April 10, 1848. — The time is rapidly
> approaching when Lieut. Carson, the Kit Carson of Fremont's
> narratives, will start for home. He goes from Los Angeles
> to Santa Fe, and thence to Saint Louis, where he will put his
> mail in the Post Office, a long and rough route to entrust papers
> to, but letters have come that way and may possibly go
> again.[136]

Of Carson's trip we fortunately have full account, from
the sprightly pen of Lieutenant G. Douglas Brewerton, late
of the Seventh New York Volunteers, who accompanied
Carson and who later proved himself to be a journalist the
equal of the more famous Albert D. Richardson, another
chronicler of a "ride with Kit Carson." [137]

The trail opened from Los Angeles, headquarters, where
Lieutenant Brewerton waited to take advantage of the Carson escort. He was "beginning to weary of the comparatively idle life which we were leading," when

> a friend informed me that Carson had arrived and would
> shortly join our party at the mess-room. The name of this
> celebrated mountaineer had become in the ears of Americans
> residing in California a familiar household word; and I had
> frequently listened to wild tales of daring feats which he had
> performed. . . .

The Kit Carson of my *imagination* was over six feet high
— a sort of modern Hercules in his build — with an enormous
beard, and a voice like a roused lion, whose talk was all of
" Stirring incidents by flood and field."
The *real* Kit Carson I found to be a plain, simple, unostenta-
tious man; rather below the medium height, with brown, curling hair, little or no beard, and a voice as soft and gentle as a
woman's. In fact, the hero of a hundred desperate encounters,
whose life had been mostly spent amid wildernesses, where the
white man is almost unknown, was one of Dame Nature's
gentlemen — a sort of article which she gets up occasionally,
but nowhere in better style than among the backwoods of
America.

Evidently it was Carson's way, born of experience, not
to assume the responsibilities of the trail before he was prepared to meet them. Only a tenderfoot relies on luck or
bravado to see him through; and the longer a woodsman,
plainsman, mountain man, or seaman follows his profession,
the greater care does he take to anticipate emergencies.
Consequently Carson had gone into camp at Bridge Creek,
fifteen miles from Los Angeles, where he assembled his
men and animals. Brewerton continues:

Many of these men were noted woodsmen, old companions
of Carson in his explorations with Fremont; while others,
again, were almost as ignorant of mountain life as myself;
knowing nothing of the mysteries of a pack-saddle, and keeping at a most respectful distance from the heels of a kicking
mule.

Lieutenant Brewerton joined Carson in the camp of
instruction; several weeks were spent in hardening the green
men and the animals. Camp was broken May 2, and moved
to Los Angeles, whence the start was to be made May 4.

In the interval we employed ourselves in making our final
preparations; drawing rations and ammunition for our men, and

dividing our provisions into bags of equal size and weight for the greater convenience of packing. The stores provided for our own mess (which had been increased to four in number by the addition of an old man, a friend of Carson's, and a citizen returning to the States), consisted of pork, coffee, brown sugar, " penole " and " atole."

Atole is a kind of meal which when prepared forms a very nutritious dish not unlike "mush" * * *. Penole is made by parching Indian corn; then grinding it, and mixing it with cinnamon and molasses. This condiment is almost invaluable to the travelers in the wilderness of the far West; as it requires no fire to cook it, being prepared at a moment's warning by simply mixing it with cold water. It has the further advantage of occupying but little space in proportion to its weight; but when prepared for use, it swells so as nearly to double in quantity. A very small portion is therefore sufficient to satisfy the cravings of hunger. In addition to these matters, we carried for our private consumption a small quantity of dried meat; this is also obtained from the Mexicans, who cut the beef into long strips and then hang it upon a line, exposing it to the influence of the sun and wind until it is thoroughly hardened. * * * Beef prepared in this way * * * is generally sold by the Mexican *vara* or yard.

On May 4 the cavalcade set out from the Pueblo de los Angeles, which Kit Carson was not to see again for half a dozen years. The mules were well laden and the Carson saddlebags stuffed with soldier letters for " home."

We numbered twenty hired men, three citizens, and three Mexican servants, besides Carson and myself, all well mounted and armed for the most part with " Whitney's rifle," a weapon which I cannot too strongly recommend for every description of frontier service, from its great accuracy and little liability to get out of order — an important point in a country where no gunsmith can be found.

Starting thus for the States, Kit Carson left behind him an Alta California pacified, with the Californians and the Fremont riflemen alike settled down to the pursuits of quiet citizenship. But on the American Fork above Sutter's Mill gold had been discovered almost four months and California was on the verge of bursting into a flame which would spread like a prairie fire throughout the whole civilized world. Just in advance of it rode Kit Carson (the news reached Monterey May 29, and reached Los Angeles soon after), his back to possible fortune, his face to further fame. Yet in this he was favored, for it is doubtful if after another month he could have held in his train a corporal's guard.

The trail from Los Angeles led past the preliminary camp at Bridge Creek and over the " Great Pass " (which doubtless was the Cajon Pass, by which the railroad today crosses the Sierre Madre 'twixt desert and interior California) for the Mohave Desert and the Spanish Trail. The first stages were without event, save accidents to poor packs, the overtaking of a trading caravan, and our tenderfoot lieutenant's trials with his muleteer.

I have heretofore briefly mentioned my Mexican servant Juan, to whom Carson had given so indifferent a character. This scapegrace had for some days shown a disposition to give trouble in various ways; but we had come to no open rupture until one afternoon, when riding in the advance, I looked back and observed the *reata* of my pack-mule dragging upon the ground. Calling Juan to secure it, I rode on, thinking that my orders had been attended to. Now it so happened at that particular moment that Señor Juan was engaged with the assistance of a Mexican friend and his cigarrito in making himself exceedingly comfortable; and upon again turning my head I found my *reata* in a worse way than before. " Now," said Kit, " that fellow is trying which is to be the master, you or he, and I should advise you to give him a lesson which he will remember; if we were nearer the settlements I would not recommend it, for he would certainly desert and carry your animals with him; but as it is, he will not dare to leave the party, for fear of Indians." As I fully concurred in Carson's opinion, and felt moreover that the period had arrived for bringing up Señor Juan with the " round turn " I had mentally promised him, I simply rode back, and without any particular explanation knocked the fellow off his mule. It was the first lesson and the last that I found it necessary to read him. Juan gave me, it is true, a most diabolical look upon remounting, which made me careful of my pistols for a night or two afterward; but he was conquered, and in future I had no reason to complain of any negligence.

*   *   *   *   *   *   *   *   *   *

Our daily routine of life in the desert had a sort of terrible sameness about it; we rode from fifteen to fifty miles a day, according to the distance from water; occasionally after a long drive halting for twenty-four hours, if the scanty grass near the camping grounds would permit it, to rest and recruit our weary cattle; among our men there was but little talking and less laughing and joking, even by the camp-fire, while traversing these dreary wastes; the gloomy land by which we were surrounded, scanty food, hard travel, and the consciousness of continual peril, all tended to restrain the exhibition of animal spirits. Carson while traveling, scarcely spoke; his keen eye was continually examining the country, and his whole manner was that of a man deeply impressed with a sense of responsibility. We ate but twice a day, and then our food was so coarse and scanty, that it was not a pleasure, but a necessity. At night every care was taken to prevent surprise; the men took turns in guarding the animals, while our own mess formed the camp guard of the party.

*   *   *   *   *   *   *   *   *   *

During this journey I often watched with great curiosity Carson's preparations for the night. A braver man than Kit perhaps never lived, in fact I doubt if he ever knew what fear was, but with all this he exercised great caution. While arranging his bed, his saddle, which he always used as a pillow, was disposed in such a manner as to form a barricade for his head; his pistols, half cocked, were laid above it, and his trusty rifle reposed beneath the blanket by his side, where it was not only ready for instant use, but perfectly protected from the damp. Except now and then to light his pipe, you never caught Kit exposing himself to the full glare of the camp fire. He knew too well the treacherous character of the tribes among whom we were traveling; he had seen men killed at night by an unseen foe, who, veiled in darkness, stood in perfect security while he marked and shot down the mountaineer clearly seen by the firelight. " No, no, boys," Kit would say; " hang round the fire if you will; it may do for you if you like it, but I do n't want to have a Digger slip an arrow into me, when I can't see him."

*   *   *   *   *   *   *   *   *   *

When the hour for our departure from camp had nearly arrived, Kit would arise from his blanket and cry " Catch up "; two words which in mountain parlance mean, prepare to start; and these words once uttered, the sooner a man got ready the better. Kit waited for nobody; and woe to the unfortunate tyro in mountain travel who discovered to his sorrow that packs would work, bags fall off, and mules show an utter disregard for the preservation of one's personal property.

They arrived at the dreaded Jornada del Muerto (Journey of Death) which the Spanish Trail, like the majority of desert trails of the West and Southwest, possessed; and this stretch of eighty waterless miles, covered in one stage from three in the afternoon until late the next morning, filled Brewerton's mind with fantasies: " Our wayworn voyagers, with their tangled locks and unshorn beards (rendered white as snow by the fine sand with which the air in these regions is often filled) had a weird and ghostlike look, which the gloomy scene around, with its frowning rocks and moonlit sands, tended to enhance and heighten."

It was the many horse skeletons bleaching along this *jornada* which prompted a tale, for the Brewerton ready ears, of old Bill Williams' raid upon the mission herds; of the pursuit; of the one thousand animals that dropped from fatigue; of the mountain men's reprisal, and of the final loss of the whole *caballada* to the Indians.

The Jornada del Muerto put behind,

our party, with few exceptions, besides the watchful horseguard, were stretched upon the ground resting wearily after the long night's ride, which we had just accomplished. Carson, who was lying beside me, suddenly raised himself upon his elbow, and turning to me, asked " Do you see those Indians? " at the same time pointing to the crest of one of the gravelly, bluff-like hills with which we were surrounded. After a careful examination of the locality, I was obliged to reply in the negative. " Well," said Kit, " I saw an Indian's head there just now, and there are a party of at least a dozen more, or I am much mistaken." Scarcely were the words out of his mouth when a savage rose to his full height, as if he had grown out of the rocks which fringed the hill top; this fellow commenced yelling in a strange guttural tongue, at the same time gesticulating violently with his hands; this he intended as a declaration of friendship; and Kit rising up, answered him in his own language, " Tigabu, tigabu (Friend, friend)."

The old Digger was persuaded to come in — and by twos and threes came in, sure enough, the dozen others whom Carson had predicted. Came in also, from the trail, and bound eastward, Captain Joe Walker with a trading company convoying horses and mules into the Utah country.

Imagine us seated in a circle on the ground, checkered red and white, with here a half naked Indian, and there a mountaineer, almost as uncouth, in his own peculiar garb. The arms of both parties, though not ostentatiously displayed (which might have interfered with our negotiation), being placed where they could be reached at a moment's warning; a pipe (Carson's own particular " dudheen ") being put into requisition for the occasion, was duly filled with tobacco, lighted, and a short smoke having been taken by Carson, Walker and myself, it was then passed to the oldest man among our Indian guests, who took two or three long whiffs, retaining the smoke in his mouth until his distorted face bore so strong a resemblance to an antiquated monkey's under trying circumstances, that I had all but disturbed the gravity of the assembly by bursting into a roar of laughter * * *. The pipe having finally gone the rounds of our parti-colored circle, found its way back into the hands of the old Indian, who, having placed it securely in his mouth, seemed to continue smoking in a fit of absence of mind, which not only induced him to refill it, but rendered him perfectly insensible to the reproving grunts of his brethren.

And this was Kit Carson's " own particular ' dudheen ' " !

The talk then commenced. Kit told as much of his route and future intentions as he thought necessary, though I doubt whether they gained much *real* information; and concluded by charging divers murders and outrages upon the members of the tribe to which the visitors belonged. The Diggers answered to the effect that there were bad Indians living among the hills who did such things, but that for themselves they were perfectly innocent, never did anything wrong in their lives, entertained a great regard for the whites in general, and ourselves in particular; and wound up, diplomatically speaking, by " renewing to us the assurances of their distinguished consideration," coupled with a strong hint that a present (a horse, or some such trifle) would not be unacceptable as an evidence of our esteem.

The Diggers remained all day, and the night travel was hedged about by smoke signals, so that the next day Carson thought best to hold a young warrior as a hostage against trouble. The camp was undisturbed, save by the lamentations, from the hills, of the young man's friends and relatives, who were quieted only by assurances from Carson and the hostage himself.

The vicinity where in the spring of '44 Carson and Godey, under Fremont, performed the ride which made them both famous was passed, and the story was retold. Indian signs by tracks and fires grew more pronounced; and the party soon passed another of the Fremont camping places, where the hunter Tabeau had been killed. This tale also was told again, for

many of our party had been friends and companions of the unfortunate Tabeau; and the exciting sensations called up by revisiting the scene of his tragic end, found vent in the deep and general feelings of indignation expressed by our mountaineers against the tribe who had committed the murder.

We had scarcely been encamped two hours, when one of our horse-guards reported that he had discovered new Indian tracks near our *caballada,* and expressed the opinion that they had just been made by some Digger spy, who had reconnoitered our position with the view of stealing the animals. With the associations connected with the spot, it will hardly seem wonderful that our line of conduct was soon determined upon. Carson, two old hunters, named Auchambeau and Lewis, and myself took our guns, and started upon the freshly-made trail. The foot-tracks at first led us through the winding paths, along the river bottom, where we were obliged to travel in Indian file; and then turned suddenly aside, ascending one of the steep sand hills which bordered upon the stream. There we lost some time from the obscurity of the trail, but finally recovered it upon the crest of the bluff. A moment after, I heard Kit shouting, " there he goes "; and looking in the direction to which he pointed, I saw a Digger with his bow and arrows at his back, evidently badly frightened, and running for his life. Such traveling through deep sand I never saw before. The fellow bounded like a deer, swinging himself from side to side, so as to furnish a very uncertain mark for our rifles. Once, he seemed inclined to tarry, and take a shot at us; but after an attempt to draw his bow, he concluded he had no time to waste and hurried on. Kit fired first, and, for a wonder, missed him; but it was a long shot, and on the wing, to boot. I tried him next with a musket, sending two balls and six buck-shot after him, with like success. Auchambeau followed me, with no better fortune; and we had begun to think that the savage bore a charmed life, when Lewis, who carried a long Missouri rifle, dropped upon one knee, exclaiming, "I'll bring him, boys." By this time the Indian was nearly two hundred yards distant, and approaching the edge of a steep cañon (as it is called) of rocks and sand. The thing was now getting exciting, and we watched the man with almost breathless care, as Lewis fired; at the crack of the rifle the Digger bounded forward, and his arm, which had been raised in the air, fell suddenly to his side. He had evidently been wounded in the shoulder; yet, strange to say, such is their knowledge of the country, and so great are their powers of endurance, that he succeeded in making his escape.

" Our adventures in the desert were eventually terminated by our arrival at ' Las Vegas de Santa Clara,' " continues

Lieutenant Brewerton; "and a pleasant thing it was to look once more upon green grass and sweet water, and to reflect that the dreariest portion of our journey lay behind us." Unknown to them while they had been traveling, all this great country of Nevada, and of the Utah which they were just entering, had changed nominal ownership; and the Spanish Trail which commenced in American territory by conquest now traversed American territory by purchase as well. Like a missing puzzle-piece the final section had been fitted into place in the old beaver West, completing to solidity the checkerboard of the United States of North America.[188] Upon the high ridges beyond Little Salt Lake the California mules first saw and felt snow — testing it gingerly with forefeet.[189] The Green was high and icy cold with the June meltings.

This formidable obstacle was to be passed, and how to overcome the difficulty I scarcely knew. Kit, however, solved the problem, by proposing a raft, and accordingly all hands set to work with a will collecting the necessary material from the neighboring woods. Kit, in his shirt-sleeves, working hard himself — instructing here and directing there, and, as usual, proving himself the master-spirit of the party. After much labor, a few logs were properly cut, notched, and rolled into the water, where they were carefully fastened together by binding them with our *reatas*, until this rude expedient furnished a very passable mode of conveyance for a light load of luggage.

Having freighted it as heavily as we dared with our packs and riding saddles, and placed the bags containing the California mails upon the securest portion, we next proceeded to determine who of our party should be the first to swim the stream. Five men were at length selected, and as I was a good swimmer, I concluded to join the expedition as captain. So taking Auchambeau as my first mate, we two plunged into the stream; and having arranged our men at their appointed stations, only waited Kit's final orders, to trust ourselves to the waters. These instructions were soon briefly given in the following words: " All you men who can't swim may hang onto the corners of the raft, but do n't any of you get upon it except Auchambeau, who has the pole to guide it with; those of you who can swim, are to get hold of the tow-line, and pull it along; keep a good lookout for rocks and floating timber; and whatever you do, do n't lose the mail bags."

The result was, that while cheered on by the detachment which remained behind, the navigators were carried down stream a mile and landed on the same side whence they had started! Brewerton was almost drowned, being saved by Auchambeau.

The river at this point was impassable on account of rapids and rocks; so that, naked except for their hats, shouldering their baggage and towing the raft, the squad must retrace their way, ascending along the stream, " and uttering more than one anathema upon the thorny plants, which wounded our unprotected feet at every step."

A second essay was successful — abeit the plucky Auchambeau had to be well rolled and rubbed, on the opposite bank, to relieve him of violent cramps from the cold water and the exertion. Buffalo robes were borrowed, for covering, from the Ute Indians who opportunely arrived; and by the Utes' assistance the raft was unloaded.

Carson and his squad crossed safely, with more baggage; but the last squad met with disaster — the raft bursting upon a snag, the men saving themselves with difficulty, and "six rifles, three saddles, much of the ammunition, and nearly all our provisions " being lost.

Under these depressing circumstances, our camp that night was anything but a lively one; the Eutaws being the only persons who seemed to feel like laughing. Indeed, I half think that our loss put them in high good-humor, as they had some prospect of recovering the rifles, when a lower stage of water should enable them to explore the bed of the river. The little that remained of our private mess stores was now the only certain dependence left to us in the way of food for our whole party. These stores were equally divided by Carson himself; our own portion being the same as that of our men, and the whole would, with economy in using, furnish but three days' scanty rations for each individual. Some of our men had lost their riding-saddles, and were fain to spread their blankets upon a mule's back, and jog along as best they might — a mode of travel which, when the animal's bones are highly developed, I take to be "bad at the best." Others of the party had lost their clothing; and I am sorry to say that the number of pairs of "nether integuments" was two less than that of the people who ought to have worn them. But this was a trifle compared with our other difficulties, for there was nobody in those regions who knew enough of fashions to criticise our dress; and as for ourselves we were in no mood to smile at our own strange costumes. Personally, I had been more lucky than the majority of my companions, having saved my precious suit of deer-skins, my rifle, and a few rounds of ammunition; but, alas! the waters of Grand [i. e., Green] River had swallowed up my note-book, my geological and botanical specimens, and many of my sketches, a most serious and vexatious loss, after the labor of collecting and preparing them.

Two days thereafter the Grand River must be similarly crossed — crossed with as much discomfort but with less loss. The party was soon down to horseflesh and muleflesh — against which the New Yorker held out for forty-eight hours, only to give in, "and for more than a week ate horseflesh regularly."

"Perhaps the reader would like to know how it tasted. I can only say that it was an old animal, a tough animal, a sore-backed animal — and, upon the whole — I *prefer beef.*"

The Rockies of Colorado were reached, at the western side. Here much game was seen, but it was exceedingly wild, evading the white hunters.

I shall not soon forget accompanying Carson, about this time, on one of our many excursions to procure venison. We had discovered a doe with her fawn in a little grassy nook, where the surrounding rocks would partially screen us from their view, while we crawled within gun-shot. Dismounting with as little noise as possible, I remained stationary, holding our horses, while Kit endeavored to approach the unsuspecting deer. We were both somewhat nervous, for our supper and breakfast depended upon our success; but we knew well from former experiences that if the doe heard but the crackling of a bush she would be off like the wind. Kit, therefore, advanced with somewhat more than ordinary care, using every caution which a hunter's education could suggest, and at length gained a point within rifle-shot of his prey. My nervousness was now at its height; why does n't he fire? thought I. But Kit was cooler, and calculated more closely than myself. At last I saw him bring his rifle to his eye, at the time showing himself sufficiently to attract the attention of the doe, who raised her head a little to get a look at the object of alarm, thus offering a better mark for his rifle; a moment more, at the report of the piece the doe made a convulsive bound, and then rolled upon the sward. To tie our horses, cut up the deer, and attach its quarters to our saddles, was the work of twenty minutes more; and then, remounting, we pursued our way, making quite a triumphal entry into camp, where Kit's luck rejoiced the hearts and stomachs of every man in the party; it was really a great event to us in those days, and we had that night a right jolly time of it.

From those rugged mountain paths we at length emerged, descending into the beautiful plains known as Taos Valley. Here we had scarcely gone a day's journey, before we discovered a great increase in the amount of " Indian sign," and also a change in its appearance, which, though hardly perceptible to an inexperienced eye, was too surely read by Carson's not to beget great uneasiness.

" Look here," said Kit, as he dismounted from his mule, and stopped to examine the trail; " the Indians have passed across our road since sun-up, and they are a war-party, too; no signs of lodge-poles, and no colt tracks; they are no friends, neither; here's a feather that some of them has dropped. We'll have trouble yet, if we do n't keep a bright lookout."

After two or three alarms, which resulted in nothing serious, the party was within eighteen miles of the outermost of the New Mexican settlements. This was a debatable country, where both Utes and Apaches were liable to be encountered.

I was just beginning to feel a little relieved from the anxious watchfulness of the last few days, and had even beguiled the weariness of the way by picturing to myself the glorious dinner I would order upon reaching Santa Fe, when Carson, who had been looking keenly ahead, interrupted my musings, by exclaiming: "Look at that Indian village; we have stumbled upon the rascals, after all." It was but too true — a sudden turning of the trail had brought us full in view of nearly two hundred lodges, which were located upon a rising ground some half a mile distant to the right of our trail. At this particular point the valley grew narrower, and hemmed in as we were upon either hand by a chain of hills and mountains, we had no resource but to keep straight forward on our course, in the expectation that by keeping, as sailors say, "well under the land," we might possibly slip by unperceived. But our hope was a vain one; we had already been observed, and ere we had gone a hundred yards, a warrior came dashing out from their town, and, putting his horse to its speed, rode rapidly up to Carson and myself; he was a finely formed savage, mounted upon a noble horse, and his fresh paint and gaudy equipments looked anything but peaceful. This fellow continued his headlong career until almost at our side, and, then, checking his steed so suddenly as to throw the animal back upon its haunches, he inquired for the "capitan" (a Spanish word generally used by the Indians to signify chief); in answer to which, I pointed first to Carson, and then to myself. Kit, who had been regarding him intently, but without speaking, now turned to me, and said: "I will speak to this warrior in Eutaw, and if he understands me it will prove that he belongs to a friendly tribe; but if he does not, we may know to the contrary, and must do the best we can; but from his paint and his manner I expect it will end in a fight anyway."

Kit then turned to the Indian, who, to judge from his expression, was engaged in taking mental, but highly satisfactory notes of our way-worn party, with their insufficient arms and scanty equipments, and asked him in the Eutaw tongue, " Who are you?" The savage stared at us for a moment; and then, putting a finger into either ear, shook his head slowly from side to side. "I knew it," said Kit; "it is just as I thought, and we are in for it at last. Look here, Thomas!" added he (calling to an old mountain man) — "get the mules together, and drive them up to that little patch of chaparral, while we follow with the Indian." Carson then requested me in a whisper to drop behind the savage (who appeared determined to accompany us), and be ready to shoot him at a moment's warning, if necessity required. Having taken up a position accordingly I managed to cock my rifle, which I habitually carried upon the saddle, without exciting suspicion.

Kit rode ahead to superintend the movements of the party, who, under the guidance of Thomas, had by this time got the pack and loose animals together and were driving them toward a grove about two hundred yards further from the village. We had advanced thus but a short distance, when Carson (who from time to time had been glancing backward over his shoulder) reined in his mule until we again rode side-by-side. While stooping, as if to adjust his saddle, he said, in too low a tone to reach any ears but mine: "Look back, but express no surprise." I did so, and beheld a sight which, though highly picturesque, and furnishing striking subject for a painting, was, under existing circumstances, rather calculated to destroy the equilibrium of the nerves. In short, I saw about a hundred and fifty warriors, finely mounted, and painted for war, with their long hair streaming in the wind, charging down upon us, shaking their lances and brandishing their spears as they came on.

By this time we had reached the timber, if a few stunted trees could be dignified with the name; and Kit, springing from his mule, called out to the men: "Now, boys, dismount, tie up your riding mules; those of you who have guns, get round the *caballada*, and look out for the Indians; and you who have none, get inside, and hold some of the animals. Take care, Thomas, and shoot down the mule with the mail bags on her, if they try to stampede the animals."

We had scarce made these hurried preparations for the reception of such unwelcome visitors, before the whole horde was upon us, and had surrounded our position. For the next fifteen minutes a scene of confusion and excitement ensued which baffles all my powers of description. On the one hand the Indians pressed closely in, yelling, aiming their spears, and drawing their bows, while their chiefs, conspicuous from their activity, dashed here and there through the crowd, commanding and directing their followers. On the other hand, our little band, with the exception of those who had lost their rifles in Grand River, stood firmly around the *caballada;* Carson, a few paces in advance, giving orders to his men, and haranguing the Indians. His whole demeanor was now so entirely changed that he looked like a different man; his eye fairly flashed, and his rifle was grasped with all the energy of an iron will.

"There," cried he, addressing the savages, "is our line; cross it if you dare, and we begin to shoot. You ask us to let you in, but you do n't come unless you ride over us. You say you are friends, but you do n't act like it. No, you do n't deceive us, we know you too well; so stand back, or your lives are in danger."

It was a bold thing in him to talk thus to these blood-thirsty rascals; but a crisis had arrived in which boldness alone could save us, and he knew it. They had five men to our one; our ammunition was reduced to three rounds per man, and resistance would have been momentary; but among our band the Indians must have recognized mountain men, who would have fought to the last, and they knew from sad experience that the trapper's rifle rarely missed its aim. Our animals, moreover, worn out as they were, would have been scarcely worth fighting for, and our scalps a dear bargain.

Our assailants were evidently undecided, and this indecision saved us; for just as they seemed preparing for open hostilities, as rifles were cocked and bows drawn, a runner, mounted upon a weary and foam specked steed, came galloping in from the direction of the settlements, bringing information of evident importance. After a moment's consultation with this new arrival, the chief whistled shrilly, and the warriors fell back. Carson's quick eye had already detected their confusion, and turning to his men, he called out, " Now, boys, we have a chance; jump into your saddles, get the loose animals before you, and then handle your rifles, and if these fellows interfere with us we 'll make a running fight of it."

In an instant each man was in his saddle, and with the *cabal-*

lada in front we retired slowly; facing about from time to time, to observe the movements of our enemies, who followed on, but finally left us and disappeared in the direction of their village.

Few situations show to better advantage Kit Carson's mountain-man abilities, or the respect in which he was held, as a leader. Even with his preparedness and bold front the party might not have escaped, for we are told that he was aided by the Indians' fear of past misdeeds and by their information that a posse was upon their trail. Now free from peril, camp was made, and rest of a day was taken.

Early upon the following day we resumed our march, and that evening terminated our wanderings, for a season, by bringing us to the Mexican village of Taos, where I was hospitably entertained by Carson and his amiable wife, a Spanish lady, and a relative, I believe, of some former governor of New Mexico.

The other members of the party again took the trail, for Santa Fe, eighty miles south; and finding in Kit Carson a disposition (under the circumstances not reprehensible) " to linger by his own fireside to the last moment which duty would permit," Lieutenant Brewerton, with promise from host to join him again in Santa Fe, also took the trail and overtook the company.

Thus ended Lieutenant G. Douglas Brewerton's " ride with Kit Carson." With that mockery of fate which so often impresses itself upon man's career, after enduring all the hardships of the trip by desert, river, and peak, our New Yorker finds himself, now arrived at Santa Fe, stricken with influenza, caught (he judges) by sleeping in a draught! Therefore, Kit Carson, riding in but little later, ready for business, and appearing as a " very gleam of sunshine, if sunshine ever came in the garb of a travel-soiled mountaineer," had to be disappointed in that companionship upon which he must have counted. However, this was not

KIT CARSON'S HAWKINS RIFLE

THE SILVER PLATE IN THE STOCK READS, "PRESENTED TO MONTEZUMA LODGE, NO. 109, A. F. & A. M., BY BROTHER KIT CARSON, MAY, 1868"

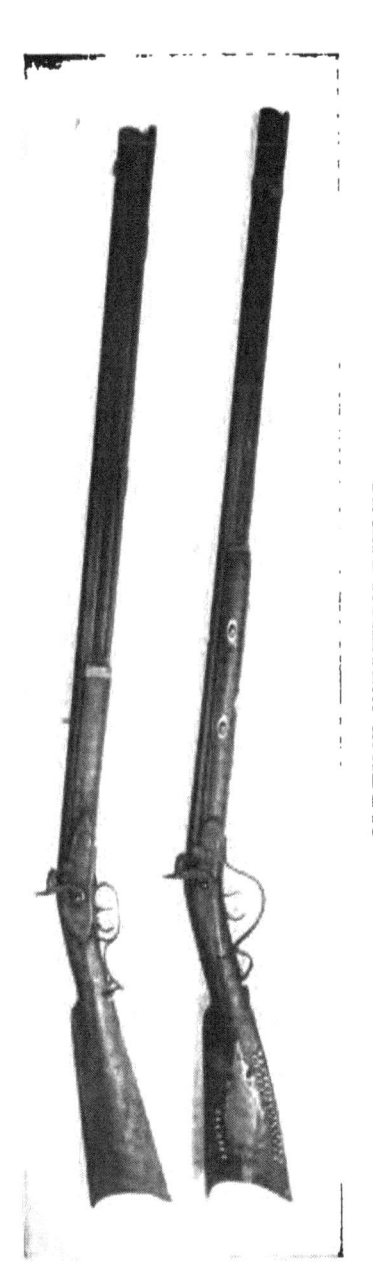

OLDTIME WESTERN RIFLES

THE LOWER GUN IS THE ONE GIVEN BY KIT CARSON TO OLIVER WIGGINS AT TAOS IN 1841. NINETEEN OF THE TWENTY-SEVEN TACKS ARE CARSON "COUPS," AND THE OTHERS WIGGINS'

(Colorado State Historical Society collection)

TOM TOBIN

CARSON'S CLOSE FRIEND AT TAOS AND ON THE TRAP TRAIL. HIS DAUGHTER
MARRIED CARSON'S OLDEST SON

(Photograph by O. T. Davis, at Fort Garland, Colo., 1905)

the only disappointment. In Santa Fe he learned for the
first time, from the lips of Colonel E. W. B. Newby of the
Illinois Volunteers, that the lieutenancy conferred a year
ago by the President never was confirmed by the Senate.

I do not know that this news was to Kit Carson a disappointment so much as it was a source of chagrin. He
says that he did not intend to retain the commission, after
the war, and this we may believe. His tendencies and his
independent training, coupled with his love of home, did
not influence him toward army life. But he had been
taught, for a year, to consider himself a commissioned
officer in the United States service, and he had presumed
that he was entitled to a lieutenant's pay. Now he must
realize that he had not been a commissioned officer, that
he had not been entitled to a lieutenant's pay, and that,
furthermore, he had no back pay and no future pay coming
to him! [140] To him here, triumphant after a long, hard,
dangerous trail upon government business, a trail followed
through successfully despite hunger, thirst, freshet, and savages, the words from Colonel Newby must have been a
blow in the face.

About this failure of President Polk's recommendation
there has centered a mystery. Why should Kit Carson
have been turned down by the Senate, particularly at this
time when appointments were called for, right and left, as
the forces in the field demanded? Many a commission in
the army has been handed to less deserving candidates. Dr.
Peters, of the army medical corps, serving soon after the
occurrence, claims that army circles did not know the reason
for the Senate's action. Nevertheless, it seems to me that
this was a little slap by the West Point and Kearny faction
at Senator Benton, who, of course, suggested to President
Polk the Carson commission.

The alleged caste of the West Point clique had long been
bitterly assailed by Senator Benton, who never minced

words; to West Point jealousy he laid all hostility against Fremont, his son-in-law, and he lost no opportunity to deride the abilities and the characters of the Government Academy graduates.

Whether the commissioned rank in the regular service resented the appointment, *per se*, of illiterate Kit Carson, who may have appealed on the trail but not in the garrison; whether it was trying to check the infusion of civilian blood amidst its Academy *sang royal* cannot now be told. In Civil War time no man who wore the United States uniform was more highly esteemed than was Colonel and General Kit Carson — although even here he was made (it is claimed) the scapegrace of army politics.[141]

As regards this lieutenancy which was not confirmed, Kit Carson betrayed no pique. It is stated by Peters that various friends, real or pretended, advised Carson not to persist with the dispatches, urging him that he was under no obligations to perform the mission. As might be expected of Carson, and as could not be expected of a man less broad in his conceptions of duty, he forebore to turn his dispatches in to the commanding officer at Santa Fe, and continued on to finish the task which he had undertaken. This is the more creditable to him, inasmuch as from Colonel Newby he had learned also that the Santa Fe Trail and the southwest plains were badly infested by the Comanches, threatening all travel.

From Santa Fe Carson returned with fresh animals to Taos, for the remainder of his trans-continental journey. Wishing, with his usual discretion, to avoid interference by the Comanches, he rode from Taos with four followers, of whom one was Oliver Wiggins (just recovered from a bullet wound received at the battle of Monterey, Mexico), and headed upon a great circuit into the north and the Platte country.

This being June, it is probable that the bulk of the Indians would be finishing their buffalo hunts on the plains — tagging the great herds northward. I should think, therefore, that Carson would have chosen the foothills trail, through Pueblo, Colorado, up the Fontaine qui Bouille, through Colorado Springs, over the divide and down to the site of the future Denver. Hereabouts he veered to the eastward, and struck the Bijou Creek which flows some fifty miles east of present Denver, through the rolling plains, for many a crooked mile deep-cut in clay or bordered by willows and cottonwoods and wild crabs, to empty into the South Platte west of old Fort Morgan.

Into the first noon camp of the Carson party, twenty-five miles from the Bijou mouth, rode seven Kiowas. I have the story from Wiggins.

No Indians of early plains days were more to be feared than the perpetually hostile Kiowas; and the arrival of the visitors indicated trouble. Although Carson's reputation among the tribes of the Southwest was undiminished, he had been absent so long that to many of the young men his face was unfamiliar. These Kiowas evidently did not recognize him. They sat, ate, and the inevitable pipe was filled, lighted, and passed.

Carson understood enough Kiowa to make out what the guttural asides meant. Said the leader to the other bucks: " These are some of those Carson men who have killed so many of us. When the smoke has gone around the third time, kill them quick."

Carson understood but betrayed no emotion other than the suave dignity which characterized the meeting; but he spoke to his companions: " Be attending to the horses. Watch what I do, and if I lift my hand, shoot."

The pipe passed, once, twice; and as Carson took it for the third pull, he remarked, pleasantly but clearly, in plain English:

"I suppose this is the last time 'round, is it? Now you will kill us."

The Indians understood enough English to interpret aright either the words or the tone. Carson's men of course sprang forward with their weapons; the startled Kiowas threw off their blankets — but they were too late. Carson berated them in Kiowa and English.

"You red dogs! You thought you could murder us. Do you know who I am? I am Kit Carson! Take a good look at me, before you die."

The Indians collapsed — not so much from alarm as from astonishment. They dropped their guns and bows.

"You're a nice set of cowards," scolded Carson. "Shame on you and your tribe. Go! Go, tell your chiefs that you have seen Kit Carson and that he let you live. Stop!" he yelled, as they slunk away. "Take your bows and arrows, so you can kill a few rabbits on your way. And next time you smoke the peace pipe with a white man, do n't plan to murder him."

The Kiowas went off, afoot. After watching them out of sight, the Carson party resumed their route, leaving the Bijou and making a short cut to the Platte. Where the South and the North Platte joined, a trading party descending from Fort Laramie were met. So Wiggins, his three comrades, and one of the traders bound southward turned back for Taos, and Carson continued with the other party of fifteen, on to St. Joe.

He reported at Fort Leavenworth, deposited his mail at St. Louis, and proceeded again to Washington, where he was entertained by the Benton and Fremont households.

Here in Washington was also Joe Meek, the mountain man, now "envoy from Oregon," arrived across country to bear the news of the Whitman massacre and to deliver the appeal of the Oregon people for government protection. But Judge J. Q. Thornton had preceded him, trav-

eling around the Horn, to present to Congress Oregon's
ideas upon the administration of her affairs. The bill for
the admission of Oregon Territory was being considered at
last.

Of Judge Thornton, the citizen, we hear little; of Joe
Meek, the messenger, we hear more, as he revels in favor of
hero-worshiping womankind, lives fatly, and occasionally
is interviewed by the more humble Carson. A strange
meeting amidst unwonted scenes was this, for both.

So long as Meek's purse was supplied, as it generally was,
by some member of the family at the White House, Carson
could borrow from him. But one being quite as careless of
money as the other, they were sometimes both out of pocket
at the same time. In that case the conversation was apt to take
a turn like this:

Carson: "Meek, let me have some money, can't you?"
Meek: "I have n't got any money, Kit."
Carson: "Go and get some."
Meek: "Hang it, whar am I to get money from?"
Carson: "Try the 'contingent fund,' can't you?"[142]

After a bitter debate upon the section which prohibited
slavery, the Oregon Bill, as approved by Judge Thornton,
passed the Senate, with all amendments, Sunday morning,
August 13 — only twenty-four hours before final adjourn-
ment.

Now appointed United States Marshal in the new territory, Joe Meek was dispatched to Newburg, Indiana, to
hand to General Joseph Lane, veteran of the late war, the
presidential warrant as governor of the northwest empire.

Kit Carson, retired to civil life (and glad of it), having
again experienced the hospitality of the Benton home, left
it, and in October was back by his own fireside at old Taos.

CHAPTER XXIX

THE RANCH AT THE RAYADO — 1849–1853

WHEN in October of 1848 Kit Carson, brevet lieutenant (so to speak) late of the United States Mounted
Riflemen, returned to home and private citizenship in Fernandez de Taos, he found that during the past decade the
frontier of the United States had not advanced an inch.
The longitude of western Missouri was still the longitude
of the American frontier.

The state of Iowa had come into the flag; the territory of
Minnesota was another new enlistment; and ranged thus,
Louisiana, Arkansas, Missouri, Iowa, Minnesota, in a solid
column, permanent and steadfast, the trans-Mississippi West
pressed against the trans-Missouri East. But the line
of cleavage was as sharply marked as the boundary between
two nations.

Of the great Louisiana Purchase of 1803 only this narrow
eastern strip between the Mississippi and the lower Missouri
was yet devoted, even in part, to the legitimate uses for
which the expanse had been created — the home of civilized
man. Ignoring its possibilities, across it were annually
trekking hundreds of people, deeming it but an interruption,
and rejoicing when they had put behind them its five hundred miles of hidden riches. It was still the Great American Desert; still accepted as an asylum for wild men and
a pasture for wild beasts; the reports of Fremont thus far
were bearing only green fruit.

Still there assembled at Westport, or at Elm Grove,
within the eastern border of present Kansas, the emigrants
for Oregon and the traders to Santa Fe reinforced, now,

by the California settlers, and soon doubly reinforced by the Forty-niners. Oregon Territory embraced all that northwest country beyond the South Pass, the country out of which was to be born not one state but three: Idaho, Oregon, Washington. As for the rest of that mighty section beyond the Shining Mountains, the present upper California, Utah, Nevada, Arizona, western Colorado, and western New Mexico, it was known vaguely as California and as "unorganized."

In October, 1848, Major (Brevet Lieutenant Colonel) John M. Washington, of the Light Artillery in the recent war, was military governor of New Mexico, succeeding Charles Bent, Donaciano Vigil, Colonel Sterling Price, Colonel E. W. B. Newby, and Major Benjamin L. Beall — a long list (equaling that of California) for two short years. New Mexico had been left largely to its own devices under the eyes of temporary tutors. "Until Congress shall provide for them a territorial government" the people of New Mexico are advised by the President "to live peaceably and quietly under the existing government *de facto;*" but addressing a letter, August 28, 1848, to "the people of California and New Mexico," Senator Thomas H. Benton advised: "Meet in convention, provide for a cheap and simple government, and take care of yourselves until Congress can provide for you."

The provisional government idea had worked well in Oregon; but minds and temperaments in Latin New Mexico were far different from those of the Saxonized Northwest. Here in *Nueva Mejico* social conditions also were different: Texas claimed the Rio Grande, and in the organization of a civil government the slave question thrust the shadow of its black arm across the pages of any prospective constitution.

If Kit Carson, back from the wars, anticipated a period of ease, he was to learn that he was one who could "consider peace only as a breathing-time." With those 650,000 square miles of territory the government of the United States had inherited the doubtful asset of 120,000 additional Indians: Navajos and Apaches, of characteristics untested, unappreciated; Utes and Comanches, known to the trapper and the trader, but a tenantry strange to the new landlord.

Against these — against the Ishmaelite Comanches ranging the Texas plains and north clear to the Santa Fe Trail; against the Utes, descending from the San Luis Valley and the foothills of Colorado to prey upon the lowlanders and to stir the plains tribes into retaliation; against the cruelest Apaches, the very thugs and holdups of the Southwest, by horse and foot ranging from central Arizona to the Cimarron of northeastern New Mexico; against the wealthy and ever haughty Navajos, " lords of New Mexico," whose open declaration was " that they would have exterminated the Mexicans long ago had it not been more profitable to use them as *herders"*; against these the Government of the United States must not only protect its own citizens, but by the treaty of Guadalupe Hidalgo, through which the savage-infested territory was acquired, did " solemnly agree " to protect Mexico also, and to redeem and return to their country the luckless Mexicans whom Apache, Comanche, and Navajo were in the habit of capturing across the border and leading back, as slaves, to the fastnesses of the North.

That was a large contract upon the part of the new owners of all this acreage and of all these chattels; how large, Mexico, two hundred heavy years helpless before the red raiders, well knew — and Mexico's successor was to find out by experience extending over forty years of hard, incessant fighting to a practical extermination of the enemy. The millions of dollars and the hundreds of lives expended by the United States to fulfill its obligations toward a conquered people form one bright spot in the western Indian wars.

So dawns in the Southwest the era of the army days, forming protection for the march onward of the white settler — a march to which the hundred forts now but idle names were stepping-stones as significant, in many cases, as the crosses beside the Mexican trails.

Not yet, indeed, had there sprung up by trail and stream, in desert and green vale, those valiant citadels, Fort Union, Fort Bliss, Defiance, Bowie, Apache, Fillmore, Massachusetts, Bascom, Sumner, Yuma, Craig, Stanton, Wingate, Webster, and others — many of them parched, forsaken places where to live was heroic.

In the North the First Regiment of Mounted Riflemen (Carson's old regiment) was about to follow the Oregon Trail to the coast, leaving behind a garrisoned Fort Laramie and Cantonment Loring beside old Fort Hall. Thus the soldier advanced into the country of the Sioux, never to be driven back. And when in October, 1848, Kit Carson returned to Taos, almost simultaneously there marched in C Company, First Dragoons, Lieutenant J. H. Whittlesey. At Fort Marcy of Santa Fe, also, there were troops. But the army days were tentative and very young. Afar stretched New Mexico — including the country north into central Colorado, west to California, east indefinitely; a country wild, diversified, hot and cold, with its deserts, chaparral and timber, its fearsome cañons, secret valleys and rugged heights, ruled by the Navajo, poisoned by the Apache. Through it, as through the North, the white race must first travel by emigrant trail to California, and after that, buy with blood the right of tilling the barren earth.

Upon the eve of the new era Kit Carson arrived " home." He was thirty-nine years old; he had a name known from California to Washington; to welcome him there were old friends: Judge Beaubien, Captain Ceran St. Vrain (about

to remove to the Mora, to conduct a store and a mill),
Lucien Maxwell, Alex Godey (about to join Fremont at
Bent's Fort, for a disastrous exploration straight west into
the heart of the Colorado mountains), Dick Owens (soon
to be married), and many mountain-man cronies of former
days.

It required time to distribute the American soldiery
through New Mexico; the volunteers had been discharged,
and recruits for the regular service, and particularly for the
mounted regiments, had to be found. The cavalry arm,
hitherto deprecated, came into its own when the army
spread through the western chaparral and desert. Meanwhile, for a year or so, the Navajo and the Apache on the
one hand and the *Americano* on the other examined one
another, appraised one another, sparred a little, skirmished
a little, and drew on to the inevitable close grip.

So, with the interruption of an occasional trip to Santa
Fe, on private business, and of one or two trips afield as
guide with Major Benjamin L. Beall, in command of the
district, in ineffectual pursuit of marauding Apaches, Kit
Carson, for a year, rested.

His household was composed of his wife, little Teresina
Bent, his niece (daughter of the murdered Charles Bent,
his friend), and Dick Owens. From this home, under date
of January 27, 1849, John Charles Fremont writes to his
wife. The fourth expedition has been a failure, and he
is resting after its fatigues.

My Very Dear Wife:
I write to you from the house of our good friend Carson.
This morning a cup of chocolate was brought to me, while
yet in bed. To an overworn, overworked, much fatigued, and
starving traveler, these little luxuries of the world offer an
interest which in your comfortable home it is not possible
to conceive. While in the enjoyment of this luxury, then, I
pleased myself in imagining how gratified you would be in
picturing me here in Kit's care, whom you will fancy con-

stantly occupied and constantly uneasy in endeavoring to make me comfortable. How little could you have dreamed of this while he was enjoying the pleasant hospitality of your father's house! The furthest thing then from your mind was that he would ever repay it to me here.

*   *   *   *   *   *   *   *   *   *

I find myself in the midst of friends. With Carson is living Owens, and Maxwell is at his father-in-law's, doing a very prosperous business as a merchant and contractor for the troops.

*   *   *   *   *   *   *   *   *   *

Mr. St. Vrain dined with us today. Owens goes to Missouri in April to get married, and thence by water to California. Carson is very anxious to go there with me now, and afterwards remove his family thither, but he cannot decide to break off from Maxwell and family connections.

At Carson's adobe house Fremont stayed three weeks. This increase in the household was nothing for the hospitable Southwest. However, Carson and his wife were anticipating a further increase; for in the spring of 1849 arrived their first-born, Charles (named for Charles Bent), who, however, survived only a few months.

At this time living in New Mexico was a problem, so scarce was money, so high were prices. The occupation of the country by the invading army had stripped it bare of resources and it had not yet shown any recuperative powers. An adobe house with dirt floor rented in Santa Fe (as Indian Agent Calhoun pathetically records) at $70 a month.

Corn is worth at this time $2 per bushel; shoeing of a horse, $4; sugar, 50 cents per pound; coffee, 37½; lumber, $65 per M; bacon and lard, none except at the commissary's; beef, exceedingly poor and coarse, 8 cents per pound; a shoat, not weighing more than 60 to 75 pounds, $8 to $10; chickens, from 25 to 50 cents each; turkeys, from $1 to $2. The necessities of life, such as we have been accustomed to in the States, and the delicacies and luxuries which we require, must all be brought from the United States.

Freight on the Santa Fe Trail from Independence to Santa Fe was ten and twelve cents a pound; horses were $125; hay, $60 a ton, and little of it at that.

Obviously, it behooved Kit Carson, not even on half pay, to engage in some business which would be a source of steady income. His beaver days were over, a resumption of his precarious hunter days could not be considered, the post of official guide for the United States Army was not created, neither would it be a sinecure; and with that fascination of opposites which stamps alike the frontiersman and the clerk, Kit Carson again bethought of farming. And, despite the attractions of California, which was then booming, he decided upon farming in New Mexico with Lucien Maxwell.

Maxwell was located upon the vast estate of his father-in-law, Judge Charles Beaubien, fifty miles east from Taos, in a valley on the Santa Fe Trail, mountain branch, from Bent's Fort south over the Raton Mountain, down to the Rayado River and on toward Santa Fe. Stretching many leagues over hill and dale, this estate comprised the celebrated "Beaubien and Miranda Grant": a sheer gift in 1841, from Governor Manual Armijo to his friends Don Guadalupe Miranda and Don Carlos Beaubien, of more than 1,700,000 acres — a principality almost as large as the state of Connecticut. Don Carlos bought out Don Guadalupe; as son-in-law of Don Carlos, Lucien Maxwell managed the domain, eventually inherited it, and here he lived in 1849, potential prince of the greatest private estate in America, "and after the vicissitudes of early frontier life, enjoyed leisure and profusion in his later days." [143]

Out of his love of home, loving his friends also, and counting Lucien Maxwell high among them, Carson "threw in" with him; eventually moved over from Taos, and put up an adobe house. Just what was his thought, in making the change, we may not know. But it was his second venture in the same place, for hereabouts upon the Cimar-roncito, or Little Cimarron, he and Dick Owens had been ranching (says Peters) when Fremont sent from Bent's Fort his call to the Third Expedition.

Encouraged by the presence of both Maxwell and Carson in this valley which Utes and Comanches made perilous, other bold spirits may have entered and squatted; there was land a-plenty for all, and the more settlers, the better. But a Deerfield or a Plymouth of old New England days was not more exposed or more precariously founded than this early Maxwell colony at the Rayado. However, all the men were Indian fighters, and the women, mainly of Mexican blood, were wonted to frontier perils.

But no sooner was Carson established than he was summoned away by an event which seems to have been noted as the first of those sickening murders that marked the American warfare with the Apache in New Mexico and Arizona.

This was the attack October, 1849, upon the family of J. M. White — a tragedy that through more than sixty years has come down to us as typical of frontier times in the Southwest. Strangely enough, all the references are simply to " Mr. White, a merchant of Santa Fe "; by this title he traveled his last trail, and by this title he died. Returning in his own carriage from Missouri, with his wife and ten-year-old daughter, near Point of Rocks on the Trail, being within 161 miles of Santa Fe and as he thought beyond danger, he pushed ahead of the slower wagon train (under F. X. Aubrey, well known trader) for home. " A German named Lawberger, an American whose name is not known, a Mexican, and a negro servant, accompanied his carriage."

While the Americans were in camp, a small party of Indians came up and demanded presents. These Mr. White refused to give them, and drove them out of the camp. They returned shortly, and were again treated in the same manner. This time they did not go away, but commenced an attack upon the party by shooting the negro and the Mexican, the latter falling upon the fire. The others made an attempt to escape, but were all killed except Mrs. White and child, who were made prisoners. The dead bodies were then laid beside the road, but were neither scalped nor stripped. A short time afterward a party of Mexicans came along and began to plunder the wagon, when the Indians, who had concealed themselves, fired upon them and wounded a boy, who was left for dead. He lay still until the Indians had left, when he got up and started toward the settlements, with an arrow sticking between the bones of his arm. He came up with a party of Americans the same day, and got in in safety.[144]

The word seems to have been taken to Taos, where Major W. N. Grier, then in command of the post, ordered his company of First Dragoons into the field, to the rescue. On their way to pick up the trail at the scene, the dragoons, guided by two Taos mountain men, Joachim Leroux and one Fisher, whose deeds have distinguished him more than his name, passed through the Rayado; and with his characteristic readiness Kit Carson joined them. However, the scouting command was vested in Leroux.

The trail was found at the spot where the deed had been committed, and for twelve days was followed southeast, to the Canadian River. Already some three weeks had passed; so that it was a cold trail to begin with, and snow had since descended. Only the mountain-man guides, experienced in Indian customs, could realize what probably had befallen Mrs. White during these three weeks.

Carson describes this as being the most difficult trail to follow he remembers ever to have undertaken, for the rascally Apaches, on breaking up their camps, would divide into parties of two and three, and then scatter over the vast expanse of the prairies to meet again at some preconcerted place, where they knew water could be had. In several of these camps the pursuers found remnants of dress and other articles, that were known to have belonged to Mrs. White. By these signs, they were led to believe that she still lived.[145]

It is probable that in hope of rescue the wretched prison captive did her best to encourage pursuit. At last, in eastern New Mexico, near where the Canadian River enters Texas, the dogged perseverance of the chase was rewarded by sight of the Apache village. Carson was ahead; well knowing the utmost importance of instant action before the Indians could form for defense or could collect their wits for aught save flight, with a yell to the soldiers to come on he rode headlong, whooping briskly.

Dr. Peters would have us believe that between the Leroux and the Carson adherents jealousy existed; and that opposing Carson's policy, guide Leroux counseled a parley; whereupon Major Grier halted his command. In this is seen that mistaken policy which for a time dominated the attitude of the Government toward the red man: the policy of temporizing, rather than of conquering.

However, in the case of Mrs. White there was room for two opinions: one, that the band could be induced to surrender her; the other, that the band could be made to surrender her. Unfortunately, while Kit Carson acted upon the latter assumption, Major Grier paused to act upon the other. Carson probably was right.

He charged alone, and seeing this, he reined up. Meanwhile, the camp had been in confusion, squaws scuttling for safety, warriors hurriedly mounting to spread for cover. But seeing the hesitation of the soldiery, they turned with a volley, and a ball struck the major in the breast, by the shock taking the breath from him. He was unable to speak. Infuriated by the wound, apparently mortal, given him, his men swept forward. The charge was too late. Only one warrior was killed, the others escaped, and the camp was deserted save for the body, yet warm, of Mrs. White, with an arrow piercing it. Having been granted a moment of grace the Indians had, as was their custom, killed their now useless captive — as menace against other pursuits, and as a means of lightening their trail.

" As God would have it," said Kit Carson, to Colonel Meline, in years afterward, " she was just dead when we reached her; and perhaps it was as well." She was " wasted, emaciated, the victim of a foul disease, and bore the sorrows of a life-long agony on her face." [146] To Surgeon Peters, Carson related:

I am certain that if the Indians had been charged immediately on our arrival, Mrs. White would have been saved. At first, the savages were much confused at our approach, and I do not hesitate to say that she saw us as quickly as any of the redskins did, for it undoubtedly was the all-absorbing topic in her mind that her rescue would be attempted by her friends and countrymen. On seeing us coming, she had attempted to run toward us, when she was shot down. Had she been liberated, she could not have long survived the brutality of hardships and vicissitudes she had experienced. Words cannot describe the bitter cup that she had been obliged to drink during her captivity.

Major Grier was found not to have been seriously injured; the ball had struck his buckskin gloves, folded and thrust inside his blouse. The Indians were pursued farther, for a few miles, until the dragoon horses, already severely pushed, began to fail. Then the company, fain to be content with the little damage that they had inflicted upon Apache life and property, could only return to the camp, give the piteous remains of the murdered woman a burial, and head for Taos.

On the way a fierce winter blizzard drove them into the timely shelter of a patch of timber near Las Vegas. Had it not been for the knowledge of their guides they might have perished; but to their sufferings there was some recompense in the tidings, later, that the Apaches, hard put through loss of their camp equipment, were decimated by this same storm.

The young daughter, who had been sharing the mother's torture, was still to be found. The Honorable Alexander H. H. Stuart, Secretary of the Interior, says in his annual report of 1850, to the President:

At the last session, Congress appropriated $1,500 to be used in procuring her release. This sum was promptly placed at the disposal of Agent Calhoun, the nearest resident agent, whose judgment and knowledge of the Indian character fit him in a peculiar manner to discharge the duty, with full power to use it in such manner as he might think best. He has also been instructed to convey information to the Indians, that unless this child be delivered up they will receive the chastisement by the military power of the government which their savage cruelty so richly deserves.[147]

But despite this fatherly admonition by the State Department, the Apaches (for obvious reasons) declined to produce the girl — whose body probably long before had been food for the wolves.

The Government at Washington was still young in Indian knowledge, still uncertain in its course toward its fickle wards: and Colonel Meline's statement, here appended, may in the main be true.

The following year a treaty of peace was made with the Apaches, and they received the "whisk" and "shoog" (whiskey and sugar) for which alone they made it. The Apache chief who represented the tribe, and who had carried off the unfortunate lady we have spoken of, came into our camp on that occasion appropriately adorned with a necklace made of the teeth of the murdered Doctor White! [148]

Of this, however, we are assured: the head chief, White Wolf (Lobo Blanco) finally met his deserts in a dramatic duel, March 5, 1854, near the Cimarron River seventy miles east of Fort Union, with Second Lieutenant David Bell, H Company, First Dragoons. The company, then on a scout, numbered about thirty men.

Bell had assigned his baggage-mules to the charge of five or six men, and held a mounted interview with White Wolf, who stood in front of twenty-two Indians on foot, well armed and in line. Bell was in front of his troopers, who were about twenty paces from the Indians — exactly equal in number and extent of line. Both parties were prepared to use firearms.
The parley was almost tediously long. * * * White Wolf was very bold, and became defiant.
At last — the chief sinking on one knee and aiming his gun, and Bell throwing his body forward and reining up his horse — they exchanged shots. Both lines, by command, followed the example, the troopers, however, spurring forward through or over their enemies. The warriors mostly threw themselves on the earth, and several vertical wounds were received by horse and rider.

The Apaches were broken, and fled; the death list (mainly Indian) was twenty-one out of the forty-six participants. Lieutenant Bell was not wounded, but

he had shot White Wolf several times, and afterwards others did so; but so tenacious of life was he that, to finish him, a man got a great rock and mashed his head.[149]

Thus were the White family avenged. But from this aftermath of that tragedy which so interested Kit Carson and his contemporaries, let us return to Kit Carson himself.
During the winter of 1849-50 Rayado (the " The " being early dropped, and today being forgotten) became a military outpost, at which were stationed a detachment of the First Dragoons. The settlement must have been growing — Lucien Maxwell and Kit Carson, both so well known, would have popularized the venture — and the protection of the soldiers would be welcomed. As an outpost Rayado

was admirably located, being across the ridge from close-
pent Taos, and within easy striking distance of the Santa Fe
Trail from the Cimarron to Santa Fe, and of the country
north and south.

Through Colonel John Munroe, commanding the Ninth
Military District (which was New Mexico) we have the
following dispatches, dated April 15, 1850, transmitted to
the adjutant general at Washington, " giving an account of
a gallant and successful affair * * * with a marauding party of Apache Indians, the troops having the valuable
experience of Mr. Kit Carson and his two associates in conducting the business " :

Taos, New Mexico, April 12, 1850.

Sir:

Herewith I have the honor to forward, for the information
of the Colonel commanding 9th military department, a report
of Sergeant Holbrook, of my company, who has lately had a
fight with a party of Apache Indians. I regard the affair as a
very handsome one, and very creditable to the sergeant and his
men.   I am informed by a creditable person from Rayado that
two of the Indians were killed with the sabre — the contest
having become so close.

The sergeant speaks of having the scalps of the Indians
whom they killed.   They were taken, I am informed, by two
or three Mexican herders who came up after the fight was
over.

I rejoined my command at this post (from Santa Fe) at 11
o'clock A. M. yesterday.

Very respectfully, &c.,
Wm. N. Grier,
Capt. and B't. Maj., Com'g at Taos, New Mexico.

Rayado, New Mexico, April 7, 1850.

Sir:

It becomes my duty to report the result of a fight between
the detachment of company " I," first dragoons, stationed
at Rayado, and a party of Apache warriors, which took place
yesterday, the 6th instant, on the opposite side of Red River,
thirty miles from this place.   The circumstances led to it as

follows: On the night of the 5th instant, Mr. Maxwell's herders' camp, which is three miles from here, was attacked by Indians, who severely wounded two of his men, and drove off nearly all of the horses and mules belonging to the citizens of this place. On the news of this, I started in pursuit, with the assistance of Messrs. Carson, Fesher, and Newell; and as soon as daylight appeared, to enable us to discover the trail, we galloped until we overtook the enemy. A charge was immediately made, which resulted in the loss on our side of one horse (that of private Richart's, shot from under him). We killed five Indians, (the scalps of which we have for a voucher), and wounded one or two others, and recovered all the animals, but four, which four Indians made their escape on. Allow me to say that every man was eager in the pursuit, and fought with that gallantry *characteristic* of the American soldier.

Very respectfully, your obedient servant,
WM. C. HOLBROOK,
Sergeant, Commanding Detachment.

MAJOR WM. N. GRIER,
    Commanding Officer at Taos, N. M.

Existence at the Rayado was therefore by no means as halcyon as might have been hoped; for when the Indians grew so vindictive as to pillage the property of mountain men as well known as Maxwell and Carson life assumed a serious aspect.

Soon after the little battle exultantly reported by Colonel Munroe, from Major Grier and Sergeant Holbrook, Kit Carson and comrade Tim Goodell (another veteran of the beaver trail) rode north with fifty mules and horses to cut the Oregon Trail at Fort Laramie. Here the animals were marketed among the passing emigrants bound for the golden West — and here, if report may be credited, the overlanders, curious to view the wearer of a name so celebrated, upon seeing Carson, roundly vented their disappointment, even declared the modest claimant a pretender. Goodell was smitten with the gold fever, and proceeded to California;

Kit Carson, more phlegmatic, and conscious of his family responsibilities, returned to Rayado, via Taos.

Again at home, and bent upon that farmer's profession which he would make a vocation, but which the fates decreed should be only an avocation, during the summer he was called, as general police officer, to take the trail of one Fox who, with some companions, was suspected of designs upon the life and money of Messrs. Weatherhead and Brevoort, Santa Fe merchants bound upon a purchasing visit to St. Louis. With a small squad of dragoons, and aided by reinforcements from the inward bound recruits under Captain R. S. Ewell (future Confederate general) encountered on the way, Carson, after a ride of some 300 miles, intercepted the caravan before the evil design upon it had been consummated, exposed the conspirators, and assisted at their arrest. Fox was taken back to Taos, and incarcerated in the *calabozo* — whence, for lack of proper witnesses to testify against him, he was soon liberated. As for Kit Carson, his tangible reward for succor rendered to honest traders was a pair of silver-mounted revolvers, engraved with " a very few, but expressive words."

Sometime in 1850 he made a trip to Missouri, and brought back with him (so claims a report) his little daughter Adaline and a niece, Susan Carson, who soon married Jesse Nelson, a member of the Rayado colony. Carson's household now consisted of his wife, his half-Indian daughter Adaline, aged about fourteen and better educated than her father, his niece, Teresina Bent, aged nine, and his new niece, Susan. In the coming year, 1851, would be born a second boy, William — the first of the seven children who lived.

Again, in 1851 (the exact season is in dispute), Carson made another trip to Missouri, as captain of a wagon train from the Maxwell rancho, conveying, probably, robes, Mexican blankets, horses and mules, for trade in the " States." He would see the beginnings of that new town called Kansas

City; and from its port of Westport Landing would descend by steamboat to St. Louis, there to purchase supplies for the Rayado establishment. Carson came back by Bent's Fort, which, now lapsed from its former glory and devoted chiefly to the wants of the gold field emigrants, was being offered in vain to the government.

With his customary fortune he ran into a band of Cheyennes enraged over the flogging of a chief by an indiscreet army officer. Here ensued a scene very much like the incident with the Kiowas, in the summer of 1848. After the pipe had gone round, Carson heard himself discussed as a prospective victim; whereupon, when his treacherous guests, not knowing him and not suspecting that he understood their words, had said their say, he arose, to accuse them.

Of his fifteen men only two were dependable. One, a Canadian, Pete, afterwards narrated to Dr. Peters:

Why, Kit knew just what was to be done, and did it, too. With any other man, we would have gone under. The Indians were more afraid of him than all the rest of us put together. There were red fellows enough there to eat us up, and at one time I could almost feel my hair leaving my head. We had two women traveling with us, and their crying made me feel so bad that I was sartin there was no fight in me. Women are poor plunder to have along when going out on a war party, but Kit talked to them and then to the Indians, and put them both finally on the right trail. Wagh! But them were ticklish times!

After having been reminded by Carson who he was, and how at Bent's Fort and elsewhere their nation had accepted his hospitality, the Cheyennes sullenly withdrew, to recover from their astonishment and to consult further. Ere their return, the train had been put in motion, and under cover of night Carson had dispatched a Mexican boy, on foot, for Rayado, over 200 miles south, with word to the dragoons stationed there.

On the second day, back came the Cheyennes, as if on mischief bent. They were told that the express had been sent, and that if harm happened to the train the soldiers would know just whom to punish. The wily Indians replied that they would look for moccasin tracks, and see whether the words were true. They found the messenger's tracks leading south from the late camp; and they promptly made tracks themselves for cover in the hills. The train was not troubled again — especially as the relief from Rayado met it near Bent's Fort, to escort it on.

About the same time, or in July of 1851, Lieutenant Colonel Edwin Vinton Sumner succeeded, in command of the Department of New Mexico, the bluff soldier, Colonel John Munroe. " His orders were to cut down the expenses of all branches, both military and civil," runs the lore of New Mexican pioneers. Probably acting upon this plan, he appointed Carson purchasing agent, at the Rayado post, for the Utes and the Apaches who were being supplied with rations from there. Maxwell, the trader, must have had the contract for supplies, and Carson could work well in conjunction with him, and not be dishonest. The Government could have had no better agent than Kit Carson — and never did.[150]

In the spring or fall of 1852 Carson, as if seeking variation, led a company of retired trappers upon an oldtime beaver hunt. The streams long had been neglected, save by a few recluse mountain men whom nothing could tempt therefrom, and nothing discourage. Consequently the hunt was a success — the more so, of course, because many of the trappers felt that it was their last. The emigrant was invading the Platte and the Green; around the Salt Lake were the Mormons; the plains were alive with wagons; there was talk of a Kansas and a Nebraska in the Great American Desert; old Fort Laramie and Fort Hall were " busted "; old Bent's had been " wiped out " — blown to smithereens by the colonel; the days that were could never come again, except in pretense.

In the early summer of 1853 Carson and Maxwell embarked in the speculation of driving sheep overland to California, there to sell them on the hoof. Below Santa Fe they bought some ten or twelve thousand, and with a band of sixty-five hundred, Carson started ahead, by way of the Laramie and the Salt Lake Trail. The northern route of course promised more water and feed; but that he and his herders managed to get the shaggy flock through the thousand miles of perils by Indian, desert, and storm, is another tribute to his absolute knowledge of western ways and means. By careful treatment of the aborigines especially, and due observance of their requirements as to toll, he landed his sheep, with little loss, on the Sacramento. They brought $5.50 a head. Maxwell, following by the same trail, was equally successful.

They found many changes in California, since the old days of the Fremont incursion and the Bear War. The miserable hamlet of Yerba Buena, which in January, 1847, under its new name had a population of 479, now in 1853, after being four times burned, had a population of 40,000 and in tonnage of its shipping ranked only after New York and New Orleans. The barren waste adjoining Sutter's Fort was covered by a mushroom growth equally wonderful — the tents and shanties and business blocks of 12,000 people collected to make Sacramento City. All the hills amidst which the Fremont men had ridden, seeing only Indians and wild horses and deer, were populous with the white race; and the straggling Pueblo de los Angeles, out of which in May, 1848, Carson had ridden with Lieutenant Brewerton, now was a chartered American city of 2,000 people.

Friends Carson probably found. Fremont, late senator from California, was in the East, having just returned from

Europe to outfit his fifth and last expedition, which would take him through the Great Basin again and to the coast.[151] But Godey was in the state; Lieutenant Beale, as Indian Agent newly appointed, arrived at Los Angeles, August 22; and while near San Francisco Carson met an old mountain-man crony and Taos fellow citizen, Jacob Beard, farming. " Kit, on seeing you I feel homesick," he exclaimed, " and I think I ought to go back with you." Carson became sympathetic at once, and said: " Well, Jake, we have only one life to live, and in living it we should make the most of our opportunities."

Whereupon for Mr. Beard "that settled the matter. I returned to the ranch, adjusted my affairs, saddled my mule, caught up with Carson's party, went back to New Mexico, and lived there for many years afterward." [152]

This expedition from the Rio Grande to the coast, with the sheep, and back was Kit Carson's last journey overland west — the last of those long trails, by pass and desert, which had occupied his time so much during twenty-five years. He was now forty-four, and in his prime; but he had drained the best that the adventurous West might offer, and although government columns on half a dozen lines were traversing the country, seeking that Pacific Railroad which yet was distant almost a decade and a half, either he was not offered the post of guide, or else he declined it. A better occupation was awaiting him. The return was evidently uneventful, and arrived in Santa Fe he received the welcome news, communicated by the delegate from the Utah Territory to Congress, that he had been appointed United States Agent for Ute Indians — "probably the most difficult Indians to manage within the territory."

CHAPTER XXX

CARSON AND THE INDIAN — 1853-1861

CARSON'S affairs at the Rayado were such that he could easily leave them (and frequently he had left them), in order to administer officially in Taos. Now for the ensuing eight years he had office and home in Taos. Indeed, Taos always may be considered as his home after his boyhood in Missouri. It was the center around which he revolved and whither he returned from his excursions. From time to time he had temporary quarters elsewhere — trapper quarters, scout quarters, ranch quarters, army quarters; but he was a Taosan from 1827 until the close of his life; and at Taos is his grave, today.

At the time of the advancement of Carson to the agency of the Utes and Apaches, the National Government was face to face with the Indian problem, which to this day never has been solved. In the Southwest the American soldiers had planted a new flag whose principles were as new, had brought new ideas to be enforced among an old race, and had made new regulations for a people hitherto unregulated. The mettle of red and white was to be tried out. And into the West, into the region by solemn pledge given to the Indian and " forever secured and guaranteed " to him against encroachment by alien, was pressing at last the white settler.

For a dozen years, he had been crossing, in constantly increasing numbers, with his teams and his firearms and his foreign virtues and vices, grazing upon the Indian's grass, burning the Indian's fuel, eating the Indian's game or driving it away, shooting the Indian himself when necessity or convenience demanded, and scattering among the natives "loathsome diseases, unknown in their primitive state." Still, amidst his unavailing protests the Indian had been recognized, in the letter if not in the spirit of the law, as proprietor of his own allotted territory.

But the crest of the westward rolling wave representing civilization was towering above the fictitious barrier erected in 1835 by President Jackson — that barrier, between the United States at the Missouri and the Great American Desert beyond — and the white spray was dashing over and on. The closer the Great American Desert was viewed, the more attractive did it appear; and in 1852 the inevitable was recognized:

One thing is certain, the condition of the various tribes located on the western border of Missouri will be speedily changed, and now is the time to determine what is best to be done for their future welfare. * * * The border tribes themselves are well aware of the fact, that there is no resting place for them, under the existing order of things; and this knowledge has had a most unhappy effect upon them. When urged to turn their attention to agricultural or mechanical pursuits, they invariably reply: "What is the use of it? In a few more years we will be driven back into the plains, or the Rocky Mountains; and what will our knowledge of agriculture, or the mechanic arts, avail us on the prairies, or in the Rocky Mountains?"[158]

In 1851 was signed at Fort Laramie the first great treaties by which the plains Indians began to relinquish the rights guaranteed to them forever. Agent Fitzpatrick's Cheyennes and Arapahos, the Shoshoni, the Sioux, the Blackfeet, and the Crows agreed to let the army in and to let the emigrant through. In 1853 Fitzpatrick met the Comanches and Apaches at Fort Atkinson on the Santa Fe Trail in present southern Kansas, wheedling them, persuading them, making "a renewal of faith, which the Indians did not have in the Government, nor the Government in them,"

So the frontier of a quarter-century duration, as if over-weighted by the yearly emigrant rendezvous, sorely pressed at the center bulged outward, threatening to break upon the easternmost tribes, and to the whites already wrestling with the red man's ethical nature add those who would encroach upon his worldly treasures as well.

By order of Congress new treaties were made — for treaties with the Indians are never exhausted. Commissioner George A. Manypenny himself spent much of the summer of 1853 holding councils with the various tribes, laboriously explaining why the old promises were worn out and why fresh ones were better. This explaining was polite, but perfunctory. Shawnee and Kickapoo, Sac and Fox, Omaha and Wea, yes, Arapaho, Pawnee, Cheyenne, and Ute were already evicted, and the Manypenny and the Fitzpatrick excuses, the sounding responses from chief high and low, all the pipes smoked, all the presents given, all the indentures exchanged, only joined other chips carried with that current which no chips could stem. The Indian of the West has had the westerner's choice: "If you do n't like bacon, help yourself to the peppersass."

So in the spring of 1854 they sign their "articles of agreement and convention;" they sign

the Omaha, Ottoe and Missouria, Sac and Fox of Missouri, Iowa, Kickapoo, Delaware, Shawnee, Kaskaskia, Peoria, Wea, Piankeshaw, and Miami Indian, all residing within the central superintendency. * * * These tribes possessed lands bounded on the east by the western boundaries of the States of Missouri and Iowa, and lying between the parallels of 37° and 42° 40′ north latitude, embracing, in the aggregate, nearly 15,000,000 acres, all of which, with the exception of about 1,342,000 acres, being the amount of their several reservations, was ceded to the government. * * *

In the recent negotiations for their lands the Indians dwelt upon the former pledges and promises made to them, and were averse generally to the surrender of any portion of their

CARSON AND THE INDIAN 361

country. They said that they were to have the land " as long as grass grew or water run," and they feared the result if they should consent to yield any part of their possessions. When they did consent to sell, it was only on the condition that each tribe should retain a portion of their tract as a permanent home. All were unitedly and firmly opposed to another removal. * * *

There they stand, the representatives and remnants of tribes once as powerful and dreaded as they are now weak and dispirited. By alternate persuasion and force, some of these tribes have been removed, step by step, from mountain to valley, and from river to plain, until they have been pushed half-way across the continent. They can go no further; on the ground they now occupy the crisis must be met, and their future determined. Among them may be found the educated, civilized, and converted Indian, the benighted and inveterate heathen, and every intermediate grade. But there they are, and as they are, with outstanding obligations in their behalf of the most solemn and imperative character, voluntarily assumed by the government.[154]

Yes, there they are; but the " crisis " which so stirred the Honorable Commissioner George W. Manypenny could scarcely be expected to create much of a furor in the halls of Congress where the red complexion of the debatable country was of far less moment than whether the complexion should be white or black; where, indeed, the resolution introduced by Senator Augustus C. Dodge of Iowa, organizing the territory of Nebraska to extend from the latitude of New Mexico north to 43° 30', in present South Dakota, from Iowa and Missouri west to the mountains, did provide that nothing in the act " be construed to impair the right of persons or property now pertaining to the Indians in that territory, so long as such rights shall remain unextinguished by treaty between the United States and such Indians": but where, this phase considered to be settled by the customary temporizing, the great Douglas was thundering in defense of his compromise Kansas-Nebraska Bill and

" squatter sovereignty "; where Chase and Sumner were denouncing the waiving of the Missouri Compromise line (the slave-district boundary of 36° 30′) as " a gross violation of a sacred pledge," " criminal betrayal of precious rights," an " atrocious plot to exclude from a vast unoccupied region emigrants from the old world, and free laborers from our own states, and to convert it into a dreary region of despotism, inhabited by masters and slaves "; and where (the pledge referred to looming above pledges forgotten) " the struggle * * * on the one side and the other in regard to this measure, heated and made more intense by so constant appeals from without, made by memorials, public meetings, and newspaper arguments, was carried on with a vehemence and passion rarely exhibited in deliberative bodies." [155]

A small chance there was for that innocent bystander, the Indian! And when, on May 30, 1854, the bill was signed creating out of that pleasant fiction the Indian Territory (" forever secured and guaranteed ") the territories of Kansas and Nebraska, the same signature dissipated the Indian. The white man had assumed control of the Great American Desert.

The organization of the Indian country into the Kansas and Nebraska territories affected Kit Carson only in that when it threw open the land, it threw open also the question : " What shall be done with the red man? " As Indian Agent, Carson now was called upon to add his opinions to the thousand other opinions, of which two rarely were harmonious. He had returned to Taos. The first year, of his seven years and a half, as agent, was 1854. In this year the hundred thousand buffalo robes descending the Missouri and the Platte were met by the inflowing five thousand settlers with their cattle; in reports to fill twelve volumes the various army officers detailed to make transcontinental surveys for a future Pacific Railroad were asserting the news (which was to Kit Carson and many another no news at all) that the continent was traversable.

Meanwhile, as a cog in the new machine which is being adjusted, Carson at Taos is agent over two tribes. He succeeds John Greiner, advanced to become secretary of state. The corps of 1854, in the honorable Indian service of New Mexico Territory was: Superintendent *ex officio*, at Santa Fe, Governor David Merriwether; agent of the Navajos, at Fort Defiance, H. L. Dodge; agent of the Southern Apaches, at Doña Ana, E. A. Graves; agent of the Capote and Tabuache Utes, at Abiquiu, James M. Smith — soon succeeded by Lorenzo Labadie; agent of the Jicarilla Apaches and Mohuache Utes, at Taos, Christopher Carson.

It seemed as though Carson was now fitted into his niche. He certainly was a man who understood Indians — even felt at home with Indians; and he was a man whom the Indians understood, and with whom they felt at home. Here in Taos, with his family and friends, and amidst familiar scenes, comfortable in his salary of $1,000, his many years of activity an inexhaustible resource upon which to draw, and the country roundabout suiting his mode of life, Carson held to his agency, and outlasted all his colleagues with whom he started. Governors changed, superintendents changed, agents changed, but he stuck fast.

At the close of 1856 the Jicarillas seem to have been transferred to the Abiquiu agency, and the Tabuache Utes attached to the Taos agency. The Carson reports are uniformly headed " Utah Agency."

As to the Utes in general and the Jicarilla Apaches with whom the Mohuache Utes, particularly, affiliated in deeds of outlawry, Superintendent Merriwether reports in 1854:

The Utahs of New Mexico are a portion of the tribe of the same name inhabiting the Territory of Utah; they speak the same language and have frequent intercourse with each other. From the best information which I have been able to obtain, that portion of the tribe properly under the charge of this superintendency numbers between five and six thousand souls; and they inhabit and claim all of that region of country embracing the sources of the northwestern tributaries of the Arkansas River, above Bent's Fort, up to the southern boundary of Utah territory, and all the northern tributaries of the Rio Grande which lie within New Mexico and north of the 37th parallel of latitude. This country is estimated to cover a space equal to twenty thousand square miles, which would give about five square miles to each soul; but they often extend their wanderings beyond these limits. This is a highly warlike tribe of Indians, are well-armed with fire-arms, and have committed many depredations upon the unoffending inhabitants of New Mexico. They do not cultivate the soil, but depend upon the chase and robbery for a subsistence. A continued feud has existed between the Utahs on the one side, and the Arapahoes and Cheyennes of the Arkansas on the other, for many years past; but latterly, the latter Indians, having been supplied with arms and ammunition by our Indian agents and traders, have proved more than a match for the former, and consequently the Utahs dare not visit the buffalo regions in search of food. This, together with the fact that game is becoming comparatively scarce in their country, has induced if not constrained the Utahs to keep up their ancient custom of theft and robbery.

The Utahs are probably the most difficult Indians to manage within the territory. They are subdivided into several small bands under petty chiefs, who acknowledge no superior, and roam over a vast extent of country, having no permanent places of residence, and hence are often difficult to be found. Occasionally, parties will come into the settlements and labor for the citizens for a short time, particularly in threshing out the grain, which they are enabled to do with their own horses and mules; they then leave, and nothing more is heard of them for months. They * * * are always ready for mischief, and hard to overtake in a retreat. Many of this tribe are understood to have made common cause with the Jicarillas in their recent difficulties. * * * They now profess to be friendly with us, but little confidence is to be placed in their professions at any time.

* * * * * * * * * *

The Jicarilla Apaches * * * claim a region of country

CARSON AND THE INDIAN 365

of indefinite space, lying west of the Rio Grande and on the head of the Chama and Puerco rivers, but they roam over other portions of the territory. It is confidently believed that no other single band of Indians have committed an equal amount of depredations upon, and caused so much trouble and annoyance to the people of this territory, as the Jicarillas. They are supposed to number about one hundred and fifty warriors, and probably five hundred souls; they own a large number of horses and mules, and whenever there is any mischief brewing, invariably have a hand in it. * * * They rely upon the chase for a subsistence; and when this fails resort to depredations upon the flocks and herds of the inhabitants.

At the time of Kit Carson's accession to the fatherhood of the Mohuache Ute and Jicarilla Apache bands, annual reports upon some 350,000 Indians were being handed in by 100 agents, teachers, and superintendents.

The Carson report for 1853 is lacking in the fifty published volumes, entitled *Indian Affairs.* He first reports " for the present month," September 26, 1855, confining himself chiefly to an attack by Indians in his district upon Mexican herders near Mora and the theft of some twelve head of cattle (valued at $12 a head) from the Maxwell Ranch, and to the rescue by Mexicans of Mexican prisoners.

The Indians that are now committing depredations are those who lost their families during the war [i. e., probably the campaign declared in 1854 against the Jicarillas and allies by the Government]. They consider they have nothing farther to live for than revenge for the death of those of their families that were killed by the whites; they have become desperate; when they will ask for peace I cannot say.

Respectfully submitted.

I have the honor to be, very respectfully, your obedient servant,

C. CARSON,
Indian Agent.

To the report Superintendent Merriwether affixes the mild reproof: " Mr. Carson does not inform me what

Indians committed these depredations, though the last part of his report would leave the impression that they were committed by the Jicarilla Apaches. * * * It is to be regretted that Agent Carson did not ascertain from the prisoners what Indians they were."

This Carson probably did; rather, certainly he did; it would be one of the first details babbled by the mouths of the frightened fugitives, and passed from mouth to mouth by the other Mexicans. But in his unaccustomed dictation he left it out.

The Carson reports as agent at Taos appear in 1855, are omitted in 1856, resumed in 1857, and continue to 1861. The reports are signed (with slight variation) " I have the honor to be, very respectfully, your obedient servant, C. Carson." In addition to preparing the reports, he must distribute and otherwise account for the annuities — blankets, knives, powder, paint, provisions; must act as judge, jury and tribal parent; must pay visits, and must satisfy both the governmental red tape and the aboriginal ideas, equally as rigid and peculiar.

The Carson home was at the northeast corner of the Taos plaza — that central square which in all frontier Mexican towns indicated the original corral whither the community animals were driven at night. The house stands today; a low one-story, flat-roofed " adobe," continuous with other houses forming a solid line, and having the customary veranda, supported by poles, along the front. Here lived Kit Carson, his wife, and their increasing family.[156]

The official agency quarters were halfway around the plaza, on the south side — being a single room in the row of adobes there. But the Indians, growing to trust their agent and being emboldened more and more to seek the town, on chance of gaining some point, frequented home and office alike.

The only fly in the ointment was the clerical duties connected with the office. At this time Kit Carson could sign his name — having been instructed in that while an army officer in California, and later by his wife; but beyond this, " reading, writing, and (save in its simplest form) arithmetic " were a *terra incognita.*[157] With fatuous and apparently suspicious insistency the Government required from all its agents a regular accounting; and to fill out the forms, to make out an annual, much more a monthly report, seriously bothered Carson.

However, he got around this difficulty without formal confession or requisition for a go-between. The Government did allow interpreters — but not for the clerical role which would have appealed to Carson.[158] Accordingly, in the matter of the monthly reports upon his Indian charges he reported in person and by word of mouth at Santa Fe. A letter to the author from Captain Smith Simpson says:

> Kit would go to Santa Fe six or eight times a year. In the office of the Superintendent of Indian Affairs there was a man named John Ward — a very intelligent man. I think that he wrote Kit's monthly reports and dated them " Taos." I do not remember to have written any reports except the quarterly accountings covering the money on hand and the money expended for corn, wheat, sheep and beef.[159]

Possibly it was through John Ward that, previous to young Smith Simpson's appearance in Taos, Agent Carson managed his quarterly accountings also; possibly Ceran St. Vrain may have helped. Then when, in the summer of 1855, the campaign against the Utes and Jicarillas having been finished, Sergeant Smith H. Simpson, of the volunteers from Santa Fe, was mustered out in Taos and concluded to stay there, Carson's accountings were simplified. Young Simpson, aged twenty-two, came opportunely into Kit Carson's life. He was also a welcome adjunct to the English-speaking society in Taos. While thereafter Carson did the quarterly dictating, young Simpson did the figuring; and from this partnership between young New Yorker and older mountain man evolved the first (or what is claimed to be the first) Kit Carson photograph.

Photographs (daguerreotypes, ambrotypes, and tintypes) became the fashion, it would seem, following the Mexican War; and during the period from 1845 to 1860 there appeared what now are our most valued mementoes of many frontiersmen. Jim Bridger, William Sublette, the Bents, Ceran St. Vrain, and their comrade veterans sat before the novel lens. But with typical aversion to publicity, and with almost Indian suspicion, some refused, among them being for many years Kit Carson, until in 1860 he had to make a virtue of necessity. The time had waxed until that bugbear, a government quarterly report, must be tackled; and Carson mildly suggested that they get to work. Simpson blandly returned that inasmuch as Carson would not favor him by having that picture taken, he did not know that he could set his hand to writing.

" Come along, then," bade Carson, accepting the Simpson challenge; and together they went to the little gallery, where before that mysterious "machine" to which, Carson had declared, he would prefer the " cannon's mouth," they singly posed. " That was December, 1860," writes Captain Simpson, now half a century after. " It cost me $7.50, for Kit's and my own taken at the same time." [160]

In the real and active duties of his agency, Kit Carson was thoroughly at home. No white man could better have interpreted to the Indians the Government, or to the Government the Indian. This was a matter independent of pen and paper. The selection of the Utes as Carson's charges was particularly happy; with the Utes he was thoroughly familiar, and, in addition, there was mutual respect. They knew him by tradition and by actual experience; he knew them, as repeats General Rusling in 1866, for " the bravest

KIT CARSON AND MASTER CHARLEY BOGGS

AN EARLY PICTURE OF CARSON, TINTYPE, DATE UNKNOWN, PROBABLY LATE
FIFTIES OR EARLY SIXTIES. THE BOY WAS THE SON OF CARSON'S FRIEND,
T. O. BOGGS OF TAOS AND THE ARKANSAS. TINTYPE GIVEN TO J. S. HOUGH
BY CARSON'S DAUGHTER, TERESINA

(Courtesy of George L. Beam, present possessor)

VIEJO CHEYENNE

SCOUT UNDER CARSON IN THE INDIAN CAMPAIGN OF 1855.
AN AGED ALIEN, CLAIMED TO BE A CENTENARIAN AT THE
TAOS PUEBLO

(Photograph by F. J. Francis)

LUCIEN R. MAXWELL

FAMED TRADER AND RANCHER OF SANTA FE TRAIL DAYS,
AND ONE OF CARSON'S CRONIES

*(From oil portrait at the M. M. Chase ranch house at
Cimarron, New Mexico)*

and best Red Skins he had ever met, in all his wide wanderings." Said General Sherman at the same time:
" These Red Skins think Kit twice as big a man as me. Why, his integrity is simply perfect. They know it, and they would believe him and trust him any day before me."

And in his report of 1857 Carson refers to the Tabuaches as being " by far the most noble of the Utah tribes," and the Mohuaches as " the most noble and virtuous tribe within our Territory."

Entire harmony seems to have prevailed between Carson and the Utes, when he could get at them and reason with them. The Apaches were " truly the most degraded and troublesome Indians we have in our department "; " we daily witness them in a state of intoxication in our plaza "; to them he was "Kit," but to the Utes he was not only " Kit," but " Father Kit " and " Uncle Kit."

The Carson Indian policy would endorse the theory of segregation from the whites, and of pride in work. However, the Government's early experiments with the native westerner, whom it displaced by the imported easterner, were vacillating and unfortunate.

Having deprived them of most that made existence [i. e., in the old way and accustomed way] possible, it took great satisfaction in furnishing a substitute, in the form of a ration system under which all Indians who were good — in other words, who stayed on their reservations and abstained from violence — would receive at stated intervals so many pounds of meat, of beans, of flour, of sugar and other edibles. * * * Nothing was demanded of the Indians in return except that they obey their Agents and keep quiet. It is true that salaried farmers were sent to the reservations to instruct them in agriculture, and that tools and fencing were offered them as rewards of industry; but what was to be gained by being industrious if one could live on the fat of the land without stirring a muscle in labor? Satan's proverbial gift for finding mischief for idle hands to do came promptly into play, and the idle hands of the Indians soon learned to reach for the whiskey bottle. Hence it came that a people once vigorous, strong-willed, untiring on the trail of anything they wanted, became debauched by a compulsory life of sloth, and within a single generation acquired among the whites a reputation for laziness, incompetence, and general degradation.[161]

This criticism, and more, Carson and a few of his associate agents proclaimed, earnestly, fifty years preceding. For his Mohuache Utes Carson advises, in his annual report, date August 29, 1857:

Humanity, as well as our desire to benefit the Indian race, demands that they be removed as far as practicable from the settlements. Have farmers, mechanics, etc., placed among them to give instruction in the manner of cultivating the soil to gain their subsistence, and learn them to make the necessary implements to carry on said labor. They would, in a few years, be able to support themselves, and not be, as at present, a burden on the general government. It is true much could not be expected of the present generation, for they have been accustomed to gain their maintenance by the chase and robberies committed on the neighboring tribes and the whites. But if the rising generation be taught to maintain themselves by honest labor, in their manhood they will not depart therefrom, and will feel proud in being able to instruct their children the manner of maintaining themselves in an honest way. Troops, for a period of time, should be stationed near them, for the purpose of protecting them from hostile tribes, and also show them that the government has the power to cause them to remain on the lands given them and not to encroach on that of their neighbors.

In the annual report of 1858, Agent Carson would explain that " it is impossible to give, as required by communication from the Department of the Interior, dated July 11, 1857, the exact number of Indians under my charge. They live in parties of ten to twenty lodges, and have no permanent residence. In agricultural or mechanical pursuits there are none engaged; by the chase, and with what is given them

by the United States and its citizens, they maintain themselves." And he adds, as if responding to another sugges-
tion:

It would promote the advance of civilization among the
Indians of this agency if it were practicable that I could live
with them. They have no particular place to reside, are of a
roving nature, and an agent could not be with them at all
times, so I have selected this place as the most proper for
them to receive such presents of food as they need, and such
will necessarily be the case until the agency buildings are
built. The Indians should be settled on reserves, guarded by
troops, made to cultivate the soil, because the required amount
of provisions to be given them cannot be procured at any of
the frontier settlements. * * *
To keep the Indians from committing depredations on citizens, food by the government must be furnished them, and
liberally, there being no game of any consequence in the
country through which they roam.

Thus the annuities were becoming only briberies, and
none knew it better than the Indians themselves. If they
were to be made dependents, the people which so decreed
should pay a price!

During the year the Indians committed few depredations;
they stole some animals from the Mexicans, and the Mexicans
also stole some from them. The Indians gave me the animals
stolen by them, and I made the Mexicans return the animals
they had stolen, thus satisfying both parties.
I have visited the Indians as often as necessary during the
year, and given them such articles as they required, principally
provisions. It being thought that the Utahs would join the
Mormons in their opposition to the entry of the United States
troops into Great Salt Lake City, I caused the allowance of
their provisions to be increased, to prevent such a course
being pursued by them. No Utah, as far as I know, aided the
Mormons.[162]

Carson's September, 1859, annual report from Taos, to
Superintendent J. L. Collins at Santa Fe, includes:

The two bands of the Muahuaches and Tobawatches, so far as regards their numerical strength, are on the decline, and the causes of this decrease in population are disease and frequent conflicts with other warlike tribes.

If any improvement has been made in their condition or prospects, it is not perceptible. They are, at the present day, as uncivilized as when the government first took them under her care, and it is my opinion they will remain in the same state until they shall be settled on reserves, and compelled to cultivate the soil for their maintenance. Not having the least particle of the pride of self-support about them, they will continue to sink deeper into degradation, so long as a generous government, or their habits of begging and stealing, afford them a means of subsistence. I have, heretofore, recommended that they be settled on farms, and I am still satisfied that it is the only practicable mode of reclaiming them from their barbarous condition.

The report refers to hostilities commenced in July against gold hunters of the Valle Salado — for into South Park of the Colorado soon to be, had penetrated the white roamer, disturbing with pick and shovel the ground long sacred to Ute dead, with rifle and voice disturbing the game long sacred to Ute living — advises that no troops have yet been furnished in response to the call for protection to the trespassers, and warns:

The consequences arising from letting these Indians go unpunished will be injurious. Other bands of Indians, seeing that depredations are committed by these with impunity, will soon follow the example so much in accordance with their habits and inclinations, and will only remain quiet so long as it suits their convenience.[163]

The last Carson report, that of August 29, 1860, reiterates the opinion of 1857:

In my opinion, the best policy the government can adopt in the regulation and management of these two bands of

Utahs would be to have them settled upon reserves, and furnished with a few good farmers and mechanics, who could and would instruct them in husbandry and the mechanic arts. Their minds are tractable, and capable of receiving impressions which would in a comparatively short time, under judicious training, enable them to obtain an honest subsistence for themselves and families. It is true that the older members of the tribes, who are confirmed in their present habits of life, might be obstinate in their resistance to the change; but they, in the course of nature, must pass away in a few years, and the young generation which is now growing up to take their places, can be educated in such a manner as to make them submit to the habits and customs of civilized life with facility. To effect this reformation will be required the labor of years, but, in my opinion, would in the end prove a measure of economy to the government and a blessing to the Indians.

*   *   *   *   *   *   *   *   *   *

If some policy of this kind is not adopted by the government, and if provisions are not furnished them in sufficient quantities to sustain them during the winter months, they will be reduced to the necessity of thieving and robbing. Their game being killed or driven off, nothing better can reasonably be expected from them. In a few years, if allowed to roam at large and visit the settlements at pleasure, they will become victims to intemperance and its concomitant vices, which will reduce them to a condition of great depravity. Humanity demands that this fate should be averted from them, and it can only be avoided by setting them apart to themselves, agricultural instruments given them, and proper instruction imparted to them, as before mentioned.

*   *   *   *   *   *   *   *   *   *

I have the honor to be, your obedient servant,

C. CARSON,
United States Indian Agent.[164]

In his correspondence Agent Carson presented no startling theories; he, perhaps unwittingly, advocated a system even then being tried farther east, where earnest, self-sacrificing people were endeavoring in school and field to make the Indian conscious of the responsibilities which he faced. Reservations had been set aside; farmer and mechanic teachers had been provided; tribes had been allotted their own tracts, to do thereon and therewith as their judgment might incline. But (save the usual exceptions) with all these thus early started upon the white man's road, as with Carson's Utes, Steck's Apaches, Fitzpatrick's and Bent's Cheyennes and Arapahos, the result was the same. The signposts of the white man's road appealing most to the red man were the white man's vices, not the white man's virtues. And at the close of his days Kit Carson himself, having witnessed the best plans of a mighty government apparently nullified by the machinations of unscrupulous servants of that government, could only blame the conditions upon " bad white men," and lament that the end was as the end must be.

CHAPTER XXXI

CAMPAIGNS OF THE FIFTIES

KIT CARSON, as " father " to the Indians, did not find it
possible to spare the rod. Among the mesas and hills
to the immediate west and northwest was Chico Velasquez,
the Apache, head of a long line of chiefs — Blanco, Chacon,
Mangas Colorado (Red Sleeves), Cochise, Delgadito (The
Slender), Cuchillo Negro (Black Knife) — who in Carson's time led upon vengeful foray Jicarilla, Mescalero,
Coyotero, Mimbreño, Pinal, Chiricahui, and other tribes still
smarting from the wholesale murders by Kirker's and Johnson's scalp hunters, and smarting also from the alleged
injustice of not being allowed to kill Mexicans as of yore.

From 1850 through more than a third of a century the
story of the Southwest is the story of incessant war, mainly
with the Apache. Carson entered with the first chapter;
but the volume writ in blood, its tale the cruelty of man
to man, continued long after he had been retired permanently from the scenes.

By 1854 the army had already started its series of historic
outposts which were to be oases in the midst of the threatening desolation. After old Marcy at Santa Fe, there were
erected, to protect the Southwest, forts Yuma and Union:
the one located in California, facing the mouth of the Gila,
where the emigrant trail crossed the Colorado; the other, ✓
built in 1851, in the opposite corner, on the Santa Fe Trail
100 miles northeast of Santa Fe, fifty miles southeast of
Taos, and maintained as headquarters of the Northern Military District of New Mexico. The line of posts stretched
down along the Rio Grande to the border; they spread on

either side into Apache country, and sent skirmishers into the north among the Navajos and the Utes. So that now in 1854 there were forts Marcy and Union; Cantonment Burgwin, nine miles north of Taos, and named for the gallant captain who fell before Big Nigger's bullet, at the battle of Taos Pueblo; Fort Massachusetts, in the midst of the San Luis Valley, which is Colorado; Fort Defiance, in the Navajo country, which is Arizona; forts Craig, Thorn, Fillmore, and Bliss, on the lower Rio Grande, reaching to the Texas line; and garrisons at the Rayado, Albuquerque, Las Lunas (Los Lunas) below, and Tucson; while Fort Conrad at Valverde below Socorro (first battle field of New Mexico in the Civil War), Fort Webster at the Copper Mines, long sacred to Apache rule, the towns of Ciboletta, Socorro, Taos, Doña Ana, El Paso, San Elizario, Las Vegas, Abiquiu, and others, had borne the Flag. Thus swiftly had marched in the American soldier where a decade before the only law was the wild will of the Apache, Ute, and Navajo.

Commanding the district of New Mexico was Colonel Thomas T. Fauntleroy of the First Dragoons. John Munroe, the martinet, Sumner, the distinguished, Fauntleroy, Garland, Bonneville, the mountain man soldier, Loring, the one-armed adviser of the Khedive, Canby, the victim of the lava beds, Carleton, the indefatigable; under these department commanders Carson served in border warfare.

Shudder as we may at the atrocities of the Apache, we must remember that it was broken faith which brought on the campaign that really opened the war. For in his initial report, from the palace at Santa Fe, September 1, 1854, Governor David Merriwether says, criticising a compact which he discovers as an onus upon the office:

It will be found that my predecessor, on the part of the United States, contracted with the Indians that they, and all others who should join in it, should be supplied with food, to consist of corn, beef and salt, for that current year and the year 1854, and to give them a reasonable amount of food (of which the agent was to be the judge) for three years thereafter, and also brood-mares, etc., etc.

The thirteenth article stipulates that this compact shall have no validity until approved by the authority of the United States; but before any approval on the part of the United States, my predecessor proceeded to carry it into effect, by assembling and locating a large number of these Indians on two farms situated near Fort Webster and the town of Abiquiu, employed farmers and laborers, and supplied all the Indians assembled with provisions. These steps so taken in compliance with the compact doubtless led the Indians to suppose that a ratification on the part of the United States had been received, nor am I informed of their having been undeceived previous to my arrival in the territory.

Confronted with the fact that not only were all the funds, save $3,000, for contingent expenses of Indian Affairs in New Mexico exhausted, but that there were claims of $10,-000 against the office; and that the compact itself not only had been left unratified but had been disapproved by the Government, Superintendent Merriwether must perforce break to the touchy Jicarillas the delicate news that it was all a mistake and that they would cease to be supplied with food. Consequently, not understanding, and not choosing to understand, the complicated methods of the new landlord whose every change of " father " meant a change of policy, the Apache took umbrage. For after all, he was of that savage simplicity which accepts the deed for the word.

It is due to these Indians that I should say, that the want of ability on my part to carry into effect the stipulations contained in the compact heretofore alluded to, left them in a destitute condition.

* * * * * * * * * *

I have found it difficult, if not impossible, to make the Indians comprehend how it is, that previous to my arrival in this country this compact was being executed on our part, and that their rations should be stopped so soon thereafter.

When I explain the thirteenth article to them, and inform them that my government, so far from ratifying, had disapproved it entirely, they then ask how it was that their former Father could satisfy them with food and carry the compact into effect, whilst their present Father could not. When I say to them that I had no money to purchase presents and provisions with, their reply is, how did their former Father get money for this purpose? [165]

The produce of the two farms being sufficient for only a few weeks' subsistence, there the Apache was moved from his hunting grounds, and given naught in their place. For this apparent trickery he made the Government pay dearly, the saving in the department resulting in the loss to the New Mexican people, September, 1853, to September, 1854, of "between forty and fifty thousand dollars and many valuable lives."

So in the spring of 1854, following a sharp rebuke, by warwhoop and bullet and arrow, to a detachment of First Dragoons who would have "watched and restrained their movements," Acting Governor and Superintendent William S. Messervy

issued a proclamation, declaring that war existed between the United States and the Jicarilla band of the Apache tribe of Indians, and all their aiders and abettors. Shortly afterward he also issued an order calling out a portion of the militia of the Territory, to assist in protecting the frontiers and prosecuting the war; and this decisive step, together with the bravery, energy, and promptness of the troops, assisted by the citizens * * * distressed the Indians very much and caused them great loss. [166]

Early were the soldiery taught the lesson that in the southwestern Apache they had no mean foe. March, 1854, saw the defeat of Lieutenant John W. Davidson, a hero of San Pasqual and an officer accustomed to the guerilla tactics employed by Mexicans and Indians alike. Sent forth by order of Major George A. H. Blake, commanding at Cantonment Burgwin, with F and I companies, consisting of sixty men, First Dragoons, "to watch and restrain" the marauding Jicarillas, along the trail to Santa Fe, Davidson came upon them in the Embudo Mountains, twenty miles southwest of Taos, "in a rocky defile of their own choosing." Consequently ensued, continues Colonel Meline, who a dozen years later passed through the vicinity (the lieutenant himself then being general in command at Fort Union), "one of the most desperate fights in our Indian record."[167]

When beset, the dragoons clambered on foot up the sides of the defile, trusting by the charge to dislodge the shrieking reds. But instead they only scattered them among the rocks. It was a style of fighting with which the Indian is much in love; and the Apaches, avid, gleeful, themselves scarcely seen, with a storm of lead and shaft smote the toiling, heavier soldiers. Now the dragoon horses were endangered; and led by Lieutenant Davidson ("as cool and collected as if under the guns of his fort," was reported to Kit Carson) the soldiers must cut their way back again. Just in time they arrived at their saddle stock, and retreat was ordered. It proved a hand-to-hand conflict, saber and pistol against lance and arrow. Leaving twenty-two men dead on the field ("I helped bury them myself," said Kit Carson), with thirty-six wounded, including the lieutenant, out of the remaining forty, the First Dragoons painfully made their way back to Cantonment Burgwin.

An express was dispatched with the news to Fort Union, sixty miles away, where Lieutenant Colonel Philip St. George Cooke was in command — a character of renown in western army annals: "a very peppery man with language," who "talked through his nose so that you could hardly understand him, but you *had* to understand him."[168]

He has spoken before in these pages. Let him speak again.

On the 31st of March, 1854, while at Fort Union, I received news from Major Blake, commanding at Camp Burgwin, of a severe action between a detachment of the First Dragoons, under Lieutenant Davidson, and the Apaches, in which the dragoons had " lost from thirty-five to forty men, and brought in seventeen wounded men." The despatch reached me about nine o'clock in the morning, and by noon of the same day I started with all the troops that could be prudently drawn from the fort, and comprising a detachment First Dragoons, under Lieutenant Sturgis, and Company H of the Second Dragoons, Lieutenant Bell. The entire command had, within sixteen hours, returned from marches of 200 miles, part of the distance through severe snowstorms. Closely following the mounted men came Company D, Second Artillery (serving as riflemen), commanded by Brevet Captain Sykes, Third Artillery.[169]

" By one of the most severe winter marches I ever undertook," Colonel Cooke now pursued the retiring Jicarillas.

In brief, we crossed the main ridge of the Rocky Mountains. Our force, increased by some of the First Dragoons from Fort Burgwin and Major Blake, together with about thirty New Mexicans and Pueblo Indians under the famous Kit Carson (then Indian agent for the Apaches), now amounted to 100 sabres and 89 rifles and irregulars. Crossing the Rio Grande, we pursued the enemy through deep snows along the margin of frightful precipices and ravines, over the roughest mountains by sheep-paths, following the devious and scarcely perceptible trail only through the wonderful sagacity of our Pueblo allies, who seemed never at fault.

Carson was chief of scouts. The captain of the scout company was James H. Quinn, Taos Irishman of much renown and president of the Territorial Council. The trail was approximately the stage trail of today, which connects Taos with the railroad at Servilleta, thirty-five miles east. The Rio Grande was swollen with melting snow and must be forded. Scouts and dragoons forced in their horses, which with great difficulty kept foothold among the rocks of the icy torrent, here rushing along between high cañon walls. The horses must then be sent back for the use of the riflemen. Aiding and inciting, Carson is said to have crossed and recrossed twenty times. Up the switchback trail which ascends the west wall, the benumbed, dripping men and horses clambered, and crossed the sagy plateau which lies between the river and Servilleta.

Beyond Servilleta the trail of the Apaches was discovered by the scouts. The soldiers followed persistently — the spirited Captain Sykes declining to mount the horse which was his by virtue of his rank, but lending it constantly to some disabled member of his foot command.

On the fourth day from Servilleta the foe, heading for the rugged, timbered region of the El Rito country (favorite with the Apache), finding that the Americans were not to be discouraged, punctuated the pursuit of 150 miles by turning at bay

in a position selected by them, and one of singular strength. It was defended by ramparts of solid rock, towering above and on either side of us. At its foot ran the Agua Caliente, a mountain stream, in most places impassible, and fringed along its banks with huge bowlders which had tumbled from the overhanging cliffs. The position could only be turned by a march of some hours.

This, then, was the Caliente or Warm Spring country to the southwest of Servilleta, in north central New Mexico. The scouts under Carson uncovered the enemy; nothing loth were the Pueblos to engage their ancient foe. Colonel Cooke ordered the Sykes riflemen to deploy as skirmishers. The captain " cheered his men from a limping walk into a sort of run," and, crossing the stream, through snow-water to their armpits, they dashed to the attack, supporting the scouts.

Lieutenant David Bell led his H Company of the First

Dragoons on a charge up the mountain side, penetrated the loose line of the Apaches, and, after dismounting his men, seized upon a ledge of rock which flanked the Indian position. Lieutenant Joseph E. Maxwell was ordered below, to intercept the pony herd, that the Apache retreat might be cut off.

Before this scientific assault the Jicarillas' tactics failed; they could not meet West Point and frontier combined.

With the commands of Captain Sykes and Major Blake, aided by Lieutenant Bell, the enemy's right was soon after turned, and they were completely dispersed with severe loss. The enemy numbered about 150 warriors, under Head-Chief Chacon. He acknowledged five killed and six wounded. Our loss, one (1) killed and one (1) severely wounded.

* * * * * * * * * *

It is scarcely necessary to say that all the officers exhibited energy and gallantry, and I would thus include Captain Quinn, of the Spy Company; and Mr. Carson showed his well-known activity and boldness.

* * * * * * * * * *

At sun-down, Brevet Major Carleton, First Dragoons, joined me with his command. Very early the next day (9th) the pursuit was renewed. I found, after some miles, that the enemy's horse-tracks converged in the snow on a mountain side. There had been broken a path two feet deep, which led over the great obstacles of a forest of aspens and pines which had been prostrated by storm; through bogs where mules had to be unpacked; up and down the steep mountain sides, from whose summit, above the growth of trees, a world of bleak snow spread unlimited to the west; over a stream half-bridged with ice and deep snow, where the horses fell and every mule had to be unpacked. The very beef-cattle were forced through the snow so slowly as to add to these delays of hours, and a horse losing his footing floundered dangerously. American horses, led in file, first broke the path of this retreat. Such was the scene of the enemy's flight by moonlight; the tracks of bare and diminutive feet left a feeble memorial of their suffering.

After three days of similar obstacles, somewhat ameliorated

by the occasional glimpses of the most stupendous scenery
* * * we came to a point where the trail, after expanding
like the sticks of a fan into twenty smaller trails, finally " ran
out " ; as I was assured by the guides, Carson, and all who
were experienced, that it was useless to pursue farther, I
gave the order to turn toward the settlements of the Chama.

The trail of the Apache is a work of art. No Indians
are more expert in flight, just as no Indians are more expert
in pursuit. Decoyed onward through the most difficult
places to be found, the Colonel Cooke command at night
would be only a few miles from the start of the morning
before. The Apaches traveled light — an *ignis fatuus*
almost but never quite overtaken — until, having exhausted
the dragoons and the foot soldiery, they dissolved in the
" twenty smaller trails expanding like the sticks of a fan."
After one or two futile sallies from Abiquiu, the historic
Mexican village on the Chama, the expedition under its
doughty colonel must return to the several posts. The
bodies of the twenty-two dragoons who fell at Embudo
might still call for vengeance (for slight had been the tab-
ulated loss in the fight at Agua Caliente) ; but in the words
of the Department Commander, General Garland, satisfaction could be taken from the fact that to the Indians had
been demonstrated something " worth more to us than
victory " that they " are not safe from pursuit in the most
inaccessible parts of the Rocky Mountains."

Back at Taos, and meanwhile performing his duties of
agent and overseeing his ranching operations at the Rayado,
Carson was called to the field by Major James H. Carleton,
against the Jicarillas.

Fort Massachusetts, far up into the mountain interior of
present Colorado and the most isolated of the frontier posts,
was made the basis of operations. In two columns, one
under that partisan volunteer, Captain Quinn, and the other
under Major Carleton himself, with Carson for guide, the

troops crossed eastward from Fort Massachusetts by Mosca Pass and Sangre de Cristo Pass into the valleys between the main range and the front range of the mountains, where they struck an Indian trail. Swinging southward, in a six days' march they were back into New Mexico at Fisher's Peak of the Raton Range between Bent's Fort and Taos. From the dry basin of the bald Fisher's Peak itself the Apaches and some few renegade Utes were driven in flight. It was on this trail to Fisher's Peak that Kit Carson made his special reputation as a scout — made it by one incident which, somehow, has gained the ascendency over many a more important incident.

On the morning of the day when the Apache camp was sighted, Carson, judging from the freshening sign in the trail, hazarded the prediction to Major Carleton that, barring accident, the Indians would be overtaken "by two o'clock this afternoon." The major, with that indulgency and that half-incredulity which is apt to stamp the regular army officer's attitude toward the less regular and apparently mysterious scout, promptly offered him a hat to prove his words. Evidently the prediction was accurate; for in due time came to Kit Carson at Taos, from the " States," "a superb hat," bearing within it the inscription:

At 2 o'Clock
K I T   C A R S O N
from
MAJOR CARLETON

The early spring and the summer of 1855 witnessed a larger campaign against the Jicarillas and the Mohuache Utes, their combined bands being under the leadership of Blanco — chief with the "lofty forehead" and features as regular as if "carved for sculptured perfection." By order of Governor Merriwether and Colonel Garland both volunteers and regulars took the field, the former organized at Santa Fe, under Ceran St. Vrain, the trader, in response to the proclamation calling for 700 men to serve six months. Volunteers and regulars were mobilized at Taos, whence, under Colonel Thomas Fauntleroy himself and Ceran St. Vrain (who wins the title of lieutenant colonel), and with Carson as chief of Taos Pueblo scouts, the expedition set forth. The command consisted of two companies of the First Dragoons, D company of the Second Artillery (afoot as riflemen), six companies of volunteers (Americans and Mexicans mingled and one in valor) under St. Vrain, and the company of Carson spies.

Among the regulars was Lieutenant Alexander McDowell McCook, just out of West Point and with a glorious career before him; Lieutenant William Magruder; Lieutenant William Craig, scarce a year from the Academy and one day to seek the governorship of Colorado. Among captains of volunteers were Charles Williams, A Company; Francisco Gonzales, B Company; Captain Charles Deüs and Captain Manual Antonio Chaves — the last, a worthy descendant of a DeVargas *conquistador* of 1690, his name dating back to the Moorish war of 1160, and he himself, when a warrior youth but sixteen years of age, pierced by seven Navajo arrows. The expedition of 1855 boasted no more distinguished member than Manual Chaves — smaller and slighter even than Kit Carson, with steely gray eyes, brown hair, a florid complexion, and a great heart for a fight.

The Mohuache Utes and Jicarilla Apaches, being well provisioned, well munitioned, after a brief period of quiet were refreshed, and ready to whip the Americans. The campaign out of Taos was first carried on in March weather below zero, in the San Luis Valley and among the engirting mountains of Colorado, with old Fort Massachusetts as a base. Carson vouches for the temperature and the travel being the worst in all his long experience, surpassing even the severities of the year before.

The hostiles were found encamped near the Saguache, at the northern end of the San Luis Park.. Deceived by the smallness of the advance guard, they swarmed from their lodges to the defense. Scarcely had the main body of the troops hastened to the front, when in a long, whooping line, shrieking their taunts, shaking their bows and lances, down the valley charged, with feathers streaming, the Indians.

A young Apache chief rode to and fro, yelling at the top of his voice and encouraging his warriors at every hand. This chief, with lance in hand, boldly charged upon Captain Chaves, who killed him with a shot from his unerring rifle; before the Indian had fallen from his horse he was dragged to the ground by Antonio Tapia and scalped with a knife, which afterwards came into the possession of Major Weightman, and was used by him when he killed Felix X. Aubrey in the Exchange Hotel, at Santa Fe. The Indians finally turned and fled, having suffered great loss.[170]

Writes to me Major Rafael Chacon, who, as a youth, served in the battalion of volunteers:

At the place called Saguache we had the first encounter with the enemy; they were undoubtedly waiting for us to give battle; they offered great resistance, and we had a regular pitched battle with them. Finally they were put to flight, and they left several of their dead on the field. On our side only one soldier, of the regular cavalry, was wounded; he had his leg broken; he did not die, but suffered great pain. Later on, after much travel and campaigning, when we reached Fort Massachusetts we put him in the hospital.[171]

In this battle the fighting surgeon, soldier and author, Lieutenant Colonel Dewitt C. Peters, whose life of Carson is the standard authority for all other biographies, accompanying the troops out of his station, Fort Massachusetts,

" met with an adventure which came near costing him his life." He tells his own story, and while the epistle scarcely would cause Kit Carson and his fellow Indian fighters to draw bated breath, we may readily appreciate that it furnished the worthy surgeon with food for serious thought.

It was my duty to follow the charging soldiers in order to be near at hand to render professional services to the wounded, should there be any. I was mounted on a young horse, and when the dragoon horses started off, he became frightened and unmanageable, and was in a short time left far behind, but not until he had fallen and thrown me into a thrifty bed of prickly pears, the thorns of which did not in the least save me from being hurt. On regaining my feet, I found that my injuries were but slight, and that I still retained my bridle rein, therefore I quickly regained my seat in the saddle and started on again, remembering the old proverb, which says, " All is fair in war ! " While riding on, I was joined by a soldier whose horse had broken down in the charge. As we now advanced together, our routes led us by some large sand hills, behind which several Indians had sought refuge, when hotly pursued.

It appears that, unfortunately and to his embarrassment, the worthy doctor possessed no Red Cross flag. Out at them dashed the warriors,

and commenced firing their arrows in fine style. My horse now became unmanageable, and by some unaccountable impulse made directly for the Indians, seeing which, they fled precipitately. [And this probably saved the doctor's life.] My horse seem determined to bring me into uncomfortably close quarters with a young warrior, who constantly turned and saluted me with his arrows. As the situation was getting decidedly unpleasant, I raised myself in the saddle, and sent a ball from my revolver through the body of the Indian, which rolled him to the ground dead; his horse, relieved of his load, galloped away furiously. As the danger was thick about them, the balance of the Indians soon left to effect their escape.

With his reputation as a fearless fighter now established among both whites and reds and his horse distanced, the doctor might pull down, to ride back to the field, and this he did.

The pursuit by the troops was continued until night, when camp was pitched at the foot of the Cochetopa Pass, westward of the Saguache. Lieutenant Lloyd Beale, of the fort's company, was detached, with the baggage and foot soldiers, to proceed east, across the valley, over Mosca Pass, and to meet the main column in the Wet Mountain country. Colonel Fauntleroy and the flying column continued on the round-up of the Indians, with the intention of making a circle.

At the Cochetopa Pass occurred another fight in which eight Indians were killed and two dragoons wounded. Here the Mohuaches and the Jicarillas divided and the two tribes took divergent routes — the Utes for the north, the Apaches for the east. Fauntleroy, Carson, and the rest pursued the Utes north, over Poncha (Punche) Pass, into the headwaters of the Arkansas.

At the place now called Salida [narrates Major Chacon], by us called the Puerto del Punche [i. e., Pass of the Punche] we had another encounter with the Indians; they did not make much resistance, and we took several prisoners. From there we followed them down along the Nepesta, now Arkansas, River, and we caught up with them at the junction of a small stream which flows to the north of the Sierra Mojada. I think the place is now called Rosita. From there we turned toward Fort Massachusetts by the Puerto del Mosca, for the purpose of taking out new rations, and to leave there the wounded soldier mentioned before, as well as the sick and prisoners.

Thus the circle was completed. By this time (the first of April) the men and horses of the command were badly worn. Many of the latter had died by exhaustion. Carson is quoted as saying that on this trip the troops " were exposed to the most intense cold weather I ever remember experiencing. We were overtaken by several severe snow storms which came near completely using us up." The Mexican volunteers especially suffered, for they were ill provided with clothing or blankets. However, the Indians were as hardly put, their camps were being destroyed, one after another, and it was the consensus of opinion given by St. Vrain, Carson, and the army officers that the campaign should not slacken.

After a brief rest at the post, where the horses were enabled to pick up on the abundant forage now uncovered by the melting snow; and after having given a short space of confidence to the Indians that they might unite their scattered squads and families, the command was divided.

April 20 Colonel St. Vrain with two companies, A and B, of volunteers, one company of dragoons, and a corps of spies under Carson was detached to scour the country to the east of the main Sangre de Cristo range, whither the Jicarillas had headed. Colonel Fauntleroy led the other troops upon the Utes again.

The St. Vrain command, with which were Carson and his Pueblos, crossed the Sangre de Cristo range by the northern pass called Veta Pass.

From there [writes Major Chacon] we turned south to the Rio del Oro in the direction of Apishapa. At the point now called Rio de los Trujillos we caught up with a band of Apaches who fled from us. And from there Captain Carson was ordered to come out to the plains with his scouts, going through the place now called Aguilar. The balance of our force kept along the draw now called Reilly Cañon, where we lost our way and came out towards Chicosa. The plains were full of deer; Captain Carson had given leave to his scouts to kill several of them, and as they were scattered about we took them (the Pueblos) for Apaches, and were about to charge on them, when they took refuge on the Chicosa hill; from there they displayed their signals, which were strips of white cloth

ı

two yards long, tied about their temples, and with the ends streaming down. This saved them from being attacked by us. From that point we again caught up with the Indians at what is now Long's Cañon. There we took several women and children prisoners, and we followed the trail up to Wootton's Ranch, where we again caught up with the warriors and again made some of their women and children captives. From that point the main force under Colonel St. Vrain went to Fort Union with the captives. My company pursued the Indians in the direction of Red River (the Canadian), to the location of Fort Bascom. In the month of July the company was disbanded, the Indians having sued for peace.

While the St. Vrain command was making this long march over the mountains and down upon the plains of southeastern Colorado beyond Trinidad city, thence to the Raton Mountains, and thence, as Company B, on down through northeastern New Mexico, Colonel Fauntleroy had pressed north from Fort Massachusetts, to the Punche Pass again. The artillery company, afoot, marched in snow and mud ankle deep, from Mosca Pass to the Punche, eighty-five miles in thirty-six hours. On the evening of April 28 the village of the Utes was discovered, twenty miles beyond the pass; a night attack was made, surprising the village, interrupting a war dance and strewing the field with over forty Indian bodies.

The dismayed Utes fled, separating into two bands, one of which took to the Wet Mountains and the east side of the Sangre de Cristo range, the other to the San Luis Valley west of the Rio Grande River.

Dividing his command again, to scour the country thoroughly, Colonel Fauntleroy followed the southeastward trail. After another skirmish at the foot of the Sierra Blanca mountain, early in May he re-entered Fort Massachusetts, to learn by express that the St. Vrain command, by fights of April 25 and 26 " at the crossing of the Huerfano," had smitten the Apache also, had killed six out of sixty, captured seven, rescued two Mexican prisoners, taken thirty-one horses, and destroyed all the camp equipage.

But the war was not finished. Detached by Colonel Fauntleroy, C company of the volunteers had set out on the trail down the San Luis Valley, past present Alamosa and along the west side of the Rio Grande. Captain Smith H. Simpson, who was sergeant quartermaster, serving with C company, writes:

After the fight at the Arkansas (Nepesta) we divided on the east and west side of the mountains. My company was ordered towards what is now Alamosa (Colorado) and Tierra Amarillo (New Mexico). We drove the Indians on to El Rito, where they attacked us. We drove them across the Rio Grande, and they took to the mountains known as the Jicarillas, the highest mountains north and east of Santa Fe. From there we drove them out again, and at last, after five months' chasing and fighting, they were forced, July, 1855, into Santa Fe, where they made a peace that they have kept ever since.

The Utes and Jicarillas had been seven times caught, and upon every occasion had been greatly worsted. " They had lost at least five hundred horses, all their camp equipage, ammunition, provisions, and most of their arms." Therefore, with Indian wisdom, they judged that it was time to quit and from hostiles change to friendlies. By June the campaign was closed, and the volunteers were honorably discharged. In the Taos plaza the valiant Pueblo scouts held a grand war dance of triumph. Superintendent and Governor Merriwether reported, September, 1855:

Early in August, a delegation on the part of these two bands presented themselves to me and sued for peace * * * and I appointed to meet both bands on the Chama River above Abiquiu, on the 10th instant; this meeting was held at the time and place designated, and resulted in treaties of peace with both bands * * * and I can now have the pleasure of informing you that peace has once more been restored to this territory.

Carson was opposed to this peace upon terms so easy for
the Indians. It was the psychological moment for impress-
ing the red wards with the fact that the Government held
the whip hand; and that he who fights and runs away is not
to be welcomed back as the prodigal son. Kit Carson by
no means stood alone in his attitude of criticism of the
government methods. The New Mexican native people
sided with him, for the agent, Don Diego Archuleta, stationed at Abiquiu over the Jicarillas, writes direct to Washington:

> The expeditions made by the commanding officers of this
> department against our neighboring savages during the last
> four years must, I venture to say, have cost the government
> at least one million of dollars, and what has been the gain?
> The Indians are at peace, no one doubts that; but how long
> will they remain so? Indians have no national faith — at least
> the Apaches and Utahs have not — and the propriety may be
> questioned to acknowledge in them the power to make treaties.
> The acknowledgement of such a power necessarily implies a
> sovereignty which these Indians do not possess, and which, if
> they did possess it, they would sell to the first purchaser offer-
> ing himself, for a piece of tobacco, a pipe, a piece of meat, or
> an old shirt. A treaty is not kept sacred by them, nor ever will.
> Whenever, in the opinion of our Indian neighbors, it appears
> that the government is tardy in making them the usual presents,
> or whenever they have some object in view which they cannot
> obtain peaceably, they will, disregarding their treaties, make
> war upon us by stealing our property, murdering and violating
> our families, knowing that the consequence will be a " treaty,"
> where they are to receive what they desire. The government,
> after an unsuccessful pursuit in a country almost inaccessible
> to our troops, will readily listen to their applications for peace.
> The Indians receive the gratifications, and sign the " treaty,"
> with the felonious intent to break it as soon as convenient.

Of the succeeding campaigns in which Agent Carson took
part, we have but little record, and that a record with only
slight variation of incident. The Jicarillas and the Utes,

CAPTAIN SMITH H. SIMPSON

OF TAOS. INDIAN FIGHTER, EXPRESS RIDER, CIVIL WAR VETERAN OF ARIZONA
SERVICE. HE HELPED CARSON THE INDIAN AGENT WITH REPORTS

MAJOR OLIVER PERRY WIGGINS AT 87
"KIT CARSON MAN" AT TAOS, 1838-50. TRAPPER, SCOUT, AND SOLDIER
(Photograph by author)

THE CARSON PLAT ON MEMORIAL DAY
(Courtesy of Dr. T. P. Martin of Taos)

their favor bought by government presents, remained on the whole harmless even if, in instances, most dangerous. Carson himself must have been busy; visiting Abiquiu, Conejos of the San Luis Valley, Fort Union, Santa Fe, Rayado; dividing his time between his charges and his business details; upon his excursions among the settlements, extending his rides even down to Albuquerque, there, in the summer of 1860, to be seen by the versatile Samuel Cozzens, as " a little weazen-faced, light-haired, active frontiersman " who did n't " fear no Injun livin'."

In 1860 Carson took a hunting trip with a party into the San Juan Mountains of southwestern Colorado. Here, while descending a steep gravelly slope and leading his horse, the animal slipped, and before he could throw the *reata* from him, he was entangled, drawn under the struggling brute, and dragged some distance. It was one of his narrow escapes from death; and it left him with an internal injury which grew steadily worse. From that maltreatment developed the enlargement of the artery which eight years later brought the end.

Carson was being retained as Indian agent; and with this and with his ranching prospects and the prospects which opened with the country, he seemed to be attaining prosperity. Then, suddenly, all the current of his life, and the current of the life about him, was interrupted by the shot fired at Fort Sumter.

CHAPTER XXXII

THE CIVIL WAR—CARSON AT VALVERDE

BY ALL accounts Kit Carson's mind wavered not one instant from the duty to which he was bound by every sentiment save that of remote birth. If in his bosom had lingered any rancor over the non-ratification of his lieutenancy, a dozen years before — a failure of the Government to recognize his services, but a failure atoned for later by its support of him as Indian agent — the wound had healed. Now, for another decade, he had been associating with the blue uniforms to which Fremont first had introduced him; he had marched with the Flag in California, and later with the guidon in New Mexico; he had been sworn ambassador to the red children, and had preached to them the doctrine of citizenship and obedience. He was of that single-mindedness which fosters loyalty through thick and thin — which cannot see two paths from right to right. And in his stand for the Union he was not alone.

When the news of Abraham Lincoln's election was announced in Taos, Carson, Captain Simpson, and other stanch retainers of the Republic, both Americans and Mexicans, hoisted the Stars and Stripes in the plaza and kept them there.[172] At the news of war Carson resigned his position as agent, and was succeeded, in July, by William F. M. Arny — the agency being removed, because of the Taos whiskey stills, forty miles east, to " Maxwell's Rancho on the Cimmeron." Here the Carson influence was still felt, for Agent Arny reported, September 24, of the same year, that " the Mohuache band of Utah Indians, for whom I am agent, are friendly disposed towards the United States, and since my arrival here have tendered their services for the protection of the citizens of this Territory." [178]

Henry Connelly, Kentuckian, Santa Fe trader, of long residence, was now governor, and firm in his allegiance. In the place of Colonel W. H. Loring, the seceding military commander, was appointed the uncompromising Colonel Edward R. S. Canby of the Nineteenth Infantry — a soldier who could be depended upon to the very end. Major General John C. Fremont, stationed at St. Louis, was in command of the Department of the West. Rumors were flying thick and fast regarding the contemplated withdrawal of this new West. But New Mexico, Colorado, Utah, Nevada, California, remained loyal. Arizona, however, unreconciled to the apparent neglect of Washington in ignoring its " Arizuma " delegate from the Gadsden purchase, south of 33° 40′, invited the Confederacy, and in August elected a delegate to the halls of the Southern Congress.

Lieutenant Colonel John R. Baylor, leading his Second Texas Mounted Rifles, C. S. A., crossed into the Mesilla Valley, and proclaimed for this Arizona, to the line of 34°, a Confederate military government and for himself the office of governor, making Mesilla his capital. Fort Fillmore at Mesilla was surrendered by Major Isaac Lynde, with scarcely a shot fired for its honor. The only other Arizona posts, Fort Breckinridge on the San Pedro, and Fort Buchanan on the border southeast of Tucson, were evacuated by their garrisons, who hastily retired; and as they marched out the Apaches swarmed in, their only flag the flag of plunder. What mattered to them the rights or the wrongs of the white man's providential strife?

The pioneer overland stage line — the Butterfield Southern Express, which through almost 3,000 miles of desert, carried the mails twice a week in spite of Indian, sun, dust, and cloudburst, between Arkansas and the mouth of the Gila — after three years of its six years contract at $600,000 a year was obliged to transfer its business to the Platte trail. Meanwhile

the Apache marauders swept down from their mountain strongholds, and carried death and destruction throughout Southern Arizona; ranches and stock-ranges were abandoned, and the few whites left in the country took refuge within the walls of Tucson. The savages indulged in a saturnalia of slaughter, and the last glimmer of civilization seemed about to be quenched in blood. The horribly mutilated bodies of men, women, and children marked nearly every mile of the road to the Rio Grande. This frightful condition of things existed for nearly a year after the withdrawal of the troops.[174]

Before the news of the battle of Bull Run had been received, in August, Colonel Canby was making desperate efforts to rally his local forces, and, under Ceran St. Vrain, its colonel, and Christopher Carson, its lieutenant colonel, the First New Mexican Volunteer Infantry was being rapidly recruited from the country roundabout Taos. The Second, Third, Fourth, and Fifth Volunteers had been called for, or else were in near prospect; and leaders such as the Pinos, the Chaves family, the Valdez family, and other Mexicans of noble blood, had come forward in their new patriotism.[175]

In August, from Fort Union, Colonel St. Vrain and Lieutenant Colonel Carson signed a protest, to be forwarded to western headquarters, against any withdrawal of the regular troops from the Territory, submitting that in the post were stores to the amount of $271,147.55 (eastern cost), and that the volunteers, unsupported by fire-tried troops, were not efficient for a modern battle. Colonel Canby endorsed this, calling the attention of Major General Fremont, who should know the New Mexicans well, to the fact that the volunteers enlisted were not *rancheros* or citizens of the better class, but were untrained, unambitious, apathetic *paisanos*, etc., of doubtful capabilities. Nevertheless, more than 6,000 New Mexicans, the majority natives, were enrolled under the banner which forbade peonage.

.So, aided by St. Vrain and Carson, Colonel Canby struggled to obtain from the higher authorities the other sinews of war.

I have heretofore called the general-in-chief's attention to the destitute condition of this department in military resources and supplies of every kind.
* * * * * * * * * *
No information has yet been received with regard to the annual supply of ordnance stores required for the troops in this department.
* * * * * * * * * *
The military operations in this department have for several months past been greatly embarrassed, and are now almost entirely paralyzed, by the want of funds in the pay department. Many of the regular troops have not been paid for more than twelve months, and the volunteers not at all.[176]

But, for the other side of the shield,

Men, money and supplies were forthcoming from the Territory, however. The Legislature authorized the governor to call into service the entire Territorial force, volunteers flocked to the standard, and Governor Connelly congratulated the people on their patriotism.[177]

In September Ceran St. Vrain resigned his colonelcy on account of ill health, and was succeeded by Kit Carson. He confined himself to his strong personal influence, and to supplying the commissary with flour from his mill.
In October the First Regiment was assembled at Albuquerque, garrisoned by six companies from the Fifth and Seventh United States Infantry, and by the First, Second and Third New Mexican Volunteers. Colonel B. S. Roberts, the incorruptible, was now in command of the Southern Military District of New Mexico, with headquarters at Fort Craig where Colonel Canby was, as fast as practicable, concentrating his Union forces. The border forts

had fallen; and General Henry Hopkins Sibley's Confederate brigade for the conquest of New Mexico to still another flag was marshalling at El Paso, to move on through the gateway of the Rio Grande, for Santa Fe and Colorado.

The First Regiment of Volunteers stayed at Albuquerque until the end of January. There was drilling, of course, and other martial routine to whip the recruits into shape. But Colonel Carson made the most of his opportunity to cement further his domestic bonds. The colonel's uniform sat lightly upon his shoulders. His wife and children came down from Taos.

He was very loving toward his family [says Major Chacon, captain under him]. I remember that he used to lie down on an Indian blanket, in front of his quarters, with his pockets full of candy and lumps of sugar. His children would then jump on top of him, and take the sugar and candy from his pockets and eat it. This made Colonel Carson very happy, and he derived great pleasure from these little episodes. His wife, Dona Josepha Jaramillo, was called by him by the pet name of " Chipita," and he was most kind to her.

The trail from Santa Fe down the Rio Grande to Socorro and on to El Paso, was the Chihuahua Trail for traders. Socorro marked the jumping-off place, below which was a southern New Mexico, uninhabited and, because of the Indians, deemed uninhabitable. But with forts Craig. Thorn, and Fillmore to form a line with Fort Bliss at El Paso of Texas, the Yankee government had boldly intruded upon this traditional solitude, and had thrust it through with the finger of the white civilization.

Fort Craig was at the head of the dreaded Jornada del Muerto, where the trail left the Rio Grande and for eighty miles traversed waterless lava and sand. In February a force of 3,810 men had been assembled there under Colonel Canby: Companies B, D, F, I, and K of the Fifth Regular Infantry; Companies C, F, and H of the Seventh Regu-

lar Infantry; Companies A, F, and H of the Tenth Regular
Infantry; Companies D and G of the First Regular Cavalry; Company G of the Second Regular Cavalry; Companies C, D, G, I, and K of the Third Regular Cavalry;
Company B, Captain Dodd, of the Second Colorado Volunteers (sent posthaste by the splendid Governor Gilpin);
eight companies of Colonel Christopher Carson's First
New Mexican Volunteer Infantry; seven companies of
the Second New Mexican Volunteer Infantry; seven
companies of the Third New Mexican Volunteer Infantry; one company of the Fourth and two companies
of the Fifth; Captain James Graydon's company of New
Mexican Spies; and 1,000 unorganized militia. Nor must
we omit the battery of two twenty-four-pound howitzers
from the Tenth Infantry, commanded by Lieutenant Robert
H. Hall, and the provisional light battery, made up of
Companies G of the Second and I of the Third Cavalry,
commanded by Captain Alexander McRae of the Third,
his subalterns lieutenants Lyman Mishler, First Infantry,
and Joseph McC. Bell. Governor Connelly himself, and
Superintendent of Indians J. L. Collins, were present also.

By orders of February 14 Colonel Carson was assigned,
for field operations, to the command of the Third Column,
composed of his First Regiment — two battalions of four
companies each, the one battalion under Lieutenant Colonel J. Francisco Chaves, the other under Major Arthur
Morrison, making altogether 512 men.

Colonel Canby was by no means an isolated example of
alleged neglect from a busy government, for through delays
and inattention which he declared to be disheartening (and
which were fatal· to his project) until the end of January
General Sibley was unable to resume his forward movement.

From Fort Bliss to Fort Craig is 160 miles — sixty miles
of it a rolling country providing wood and water, and eighty
miles of it the bare Jornada del Muerto. But it was do or

die with the Confederates; for the country, instead of welcoming them, seemed to be combining against them, and now, from the west, was pressing eastward the California Column of 2,350 men under Colonel James H. Carleton. Thus not only had the disaffection hoped for in California proved a disappointment, but from that state the flag carried there by desert march of Kearny's dragoons was coming back to reassert itself along the same historic Gila trail. The Confederate Arizona of " Governor " Baylor was short-lived. The " Second Texas Mounted Rifles, C. S. A.," and the reinforcements from Sibley were quickly retired; and post after post was re-occupied by the Union.

Reinforced by Baylor, the Sibley column of some 2,600, whose apparent lack in numbers was more than balanced by the equipment of experience, marched up along the Rio Grande. All were American fighters, wonted to Indian warfare; whereas on the other side fully half the Canby troops were not only of peasant class but had not been bred by custom to meet fighting. Yet, when well led, they could endure much and dare much, as was proved in the severe mountain campaign of 1855. Colonel Canby knew, however, of the timid element among his forces and so he designed that the volunteers and militia should not be maneuvered under fire, a scheme which was thwarted by his opponent officers who knew this element as well as he did.

With column depleted by illnesses, and with mules so thirsty and famished that on the 20th some 200 of them deflected to the river and to the fort, on the 18th of February the Confederate advance appeared below Fort Craig.

The course of the Rio Grande here is between ridges of drifting sand, and of lava outcrops usually parallel to the stream, thereby affording excellent cover for troops. Below and across from the post was a basaltic mesa from forty to eighty feet high, almost inaccessible by horse or artillery, but running down to the river in a point which, at 1,000 yards, commanded the interior of the post. Two and a half miles above it, began the higher Mesa del Contadero, 300 feet high, three miles long and two wide. At either extremity of it the valley of the river was accessible, with a ford at the upper end.

Any hope on the part of Colonel Canby that the enemy would attempt to reduce the post, and that he would be enabled to fight his volunteers from behind the walls, was dissipated; for it was evident that General Sibley's plan was to turn the position by marching around it. On the 20th, at the Panadero Ford below the fort he unexpectedly crossed from the west bank to the east bank, and cleverly sidestepping the defenses, although hampered by the deflection of his thirsty mules, moved northward, up the rougher east side, between the mesa, unscalable, and the river, now turgid and rising. His column, keeping three and four miles distant, could be seen from the fort.

Thus the defenders were drawn from their base, and compelled to fight upon ground of the enemy's choosing.

About five miles above the fort, at Valverde, a ruinous, deserted settlement, the river was to be crossed again, from east to west. Seeing that the Sibley forces were evidently making for this point, Colonel Canby dispatched to the east side of the river Graydon's spies, and 500 mounted militia and volunteers under colonels Pino and Stapleton, to threaten the enemy's flanks and impede him. But the volunteers, as Canby remarks in disgust, were thrown into confusion by a " few harmless shells," and this movement failed. However, by the demonstration the Confederates were held all that night in position. At eight o'clock on the morning of the next day, the 21st, they advanced again.

As the battle was inevitable, and as Sibley was outmaneuvering him, Colonel Canby had dispatched Lieutenant Colonel Roberts along the west bank to the ford with regular cavalry and mounted volunteers to occupy and hold the crossing. He was followed at five in the morning by the McRae and Hall batteries, supported by Brotherton's company of the Fifth Infantry, Ingraham's of the Seventh, and two companies of volunteers; and these by Selden's battalion, eight companies of regulars, the company of Colorado Volunteers, and Carson's First Regiment.[178]

So here, in the Southwest, with little attention from the great armies maneuvering in the East, where the fate of a national principle was to be decided, was waged the first of the two or three battles that settled not so large a question as the national one, but one that nevertheless bore definitely upon the affairs of half a continent. Had the Confederate project of investing the Rocky Mountain country met with only a measure of success, it would have started in the flesh of the Republic a malignant sore of guerilla warfare more virulent than ever yet has been prescribed for. White and red against white and red — thus the fever would have swept desert, pass, plain, and vale.

Fairly planned, but poorly executed, were the Federal operations in the battle of Valverde, New Mexico, February 21, 1862. Colonel Canby gained less credit from the contest than his subalterns; yet there was truth in his complaint:

> The battle was fought almost entirely by the regular troops (trebled in number by the Confederates), with no assistance from the militia and but little from the volunteers, who would not obey orders or obeyed them too late to be of any service. The immediate cause of the disaster was the refusal of one of the volunteer regiments to cross the river and support the left wing of the army.
>
> The contemporary operations of the right wing were eminently successful.

Although the ground had been surveyed a month before, says Colonel Roberts, and the importance of the Valverde ford had been recognized, upon arrival there he now found himself too late; the passage had been pre-empted by the invading column, which was being posted to cover the crossing. However, Colonel Roberts was a fighter; and so acting promptly he succeeded in seizing, by desperate work of the McRae battery and Major Duncan's cavalry, the little *bosque* or copse that commanded the ford — the key to the situation.

When the Carson regiment arrived at nine o'clock, the booming of the cannon and the rattle of the small arms were incessant. None recognized better than Carson how uncertain a quality the New Mexican green volunteers were; and he had wisely asked of Colonel Canby that the First Regiment be held back as long as practicable — probably with a view to arousing its spirit. Now, upon reporting to Colonel Roberts, he was ordered to take position on the left, in a *bosque* there, and to watch the Confederate right. This he did, and "moved along up the west side of the Rio Grande as the enemy extended his right in the same direction."

Thus, previous to the arrival of Colonel Canby himself with fresh troops to relieve the Roberts companies, the Carson men "had remained on the west side of the river and had taken no part in the battle."

About 1 o'clock in the afternoon I received from Colonel Canby the order to cross the river, which I immediately did, after which I was ordered to form my command on the right of our line and to advance as skirmishers toward the hills. After advancing some 400 yards we discovered a large body (some 400 or 500) of the enemy ·charging diagonally across our front, evidently with the intention of capturing the 24-pounder gun, which, stationed on our right, was advancing and doing much harm to the enemy. As the head of the enemy's column came within ·some 80 yards of my right a volley from the whole column was poured into them, and the firing being kept up caused them to break in every direction. Almost at the same time a shell from the 24-pounder was thrown among them with fatal effect. They did not attempt to reform, and the column supported by the gun on the right, was moving forward to sweep the wood near the hills, when I received the order to retreat and recross the river. This movement was executed in good order. The column, after crossing the river, returned to its station near Fort Craig, where it arrived about 7 o'clock in the evening.[179]

This is Carson's report of his part at Valverde, where West Pointer was arrayed against West Pointer, and where for the first and only time he witnessed American battle tactics opposed to American battle tactics, American arms opposed to American arms. To him, the battle was going well for the Union forces, and his own advance had been successful; but to the more practiced eye the aspect was different.

When at 2:45 (according to Colonel Roberts) Canby took command on the field, having left a rear guard at the fort and sent forward every other available man, he found that the Confederate movement had been entirely uncovered, that the ford was the focus, and that Colonel Roberts' occupation of the *bosque* was precarious. Sibley, practically abandoning his supply train, was rushing up more men; his position, in a swale between two sand ridges, was very strong, and an assault upon him all along the line would have been risky.

Colonel Canby determined, as a last measure, to force the Confederate left by advancing the Federal right and center with his own left as a pivot — a change of front, at a right angle, which would rake the swale and reverse the advantage.

For this movement, the McRae battery at the river, strongly supported, formed the Federal left; Selden's Regulars and Carson's Volunteers formed the center; Hall's battery, with its support, and Major Duncan's dismounted regular cavalry formed the right. The Pino Second Regiment of Volunteers, a squadron of the First Cavalry, and Colonel Valdez' Volunteers formed the reserve.

" Accordingly, Carson's regiment, which at his own request had not hitherto been brought into action, was ordered to cross the river." It was just in time to join in repulsing a charge on Hall's battery, and " by a well-directed fire added to the discomfiture of the enemy."

The charge, which was in the nature of a feint, drew the Carson regiment into pursuit. So they followed (as Carson reports), flushed with seeming victory. But behind, at the ford, two masked batteries, concealed in an arroyo, or portion of the old river bed, from about one hundred yards had opened upon the McRae battery.

The formation of this old river-bed gave ample protection to their guns and gunners, while their enfilading fire on our entirely exposed command was most destructive to men and horses. This terrific fire of canister swept through us for some time (the battery supports meantime lying protected in our rear, as their presence could be of no assistance), when a body of the enemy, numbering some twelve or fifteen hundred men, rose from behind the old river-bank and charged us. To describe this charge would be but to tell of many similar ones during the war, in which wild ardor and determination were the moving features.[180]

Colonel Canby, watching the field, noted these dismounted Texans (1,000, he states) stealing forward under cover of the sand hills. He hastened, himself, to warn the battery support, but before he could deliver the word the charge had developed; " on they came, without order, each man for himself, and ' the devil for the vanquished,' in true ' Ranger' style, down to almost the muzzles of our guns." At the sight and the yells, the Mortimore and Hubbell companies of the Third New Mexican Volunteers broke and fled, tearing their way through the companion support of Captain P. W. L. Plympton's Regulars and the Colorado company, "leaving their gallant Colonel * * * and a few of his officers to do independent service in the battery." [181]

Letting the New Mexicans go, the regulars and the Coloradans rallied, pressed forward, and aiding the cannoneers by fierce volleys drove back the Texan advance. But, as says the gallant Bell, serving with these cavalrymen turned artillerists:

> Then again the Texan batteries opened with the same unsavory diet of canister, and we replied in kind, preparing for the next onslaught that was sure to come. And it did come, with larger numbers and more violence than before.

> The wild Texan wave surged forward, deploying in a long fan-shaped line, and converging while it poured a furious fire from rifles, revolvers, and shotguns loaded with buckshot.

> And again, with double-shotted guns, they were driven back, but leaving us little able to resist successfully such another effort. In this second charge Captain McRae (this officer refused to surrender, but, seated upon a gun, coolly emptied his pistols, each shot counting one Texan less, until covered with wounds, he expired at his post) and Lieutenant Mishler were killed, Lieutenant Bell thrice wounded, and certainly one-half the men and two-thirds of the horses either killed or *hors de combat*. The charging party of the enemy regained their position behind the old river-bed, we were again treated to another and more continuous fire from their batteries, which we feared was but the introduction to another charge from their reinforced numbers. We hadn't long to wait for the *coup de main*. Down they came upon us, rushing through the fire poured into them, with maddened determination, until the whole force was inside the battery, where, hand-to-hand, men were slaughtered. Simultaneously with this third charge, a column of the enemy's cavalry moved upon our left flank, which commanded the attention of our infantry supports, leaving our thinned but enthusiastic battery-men to resist as well as possible the Texan force among us.[182]

All was confusion. The available Federal cavalry, a small squadron under Lieutenant Lord of the volunteers, were summoned to the scene to occupy, if possible, the battery until the Fifth Infantry, from another part of the field, could arrive. But amid the struggling mass they were unable to distinguish friend from foe, and had to be sent to the rear again. But the Captain Wingate battalion of regulars, arriving at double-quick, by rapid volleys threw the Texans into momentary disorder. Seizing upon this, and still trusting to turn the scale, Colonel Canby (three horses having been shot under him), dispatched his messages recalling the Carson and other troops from the vain pursuit and rallying the reserves.

The right wing, with which Carson's command had coalesced, was far and scattered; the Union troops had been fording and re-fording, where the water was swift and cold, and were worn out; the reserves were panic-stricken, inextricably mixed with fugitives, and at the last

Pino's regiment, of which only one company (Sena's) and part of another could be induced to cross the river, was in the wildest confusion, and no efforts of their own officers, or of my own staff, could restore any kind of order. More than 100 men from this regiment deserted from the field.[188]

The day was lost to the Union forces; the capture of the McRae battery settled the possession of the ford. From the Confederate supply train more men, swelling the reinforcements to 500 (according to Canby) were hastening up; the hour was five o'clock, dusk was near, and " with a large number of our men killed and wounded, horses dead and disabled, our supports badly thinned, and the enemy massing their forces upon us, General Canby gave the orders to fall back. It was not possible to carry the whole of the battery with us, and but two guns and three caissons were taken across the river, under the fire that was poured into us by the Texan troops lining the east bank of the stream." [184]

The Canby army retired to Fort Craig; crippled by the victory dearly won, the Sibley army pressed wearily on, to leave their wounded at Socorro, twenty-seven miles above, and thence to hasten for Albuquerque, Santa Fe, and Fort Union, which none reached save as prisoners.

The Confederate loss was reported by Sibley as forty killed and 100 wounded — and this is supplemented by the report of his field officers, who place the loss at thirty-six killed and 150 wounded. Union casualties, sixty-eight killed, 160 wounded, thirty-five missing; total 263. The Carson First Regiment's quota was one man killed, one wounded, and eleven missing.

Colonels Miguel E. Pino and Christopher Carson, lieutenant colonels J. Francisco Chaves and Manual Chaves, and others of the volunteer officers, the majority of whom seem to have led bravely, were mentioned in dispatches.

CHAPTER XXXIII

CORRALLING THE APACHE — 1862–1863

WITH the subsequent war between whites and whites in New Mexico we have naught directly to do. History records how the battered Sibley column marched on to Albuquerque, occupied Santa Fe, and pushed for the $300,000 cache of Fort Union; how hurrying from the north, with one march of sixty-four miles in twenty-four hours, the First Regiment, Colorado Volunteer Infantry, under Colonel Slough and the fighting parson, Chivington, arrived in time to place the post, already mined by the weak garrison, out of immediate danger; how from the fort regulars and volunteers sallied to the south, and how from Fort Craig the chagrined Canby sallied to the north, and the Texans were between. It records how on March 26 at historic Apache Cañon, on the overland trail from Fort Union to Santa Fe, the Texans were encountered by the Colorado " Pike Peakers "; how the Texans were driven from the field; how on the 28th another battle, and a larger one, was fought by the two main armies at Pigeon's Ranch; and how the doughty Chivington, under guidance of Lieutenant Colonel Manual Chaves, flanked the Texans and compelled them to retreat to Santa Fe; how from Santa Fe the invaders fell back to Albuquerque; and how, dogged by the allied forces under Canby from the south and Chivington and Paul from the north, the shattered Texans, 1,200 men and thirteen wagons out of the 3,800 men and 327 wagons, perforce retraced their way down the Rio Grande, fighting for the lead and to prevent the Federals from crossing, until finally, above Fort Craig, they found a by-trail which conducted them to safety.

In naught of the foregoing did Colonel Christopher Carson take part. After Valverde the battles for free or slave supremacy in the Southwest were fought by the other commands, and the campaign up along the Rio Grande was conducted without his active help. For when Canby was ready to leave Craig, for vengeance upon the Sibley column, he made secure his base with the following order:

HEADQUARTERS DEPARTMENT OF NEW MEXICO.
FORT CRAIG, N. MEX., March 31, 1862.

COL. C. CARSON:

Colonel: You are charged with the duty of holding this post. Your command will consist of seven companies of your own regiment, two of the Second, and one of the Fourth Regiment New Mexican Volunteers. The convalescents, as they become effective, will add to your strength, and I am instructed by the colonel commanding to say that the objects in view of the plan of operations require that it should be held to the last extremity. The manner of doing this is left to your judgment and discretion, in both of which he has the utmost confidence. The force of the enemy in Mesilla will not allow him to make a regular attack upon the post, but it may be attempted by surprise. To guard against this he desires that you will exercise yourself and exact from all of your command the most unremitting vigilance.

The sick and wounded left in your care will of course receive every attention, and the colonel commanding desires me to say that any expenditures that will add to their comfort or conduce to their recovery will be fully authorized.

Very respectfully, sir, yr obed serv't,
WM. J. L. NICODEMUS,
Captain Twelfth Infantry, Actg. Asst. Adj't. Gen.

On this same date Colonel Canby was appointed, at Washington, brigadier general of volunteers; on the next day he rode with his column for the north. In this March, also, of 1862, before the National House was introduced that bill creating the Arizona of today, which passed the Senate a year later.

After the departure of General Canby no news of importance emanated from Fort Craig. That Kit Carson was there seems to have inspired confidence throughout the Territory.

As colonel of infantry Carson was now credited to monthly pay of $95, to six rations a day of monthly cash value of $54, to two servants of the monthly commutation value of $45, and to horse forage of monthly value of $4 in war and $2 in peace. His income therefore totalled, if he could so manage it, $198. As he did not have his family with him to require the servants and to consume the rations, he probably sent home much of both allowance and pay. He was colonel, in the field most of the time, for four years.

On May 31, the First, Second, Fourth, and Fifth New Mexican Volunteer Regiments were consolidated to form the First New Mexican Volunteer Cavalry, with Carson commanding. His income as mounted officer was now raised by $18 — his pay being $110, his servant hire $47, and his horse forage, in war, $5. General Canby was relieved by orders of August 5, 1862, and called to report at Washington; thence to enter upon a distinguished army career amidst the large operations of the East. General James H. Carleton of the California Column had already arrived at his destination, the banks of the Rio Grande; and on September 18 he succeeded General Canby in command of the Department of New Mexico which included the district of Arizona then to the south but soon to be on the west.

Behold then, Carson's commander for the next four years: James H. Carleton, aged forty-eight, Maine born and raised, appointed from Maine to the First Dragoons, 1839; brevetted major for gallantry at Buena Vista, major of the First Dragoons, and as such paying to Carson, his chief scout, the tribute of a hat; colonel of the First Cali-

fornia Infantry, brigadier general for the Department of
New Mexico. Carleton was a fighter, a gentleman and a
Christian, at once soldier and citizen, to whom the Southwest owes more than it yet has acknowledged. The records
of the Carleton rule, 1862-1866, in New Mexico, as compiled amidst the plainly bound tomes which form the reports
of general officers during the Rebellion, are convincing
token of the wonderful activity of the man. A very dynamo
of energy, relentless as a chastiser, kindly as an adviser, un-
wavering in policy yet charitable in performance, with mind
broad enough to see that he was building a state and not
merely occupying it, he was a chief most fitting to help
shape aright the character of Carson, new to army
command.[185]

General Carleton was not slow to appreciate that in his
command he had perhaps the most skillful Indian fighter in
the West; and upon Colonel Christopher Carson devolved
the campaign, first, against the Mescalero tribe, or the
White Mountain Apaches, whose range was that rolling
region from the lower Rio Grande, say at Fort Craig, east
to the Pecos. The Mescaleros were not so vicious as other
Apaches, but the Texan retreat had bequeathed the victors
a legacy of quarrel, and to the Mescalero, once incensed, all
whites looked alike.

From his command at Fort Craig, during the summer,
Colonel Carson had advanced up the river, as if gravitating
toward that home which was so often uppermost in his
mind. In September he was at Los Lunas, just below Albuquerque, with A and G companies — seven officers, ninety-
four men — of his First New Mexican Cavalry. Again
in the fall he was at Albuquerque. But this respite, this
approach to the ease of peace, was effectually broken by
Special Orders No. 176 from headquarters, where sat a
soldier who brooked no rest in anybody until rest was
further earned.

DEPARTMENT OF
NEW MEXICO, ASSISTANT ADJUTANT GENERAL'S OFFICE
SANTA FE, N. M., September 27, 1862.
*   *   *   *   *   *   *   *   *   *

III. Fort Stanton, on the Bonito River, in the country of the Mescalero Apaches, will without delay be reoccupied by five companies of Colonel Christopher Carson's regiment of New Mexico Volunteers. *   *   * Colonel Carson will receive instructions as to the particular duties of his command while serving in the Mescalero country. The world-wide reputation of Colonel Carson as a partisan gives a good guaranty that anything that may be required of him, which brings into practical operation the peculiar skill and high courage for which he is justly celebrated, will be well done.
*   *   *   *   *   *   *   *   *   *

By command of Brigadier General Carleton:
BEN C. CUTLER,
First Lieutenant, C. V., A. A. A. General.
Official: BEN C. CUTLER,
Assistant Adjutant General.

General Carleton explained the order in his report to the Adjutant General of the Army:

I find that during the raid which was made into this territory by some armed men from Texas, under Brigadier General Sibley, of the army of the so-called Confederate States, the Indians, aware that the attention of our troops could not, for the time, be turned toward them, commenced robbing the inhabitants of their stock, and killed, in various places, a great number of people; the Navajoes on the western side, and the Mescalero Apaches on the eastern side of the settlements, both committing these outrages at the same time. *   *   *
To punish and control the Mescaleros, I have ordered Fort Stanton to be reoccupied. That post is in the heart of their country, and hitherto when troops occupied it those Indians were at peace. I have sent Colonel Christopher Carson (Kit Carson), with five companies of his regiment of New Mexican Volunteers, to Fort Stanton.

Against the Mescaleros marched Colonel Carson, over-taken en route by a dispatch from headquarters giving him free hand and tight rein. " All Indian men of that tribe are to be killed whenever and wherever you can find them."

*   *   *   *   *   *   *   *   *   *

If the Indians send in a flag and desire to treat for peace, say to the bearer that when the people of New Mexico were attacked by the Texans, the Mescaleros broke their treaty of peace, and murdered innocent people, and ran off their stock; that now our hands are united, and you have been sent to punish them for their treachery and their crimes; that you have no power to make peace; that you are there to kill them wherever you can find them; that if they beg for peace, their chiefs and twenty of their principal men must come to Santa Fé to have a talk here; but tell them fairly and frankly that you will keep after their people and slay them until you receive orders to desist from these headquarters; that this making of treaties for them to break whenever they have an interest in breaking them will not be done any more; that that time has passed by; that we have no faith in their promises; that we believe if we kill some of their men in fair, open war, they will be apt to remember that it will be better for them to remain at peace than to be at war. I trust that this severity, in the long run, will be the most humane course that could be pursued toward these Indians.

You observe that there is a large force helping you. I do not wish to tie your hands by instructions; the whole duty can be summed up in a few words: The Indians are to be soundly whipped, without parleys or councils except as above. Be careful not to mistake the troops from below for Texans. If a force of rebels comes, *you* know how to annoy it; how to stir up their camps and stock by night; how to lay waste the prairie by fire; how to make the country very warm for them, and the road a difficult one. *Do this,* and keep me advised of all you do.

At Fort Stanton, vacant after the retirement of the Texans, the flag was again raised. The results were prompt. Captain William McCleave of the California Volunteers found the Mescaleros, mustering 100 warriors, opposing him at the portal Dog Cañon, and with his two companies he drove them in flight. At the end of October

"WEDDING OF THE EAST AND THE WEST"

MEETING OF THE ENGINES AFTER LAYING THE LAST RAIL OF THE TRANSCONTINENTAL RAILROAD LINE, PROMONTORY POINT, UTAH, MAY 10, 1869

(From a photograph owned by General Granville M. Dodge, who was Chief Engineer of the Union Pacific Survey)

Captain Thomas Graydon (who commanded the Spy Company at Valverde) while on a scout with his company met old Manuelito, head chief of the Mescaleros, and his band. Although they were already bound for Santa Fe to ask peace, he fired upon them, killed outright Manuelito, four warriors, and a woman; and, in pursuit, shot down others.

Astounded and alarmed by this precipitate campaign which was invading their fastnesses with its diamond-cut-diamond policy, the Mescalero leaders now did not venture to take time for the required trip to Santa Fe, but in hope of safety and out of faith in the well-known Kit Carson, they made straight for Fort Stanton. As they had trusted, Carson did not murder them. He told them, however, that he had no authority to make treaties with them as in previous days, but that they must go up to Santa Fe and submit to the irascible " big chief " there. So he sent them along, five of them, under escort; and they arrived in safety about November 23.

You are stronger than we (thus is reported the speech of Gian-nah-tah to General Carleton). We have fought you so long as we had rifles and powder; but your weapons are better than ours. Give us like weapons and turn us loose, we will fight you again; but we are worn out; we have no more heart; we have no provisions, no means to live; your troops are everywhere; our springs and water-holes are either occupied or overlooked by your young men. You have driven us from our last and best stronghold, and we have no more heart. Do with us as may seem good to you, but do not forget we are men and braves.

Already, under General Orders No. 193, date November 4, a board of officers had been ordered to locate in that region on the upper Pecos — northeast of Fort Stanton, 150 miles southeast of Fort Union and 165 southeast of Santa Fe — called the Bosque Redondo (Round Grove), a new fort, of which the title should be Fort Sumner.

Thither the Mescaleros were sent, with orders that they
be housed and fed, until, when the whole tribe should be
assembled, "we can then conclude a definite treaty, and
let them *all* return again to inhabit their proper country."

The Graydon affair brought an official investigation and
reprimand for that overzealous officer; but the result could
not be gainsaid. Manuelito and Jose Largo (Big Joe) his
cooperator were dead — and with nine companies of Indian
haters, New Mexicans and Californians, searching the chaparral with Sharp's carbines, and looking for scalps and
booty rather than prisoners, the day of the Mescalero
seemed early eclipsed. In lieu thereof rose the day of the
Bosque Redondo — that fond colonization scheme of General Carleton's, which, like many another dream solving the
Indian problem, proved to be, after all, one of vain hopes.

However, as driven or persuaded in, band by band forwarded from Fort Stanton to new Fort Sumner, the Mescaleros were rapidly concentrated at the Bosque Redondo;
and although outlawed squads of the Apaches continued to
make the whole territory from the Mesilla Valley of the
border up to Fort Union of the Santa Fe trail perilous
for soldier and citizen alike, on March 19, 1863, General
Carleton was emboldened to report to Washington:

GENERAL: I have the honor to inform you that the operations of the troops against the Mescalero Apaches have resulted
in bringing in as prisoners about four hundred men, women
and children of that tribe, from their fastnesses in the mountains about Fort Stanton, to Fort Sumner, at the Bosque
Redondo, on the Pecos River. This leaves about one hundred,
the remainder of that tribe, who are reported as having fled
to Mexico and to join the Gila Apaches. Against these last,
the Gila Apaches, vigorous hostilities are prosecuted, as I have
already informed you. Want of troops and of forage has prevented any operations against the Navajoes. Now that the
Mescaleros are subdued, I shall send the whole of Colonel
Carson's regiment against the Navajoes, who still continue

to plunder and murder the people. This regiment will take the field against them early in May. Already I have commenced drawing the companies in from the Mescalero country preparatory to such movement.

And he seals the fate of the Mescalero by adding:

It is my purpose to induce the Mescaleros to settle on a reservation near Fort Sumner at the Bosque Redondo, on the Pecos River. The superintendent of Indian affairs for New Mexico and myself proceed to that point, starting today, to have " the talk " with them with reference to this matter. My purpose is to have them fed and kept there under *surveillance;* to have them plant a crop this year; to have them, in short, become what is called in this country a *pueblo.* If they are once permitted to go at large again, the same trouble and expense will again have to be gone through with to punish and subdue them. They *will* murder and rob unless kept from doing it by fear and force.

At the same time Colonel Christopher Carson, whose office has largely been that of commander directing from headquarters at the fort, and of forwarding agent, was given short leave (which he never was in mood to decline) to visit his family.

CHAPTER XXXIV

THE NEMESIS OF THE NAVAJO — 1863-1864

THE name Navajo has come down to us almost white as compared with the crimson name Apache. But the Mexicans knew the title well as that of an ogre by which other than children were to be frightened. When from their northern cañons and plateaus rode these "Lords of the North," and through the Mexican villages pealed the cry "Navajo, Navajo!" uttered by a score of savage throats, how quickly the inhabitants blanched and fled! The Navajo recked no master. As Superintendent Amos Steck reports in September, 1863, "Not since the acquisition of New Mexico in 1847 have the Navajos been at peace." Six treaties with them were broken even before they had been ratified. Out of this condition

four campaigns against the Navajoes resulted, in three of which our army failed of either success or glory. In the fourth the Indians succumbed to the superior strategy of the renowned Kit Carson, and were compelled, by hunger, to surrender.[186]

True Bedouins were the Navajos — true Ishmaelites, their hand against every man and every man's hand against them. With their flocks and their herds, their looms and their orchards, and their kindly treatment of their women, yet with the migratory instincts which forbade any settled village, sending them hither and yon through the summer, and housing them in rude hogans and the cañons in the winter, they stand out distinct as an independent, aboriginal people. Strange, that a pastoral folk, today wealthy as compared with other tribes, still aloof and united, troubling not the white world and of the white world asking naught, should have so scourged the Southwest.

General Kearny in 1846 found the Navajos at war with the country; he promised protection for the citizens, subjugation for the enemy — and scarcely had he thus given his pledge when, in his very sight, the underrated Lords of the North drove off some of his stock.

Thereupon the doughty Missourian, Colonel Doniphan, and the fighting statesman, William Gilpin, proceeded against the Navajo, and made a treaty. In 1847 Major Walker, in 1848 Colonel E. W. B. Newby, in 1849 Colonel John M. Washington successively marched to the Cañon de Chelly, made treaties, and marched back again. As for the Washington treaty

a party of the same Indians who were present when the treaty was signed, reached the settlements in advance of the colonel's command, and stole a large number of mules that were grazing near this place, almost in sight of the flag staff which stands in the Plaza.[187]

In the winter of 1851-52 Colonel E. V. Sumner, sent out by the Government to organize this troublesome and costly New Mexico, settle the Indian question, and cut down expenses, had the doubtful pleasure of obtaining from the Navajos still another treaty. Thereafter he, also, marched against them, as far as the Cañon de Chelly; but " believing his force insufficient to meet the enemy, concluded to retreat, which, it is thought by some, he did rather hurriedly." This doubtless was one of those experiences which prompted the colonel to advise, in May, 1852, that the territory of New Mexico was not worth retaining, and that it would be a good stroke of the United States to " withdraw all the troops and civil officers " and to exercise merely a protectorate.

Fort Defiance was established, in the very midst of the Navajo country, " and for a time produced more effect upon the Indians than all the expeditions that had been made against them."

Colonel Edward R. S. Canby had been the last man, before General James H. Carleton, to proceed against the Navajos. In the winter of 1860-61, by the most successful of all the army campaigns up to that date he had brought the enemy not only to another treaty but also apparently to a realization that the American soldiery was a new and stern kind of foe. To this treaty twenty-two chiefs appended their marks — " a greater number than on any previous occasion."

From this fact and other concurrent causes, it was believed that permanent peace and security was at last bestowed on the Territory, and commensurate to the boon was the joy of the people. Grain and other seeds were given to the Indians, and they made gardens after their own mode and fashion * * *.[188]

But the Navajos were a pastoral rather than an agricultural people, and their herds, as well as their crops, had been badly decreased through the incessant wars. So, pending the time when they would be again self-supporting, they broke the truce of a year, and the treaty also, and by 1862 were more active than ever. Their raids extended from their central base, where northern Arizona and New Mexico meet, as far as the lower Rio Grande and into the country of the Mescaleros. Indeed, they boldly stampeded stock from the Bosque Redondo itself.

With the same thoroughness with which he would clean his house of the Apache, General Carleton in the spring of 1863 started in to clean his house of the Navajo.

Again the Bosque Redondo was to be the concentration point; and the Navajos as well as the Apaches were to be herded under surveillance. September 6, Carleton thus announced his plans to Adjutant General Lorenzo Thomas, at Washington:

> The knowledge of the perfidy of these Navajoes, gained after two centuries of experience, is such as to lead us to put no faith in their promises. They have no government to make treaties. They are a patriarchal people. One set of families may make promises, but the other set will not heed them. They understand the direct application of force as a law. If • its application be removed, that moment they become lawless. This has been tried over and over, and over again, and at great expense. The purpose now is never to relax the application of force with a people that can no more be trusted than you can trust the wolves that run through their mountains; to gather them together, little by little, on to a reservation, away from the haunts, and hills, and hiding-places of their country, and then to be kind to them; there teach their children how to read and write; teach them the arts of peace; teach them the truths of Christianity. Soon they will acquire new habits, new ideas, new modes of life; the old Indians will die off, and carry with them all latent longings for murdering and robbing; the young ones will take their places without these longings; and thus, little by little, they will become a happy and contented people, and Navajo wars will be remembered only as something that belongs entirely to the past. Even until they can raise enough to be self-sustaining, you can feed them cheaper than you can fight them.

Such was the plan, to the spirit of which no one may take exception; and as the truant officer, so to speak, Kit Carson was naturally selected. Not until June were the arrangements completed, although there was correspondence with Carson at Taos, in April, when he was advised from headquarters to hire as guide for the proposed expedition one Manzaneres, of Abiquiu, former captive among the Navajos, and also ten "of the *best* Ute warriors, and say four of the *best* Mexican guides, as spies and guides." In May Colonel Carson was at Santa Fe for a council with the department commander over details of the campaign. And next were issued the decisive General Orders No. 15:

HEADQUARTERS DEPARTMENT OF NEW MEXICO,
SANTA FE, N. M., June 15, 1863.

I. For a long time past the Navajo Indians have murdered and robbed the people of New Mexico. Last winter, when eighteen of their chiefs came to Santa Fé to have a talk, they were warned, and were told to inform their people that, for these murders and robberies, the tribe must be punished, unless some binding guarantees should be given that in future these outrages should cease. No such guarantees have yet been given; but, on the contrary, additional murders and additional robberies have been perpetrated upon the persons and property of our unoffending citizens. It is therefore ordered that Colonel Christopher Carson, with a proper military force, proceed without delay to a point in the Navajo country known as Pueblo Colorado, and there establish a defensible depot for his supplies and hospital, and thence to prosecute a vigorous war upon the men of this tribe until it is considered, at these headquarters, that they have been effectually punished for their long-continued atrocities.

The following comprises the force alluded to above:

FIELD AND STAFF.

Colonel Christopher Carson, 1st New Mexico volunteers, commanding.

Captain A. B. Carey, United States army, chief quartermaster.

First Lieutenant Richard S. Barrett, 1st infantry California volunteers, chief commissary.

First Lieutenant Lawrence G. Murphy, adjutant, 1st New Mexico volunteers.

Major Joseph Cummings, 1st New Mexico volunteers.

Major Arthur Morrison, 1st New Mexico volunteers.

Surgeon Allen F. Peck, 1st New Mexico volunteers.

Rev. Damaso Taladrid, chaplain 1st New Mexico volunteers.

* * * * * * * * * *

Companies K, L, and M will proceed from Fort Union, New

Mexico, to Los Pinos, New Mexico, starting the day after the military commission adjourns which has been ordered to assemble at Fort Union.

Companies A, H, and G have heretofore been ordered to rendezvous at Los Pinos.

Companies B and C, now at Fort Wingate, will be in readiness to move at a day's notice.

Colonel Carson will require, and receive, two mountain howitzers on prairie carriages, with an adequate supply of ammunition, etc., to be used in defence of his depot at Pueblo Colorado.

These troops will march from Los Pinos for the Navajo country on Wednesday, July 1, 1863.

The chiefs of the quartermaster, subsistence, medical, and ordnance departments will furnish, on Colonel Carson's requisition, such spies and guides, means of transportation, intrenching tools, quartermaster property, clothing, camp and garrison equipage, subsistence stores, hospital stores, medicines, arms, and ammunition as may be necessary to equip and provide completely for his command to insure to it the cardinal requirements of health, food, mobility, and power.

*   *   *   *   *   *   *   *   *   *

III. A board of officers, to consist of Colonel Christopher Carson, 1st New Mexico volunteers; Major Henry D. Wallen, United States army, acting inspector general; Surgeon James M. McNulty, United States volunteers, medical inspector; Brevet Captain Allen L. Anderson, United States army, acting engineer officer; and Captain Benjamin C. Cutler, assistant adjutant general United States volunteers, will proceed with Colonel Carson's command to the locality known as Pueblo Colorado, in the Navajo country, and select and mark out, at or as near that place as practicable, the exact site for a military post, to be garrisoned by four companies of cavalry and four companies of infantry.

A map of the surrounding country will accompany the report of the board, as well as a ground-plan of the post, an estimate of its cost, and its measured distance from the Rio Grande. The geographical position of the post will be fixed instrumentally.

Unless otherwise ordered by competent authority, this new post will be known as Fort Canby, in honor of Brigadier

General E. R. S. Canby, United States army, the recent commander of the department of New Mexico.

By command of Brigadier General Carleton.

BEN. C. CUTLER,
Assistant Adjutant General.

F. P. Abreü, A. H. Pfeiffer, J. L. Barbey, Charles Deüs, John Thompson, Joseph Birney, Francis McCabe, Eben Everett, and Jose de Sena were the company commanders. The force consisted of twenty-seven officers, 709 men, and 260 were unmounted.

On June 23, Lieutenant Colonel J. Francisco Chaves, commanding at old Fort Wingate on that Gallo River the name of which appears to have survived in the station of Gallup (Arizona), was directed by Carleton to inform the Navajo chiefs upon the proposed war, which was to be for submission or extermination. All Navajos who claimed to desire peace and who were " good Navajos " must come into Wingate, at once, there to be given transportation to the Bosque Redondo, their future home.

Send for Delgadito and Barboncito again and repeat what I before told them, and tell them that I shall feel very sorry if they refuse to come in; that we have no desire to make war upon them and other good Navajoes; but the troops cannot tell the good from the bad, and we neither can nor will tolerate their staying as a peace party among those against whom we intend to make war. Tell them they can have until the twentieth day of July of this year to come in — they and all those who belong to what they call the peace party; *that after that day every Navajo that is seen will be considered as hostile and treated accordingly;* that after that day the door now open will be closed. Tell them to say all this to their people, and that as sure as that the sun shines all this will come true.

Some came in; more did not. And at the dry-wash of the Rio Pueblo Colorado (Red Town River), in northeastern Arizona, west of Fort Defiance, Colonel Carson established Fort Canby the last week in July.

For the majority of the companies, the orders indicated a hard march, without adequate water, from the Rio Grande into the Navajo field. The first stage was to the Rio Puerco, by the trail fifty miles; the next was to old Fort Wingate, sixty miles. Carson accompanied the main command from Albuquerque. A short halt was made to organize at Fort Wingate.[189]

The command arrived late in the afternoon, and after getting settled down, one of the men went to the company clerk, and asked him to write an order on the post commissary, that he might purchase a quart of molasses; the order was required to be signed by the commanding officer of the post, who was then Colonel Carson. The man went over to the colonel's quarters, and presenting his order asked him to sign it as he was not well — explaining to the colonel the purport of the order. The colonel, who was always the best-natured of men, signed it, and the man got his molasses. The man upon his return to his quarters, informed his friends that he believed the colonel could not read manuscript, and related his experience. It was the regulations of the post that no enlisted man could purchase whiskey at the sutler's except upon the order of the commanding officer. So one of the men, who was anxious to get some whiskey, thought that he would try and see what he could do with the colonel in this direction. He had the company clerk write an order on the sutler for a canteen of whiskey (price of which was $5). He accordingly appeared with it before the colonel and told him that he was not feeling well and that he would like to get some molasses at the commissary's. The colonel signed the order as before, and the man obtained the canteen of whiskey at the sutler's and paid for the same. The news soon spread through the company and for the next two weeks there was a brisk business at the sutler store. It happened that then Colonel Carson made a visit to the sutler's and looking around asked, kindly: " Well, John (the sutler's name was John Waters), how 's business? " John answered that it was fine — he had sold two barrels of whiskey by the canteen, to H company! Upon this the colonel waxed warm, and said: " John, do n't you know that it 's agin regulations to sell whiskey to enlisted men of the post without the written order of the commanding officer?" Waters replied that he knew it very well; and he added that every sale had been made upon written order. To prove it, he went behind the counter and showed his order string — a wire set in a block of wood and holding already a foot of orders! After this Colonel Carson would not sign an order until his adjutant, Lieutenant Lawrence Murphy, had read it first.[190]

This being Kit Carson's first large command in the field, he was somewhat bothered in the handling of it. He was fortunate in having at his elbow Captain Carey, Regular, who could and did advise him. The rules of discipline were what embarrassed him the most. He must be refused, kindly but emphatically, his ill-timed requests for leave of absence; and, on September 19, he is informed by orders from headquarters:

COLONEL: By custom of service, no officer who is not competent to order a general court-martial can order a court of inquiry, excepting in the case of an enlisted man, when a colonel commanding a regiment may order the court (DeHart, 272, 273). You will, therefore, annul all proceedings of any such court in the case of Lieutenant Hodt.

Non-commissioned officers must not be reduced to the ranks within your regiment by any person's orders but your own. The regulations must be your guide in all such matters, or the discipline of your regiment will be bad.[191]

The campaign has gone down into history as a spectacular achievement. But as a matter of fact the character of the country and of the foe, together with the character of the officer commanding in the field, forbade the spectacular; and the crowning effort of all — that passage of the Cañon de Chelly — which alone was spectacular, fell to the lot of a subordinate, Captain Albert Pfeiffer. The campaign

was one of constant hard scouting with now and then a skirmish; the idea being to wear the Indians out by capture of their herds of sheep and ponies (they had no other live stock), the destruction of their fields of corn, beans, pumpkins, etc.; the covering by occupancy by small detachments of troops, of all water supply, which in the end would result in acceptance by them of General Carleton's terms.   The same policy was pursued in the campaign of 1860-61 commanded by Col. E. R. S. Canby when the Navajoes were pushed in the same way to final surrender, the only difference being that peace was made by General Canby, the Indians remaining in their own country, whereas in the campaign of 1863-64 they were sent out of their own country under guard, and kept under guard and fed at a specified place.   True, Carson's campaign was a great success, indeed it was the last war against the Navajoes, and to General Carleton belongs the credit of its great success, inasmuch as he pursued them to a reservation and confined them to it.[192]

To carry out such a policy for a campaign, Kit Carson, thorough plainsman and mountaineer, and as thoroughly versed in all the wants, likes, and dislikes of the Indian, was the very man.   With the 1,000 troops operating out of Fort Wingate and Fort Canby as bases, results were prompt.

To stimulate the zest of the troops and employees, a bonus of $20 was authorized by General Carleton as prize money for every sound and serviceable horse or mule cap-tured and delivered to the quartermaster; one dollar a head was allowed for sheep.   But the naïve suggestion from Colonel Carson (dated July 24) that to stimulate and reward the Ute scouts they be permitted to keep the women and children captured by them was repudiated with proper emphasis.[193]

The reports of scouting operations are brief.[194]

August 19.—Colonel Christopher Carson reports that he left Camp Cañon Bonita, August 5, 1863, on a scout for thirty days.   On the first day out sent Sergeant Romero with fifteen men after two Indians seen in the vicinity; he captured one of their horses; the Indians made their escape.   On the night of the 4th instant Captain Pfeiffer captured eleven women and children, besides a woman and child, the former of whom was killed in attempting to escape, and the latter accidentally. Captain Pfeiffer's party also captured two other children, one hundred sheep and goats, and one horse. The Utes captured in the same vicinity eighteen horses and two mules, and killed one Indian. Captain Pfeiffer wounded an Indian, but he escaped. On the 16th, a party who were sent for some pack-saddles brought in one Indian woman. At this camp the brave Major Cummings, 1st New Mexico Volunteers, was shot through the abdomen by a concealed Indian, and died instantly. One of the parties sent out from this camp captured an Indian woman. Total Indians killed, three; captured, fifteen; wounded, one; twenty horses, two mules, and one hundred sheep and goats captured. Troops, one commissioned officer killed.

August — . — Colonel Christopher Carson with his command left Pueblo Colorado on the 20th day of August for Cañon de Chelly with the main force, secreting twenty-five men under Captain Pfeiffer in the cañon to watch for Indians. Soon after, two Indians were seen approaching the cañon, and were fired upon, and although badly wounded succeeded in getting away. On the same day the advance guard pursued and killed an Indian. On the 31st the command returned to Fort Canby. Indian loss, one killed, two wounded.

October 5. — Colonel Carson reports that on the 22d of September his command pursued a party of Indians, but, owing to the broken-down condition of his animals, they only succeeded in capturing one. On the 2d day of October discovered a small Indian village which had just been abandoned; this was destroyed, nineteen animals captured, seven of which got away. Three men left camp to hunt up the animals which had escaped; they did not return until after the command had returned to Fort Canby; they state that they were attacked by a party of Indians when within five miles of the post, one of whom they killed. One of the men, named Artin, was severely wounded and the Indians captured his mule. On the 3d day of October Lieutenant Postle discovered an Indian, pursued him and wounded him in three places; the lieutenant was slightly wounded by the Indian. Indian loss, one killed, one wounded, and one captured, twelve animals captured. Our loss, one officer and one private wounded and one mule lost.

November 15. — Colonel Carson with his command left Fort Canby for the country west of the Oribi villages, for the purpose of chastising the Navajo Indians inhabiting that region. On the 16th a detachment, under Sergeant Andres Herrera, overtook a small party of Indians, two of whom were killed and two wounded; fifty sheep and one horse were captured; Colonel Carson speaks in high terms of the zeal and energy displayed by Sergeant Herrera.

On the 25th the command captured one boy and seven horses and destroyed an encampment; on the same day captured one woman and one child, and about five hundred head of sheep and goats, seventy horses, and destroyed an Indian village. On the 3d of December surprised an Indian encampment, capturing one horse and four oxen. The Indians escaped. Indian loss, two killed, two wounded, three captured; 550 sheep and goats, nine horses, and four oxen captured.

Operations were carried on at the same time out of Wingate, Craig, Los Lunas, Sumner, McRae, and other forts. The Fort Canby reports show that the soldiery were by no means uniformly successful, and it is not difficult to cull other reports favorable to the cause of the red man:

August 6. — Captain E. H. Bergman reports that a party of company I, 1st New Mexico Volunteers, in charge of a herd of beef cattle, were attacked by a body of Navajoes on the 22d July, near Conchas springs. The party consisted of Sergeant Jose Lucero and Privates Juan F. Ortiz and Jose Banneras, who fought the Indians from 11 a. m. until after sundown, killing and wounding several of them. The Indians succeeded in killing Sergeant Lucero and Private Ortiz. Private Banneras, being severely wounded by eight arrow-shots, gathered up the muskets and pistols of his dead comrades and threw them into the springs. The Indians fractured his skull with rocks and left him for dead, but he recovered towards morning and made his way to Chaparita. The Indians drove off the cattle; (number not stated).

January 3 (1864). — Wagonmaster Russell's train *en route* to Fort Canby, New Mexico, was attacked near the Puerco by

about one hundred and fifty Navajo Indians. Mr. Russell
was killed; Mr. Strong and two teamsters wounded. The three
leading wagons were cut off and twenty mules were taken by
the Indians, together with some corn, blankets, &c. This
information was forwarded to the commanding general of the
department by Major John C. McFerran, chief quartermaster,
with the following remarks: " Respectfully referred to the
department commander for his information. This Wagonmaster Russell is Powell Russell, who entered the service of the
Quartermaster's department as a teamster, a poor, illiterate boy,
in 1853. By his honesty, industry, modesty, truth, and energy,
he rose to be principal or head wagonmaster in the department.
This position he has filled to the perfect satisfaction of every
one, and has now fallen like a true man, as he was, at his
post and doing his duty. It will be very, very difficult to
replace him."

But while the campaign had its setbacks, and while for
a time a very hornets' nest of Navajos seemed to have
been aroused, so that even the posts were beset, the moral
effect soon became evident.

In the first week of September, General Carleton was
enabled to report to Adjutant General Thomas, of Army
Headquarters at Washington, that a first detachment of
fifty-one Navajos, men, women and children, had been sent
to the Bosque Redondo. By September 10 the Navajos
began to treat for peace, and were given by Carson, through
fresh instructions from Carleton, the Grant terms of
" unconditional surrender." These they digested. Meanwhile the stern war went on — attack and foray and reprisal,
with the Indians steadily losing.

Another month, and a delegation of the chiefs appeared
at Wingate, to test out the temper of their " father " there,
whose query to headquarters received the admonition from
Carleton's assistant adjutant general: " The department
commander having decided that all Navajo Indians who
desire peace must go to the Bosque Redondo, he directs

me to say that further correspondence on this subject is unnecessary.

In another month, or by the middle of November, 188 Navajos had surrendered at Fort Wingate, for transportation to the Bosque Redondo. Although a pitched battle between troops and bold Navajo raiders occurred December 16 within thirty-five miles of Fort Sumner itself at the Bosque Redondo, and although at the same time the same tribe ran off from Fort Canby thirty-eight of Colonel Carson's best mules, at the close of the year of 1863 the Navajo influx actually had commenced. Colonel Carson evinced a strong desire for a few days' respite from the field and outpost duty and at this time came the following message:

The department commander congratulates the troops and the people on the auspicious opening of the year 1864. For one hundred and eighty years the Navajo Indians have ravaged New Mexico, but it is confidently expected that the year 1864 will witness the end of hostilities with that tribe. Then New Mexico will take a stride towards that great prosperity which has lain within her grasp, but which hitherto she has not been permitted to enjoy.

General Carleton did not reckon without his host. Nor did Colonel Carson, hoping for a change of scene, reckon without his, although the leave for which he applied was not in accordance with those ironclad army regulations the intricacies of which he, as a civilian in the volunteer service, had some difficulty in mastering. December 6 his general addresses him: "As I have before written you, I have not the authority to grant you a leave. * * * Please forward no more applications for leaves of absence."

But a consultation "about future operations" was permissible, and "therefore, as soon as you have secured one hundred captive Navajo men, women and children, you will turn over the command of the troops and post of Fort

Canby to Captain Carey, United States Army, and come
with those captives to Santa Fe. * * * It is desirable
that you go through the Cañon de Chelly before you come."
This cañon, "thirty miles in length, with walls a thousand feet high," located some fifty miles north of old Fort
Defiance, Arizona, and about the same distance from Fort
Canby, is one of the most noted of those natural donjons
which the land of the Navajo boasts, and which Kit Carson
regarded, even after he had conquered the defenders, as
impregnable to direct attack. Investment by siege was the
only successful course.

In the main Cañon de Chelly they had some two or three
thousand peach trees, which were mostly destroyed by my
troops. Colonel Sumner, in the fall of 1851, went into the
Cañon de Chelly with several hundred men, but had to retreat
out of it at night. In the walls of the cañons they have regular
houses built in the crevices from which they fire and roll down
huge stones on an enemy. They have regular fortifications,
averaging from one to two hundred feet from the bottom, with
portholes for firing. No small-arms can injure them, and
artillery cannot be used. In one of the crevices I found a two-
story house. I regard these cañons as impregnable. General
Canby entered this cañon, but retreated out the next morning.
When I captured the Navajoes I first destroyed their crops,
and harassed them until the snow fell very deep in the cañons,
taking some prisoners occasionally * * * I took twelve
hundred sheep from them at one time, and smaller lots at
different times. * * * It took me and three hundred men
most of one day to destroy a field of corn.[195]

There are other cañons in Navajo land. The Cañon
Chaco, at the east border of the present reservation, in
northeastern New Mexico, is as celebrated for its grandeur
and its ruins. But the Cañon de Chelly had long been considered as the chief fastness of the tribe. Like all cañons in
the plateau country, it consists of a main artery, with side
cañons coming in. The houses and forts to which the Car-

son extract refers were not built by Navajo hands, but long antedated the Navajo possession of the country.

Before the march through it by Captain Pfeiffer's column, on January 12 and 13, 1864, the cañon had indeed been traversed by an American detachment; but not (as Colonel Carson himself remarks in his report) in time of war. In July, 1859, Lieutenant Walker of the Mounted Rifles, with a scouting party and accompanied by Alexander Baker, agent at Fort Defiance, entered the cañon about two miles from its head and followed it to its mouth. The Navajos, then cultivating their corn, were hospitable to civilians, but objected to showing the country to the riflemen.[196]

The reports of rock-niche fortresses, of huge stones to be rolled down, of heights, manned by the Navajo, but so beetling that arrows were spent before they reached the bottom, of narrow defiles where only one man at a time could squeeze through — these made the Cañon de Chelly sound formidable. And Colonel D. S. Miles, who had investigated a portion of it, left the word: " No command should ever again enter it."

However, Kit Carson's reputation was at stake; and he was now under orders. Replying to the dispatch of General Carleton he announced from Fort Canby, date of December 26, 1863:

> I have the honor to report for the information of the general commanding that I have made all the necessary arrangements to visit the Cañon de Chelly and will leave this post for that purpose with my command on the third or fourth of next month. * * * Of one thing the General may rest assured, that before my return all that is connected with this cañon will cease to be a mystery. It will be thoroughly explored, if perseverance and zeal with the numbers at my command can accomplish.

The now celebrated Cañon de Chelly expedition left Fort Canby on the morning of January 6, 1864. Carson, attacking the problem methodically, preceded his column with an ox train of supplies for the prospective headquarters camp to be established at the west end of the cañon. But the snow, upon which he counted as an ally, impeded the oxen and in a march of twenty-five miles, hauling the wagons through the drifts, twenty-seven animals perished from exhaustion.

Simultaneously with leaving Fort Canby for the west opening of the cañon, Colonel Carson detached Captain Pfeiffer with H Company and thirty-three men of E Company, First New Mexican Cavalry (which had been ordered to Canby from Wingate), in all about 100, rank and file, for the east opening, to assist him from there in bottling the Navajos.

The laboring and miserable ox train was overtaken as it toiled along at the rate of five miles a day. Loads were lightened; and with the train and his command Colonel Carson pushed on, arriving at the west end of the cañon on January 12. Sergeant Andres Herrera, of C Company, and a detachment of fifty men inaugurated the campaign by a brisk skirmish with a squad of Navajos who were making for a side entrance to the cañon. They killed eleven and captured two women, two children, and 130 sheep and goats.

On the morning of the 13th Colonel Carson, having established his camp as a base and a receiving depot, assigned his command into two columns, one under Captain Carey, the other under Captain Joseph Birney of the volunteers, for the purpose of a preliminary scout to reconnoitre either rim of the great crevasse; to see what was the practicability of descending midway, and what the practicability of flanking. The south rim proffered only a sheer depth of 1,000 feet, but it was unbroken by side cañons and therefore admitted of a flanking movement which might sweep that verge. While investigating this, Colonel Carson kept a sharp lookout for the Pfeiffer command. When at last he reached a point on the south rim which gave a view down through to the east opening, no trace of the Pfeiffer column could be perceived.

Alarmed and mystified, the column, owing to lack of sufficient grass for the animals, had to retrace their trail, to camp. However, while the main detachments were thus riding around the cañon, on the outside, Captain Pfeiffer had been going through it on the inside!

A frontiersman almost of the dime novel type was Albert H. Pfeiffer, who as captain and as major served under Kit Carson. In all that goes to make for recklessness and for daring he stood forth prominent even in those reckless, daring days. " A fighter, who never got into a scrape with the Indians without being wounded," is the tribute paid to him by one who served upon his staff in the Navajo and Kiowa campaigns. For this recklessness Captain Pfeiffer could refer to a fount, within him, of bitter hate — the hate which, engendered by the murder of wife and family, many another frontiersman cherished throughout a lifetime.[197]

Under orders to proceed from Fort Canby to the east end of the cañon, and there to operate carefully, Captain Pfeiffer and his men, traveling light with a pack train, reached the point of destination on the 11th, and made camp. The snow was two feet deep and two men suffered frozen feet. But without waiting to reconnoitre, Captain Pfeiffer, after a brief rest of preparation, immediately plunged into the depths — plunged in with the anticipation of a Fremont. Evidently he wanted to be first.

He divided his command into three parties, with an advance of pioneers bearing picks and shovels for clearing the trail. The first twelve miles must be traversed in the icy bed of the stream, through which the animals frequently broke. On the 12th they traveled eight miles, the Indians " whooping and cursing, shooting and throwing rocks." Ruins were seen; one set was named Carey Castle, in honor of Captain Carey. The cañon sides were so steep that the Indians could not be pursued; and the distances so vast that even the carbines were inadequate. The cañon waxed to depths of 1,200 and 1,500 feet — in places spreading out into beautiful savannas, cultivated to fields and orchards, in others closing in a narrow zigzag, with fastnesses 300 and 400 feet up among the snowy crags. Reads the sprightly Pfeiffer report:

Here the Navajoes sought refuge when pursued by the invading force, whether of neighboring tribes or of the arms of the government, and here they were enabled to jump about on the ledges like mountain cats, hallooing at me, swearing and cursing and threatening vengeance on my command in every variety of Spanish they were capable of mustering. A couple of shots from my soldiers with their trusty rifles caused the red-skins to disperse instantly, and gave me a safe passage through this celebrated Gibraltar of the Navajoes. At the place where I encamped the curl of the smoke from my fires ascended to where a large body of Indians were resting over my head, but the height was so great that the Indians did not look larger than crows, and as we were too far apart to injure each other no damage was done except with the tongue, the articulation of which was scarcely audible.[198]

The cañon rose and sank, widened and narrowed; and on the 13th, or the second day, after a march estimated by him as thirty miles, Captain Pfeiffer emerged at the other end. So that, returning to camp from the scout along the south rim, to his " great surprise and gratification " Colonel Carson found here the likewise gratified captain,

having accomplished an undertaking never before successful in war-time, that of passing through the Cañon de Chelly from east to west, and this without having had a single casualty in his command. He killed three Indians (two men) and brought in ninety prisoners (women and children). He found two bodies of Indians frozen to death in the cañon.[199]

CAPTAIN GEORGE H. PETTIS

WHO COMMANDED THE HOWITZERS UNDER
CARSON AT ADOBE WALLS

SET-INKIA OR STUMBLING BEAR

LEADER IN THE DEFENSE OF THE KIOWAS
AT ADOBE WALLS

(*Photograph by Soule, 1870. Courtesy of
the Bureau of American Ethnology*)

MAJOR ALBERT H. PFEIFFER

WHO MADE THE FIRST PASSAGE OF CANON
DE CHELLY IN THE NAVAHO CAMPAIGN,
1864

*(From photograph loaned by his son.
Albert H. Pfeiffer, Jr.)*

SET-T'AINTE (SATANTA)
OR "WHITE BEAR"

FAMOUS KIOWA CHIEF, WHO IS SAID TO
HAVE SOUNDED THE BUGLE CALLS ON THE
INDIAN SIDE AT ADOBE WALLS

*(Photograph by Soule. Courtesy of the
Bureau of American Ethnology.)*

There seems to be no indication that Kit Carson himself ever traversed this cañon. He must have shared the keen curiosity of his command; but after Captain Pfeiffer had rent the vail of mystery, Carson resisted any temptation to try for personal honors, and, instead, delegated to Captain Carey, who deserved the privilege, the second passage of the defile.

This command of seventy-five men, I conferred upon Capt. Carey at his own request, he being desirous of passing through this stupendous cañon. I sent the party to return through the cañon from west to east, that all the peach orchards, of which there were many, should be destroyed, as well as the dwellings of the Indians. I sent a competent person with the command to make some sketches of the cañon, which, with a written description of the cañon by Capt. Carey * * * I respectfully enclose.

As for the colonel himself, he very properly shelved the active and the spectacular in favor of those responsibilities which were his as commanding officer. The prime object of the campaign was to collect and forward the Navajos; and for this purpose he returned to Fort Canby. Sixty refugees, besides those prisoners brought in, already were at the camp; 110 were found, the fruits of the Carey scout, at Canby.

" Result of this expedition: Indians killed, twenty-three; wounded, five; prisoners, thirty-four; voluntarily surrendered, two hundred; and two hundred head of sheep and goats captured."

So read the report by General Carleton; but the results were wider reaching than this. After two centuries the Navajos were subdued; the back of their resistance had been broken. By hundreds they came in, submitting to that will of the *Americano* which intended not torture nor slavery but protection, even succor, ill advised though that succor proved to be.

Within three weeks, or on February 14, there were 1,000 Navajos at Fort Canby; another ten days, and there were 1,500 and 3,464 had been forwarded to Los Pinos, from Canby and Wingate, for the Bosque Redondo. On March 4 some 2,138 more were started from Canby.

The Carleton-Carson combination had worked well; and back at Canby, enabled to send in his report of success, Colonel Carson now was entitled to make that postponed trip to Santa Fe. Accordingly we find him leaving Canby, with 253 of the Navajo prisoners, the last week of January (following his report), and arriving at Los Pinos, near present Peralta, on the Rio Grande, south of Albuquerque, early in February. Here he turned the charges over to Lieutenant George H. Pettis (now of K Company, First California Infantry) who on the 8th set out for the Bosque Redondo. The colonel arrived at Santa Fe, for conference with General Carleton. And after an eighteen-days march, across country, the lieutenant arrived at Fort Sumner with one more Indian than he had receipted for!

Although, as in the case of the Mescaleros, outlaw bands of Navajos continued to vex both soldiers and citizens, the Navajo campaign was considered to have accomplished its purpose. And while warning the post commanders that the operations in the field were not to be discontinued, a postscript was added, enjoining caution lest refugees be mistaken for hostiles; and on February 27 the outgoing mail for Washington bore the letter, from Carleton to the adjutant general:

What with the Navajos I have captured and those who have surrendered we have now over three thousand, and will, without doubt, soon have the whole tribe. I do not believe they number now much over five thousand all told. You have doubtless seen the last of the Navajo war — a war that has been continued with but few intermissions for one hundred and eighty years, and which, during that time, has been marked by every shade of atrocity, brutality, and ferocity which can be imagined or which can be found in the annals of conflict between our own and the aboriginal race.

*   *   *   *   *   *   *   *   *   *   *   *

I beg to congratulate you and the country at large on the prospect that this formidable band of robbers and murderers have at last been made to succumb. To Colonel Christopher Carson, first cavalry New Mexico volunteers, Captain Asa B. Carey, United States army, and the officers and men who have served in the Navajo campaign, the credit for these successes is mainly due. The untiring labors of Major John C. McFerran, United States army, the chief quartermaster of the department, who has kept the troops in that distant region supplied in spite of the most discouraging obstacles and difficulties — not the least of these the sudden dashes upon trains and herds in so long a line of communication — deserves the especial notice of the War Department.

CHAPTER XXXV

THE BATTLE OF ADOBE WALLS — 1864

COLONEL CARSON arrived in Santa Fe after his Navajo campaign about February 10. His commanding general had already written to Washington: "I respectfully request the government will favorably notice that officer, and give him a substantial reward for this crowning act in a long life spent in various capacities in the service of his country in fighting the savages among the fastnesses of the Rocky Mountains."

Very likely Carson was granted a thirty-day respite from field duty, but by March 16 he was again being addressed through Captain Carey, at Fort Canby, and evidently he had resumed his post as "commanding Navajo expedition."

Within another fortnight, on April 1, the indefatigable General Carleton, expressing the belief that the Navajo grist has been taken to the mill, announced that he should attend to the Apaches of the Gila. By dispatch of April 17 he ventured the hope:

It is very fortunate that the Navajo war is at that point toward a final ending as to give but little further uneasiness. If, by the help of Providence, we can have the same fortune in our demonstrations against the Apaches of Arizona, the great drain upon the treasury, which has been kept up by these Indian wars, will forever cease.

In the far East the fortunes of the Confederacy were now on the wane. Gettysburg had been fought, Vicksburg had fallen. But few of the operations of Grant and Sherman,

440

Lee and Johnston, and those other " hard and fast fighters," appear to have affected the surface of events in New Mexico and Arizona, where Carleton and Carson, Delgadito, Cochise, and Manuelito, had their hands full with internal affairs. Meantime, stung by white aggression upon their hunting grounds, the Cheyenne and Arapaho of the Great American Desert had risen in the north and the proud Sioux was on the warpath. From panicky Denver to ravaged Minnesota reached a broad trail of blood and plunder.

With the Carleton campaign against the Apaches in Arizona we have little to do. By dispatch of April 1, 1864, Colonel Carson at Fort Canby was asked to send out a picked force of 100 men, for fifty days, against marauding Apache bands in the Mogollon Mountains, south at the head of the Rio Pueblo Colorado. He did not accompany them, himself. The trail no longer had its former attraction for him. Now at fifty-four he was well content to rest upon his honors, wrung by almost forty years of incessant activity amid all the perils known to the western wilderness. Therefore April 24, General Carleton transmits to Washington this report:

1st. A copy of an official letter from Colonel Christopher Carson, 1st cavalry New Mexico volunteers, dated the 10th instant. In this letter the colonel expresses his conviction that we have not yet got one-half of the tribe of Navajoes. In this, from all I can learn, I think the colonel overestimates the number of those not come in. In my belief the *Ricos* not yet surrendered, but who, it is said, will soon come in, do not number over two thousand. We have now, in round numbers, six thousand, which would make the whole number of the nation to be eight thousand — a full estimate, I think. See in this letter what Colonel Carson says of the " wisdom " displayed in moving these Indians. I use the word wisdom without any reference to myself, but merely to contrast it against the utter folly of any measure looking toward putting the Navajoes on a reservation in the Navajo country.

2d. An official copy of a private letter from Colonel Carson, in which he speaks more fully of the propriety of removing the Indians, and of his desire to be at some post where he can have his family with him. Colonel Carson has labored hard, and is deserving of some respite. I sincerely trust the War Department will recognize his services in some substantial manner.

After some detail work, Carson is next sent to Fort Sumner and the Bosque Redondo, in pursuance of a project outlined by letter of March 12 from General Carleton to the adjutant general at Washington, saying that when the *ricos*, or wealthy refugees from the Navajos, have been persuaded from their cañon home, " Colonel Carson will himself come in from the Navajo country, and go down to the Bosque Redondo to give the Indians the counsel they so much need just at this time as to how to start their farms and to commence their new mode of life."

So Carson reports on July 11 that he has arrived; that conditions there among both Apaches and Navajos are favorable; that the captives number 6,309, and that soon this total will be increased, by prisoners on the way, to 7,353. The great majority of the captive Indians, of course, are Navajos, marched hither under soldier escort. Of them, General Carleton speaks well:

The exodus of this whole people from the land of their fathers is not only an interesting but a touching sight. They have fought us gallantly for years on years; they have defended their mountains and their stupendous cañons with a heroism which any people might be proud to emulate; but when, at length, they found it was their destiny too, as it had been that of their brethren, tribe after tribe, away back toward the rising of the sun, to give way to the insatiable progress of our race, they threw down their arms, and, as brave men entitled to our admiration and respect, have come to us with confidence in our magnanimity, and feeling that we are too powerful and too just a people to repay that confidence with meanness or neglect — feeling that for having sacrificed to us their beautiful country, their homes, the associations of their lives, the scenes rendered classic in their traditions, we will not dole out to them a miser's pittance in return for what they know to be and what we know to be a princely realm.

But the Bosque Redondo was doomed — as might be expected of any policy of concentration, no matter how well intended. To be sure, an acequia seven miles long was opened, and some 1,500 acres of land were planted to grain, squash, and other produce. Then the army worm and corn worm came, and hail and frost, while ploughs and shovels, blankets and clothing, did not come. Besides the " acts of God," there were the defects of man: antipathy of Apache and Navajo, who were hereditary enemies, and the curse of unprincipled whites. Therefore the Bosque Redondo reservation scheme was doomed, and Kit Carson, although one of its firm supporters, did not linger to attend upon its death struggles.

The Comanches have, within a few days, killed five Americans at lower Cimarron Springs, and have run off cattle from a train of five wagons belonging to Mr. Allison, of this city. * * * Will two hundred Apaches and Navajos go with troops to fight Comanches in case of serious trouble with the latter Indians?

Thus to Acting Superintendent Carson at the Bosque Redondo wrote General Carleton, August 15. The query was portentous.

Portentous also were the orders which were issued within the same week, that the completion of Fort Bascom, on the Canadian River in eastern New Mexico, at the border of the Comanche country, should be pushed through, and that Captain Bergman of the First New Mexican Cavalry and Major Joseph Updegraff, commanding Fort Marcy (Santa Fe) should cooperate with outposts protecting the Santa Fe Trail. For the Kiowas and Comanches, working together, as usual were emulating the feats of Cheyenne, Arapaho, Sioux, and Apache, and were pillaging the frontier from central Kansas almost to Santa Fe. The interruption of traffic, civil and military, along the Santa Fe Trail, when such traffic was necessary to the struggling Southwest, stung afresh the doughty Carleton; stung him the keener because it delayed supplies which were the very life of the Bosque Redondo.

He was not a man who minced matters. He directed the commanding officer at Fort Bascom to inform the Kiowas and Comanches, visiting there under flag of truce, that "their hearts are bad," that "they talk with a forked tongue," that "we put no confidence in what they say," and that "we regard them not as friends." He promptly took issue with Superintendent of Indian Affairs, Matthew Steck, who would have questioned the guilt of these notorious bandits, and declared to the superintendent: "I should be derelict of my duty if I should refrain from making at least an attempt to avenge our slaughtered and plundered citizens." And he ordered Kit Carson into the field.

[General Orders No. 32.]
HEADQUARTERS DEPARTMENT OF NEW MEXICO,
SANTA FE, N. M., October 22, 1864.

An expedition will be organized, without delay, to move against the Kiowa and Comanche Indians, who, during the last summer, attacked trains on the roads leading from New Mexico to the States. This expedition is designed to co-operate with one moving from near Fort Larned, under the command of Major General Blunt, with a view to the punishment of the same Indians. Its organization will be as follows:

Colonel Christopher Carson, 1st cavalry New Mexico volunteers, commanding.

Lieutenant Colonel Francisco P. Abreü, 1st infantry New Mexico volunteers, to command the infantry.

Major William McCleave, 1st cavalry California volunteers, to command the cavalry.

First Lieutenant Benjamin Taylor, Jr., United States 5th infantry, acting assistant quartermaster and acting commissary of subsistence.

Assistant Surgeon George S. Courtright, United States volunteers.

Captain Birney's company, mounted................. 42

Lieutenant Heath, with all of Johnson's men now at Fort Union and at Fort Bascom...................... 39

Captain Witham's cavalry, now *en route* to Fort Union.. 66

Captain Fritz, with thirty of the best cavalry from Fort Sumner, New Mexico........................... 30

Captain Deüs' company at Fort Bascom............... 69

Lieutenant Edmiston, with the effective men of company A, 1st veteran infantry California volunteers........ 62

Lieutenant Pettis, with all the effective men of company K, 1st infantry California volunteers, with two mountain howitzers................................ 45

Total, say............................... 353

To these will be added, of Ute Indians and Jicarilla Apache Indians, say 100. These will proceed to Fort Bascom, New Mexico, direct from Mr. Maxwell's ranche, on the Cimarron, and there join the troops.·

Captain Marion's company C and Captain Baca's company E, 1st cavalry New Mexico volunteers, and Captain Bergmann's men, now on the plains, will garrison Fort Bascom until further orders. All these troops will concentrate at once at Fort Bascom, and have that post as their base of operations, and thence commence the movement against the Kiowas and Comanches. As the season is now getting late, every moment becomes more and more precious. Every officer and soldier must therefore do his utmost, not only to take the field promptly, but to accomplish all that can be accomplished in punishing these treacherous savages before the winter fairly sets in. They have wantonly and brutally murdered our people without cause, and robbed them of their property; and it is not proposed that they shall talk and smoke and patch up a peace until they have, if possible, been punished for the ·atrocities they have already committed. To permit them to do this would be to invite further hostile acts from them as soon as the spring opens and our citizens once more embark in their long journeys across the plains.

The various chiefs of the staff departments will furnish

Colonel Carson with the means of transportation and supplies necessary to give this order practical effect.

By command of Brigadier General Carleton:

BEN. C. CUTLER,
Assistant Adjutant General.

Between these decisive general orders and that first intimation of August 15, considerable correspondence and travel of a preparatory nature had intervened. This referred largely to those allies, the Utes and Jicarilla Apaches, Colonel Carson's proteges. By letter of September 18 Colonel Carson, again at Taos, was instructed to proceed to " Mr. Maxwell's place on the Little Cimarron," and there enlist, for expedition against the Kiowas and Comanches, 200 Utes — terms of payment in rations and plunder to be specified. With these Maxwell Agency Indians were to be combined, if possible, Apaches and Navajos from the Bosque Redondo.

The Utes and Jicarillas of the agency at Maxwell's proved susceptible to negotiations; they would be pleased to have the Mescalero Apaches from the Bosque join with them, but they objected to the Navajos; they would appreciate being favored, when upon the march, with sugar and coffee, like other soldiers; and desired that during their absence their families be fed, at Maxwell's, by daily rations of meat and flour. In consideration thereof, by letters of October 10 and 18 Carson, from Maxwell's, reported that he could get about 100 Indians. He asked for them an equipment of 100 rifles with ammunition, 120 blankets and shirts, and for Chief Ka-ni-at-ze one extra horse. For himself he requested two pieces of artillery and at least 300 mounted troops.[200]

General Carleton agreed to the arms, the blankets and shirts, even to the much-prized coffee and sugar, and probably to the " extra horse " for old Ka-ni-at-ze; but he delegated to the Indian department the issuance of those family rations. " I believe you will have big luck," he encouraged Colonel Carson; and — " If the Utes will not agree to remain in the field forty-five days they had better not go." About the same time (October 22), he sent a dispatch to Major General James G. Blunt, who also was organizing an expedition, out of Fort Larned of Kansas, against these same allied tribes:

This is to inform you that a report has reached me, coming through Mexicans, that the Kiowas and Comanches are now encamped on a creek called Palo Duro, some two hundred miles in a northeasterly direction from the mouth of Utah creek, on the Canadian or Colorado river, east of Fort Union, New Mexico. This would make them about, say, two hundred miles south of Fort Larned, or southwardly from that post.

I shall, within ten days, send a force of three hundred volunteer troops, two hundred mounted and one hundred on foot, with two mountain howitzers, and, say, one hundred Ute and Apache Indians, *i. e.*, four hundred in all, under Colonel Christopher Carson, to attack the Kiowas and Comanches. This force will move down the Colorado to within fifteen miles of Ute creek and there doubtless take a road running northeast toward the States, which road is said to come into the Arkansas from the southwest near the mouth of Walnut creek.

I hope you may be able to time your movements so as to reach the Indians on the Palo Duro or near there at the same moment with Colonel Carson, so that a blow may be struck which those two treacherous tribes will remember.

With true Indian shrewdness the Navajos of the Bosque Redondo declined the proffered warpath, reminding the authorities, " We have been told that we should work, not fight ! " The author finds no record that any of the Mescalero Apaches of the Bosque went. The Utes and the Jicarillas of the Maxwell Agency went, following their Father Kit. They went — and they bargained to the last, influencing Carson himself.

CIMARRON, N. MEX., November 3, 1864.
BRIG. GEN. JAMES H. CARLETON,
  Santa Fe, N. Mex.
GENERAL:

I leave this morning with sixty-five Utes and Jicarilla Apache Indians, after having had the greatest kind of trouble to get them started, and had to tell them that I would write to you recommending to your favorable consideration that the families of these Indians going with me should be fed one pound and a half of meat and flour daily by Mr. L. B. Maxwell until they return from the campaign. The snow has been so deep for the last four days that I was doubtful of any of them to go with me. I therefore most respectfully solicit you to send to Mr. L. B. Maxwell an order to issue the above rations, and also to instruct the chief commissary to pay for said subsistence. I deem it a good policy to do it, as we may need their services in future time.

I am, General, very respectfully,
    Your obedient servant,
                    C. CARSON,
        Colonel 1st N. M. Vols., Commanding.

P. S. — Since my writing seventeen more Indians have joined my command, making in all eighty-two. All of them have families, which are suffering very much, and would be very glad if you approve the subsistence to be issued by L. B. Maxwell as heretofore mentioned in the within.

Whether the general succeeded in persuading the Indian department of the territory, with which he was at outs, to ration the families of these red children whose enlistment it had opposed, I do not know; but I doubt it. Superintendent Steck likely enough seized upon the opportunity to let General Carleton shoulder (as he had expressed himself willing to do) " all the consequences which may follow my acts." He who sent the men upon the warpath must provide for the women at home.

On November 10, Colonel Carson and his Indians arrived at Fort Bascom where he " found all the companies composing the expedition in readiness to move at any moment."

On the 12th he set out from Bascom " with * * * a total of fourteen officers and 321 enlisted men and seventy-five Indians," all subsisted for forty-five days, or until the first of the year. The quartermaster supplies were transported in twenty-seven wagons and an ambulance. It was the Carson plan to establish a base at Adobe Walls, and thence operate with pack animals. Thus equipped with infantry, cavalry, artillery, scouts, rations, and, best of all, a free hand, Carson the experienced, at the head of experienced fighters, well might anticipate the success expected of him by General Carleton:

As you see, I have given you more men than you asked for, because it is my desire that you give those Indians, especially the Kiowas, a severe drubbing. * * * I do not wish to embarrass you with minute instructions. You know where to find the Indians; you know what atrocities they have committed; you know how to punish them. The means and men are placed at your disposal to do it, and now all the rest is left with you.

The allied Kiowas and Comanches with a number of Kiowa Apaches and of Arapahos, totalling between 4,000 and 5,000 adults, were in winter camp about 200 miles down the Canadian from Fort Bascom, in the rich bottoms well supplied with wood and game, along the river in present Hutchinson County, of the Texas Panhandle. The principal villages were located on either side, east and west, of the old Bent's trading posts of Adobe Walls.

A portion of the command being afoot, and the wheels of the gun-carriages being small, advance was slow. Moreover, the line of march was projected through a country little known, seldom traversed, infested with the most dreaded Indians of the plains, and Carson was too wary a frontiersman unduly to expose his column. Therefore the march was by easy stages, with the certainty of finding the foe in winter camp at the end.

According to the account by Lieutenant George H. Pettis, commanding the twelve-pounder howitzer detachment, on the third or fourth day out of Bascom was passed the place where, in the fall of 1849, the troops led by Carson and Leroux had surprised the Apache captors of the wretched Mrs. White.

Carson explained to us how the attack was made, the position of the Indian camp, where the bodies were found, etc., in his usual graphic manner.[201]

The march was further enlivened by the Ute and Apache scouts, who

every night after making camp, being now on the warpath, indulged in their war dance, which, although new to most of us, became almost intolerable, it being kept up each night until nearly daybreak, and until we became accustomed to their groans and howlings incident to the dance, it was impossible to sleep. Each morning of our march, two of our Indians would be sent ahead several hours before we started, who would return to camp at night and report.

Thus with advance scouts and with flankers, Colonel Carson proceeded cautiously, twelve days (delayed two, however, by snowstorms), along the old trader road, upon the north of the Canadian, between Albuquerque, or Santa Fe, and Arkansas. On the afternoon of November 24, after a march of eighteen miles, camp was made at Mule Spring, or Arroya de la Mula, about thirty miles from Adobe Walls, lying east. Narrates Lieutenant Pettis:

We had arrived at Mule Spring early in the afternoon; had performed our usual camp duties, and as the sun was about setting, many of us being at supper, we were surprised to see our Indians, who were lying around the camp, some gambling, some sleeping, and others waiting for something to eat from the soldiers' mess, spring to their feet, as if one man, and gaze intently to the eastward, talking in their own language quite excitedly. Upon questioning Colonel Carson, why this tumult among our Indians, he informed us that the two scouts that he had dispatched that morning, had found the Comanches, and were now returning to report the particulars. Although the returning scouts were at least two miles distant, and, mounted on their ponies, were hardly discernible, yet the quick, sharp eye of our Indians made them out without difficulty. I must confess that I failed to see them, until an Indian pointed out to me, away off on the hill side, two mere specks moving towards our camp. And what was more remarkable, they had, by a single shout, in that rarefied, electrical atmosphere, conveyed the intelligence that they had found the enemy, and that work was to be done. But a short time elapsed before the two scouts arrived, and rode leisurely through camp, without answering any questions or giving any information, until they had found the Colonel, when they reported that they had, about ten miles in advance, found indications that a large body of Indians had moved that morning, with a very large herd of horses and cattle, and that we would have no difficulty in finding all the Indians that we desired. Carson immediately ordered all the cavalry, and the section of mountain howitzers, to be ready to move without delay. The Infantry, Company A, 1st California Infantry, under command of Colonel Abreü, was ordered to remain as escort to the wagon train, which was to stay in camp that night, and on the morrow was to move on and follow the trail of the command, until they overtook it.

At dusk Carson, with his mounted force and the battery, in all thirteen officers and 246 men, descended from the camp into the valley of the Canadian, and found there " the deep-worn, fresh trail of the hostile Indians." Having covered fifteen miles by midnight, a halt was made, to wait until morning.

* * * no talking was allowed (the few orders that were necessary, were given in a whisper), lighting of pipes and smoking was prohibited; each officer and soldier, upon halting, only dismounted, and remained holding his horse by the bridle rein until morning; and to add to our discomforts a heavy frost fell during the night.

As the first gray streaks of dawn appeared in the eastern skies, we mounted our horses, and proceeded on our new-found trail. * * * We had been moving but a few minutes, when I was informed that Carson wished to see me at the head of the column. I urged my horse forward as quietly as I could, and reported to him. As I did so, I remarked the funny appearance of his Indians, all of whom were mounted in their peculiar manner, with their knees drawn up nearly at right angles, and being cold, they were each of them enveloped in their buffalo robes, standing high above their heads, and fastened by a belt at their waist. Such a sight was ludicrous in the extreme. Carson commenced to say to me, in his own quaint way: "I had a dream the night before, of being engaged with a large number of Indians; your cannons were firing," — at this point of his recital, we heard a voice in Spanish, on the opposite side of the river, cry out "Bene-aca," "Bene-aca," — "Come here," "Come here." We knew that we had found a picket of the enemy. Carson hastily ordered Major McCleave, and B Company First California Cavalry, with one of the New Mexico detachments, to cross the river, as it was easily forded. Our Indians, who had been riding leisurely along, at the first cry charged into a clump of chapparel which was near by, and in a moment, as it seemed, came riding out again, completely divested of buffalo robes and all their clothing, with their bodies covered with war paint, and war feathers in abundance, and giving a war-whoop they dashed wildly into the river towards the enemy. I was wondering at the wonderful transformation of our Indians, entirely forgetful of the enemy, when Carson gave orders for us to move down on our side of the river, he being satisfied that the village would be found within a short distance.

At the sound of shots and the sight of three Indian pickets or pony guards racing away for their camp, Colonel Carson urged his main force to the attack before the village should be prepared; with Lieutenant Heath's company of First California Cavalry, he stayed as escort to the battery. Evidently upon the battery he placed chief dependence; and this dependence was justified.

The cavalry disappeared in the cottonwood clumps and the tall grass covering the river bottoms; the battery hastened after, its carriages constantly impeded and its dismounted cannoneers panting in the rear. Stolen cattle were passed; and presently were to be seen the scouts already enjoying the fruits of their labors, in shape of the enemy's pony herds, each fortunate Ute and Jicarilla having collected from twenty to fifty animals, as individual property. The scouts were rapidly changing riding pads, and, upon new mounts, were scurrying again for the fight.

Three or four miles had been covered by the laboring battery, and the firing in the front had receded, indicating that the enemy was driven back. About nine o'clock Colonel Carson, still with the battery, saw the first one of the Indian villages, five miles ahead, just beyond a long low bluff extending into the valley. The tipis, of whitened buffalo hides, deceived the battery and escort into thinking them to be Sibley army tents. Carson, knowing better, explained.

The village, of some 170 tipis, had been abandoned — its warriors put to retreat, its women and children driven to the brush, by the precipitate charge of the Carson advance. A short distance down the river the warriors had rallied, to make a stand, and were stubbornly contesting the invaders. As says the Carson official report: " They made several severe charges on Major McCleave's command before my arrival with the artillery and the other companies, but were gallantly repulsed."

The breath of conflict in his nostrils, Colonel Carson remarked to Lieutenant Pettis of the battery that if the fight was not over by the time they arrived it soon would be, after which the lodges could be burned. " At the same time," relates Pettis,

he threw his heavy military overcoat on a bush alongside the road, and advised me to do the same, as we should return in a few minutes and get them again. I did not do so, however.

Some of my men wished to take their overcoats and blankets from the guns and leave them, but I would not allow them to do so, and for once, my judgment was better than Carson's, for he never saw that coat of his again, while my own and those of my men did good service, afterward. But as we pushed on, the firing seemed no nearer, until after we had made about four miles from the village, when we saw our men, dismounted and deployed as skirmishers, with their horses corralled in an old, deserted, adobe building, known by all frontiersmen as the Adobe Walls. When we were within about a thousand yards of this point, Carson, with Lieutenant Heath and his detachment, put spurs to their horses and charged forward to join in the fray. My men seemed to get new life, and forgot all their fatigues, at the prospect of going into action, and but a few minutes elapsed before we came into the center of the field at a gallop, and touching my cap to Carson, I received from him the following order: " Pettis, throw a few shell into that crowd over thar." The next moment, " Battery, halt! action right — load with shell — LOAD! " was ordered.

It was now near ten o'clock in the morning, the sky was not obscured by a single cloud, and the sun was shining in all its brightness. Within a hundred yards of the corralled horses in the Adobe Walls, was a small symmetrical conical hill of twenty-five or thirty feet elevation, while in all directions extended a level plain. Carson, McCleave, and a few other officers, occupied the summit, when the battery arrived and took position nearly on the top. Our cavalry was dismounted and deployed as skirmishers in advance, lying in tall grass, and firing an occasional shot at the enemy. Our Indians, mounted and covered with paint and feathers, were charging backwards and forwards and shouting their war cry, and in their front were about two hundred Comanches and Kiowas, equipped as they themselves were, charging in the same manner, with their bodies thrown over the sides of their horses, at a full run, and shooting occasionally under their horses' necks; while gathered just beyond them twelve or fourteen hundred, with a dozen or more chiefs riding up and down their line haranguing them, seemed to be preparing for a desperate charge on our forces. Surgeon Courtright had prepared a corner of the Adobe Walls for a hospital, and was busy, with his assistants, in attending to the wants of half a dozen or more wounded. Fortunately, the Adobe Walls were high enough to protect all our horses from the enemy's rifles, and afford ample protection to our wounded. Within a mile of us, beyond the enemy, in full and complete view, was a Comanche village of over five hundred lodges, which, with the village that we had captured, made about seven hundred lodges, which allowing two fighting Indians to a lodge, which is the rule on the frontier, would give us fourteen hundred warriors in the field before us.

This was the prospect when the battery came on the ground. A finer sight I never saw before, and probably shall never see again.

The Indians seemed to be astonished when the pieces came up at a gallop and were being unlimbered. The pieces were loaded in a few seconds after the order was given, and were sighted by the gunners, when the command " Number one — Fire! " was given, followed quickly by " Number two — Fire! " At the first discharge, every one of the enemy, those that were charging backwards and forwards on their horses but a moment before as well as those that were standing in line, rose high in their stirrups and gazed, for a single moment, with astonishment, then guiding their horses' heads away from us, and giving one concerted, prolonged yell, they started on a dead run for their village. In fact when the fourth shot was fired there was not a single enemy within the extreme range of the howitzers.

The artillery having given the white force the *morale* (that potent military expedient) over the astonished reds, Colonel Carson might deem the combat decided. He declared that the Indians would not make another stand; and ordered his command to unsaddle, unharness, to water and to stake the horses, and to eat breakfast. After breakfast he purposed moving upon the villages farther down river, or, as the Pettis account states, returning to destroy the village already abandoned.

Scarcely had the men eaten their haversack rations of raw bacon and hard-tack, when, while they yet were boisterously relating adventures, looking through my glass (reports Carson) I discovered a large force of Indians advancing from another village about three miles east of Adobe fort. In this village there were at least 350 lodges. I immediately ordered the command to saddle and the companies to take position. In a short time I found myself surrounded by at least 1,000 Indian warriors mounted on first-class horses. They repeatedly charged my command from different points, but were invariably repulsed with great loss.

The battle, renewed, lasted throughout the afternoon. By their customary rapid movements and by open order the Kiowas and allies avoided the howitzer shells, so formidable in their strange explosions. One shell passed through a horse being ridden at full speed by a Comanche. Down pitched the horse, sending his painted master twenty feet through the air, sprawling and senseless. Instantly two other warriors raced for him, and from their saddles seizing him, each by an arm, amid a shower of rifle balls dragged him to safety. Lieutenant Pettis narrates:

Quite a number of the enemy acted as skirmishers, being dismounted and hid in the tall grass in our front, and made it hot for most of us by their excellent markmanship, while quite the larger part of them, mounted and covered with their war dresses, charged continually across our front, from right to left and *vice versa,* about two hundred yards from our line of skirmishers, yelling like demons, and firing from under the necks of their horses at intervals. About two hundred yards in rear of their line, all through the fighting at the Adobe Walls, was stationed one of the enemy who had a cavalry . bugle, and during the entire day he would blow the opposite call that was used by the officer in our line of skirmishers. For instance, when our bugle sounded the " advance," he would blow " retreat;" and when ours sounded the "retreat," he would follow with the " advance;" ours would signal " halt;" he would follow suit. So he kept it up all the day, blowing as shrill and clearly as our very best buglers. Carson insisted that it was a white man, but I have never received any information to corroborate this opinion. All I know is, that he would answer our signals each time they were sounded, to the infinite merriment of our men, who would respond with shouts of laughter each time he sounded his horn.[202]

The Kiowas, principals in the fight, were under command of the elderly chief Dohasan, or Sierrito (Little Mountain). Prominent as his aides were Set-imkia (Stumbling-bear), and the notorious Set-t'ainte (White Bear), known commonly as Satanta. Among the Apache chiefs was Iron Shirt — killed at the door of his lodge which he refused to desert.

According to the Kiowa statement, most of the younger men were away on the warpath at the time, having left their families in the winter camp in charge of the old chief Dohasan. Early one morning some of the men had gone out to look for their ponies, when they discovered the enemy creeping up to surround them. They dashed back into camp and gave the alarm, and the women, who were preparing breakfast, hastily gathered up their children and ran, while the men mounted their horses to repel the assault. The Ute scouts advanced in Indian fashion, riding about and keeping up a constant yelling to stampede the Kiowa ponies, while the soldiers came on behind quietly and in regular order. Stumbling-bear was one of the leading warriors in the camp at the time and distinguished himself in the defense, killing one soldier and a Ute, and then killing or wounding another soldier so that he fell from his horse. Another warrior named Set-tadal, " Lean-bear," distinguished himself by his bravery in singing the war song of his order, the Tontonko, as he advanced to the charge, according to his military obligation, which forbade him to save himself until he had killed an enemy. Set-t'opte, then a small boy, was there also, and describes vividly how he took his younger brother by the hand, while his mother carried the baby upon her back and another child in her arms, and all fled for a place of safety while Stumbling-bear and the warriors kept off the attacking party.[203]

So much for the Indian account of the battle. The Kiowas, engaged first by that attack upon their village above the Adobe Walls, quickly were reinforced by Comanche, Apache, and Arapaho. From the Adobe Walls the troops could see for a dozen miles down the river; still other villages were visible, and each was dispatching its quota of vengeful warriors. All the afternoon they were arriving in parties of from five to fifty, until by white estimate fully 3,000 were upon the field. By no means "poor" Indians were these; they were Indians enriched by forays upon caravans to the north and upon Mexican villages to the south; by herds of fat ponies, and by supplies of guns, powder, and lead furnished them through the hands of white and Mexican traders.

The Sioux who wiped out Custer's soldiery at the Big Horn were not better equipped, and they were not as many. The claim by the Carson men that this was the "biggest fight," in point of Indian strength, that ever occurred west of the Mississippi River, hardly can be gainsaid.

The Indians were not only gathering upon the field, but they were also making circuit and reentering their village above, there rescuing their stock and other movable property, and hustling their families away with it. Above the village was the Carson wagon train, protected by only seventy-five men; this might be cut off and overwhelmed, and the main force put in bad plight.

Although the village ahead was a great temptation, and the majority of the officers and men wished to fight through and capture it, the cautious Carson decided that with an enemy so determined he ought to make sure of his rear. In this he was supported by the Ute and Jicarilla chiefs, who were witnessing their booty being swiftly disintegrated. To the allies (as to any Indian) plunder was a great glory of battle.

Accordingly, "after some hesitation (narrates Lieutenant Pettis) and against the wishes of most of his officers, at about half-past three Carson gave orders to bring out the cavalry horses, and formed a column of fours — the number four man of each set of fours to lead the other three horses — with the mountain howitzers to bring up the rear of the column." The dismounted men were deployed in rear and on right and left. Then, as reports Colonel Carson:

> In this manner I commenced my march on the village. The Indians, seeing my object, again advanced, with the evident intention of saving their village and property if possible. The Indians charged so repeatedly and with such desperation that for some time I had serious doubts for the safety of my rear, but the coolness with which they were received by Captain Berney's command, and the steady and constant fire poured into them, caused them to retire on every occasion with great slaughter.
>
> The Indians now finding it impossible to impede my march by their repeated charges, set fire to the valley in my rear, which was composed of long grass and weeds, and the wind being favorable it burned with great fury and caused my rear to close up at double quick. I immediately saw their object and had the valley fired in my front to facilitate my march. I then retired to a piece of elevated ground on my right flank upon which the grass was short, and upon which I knew I was out of danger from the fire. Here the Indians again advanced under cover of the fire and smoke which raged with great fury, but my artillery being in position they were again repulsed with great slaughter.

Captain Pettis declares that occasionally, where the smoke was thick, the red horsemen would charge until within a few yards of the beleaguered line, deliver their fire, and then escape. The only scalp of the day was taken in the return march, by a Mexican youth who in the morning had been bitten by a rattlesnake. In the smoke a Comanche made his charge, and by a gust of wind was revealed within twenty feet of the boy. Indian and Mexican fired, and the Indian fell. While the Indian's friends vainly attempted the rescue of the corpse, protected by the rifles of his comrades the

Mexican snatched the scalp. The fact that this was the only scalp taken by the attacking force, bespeaks the furious character of the fray. For obvious reasons Colonel Carson, on this return march, did not pause to pick up his overcoat. " Just before sundown," narrates Lieutenant Pettis,

we reached the village, which we found full of Indians trying to save their property from destruction. A couple of shells, followed by a charge of our men, drove them into the far end of it, when the work of destruction commenced, about half of the command being detailed to set fire to the lodges, while the rest of us were to keep the enemy in check.
＊　　＊　　＊　　＊　　＊　　＊　　＊　　＊　　＊　　＊
The lodges were found to be full of plunder, including many hundreds of finely finished buffalo robes. Every man in the command took possession of one or more of these, while the balance were consumed in the lodges. There were found some white women's clothing, as well as articles of children's clothing, and several photographs; also a cavalry sergeant's hat, with letter and cross-sabres, cavalry sabre and belts, etc.

The 176 lodges (or, according to the Carson official report, about 150) contained also much dried meat, berries, powder, and cooking utensils. Among the women's clothing were bonnets and shoes. A buggy, a spring wagon, and several sets of harness, reputed to be the proud possessions of Sierrito himself, were confiscated and burned with the other property.

Two old squaws, attached to the Ute and Jicarilla contingent, proved their feminine valor by gleefully disclosing to the detail firing the lodges four Kiowas, two blind and two crippled, who had been cut down with axes by these ruthless harpies.

By the time the village had been destroyed, darkness had gathered. Now the column must proceed, in search of the wagon train, a measure the more imperative in that the company commanders reported their ammunition to be nearly expended. Says Pettis:

> The two gun carriages and the two ammunition carts were loaded with the most severely wounded, while the slightly wounded retained their horses. The march now became the most unpleasant part of the day's operations. The wounded were suffering severely; the men and horses were completely worn out; the enemy might attack us at any moment, unseen; and the uncertainty of the whereabouts and condition of our wagon train, for you will remember that we were now nearly two hundred and fifty miles from the nearest habitation, or hopes of supply, with the whole Comanche and Kiowa nations at our heels — all combined to make it anything but a pleasant situation to be in. We had been moving slowly on our return from the destroyed village about three hours, when we saw away off on our right several camp fires burning dimly, and approaching cautiously, we were soon welcomed by the challenge of a sentinel, in good, clear, ringing Saxon, " Who comes there? "

The train was intact and unmolested, here encamped and prepared for defense, within clear sound of the battle. After almost thirty hours of marching and fighting upon a few mouthfuls of hard-tack and salt pork or raw bacon the column was completely exhausted; even the Indian scouts being so spent

that they adjourned their " scalp dance," and sought the comfort of their buffalo robes; but, as we had been entertained every night until the fight by their " war dance," so for twenty-one days after, or as long as they remained with us, the monotony of the march was diversified by their own peculiar " scalp dance," and that with only one scalp, which they had purchased of the Mexican soldier whose exploit I have before mentioned.

Colonel Carson, apprehending the customary daybreak attack, had ordered the reveille to be sounded before dawn.

The command, rested and refreshed, was soon prepared to fight again. The Indians failed to close in; although throughout the day, while the soldier camp took its ease, they hovered about, on the hills, evincing, however, a proper respect for the howitzers.

After early breakfast, the next morning, the 27th " orders were issued," narrates Lieutenant Pettis, " by Colonel Carson to saddle up, and commence the return march, much to the surprise and dissatisfaction of all the officers, who desired to go to the Comanche village that we had been in sight of, on the day of the fight." It was said that the Indian scouts had advised their colonel to take the Bascom Trail; but he knew as well as they; he knew that the valley of the Canadian was no place in which, with his twenty-five wounded men and many wounded animals, to tempt fortune farther. Says Carson's official report:

I now decided that owing to the broken-down condition of my cavalry horses and transportation and the Indians having fled in all directions with their stock that it was impossible for me to chastise them further at present. Therefore, on the morning of the 27th, * * * I broke camp and commenced my return trip.

Having safely extricated his column from the dangerous territory, he might reveal his private opinion by his dispatch, December 16, from camp near Fort Bascom, requesting reinforcements of animals, of 700 mounted men, two six-pounder and two twelve-pounder guns, and of supplies for issued in General Orders No. 4, February 18, 1865, giving a resume of the important engagements of the previous year, runs:

November 25 — Colonel Christopher Carson, 1st cavalry New Mexico Volunteers, with a command consisting of fourteen commissioned officers, three hundred and twenty-one enlisted men and seventy-five Indians, Apaches and Utes, attacked a Kiowa village of about one hundred and fifty lodges, near the Adobe Fort, on the Canadian River, in Texas, and after a severe fight compelled the Indians to retreat, with a loss of sixty killed and wounded. The village was then destroyed. The engagement commenced at 8½ a. m., and lasted without intermission until sunset. * * *

Colonel Carson, in his report, mentions the following officers as deserving the highest praise: Major McCleave, Captain Fritz and Lieutenant Heath, of the 1st Cavalry California Volunteers; Captain Deus and Berney, 1st Cavalry New Mexico Volunteers; Lieutenant Pettis, 1st Infantry California Volunteers; Lieutenant Edgar, 1st Cavalry New Mexico Volunteers, and Assistant Surgeon George S. Courtright, United States Volunteers.

The Kiowas claimed that in the attack upon the village only five, two of them being women and one an aged Apache, abandoned by mistake, were killed. Afterwards many more, of course, met their death, in the " great slaughter " frequently referred to in the Carson official report, and finally summed as sixty! In this report Colonel Carson admirably " covers up "; naturally, he could no more confess to any misgivings upon the way the battle went, than could the Indians confess their losses.

"I flatter myself that I have taught these Indians a severe lesson." asserts the lucky colonel. "

The reason for such effort became known to plains circles. As Colonel (Brevet Brigadier General) James H. Ford testifies, at Fort Larned, May 31, 1865:

I understand Kit Carson last winter destroyed an Indian village. He had about four hundred men with him, but the Indians attacked him as bravely as any men in the world, charging up to his lines, and he withdrew his command. * * * Carson said if it had not been for his howitzers, few would have been left to tell the tale. This I learned from an officer who was in the fight.

George Bent, who, as half-breed son of William Bent, was so intimate with plains conditions among both whites and Indians, writes, about 1900:

The Kiowas, Comanches and Apaches were not in one village. Little Mountain was head chief of the Kiowas, One-Eyed Bear of the Comanches, and Iron Shirt of the Apaches. It was the Apache village that Carson struck, and he burned part of it. Iron Shirt was killed at the door of his lodge. He refused to leave his lodge. His son and wife are still living down here (Oklahoma). Kit Carson told me in 1868, three weeks before he died, that the Indians whipped him in this fight. What saved him was Adobe Fort. When the Indians attacked him he ran back to the old fort to make his stand. Buckskin Charley, the Ute chief, was with Carson in this fight. He says the Kiowas, Comanches and Apaches had Carson whipped. He told me they had to fight fire to keep from being burned up. I bought a race horse from Kit Carson in 1868, the horse he rode during the fight. The Indians followed Carson two or three days after leaving Adobe Fort. This horse I bought had white spots on each side of his back. Carson told me he had the saddle on the horse four days during this fight, and when he took the saddle off the skin came with it.

Captain Pettis also adds to the aftermath of well-endorsed rumor:

In 1867, about three years after the events narrated here, I was residing in a little Mexican village on the Rio Grande, Los Algodones, about forty-five miles south of Santa Fe, where I became acquainted with a couple of Mexicans who were trading with the Comanche and Kiowa Indians in the fall of 1864, and they informed me that they were at the Comanche village which we were in sight of, and that when the fight commenced they were held as prisoners and kept so for several days after we left that neighborhood; that in the village on the day of the fight there were seven white women and several white children, prisoners; they also informed me where the women and children of the village were hid when we passed through the Kiowa village on the morning of the fight, and that our enemy sustained a loss on that day, of nearly a hundred killed and between one hundred and one hundred and fifty wounded, making a difference with the official report, which guessed at thirty killed and thirty wounded. They also said that the Indians claimed that if the whites had not had with them the two guns that shot twice, referring to the shells of the mountain howitzers, they would never have allowed a single white man to escape out of the valley of the Canadian, and I may say, with becoming modesty, that this was also the often expressed opinion of Colonel Carson.

Even the hero worshiper, Surgeon Peters, speaking of this fight, admits that " at Stone Wall (?) near the Red River, Carson met his match, being overpowered and badly defeated."

Nevertheless, that Carson took the back trail, and considered himself fortunate so to do, deprives him no whit of glory. Any leader only less wise than he, would have been annihilated despite the howitzers. Bringing in a column, with baggage train, more than 200 miles, he actually surprised the camp of 5,000 watchful Indians, destroyed a portion of it, and suffered no Custer or Fetterman defeat. As in the case of other army officers in the West, he met a red enemy well munitioned by the white government. In his dispatch of December 16, following the fight, he complains that he found tracks of traders' wagons, pointing down the river, for the Indian camp; and he had no doubt that in this fight his men were killed or wounded by powder and ball supplied thus.

The headquarters encomium is not misplaced:

This brilliant affair adds another green leaf to the laurel wreath which you have so nobly won in the service of your country. That you may long be spared to be of still further service, is the sincere wish of your obedient servant and friend,

JAMES H. CARLETON,
Brigadier General, Commanding.

CARSON IN COLONEL'S UNIFORM

ENGRAVING OF A WARTIME PHOTOGRAPH BY BRADY OF WASHINGTON. ONE
OF THE FEW PICTURES OF CARSON SHOWING HIM CLEAN SHAVEN

(Courtesy of the Century Magazine)

CARSON AS INDIAN AGENT

COPY OF A TINTYPE TAKEN AT TAOS DECEMBER, 1860,
ACCORDING TO THE RECOLLECTION OF CAPTAIN SIMPSON, WHO
SAT AT THE SAME TIME

CARSON IN 1847

(From an oil painting owned by Gov. William Gilpin of Colorado)

CHAPTER XXXVI

PLAINS AND MOUNTAIN SERVICE — 1865–1867

FOR Colonel Christopher Carson ensued another brief period of rest. He and his command spent Christmas of 1864 at Fort Bascom, waiting for the next movement of Kiowas, Comanches, or other hostile tribes. The allied tribes of the Canadian country had been staggered by the hard, if not altogether decisive, blow so boldly dealt them; and were the more alarmed by the tidings that almost at the same time, on November 29, their fellows to the north, the Cheyennes and Arapahos of the Arkansas, had met more wholesale destruction at the attack of Sand Creek. Indeed it would seem that the white chief, Governor Evans of Colorado Territory, had spoken truly when he said to the Cheyennes and Arapahos: "Now the war with the whites is nearly through, and the Great Father will not know what to do with all his soldiers, except to send them after the Indians on the plains." [204]

Fort Bascom waited in peace; the Carleton supplies for the Department of New Mexico came through little molested, upon the Santa Fe Trail; Comanche, Kiowa, Cheyenne and Arapaho warfare was desultory; and on December 26 went forward to Colonel Carson the fresh orders that if there was no danger to Fort Bascom his force was to be distributed or disbanded, and that he himself might proceed to Taos and Ojo Caliente until further orders.

This he did. The enlistments of the New Mexico Volunteers were rapidly expiring; the three year term of the original members of the First Regiment had expired July 31, 1864. However, the veterans and the recruits were retained, as a nucleus still to bear the guidons of the First New Mexican Cavalry. Colonel Carson was also entitled to resign; his officers were dropping away, to return to civil life, and by reason of health and inclination he fain would do the same. On the other hand, he was needed and appreciated where he was, and that being so, to doff his uniform would not have been in keeping with his character.

From Fort Union, on his way to Taos, he evidently took occasion to quiet any misgivings as to his intentions. The reply from the generous Carleton must have pleased him.

HEADQUARTERS DEPARTMENT OF NEW MEXICO,
SANTA FE., N. M., January 30, 1865.
COLONEL CHRISTOPHER CARSON,
 Taos, N. M.
COLONEL:
I received your letter from Fort Union, and it gratifies me to learn that you will not leave the service while I remain here. A great deal of my good fortune in Indian matters here — in fact nearly all with reference to the Navajos, Mescalero Apaches, and Kiowas — is due to you, and it affords me pleasure always to acknowledge the value of your services,
* * * * * * * * * * * *
JAMES H. CARLETON,
Brigadier General, Commanding.

Wider recognition came when, by Washington orders of March 13, 1865, Colonel Carson was brevetted brigadier general of volunteers, for "important services in New Mexico, Arizona, and the Indian Territory."

By the surrender, April 9, of General Lee's Army of Northern Virginia, the war in the East was virtually finished. The war in the West, apparently the lesser war, continued. General Carson had been at his Taos home over three months when, May 4, he was notified that he would be in charge of a military summer camp, on the Cimarron desert cut-off of the Santa Fe Trail, some 300 miles out of

Santa Fe, for the protection of the trail, and in hopes that
" you will be able to have a talk with some of the chiefs of
Cheyennes, Kiowas, and Comanches, and impress them with
the folly of continuing this bad course."
Carson made answer on May 6. The formal order was
dispatched to him May 8:

[Special Orders No. 15.]
DEPARTMENT OF NEW MEXICO, ASSISTANT ADJUTANT
GENERAL'S OFFICE,
SANTA FE, N. M., May 7, 1865.
* * * * * * * * * * * *
IV. Colonel Christopher Carson, with Major Albert H.
Pfeiffer and companies C and L of his regiment and company
F, first cavalry California Volunteers, will proceed from Fort
Union, New Mexico, starting on the 20th instant to Cedar
Bluffs or Cold Spring, on the Cimarron route to the States,
where, at or near one of these places, Colonel Carson will
select and establish a camp to be occupied until the first day
of November next, unless otherwise ordered from these headquarters. The object of establishing this camp is to have
troops at that dangerous part of the route, in order to give
protection to trains passing to and from the States. The details as to how this force can best effect that object are left
entirely with Colonel Carson.
* * * * * * * * * * * *
By command of Brigadier General Carleton:
BEN C. CUTLER,
Official.   Assistant Adjutant General.

The letter which accompanied this order again illus-
trates how thoroughly dependence was placed upon this
quiet, homely little man.

COLONEL:
I received last evening your note of the 6th instant,
and enclose herewith the order for your movement. In my
opinion your consultations and influence with the Indians

of the plains will stop the war. Be sure and move on the appointed day. I have full faith and confidence in your judgment and in your energy.

Nevertheless, the careful Carleton could not forget that here he was establishing a plains camp, liable to be quiet, monotonous, and under the easy-going Carson of democratic ways and the Major Pfeiffer of social tendencies. So, in kindly language he advised:

To have a fine camp, with ovens; a comfortable place for the sick; good store-rooms; some defences thrown up to prevent surprise; pickets established at good points for observation; hay cut and hauled to feed of nights or in case the Indians crowd you; large and well-armed guards, under an officer, with the public animals when herding; promptness in getting into the saddle and in moving to help the trains; a disposition to move quick, each man with his little bag of flour, a little salt and sugar and coffee, and not hampered by packs; arms and equipments always in order; tattoo and reveille roll-calls invariably under arms, so that the men shall have their arms on the last thing at night and in their hands the first thing in the morning; to have an inspection by the officers at tattoo and at reveille of the arms, and to see that the men are ready to fight, never to let this be omitted; to have, if possible, all detachments commanded by an officer, to report progress and events from time to time — these seem to be some of the essential points which, of course, you will keep in view. * * * Keep up discipline from the start and all the time. After you have established your camp and got matters in training, please report in full.

As far as may be ascertained, no news of importance came in from this summer Camp Nichols, where the Cimarron cuts through the Oklahoma panhandle. Although this portion of Oklahoma was, in 1865, an adjunct of the Indian Territory, General Carson on June 19 reported his estate as being " Camp Nichols, New Mexico." Political lines in the Indian West were still a little vague.

It may be accepted that as pacifying agent Camp Nichols was a success; but life here was not enviable. The stages had ceased running, until after the Indians should be under control; there was neither station nor ranch habitation: for this was the Cimarron Desert, the most dreaded and dangerous portion of the trail.

Colonel Meline, traversing it in 1866, says:

Since 1861 it (i. e., the route) has been almost abandoned on account of the Indians, and is only just now being resumed. This part of the plains, running down further south into Texas, * * * still remains almost in its primitive geographical seclusion and isolation. Maps have done little or nothing for it, and we find it difficult to locate ourselves day by day when we halt.[205]

Colonel Meline's reference, a little later in this chapter, to the camp, indicates that the occupants did not lead a lethargic existence; for, aside from their scouting operations, they erected stone quarters. Nevertheless, existence could not have been much varied; the bulk of travel was along the Arkansas River route to old Bent's Fort, and the mountain branch by the Raton Pass and Maxwell's of the Cimarron, near Rayado.

Carleton's activities were being devoted chiefly to herding his now restless Navajos. What councils General Carson may have held with the red men assigned to his provinces we do not know; but before the establishment of his Camp Nichols, councils in which he was to have prominent part were brewing.

By resolution of March 3 the Congress of the United States really had taken an intelligent step in this Indian problem so long delegated to hired help. A joint special committee was appointed, composed of three members of the Senate, four of the House, for the purpose of " directing an inquiry into the condition of the Indian tribes and

their treatment by civil and military authorities of the
United States."

To Messrs. Doolittle, Foster, and Ross was assigned the
duty of inquiring into Indian affairs in the State of Kansas,
the Indian Territory, Colorado, New Mexico, and Utah.

To Messrs. Nesmith and Higby the same duty was assigned
in the States of California, Oregon, and Nevada, and in the
Territories of Washington, Idaho, and Montana.

To Messrs. Windom and Hubbard the same duty was assigned in the State of Minnesota and in the Territories of
Nebraska, Dakota, and upper Montana.[206]

No junketing trips were these. They entailed much labor
and much discomfort, for "the work was immense, covering a continent," and it was carried on before the days
of Pullman cars and buffet attachments.

At last it would appear that the western aborigine, sorely
tossed between the Scylla and Charybdis of military force
and civil duplicity, was to have his alleged rights and
wrongs adequately handled. Here in the Southwest were
enlisted in his favor such authorities as William Bent, the
trader, and Kit Carson, the fighter, now about to give testimony direct to the very fountain head of National
Government.

Just when Kit Carson made his deposition at Fort Lyon
of Colorado, in reference to the conduct of the war as exemplified by the Sand Creek "Chivington massacre," we may
not fully determine. Probably it was in June, 1865; he
must have made a hasty trip down the trail, during the
founding of Camp Nichols. Here at Lyon he was simply
among the other experts and alienists summoned to give
evidence; but appreciation of his intrinsic abilities was
traveling on.

The congressional committee performed no wiser act
than that when they selected him to be mediator-in-chief

among the tribes of the southwest plains. In congratula-
tion he is addressed, at Fort Union, by his commanding
general, who grants him the leave, in a generous measure
of commendation.

HEADQUARTERS DEPARTMENT OF NEW MEXICO,
SANTA FE, N. M., August 6, 1865.
COLONEL:
 I had the honor to receive your letter of August 2, 1865,
enclosing a letter to yourself from the Hon. J. R. Doolittle,
United States Senate, chairman of the congressional committee to inquire into Indian affairs, and also enclosing two
telegraphic despatches from the Secretary of War to Mr. Doolittle, with reference to holding councils with the Indians. Mr.
Doolittle's letter, and Mr. Stanton's despatches, I herewith
return for your guidance in your special mission upon the
plains, made at the request of Mr. Doolittle. Your knowledge
of what Mr. Doolittle desires and hopes you will be able to
effect with the Indians of the plains, which knowledge you
have derived in conversation with that gentleman, precludes
the necessity of special instructions from me, indeed, in this
matter, where, as I understand it, the great object to be had
in view by yourself is to make preliminary arrangements, if
possible, with the Comanches, Kiowas, and Cheyennes and
Arapahoes, so that hostilities on their part will cease, and so
that their chiefs and principal men will meet commissioners
in council to make a treaty of peace. Your great knowledge
of the Indians — your knowledge of what is desired on the
part of the government — your knowledge of the danger to
be apprehended that the Indians may believe our overtures
proceed rather from our fears of them than from a sincere
desire not to make war upon them on our part, unless they
compel us to do so — your knowledge of how to talk with
them, so that they may not suffer from any such delusion —
these considerations you understand so much better than myself, that it is unnecessary for me to give you, or attempt to
give you, any instructions in the case.
* * * * * * * * * * * *
 I enclose herewith the order for your escort, and for Adjutant Tanfield to join you. That you may have good luck and

return in health and safety, is the earnest wish of your sincere friend,

JAMES H. CARLETON,
Brigadier General, Commanding.
COLONEL CHRISTOPHER CARSON, Fort Union, N. M.

That sub-committee to whom was assigned the southwestern plains territory was working eastward, having been at Fort Larned, Kansas, in May, arriving there just in time to frustrate a military movement southward into the Comanche country, which likely would have started a war of two or three years' duration, requiring 10,000 men and $30,000,000.[207] Such a complication would badly have interfered with this early Hague Conference.

Kit Carson, armed with his leave of absence and supplied with his escort, proceeded from Fort Union over the trail to Fort Lyon, at the upper end of the Big Timbers along the Arkansas. Under date of August 19, he reported from Fort Lyon. Camp Nichols remained in charge of Major Pfeiffer, pursuing the even tenor of its ways, but was to terminate within the compass of a year. Colonel Meline, en route from Santa Fe to Missouri in August, 1866, says:

Our camp, yesterday evening, was among the ruins (new ruins of a structure not old) of Fort Nicholson — a cantonment erected by a few companies of a California and a New Mexico cavalry regiment, two years ago, for the protection of this route. For a small force, they effected a great deal, and put up their quarters, corral, field-work, etc., of stone.

The remains of the walls, and a grave on the hill, covered with a monumental pile of heavy stones to protect it from the wolves, and a massive cross of rock, with the name " Barada, private, First New Mexico Cavalry," are all that survive their labors.[208]

The special commission upon which Kit Carson now served was appointed by order of the President, through the congressional joint committee, to meet the tribes of the

Arkansas River country and treat with them. The military commander of the district of the upper Arkansas was General John B. Sanborn; the agent for the Kiowa, Comanche and Apache bands of the lower Arkansas was Colonel Jesse H. Leavenworth. By their joint efforts the commission and the Indians came together at Bluff Creek, forty miles south of the Little Arkansas River, Kansas.

Here, October 14, 1865, with the "confederated tribes of Arapahoe and Cheyennes of the upper Arkansas River" was signed a treaty, the representatives of the United States being General Sanborn, Colonel Leavenworth, Special Commissioner Kit Carson, William Bent, James Steele, and Thomas Murphy. No Indians ever had fairer overtures extended them; substantial apologies were proffered for the overzealous attack at Sand Creek; the white soldiers were strongly censured; and the privilege of roaming about was granted, upon the naïve understanding that no camp was to be placed within ten miles of a main traveled road!

As was customary, a portion of the tribes did not sanction the treaty, which (also as customary) led to protests *vi et armis* and *viva voce* from all concerned, the protests culminating in Custer's charge, November 27, 1868, upon Black Kettle's camp of Cheyenne, Arapaho, Kiowa, Apache, Comanche, and Sioux, assembled in winter array twelve miles long, beside the Washita.

However, with these subsequent events Kit Carson had little to do. The soldiery trained to the minute in actual war had come upon the plains, and Sherman, Sheridan, Hancock, Custer and their like were there to "make peace" in their own effectual way.

This fall of 1865 was prolific of peace treaties, October itself seeing experimental amnesty and rights given to Kiowa, Cheyenne, Apache, Comanche, Arapaho and Sioux. October 14 witnessed the Carson treaty with the Arapahos and Cheyennes; October 17, a treaty with the Arapahos,

Cheyennes and Apaches; October 18, a treaty with Comanche and Kiowa; and so forth — the texts, with other contemporary texts, numbering almost 400, to be found compiled in the Government " Statutes at Large," and in the Indian Affairs " Laws and Treaties." [209]

It must have been while serving upon this special commission of the fall of 1865 that Kit Carson proceeded on to Fort Leavenworth (as is later related in this chapter) and thence visited General Sherman at St. Louis. How much farther eastward he went we do not know. General Fremont was at this time in New York and vicinity, and rumors would take General Carson even to Washington — a trip not unlikely. A photograph or two alleged to date hereabouts seems to substantiate the rumors.

During the first half of 1866 Kit Carson divided his time between Taos, where his family stayed when not briefly in camp and garrison; Cimarron, where the Maxwell manor house, now approaching its zenith, was always open to him; and Fort Union, where it would appear that he nominally was in command. He was occasionally on the trail elsewhere; to Santa Fe and Albuquerque, about official business; to the mouth of the Purgatory, at the Arkansas, where William Bent's ranch was prospering and where, at Boggsville, he himself was to locate, sick unto death; no doubt to Denver; and of course incidentally to Mora, where, only eighteen miles east from Union, Ceran St. Vrain was prospering.

The author finds no department order assigning Carson to command at Fort Union, and any tenure here by him must have been of short duration. In July, 1866, Colonel Meline, passing through, speaks of Union as being more of a military depot than a garrison station. General John Wynne Davidson, Second Cavalry, lieutenant with Carson at San Pasqual, and hero of the disastrous battle, March, 1853, with the Jicarillas in the Embuda cañon, was com-

mander of the post in the summer of 1866, and by Colonel
Meline's reference had been commander for some time.
Colonel Meline, writing at Santa Fe, under date of August
11, records:

The pleasantest episode of my visit here has been the society
of Kit Carson, with whom I passed three days, I need hardly
say delightfully. He is one of the few men I ever met who
can talk long hours of what he has seen, and yet say very little
about himself. He has to be drawn out. I had many questions to ask, and his answers were all marked by great distinctness of memory, simplicity, candor, and a desire to make some
one else, rather than himself, the hero of his story. In answer
to queries concerning Indians, he would frequently reply —
unlike so many I have met who knew *all* about them — " I
don't know," — " I can't say," — " I never saw that."

* * * * * * * * * *

He cares but little for a title, and when some one at the
table apologized for calling him Colonel, instead of General,
" Oh, call me Kit at once, and be done with it," was his reply.

* * * * * * * * * *

General Carson (he is Colonel of the First Regiment New
Mexican Cavalry, and Brevet Brigadier-General) usually resides at Taos, but is now in command at Fort Garland. He
has been married many years to a Mexican lady * * *
and has a family of three boys and three girls. I find that he
is beloved and respected by all who know him, and his word is
looked upon as truth itself.

The assignment to command at Fort Garland may be accepted as a straight compliment to Carson. The volunteer
rank and file was being mustered out by wholesale — a
final cleaning up. But Major-General John Pope, on tour
of inspection of his Department of the Missouri, writes on
August 11 from Fort Union to his chief, Major-General
W. T. Sherman of the Military Division of the Mississippi,
and now in Denver:

For the garrison of Fort Garland, by far the most important
post on the Ute frontier, I have authorized the retention

until their term of service expires of four companies of New Mexican volunteers, to be consolidated from other companies of the regiment under the command of Kit Carson, who is now the colonel, but who will be reduced to lieutenant colonel. I need not say that Carson is the best man in the country to control those Indians and to prevent war if it can be done. He is personally known and liked by every Indian of the bands likely to make trouble, and the men he will retain are perfectly familiar with the Indians and the country. * * * Peace with these Indians is of all things desirable, and no man is so certain to insure it as Kit Carson.

Fort Garland of Colorado territory, christened in honor of the former department commander in New Mexico, was built in the spring and summer of 1858 as successor to that pioneer post, Fort Massachusetts, nine miles north. To the north of the fort, as today, Sierra Blanca lifted its crest, third in height and among the most majestic in appearance of the peaks of the American Rockies. Taos was about eighty miles south. The post was at the eastern verge of the great valley known as San Luis Park.

This was distinctly the country of the Tabeguache or Uncompahgre Utes, now restive under the gold-seeking white men who persisted in penetrating through the barrier ranges to frighten game and spoil trails. The head of the Uncompahgres was Ouray (The Arrow), a statesman, financier, a Logan, and altogether a shrewd, noble-hearted, level-headed so-called savage, fitting cooperator with Kit Carson.

Garland was what might be designated a battalion post; and even at that the garrison usually consisted of only three or four companies. The volunteers stationed there were infantry and cavalry, the remnants of the two First New Mexican regiments, foot and horse, coalesced by transfer and consolidation of August 31, 1866, to form the First Battalion, Veteran New Mexican Volunteers. General Carson's staff was composed of his close brothers-at-arms,

Major Albert H. Pfeiffer, Major John Thompson, Captain Joseph Birney, Captain Donaciano Montoya, with all of whom he had been associated in camp and field, since 1861.

Life at the post was not arduous. The region roundabout is beautiful, with peak and vale, timber and grass. Game abounded (to use an expression much abused, but here appropriate), and the Trinchera Creek, upon which the fort stood, was a reservoir of speckled trout in such numbers that the soldiers scooped them out with blankets. Below the post were the Mexican hamlets of San Luis de Culebra (only fifteen miles distant), Conejos, Costilla, and others; and north of the post, but well up toward the head of the park, was the ranch of one hardy Russell. For the park had its population of settlers, even of ranchers, to be estimated, Kit Carson himself claimed, at five or six thousand.

Meanwhile, down on the plains " Hell on Wheels," as the advancing terminal town of the Union Pacific was styled, was being pushed 300 miles into the Great American Desert; and the Atlantic & Pacific had been subsidized, to head for California by way of Albuquerque.

By recollection of Mr. Ferd Meyer, post trader, the main duty devolving upon Fort Garland during the Carson regime of one year was the pacification of drunken Indians.[210]   Ouray himself, with several other chiefs who had been impressed, through a trip to Washington, in 1862, with the number of the white man's soldiery, aided in these pacifications. The Uncompahgre Utes made of Fort Garland, where Father Kit reigned, and of Conejos village, where Agent Lafayette Head reigned, their official quarters. The principal dangers were from drink, which incited anew the feeling of resentment against the prospecting whites, and forays by the plains bands, which provoked retaliation.

Several times Denver " City " (that wonder of the plains, claiming in the fall of 1866 to have 7,000 citizens and 250 new brick and stone houses) reported Fort Garland, Colorado's frontier post, as besieged by the Utes, even demolished, Kit Carson and all; but invariably the facts were disclosed to be only some alcoholic quarrel, Mexican versus Indian, or at most (as instanced by General Rusling) the finding of a Ute killed by lightning.

In September, 1866, Fort Garland entertained distinguished visitors in the persons of General Sherman himself, commanding the Military Division of the Mississippi, which included the Department of the Missouri; Alexander Cummings, Governor of Colorado territory; General James F. Rusling, of the quartermaster general's department, Washington; and their escorts.

General Sherman was upon a tour of the frontier posts in his division, better to comprehend the Indian question, his greatest problem; Governor Cummings accompanied him to Garland, in hopes of negotiating a treaty with the Utes; General Rusling, now on an inspection trip principally of western supply depots, was invited to join the party.

One of the most attractive chapters in the written story of the mountains and plains of the West is that chapter, in General Rusling's journal, descriptive of the Fort Garland country, Kit Carson, and the Utes. Naturally, much interest centered about Carson, to whom General Rusling, now meeting him for the first time, became greatly attached.

We found him in log quarters, rough but comfortable, with his Mexican wife and half-breed children around him. We had expected to see a small and wiry man, weather-beaten and reticent; but met a medium sized, rather stoutish, florid, and quite talkative person instead. He certainly bore the marks of exposure, but none of the extreme " roughing it," that we had anticipated. In age, he seemed to be about forty-five. His head was a remarkably good one, with the bumps of benevolence and reflection well developed. His eye was mild and blue, the very type of good nature, while his voice was

as soft and sympathetic as a woman's. He impressed you at
once as a man of rare kindliness and charity, such as a truly
brave man ought always to be. As simple as a child, but
brave as a lion, he soon took our hearts by storm, and grew
upon our regard all the while we were with him. We talked
and smoked far into the night each evening we spent together,
and we have no room here for a tithe of what he told us.
* * * In talking, I observed, that he frequently hesitated
for the right English word; but when speaking bastard Spanish
(Mexican) or Indian, he was as fluent as a native. Both
Mexican and Indian, however, are largely pantomime, which
may have helped him along, somewhat. The Utes seemed to
have the greatest possible confidence in him, and invariably
called him simply " Kit." Said Sherman, while at Garland,
" These Red Skins think Kit twice as big a man as me. Why,
his integrity is simply perfect. They know it, and they would
believe him and trust him any day before me." And Kit
returned this confidence, by being their most steadfast and
unswerving friend. He declared all our Indian troubles were
caused originally by bad white men, and was terribly severe
on the barbarities of the Border. He said he was once among
the Indians for two or three years exclusively, and had seen
an Indian kill his brother even, for insulting a white man in
the old times. He protested, that in all the peculiar and
ingenious outrages for which the Indians had been so much
abused of late years, they were only imitating or improving
upon the bad example of wicked white men. His anathemas
of Col. Chivington, and the Sand Creek massacre of 1864,
were something fearful to listen to. He pleaded for the Indians,
as " pore ignorant creatures," whom we were daily dispoiling
of their hunting grounds and homes, and his denunciations
of the outrages and wrongs we had heaped upon them were
sometimes really eloquent.

Said he, " To think of that dog Chivington, and his hounds,
up thar at Sand Creek! Whoever heerd of sich doings among
Christians! The pore Injuns had our flag flyin' over 'em,
that same old stars and stripes thar we all love and honor,
and they 'd bin told down to Denver, that so long as they kept
that flyin' they 'd be safe. Well, then, here come along that
durned Chivington and his cusses. They 'd bin out several
days huntin' hostile Injuns, and could n't find none no whar,

and if they had, they'd run from them, you bet! So they just pitched into these friendlies, and massa-*creed* them — yes, sir, literally massa-*creed* them — in cold blood, in spite of our flag thar — women and little children even! Why, Senator Foster told me with his own lips (and him and his committee investigated this, you know) that that thar d — d miscreant and his men shot down squaws, and blew the brains out of little innocent children — even pistoled little babies in the arms of their dead mothers, and worse than this! And ye call *these* civilized men — Christians; and the Injuns savages, du ye?

"I tell ye what; I do n't like a hostile Red Skin any better than you du. And when they are hostile, I 've fit 'em — fout 'em — as hard as any man. But I never yit drew a bead on a squaw or papoose, and I loathe and hate the man who would. 'Tain't nateral for brave men to kill women and little children, and no one but a coward or a dog would do it. Of course, when we white men du sich awful things, why, these pore ignorant critters do n't know no better, than to follow suit. Pore things! I 've seen as much of 'em as any white man livin', and I can't help but pity 'em. They 'll all soon be gone, anyhow."

Poor Kit! He has already "gone," himself, to his long home. But the Indians had no truer friend, and he would wish no prouder epitaph than this. He and Sherman were great friends, and evidently had a sincere regard for each other. They had known each other in California in '49, when Sherman was a banker there, and Kit only an Indian guide. [General Rusling here errs, as Sherman and Carson had met at Los Angeles in 1847-1848, when both were lieutenants.] In '65, when Kit was at Leavenworth, Sherman sent for him to come down to St. Louis, and they spent some time together very pleasantly. Now Sherman returned his visit, by coming to Fort Garland, in the heart of the Rocky Mountains.[211]

Of this visit at Fort Garland General Sherman says:

I stayed with him [Carson] some days, during which we had a sort of council with the Ute Indians, of which the Chief Ouray was the principal feature, and over whom Carson exercised a powerful influence.

Carson then had his family with him — wife and half a dozen children, boys and girls as wild and untrained as a brood of Mexican mustangs. One day these children ran through the room in which we were seated, half clad and boisterous, and I inquired, " Kit, what are you doing about your children? "

He replied: " That is a source of great anxiety; I myself had no education (he could not even write, his wife always signing his name to his official reports). I value education as much as any man, but I have never had the advantage of schools, and now that I am getting old and infirm, I fear I have not done right by my children."

I explained to him that the Catholic College, at South Bend, Indiana, had, for some reason, given me a scholarship for twenty years, and that I would divide with him — that is let him send two of his boys for five years each. He seemed very grateful and said he would think of it.[212]

To have the high regard of soldiers such as General Sherman and General Rusling, surely bespeaks the sterling character of plain, uncultured Carson.

A preliminary council with the Utes was held by General Sherman and Governor Cummings on the afternoon of September 21, in the commandant's quarters at the fort. Another talk, at which a treaty was essayed, was held, September 23, by Governor Cummings and Agent Head, with the chiefs, on the banks of the Rio Grande about thirty miles northwest of the fort. The overtures from the Government were " interpreted by Kit Carson into Mexican, with profuse pantomime, after the Indian fashion, and then re-interpreted by Ouray into Ute for the benefit of his red brethren."

Another episode of more than passing interest, to break the routine of Fort Garland, was the revolt, in the summer of 1867, of Carson's former ally, Kaniatse. This Ute chief, for whom an extra horse had been asked, in the Kiowa expedition of November, 1864, here three years later ran amuck, raiding the cornfields along the Purgatoire, and encountering troops from the foothills post of Fort Stephens.

Heading toward the San Luis park, he invited Ouray and the Uncompahgre Utes to join him.

Instead of joining him, however, Ouray placed all his people under the surveillance of Fort Garland, commanded by Col. Carson, and repaired to the Purgatoire to warn the settlers. The enemy was met by a small force of Tabaquaches [Tabeguaches], under Shawno [Shavano], one of their chiefs, whom Carson sent to bring in Kaneache [Kaniatse], dead or alive. The order was obeyed, Kaneache and another hostile leader being captured and taken to Fort Union.[218]

Indeed, to Carson and Ouray, working together, did the settlers of mountain Colorado and New Mexico owe much.

COMMISSION

WHICH ACCOMPANIED THE DELEGATION OF UTE INDIANS TO WASHINGTON
IN 1868

(Photograph by Brady, Washington, March, 1868. Signatures by each man. Original loaned by Judge H. P. Bennet of Denver, who was clerk to the Commission)

CHAPTER XXXVII

CARSON AT WASHINGTON — 1868

$\mathbf{D}$ EPARTMENT returns in the report dated September
30, 1867, refer to Fort Garland as garrisoned by
B Company cavalry, C and D companies infantry, New
Mexican Veterans, still under Lieutenant Colonel (Brevet
Brigadier General) Christopher Carson, New Mexican
Volunteers.

However, in July General Carson had resigned from the
service: reason, ill health.[214]   The injury of 1860, when
his horse had dragged him, had developed into an aneurysm   .
— a ruptured wall of the aorta, or great artery, pressing
against the trachea at the upper chest.   He complained of
pain in the chest, a tendency to cough, and distress when
lying flat.   The hard campaigns of the 'sixties had told upon
him heavily.   Formerly a fearless, reckless horseman, of
late he had done his journeying in an army ambulance.

From Fort Garland he removed his family to Taos, or
possibly to Boggsville, and later followed, himself.   Through
his wife, whose uncle had been of the Vigil family, he
had possessed some land in the Vigil and St. Vrain Spanish
Grant in southern Colorado.   This, it would seem, he had
deeded to the young son of his comrade, Major Pfeiffer.   He
owned other land, in the Taos Valley, and he had clung
to a few cattle — of which the brand was CC on the left
hip, or cross J (+J) on the left hip.   The house and lot
in Taos were his; and there were horses and carriage, and
a certain amount of other trail and ranch conveniences and
chattels.   But he had by no means a competence.   His life
had been a roving one, and he was rearing a large family.

The widow and children of Charles Bent had been much in his household; he had assumed the care of a lad, Nicanor Jaramillo, nephew of his wife; and there must not be omitted his own children. To be sure, his pay in the army had been certain and fairly liberal, and his expenses small; but he was too generous to be a good accumulator.

Santa Fe, Maxwell's rancho, and Denver City saw him, as he pursued various errands; and in October he practically took up quarters at the settlement of Boggsville, near the mouth of the " Purgatory " or Las Animas River, in the southern plains of Colorado. It was but a few miles down the Arkansas from the old stamping ground of Bent's Fort. A ranch had been located here by Thomas O. Boggs, nephew of Charles Bent, son-in-law of Mrs. Bent, a Santa Fe Trail trader out of Missouri and Taos, and one of Carson's intimates.

Mr. John S. Hough, who shared quarters with the Carson family, at early Boggsville, writes, of that period:

In the summer of 1867 we made a settlement on the Purgatoire River near its mouth, about two miles from the present city of Las Animas, in Bent County, Colorado. Colonel William Bent claimed the land between our place and the mouth of the river where it enters into the Arkansas. The settlers were Thomas O. Boggs and L. A. Allen, who brought in a herd of sheep from New Mexico; my brother-in-law John W. Prowers, who had a herd of cattle; William Ritz, who did some farming and whose wife was, I think, a niece of Mrs. Carson's; myself, wife and children. I brought in a large stock of merchandise, having been informed that a new fort was to be built near. In the spring of 1868 Carson moved over from Taos, bringing his family. Major Pfeiffer, his old friend, accompanied him. Tom Boggs had during the previous winter put up quite a number of buildings of the Mexican adobe variety, on the bank of the Purgatoire (the Las Animas). I secured three of the rooms, and Carson the other three, in one building or row, until such time as we could erect our own houses. My wife was the only American woman in the settle-

ment, Mrs. Prowers being a Cheyenne, and the three other
women being Spanish. Carson's health at that time was very
bad. Not being able to ride about he spent most of his time
keeping me company, my trading store being only a few feet
away from our quarters. He and I were born on the same day
— Christmas; which he considered remarkable, and in reference to which he was wont to declare but not irreverently,
that he knew of only *three* birthdays being on Christmas!
I of course took an interest in doing everything that I could,
to be of service to the family, for besides living in the same
row with them I thought a great deal of them. In fact, we all,
at Boggsville, were pretty close together, on account of the
Indian troubles.[215]

Major Pfeiffer and the other personages at the settlement could see that " the General," as he was affectionately
called, was in a critical state. He probably consulted medical authorities at Santa Fe and Denver, who, however,
gave him no relief. Surgeon H. R. Tilton, of the army,
relates:

I first met him at the house of a mutual friend, not far from
Fort Lyon, C. T. [this must have been Bent's ranch, or else
Boggsville] late in the fall of 1867. He had then recently left
the service of the U. S., having been colonel of a regiment
of New Mexican volunteers during the War of the Rebellion.
As I was a successful amateur trapper, he threw off all
reserve, and greeted me with more than usual warmth, saying,
" the happiest days of my life were spent in trapping." He
gave me many practical hints on trapping and hunting.
He was then complaining of a pain in his chest, the origin
of which he attributed to a fall received in 1860.[216]

Dr. Tilton, who was Carson's constant adviser in a
medical capacity, could effect no cure. The aneurysm apparently had progressed beyond remedy. Carson now was in
his fifty-eighth year. His malady prevented him from engaging in active employment; and he was not entitled to a
pension or invalid half pay. William, his eldest boy, was

only sixteen. So, with his enforced idleness, his ill health, and his dubious prospects, these must have been Kit Carson's hardest days.

Both for diversion and medical treatment he made frequent trips down to Fort Lyon, about five miles east. Here he was welcomed, and found congenial spirits in the army company. This, the second Fort Lyon of the Arkansas River country, was known as " new " Fort Lyon, in distinction from the preceding Fort Lyon, which, originally christened Fort Wise, had succeeded to the second Bent's Fort buildings, twenty-five or thirty miles down river. " New " Fort Lyon had been occupied in June of 1867, the immediate occasion for the change being a spring freshet which flooded the Fort Lyon at the Big Timbers.

In February of 1868, by order of the Commissioner of Indian Affairs, a delegation of Ute Indians were invited to Washington, that they might present their grievances direct, and talk over another treaty. In word from Washington, Carson was urgently requested to accompany the chiefs and escort, that both parties might have the benefit of his well-known experience. Moreover, it was felt that his presence would inspire the Utes with confidence.

He hesitated much over attempting the journey; his strength was impaired, and Mrs. Carson was soon to be confined with another child. Finally he consented, out of a sense of civic duty, regard for the welfare of the Indians, and a desire to consult eastern specialists regarding his disease.

The commission escorting the Indians consisted of Governor A. C. Hunt of Colorado (Indian agent *ex officio*); Major Lafayette Head, agent of the Uncompahgre Utes; Major D. C. Oakes, agent of the Uintah Utes; General Carson and Colonel Albert Gallatin Boone, special commissioners; Uriah M. Curtis, interpreter from the San Luis Valley; Hiram P. Bennet, clerk to the commission; and

W. J. Godfroy and E. H. Kellogg, Denver citizens. The Indians were Chief Ouray, Capote, Waro, Jack, Sa-wa-ish, Su-ru-ipe, Pe-a-ah, An-ko-tash, and two others, representing the "Tabaguache, Muache, Capote, Weeminuche, Yampa, Grand River and Uintah tribes" of Utes.

The whole party, except Carson, went from Denver by stage to Cheyenne — a wide-open town of 10,000 people, then the farthest-west railroad terminal; from it, however, the Union Pacific was again about to push still farther west. From Cheyenne they rode luxuriously by train to the Union Pacific terminal at Omaha, crossed the Missouri by ferry, and continued on from Council Bluffs, by the new North Western Railroad, to Chicago.

Carson himself chose for his stage journey the route from Fort Lyon to Fort Hays, there to take railroad for St. Louis. Here he was joined by Colonel Boone (grandson of Daniel Boone, formerly special Indian Agent at the upper Arkansas) who likewise, by his years and counsel, was to aid the negotiations.

The photographs of Carson, made during this, his last visit to the far East, show him much reduced in flesh, and feeble in appearance. To members of the commission he complained of a vein in his neck. However, it did not prevent his having a royal good time. The commission stopped at the Washington House; General Fremont called on Carson, and so did many other notables, both of army and civil life. In fact, he was so much lionized that in his weakened condition he evinced, for the first time on record, a trace of elation and self-importance. When the commission proposed to have their pictures taken in company with the Indians, they were astounded and amused, to hear "the General" remark, "with his chin up" (as was related to me by a survivor): "Oh, I guess I won't be in it, this time," and to see him rather contrarily stroll away.

There was some suspicion that having just been photo-

graphed in company with General Carleton and former
staff (a group reproduced in this volume), he was too proud
to sit with civilians.   However, the next morning, as if
ashamed, he sought out his three favorites in his party, to
proffer in brusque apology: " Boys, let 's us four go out and
have those pictures! "

So they went. He now was the mild, affable Kit of old.
When the prints had been mounted, it was proposed that
each man sign his name.   " Shall I sign Christopher, or
just Kit? " queried the General, poising the pen.

" Kit, by all means! " they cried.   And this of course
pleased him, as intended.

With care he wrote his " Kit Carson " — a labored scrawl
which at first had been an imitation, as a child or an Indian
imitates, but which by this time was known to him in its
component letters.[217]

The treaty was concluded March 2, and the New Mexico
and Colorado Utes agreed to remove to a reservation of
15,120,000 acres, in western Colorado, extending from the
White River on the north to the Rio de los Pinos on the
south.

The United States now solemnly agrees that no persons,
except those herein authorized so to do, and except such officers,
agents, and employes of the government as may be authorized
to enter upon Indian reservations in discharge of duties enjoined
by law, shall ever be permitted to pass over, settle upon, or
reside in the territory described in this article.

Thus read the promise; and it is strange that Kit Carson
— whose forty years' experience had shown him how futile
were any barriers set by nature or by ethical law against
the white adventurer, who had witnessed the Great American Desert spanned to the foothills, and had heard the
pick in the recesses of the ranges — should gravely expect
to withhold from greed and civilization this one-quarter

A REUNION PICTURE

CARSON AND SOME OF HIS OLD COMPANIONS-AT-ARMS, WASHINGTON, SPRING OF 1868.
(1) COL. EDWARD H. BERGMAN, U. S. VOLS. (2) HON. C. P. CLEVER, NEW MEXICO. (3) GEN.
N. H. DAVIS, U. S. A. (4) COL. H. M. ENOS, U. S. A. (5) SURGEON BASIL NORRIS, U. S. A. (6)
GEN. J. C. MCFERRAN, U. S. A. (7) COL. ALBERT GALLATIN BOONE, GRANDSON OF DANIEL BOONE.
(8) GEN. D. H. RUCKER, U. S. A. (9) GEN. KIT CARSON. (10) GEN. JAMES H. CARLETON.
OF THESE, ALL THE OFFICERS HAD SERVED WITH CARSON IN NEW MEXICO.
(Copy of original print in possession of Robert C. Mowry, New York)

LAST PHOTOGRAPH OF KIT CARSON

of a rich, energetic Territory. As a matter of history, the promise was null and void almost from the start.

The treaty having been concluded, to the satisfaction of all, the commission returned to the West, Clerk Bennet only remaining, to wait for the confirmation of the articles by the Senate.

Captain Pettis wrote to the author in 1908:

In March, 1868, I was in Rhode Island on a visit to my old home, having been absent fifteen years. While there I heard that Carson was at Washington with a number of Ute Indians. He visited Philadelphia, and was in New York when I was ready to start back to the "Land of Sunshine." I expected to meet him in New York. When I arrived there I found that we had passed each other in the night, he being on his way to Boston. I did not turn about, but kept on, being anxious to get back to my family at Los Algodones, New Mexico. Upon leaving the train at Fort Hays, Kansas, we took the stage coach for Santa Fe, and one afternoon we drove to the sutler's store at new Fort Lyon. Colonel Pfeiffer opened the stage door, and recognizing me said: "Well, Pettis, where's Colonel Carson?" I gave him all the information that I had, and he said that they had been expecting him by that coach. Now, at this moment he was just up the river at a place called La Junta, where his wife was awaiting him.

In Philadelphia, New York, and Boston the General had consulted medical specialists. None had given him much hope. In Boston he sat for the last protograph ever takén of him. Thence he had returned West by way of Chicago, over the North Western Railroad to Council Bluffs, and over the new Oregon Trail route of the Union Pacific to Cheyenne. The stage from Cheyenne landed him in Denver about the end of March.

Carson was so much exhausted from his long trip that he stayed at the Planter's House in Denver for two or three days, part of the time being in bed in his room. His Denver friends, of course, attended to his comfort. He was still suffering from pain in chest and neck; and he alluded also to pain in the legs, which he thought might be due to some veins enlarged once in a foot race which he had run many years before to escape Blackfeet Indians. While East he had caught a severe cold, which added to his troubled condition.[218]　Having at last recuperated by resting, he proceeded by stage to La Junta, above Boggsville, where his solicitous wife met him. The time must have been the first week of April, 1868.

CHAPTER XXXVIII

LAST DAYS OF "THE GENERAL" — 1868

NO ONE could fail to note that Kit Carson had come home a very ill man. Seeing him shortly after the return, Dr. Tilton of Fort Lyon remarked that his disease

had progressed rapidly; and the tumor pressing on the pneumo-gastric nerves and trachea, caused frequent spasms of the bronchial tubes which were exceedingly distressing.[219]

It would seem that, as is strangely the case with many men and women, when he had apparently earned peace and comfort "the General" had fallen into evil days; for unexpectedly Mrs. Carson, the younger and stronger, was taken from him. Aged but forty-one, she died on April 23, leaving him with seven children, the last being the new babe, only fifteen days old, and named Josefita, for its mother.

Mrs. Carson ("a very good wife and the best of mothers," is her eulogy) was interred in the yard at Boggsville, about 500 feet from the Carson-Hough quarters.

The children thus made motherless were William, Teresina, Kit, Charles, Rebecca (for Carson's own mother), Estella, and Josefita or Josephine; thus are they recorded, in line of birth. The eldest, William, was born in 1851, and therefore was now scant seventeen.

So suddenly deprived of his wife of a quarter century, who lately had more than ever been his dependence, General Carson was much depressed. He survived her just a month. However, it is doubtful, if her death much hastened the irresistible march of his disease.

493

When Mrs. Carson died [related Mrs. Scheurich to the author], the General wrote to Mr. Scheurich, my husband, that he wished my mother and myself to go to him, as he was very sick and his children were so small. So he sent a man by the name of Willy Betts on horseback from Boggsville or West Las Animas to Taos, as the mail came through only once a month in those days. This man made the trip on horseback, and in five days had covered the 300 miles to Taos; and in three days afterward we left Taos. When we got to Boggsville Mr. Carson had been removed to Fort Lyon. So after dinner Mr. Scheurich went down to the fort to see the General. He found him very sick. Mr. Boggs came back and told me that the General did not want Mr. Scheurich [who was a godfather to his children] to leave him, but must stay with him; and he sent us word that mother and I should take care of his children, but that he was so weak that he could not stand it to see us, and to think that they were to be orphans. Mr. Scheurich stayed with him until he died, which was in ten days.[220]

According to Surgeon Tilton's statement, it was May 14 when General Carson was removed from his Boggsville quarters to Fort Lyon, five miles eastward. He needed medical attention so frequently (at the last, declares Mrs. Scheurich, every hour) that, as the Arkansas was rising with the snow water from the upper country and fording was difficult, the doctor advised the change.

This [records the doctor] enabled me to make his condition much more comfortable. In the intervals of his paroxyms, he beguiled the time by relating his past experiences. I read Dr. Peters' book, with the hero for my auditor; from time to time he would comment on the incidents of his eventful life.

It was wonderful to read of the stirring scenes, thrilling and narrow escapes, and then look at the quiet, modest, retiring, but dignified little man who had done so much.

* * * * * * * * * *

His disease rapidly progressed and he calmly contemplated his approaching death. Several times he repeated the remark:

" If it were not for this," pointing to his chest, " I might live to be a hundred years old."

I explained to him the probable mode of termination of his disease: " that he might die from suffocation or more probably the aneurism would burst and cause death by hemorrhage." He expressed a decided preference for the latter mode. His attacks of dyspnoea were horrible, threatening immediate dissolution. I was compelled to give him chloroform to relieve him, at considerable risk of hastening a fatal result; but he begged me not to let him suffer such tortures, and if I killed him by chloroform while attempting relief, it would be much better than death by suffocation.

Once he remarked: " What am I to do? I can't get along without a doctor."

I replied: " I'll take care of you."

He, smiling, said: " You must think I am not going to live long." [221]

Captain (Brevet Brigadier General) W. H. Penrose commanded the post of Fort Lyon in the spring of 1868. The troops then stationed there were A Company, Fifth Infantry, Captain (Brevet Major) James Casey, First Lieutenant Charles Porter, Second Lieutenant J. W. Pope; I Company, Third Infantry, Captain Gageby, First Lieutenant Bonsall, Second Lieutenant John W. Hannay; G. Company, Third Infantry, First Lieutenant J. W. Thomas (commanding), Second Lieutenant Briggs; Troop L, Seventh Cavalry, Captain Gillette, First Lieutenant Berry, Second Lieutenant John F. Weston.

New Fort Lyon was at this time one of the rudest and dreariest of frontier posts. It was, of course, unenclosed, after plains fashion of army days — its buildings being grouped about the sun-baked parade ground. The " officers' row " was composed of small four-room houses, some occupied by, two families; built of rough stone blocks chinked with mud, the floors unfinished lumber, the wood partitions between rooms being in many instances only eight or nine feet high, with the remaining space to the rafters filled in with flour sacking. There were no ceilings. The roofs were of long boards, in the rough, and untrimmed, so that their ends projected irregularly, as eaves. The Tilton quarters were next to the foot of the row, the chaplain's being last.[222]

The presence of Kit Carson at the post was a diversion of much interest to the garrison, relieving a routine usually monotonous. The officers paid him marked attention, of mingled respect and admiration; he need never be without callers.

The day after his arrival at the fort, or May 15, he made his will. A bed of blankets and buffalo robes had been laid for him upon the floor of the Tilton quarters. Here he reclined in a half-sitting posture, his head well bolstered so that he might breathe at his easiest. Beside him slept, at night, when not on duty, the surgeon and Mr. Scheurich.

The night preceding death he spent more comfortably than he had for days before. He was obliged to sit up nearly all the night time. He coughed up a little amount of blood during the night, and a very little in the forenoon.[223]

He had been told that a grave token in the progress of his disease would be blood in the sputum — indicating that the aneurysm was breaking through into the trachea. Therefore he was accustomed (so once related Mr. Scheurich) to watch his sputum and comment upon it. About mid-afternoon, of May 23, he said that he was hungry, and he asked Mr. Scheurich to cook him a good dinner; he wanted something prepared by his dear *compadre*; he was tired of what had been given him.

Accordingly, Mr. Scheurich (husband to Carson's favorite niece, Teresina Bent, Santa Fe Trail trader, and *compadre* or godfather in the Carson household) went to the kitchen, under approval of Dr. Tilton — who knew that the end could not be far — cooked a substantial steak and made

HOUSE WHERE KIT CARSON DIED

THE SURGEON TILDEN QUARTERS AT OLD NEW FORT LYON, NOW U. S. NAVAL SANITORIUM NEAR LAS ANIMAS, COLORADO

THOMAS O. BOGGS
OF MISSOURI AND TAOS. A NOTED EARLY DAY CHARACTER AND INTIMATE
OF CARSON

*(From large crayon portrait at the M. M. Chase ranch house,
Cimarron, New Mexico)*

coffee, and brought them in; and General Carson dined heartily.

Then he called for a pipe. Which pipe would he have? There was the fine pipe, gift to him from General Fremont, and there were other pipes of good quality. No; he wished his old clay pipe, and while he smoked it he and his *compadre* would talk of old times.

The doctor and Mr. Scheurich were glad to humor him. He smoked; Mr. Scheurich chatted; Surgeon Tilton listened. Suddenly the General coughed (as Mr. Scheurich recollected, in telling), his saliva came red. " I'm gone," he uttered. " Goodby, doctor. *Adios, compadre.*" He grasped Mr. Scheurich's hand, and held it to the end, which arrived quickly.[224]

With this account Surgeon Tilton's report substantially agrees:

In the afternoon, while I was lying down on the bed, and he was listening to Mr. Sherrick, he suddenly called out, " Doctor, *Compadre, Adios!* "

I sprang to him, and seeing a gush of blood pouring from his mouth, remarked, " This is the last of the general "; I supported his forehead on my hand, while death speedily closed the scene.

The aneurism had ruptured into the trachea. Death took place at 4:25 p. m., May 23, 1868.[225]

Thus after over forty years of peril by camp and trail passed Kit Carson, peacefully, of natural cause, in his bed, holding to the hand of one friend, ministered to by the hand of another. He passed, knowing that he was beloved and honored to the extent even of his need. Death might have been much worse.

Releasing himself, Mr. Scheurich rushed out and encountered the officer of the day. " The General is dead! General Carson is dead! " he reported, half distraught.

The officer, a young subaltern, seemed to have his mind upon matters afar, and his first response was " Very well, sir"; but instantly realizing, he, likewise, was strongly moved, and carried the word to headquarters. General Penrose, commanding officer of the post, ordered the funeral for ten o'clock, the next morning, May 24. Sergeant Luke Cahill, who was non-commissioned officer of A Company, Fifth Infantry, writes to me:

As soon as his death was announced the flag was lowered to half-mast. All troops off duty were ordered to attend the funeral. The funeral commenced as ordered; marched one mile west of the fort; music was furnished by three fifers and three drummers of the infantry; three volleys were fired by cavalry and infantry; taps were sounded by the 7th Cavalry bugler; the napoleon guns at the fort were fired each minute during the march and ceremony.[226]

The post chaplain officiating was the Reverend Gamaliel Collins, who bore the customary soubriquet of the army service, " Holy Joe." To contribute to the simple ceremony, the women of the post gave the white paper flowers from their bonnets; no more suitable floral offerings were available. To line the rough board casket Mrs. Casey, the wife of Captain Casey, gave her wedding gown.

At a mile from the post the body was consigned to the relatives and friends from Boggsville; and, conveyed thither under military escort, was interred beside the remains of the wife who had preceded him by only a month. Carson's request had been that he and Mrs. Carson be buried in the cemetery at Taos. The removal, however, was not made until more than a year had elapsed. Then, both bodies were taken over the Raton Pass, by wagon and team, and on through Maxwell's at Cimarron to Taos. In the quaint Taos cemetery they rest, today. For forty years the two graves, enclosed by wooden palings, were neglected, except on Memorial Day. The General's mound was marked by a headstone, inscribed:

KIT CARSON
Died May 23rd, 1868
Aged 59 Years.

Mrs. Carson's mound was designated only by a small wooden cross. But on July 8, 1908, the Grand Lodge of Masons of New Mexico dedicated an iron fence, erected by them, and saw to the rehabilitation of the graves, themselves. The Carson stone was set upon a new base, and a tasteful granite stone was planted at the head of his wife's mound. It reads:

JOSEPHINE,
wife of
KIT CARSON
Born March 19, 1828,
Died April 23, 1868.

The death of Kit Carson was communicated at once to Denver, the nearest newspaper point, and thence was sent broadcast by telegraph. This dispatch and comment appear in the *Rocky Mountain News* of May 27:

FT. LYON, C. T., May 23, '68.
Ed. News — General Kit Carson died at this post between the hours of four and five o'clock, afternoon, this day, from disease of the heart, under which he had been laboring since his return from the East. He had been removed to the fort some ten days since, so that Doctor Tilton, the post surgeon, could give him better attention than if he had remained at his brother-in-law's, Mr. Boggs, some five miles distant.
E.

*   *   *   *   *   *   *   *   *   *

Over what an immense expanse of plains, of snow-clad sierras, of rivers, lakes and seas, has he cut the first paths, into which now the locomotives, the steamships, the organized two halves of human society, are massing the activity, the power, the condensed energy of ancient and modern times?

To his companions Carson has been always known as the most genial and excellent of men — of sleepless activity whereever a charitable act has been within his reach. Daring, devoted and sincere, his fidelity has been unblemished in every hour of his life, and in every relation. Citizen, soldier, husband, father, neighbor — in all these relations his guiding instinct has been an innate chivalry, from the practice of which nothing has ever deflected him. He had in him a personal courage which came forth when wanted, like lightning from a cloud — at other times, unobtrusive and unnoticed.

On May 26 the Democratic Club of Pueblo (Colorado) passed resolutions:

Whereas, it has pleased the Supreme Ruler to remove from our midst one of the most honored of our associates, in the person of General Kit Carson, therefore —

Resolved — That in the death of General Carson, Colorado mourns the loss of a single man, true-hearted patriot, who, whether in the character of citizen or soldier, was stainless and above reproach.

Resolved — That, as citizens of Colorado, we cherish with deep reverence the memory of General Carson, as the great path-finder; as a model of unobtrusive heroism; a pattern of true chivalry; as a true representative man of the West — whose character and services are justly the pride of his country-men.

Resolved — That as members of this Association we have sustained the loss of a distinguished associate, whose life was devoted to the maintenance of the cherished principles of our party, and whose pure and stainless character as a man attested the sincerity and unselfishness of his political creed.

The secretary was directed to transmit for publication a copy of these resolutions (which provoked tart rejoinder from political pens opposing their claim) to the papers of the Territory; to the *World,* of New York; to the *Missouri Republican,* of St. Louis; and to the *Intelligencer,* of Washington.[227]

When the news of the death reached Fort Garland, the

officers and residents there drew up resolutions also, signed by Albert H. Pfeiffer, late major, and brevet lieutenant colonel, First New Mexican Cavalry; John Thompson, major, First New Mexican Cavalry; John Buford, first lieutenant, 37th United States Infantry; H. B. Fleming, major, 37th Infantry, presiding; and Randolph Schmieding, secretary. These resolutions were sent to the *Army and Navy Journal,* as well as to other publications.

The Pueblo *Chieftain,* in its first issue, which was June 1; the Santa Fe *New Mexican;* the Deseret (Utah) *News,* and other western journals paid tribute to the great scout, while the large eastern papers were not less liberal in their praise. Appleton's *Annual American Encyclopaedia* for 1868 devoted to him a column — more than assigned to many higher officers, and to many scientists, jurists, and philanthropists.

The Carson will, made on May 15, or immediately after his arrival at the Tilton quarters indicates only a modest estate, of "one hundred to two hundred" head of cattle; seven yoke of steers; two ox wagons, four horses and a carriage; house and lot at Taos, valued at $1,000; the furniture in the house there; "two or three pieces of land" in the valley of Taos; a promissory note of $3,000, signed by Lucien Maxwell; and "any moneys which may be due me from Mr. Myer of Costilla, C. T., and Mr. Rudolph, the sutler of Fort Garland." Mr. Meyer informed the writer that in obedience to these instructions he turned over to the estate about $1,200.

The estate, for which his friend, Tom Boggs, was named by Carson as executor, has been figured up at $9,000. A reminder of it are the Cross J cattle still existing (1912) in the Las Animas country of southern Colorado, where they perpetuate the Carson brand, and where for many years they formed the herd of Jesse Nelson, the pioneer settler, who married a niece of Carson's.

The Carson children were taken care of by relatives and friends. Tom Boggs took some of them. Teresina was adopted by Mr. Hough, and reared and educated by him. William, the eldest, was billeted to General Sherman; the Sherman promise made at Fort Garland had not been forgotten by the father.

Accordingly [writes Sherman], some time about the spring of 1868 there came to my house, in St. Louis, a stout boy with a revolver, "Life of Kit Carson" by Dr. Peters (United States Army), about $40 in money, and a letter, from Boggs, saying that in compliance with the request of Kit Carson, on his death-bed, he had sent William Carson to me.[228]

General Sherman put William through three years at the Catholic College at South Bend, Indiana, (today Notre Dame University), but at the end found that the lad " had no taste or appetite for learning." He transferred his charge to the more congenial atmosphere of Fort Leavenworth, to work and study; and certainly no youth had better incentive toward an army career. Lieutenant Beard, post adjutant, instructed him for a commission; and when William was twenty-one, Sherman

applied in person to the President, General Grant, to give the son of Kit Carson the appointment of Second Lieutenant, Ninth United States Cavalry, telling him somewhat of the foregoing details. General Grant promptly ordered the appointment to issue, subject to the examination as to educational qualifications, required by the law.

But William was found " deficient in reading, writing, and arithmetic "; and General Sherman, head of the Army, could only advise him to return to the Boggs ranch on the Purgatoire.[229]

FIRST MONUMENT TO KIT CARSON

IN KIT CARSON PARK, TRINIDAD, COLO., ON THE MOUNTAIN BRANCH OF
THE SANTA FE TRAIL

*(Augustus Lukeman of New York, in consultation with Frederick G. R.
Roth, sculptor)*

CARSON IN SCULPTURE AT DENVER

THE PIONEER MONUMENT IN THE DENVER CIVIC CENTER (BY MAC MONNIES)
THE FIGURE ON THE PEDESTAL IS KIT CARSON

CHAPTER XXXIX

KIT CARSON

KIT CARSON was not a great man, nor a brilliant man. He was a great character; and if it was not his to scintillate, nevertheless he shone with a constant light. It is pleasant to know that he was thoroughly appreciated by Government and nation. Education might have given him more material advancement, but it could not have given him more regard.

His personal appearance has been described in the words of his contemporaries, in the foregoing pages. " A perfect Saxon," records Mrs. Fremont, " clear and fair, with light and thin ' baby ' hair, blue eyes, light eye-brows and lashes and a fair skin. He was very short and unmistakably bandy-legged, long-bodied and short-limbed." His official biographer, Dr. Peters, who might be expected, through careful observation, to describe him best, says of him — " small in stature, but of compact frame-work. He had a large and finely developed head, a twinkling gray eye, and hair of a sandy color, which he combed back à la Franklin mode." He was about five feet eight, and weighed a mean of about 145 pounds.

What he lacked in inches he made up in agility. His eyes, gray in peace, flamed to steely turquoise in excitement, when, according to Oliver Wiggins, " they were terrible — they blazed like a rattlesnake's." His hair, in later years, became thin and faded.

He was fond of his pipe, that companion of camp and march. In the use of alcohol he was exceedingly circumspect. Mr. Hough says: " Carson was not a drinking man, and did not approve of drinking." Captain Simpson says that " a spoonful of whisky in a glass of water was about his extent." Mr. Robert C. Lowry, of New York City, who was in the Carson mess at Fort Union, in the 'sixties, states that he was " not a drinker, nor yet was he a teetotaler." He had no objection to a pipe, a bowl of hot punch, and a circle of cronies about a blazing hearth, in winter. At such a time, in garrison or at Maxwell's " manor," he would drop his habitual reticence, and would vie with the others at story-telling and anecdote.

Much emphasis has been placed upon his aversion to all display or personal assertion. " Quick to act, and never known to boast," is the Peters epigram, well phrased. Carson's voice was low and mild, in keeping with his mild appearance. He was also sparing of words, although in his later years, as his hair silvered, he grew more mellow and genial, so that at Fort Garland General Rusling found him even talkative.

" A man of the most kindly and gentle spirit; unassuming, quiet, and the last person that one would suppose to be possessed of qualities that made him famous," out of his lively recollections writes Mr. Lowry to the author; and continues:

He was a very genial man, and there were one or two funny stories that I used to tell him that amused him greatly, especially one that described a fight between two camp-women at Fort Union. I lived in Santa Fe the winter of 1863 and 1864, and he was there at the time, and almost always when I met him he would stop and make me tell him that story. He also used to lend me his horse to ride. It was a very ordinary looking yellow horse, and a pacer, and by no means the prancing steed that he is always pictured as mounted upon. He was so unassuming and kind-hearted that he won me completely, for I was only a boy of seventeen or eighteen, and to have Kit Carson notice me and seem attracted to my yarns meant a great deal to me.

An oft-repeated anecdote is that which relates of an army officer, somewhat of a hero-worshiper, who, upon meeting Carson, exclaimed, effusively: " So this is the great Kit Carson, who has made so many Indians run! " " Yes," drawled Carson, "sometimes I run after *them*, but most times they war runnin' after *me.*"

An old trapper whom I encountered in San Diego declared that during the 'sixties he was with Carson on the veranda of an Omaha hotel. Carson was en route either to or from the East. A Jewish traveling man urged the General for a story, and finally Carson drawled:

" Well, I 'll tell ye. I war down on the plains, an' the Comanches got after me. Thar war 'bout five hundred of 'em, an' they chased me. We run an' we run, an' my hoss war killed an' I clum a sort o' butte. Thar war a leetle split or cañon in it, an' I run up this. One big red rascal kep' right on my heels; my gun war busted, but I had my knife. The split narrered an' narrered, an' got smaller an' smaller, an' suddenly it pinched out; an' thar I war, at the end. So I turned, with my knife, an' when he come on I struck at him. But the walls o' the split war so near together that I hit the rock, an' busted my knife squar' off at the hilt. When he seed that he give a big yell, for my scalp, an' at me he jumped."

Here Carson stopped, reflectively, and spat. The interrogator waited, breathless, until the suspense was beyond endurance.

" Yes! And then what, General? " he demanded.

" Wall," drawled Carson, calmly; " then the Injun killed me."

Considering that this episode is also attributed to Jim Bridger, as a favorite in his wide repertoire, we may accept the new version of it as " trapper's talk." However, the retort is like Kit Carson.

Captain Simpson recalls that when Carson visited at Taos,

during active army service, he was wont to doff his uniform and modestly return to citizen garb. It always irritated him to be addressed with a title. "Oh, call me 'Kit,' boys. Plain Kit's good enough for me," he would direct — in the same tenor as remarked by Colonel Meline at Santa Fe. He was likewise prone to deprecate the Peters language, in the official biography, and complain, humbly, that "Peters laid it on a leetle too thick."

Carson was eminently a self-made man. What he acquired, beyond the intrinsic character which was his by birthright, he acquired through observation and assimilation. Concerning his ability in letters there has been much dispute. Until past middle age he could not read or write. Captain Pettis says that when he knew him, in the 'sixties, the most that he could accomplish was to scrawl his name "after much twisting about in his chair, and turning his head in forty directions." Another authority says that he could pick out a few printed words, as a child would pick them out. Mr. Hough says that at Boggsville he could both read and write. Captain Simpson solves the discussion by saying that all are correct. "Kit Carson before the war could but write his name, and read but a word or two. But from the time when he went out as an army officer with other army officers, by association and by application he learned more, so that when I was last with him he was a fair reader and writer, but was not 'stuck on the job.' I noticed quite an improvement in his dress, his speech and his whole being. The war developed him, so that in my opinion there were two Kit Carsons — one before the war, and one after."

"He would frequently get his grammar wrong, and his speech was the patois of the Border," narrates General Rusling. "But there was an eloquence in his eye and a pathos in his voice that would have touched a heart of stone."

The war seems to have made him more affable. He

dropped the careful reserve engendered by years of watchfulness and hardships on the lone trail. Mr. Lowry relates:

When Carson was organizing the First Regiment of New Mexico Volunteers, and was at Fort Union, he was a member of our mess, which consisted of Captain P. W. L. Plympton, now deceased, Captain (General) A. B. Carey, now retired, two or three others, and myself. I was only a government clerk. In the cold winter evenings, over a roaring fire-place and a steaming bowl of punch we smoked our pipes and told stories. Carson was usually reticent and sparing in speech, but whenever he got warmed up a little with a sip or two of punch his tongue would loosen itself somewhat and he would join in the " story telling." He had one account of a buffalo hunt, to the effect that somewhere down on the lower Cimarron, on a scout with General Carleton, the soldiers kept returning empty-handed to camp, with reports of poor shooting and bad luck, etc. Carson told them that he would wager he could go out and kill ten buffalo with ten balls. He went out, and killed the ten buffalo with *nine* balls, having got two of the animals in line and killed both with the one shot!

Like many another frontiersman, Carson possessed a great thirst for and a keen, practical appreciation of good literature. The realm of books was to him a fascinating fount. It is recorded that " old " Jim Bridger, excited by long months in camp with the cultured Sir George Gore, and by the Shakespeare to whom Sir George introduced him, bought from an emigrant train a Shakespeare in trade for a yoke of oxen, and then hired a boy at forty dollars a month to read it to him. Literature was a new trail. As for Carson — Captain A. W. Archibald, Trinidad, Colorado, says:

Talking with him one day he said to me that nobody whose writings had been read to him had ever fully described life along the trail, western life, or the experiences of a hunter. I happened to quote to him the beginning of Scott's " Lady of the Lake "—
/" The stag at eve had drunk his fill," etc. Immediately he

asked me who wrote that and what was the poem. He begged me to find a copy of the entire poem, which I did, and every night for three weeks I read it to him. He regarded it as the finest expression of outdoor life that he had ever heard, and frequently afterward quoted with genuine approval stanzas from it.

In common with westerners, and particularly borderers — especially as is the case with the half-Indian life, of the trapper — Carson was passionately fond of horse racing, or, more definitely, pony running. A natural amphitheater, like a basin, on the outskirts of Denver, where the Arapahos were prone to run their ponies, is pointed out as one of the Carson race courses.

He also enjoyed the old draw poker of the frontier in army days. "He gambled to the extent of playing with beans for chips," related to me Captain Pettis, "and he always paid his losses, if any. But whenever I called a hand, he was apt to reply ' two pair ' (which usually meant fours), when he would haul in the pot, and looking at me over the tops of his glasses would say, ' Pettis, you can't play poker' — in which assertion he was correct as he was in other assertions."

When he died he had long been a member of Montezuma Lodge, A. F. & A. M., Santa Fe, to which he presented his Hawkins rifle. He is reported as having claimed that among the Pueblos and other tribes he observed traces of Masonic rites. He is enrolled as a charter member of Kit Carson Post No. 2, G. A. R., of Washington.

A monument has been erected to him by the New Mexico Grand Army, in the plaza at Santa Fe. His figure crowns the Pioneer Monument in the Civic Center at Denver. Trinidad has a Kit Carson Park, donated by Mayor Daniel L. Taylor, who knew him; and a monument, bearing his figure, is to be erected there also. Kentucky and Missouri have signified a determination to erect other monuments to his memory. Thus will three communities, those wherein respectively he was born, raised, and where he worked, do him honor. Surely Kit Carson cannot complain of ingratitude.

It has been proposed to make of his house in Taos a shrine, where visitors may view relics of his life; and the Daughters of the American Revolution have proposed to dedicate, similarly, the house wherein he died, at Fort Lyon which is now the United States Naval Sanatorium.

So the glamour of his name continues; increasing rather than failing. About it there is nothing false; fact and tradition alike are pleasant and wholesome; and as time wears on, the assertion of the *Santa Fe Gazette* correspondent, November 18, 1864, still holds good:

" As loyal a gentleman and as truthful a citizen as ever honored any country or age."

CARSON MONUMENT AT SANTA FE

ERECTED BY COMRADES OF THE G. A. R.

KIT CARSON II

SECOND OF THE CARSON BOYS, NAMED AFTER HIS FATHER,
LIVING AT TRINIDAD, COLO. RESEMBLES HIS FATHER

*(This picture was chosen for features for the Carson
monument at Trinidad, Colo.)*

WILLIAM CARSON

THE CARSON OLDEST SON, RESEMBLING MORE HIS MOTHER
THAN HIS FATHER

*(Copied from picture of his widow's home,
Alamosa, Colo.)*

APPENDIX

I

CAPTAIN JEDEDIAH STRONG SMITH: A Eulogy of That
Most Romantic and Pious of Mountain Men, First
American by Land into California.

(From the *Illinois Magazine*, June, 1832)

Some remarks concerning the Columbia River, in a late
number of this Magazine, bring strongly to mind the gentleman whose name is several times mentioned in that article;
and the writer has been induced to inquire, with much interest, what notice has been taken of him at St. Louis, his
place of residence when in the United States. With not a
little concern and surprise, it has been ascertained that the
death and character of our distinguished countryman, J. S.
Smith, have been entirely unnoticed there.

It has become the duty, then, of one of his latest friends,
to say a few words of a man whose memory ought to be
cherished by every American. Our country has produced
but few travellers; let it not be told, then, that we are un-
willing to render the meed of praise where it is justly due.
Let us not cast into oblivion the memory of one so richly
deserving an imperishable monument — so worthy to be
called the greatest American traveller. Ledyard has had his
biographer, and he well deserved one. His intentions were
noble, and his plans most extensive, both to open new
sources of wealth and commerce for his country, and to
trace out analogies in the manners, customs, and language
of different nations. Had Ledyard succeeded in accom-

plishing that for which he traversed nearly the whole of the Russian empire, he would have done much that we are now proud to ascribe to Smith.

There is a marked resemblance in the characters of these two men; the same moral courage and untiring energy — the same perseverance and indifference to personal privation and suffering. But Ledyard had the advantages of a college education — Smith merely those of the common schools in the interior of New York; Ledyard made the whole world the theatre of his travels — Smith, more truly American, traversed the vast country west of the United States, between the Russian settlements, on the north, and the Spanish possessions, at California; Ledyard failed in all his great attempts — Smith, in his, succeeded perfectly. We are ready to weep for poor Ledyard, when, after so many difficulties and disappointments, he falls a victim to disease in Africa; but we are struck with horror, when, at the age of thirty-three, Smith falls beneath the spears of the savage Cumanchees, in the wilds between Missouri and Santa Fe.

The writer of this notice is little acquainted with the early history of Smith. It may, however, easily be obtained. He was born in Bainbridge, Chenango county, New York, 24th June, 1798.

He came to St. Louis, in 1821, with the intention, it is said, of accompanying an expedition of hunters to the Rocky Mountains. He enlisted in the service of Gen. Ashley, as a hunter, and started with the company in the spring of 1822.

"Few men have been more fortunate than I have," said Mr. Smith to the writer, in March, 1831. "I started into the mountains, with the determination of becoming a first-rate hunter, of making myself thoroughly acquainted with the character and habits of the Indians, of tracing out the sources of the Columbia River, and following it to its mouth; and of making the whole profitable to me, and I have perfectly succeeded." Indeed, he did much more than he had planned out. For nine years and a half he was almost constantly traveling. He became well acquainted with the sources, direction, and length of most of the tributaries of the Missouri and Columbia rivers, and of the numerous tribes of Indians that dwell on their banks. He traversed the Rocky Mountains in every direction, found out the best hunting grounds and the best passes through the mountains. The salt lake, salt plains, and caves of solid salt were familiar to him. He had visited whole tribes of Indians that had never before seen a white man or a horse — people more rude and barbarous probably than any that have ever been described. There is no written notice of these people anywhere except in the notes of Mr. Smith. He was a close and accurate observer and a student of nature. He thought nothing in the works of God unworthy of his notice, and from constant observation he had amassed an immense fund of knowledge, exceedingly useful and interesting in every branch of natural history. More than this, by his intimate knowledge of the geography of that immense tract of country, he had found that all the maps of it were full of errors, and worse than useless as guides to travellers. Compare his travels with those of all who had gone before him, of all who have published anything of that country, and it will appear how much, I had almost said infinitely, greater his opportunities have been than all theirs, however great may have been their pretensions.

We have read with delight and instruction, expeditions and travels to the mountains, and the Pacific Ocean. The difficulties and dangers to be encountered, the perilous adventures, and hairbreadth escapes of which we have read and heard, have thrown over that whole land a fearful kind of romance — and the hunters themselves we have looked on as most daring, intrepid, persevering men; and so, indeed, many of them are. But where shall we find another who has braved and overcome more dangers and perils than

Smith? Where one who has suffered so much, and still
with an unbroken spirit? Much as we feel for Capt. Franklin and his party, in their travels to the Polar Seas, the
Hudson Bay Company, with whom Smith spent a winter,
and who were acquainted with the circumstances of both,
will tell us that the exertions and sufferings of Smith were
not exceeded by those of Capt. Franklin.

If there is any merit in untiring perseverance and terrible
suffering in the prosecution of trade, in searching out new
channels of commerce, in tracing out the courses of unknown rivers, in discovering the resources of unknown
regions, in delineating the characters, situation, numbers,
and habits of unknown nations, Smith's name must be enrolled with those of Franklin and Parry, of Clapperton and
Park.

Is there one, then, who would detract one iota from his
deserts? Can there be found one who, in danger, distress,
and want shared his hospitality in the mountains, that would
appropriate to himself the least portion of honor due to
Smith, or would refuse him just praise and gratitude? For
the honor of our country, let us trust there is not one.

It will certainly be gratifying to our literary men, as well
as to all those engaged in the fur trade, to know that Smith
took notes of all his travels and adventures, and that these
notes have been copied, preparatory for the press. There
may be some omissions in them, for reasons which will probably appear in the book itself. That country is attracting,
every day, more and more attention. And particularly at
this time, when people begin to talk of making an establishment near the mouth of the Columbia, where Smith spent
a winter, and from whose communication to the secretary
of war is derived the most authentic information we have
of Fort Vancouver, such information as may be obtained
from Smith's notes must be of immense interest and importance. This, however, is not all; convinced, as Smith was,

of the inaccuracy of all the maps of that country, and of the little value they would be to hunters and travellers, he has, with the assistance of his partners, Sublitt and Jackson, and of Mr. S. Parkman, made a new, large, and beautiful map, in which are embodied all that is correct of preceding maps, the known tracks of former travellers, his own extensive travels, the situation and numbers of various Indian tribes, and much other valuable information.* This map is now probably the best, extant, of the Rocky Mountains and the country on both sides, from the States to the Pacific. . . . It will be published, and exactly as Smith left it. This is perfectly proper, for it is very doubtful whether there is a man in our country, who is competent to mend it, where it may be erroneous, or supply its deficiencies where any exist.

A narrative of five or six years' residence on the banks of the Columbia, by Mr. R. Cox, is announced as about appearing in London. The American public will doubtless receive it greedily. No map is mentioned in connection with his work. It gives us pleasure to know that the whole of that region is about to be unlocked to the knowledge of the civilized world, and that one of our own countrymen is to have so much of the honor of doing it.

The circumstances of Mr. Smith's death, as nearly as they could be collected, are the following:

He left St. Louis on the 10th of April, 1831, at the head of a party of Santa Fe traders. On the 27th of May, about three hundred miles from Santa Fe, the party had been nearly three days without water, and as many as could be spared were sent in different directions in search of it. Smith, with Mr. Fitzpatrick, went forward in a south direction, the same the party were then travelling. They came to a deep hollow, in which water had usually been found by former parties, but it was then dry. Smith left Fitzpatrick

* " Parkman " means, of course, Rev. Samuel Parker, the missionary. " Sublitt " is properly Sublett. — E. L. S.

to wait till the party should come up, with directions to dig for water, while he would push on a few miles further south, to some broken ground, visible in that direction. He was last seen, by a spy-glass, about three miles from Fitzpatrick. It seems that he came to the head of a stream, which was afterwards ascertained to be the Cimeron, and imprudently descended to it. He was discovered by some Indians, who kept themselves concealed from him, till they were sure of cutting off his retreat. He discovered them approaching, when they were within half a mile's distance; and knowing that it was too late for flight, he rode directly towards them. At a short distance, they halted at his order, and made efforts to frighten his horse, wishing to fire on him when he was turned from them. After conversing among themselves about fifteen minutes, in Spanish, which Mr. Smith did not understand, they succeeded in scaring and turning his horse, when they immediately fired. A ball entered his body, near the left shoulder. Smith turned, levelled his rifle, and with the same ball shot the chief and another Indian, who was immediately behind him, and before he could get command of his pistols, they rushed upon him, and despatched him with their spears. His body was probably thrown into a ravine, as nothing could be found of it, when search was made for it two days afterwards. This information was obtained of the Indians, by a Spanish Indian trader, after the party arrived at Santa Fe.

All who were intimately acquainted with Mr. Smith must look upon his death as a public calamity. No man was better able to give the government information of the character, numbers, and strength of the different Indian tribes, of the value of the lands they inhabit, the value of the lands of the Columbia, the best places for settlements, the resources of the new settlers, should a colony be established there, the dangers they would have to encounter, and the best means to meet them. He could have proposed practicable plans for ameliorating the condition of the Indians, infinitely superior to the theories of kind hearted philanthropists, who are little acquainted with the Indian character; for he was fully aware of many causes operating against their improvements, which are not sufficiently estimated, if at all; such as the pernicious effects of different hunting and trading companies with opposing interests; of English and Spanish influence, as opposed to us; of their perpetual hostilities among themselves. We need the experience of such men, in devising any plans of civilization among them.

In reflecting on the character of Mr. Smith, when we recollect how and where, and in what company he had spent the last ten years of his life, we are filled with admiration and delight. There was none of the uncouth roughness of a hunter — he was gentle and affable. Exposed as he had been, as captain or chief of a party, in that lawless country, to many and great temptations, he held fast his integrity; with his ears constantly filled with the language of the profane and dissolute, no evil communication proceeded out of his mouth. He was exact in his requisitions of duty, determined and persevering, always confident of success. When his party was in danger, Mr. Smith was always among the foremost to meet it, and the last to fly; those who saw him on shore, at the Riccaree fight, in 1823, can attest to the truth of this assertion. In all his dealings with the Indians, he was strictly honorable, and always endeavored to give them favorable ideas of the whites. He made it a sacred rule, never to molest them, except in defence of his own life and property, and those of his party. He was kind, obliging, and generous to a fault. Without being connected with any church, he was a Christian. The lone wilderness had been his place of meditation, and the mountain top his altar. He made religion an active, practical principle, from the duties of which nothing could seduce him. He affirmed it to be " the one thing needful," and his greatest happiness; yet was he modest, never obtrusive, charitable, " without guile."

Such is a feeble sketch of J. S. Smith, a man whom none could approach without respect, or know without esteem. And though he fell under the spears of the savages, and his body has glutted the prairie wolf, and none can tell where his bones are bleaching, he must not be forgotten. One, at least, who knew his worth, and who had listened with childlike delight to his tales of daring deeds, and perilous adventure, can never forget him. But after all, his character as a traveller — as the greatest American traveller — must depend upon his works. When they are published, exactly as he left them, there are thousands in our country, who, thirsting for more knowledge of the " farthest west," will delight to render him all the honor that is justly due him.

Alton, March, 1832.

II

CARSON REPORTS AS INDIAN AGENT, 1855

UTAH AGENCY, TAOS, N. M., September 26, 1855.
SIR:

I have the honor to report the following in regard to Indian affairs in my agency during the present month.

On the 2nd instant, near Mora, two pastors were captured and one man killed. One of the pastors has made his escape from the Indians; he was in captivity four days. On the same day two pastors in the employ of Señor Juan Maus, on Rio Acate, were captured, and twelve head of cattle, average value twenty-five dollars per head, the property of Lucien B. Maxwell, was driven off from the Rayado. The two pastors captured on the Acate remained in captivity some fifteen days. They say that the Indians brought them and other property to the cañon of Red River, and there concealed the animals they had, and proceeded to the neighborhood of the San Miguel for the purpose of stealing. The larger boy at the cañon of Red River made his escape, and, arrived at San Miguel, informed the Mexicans of the animals concealed in cañon of Red River. A party returned with him, and found animals as he had stated, and on their return to San Miguel they met the party of Indians, which the boy had informed them had gone to the neighborhood of San Miguel for the purpose of stealing. They had with them several animals. The Mexicans attacked them and rescued the boy that was still in their possession, who had been captured at Acate.

On the 8th instant I left my agency for the purpose of attending the treaty to be held at Abiquiu on the 10th. I made it my duty to pass by Embudo and Rio Arriba, for the purpose of ascertaining the whereabouts of the Utah captive reported to have been sold, but without success.

On the 10th and 11th I attended the treaty. I think the Mohuaches and Jicarillas that were present were serious in that which they said, and in all probability will remain friendly for a long period. The Indians that are now committing depredations are those who have lost their families during the war. They consider they have nothing further to live for than revenge for the death of those of their families that were killed by the whites; they have become desperate; when they will ask for peace I cannot say.

Respectfully submitted.

I have the honor to be, very respectfully, your obedient servant,   C. CARSON,
                                                                Indian Agent.

HON. D. MERRIWETHER,
   Supt. Indian Affairs, Santa Fe, New Mexico.

Mr. Carson does not inform me what Indians committed

these depredations, though the last part of his report would leave the impression that they were committed by the Jicarilla Apaches. I am of the opinion that the Comanches are the guilty party, because it is scarcely probable that the Apaches would be guilty of such acts after they had sued for peace, and before peace was made, and then meet me in council but a few days thereafter. In addition to this it is positively known that the Comanches had been about the cañon of Red River both before and after the date of these depredations, and the Comanches and Jicarilla Apaches are hostile to each other. It is to be regretted that Agent Carson did not ascertain from the prisoners what Indians they were.

D. MERRIWETHER,

Gov. and Supt. Indian Affairs, New Mexico.

1857

UTAH AGENCY, TAOS, N. M., August 29, 1857.

SIR:

In compliance with the regulations of the Indian department, under which I have the honor to act, I submit the following report of the condition of this agency during the past year:

It gives me pleasure to state that the Mohuache band of Utah Indians, for whom I am agent, are at this present date in a more prosperous condition than for years past. They are friendly disposed towards the United States, and are well satisfied with the treatment they receive from government.

On the 18th of this month their yearly presents were delivered them at Abiquiu, and I can assure you that they never departed from a place more contented. They all were apparently happy and well satisfied with the presents they received. Heretofore they departed from the place that they received their presents in a state of discontentment;

and after receiving their presents, in the year 1854, they immediately commenced hostilities. They are now more favorably disposed towards the whites than ever known heretofore. The citizens have no cause of complaint. I hear of no robberies being committed, and have ardent hopes of their remaining in a friendly state.

The Mohuache Utahs are not Indians that are addicted to the use of ardent spirits. But I fear, if they are permitted to visit the settlements as they desire, that in a few years they will become accustomed to the use of ardent spirits; and as Indians generally learn the vices and not the virtues of civilized men, they will become a degraded tribe, instead of being, as they are now, the most noble and virtuous tribe within our Territory. Prostitution, drunkenness, and the vices generally are unknown among them. Humanity, as well as our desire to benefit the Indian race, demands that they be removed as far as practicable from the settlements. Have farmers, mechanics, etc., placed among them, to give instruction in the manner of cultivating the soil to gain their subsistence, and teach them to make the necessary implements to carry on said labor. They would, in a few years, be able to support themselves, and not be, as at present, a burden on the general government. It is true much could not be expected of the present generation, for they have been accustomed to gain their maintenance by the chase and robberies committed on the neighboring tribes and the whites. But if the rising generation be taught to maintain themselves by honest labor, in their manhood they will not depart therefrom, and will feel proud in being able to instruct their children the manner of maintaining themselves in an honest way. Troops, for a period of time, should be stationed near them, for the purpose of protecting them from hostile tribes, and also show unto them that the government has the power to cause them to remain on the lands given them, and not to encroach on that of their neighbors.

The Mohuaches maintain themselves by the chase, and, as game is becoming more scarce, the government must furnish them provisions, more especially in the winter season, when, on account of the weakness of their animals and the depth of the snow in the mountains, it is utterly impracticable for them to proceed to their hunting grounds.

During the year the Mohuaches have acted as well as could be expected of an uncivilized nation. They had but one cause of complaint, and that was in February last. A Mexican killed an Indian and squaw of their band, and they, knowing no other law but that of restitution, demanded payment for the Indians murdered. I could not comply with their demand. They stole some fifteen head of horses and mules from the settlements of Rio Colorado and Culebra. They have returned them, with the expectation that justice, some day, will be rendered them, either by punishment of the murderer or payment for the murdered. Every means has been used to apprehend the murderer, but without effect. I have been informed that he has left the Territory, so I have but little hopes of ever being able to turn him over to justice.

I can only give you a rough estimate of the number of the band. They are seldom together, being dispersed among the different lands of the tribe. I am of opinion that of the Mohuache band of Utahs there are three hundred and fifty males and four hundred females. They maintain themselves by the chase, and such provisions as are given them by government. They are a very tractable race, and I have no doubt but that, by kind treatment, they might be brought to a state of civilization in a short period.

During the past and present months, some one hundred and fifty lodges of the Tobawache band of Utahs have visited this section of the country. They expected to receive presents on the 18th of this month, but as they are not included within the superintendency, little could be given them. They are by far the largest band of the Utahs. Their main hunting grounds are within the limits of this Territory. They range from Grand River west to the headwaters of the Del Norte east. It is impracticable for them to go to the Salt Lake to receive presents, on account of the barrenness of the country over which they would have to travel, and the scarcity of game. They have never joined any of the bands of Utahs that have waged war against the citizens of this Territory. I would respectfully suggest that an agent or subagent be appointed to reside among them. They are by far the most noble of the Utah tribes. They have not, as yet, been contaminated by intercourse with civilized man.

Respectfully submitted.

I have the honor to be, very respectfully, your obedient servant, C. CARSON,

Indian Agent.

JAMES L. COLLINS, ESQ.,
Superintendent of Indian Affairs, Santa Fe, New Mexico.

1858

UTAH AGENCY, TAOS, N. M., August 31, 1858.
SIR:

I have the honor to submit for your examination my annual report of operations, as required by the regulations of the Indian department.

In my annual report dated August 29, 1857, I stated there were within this agency, under my charge, seven hundred and fifty Indians, male and female.

The Tobawache band of Utahs have since then been attached to this agency. They number seven hundred males. It is impossible to give, as required by communication from the Department of the Interior, dated July 11, 1857, the exact number of Indians under my charge.

They live in parties of ten to twenty lodges, and have no permanent residence.

In agricultural or mechanical pursuits there are none engaged; by the chase, and with what is given them by the United States and its citizens, they maintain themselves.

During the year the Indians committed few depredations: they stole some animals from the Mexicans, and the Mexicans also stole some from them. The Indians gave me the animals stolen by them, and I made the Mexicans return the animals they had stolen, thus satisfying both parties.

I have visited the Indians as often as necessary during the year, and given them such articles as they required, principally provisions. It being thought that the Utahs would join the Mormons in their opposition to the entry of the United States troops into Great Salt Lake City, I caused the allowance of their provisions to be increased, to prevent such a course being pursued by them. No Utah, as far as I know, aided the Mormons.

It would promote the advance of civilization among the Indians of this agency if it were practicable that I could live with them. They have no particular place to reside, are of a roving nature, and an agent could not be with them at all times, so I have selected this place as the most proper for them to receive such presents of food as they need; and such will necessarily be the case until agency buildings are built. The Indians should be settled on reserves, guarded by troops, and made to cultivate the soil, because the required amount of provisions to be given them cannot be procured at any of the frontier settlements. I have purchased all the grain issued during the year as near their haunts as I could.

To keep the Indians from committing depredations on citizens, food by the government must be furnished them, and liberally, there being no game of any consequence in the country through which they roam.

I have in the employ of the Indian department John Mostin, as interpreter, a native of Clinton county, State of New York, aged 29 years, at a salary of $500 per annum. He was appointed June 1, 1857, at this agency.

I have the honor to be, very respectfully, your obedient servant, C. CARSON,
Indian Agent.

HON. JAS. L. COLLINS,
Superintendent Indian Affairs, Santa Fe, N. M.

1859

UTE AGENCY, TAOS, N. M., March 31, 1859.
SIR: * * * The Indians at this agency have always depended on the chase for a subsistence, and as game is fast disappearing, and their hunting grounds either being settled by the whites, or invaded by their hereditary foes, the Indians of the plains, it behooves the General Government to do something for them if it wishes that they be perpetuated. I only know of one mode of saving them from annihilation. It is this: Remove them as far as practicable from the settlements; settle them on a reservation, that by its cultivation they may be able to raise produce for their maintenance; also cattle to stock their farms; have troops stationed on the reserve, not only for the purpose of guarding them from their enemies but to deter them from leaving the homes the Government chooses to assign for their habitation; with Indians arrived at the age when habits of life are permanently made, compulsion to retain them on the reserve will be required; but the benefit to be received by the rising generation will justify such a course.

I am confident that many of these Indians can be made to support themselves; but the Government must render them assistance. Give good land; have comfortable houses built, and allow no persons to remain among them excepting those employed as their instructors, and such others as the Indian Department may consider uninjurious to their welfare; and, before the expiration of twenty years, the Indian that to the Government is now a cost will be able to render aid, etc., as any citizen.

Liquor is the cause of great destruction to these Indians. So long as they are permitted to visit the settlements they can always procure it. There are disreputable men living in each settlement who for a blanket or, in fact, any article that the Indian may have, are ready to furnish liquor.

On the 6th of this month, at the ranches three miles from here, arrived three Jicarillas Apaches; a Mexican of said place joined them; and, I presume, entered into the traffic of liquor. He was not long in their company when a difficulty arose; liquor the main cause; the consequence being that the Mexican was shot dead by one of the Indians; Indian tried to make his escape; Mexicans, hearing of the murder, and perhaps not knowing the cause, pursued him. He was overtaken and carried here, to be turned over to civil authority; died a few minutes after his arrival; cause, mal-treatment from the hands of his captors. The deceased Mexican was a man of the lowest character, and the Indian the same. I have stated the circumstances to some of the principal Jicarillas, and they consider the case properly disposed of, life for a life being justice.

Difficulties of the above description will often occur if the Indians continue, as heretofore, in the settlements, and perhaps never again be so easily settled. If the deceased had been a Muahuache I am satisfied that the band would at least have killed four or five Mexicans and stole a number of horses to pay the friends of the deceased.

I will do all in my power to keep them out of town.

I have the honor to be, very respectfully, your obedient servant, C. CARSON.

1859

UTAH AGENCY, TAOS, N. M., September 20, 1859.
SIR:

In conformity with the regulations of the Indian department, I have the honor to present the following report of the
condition and conduct of the Indians under my charge during the past year.

The two bands of the Muahuaches and Tobawatches, so
far as regards their numerical strength, are on the decline,
and the causes of this decrease in population are disease
and frequent conflicts with other warlike tribes.

If any improvement has been made in their condition or
prospects, it is not perceptible. They are, at the present
day, as uncivilized as when this government first took them
under her care, and it is my opinion they will remain in the
same state until they shall be settled on reserves, and compelled to cultivate the soil for their maintenance. Not having the least particle of the pride of self-support about them,
they will continue to sink deeper into degradation, so long
as a generous government, or their habits of begging and
stealing, afford them a means of subsistence. I have, heretofore, recommended that they be settled on farms, and I
am still satisfied that it is the only practicable mode of reclaiming them from their barbarous condition.

In July last hostilities were commenced by these Indians
against the whites who were then entering the Valle Salada
in search of gold, and many murders, as well as other depredations, were committed by them. Seven whites are reported to have been killed, and many Indians were killed by
the whites in the defense of their lives and property. The
Muahuaches came to the agency immediately after the commission of the first murders, and reported to me faithfully
all the circumstances of the difficulty. They said that
among the murderers was a single Muahuache, who was an

outcast from the band; that they did not desire war, but hoped to remain on friendly terms with us. The principal men, and indeed the whole band, are opposed to war, and have determined to remain in the vicinity of the agency to prove their good faith, and that I may be satisfied they take no part with the perpetrators of these outrages.

The proceedings of the Tobawatches have been different. After the commission of the murders, they moved to their own country, on the waters of Grand River, and, having encamped there until joined by other bands of the same nation from Utah, they sent me word that the murderers of the white men were with them; that troops should be sent after them, if it was thought necessary to take them; and that they would await the arrival of the troops. Their conduct was duly reported to you, and by you laid before the proper officer. Nothing has been done to make them cease from the commission of hostilities, or to teach them that when they rob and plunder our citizens they should expect a prompt and severe punishment; the reason, I believe, being that the troops are now absent on service in the country of the Navajos.

The consequences arising from letting these Indians go unpunished will be injurious. Other bands of Indians, seeing that depredations are committed by these with impunity, will soon follow an example so much in accordance with their habits and inclinations and will only remain quiet so long as it suits their convenience.

The Tobawatches will not be able to do much injury in this country during the winter, even if they are so inclined, the mountains being impassable; but I have every reason to fear that in the spring they will visit us, and do much damage to the unprotected northern settlements of this Territory, in which marauding expeditions they will be joined by the Muahuaches, if the latter band is not well treated during the winter.

Few thefts have been committed during the past year, and in those which have been committed, I have succeeded in recovering the animals stolen by the Indians, and returning them to their respective owners. I have horses and mules to the number of eight now in my possession, which I have received in this manner, and will properly dispose of. In making these exchanges of property between the Mexicans and Indians, I meet with much more difficulty in tracing and recovering stock stolen from the Indians by Mexicans than from the Indians; the Mexicans seem mostly to have the advantage in these thefts.

On the 17th instant, the annual presents for the Muahua-ches were distributed to them at the Conejos, and they con-ducted themselves throughout the whole with order and propriety, seeming satisfied with the quantity and quality of the presents.

The presents for the Tobawatches have been retained, and are stored with Mr. Head, of Conejos, for safe keeping.

The Muahuaches have now received their presents, will leave the settlements, and will not again return until com-pelled to do so by hunger.

All of which is respectfully submitted.

Very respectfully, your obedient servant,

C. CARSON,
Indian Agent.

J. L. COLLINS, ESQ.,
Superintendent Indian Affairs, Santa Fe, New Mexico.

1860

TAOS AGENCY, August 29, 1860.

SIR:

In compliance with the regulations of the Indian department, under which I have the honor to serve, I submit the following report of the condition of this agency during the last year:

It gives me pleasure to state that the Indians under my charge have continued during the year in the peaceful pursuit of their vocation, which is the chase, and are on friendly terms with all the citizens.

The hunting grounds of the Tabahuaches being in the section of country where the whites are in search of gold, their game is becoming exceedingly scarce; much of it having been killed by the settlers, and a great deal of it driven from the country. Hence it will be absolutely necessary to feed them during the approaching winter months. Although the whites are scattered all over their usual hunting grounds, which extend from the St. Louis Pass and the Valle Salada west to the Grand River, the Indians do not molest them but permit them to pass and repass undisturbed. They, however, do not appear to be entirely satisfied with the encroachments which are thus being made upon what they are accustomed to consider their rights; but as long as the whites do not interfere with them or sell them intoxicating beverages, I think they will continue friendly with the people, both of the mines and the Territory. Their number of all ages and sexes is about 1,800.

The Mohuache band of Utahs are not as numerous as the Tabahauches, they numbering about 850 or 900 souls. They live much nearer the settlements; and from their intercourse with the people of the Territory are constantly becoming more and more addicted to the use of ardent spirits. I have used every exertion in my power to discover the guilty persons who sell them spirituous liquors, but all my efforts have proved unavailing. These Indians do not follow the chase as closely as the Tabahuaches, and are consequently more frequently seen in the settlements.

In my opinion, the best policy the government can adopt in the regulation and management of these two bands of Utahs would be to have them settled upon reserves, and furnished with a few good farmers and mechanics, who could and would instruct them in husbandry and the mechanic arts. Their minds are tractable, and capable of receiving impressions which would in a comparatively short time, under judicious training, enable them to obtain an honest subsistence for themselves and families. It is true that the older members of the tribes, who are confirmed in their present habits of life, might be obstinate in their resistence to the change; but they, in the course of nature, must pass away in a few years, and the young generation which is now growing up to take their places, can be educated in such a manner as to make them submit to the habits and customs of civilized life with facility. To effect this reformation will be required the labor of years, but, in my opinion, would in the end prove a measure of economy to the government and a blessing to the Indians.

For a period it would be necessary to keep a small body of troops near their reserves to protect them from the incursions of the roving bands on the great plains, with which they are often at war, as well as to show them that government has the power to compel them to keep within their own limits, and not encroach upon the rights of others.

If some policy of this kind is not adopted by the government, and if provisions are not furnished them in sufficient quantities to sustain them during the winter months, they will be reduced to the necessity of thieving and robbing. Their game being killed or driven off, nothing better can reasonably be expected from them. In a few years, if allowed to continue to roam at large and visit the settlements at pleasure, they will become victims to intemperance and its concomitant vices, which will reduce them to a condition of great depravity. Humanity demands that this fate should be averted from them, and it can only be avoided by setting them apart to themselves, agricultural instruments given them, and proper instruction imparted to them, as before mentioned.

On Monday the 18th of August I left this agency to go to the Conejos, which is about eighty miles northwest of Taos, to deliver the presents to the Mohuaches and Taba- huaches. I arrived there on the 19th, and found them all assembled and awaiting my appearance. The following day the superintendent arrived, and on the 21st we made the distributions, the Indians conducting themselves with great propriety and receiving the presents with evident satisfac- tion. About the middle of the afternoon, after having given them some provisions, we dismissed the Indians, who went to their homes, contentment being visible on the faces of all.

The Jicarilla Apaches number about nine hundred and fifty souls. They live in the vicinity of the agency, and the chase is their only means of support. They are rapidly degenerating, their associations with the citizens of this Territory proving to be a great bane to their naturally not very correct morals. We daily witness them in a state of intoxication in our plaza. No sacrifice is considered by them too great to be made in order to procure whisky. Not being allowed to buy it themselves they are always able to find those who will buy it for them. Some time since the territorial legislature passed an act exempting the Pueblos from the conditions of the law which prohibits the whites from selling intoxicating liquors to the Indians, and the Apaches furnish them the means to buy whisky, when all get drunk together. Both the Apaches and Pueblos in this agency will part with everything they have to gratify their appetites for whisky.

The Apaches have caused me more trouble this year than all the balance of the Indians under my charge. They are truly the most degraded and troublesome Indians we have in our department. A few days since, one of them was killed in a drunken spree by being stabbed by one of his own tribe with a large butcher knife. This occurrence

placed a temporary check upon them, but they are already
conducting themselves with as little restraint as before.

Something must be done soon to remove them from contact with the settlements if we would avoid their utter ruin.
If permitted to remain as they are, before many years the
tribe will be entirely extinct.

I have the honor to be, your obedient servant,

C. CARSON,
United States Indian Agent.

J. L. COLLINS, ESQ.,
Superintendent of Indian Affairs, Santa Fe, N. M.

III

THE BATTLE OF VALVERDE: February 21, 1862

(By Major Rafael Chacon, Who was Captain in the Kit
Carson Regiment)

During the Civil War of 1861-5 the First Regiment of
New Mexico Volunteers was organized as infantry under
Colonel Ceran St. Vrain. He resigned, and Kit Carson
remained in his place as colonel. In October of 1861 the
regiment went to Albuquerque; there we remained until
the end of January, 1862, when we went down to Fort
Craig, where the Battle of Valverde was fought by our
troops with the rebel forces under Sibley, on the 21st day
of February, 1862.

In this battle my company, because it was mounted, was
assigned to the cavalry service; the rest of the regiment
under Colonel Carson fought bravely as infantry (the Deus
company, however, being mounted) on that portion of the
field assigned to them, and they would have retaken the guns
which the enemy had captured from our side if the retreat
had not been sounded just as they were advancing on the
enemy for that purpose.

Just before sunrise on the day of February 21, my mounted company of the Carson regiment, and Graydon's mounted company (Graydon's was an independent company mustered in to serve three months) were ordered to march from Fort Craig, to cross the river at the ford of Valverde, above, and to resist any fording here by the rebel troops. Colonel Roberts, in command in the field, gave us our orders to cross the river, and then he proceeded to place his artillery in position on the west bank of the river. As we crossed the river, an advance guard of the Texan troops received us with a discharge of carbines; we replied, and this skirmish, beginning just before sunrise, lasted about an hour; the sun was above the horizon when it ceased. We compelled this advance detachment of the rebels to withdraw and to join their main army. Our artillery, already in position, supported us during this skirmish by firing into the enemy. Graydon and myself maintained our positions across the river. About 9 o'clock a. m. we were reinforced by Captain Morris with his dragoons of regular cavalry, and he at once assumed command of all our troops east of the river. About 9:30 a. m. Colonel Valdez, with the Third Regiment, arrived and took up a position near my company. Graydon had in the meantime shifted his position. Near me were the companies of Captain Pedro Sanches, Captain Branch and other companies of their regiment.

About 10 a. m. Captain Wingate arrived with a battalion of infantry and two companies of Pike's Peakers; we so called them because they were of the Colorado Volunteers, of the regiment of Colonel Slough. Immediately with all these reinforcements we engaged a portion of the Texas cavalry. These Texans were of the best in the rebel army, and were armed with lances and sabers. I joined the attack. All our troops then east of the river — the mounted forces with drawn sabers, and the foot soldiers with fixed bayonets — delivered a telling blow on the enemy. In about fifteen minutes we had swept over their position, leaving their horses and men dead and dying on the field; almost all the forces then opposing us at that point were annihilated by the severity of our attàck.

After this charge, the battle continued to rage with desultory firing from both sides at various points of the battle field. Those of us who were thus engaged in this firing were protected by the thick grove, each side awaiting developments before making any advance move. Our artillery, posted on the west bank of the river, all this time kept up a heavy cannonade, raking the timbers, and so close to us did the balls strike, that many of the shattered branches and limbs of the trees fell almost at our feet.

About one o'clock p. m. one solitary piece of rebel artillery, stationed at the foot of the Mesa, opened a steady fire on us; it seemed to me that the fire was deliberately aimed at the point where I was stationed with my company. I also noticed that our artillery gave no response to this firing, and that my company was left without support. Thereupon, in order to silence this annoying fire which was deliberately aimed at me, I ordered my men to charge this one-piece battery. The men serving that gun did not stand their ground, but fled upon seeing our advance, without firing another shot, and abandoned their gun. One of my men, Corporal Leyba, with three or four others, then rushed upon the gun and seized it; they lassoed it and hauled it cowboy fashion to our lines. We kept this gun within our lines all day, long after that, until, in obedience to superior orders we were compelled to fall back and abandon the battle field at sunset.

General Canby, on assuming personal control of the operations on the battle field about two p. m., had ordered the artillery to cross the river, together with all the reserves which he had brought with him from the Fort Craig on the bluffs west of the river. By this time I, with my company, had already rejoined my regiment. General Canby had all three arms move forward and deploy in line of battle for a general action, and he himself personally gave all orders from that hour. He rearranged the various troops and gave them new positions. My regiment (Kit Carson's) formed the right wing of the line of battle. All our forces, except the militia and the Second Regiment, had by this time penetrated into the enemies' zone. The rebels, when they saw that the General was on the field, distinguishing him by his brilliant staff, at once opened up the battle anew with greater energy, directing a most terrific fire upon the point occupied by the General. Our side replied with equal vigor. The fighting became general from that moment, and it was so severe that General Canby was in great peril on several occasions, and he had three horses killed under him that day.

About four or five o'clock p. m., the main body of the rebel cavalry charged upon the position held by our regiment, but we repulsed them with heavy loss on their side. Falling back they reformed, and this time advanced and sought to charge the center of our line of battle where the General was in person commanding the operations. Our right wing then received the order to advance; we moved forward and delivered a flank attack upon the advancing cavalry of the rebels. We checked them, pushed them back, and pressing onward we put them to flight and drove them clear into the hills. But fate was not with us on that day. At the same time we were carrying on this flanking attack to a brilliant issue, upon another part of the field our artillery had fallen into the hands of the enemy. Our gunners fought heroically, but they were overpowered by superior numbers.

About the hour of sunset the retreat was sounded. I, with my mounted company, had driven far into the enemies' lines. For the moment I could not understand the signals to retreat, for we considered that our charge upon the enemy's main cavalry had won the battle. I was so loath to leave the field that my company was the last of our army to recross the river. I mounted a wounded horse taken from the enemy; it was a splendid horse. My own mount, tired and fagged, was led by the bridle after me by one of my men. We recrossed the river under the cannon fire of the enemy. They were now shelling us with our own guns, but their fire fell short and did us no harm.

The militia regiments did not take part in the battle of that day. They remained on the bluffs watching the fighting below. In the evening, when the order for retreat was being carried out, these regiments became panic-stricken, and deserting their officers and their colors, they returned to their homes.

Personally I have always disliked to speak of matters that might be construed into self-praise. In my own affairs I have always preferred to let others speak for me. But there are times, and this is one of them, when we must speak on behalf of truth to correct all erroneous impressions given out about the Battle of Valverde. That was a bloody battle, not yet sufficiently understood and not yet sufficiently appreciated.

As you are in possession of the official reports and of the letter of Lieutenant Bell, I have only to state to you that *not a single man of the Kit Carson regiment had been ordered or placed in support of the battery of McRea at the battle of Valverde,* and you are correct in your impression that *the Mortimer and Hubbell companies of the Third Regiment (which whole said regiment was in support of the battery), were the ones to be put to flight close to the guns by the charge of the enemy on that day.*

Yours very truly,

RAFAEL CHACON, Late Major 1st N. M. Vol. Cav.

November 30, 1911.

IV

CARLETON DISPATCHES TO CARSON
(Being extracts from Civil War Orders)

1862

HEADQUARTERS DEPARTMENT OF NEW MEXICO,
SANTA FE, N. M.,
October 12, 1862.

COLONEL:

Enclosed you will find a confidential communication to Colonel West, commanding the district of Arizona; it is dated the 11th instant, and directs him to send two expeditions against the Mescalero Apaches, starting them on the 15th of next month.

I desire you to send one of your mounted companies down to the junction of the Rio Hondo with the Pecos, to act as an outpost to this country; to keep scouts well down the river toward Delaware Creek to see that no force advances up the Pecos from the direction of Fort Lancaster, in Texas, without your having timely notice of the fact, so that you can send me word.

As your scouts from this company come near the mouth of the Peñasco they will, doubtless, find a plenty of Mescaleros. It was near that point where Captain Stanton was killed by them. In this case you could, if you thought it advisable, move the company down to the mouth of the Peñasco to produce an impression upon the Indians, at the same time it watched the approaches to New Mexico by the way of the Pecos; but under no circumstances will it leave the valley of the river unwatched.

The other three companies you can divide as you please, but with these you will make war upon the Mescaleros and upon all other Indians you may find in the Mescalero country, until further orders. All Indian men of that tribe are to be killed whenever you can find them. The women and children will not be harmed, but you will take them prisoners, and feed them at Fort Stanton until you receive other instructions about them. If the Indians send in a flag and desire to treat for peace, say to the bearer that when the people of New Mexico were attacked by the Texans, the Mescaleros broke their treaty of peace, and murdered innocent people, and ran off their stock; that now our hands are untied, and you have been sent to punish them for their treachery and their crimes; that you have no power to make peace; that you are there to kill them wherever you can find them; that if they beg for peace, their chiefs and twenty of their principal men must come to Santa Fe to have a talk here; but tell them fairly and frankly that you will keep after their people and slay them until you receive orders to desist from these headquarters; that this making of treaties for them to break whenever they have an interest in breaking them will not be done any more; that that time has passed by; that we have no faith in their promises; that we believe if we kill some of their men in fair, open war, they will be apt to remember that it will be better for them to remain at peace than to be at war. I trust that this severity, in the long run, will be the most humane course that could be pursued toward these Indians.

You observe that there is a large force helping you. I do not wish to tie your hands by instructions; the whole duty can be summed up in a few words: The Indians are to be soundly whipped, without parleys or councils except as above.

Be careful not to mistake the troops from below for Texans. If a force of rebels comes, *you* know how to annoy it; how to stir up their camps and stock by night; how to lay waste the prairies by fire; how to make the country very warm for them, and the road a difficult one. *Do this,* and keep me advised of all you do.

I am, colonel, respectfully, your friend,

JAMES H. CARLETON,
Brigadier General, Commanding.

COLONEL CHRISTOPHER CARSON,
1st New Mexico Vol., en route to Fort Stanton, N. M.
Official: ERASTUS W. WOOD,
Captain 1st Vet. Inf. C. V., A. A. A. General.

HEADQUARTERS DEPARTMENT OF NEW MEXICO,
SANTA FE, N. M., November 25, 1862.

COLONEL:

I have the honor to acknowledge the receipt of your letter in relation to the Mescalero chiefs who have come to this city with Mr. Labadie, the Indian agent, to sue for peace.

Yesterday, in presence of the governor, the superintendent of Indian affairs, and other gentlemen, I had an interview with the chiefs above alluded to, and told them that if they and their part of the tribe desired to have peace they must come out of the Mescalero country, so that we should not mistake them for those who were hostile, and so that we would be sure that they conveyed no intelligence of our movements to those who did not come in. I told them I would send them and their families to Fort Sumner, at the Bosque Redondo, on the Pecos River, and there feed and protect them until we had punished those who were still at war, and until these latter come in and beg for peace likewise.

A train of government wagons will leave Fort Union, with subsistence stores, for Fort Stanton, in a few days. When this train starts to return, have all the Mescalero men, women and children, *of the peace party,* with all of their effects, come with this train. The women and children and baggage will be hauled in the wagons, and you will see that they have provisions enough to last them all to the Bosque Redondo, by the way of Agua Negra. The meat portion of the ration will be beef on the hoof. The commanding officer at Fort Sumner will be instructed to feed and protect them after their arrival at the Bosque Redondo.

After these Indians have been sent to the Bosque Redondo you will continue to make war on the others, as heretofore instructed. If they sue for peace (any one small band of the Mescaleros), send that band to Fort Sumner to await there until the remainder come in. The result of this will be that, eventually, we shall have the whole tribe at the Bosque Redondo, and then we can conclude a definite treaty, and let them *all* return again to inhabit their proper country.

If you are satisfied that Graydon's attack on Manuelita and his people was not fair and open, see that all the horses and mules, including two said to be in the hands of one Mr. Beach, of Manzana, are returned to the survivors of Manuelita's band.

These arrangements seem to be just. When any band comes in for peace, send me a list of the names of all the men, and the number of the women and children, so that I may know the additional number to provide for at Fort Sumner.

I am, respectfully,

JAMES H. CARLETON,
Brigadier General, Commanding.

COLONEL CHRISTOPHER CARSON,
Commanding Expedition against the Mescalero Apaches, Fort Stanton, N. M.

Official: ERASTUS W. WOOD,
Captain 1st Vet. Inf. C. V., A. A. A. General.

HEADQUARTERS DEPARTMENT OF NEW MEXICO,
SANTA FE, N. M., April 11, 1863.

COLONEL:

There is said to be a man in Taos, or near there, who was for a great many years a captain with the Navajo Indians, against whom you are about to take the field. Mr. Manzaneres, of Abiquiu, says he knows their country thoroughly; it will be well for you to secure his services as a guide. Some of the Ute Indians from the neighborhood of Abiquiu would like to be employed as trailers, etc. You have my authority to secure the services of, say, ten of the *best* Ute warriors, and say four of the *best* Mexican guides, as spies and guides for the contemplated campaign against the Navajos, their services to commence when the campaign commences; a reasonable compensation will be allowed them. It is said several fine guides lives near Abiquiu; we will have none but the best; our work is to be thorough, and we must have *men* to do it.

I shall leave for Fort Wingate on the 13th instant, and shall be gone some twelve days. When I return you will doubtless be in Santa Fe.

I am, colonel, very respectfully, your obedient servant,

JAMES H. CARLETON,
Brigadier General, Commanding.

COLONEL CHRISTOPHER CARSON,
1st New Mexico Volunteers, Taos, N. M.

Official: ERASTUS W. WOOD,
Captain 1st Vet. Inf. C. V., A. A. A. General.

HEADQUARTERS DEPARTMENT OF NEW MEXICO,
SANTA FE, N. M., August 7, 1863.

COLONEL:

I have heard a rumor that you have had some success

against the Navajos, and have felt surprised that an official report from you on the subject could not have reached me as soon as the rumor.

Make a note of this: You will send me a weekly report, in *detail*, of the operations of your command, a certified copy of which I desire to send to Washington by each mail, if possible. Let me know all about the crops destroyed, their extent and location; all about the stock captured — when, where, by whom, and the kind and number; all about the Navajoes killed, and the exact number of captured women and children. The prisoners are all to be sent to Santa Fe, to my care, by every safe and practicable opportunity. Be sure and make *timely* requisitions for supplies.

Keep me advised of just how you are getting along in all respects.

Major Morrison will be required to state what reason he had for delaying his command so long at and near Las Lunas. That officer will be kept in the field until he has become an experienced Indian fighter. When you can, pray give Major Blakeney a chance for distinction.

The value of time cannot be too seriously considered. Make *every* string draw. Much is expected of you, both here and in Washington.

I am, colonel, very respectfully, your obedient servant,
JAMES H. CARLETON,
Brigadier General, Commanding.
COLONEL CHRISTOPHER CARSON,
Commanding Fort Canby, N. M.
Official: ERASTUS W. WOOD,
Captain 1st Vet. Inf. C. V., A. A. A. General.

HEADQUARTERS DEPARTMENT OF NEW MEXICO,
SANTA FE, N. M., August 18, 1863.
COLONEL:
I have the honor to acknowledge the receipt of your letter

of the 24th ultimo, in relation to the disposition to be made of the captured Navajo women and children, and to say, in reply, that *all* prisoners which are captured by the troops or employes of your command will be sent to Santa Fe, by the first practicable opportunity after they are, from time to time, brought in as prisoners. *There must be no exception to this rule.* Here, the superintendent of Indian affairs and myself will make such dispositions as to their future care and destination as may seem most humane and proper.

All horses, mules, or other stock which the troops or employes under your command may capture belong to the United States, and will be reported to department headquarters. The horses and mules will be turned over to your chief quartermaster, who will have them carefully branded " U. S.," and used in the public service. These he will account for on his property returns. But to stimulate the zeal of the troops and employes who have captured horses and mules from the Navajoes, or who may hereafter make such captures from those Indians, a bonus of twenty dollars apiece will be paid to their captors as prize-money, on the delivery to the chief quartermaster of every sound, serviceable horse or mule. These will be accounted for as purchased.

All sheep captured will be turned over to the chief commissary of your expedition. These will be taken up on the returns of provisions; will be properly marked; will be killed from time to time and issued as fresh meat to the troops and employes. The chief commissary is authorized to pay the captors of such sheep one dollar per head as prize money, and as an encouragement to renewed exertions. Every lot captured will at once be reported to department headquarters. The sheep paid for, as here set forth, will be taken up as purchased.

All other property captured from the Indians will be

reported, when orders will be given as to what disposition shall be made of it.

I am, Colonel, very respectfully, your obedient servant,

JAMES H. CARLETON,
Brigadier General, Commanding.

COLONEL CHRISTOPHER CARSON,
Commanding Expedition against the Navajoes, Fort Canby, N. M.

Official: ERASTUS W. WOOD,
Captain 1st Vet. Inf. C. V., A. A. A. General.

HEADQUARTERS DEPARTMENT OF NEW MEXICO,
SANTA FE, N. M., September 19, 1863.
COLONEL: * * *

I recommend, unless you can produce the same result by more gentle measures, that you seize six of the principal men of the Zuñi Indians, and hold them as hostages until all Navajoes in and near their village are given up, and all stolen stock surrendered. You will assure the Zuñi Indians that if I hear that they help or harbor Navajoes, or steal stock from any white men, or injure the person of any white man, I will as certainly destroy their villages as sure as the sun shines.

I have received the report of your operations in the vicinity of Cañon de Chelly. If any Indians desire to give themselves up, they will be received and sent to Fort Wingate, with a request that from that post they be sent to Los Pinos. No Navajo Indians of either sex, or of any age, will be retained at Fort Canby as servants, or in any capacity whatever. All must go to the Bosque Redondo.

You are right in believing that I do not wish to have those destroyed who are willing to come in. Nor will you permit an Indian prisoner, once fairly in our custody, to be killed, unless he be endeavoring to make his escape. There is to be no other alternative but this: Say to them

— " Go to the Bosque Redondo, or we will pursue and destroy you. We will not make peace with you on any other terms. You have deceived us too often and robbed and murdered our people too long to trust you again at large in your own country. This war shall be pursued against you if it takes years, now that we have begun, until you cease to exist or move. There can be no other talk on the subject."

As winter approaches you will have better luck. I send your report to Washington.

I am, Colonel, very respectfully,

Your Obedient Servant,

JAMES H. CARLETON,
Brigadier General, Commanding.

COLONEL CHRISTOPHER CARSON,
Commanding Expedition against the Navajoes, Fort Canby, N. M.

Official: ERASTUS W. WOOD,
Captain 1st Vet. Inf. C. V., A. A. A. General.

HEADQUARTERS DEPARTMENT OF NEW MEXICO,
SANTA FE, N. M., September 19, 1863.

COLONEL CHRISTOPHER CARSON,
Commanding Expedition against the Navajoes, Fort Canby, N. M.

COLONEL:

By custom of service, no officer who is not competent to order a general court-martial can order a court of inquiry, excepting in the case of an enlisted man, when a colonel commanding a regiment may order the court (DeHart, 272, 273). You will, therefore, annul all proceedings of any such court in the case of Lieutenant Hodt.

Non-commissioned officers must not be reduced to the ranks within your regiment by any person's orders but your own. The Regulations must be your guide in all such matters, or the discipline of your regiment will be bad.

* * * * * *

JAMES H. CARLETON,
Brigadier General, Commanding.
Official: ERASTUS W. WOOD,
Captain 1st Vet. Inf. C. V., A. A. A. General.

HEADQUARTERS DEPARTMENT OF NEW MEXICO,
SANTA FE, N. M., December 5,. 1863.
COLONEL:

As I have before written to you, I have not authority to grant you a leave, but it is important that before long we have a consultation about further operations against the Navajoes. Therefore, as soon as you have secured one hundred captive Navajo men, women, and children, you will turn over the command of the troops and post of Fort Canby to Captain Carey, United States army, and come with those captives to Santa Fe. You will take all captives which may then be at Fort Wingate, and bring them in as well.

Major Sena, with Captain Pfeiffer, and Lieutenant Abeyta and Dr. Short, may come as part of the escort to the Indians.

It is desirable that you go through the Cañon de Chelly before you come. It is also desirable that you try that murderer and have your court adjourn *sine die*. No other officers than those named will come with you. Captain Carey will be instructed to press the campaign against the Navajoes to the best of his ability while you are absent. If you have more than a hundred captives bring them all. Do not leave in Fort Canby, as servants or otherwise, one single Indian man, woman, or child of any tribe; and when you come by Fort Wingate, make a clean sweep of every Indian man, woman, or child, whether held as servants or otherwise, at that post. Please forward no more applications for leaves of absence.

I am, Colonel, very respectfully, your obedient servant,

JAMES H. CARLETON,
Brigadier General, Commanding.

COLONEL CHRISTOPHER CARSON,
Commanding Navajo Expedition, Fort Canby, N. M.

Official: ERASTUS W. WOOD,
Captain 1st Vet. Inf. C. V., A. A. A. General.

HEADQUARTERS DEPARTMENT OF NEW MEXICO,
SANTA FE, N. M., December 31, 1863.

COLONEL:

I regretted to hear that the Indians have run off thirty-eight of your best mules. It appears to me that if they prowl around your herds in this manner some stratagem might be used so as to decoy them to the neighborhood of a force strong enough to destroy them. It is hoped, hereafter, your command will be able to protect its own stock.

If Captain Carey can furnish mules to carry provisions for the expedition through the Cañon de Chelly, but not the men's blankets, you will not delay the expedition on account of lack of transportation. You will have the men carry their blankets and, if necessary, three or four days' rations in haversacks. The army of the Potomac carries eight days' rations in haversacks. Unless some fatigue and some privations are encountered by your troops the Indians will get the best of it.

Captain McFerran will soon send you some more mules. I sincerely hope we have had the last report of the Indians running off stock in the Navajo country.

Now, while the snow is deep, is the true time to make an impression on the tribe. You will give your chief quartermaster positive orders that, when expeditions leave Fort Canby for scouts, not to exceed twelve days, the men will be required to carry their blankets and greatcoats for the first eight days.

There is now a large party of citizens and Utes in the Navajo country after Indians. They started from Abiquiu.

I am, colonel, very respectfully, your obedient servant,

JAMES H. CARLETON,
Brigadier General, Commanding.

COLONEL CHRISTOPHER CARSON,
Commanding Navajo Expedition, Fort Canby, N. M.

Official: ERASTUS W. WOOD,
Captain 1st Vet. Inf. C. V., A. A. A. General.

1864

HEADQUARTERS DEPARTMENT OF NEW MEXICO,
SANTA FE, N. M., April 1, 1864.

COLONEL:

There are many Apaches returned from Chihuahua, and are now in the Mogollon and White mountains, at the head of the Little Colorado, due south of Fort Canby. A few days since they stole seventy mules and horses from one of our trains at Cow Springs. Is it possible for you to send a force of one hundred picked men into these mountains, to scout for them, for, say, fifty days? If so, do it at once. Two parties will be out from Craig, and two others from McRae, and one from the Mimbres. You will find some Navajoes in that way who have stock. The men should take mainly cattle or sheep on the hoof for food, a very little flour and sugar and coffee and salt. This is the way they will go from the other posts: as light as possible; as silently as possible; with spies well to the front; with flankers; with a few men secreted in camps to ambush Indians following the trail.

I think you overrate the numbers of the Navajoes. Get all the information you can from prisoners, Zuñi Indians,

Moquois, of where they are; have this written down, and the probable numbers. We will then see what the chiefs at the Bosque say. Some of those we can then get for guides, and lay all our plans understandingly. You can send on 7,500 Navajos, including what we have. That number we can feed.

* * * * * *

Respectfully, I am, Colonel, your obedient servant,

JAMES H. CARLETON,
Brigadier General, Commanding.

COLONEL CHRISTOPHER CARSON,
Commanding Navajo Expedition, Fort Canby, N. M.

Official: ERASTUS W. WOOD,
Captain 1st Vet. Inf. C. V., A. A. A. General.

HEADQUARTERS DEPARTMENT OF NEW MEXICO,
SANTA FE, N. M., April 8, 1864.

COLONEL:

I have noted what you have said about the rich Navajoes. If they can feed themselves you can send in even 10,000. If not, send in not over 8,000, including what we have. Those who have stock and can support themselves had better be told again that, if they come in, they shall have their own stock. If they compel us to force them in, we will have all we can take. I cannot believe but that 8,000 will cover all the tribe; and we can manage to feed that number. The Ricos can live on their stock at the Bosque as well as in their own country. Transfer your command to Captain Carey when you come in on the court that is to try Captain Everett.

I am, Colonel, very respectfully, your obedient servant,

JAMES H. CARLETON,
Brigadier General, Commanding.

COLONEL CHRISTOPHER CARSON,
Commanding Navajo Expedition, Fort Canby, N. M.

NOTE.— Captain Murphy can come. Captain Pfeiffer

must stay with his company. Send in Indians by every opportunity. If the Ricos come in soon they can plant some this year.

Official: ERASTUS W. WOOD,
     Captain 1st Vet. Inf. C. V., A. A. A. General.

HEADQUARTERS DEPARTMENT OF NEW MEXICO,
SANTA FE, N. M., September 18, 1864.
COLONEL:

I have received, through Brigadier General Crocker, United States Volunteers, a message from ·Mr. Lucien B. Maxwell that some two hundred or more Ute Indians, now near Mr. Maxwell's place on the Little Cimarron, are willing and anxious to go out on the plains and attack the Kiowas and other Indians now depredating upon our trains and killing our people who are en route to and from the States and New Mexico, provided that they, the Utes, can be furnished with some rations, ammunition, perhaps a blanket apiece, and provided they may have whatever stock or other property they may be able to capture from the hostile Indians alluded to. I desire that you proceed without delay to Mr. Maxwell's, and if a strong party of these Utes, say two hundred, are willing to go on the service alluded to, under your direction and command, I wish them to do so on the terms above indicated, except that if they capture from the Indians of the plains any stock belonging to the United States or to the citizens, such stock shall be restored to the rightful owners on the owners paying to the said Utes a fair sum for the recovery of the animals, which sum per head must be agreed upon between yourself and the said Utes before they start upon the expedition. All stock belonging to the hostile Indians themselves, and which has not been captured from the United States troops or trains, or from citizens, the Utes shall receive as their own in case they can take it from the said hostile Indians. It is important to have these Utes start at once in case they go at all, and I desire that you should lead them. There are fifty cavalry and thirty infantry at or near Cold Spring, under Captain Bergmann, and fifty cavalry and fifty infantry at the lower Cimarron Spring, under Major Updegraff, and a like force at the crossing of the Arkansas, under Captain Davis; there is also a company of infantry on the road near Gray's ranch.

Any one of these parties will cooperate with you on showing this authority to its commander.

In case the Utes will go, you will proceed to Fort Union and report to me the number and the length of time for which they should draw subsistence, etc. It is important that there be no unnecessary delay in this matter. It is believed that a demonstration of this kind, made at this time, will be productive of good results. The main object is to have the Utes commit themselves in hostility to the Indians of the plains, that there may be less chance for them to join in any league which the latter Indians may attempt to make for a general war by all the Indians between the mountains and the Missouri upon the whites.

Your knowledge of the haunts of the Indians of the plains, and the great confidence the Ute Indians have in you as a friend and as a leader, point to yourself as the most fitting person to organize, direct, and bring this enterprise to a successful issue.

I am, Colonel, very respectfully, your obedient servant,

JAMES H. CARLETON,

Brigadier General, Commanding.

COLONEL CHRISTOPHER CARSON,

1st Cavalry New Mexico Volunteers, Taos, N. M.

Official: ERASTUS W. WOOD,

Captain 1st Vet. Inf. C. V., A. A. A. General.

HEADQUARTERS DEPARTMENT OF NEW MEXICO,
SANTA FE, N. M., October 14, 1864.

COLONEL:

` I have received your letter of the 10th instant in relation to the Utes and Apaches. You will issue to the men of those tribes, who will be sure to go, one and a quarter pound of beef and one pound of breadstuffs per man, each day, and the necessary amount of salt. You will send to Fort Union for the salt and get the meat and breadstuffs from Mr. Maxwell. Captain Bell will write to you on the subject. The amount of issues must not exceed the number of your party. Send me an exact list of the number who will be sure to go. As soon as I get off the Arizona mail and make arrangements for Thompson's company and a train of supplies which are to go to Fort Whipple, I will commence the organization of your party. General Crocker writes that some of the Apaches from the Bosque will go. They are the best fighting Indians we have. It is possible you will not be able to get off quite so soon as we talked, as I may have to wait for Bergmann to come back. But this I shall know in two or three days, and will write you by mail. The guns, ammunition, blankets and shirts will be sent to you. At Taos we agreed on two hundred men and one hundred Indians as the strength of the party. You now say three hundred men. These I will try to raise, but the Apaches from Fort Sumner will have to be included. I will write by mail. Give me positive information of the number of Indians who will go. I believe you will have big luck.

Very respectfully, your obedient servant,

JAMES H. CARLETON,
Brigadier General, Commanding.

COLONEL CHRISTOPHER CARSON,
At Maxwell's, on the Cimarron, N. M.

Official: ERASTUS W. WOOD,
Captain 1st Vet. Inf. C. V., A. A. A. General.

HEADQUARTERS DEPARTMENT OF NEW MEXICO,
SANTA FE, N. M., October 20, 1864.

COLONEL:

I have just received your letter of the 18th instant. It is impossible for me to issue rations to the families of the Utes; I have not the means or the right. The Indian department should do this. If the Utes will not agree to remain in the field forty-five days they had better not go.

You will be informed what troops will form your command as soon as I can get an express from Sumner and Bascom replying to communications sent there some four or five days since. I approve of Lieutenant Haberkom's going with you if Colonel Selden can spare him. You can have Lieutenant Taylor for your commissary and quartermaster; I cannot conjecture why he expected to go. But he is a capable officer, and if he tries can be distinguished. Your Utes and Apaches should have sugar and coffee from Fort Bascom. I will try to get the Apaches, some fifty, to go with you from Fort Sumner. An order was given to the quartermaster's department for the blankets and shirts to be sent to you. It has doubtless been received at Fort Union. Call on Captain Shoemaker for the rifles; show him this letter as your authority. Send me an exact list of all you receive for the Utes. Talk with Captain Carey how few mules you will want to go from Maxwell's to Bascom. Reduce the number down to the lowest. Your own things which you may need at Bascom had better be sent to Fort Union to go down on a wagon.

In haste, respectfully, your obedient servant,

JAMES H. CARLETON,
Brigadier General, Commanding.

COLONEL CHRISTOPHER CARSON,
1st Cavalry New Mexico Volunteers, Fort Union, N. M.

Official: ERASTUS W. WOOD,
Captain 1st Vet. Inf. C. V., A. A. A. General.

HEADQUARTERS DEPARTMENT OF NEW MEXICO,
SANTA FE, N. M., October 23, 1864.

COLONEL:

Enclosed herewith please find General Orders No. 32, current series from these headquarters, which organizes an expedition under your command to proceed against hostile Kiowas and Comanches. As you see, I have given you more men than you asked for, because it is my desire that you give those Indians, especially the Kiowas, a severe drubbing. Enclosed is also a copy of a letter which I sent by mail to General Blunt. I do not wish to embarrass you with minute instructions. You know where to find the Indians; you know what atrocities they have committed; you know how to punish them. The means and men are placed at your disposal to do it, and now all the rest is left with you.

I need not repeat to you the orders given to all commanders whom I have sent out to fight Indians, that women and children will not be killed — only men who bear arms. Of course, I know that in attacking a village, women and children are liable to be killed, and this cannot, in the rush and confusion of a fight, particularly at night, be avoided; but let none be killed wilfully and wantonly.

We make war upon men who have murdered and robbed our people.

I have written to General Crocker that if thirty of the Mescalero Apaches wish to go under Cadetta, they can come to Bascom with Captain Fritz and join you there. In this case the general will give them a blanket and shirt apiece and arm them. They complain that their horses are poor. They will be told that they can get better ones from the Kiowas. You had better come at once to Fort Union and see everything started to suit yourself, and then return to Maxwell's and go on with the Utes. Remember to take everything from Union which you will require for packing, as at Fort Bascom you will find little or nothing belonging to the post for this purpose.

Should you get among the buffaloes you can stay out, if necessary, a much longer time than you otherwise could.

Be sure and take some spades and axes, so as to form an intrenched camp for wounded men, and supplies, if necessary.

I am, colonel, very respectfully,

Your Obedient Servant,

JAMES H. CARLETON,

Brigadier General, Commanding.

COLONEL CHRISTOPHER CARSON,

At Maxwell's Ranch on the Cimarron River, N. M.

NOTE.— I enclose a copy of a letter to Major General Blunt, dated the 22d instant.

Official: ERASTUS W. WOOD,

Captain 1st Vet. Inf. C. V., A. A. A. General.

HEADQUARTERS DEPARTMENT OF NEW MEXICO,

LAS CRUCES, N. M., December 15, 1864.

COLONEL:

I had the pleasure to receive your very interesting and satisfactory report of your battle with the Kiowas on 25th ultimo, and have sent a copy of it to the War Department.

I beg to express to you and to the gallant officers and soldiers whom you commanded on that occasion, as well as to our good auxiliaries, the Utes and Apaches, my thanks for the handsome manner in which you all met so formidable an enemy and defeated him. Please to publish an order to this effect.

This brilliant affair adds another green leaf to the laurel wreath which you have so nobly won in the service of your country.

That you may long be spared to be of still further service, is the sincere wish of your obedient servant and friend,

JAMES H. CARLETON,
Brigadier General, Commanding.

COLONEL CHRISTOPHER CARSON,
Com'dg Expedition against the Kiowa and Comanche Indians, Fort Bascom, N. M.

Official: ERASTUS W. WOOD,
Captain 1st Vet. Inf. C. V., A. A. A. General.

1865

HEADQUARTERS DEPARTMENT OF NEW MEXICO,
SANTA FE, N. M., May 4, 1865.

COLONEL:

I received your note of the 12th of April. It is my purpose to establish a camp of three companies during the summer at or near Cedar Bluffs or near Cold Spring, on the Cimarron route, to give assistance to trains en route to and from the States. I believe if you go upon duty at that point you will be able to have a talk with some of the chiefs of Cheyennes, Kiowas, and Comanches, and impress them with the folly of continuing this bad course. The troops would have been ordered out to that point before now, but the spring was so backward the grass would not sustain the animals. Pfeiffer, perhaps, may be spared to go. It would be well for you to get ready to go from Fort Union by the 20th instant.

Please talk with Colonel St. Vrain about purchasing the beaver skins for me.

Respectfully, your obedient servant,

JAMES H. CARLETON,
Brigadier General, Commanding.

COLONEL CHRISTOPHER CARSON, Taos, N. M.

NOTE — It would be well if Mr. Beuthner would send out

to your camp some necessaries to sell to your soldiers, and canned fruit, which would keep them healthy. Besides, he would sell much to passing companies and trains.

Official: ERASTUS W. WOOD,
        Captain 1st Vet. Inf. C. V., A. A. A. General.

HEADQUARTERS DEPARTMENT OF NEW MEXICO,
        SANTA FE, N. M., May 8, 1865.
COLONEL:

I received last evening your note of the 6th instant, and enclose herewith the order for your movement. In my opinion your consultations and influence with the Indians of the plains will stop the war. Be sure and move on the appointed day. I have full faith and confidence in your judgment and in your energy.

To have a fine camp, with ovens; a comfortable place for the sick; good store-rooms; some defences thrown up to prevent surprise; pickets established at good points for observation; hay cut and hauled to feed of nights or in case the Indians crowd you; large and well-armed guards, under an officer, with the public animals when herding; promptness in getting into the saddle and in moving to help the trains; a disposition to move quick, each man with his little bag of flour, a little salt and sugar and coffee, and not hampered by packs; arms and equipments always in order; tattoo and reveille roll-calls invariably under arms, so that the men shall have their arms on the last thing at night and in their hands the first thing in the morning; to have an inspection by the officers at tattoo and at reveille of the arms, and to see that the men are ready to fight, never to let this be omitted; to have if possible, all detachments commanded by an officer, to report progress and events from time to time — these seem to be some of the essential points which, of course, you will keep in view. If the Indians behave themselves, that is all the peace we want, and we shall not molest them; if they do not, we will fight them on sight and to the bitter end. The war is over now, and, if necessary, 10,000 men can at once be put into the field against them. Tell them this. It is a short speech, but it covers all the ground. You know I don't believe much in smoking with Indians. When they fear us, they behave. They must be made to fear us or we can have no lasting peace. They must not think to stop the commerce of the plains, nor must they imagine that we are going to keep up escorts with trains. We do this now until we learn whether they will behave or not. If they will not, we will end the matter by a war which will remove any further necessity for escorts. Keep up discipline from the start and all the time. After you have established your camp and got matters in training please report in full.

Very respectfully and truly,

JAMES H. CARLETON,
Brigadier General, Commanding.

COLONEL CHRISTOPHER CARSON,
1st Cavalry New Mexico Volunteers, Taos, N. M.

Official: ERASTUS W. WOOD,
Captain 1st Vet. Inf. C. V., A. A. A. General.

HEADQUARTERS DEPARTMENT OF NEW MEXICO,
SANTA FE, N. M., August 6, 1865.

COLONEL:

I had the honor to receive your letter of August 2, 1865, enclosing a letter to yourself from the Hon. J. R. Doolittle, United States Senate, chairman of the congressional committee to inquire into Indian affairs, and also enclosing two telegraphic despatches from the Secretary of War to Mr. Doolittle, with reference to holding councils with the Indians. Mr. Doolittle's letter, and Mr. Stanton's despatches, I herewith return for your guidance in your special mission upon the plains, made at the request of Mr. Doolittle.

Your knowledge of what Mr. Doolittle desires and hopes you will be able to effect with the Indians of the plains, which knowledge you have derived in conversation with that gentlemen, precludes the necessity of special instructions from me, indeed, in this matter, where, as I understand it, the great object to be had in view by yourself is to make preliminary arrangements, if possible, with the Comanches, Kiowas, and Cheyennes and Arapahoes, so that hostilities on their part will cease, and so that their chiefs and principal men will meet commissioners in council to make a treaty of peace. Your great knowledge of the Indians — your knowledge of what is desired on the part of the government — your knowledge of the danger to be apprehended that the Indians may believe our overtures proceed rather from our fears of them than from a sincere desire not to make war upon them on our part, unless they compel us to do so — your knowledge of how to talk with them, so that they may not suffer from any such delusion — these considerations you understand so much better than myself, that it is unnecessary for me to give you, or attempt to give you, any instructions in the case.

I wish you to keep a journal of each day's march, and of each day's events, and of what Indians you meet. Please report your talks with them, and all they say in reply. This information is required for the War Department.

If you go by Fort Bascom, you have my authority to take Mr. DeLisle, the guide at that post, with you. He knows well the country between the Canadian and the Arkansas rivers.

Please look well to the country you pass over, with an eye to the site of a large post to be built in the place where the Kiowas and Comanches spend their winters — a ten-company post, with six of the companies cavalry.

I enclose herewith the order for your escort, and for Adjutant Tanfield to join you. That you may have good luck and return in health and safety, is the earnest wish of your sincere friend,

JAMES H. CARLETON,
Brigadier General, Commanding.

COLONEL CHRISTOPHER CARSON,
Fort Union, N. M.

Official: ERASTUS W. WOOD,
Captain 1st Vet. Inf. C. V., A. A. A. General.

V

THE NAVAJO CAMPAIGN : Kit Carson Reports, Reports of Captain Pfeiffer and Captain Carey, Report of General Carleton.

HEADQUARTERS, NAVAJO EXPEDITION,
CAMP AT PUEBLO COLORADO, N. M., July 24, 1863.
To the A. A. Adjutant General, Hdqrs. Dept. of N. M.,
Santa Fe, N. M.

SIR:

I have the honor to report that in obedience to General Orders No. 15, current series, Hdqrs. Dept. of N. M., I left camp near Los Lunas, N. M., July 7, 1863, en route to Pueblo Colorado, N. M., with Companies " D," " K," " L " and " M," 1st Cav. N. M. Vol., the only companies of the expedition which had arrived at the place of rendezvous up to that time.

I arrived at Fort Wingate on the 10th inst., where I remained three days, receiving supplies and some necessary articles of outfit for my command.

Having ascertained that there were two trains with supplies for my command shortly to arrive at this post, I directed that Companies " B " and " C," 1st N. M. Vol., should remain at the post until their arrival, to escort them to the Depot. They have not yet joined.

Left Fort Wingate on the 14th and arrived at Ojo del

Oso on the night of the 16th. Owing to a scarcity of water on the route my animals suffered a good deal, and many of the mules were completely broken down and unable to travel; I therefore concluded to give them a rest, and remained in camp on the 17th, 18th and until 2 o'clock p. m. on the 19th inst. There were two small fields of wheat near the camp, which I had fed to the animals on the 17th. I found some wheat at a spring about two miles west of the camp, which I sent for. The wheat found at the camp and at the west spring amounted to about forty thousand pounds, and with the grass, which at this place was abundant and of good quality, put my animals in good condition.

I was joined at this place on the 19th by Capt. Carey, Chief Quartermaster, and Lieut. Cook, Chief Commissary, with a supply train, escorted by Capt. Sena's Company ("C"), 1st N. M. Vol., but as his animals also needed rest I left him behind for this purpose.

I arrived with my command at Fort Defiance on the 21st inst., where I found a large quantity of wheat — say one hundred thousand pounds, which was also fed to the public animals. The Utah Indians, that preceded me on this day's march, killed one man (Navajo) and captured twenty sheep. Shortly after camping I was joined by nineteen Ute warriors, who had been operating against the Navajoes on their own account. They report having met a party of Utes returning to their country having eleven captives (women and children) and that there are two other parties now in this country. They themselves saw no Navajoes. I have hired five of the party as spies.

I remained at Fort Defiance on the 21st. On the 22d I left for this place with the board appointed to select a site for Fort Canby, taking with me the Field and Staff and 70 men of the command, and the Ute Indians. About one-third the distance from Defiance I left the command and pushed on with the Utes. When about nine miles from this point, and on the Rio de Pueblo Colorado, we came on a small party of Navajos and killed three men. From a Pah-Ute woman captured I ascertained that a strong party of Navajoes, with a large herd of sheep, cattle and horses, were at a pond of water about 35 miles west of here, and would remain there all night. I immediately determined to pursue them with the command as soon as possible after its arrival. It reached here about 5 o'clock p. m. and at 7:30 p. m. I started. At 5 o'clock next morning (23d) I arrived at the water, only to find that the Navajoes with their stock had left the previous evening.

I followed their trail for two hours, and until many of the horses had given out, and only returned on my own conviction, supported by the superior knowledge of Kan-a-at-sa, that it would be impossible to overtake them without to travel some ninety miles without water, and this my horses could not do.

On my return route the Ute Indians killed eight Navajoes, making a total of twelve killed since my arrival in this country.

I arrived at this place with the party yesterday evening, at 5 o'clock, having been nearly thirty-six hours continuously in the saddle.

The remainder of the command left behind at Fort Defiance arrived here yesterday at 4 o'clock, in the afternoon, also Capt. Carey and Lieut. Cook.

I would respectfully call the attention of the General commanding the Department to the valuable services rendered by the Ute Indians, and earnestly request that I may be authorized to send an officer to their country to employ at least thirty more Utes as spies for the expedition.

I am, Captain, very respectfully,
Your most obedient servant,
C. CARSON,
Colonel 1st Cav. N. M. Vol., Commanding.

Camp at Pueblo Colorado, N. Mex., July 24, 1863.
Dear General:

I send by Captain Cutler the official report of the operations of my command since leaving Los Lunas, but in it have made no mention of the women and children captured by the Utes (4 women and 17 children). It is expected by the Utes, and has, I believe, been customary, to allow them to keep the women and children and the property captured by them for their own use and benefit, and as there is no other way to sufficiently recompense these Indians for their invaluable services, and as a means of insuring their continued zeal and activity, I ask it as a favor that they may be permitted to retain all that they may capture. I make this request the more readily as I am satisfied that the future of the captives disposed of in this manner would be much better than if sent even to the Bosque Redondo. As a general thing, the Utes dispose of their captives to Mexican families, where they are fed and taken care of, and thus cease to require any further attention on the part of the Government. Besides this, their being distributed as servants through the Territory causes them to lose that collectiveness of interest as a tribe which they will retain if kept together at any one place. Will you please let me know your views on this matter as soon as possible, that I may govern my conduct accordingly?

The Utes more than come up to the expectations I had formed of their efficiency as spies, nor can any small straggling parties of Navajoes hope to escape them. I trust you will grant me permission to send Captain Pfeiffer to their villages to employ some more of them. I am very badly off for guides, and intend to employ some Zuni Indians as such in a few days, when I shall visit their village.

The Navajoes have planted a large quantity of grain this year. Their wheat is as good as I have ever seen. Corn is rather backward, and not so plentiful.

I have directed Major Cummings to send out a party to-morrow to bring in all the grain on this creek, which will amount to over 75,000 pounds of wheat and a large amount of corn. The latter, when dried, will answer for fodder for the animals in the winter. I would have permitted all the grain in this vicinity to have ripened, but that it is hoped you will change the location of the depot, there being neither grass, timber, nor anything like a sufficiency of water any place in this neighborhood for this purpose.

I forwarded with Captain Cutler the resignations of Chaplain Taladrid and Captain McCabe, and request that you will accept them, as well as all others which I may forward to you, as I do not wish to have any officer in my command who is not contented or willing to put up with as much inconvenience and privations for the success of the expedition as I undergo myself. I respectfully urge that, in the event of your accepting the resignation of Captain McCabe, Lieutenant Brady be promoted to the vacant captaincy.

Respectfully yours,

C. CARSON,
Colonel First New Mexico Volunteers.

BRIG. GEN. JAMES H. CARLETON,
Commanding Department of New Mexico, Santa Fe.

HEADQUARTERS NAVAJO EXPEDITION,

CAMP AT PUEBLO COLORADO, N. MEX., August 19, 1863.
CAPTAIN:

I have the honor to report that on the 5th instant I left my camp, 7 miles south of Cañon Bonito, with companies B and H, First New Mexico Volunteers, dismounted, and D, G, K, and M, mounted (total strength, twelve companies, and 4 field and staff officers, and 333 enlisted men), on a scout for thirty days.

Companies G and H arrived at Defiance on the 2d instant

with their horses in very poor condition. Those of Captain Pfeiffer's company (H) were so broken down that I was reluctantly obliged to dismount his men, and leave his horses at Defiance to recruit. All of my animals showed plainly the want of grain, none of which they have had since leaving the Rio Grande, excepting such as was found growing — the property of the Navajoes.

After leaving camp, I took a direction south, toward Zuni, intending to visit that village, procure some guides, thence to scour the country to the Moqui and Oribi villages, and return by the Cañon de Chelly. When about two hours from camp, we found and destroyed about 70 acres of corn. Three hours afterward encamped in wheat and corn fields. The wheat, about 15 acres, was fed to the animals, and the corn, about 50 acres, was destroyed. Sent Sergeant Romero, of Company D, with 15 men after 2 Indians seen in this vicinity. He captured one of their horses. Distances between camps, about 15 miles.

On the night of the 4th instant, I detached Captain Pfeiffer, with Lieutenant Fitch, with 100 enlisted men, 25 of whom were mounted, and the Ute Indians, to examine the country to the right and left of the line of march.

On the 6th, after traveling about 17 miles, I found part of his detail encamped, having in charge 11 women and children, 5 of whom were taken by Captain Preiffer's detail, besides a woman and child, the former of whom was killed in attempting to escape, and the latter accidentally, and 100 head of sheep and goats. When I arrived, Captain Pfeiffer, with the balance of his party, were out scouting. He returned about 12 o'clock at night with 2 children and 1 horse, captured. About an hour before reaching camp, found and destroyed 5 acres of corn.

Next morning I sent to Fort Defiance, with an escort of 10 men, the 7 prisoners captured by Captain Pfeiffer, with directions to the commanding officer to forward them by the first convenient opportunity to Fort Wingate, and to request the commanding officer of that post to forward them to Los Pinos. Continued the direction toward Zuni on the 7th, until, within about 15 miles from the village, we captured 5 Moqui Indians, who, when questioned, stated that there were Navajoes with large herds in the vicinity of their villages. I immediately changed the direction west for Moqui, and, after traveling some distance, encamped in a rain-storm.

On the 8th instant it commenced raining before we left camp, and continued steadily until 2 p. m.; at 1 p. m. we encamped. Distance traveled, about 18 miles. Shortly after leaving camp on the 9th, destroyed about 12 acres of corn, marched about 15 miles, and encamped. At 5 p. m. I left this camp with Companies D, G, and K, 75 men of Companies H and M, dismounted, and 30 mounted men of Company M, and the Utes. Took but 1 pack animal to each company, and three days' cooked rations for the men; the remainder of the pack animals were left with Captain Everett's company, to follow up next day. Marched all night, and arrived at 10 a. m. next morning at a cañon a little west of Moqui. Here the Utes took 2 women and 3 children prisoners, and Captain Berney's company (D) captured 25 head of horses; there were also captured 100 sheep and goats. While Captain Berney was after the horse herd, Captain Pfeiffer, with 30 cavalry, pursued and captured 1,000 head of sheep and goats; some of the Utes captured in the same vicinity 18 horses and 2 mules, and killed 1 Indian. Captain Pfeiffer severely wounded an Indian, but he contrived to secrete himself in the rocks.

The Utes here left the command to return to their homes, ostensibly because they could not get the herds captured by Captains Berney and Pfeiffer, as they stated that it was the understanding with the general that they were to receive all the stock captured during the campaign. The real cause, however, was the fact that they had now sufficient stock and captures. Marched about 3 miles farther west to spring in cañon, and encamped on table-land above; horses very much broken down. At retreat, Lieutenant Hubbell and a private of Company M are missing. Some Moqui Indians report the death of the Indian wounded by Captain Pfeiffer, and say that he was not only one of the most powerful, but the worst chief of the nation. I intended to remain at this camp on the 11th, but as Lieutenant Hubbell and the private had not yet come in, I made a detail of 50 men to accompany me in search of him. Just as I had the detail ready to start, an Oribi Indian brought me word that a party of Navajoes, with large herds, had passed their village, 12 miles distant, just as he left with the information. I increased the detail to 100 men, under Captain Thompson, who volunteered to accompany me, and followed in pursuit. I continued it a distance of 25 miles without overtaking them, when night came on; I could no longer keep the trail. I then encamped, and it being useless to continue the pursuit returned next day. During my absence, and while Major Morrison was in command, 7 public mules strayed from the camp and were taken by the Navajoes. On inquiry, I found that Major Morrison is blameless. The pack train arrived shortly after my departure from camp, as did also Lieutenant Hubbell and the soldier, the mules nearly broken down for want of water. On my return, I directed the command, excepting that portion which was with me, to proceed immediately to some springs, reported by the Indians as but a short distance off, the water at this camp having become insufficient. Next morning I proceeded to join them, and found them encamped in a cañon about 12 miles west of Moqui, where there was an abundance of good water and grass; fed to animals about an acre of corn found here. I laid over on the 14th to recruit my animals. At about 2 a. m. on the morning of the 15th, the camp was aroused by the whooping of a party of Navajoes, who made an unsuccessful attempt to drive off our herd. They retired after a few volleys from our pickets. Owing to the darkness, it is not known whether any of them were injured by our fire. After leaving this camp, took northeast direction, so as to strike this stream some distance south of the Pueblo Colorado. While en route on the 16th, destroyed about 50 acres of corn; several of my animals gave out and were shot.

17th — Sent a party this morning to bring in some packmules which were left behind yesterday. They returned this evening with the packs, and 1 woman captured.

This forenoon I arrived at this camp, rendered memorable by the death of the brave and lamented Major Joseph Cummings, who fell, shot through the abdomen by a concealed Indian. At the time of his death he was almost alone, having with him an unarmed citizen, and, having left the command some time previous, contrary to my positive instructions, his death is the result of his rash bravery. I sent his body to Defiance this morning. I sent, at dark yesterday evening (dismounted), two parties of 40 men each, to examine the country in the vicinity. Before leaving the valley, one of the parties captured a woman, who was sent into camp. This morning the parties returned without having seen any Indians.

Captain Deus captured 5 horses yesterday. To-day I have sent to Defiance to recruit all the animals unable to travel, retaining only about 60.

From all I could learn from the Moqui Indians, and the captives taken, the majority of the Navajoes, with their herds, are at the little Red River, and this is confirmed by my own observation. My next scout will probably be in that direction, and will, I trust, be more successful.

I am, captain, very respectfully, your obedient servant,

C. CARSON, Colonel Commanding.

CAPT. BENJ. C. CUTLER, A. A. G., Hdqrs. Dept. of N. M.

HEADQUARTERS NAVAJO EXPEDITION,
FORT CANBY, N. MEX., August 31, 1863.
CAPTAIN:

I have the honor to report, for information of the general commanding, that, on the morning of the 20th instant, the command left Pueblo Colorado, to make an examination of the country north of that place, including the neighborhood of the Cañon de Chelly. About 5 miles from camp found and destroyed about 10 acres of good corn; at the night camp, some 10 miles farther, found a patch of corn, which was fed to the animals.

On the 21st instant, returned on the route of the previous day, about 2 miles, to the Cañoncito de los Trigos, which I had explored the night previous. This cañon runs to northeast and southwest, with a small stream of clear water running through it; its sides are nearly perpendicular, averaging 150 feet high; its width about 300 feet; it is about 3 miles in length; found large quantities of pumpkins and beans, the latter quite ripe, and about 50 acres of corn. Left this cañon about 4 o'clock p. m., and returned to the camp of the 20th, taking with me packed on the animals all the grain not previously consumed by them or destroyed by the command. When leaving the cañon, I secreted 25 men, under Captain Pfeiffer, in two parties, believing that the Indians who owned this farm would return as soon as the troops had left. In this I was not disappointed, as but a short time elapsed before 2 Indians came to the fields. They were allowed to pass the first party, but, before getting in range of the second party, it fired on them. They were now between the two parties, when a chase ensued, and, although badly wounded, I am sorry to say the Indians escaped.

While en route on the 22nd, discovered the bodies of 2 Indians killed by a party of Utes some short time since. About 10 o'clock a. m., the command arrived at a large bottom, containing not less than 100 acres of as fine corn as I have ever seen. Here I determined to encamp, that I might have it destroyed. Just as the advance guard reached the cornfield, they discovered a Navajo, whom they pursued and killed. He slightly wounded 1 horse, with an arrow, in the neck. Lieutenant Fitch was in charge of the guard.

At 8 a. m. on the 23rd, arrived at the west opening of Cañon de Chelly, but could find no water; about 12 miles farther found abundance of running water and good grass, and encamped. I made a careful examination of the country on this day's march, particularly in the immediate neighborhood of Cañon de Chelly, and am satisfied that there are very few Indians in the cañon, and these of the very poorest. They have no stock, and were depending entirely for subsistence on the corn destroyed by my command on the previous day, the loss of which will cause actual starvation, and oblige them either to come in and accept emigration to the Bosque Redondo, or to fly south to Red River to join the wealthy bands now there. I am inclined to think they will adopt the first of these courses.

On the 24th, I encamped on a bottom of very fine grass, which my animals were very much in need of. My guide informed me that General Canby encamped here with his command for several days when on his campaign of 1860, at which time the Indians were very numerous and bold, coming in sight of the troops in large numbers on the high mesas to the left of the route. Now there is not one to be seen, nor has there been any in this vicinity for a long time.

On the 25th, changed the direction of the line of march to northeast; we had heretofore been traveling due north; marched 15 miles; good grass and water.

On the 26th, traveled about 12 miles in southeast direction over a fine stock-raising country.

On the 27th, about 12 miles from the camp of the previous evening, crossed the stream that runs through the eastern opening of the Cañon de Chelly; encamped on a branch of this stream 4 miles farther on. I am of the opinion that in a very short time both these streams could be turned off, were it necessary to do so, and thus compel any Indians who might take refuge in that stronghold to abandon it for want of water; general direction of this day's march east-southeast.

August 28, left camp at 6 a. m.; when about 7 miles out, I sent a detachment, composed of Companies D and H, to a wheat field 5 miles east of the line of march, where they killed an Indian; marched 3 miles farther and encamped; sent at night two detachments, one under Captain Everett toward Cañon de Chelly, and one under Lieutenant Dowlin to examine mountains east of the day's route; both parties returned next day. The party under Lieutenant Dowlin discovered 1 Indian mounted, but owing to the excitability of 3 of the men, he discovered the party in time to effect his escape; his horse was captured, having a wound in his back, caused by a ball passing through the saddle, and which, I think, must have injured the rider. Captain Everett saw no Indians or signs.

On the 31st, I arrived at this post.

On the 8th instant, an employe of the quartermaster's department at this post, named Hoffstetter, captured and brought into post an Indian, who stated that he came in to have a talk with his white brethren; his statement not being believed by the post commander, he was confined. While attempting to escape on the night of the 12th instant, he was killed.

I respectfully call the attention of the general commanding to Major Blakeney's report of the killing of 1 Indian and the capture of 3 others, 2 of whom escaped. From all I can learn, these Indians came in with a flag of truce, and I cannot but regret that they were not better received (when received at all), and kept until my arrival. The

Indian who was here on my arrival is about seventy years of age, and is called Little Foot. I have examined him, and he states that he came from the salinas southwest of Zuni to Chusco, where his people live, and that he came here to make arrangements to comply on the part of his people with the wishes of the general commanding, and that his people were destitute, and were ready to go to the Bosque Redondo, or anywhere else the general was disposed to send them. I believe him to have spoken in good faith, and have set him at liberty, giving him twelve days to return with his people, at which time he promises to be here.

In summing up the results of the last month's scout, I congratulate myself on having gained one very important point, viz., a knowledge of where the Navajoes have fled with their stock, and where I am certain to find them. I have also gained an accurate knowledge of a great portion of the country, which will be of incalculable benefit in our future operations. I have ascertained that a large party of Navajoes are on Salt River, near the San Francisco Mountains, among the Apaches, and within easy striking distance of Pima Villages.

I would respectfully suggest that a force operating against them from that point would greatly facilitate the entire subjugation of the Navajo nation.

I am about to send the command just returned to the camp 7 miles south of this post, where they will remain a few days to recruit their animals and refit, previous to proceeding to Red River.

Very respectfully,
Your Obedient Servant,
C. CARSON,
Colonel First New Mexico Volunteers, Commanding.

CAPT. BENJ. C. CUTLER,
Asst. Adjt. Gen., Hdqrs. Dept. of New Mexico, Santa Fe, N. Mex.

HEADQUARTERS NAVAJO EXPEDITION,
FORT CANBY, N. MEX., October 5, 1863.

CAPTAIN:

I have the honor to report, for the information of the general commanding, my arrival at this post to-day, off a scout of twenty-seven days.

On the 9th ultimo, I left camp at the Cienega Amarilla, 7 miles south of this post, with Companies D, G, H, K, L, and M, numbering 10 officers and 395 enlisted men and 192 horses.

On the 11th, I arrived at Zuni, where I met Surveyor General Clark and escort returning from the newly discovered mines. From Captain Pishon, First Cavalry, California Volunteers, who was in command of the escort, I learned that he had seen no fresh trails of Navajoes on the Little Colorado; but nevertheless I determined to examine that section of country, with a view to future operations, and hoping that by proceeding some distance below, where the road leaves the river, I might surprise some party, who, calculating upon the fact that no previous expedition had penetrated that portion of the country, would be there with their herds in fancied security. The Governor of Zuni furnished 3 men as guides to the river, and I was accompanied by 20 others, who desired thus to show their friendship to the whites and their enmity to the Navajoes. That they are not on friendly terms with the Navajoes, and are desirous to aid us in every possible manner, I am fully satisfied, not alone from their professions, but from having seen the dead bodies of some Navajoes, whom they had recently killed in an engagement, and from other facts which have come under my observation. They have a considerable quantity of corn, which they are willing to sell to the Government, and my chief quartermaster is making the necessary arrangements for its purchase.

I encamped 4 miles southwest of their village, and re-

mained in camp until 4 p. m. next day, when I started, traveling all night, and arriving at next water (Jacob's Well), 35
miles from Zuni, about 3 a. m. on the 13th.

The grass in this vicinity was not good, and in the afternoon I moved to a spring 9 miles farther. Before leaving
camp, I sent some infantry with the Zuni Indians to examine
the mountains south and east of our route. From these
springs the road to the Little Colorado leads for 30 miles
over the finest grass country I have ever seen; but there is
no permanent water.

Encamped about 7 p. m. on the edge of an arroyo, where
we found some water-holes: little water and very muddy.
Moved camp next day 2 miles to some more holes of same
description. Here I left the packs and infantry, under
Capt. F. McCabe, directing him to proceed to the river next
day, it being but 15 miles distant, while I proceeded with the
mounted men of my command to examine the country
northwest of our line of march. I left camp at sundown,
under the guidance of an enlisted man of Company M, who
professed knowing the country. About 10 p. m. found my
guide ignorant of our whereabouts, and encamped. About
4 p. m. next day, found some very muddy rainwater, and
encamped; about 40 miles since previous evening. I saw
no indications of Indians. On the 17th, joined the pack
train on the river, having marched about 35 miles. Learned
from Captain McCabe that the Zuni Indians had returned
to the village, having taken about 50 head of sheep and
goats from the Navajoes. The 3 guides returned with
them. On the 22nd, some fresh signs reported by my spies.
I sent forward in the evening Captains Pfeiffer and Deus
and Lieutenants Hodt, Hubbell, and Postle, with 126 enlisted men, with directions to march all night, so as to get
to the Rapids near daylight. I myself followed up next
morning with the remainder of the command. On the 24th,
was joined by Captain Pfeiffer's party. At the Rapids they

saw and pursued 7 Navajoes with about 15 horses; but, owing to the broken down condition of our horses, the Indians escaped. They captured 1 child. I examined the river thoroughly a distance of 85 miles from where the California road first strikes it, and am satisfied that no Indians have been on the river within this distance since last spring, excepting this party of 7 seen by Captain Pfeiffer. On the 25th, commenced our return march on the river. On the 27th, I selected the best of the animals (horses and mules), and, with 7 officers and 148 enlisted men, determined to explore the country from the Colorado north to Fort Canby.

The remainder of the command, under Capt. J. Thompson, I directed to return to the post by easy marches on the route we came.

Marched 15 miles up the river, and encamped until 6:30 p. m., when we left the river.

On the 30th, about 60 miles from the river, we arrived at our fourth camp of the previous scout, when en route for Moqui. At quarter to 7 a. m., on the 2nd instant, halted in a small cañon to breakfast, and to rest and water the animals. Saw fresh Indian signs, and had the country in the vicinity examined; discovered a small village, which had just been abandoned. This I had destroyed. We found in it 6 saddles and bridles, 1 rifle, some blankets and other property, which we destroyed. The parties I sent out captured 19 animals, part of which were wild mares; 7 of the latter got away, and, with my broken-down animals, I was unable to recover them. No Indians were discovered. Three men left the camp, without my knowledge, to hunt up the mules. They did not again join the command until its arrival at this post, where they arrived yesterday evening. They were attacked by a party of Indians when within 5 miles of this post, one of whom they killed. One of the men named Artin, a private of Company G, being a little in advance, was very severely wounded, though it is expected he will recover. The Indians captured his mule.

On the 3d of October, I arrived at the Jara, about 8 miles south of the Pueblo Colorado. Lieutenant Postle here discovered an Indian, whom he pursued with 6 men. Being in advance of this party, he overtook the Indian, whom he wounded in three places, when he was himself slightly wounded by the Indian.

Captain Thompson's command has not yet arrived, but it is expected on the 7th instant.

This scout, I am sorry to say, was a failure as regards any positive injury inflicted on the Navajoes; but the fatigues and hardships undergone by my command are fully compensated for by increased knowledge of the country, and of the haunts of the Navajoes with their stock.

I would respectfully call the attention of the general commanding to the fact that since leaving the river the animals of my command have had but five days' rations of corn; that since that time they have been almost constantly in the field, and operating in a country where grass has only been found at long intervals, and where the supply of water is uncertain and too irregular for marching columns. The only exception to this has been while east of Cañon de Chelly and on the Little Colorado; and that at no time since their arrival in this country have they been in an efficient condition for field service. The result of all this is, that I cannot again this winter take the field with a mounted force; and as I believe the animals to be too poor to stand the rigors of a winter at this place, I respectfully suggest the economy of having them wintered on the Rio Grande. I am now about to operate in detached parties on foot, which plan of campaign I shall continue during the winter. One party of 75 men will leave this post tomorrow morning.

Little Foot did not come in as promised, and I shall send a party immediately to hunt him up at Chusco.

I am, captain, very respectfully, your obedient servant,

C. CARSON,

Colonel First New Mexico Cavalry, Commanding Exped.

CAPT. BENJ. C. CUTLER,

    Asst. Adjt. Gen., Hdqrs. Dept. of New M., Santa Fe, N. Mex.

HEADQUARTERS NAVAJO EXPEDITION,

FORT CANBY, N. M., December 6, 1863.

CAPTAIN BEN C. CUTLER, A. A. GENERAL, HDQRS. DEPT. OF NEW MEXICO, SANTA FE, N. M.

CAPTAIN:

I have the honor to report for the information of the Department Commander, that on the 15th inst., I left this post with Co. C, D, G, H and L, 1st Cav. N. M. Vol., dismounted, for the purpose of exploring the country west of Oribi villages, and, if possible, to chastise the Navajoes inhabiting that region.

On the 16th I detached thirty men with Sergeant Andres Herrera, Company C, 1st Cav. N. M. Vol., on a fresh trail which intersected our route. The sergeant followed the trail for about twenty miles, when he overtook a small party of Navajoes, two of whom were killed, wounded two, and captured fifty head of sheep and one horse. En route the party came on a village lately deserted, which they destroyed. The energy and zeal displayed by the sergeant and his party on this occasion merits my warmest approbation.

On the 21st arrived at the Moqui village. I found on my arrival that the inhabitants of all the villages, except the Mibis, had a misunderstanding with the Navajoes, owing to some injustice perpetrated by the latter. I took advantage of this feeling and succeeded in obtaining representatives from all the villages — Oribi excepted — to accompany me on the war path. My object in insisting on parties of these people accompanying me was simply to involve them so far that they could not retract; to bind them to us, and place them in antagonism to the Navajos. They were of some service and manifested great desire to aid us in every respect.

While on this subject I would respectfully represent that these people, numbering some four thousand souls, are in a most deplorable condition, for the fact that the country for several miles around their villages is quite barren, and is entirely destitute of vegetation. They have no water for purpose of irrigation, and their only dependence for subsistence is on the little corn they raise when the weather is propitious, which is not always the case in this latitude. They are a peaceable people, have never robbed or murdered the people of New Mexico, and act in every way worthy of the fostering care of the Government. Of the bounty so unsparingly bestowed by it on the other Pueblo Indians — aye even on the marauding bands — they have never tasted. And I earnestly recommend that the attention of the Indian Bureau be called to this matter. I understand that a couple of years of annuities for the Navajoes not distributed are in the possession of the Superintendent of Indian Affairs at Santa Fe, and I consider that if such an arrangement would be legal, these goods should be bestowed on these people.

Before my arrival at Oribi I was credibly informed that the people of that village had formed an alliance with the Navajoes, and on reaching there I caused to be bound their governor and another of their principal men and took them with me as prisoners. From the Oribi villages I marched my command sixty-five miles, with but one halt of two hours, and at two o'clock a. m. on the 24th I arrived at a running stream — a tributary of the Little Colorado. Next day my command captured one boy and seven horses and destroyed an encampment. The mounted party while out scouting that day had two horses give out, and when the riders were returning to camp they passed three concealed

Indians, one of whom fired off his rifle *in the air,* and then rode towards them. On his approach the soldiers were going to shoot him, but owing to his gesticulating they allowed him to draw nigh. He had two rifles on his saddle, both of which the soldiers took, after which they allowed him to depart as he came. One of the rifles was recognized by the Moquisas as belonging to Manuelito, a chief of great influence. It is more than probable that the Indian, whoever he was, desired to have an interview with me, but was deterred by the hostile attitude of the soldiers.

On the 25th we captured one woman and child, about five hundred head of sheep and goats, and seventy head of horses, and destroyed another Indian encampment. There were five Indians with this herd, but on our approach they fled. About three miles from this encampment the spies gave us the information. The mounted party and a few of the officers immediately rode forward. Captain McCabe, Lieutenant Dowlin, Mr. J. C. Edgar, myself and Lieutenants Murphy and Montoya, with those of the mounted party, were the first to arrive at the herds, but only in time to see the Indians climbing the very steep sides of the Cañon of the Little Colorado where the herd was, and out of our reach. The conduct of the above named gentlemen on this occasion is worthy of commendation. Had our horses been in a fit condition there is no doubt but that we would have been enabled to overhaul these Indians, but they were unable to travel sufficiently quick, owing to the fact that they had been the three days previous without sufficient rest, and with but little grass. I encamped on the table lands of the river, and that night sent out spies, who, on their return, informed me Navajoes were in the vicinity.

At daylight next morning I sent out two parties of fifty men each under the command of Captains Pfeiffer and McCabe to examine the localities indicated by the spies as occupied by the Navajoes. The parties returned to camp late at night without having found any Indians, although they found every indication of where they had been recently. In some places the fires were still burning. From this place to where the Navajoes went is three days without water, as I am informed by a Mexican boy, taken captive some time since by the Navajoes, and recaptured by Captain McCabe. This my animals could not stand, and I was reluctantly obliged to let them go unmolested. Our camp of this day is about twenty-five miles northeast of the San Francisco Mountains.

On my return to Moqui I took a different route from the one I came, but on neither road is water to be found for a distance of fifty miles. While enroute on the morning of the third I discovered at a distance the smoke of an Indian encampment. I took with me the mounted party and fifty infantry, with the hope of being able to surprise them. After a rapid march of about eight miles we came to the valley, at the opposite side of which were the Indians, but, being obliged to descend a steep hill in view, the Indians, of which there were five, managed to escape. They left behind them their shields, clothing, etc., and we captured one horse and four oxen.

I arrived yesterday at the post and as soon as the animals are sufficiently rested I shall send a command to examine the Cañon de Chelly, and the smaller Cañons that intersect it. Were I not of the opinion that but few if any Navajoes are in the Cañon, I should have paid it a visit long since, but of that I convinced myself while in that vicinity in September.

To the Zuni Indians whom I employed as spies, I am greatly indebted for the zeal and ability displayed by them, particularly the Governors Mauana and Salvadore, the latter of whom acted as my interpreter with the other Indians.

The boy who was taken by us on the 24th I allowed to go off that he might communicate to the Navajoes the intentions of the general commanding in regard to them, of which I took particular pains to inform him.

It is quite possible that owing to the extended operations of our armies elsewhere, that those of my command may be overlooked, but I will venture to assert that no troops of the United States have ever been called upon to endure as much hardship as did the men of my command on this scout; and I am proud to say that all was borne with the utmost cheerfulness, both by officers and men.

I enclose herewith the report of Major F. T. Abreu, commanding Fort Canby, and sub-reports showing his operations at the post during my absence on scout.

I am, Captain, very respectfully,

Your most obedient servant,

C. CARSON,
Colonel 1st Cav. N. M. Vol., Commanding.

HEADQUARTERS NAVAJO EXPEDITION,
FORT CANBY, N. M., December 20, 1863.
CAPT. BEN C. CUTLER, A. A. GENERAL, HDQRS. DEPT.
OF NEW MEXICO, SANTA FE, N. M.
CAPTAIN:

I respectfully represent that unless some measures are taken outside of this command the express between this post and Fort Wingate will be very likely to cease running. The chief quartermaster has but one or two animals fit for this purpose, and I do not feel myself justified in ordering one or two soldiers on this very dangerous duty. The last express was attacked in the vicinity of the Ojo del Oso (Bear Springs), and, though he succeeded in making his escape unhurt, to render him again willing to take the risk it is necessary to give him such a compensation as will make it an object.

Captain Carey assures me that he has used every endeavor to hire a citizen or two for this purpose, at good wages, but he could not succeed. I therefore respectfully ask that he be authorized to pay a compensation to the soldier who may be found to carry the express. This I understand was done under like circumstances in the Florida war, and by General Canby during the late invasion of this Territory by the Texans.

If the chief quartermaster has a sufficient number of mules in good order an ambulance with sufficient escort could be used for the purpose.

Until the action of the General commanding is made known, the officers of the command have agreed to subscribe from their pay a sufficient compensation, and I trust that speedy measures will be taken to relieve them from an expense not expected of them by the Government.

I am, Captain, very respectfully,

Your most obedient servant,

C. CARSON,

Colonel 1st Cav. N. M. Vol., Commanding.

HEADQUARTERS NAVAJO EXPEDITION,

FORT CANBY, N. M., December 26, 1863.

CAPTAIN B. C. CUTLER, A. A. GENERAL, HDQRS. DEPT.

OF NEW MEXICO, SANTA FE, N. M.

CAPTAIN:

I have the honor to report for the information of the General commanding that I have made all the necessary arrangements to visit the Cañon de Chelly and will leave this post for that purpose with my command on the third or fourth of next month. To enable me to do this I will be compelled to use the ox train en route to this post with Company E to transport my stores to the west end of the cañon, where I shall establish a depot from whence to operate. I will send a command to the east opening to cooperate with that at the west. This command I will be able to furnish with pack animals.

The command sent out under Major Jose D. Sena returned, I am sorry to say, without having overtaken the Indians. I respectfully transmit his report.

I have in the field at present two parties of fifty men each operating in the vicinity of the Mesa la Vasca, where I have good reason to believe there are Indians, whom I trust will be captured.

In the last few days we have had a considerable fall of snow, which shall greatly facilitate my operations against the Cañon de Chelly. Of one thing the General may rest assured, that before my return all that is connected with this cañon will cease to be a mystery. It will be thoroughly explored, if perseverance and zeal with the numbers at my command can accomplish.

I am, Captain, very respectfully,

Your most obedient servant,

C. CARSON,

Colonel 1st Cav. N. M. Vol., Commanding.

HEADQUARTERS NAVAJO EXPEDITION,

FORT CANBY, N. M., January 23, 1864.

CAPTAIN BEN C. CUTLER, A. A. GENERAL, HDQRS. DEPT. OF NEW MEXICO, SANTA FE, N. M.

CAPTAIN:

I have the honor to report for the information of the General commanding that on the 6th inst., I left this post on an expedition to the Cañon de Chelly with 14 commissioned officers and 375 enlisted men. Owing to the depth of the snow on the mountains which divides the valleys of this section with those of the Pueblo Colorado, it took my command three days to reach that place, a distance heretofore accomplished in one day. While enroute on the 8th inst. my escort killed one warrior. On my arrival at the Pueblo Colorado, I was joined by the ox train and its escort under Major Jose D. Sena, which I had sent forward on the 3rd with the expectation that he would have time to recuperate his animals before the arrival of my command. In this I was disappointed, as it took his command five days to make twenty-five miles, and with a loss of twenty-seven oxen. This made it necessary for me to lighten the loads and leave one wagon, to enable me to accomplish my object, which I did, leaving behind ten days' rations for my command and twenty-five men as a guard.

On the 12th I arrived at the west opening of Cañon de Chelly. In the morning I made a detour to the right of the line of march with my staff and escort, and struck the cañon about six miles from the mouth. Wishing to reconnoiter a little previous to commencing operations, I proceeded up the cañon on the south side some four or five miles further, but could find no means of descending to the bottom of the cañon, the height of the sides averaging about one thousand feet and nearly perpendicular. I saw several Indians on the opposite or north side of the cañon, but out of range of our small arms. Shortly after my return to the camp, Sergeant Andres Herrera of Co. C, whom I sent out with fifty men the previous night, returned, bringing in two women and two children prisoners and one hundred and thirty sheep and goats, and having killed eleven Indians. As I expected, at daylight he discovered a faint trail, and following it up rapidly overtook the Indians as they were about to enter the Cañon de Chelly — when he immediately attacked them, with the result as above stated. This is the second occasion which I have had to record my sense of the energy and ability displayed by the Sergeant in the successful carrying out of my orders, and I respectfully recommend him to the favorable notice of the General commanding.

On the morning of the 13th I sent out two commands to operate on each side of the cañon, with three days' rations in haversacks. The first consisting of Companies

B and G, 1st Cav. N. M. Vol., under command of Captain A. B. Carey, 13th U. S. Infty., on the south, and the second command composed of Companies E and D, 1st Cav. N. M. Vol., under command of Captain Joseph Berney, 1st Cav. N. M. Vol., on the north side. I accompanied the former party, being very anxious about the safety of Captain Pfeiffer's command, whom I had sent out from Fort Canby to operate from the east opening, and wishing to gain a knowledge of the topography of the cañon, with a view to operating within it. I discovered the place where Sergeant Herrera had the fight the day previous. Found eleven dead bodies and five wounded (two mortally). The other three, though badly wounded, owing to the skill and care bestowed on them by Dr. Short, will no doubt recover.

On the 14th the command continued its march to a point whence a view of the cañon was unobstructed to near its eastern outlet; and being unable to discover any signs of Captain Pfeiffer's command, or any fresh sign of Indians, and there being no grass for the animals of my escort, I determined to return. I also satisfied myself of the feasibility of flanking the south side of the cañon from west to east, without much trouble, there being no intersecting cañons of any extent. On my return to the main camp on the evening of this day, I found to my great surprise and gratification, Captain Pfeiffer and his party in camp — having accomplished an undertaking never before successful in war time — that of passing through the Cañon de Chelly from east to west, and this without having had a single casualty in his command. He killed three Indians (two men) and brought in ninety prisoners (women and children). He found two bodies of Indians frozen to death in the cañon. I respectfully enclose his report (marked " A "), which is very interesting.

While enroute on my return to camp I was joined by three Indians with a flag of truce, requesting permission to come in with their people and submit. I told them, through my interpreter, that they and their people might come unmolested to my camp up to 10 o'clock a. m. next day, but that after that time if they did not come my soldiers would hunt them up, and the work of destruction recommence. Accordingly, next morning, before the time appointed, sixty Indians arrived. They had made known to them the intention of the Government in regard to them, and expressed their willingness to immigrate to the Bosque Redondo. They declare that owing to the operation of my command they are in a complete state of starvation, and that many of their women and children have died from this cause. They also state that they would have come in long since, but that they believed it was a war of extermination, and that they were agreeably surprised and delighted to learn the contrary from an old captive whom I had sent back to them for this purpose. I issued them some meat and they asked permission to return to their haunts and collect the remainder of their people. I directed them to meet me at this post in ten days. They have all arrived here according to promise, and many of them with others joining and traveling in with Captain Carey's command. This command of seventy-five men, I conferred upon Captain Carey at his own request, he being desirous of passing through this stupendous cañon. I sent the party to return through the cañon from west to east, that all the peach orchards, of which there were many, should be destroyed, as well as the dwellings of the Indians. I sent a competent person with the command to make some sketches of the cañon, which, with a written description of the cañon by Captain Carey, in the shape of a report (marked " B "), I respectfully enclose.

This evening (the 15th) Captain Berney returned with his command, having accomplished the object of his scout, with his usual energy and ability. His party surprised and killed two Indians and captured four.

Having accomplished all that was possible in this vicinity, I determined to return to Fort Canby for the purpose of being present to receive the Indians as they arrived, and take measures to send out expeditions in other directions, as I feel certain that now is the time to prosecute the campaign with vigor and effect: The speedy removal of all Indians north and west of the Little Red River.

On my first return to camp I was visited by four warriors, who stated that they came from the vicinity of the Juanica Mountains; that they had great fears of being killed on approaching our camp, but that their necessities overcame their fears. They say that many rich Indians would come, but that they were afraid. He who appeared to be the most intelligent I furnished with provisions, and evidence of his having been in my camp, and he willingly agreed to go to those Indians and assure them of the protection of the troops, provided that they came in with the bona fide intention of immigrating. At this camp I left the captives, with three companies and the ox train under Major Sena, and pushed ahead myself with two companies and the mule train. I directed Major Sena to remain four whole days at the Pueblo Colorado to recuperate his animals. He has not yet arrived.

I arrived at this post on the 21st inst., after an absence of sixteen days. I found on my arrival about one hundred and ten (110) Indians who accompanied Captain Carey's command. Since then several parties have arrived, until the number now drawing rations is one hundred and seventy (170). This does not include small children. I have been anxiously looking for a train which should have arrived here two days since. Should it not arrive by Friday, I shall send those Indians by transportation from the post. In summing up the immediate results of my operations on this expedition, I find: Killed, 23; prisoners, 34; voluntarily surrendered, 200 souls; captured, 200 head of sheep.

In addition we have thoroughly explored this heretofore unknown stronghold, and Cañon de Chelly has ceased to be a mystery.

But it is to the ulterior effects of the expedition that I look for the greatest results. We have shown the Indians that in no place, however formidable or inaccessible in their opinion, are they safe from the pursuit of the troops of this command; and have convinced a large portion of them that the struggle on their part is a hopeless one. We have also demonstrated that the intentions of the Government toward them are eminently humane, and dictated by an earnest desire to promote their welfare; that the principle is not to destroy, but to save them if they are disposed to be saved.

When all this is understood by the Navajoes generally, as it soon will be, and they become convinced that destruction will follow on resistence, then they will gladly avail themselves of the opportunities afforded them of peace and plenty under the fostering care of the Government; as do all those with whom I have had any means of communicating. They are arriving almost hourly, and will, I believe, continue to arrive until the last Indian in this section of country is enroute to the Bosque Redondo. The benefits to the Government, and the Territory, of the wise policy induced by the General commanding with regard to these Indians can not be too highly estimated. That any treaties hitherto made with the people — so long as they were permitted to remain in their country, were entirely disregarded so soon as the force applied to them was removed and both from inclination and from want they recommenced to murder and rob the citizens. The policy of placing them on a reservation changes all this. The force will still bear upon them; and their wants will be supplied, until such time as they by their industry are able to supply themselves.

In the accompanying communication from Captain A. B. Carey, Chief Quartermaster (marked " C "), you will perceive that Sgt. Martin Bird of Company K of my regiment has had a fight with a party of Navajoes at Ojo del Oso, in which he was successful. The conduct of the Sergeant is deserving of praise.

To the officers and men of my command I return thanks, for the zealous and efficient manner in which they have seconded my efforts on this, as on all previous occasions.

To Captain A. B. Carey, my chief quartermaster, I am greatly indebted not only for the able and efficient manner displayed by him in the management of his department, but for the valuable assistance on other occasions; as also to my Chief Commissary Lieutenant F. Cook, 5th Infty. U. S. A.

I am especially indebted to the zeal and intelligence of my acting Assistant Adjutant General, Lieutenant L. F. Murphy, 1st Cav. N. M. Vol., and I particularly recommend him to the favorable notice of the General commanding as a most efficient and energetic officer.

My thanks are due Surgeon A. F. Peck, and Assistant Surgeon J. H. Short, for their untiring attention to their duties.

' I am, Captain, very respectfully,

Your most obedient servant,

C. CARSON,

Colonel 1st N. M. Vol., Commanding.

HEADQUARTERS NAVAJO EXPEDITION,

FORT CANBY, N. M., January 23, 1864.

SIR :

I have the honor to report the arrival, late this evening, of Major Sena's command. He brought with him 344 Navajoes, including the 34 prisoners referred to in my report of this date. Cabara Blanco, a chief, and one of this party, assures me that Navajoes from various points, to the number of over 1,000, are en route to this post to emigrate. I have now over 500 Navajoes at this post, but shall have them en route to Santa Fe in two days at farthest. I do not think I am premature in congratulating the general commanding on the speedy and successful result of his measures to restore permanent peace and security to the people of New Mexico.

Very respectfully, your obedient servant,

C. CARSON,
Colonel First Cavalry, New Mexico Vols., Comdg.
ASSISTANT ADJUTANT-GENERAL,
Headquarters Department of New Mexico.

REPORT OF CAPT. ALBERT H. PFEIFFER

FORT CANBY, N. M., January 20, 1864.
SIR:

In pursuance to General Orders, No. 29, headquarters Navajo Expedition, dated January 2, 1864, I left Fort Canby, N. Mex., on the morning of the 6th instant, with Company H and 33 men of Company E First Cavalry, New Mexico Volunteers, en route for the east opening of Cañon de Chelle.

On the first day I marched to the wheat fields, but saw nothing unusual or of importance; distance traveled 9 miles. On the 7th instant marched to the second hay camp, a distance of 16 miles. During the journey I saw a few Indian tracks and sent Lieut. C. P. Ortiz with a party of men to reconnoiter, and see if he could discover any Indians or overtake them, if discovered. Snow about 6 inches deep, and hard marching for the men (having had to pack their blankets and overcoats from the time they started until they met the main body of the expedition), which they endured with heroic resolution. On the 8th, I marched about 10 miles, to a creek near the Cienego Juanico. As we approached the mountain range the snow became deeper and the marching more irksome and fatiguing. On the 9th, with the snow very deep, I traveled about 10 miles. On the 11th, marched about 11 miles, to the east entrance of Cañon de Chelle, where we encamped. During the trip, on account of the deep snow, which increased in volume as we journeyed along, and which had fallen to the depth of 18 inches or 2 feet deep, I lost the trails several times, which somewhat impeded the march. Having observed a smoke in the distance I dispatched Sergeant Trujillo, of Company H, with 15 men, to discover, if possible, the locality from which the smoke arose. He returned and brought back with him 8 Indian prisoners (women and children) in an almost famished condition. It being severely cold two of my men had their feet frozen.

On the 11th, I divided my command into three parties, with an advance guard of 15 men, with picks and shovels, as pioneer sappers and miners, the main body and my animals being in the rear guard. To each party I assigned a lieutenant (Lieutenants Hubbell, Ortiz, and Laughlin), with instructions to keep as closely connected as possible, and to move as one body, my presence being required at the most dangerous points, where I could move free and observe the stratagems of the concealed foe. My travel through the cañon, for the first 12 miles, was accomplished on the ice of the bed of the stream which courses through it. During the passage of the cañon I observed plenty of oak, cotton-wood, and scrub-oak, which grew on both sides on the mountain's declivity, the hillsides at the entrance and for the first 12 miles jutting down almost perpendicular to the level of the cañon, which was very narrow and confined to the channel of the creek. The advance party on that day, under Lieutenant Laughlin, who volunteered to take precedence, caught 4 prisoners. Lieut. C. M. Hubbell, who was in charge of the rear, had a great deal of trouble in proceeding with the pack trains, as the mules frequently broke through the ice and tumbled down with their loads. All the Indian prisoners taken thus far were half starved and naked. The cañon has no road except the bottom of the creek. We traveled mostly on the ice, our animals breaking through every few minutes, and one mule split completely open under the exhausting fatigue of the march. On the 12th instant traveled about 8 miles; had several skirmishes with the enemy. Indians on both sides of the cañon whooping, yelling, and cursing, firing shots and throwing rocks down upon my command. Killed two buck Indians in the encounter and 1 squaw, who obstinately persisted in hurling rocks and pieces of wood at the soldiers. Six prisoners were captured on this occasion. Lieutenant Hubbell followed up some Indians in a tributary cañon, but could not overtake them on account of the steepness of the hillsides, where nothing save an Indian or a mountain goat could make their way. I encamped that evening in a secure place, where plenty of wood was to be obtained — the remains of the old Indian lodges. Here I saw several castles or villages, one of which I named Castle Carey, in honor of Capt. A. B. Carey, chief quartermaster of the expedition, which was located high up among the rocks, solidly built, and remarkable for its substantial and beautiful masonry, and denoting taste on the part of the rude barbarians, where most probably some of the chiefs of the tribe resided in the summer, the village being inaccessible to the footprints of the white man; and near to it in the cañon was a large orchard of peach trees, but on account of the fighting and the necessity of being on the constant lookout I was unable to destroy them. From this point westward the cañon widens, the rocky precipice being about 1,200 or

1,500 feet high. At some places it spreads out like a beautiful savanna, where the corn-fields of the savages are laid out with farmer-like taste, and supplied with acequias for irrigation. At other places the cañon is confined to a narrow compass in a zigzag, meandering course, with high projecting rocks and houses built thereon, perforated with caverns and mountain fastnesses 300 or 400 feet above the ground as hiding places. Here the Navajoes sought refuge when pursued by the invading force, whether of neighboring tribes or the arms of the Government, and here they were enabled to jump about on the ledges of the rocks like mountain cats, hallooing at me, swearing and cursing and threatening vengeance on my command in every variety of Spanish they were capable of mastering. A couple of shots from my soldiers with their trusty rifles caused the red-skins to disperse instantly, and gave me a safe passage through this celebrated Gibraltar of Navajodom. At the place where I encamped the curl of the smoke from my fires ascended to where a large body of Indians were resting over my head, but the height was so great that the Indians did not look larger than crows, and as we were too far apart to injure each other no damage was done, except with the tongue, the articulation of which was scarcely audible.

On the 13th, traveled about 10 miles, making 30 miles in all — the whole length of the cañon, more or less — according to my estimate of distances. As I proceeded west the cañon became more gently sloping and spreading out wider, but mostly overflowed by the river, which runs in a westerly direction and rises and sinks every few alternate miles until it disappears in the bosom of the earth. At the mouth of woman) under a flag of truce — Drapeau Blanc, Drapeau Lous, Tache — arrived and saluted me. I received them kindly, friendly, and frankly, and treated them accordingly until Major Sena arrived, to whom I turned them over with the flag. Colonel Carson arrived the same day, and my mission was ended. Prisoners captured, 19.

In conclusion, I have to observe that my thanks are due to Lieutenants Hubbell, Ortiz, and Laughlin,* and the men of my command, who obeyed orders with alacrity, for the signal aid they rendered me on the trying occasion, they having all determined to perish or force their way through this strong defile, which they gallantly accomplished without loss of life or limb.

I am, sir, very respectfully, your most obedient servant,

A. H. PFEIFFER,

Captain, First Cavalry, New Mexico Volunteers.

LIEUT. LAWRENCE G. MURPHY,

Acting Assistant Adjutant-General, Navajo Expedition.

———

REPORT OF CAPT. ASA B. CAREY

FORT CANBY, N. M., January 21, 1864.

SIR:

I have the honor to report that, in compliance with orders received from the colonel commanding Navajo expedition, on the 16th instant I left the west opening of Cañon de Chelle in command of Capt. A. H. Pfeiffer's company (H, First Cavalry, New Mexico Volunteers), and detachments

* This Lieutenant "Laughlin" afterward became the veteran, Joseph Loughran, prominent in G. A. R. circles, and (1911) long employed in the Bureau of Pensions, Washington. — E. L. S.

attached, on scouts against the Navajo Indians. I marched up the main Cañon de Chelle a distance of 4 miles, to a point where the cañon branched, the north branch running about five degrees north of east, the south branch nearly due east. As I was totally unacquainted with the country, I was undecided which of the cañons to follow, but on consulting Captain Pfeiffer I found that the north branch was his route from the east end. A knowledge of this almost unknown stronghold of the Navajoes being a valuable acquisition for future operations, I decided to travel the south branch. After marching up the cañon for 2 miles, several Indians were discovered on the north side, on the cliffs almost immediately above us, and beyond rifle-shot. I halted for the purpose of ascertaining if the side of the cañon could be ascended, but found it impossible. In the meantime the number of Indians on the rocks above us increased, and by signs and gestures indicated that they desired to come to me. I had with me a Navajo Indian, and through him I communicated to them that if they desired to come to me they could do so, when I would make known to them the intentions of the department commander concerning them. They then told me they would come into the cañon at a point higher up. I resumed my march, and at 4 p. m. encamped in a wide bottom, each side of the cañon being about 300 yards from my camp, and the estimated height of the sides 1,000 feet. The distance marched this day I estimated at 18 miles, and over a good trail.

The Indians in the mean time had followed my line of march, and soon came into camp in large numbers, and were disposed of in such manner as to prevent injury to my command should they prove treacherous. That night I counted 150 full-grown Indians in my camp, besides many children. I informed them of the humane intentions of the department commander concerning them, and that a full and complete submission to his wishes were required, and that under no other circumstances would they be treated with, except as enemies to be fought. They then said they surrendered themselves to me, and would accompany me wherever I desired, but many wished to return to their homes in the mountains to collect and bring in their families. I gave all who desired to leave free permission to do, stating to them that within ten days they must report themselves with their families at Fort Canby. They seemed well pleased, and many left stating that within the time indicated they would comply with my directions. On the morning of the 17th instant I resumed my march and marched about 2 miles in the cañon, when I commenced the ascent to gain the table-land on the south side of the cañon by the only practicable trail leading out of this branch. The trail was very difficult, and I found it necessary to unpack my mules in order to enable them to go up the trail, the men carrying the loads. After leaving the east opening of the cañon, I marched in a direct line for this post over a broken country covered with pine and piñon, very little grass and no water. Snow from 6 to 8 inches deep, making it hard marching for the men. Encamped at 4:30 p. m. in a large, open bottom; very good grass, but no water. The distance traveled about 20 miles. On the 15th instant I resumed my march, and at 3 p. m. arrived at this post. My route the first 10 miles was through pine forest, the snow from 1 foot to 18 inches deep, and covered with a broken crust not sufficiently hard to bear up the weight of a man, which made the marching exceedingly hard. No water on the line of march until I arrived at a point known as Ewell's hay camp, about 10 miles from the post, where grass and water are abundant.

I have the honor to state that I brought into this post 105 full grown Navajo Indian prisoners, besides some children, and since my arrival they have been coming in parties of from 3 to 10, following up my line of march. In marching through this cañon, celebrated for its length and depth and for being an almost impregnable stronghold of the Navajoes, I made such observations as my limited time and duties would permit. The main cañon commences on the west of the Pueblo Colorado Mountains, and runs almost due east, with one short side cañon on the south and two on the north. The average width of this I estimated at about 800 yards, and no permanent water within 2 1-2 miles of its mouth, and no land which has ever been cultivated. At the point where the main cañon branches the streams of the north and south cañons unite, and seem to be permanent. I was informed by all the Indians I questioned that the south branch is the main cañon, and from the point where the north and south branches separate to the only practicable point of exit I estimated at 22 miles. From the point where the north and south cañons branch the average width of the south cañon was about 600 yards, though at some points it is not more than 50 yards in width, and the estimated height of the sides from 1,000 to 1,500 feet of perpendicular, and in many cases overhanging, rocks. The number of side cañons on the south are three and on the north five, which do not, as far as I could observe, extend more than about 1,000 yards on the south, but the north branches are much longer. At points in this branch of the cañon where it widens I saw signs of extensive cultivation of both wheat and corn. The water appears to be permanent, and from the signs which I observed in spring time a large amount of water must flow through this cañon. The only timber growing in this branch is cotton-wood and box-elder. This cañon is practicable for wagons to the point where the trail commences, a distance of about 22 miles from the west end. I have the honor to inclose herewith views of the east and west openings, and view at my camp, 18 miles from the west opening, executed by Sergeant Van Reen, of Company C, First Cavalry, New Mexico Volunteers.

To the officers and men of the command are due my

thanks for the manner in which they performed their duties while under my orders.

I am, sir, very respectfully, your obedient servant,

A. B. CAREY,

Captain, Thirteenth Infantry, Commanding Scouts.

LIEUT. L. G. MURPHY,

Acting Assistant Adjutant-General, Navajo Expedition.

CARSON FINAL CAMPAIGN REPORT

HEADQUARTERS NAVAJO EXPEDITION,

FORT CANBY, N. M., April 10, 1864.

GENERAL J. H. CARLETON, COMD'G DEPT. OF NEW MEXICO,

SANTA FE, N. M.

GENERAL:

I have the honor to acknowledge the receipt of your communication of the 1st inst., a copy of which I respectfully enclose as you requested.

On the 13th inst. I shall send from here all the Indians who may be here at that time. I have now here two hundred and sixteen. As they are poor the sooner they go to work to raise grain the better.

I have unofficially learned that Captain McCabe lost while en route by desertion one hundred Indians, headed by a son of the late Chief Juanico; cause, want of sufficient to eat. I would respectfully suggest to you the propriety and good feeling of giving to the Indians, while at Fort Canby and Wingate, and while en route to the Bosque Redondo, a sufficiency to eat. It is here and when en route that we must convince them by our treatment of them of the kind intentions of the Government towards them, otherwise I fear that they will lose confidence in our promises, and desert also.

As suspicion enters so largely into the composition of the Indian character the greatest possible care must be taken not to awaken it by acts contrary to the promises. I think one pound of beef or of flour, wheat or corn, as entirely too small an allowance for an able bodied Indian for one day.

The strength of this command for duty is nine officers and two hundred and seventy-three enlisted men. Of this number one officer and thirty soldiers are in the field as a protection to the Navajoes enroute from south of the Red River against attacks from the Pueblo Indians or the Apaches. There is also a force at the herd camp. All the available transportation at the post will be sent away on Wednesday with the Navajoes then here; and an escort will leave to accompany it; it will, therefore, be impossible for me, at present, to send a force against the Apaches.

I presume you have not received my last letter relative to the strength of the Navajoes, when yours of the 1st inst. was written. All the information which I can collect on the subject confirms my belief that we have not as yet *one-half* the tribe at the Bosque Redondo. I have no exact information as to their actual numbers, nor can this information be got from either the prisoners, the Zuni or the Moqui Indians, all of whom I have questioned; nor can I point out their exact locality; but I know the section of country which they inhabit, and were it necessary I think I could very easily find them. I do not think, however, that it will be necessary to go after them, as I am satisfied that they will all come in of their own account, as soon as they can. The vigor and energy which has characterized this campaign has fully convinced them of the folly of further resistence; and the hostility of the Pueblo and surrounding tribes of Indians, warn them that their only security is in that protection which the Government offers them.

I have the honor to enclose a list of the Navajo Chiefs

who signed the Treaty of Peace made with them by General
Canby, with such remarks opposite each as I have been
able to collect. It is probable that Herrera Grande may be
able to tell you the number of each Chief's followers, and
so arrive at an approximation of their strength.

The wisdom of removing the Navajoes from this country
cannot be too highly appreciated, nor do I think that any
better location could be found for them than their present
Reservation. Aside from the fact that there is no one
place in this country sufficiently large, combining all the
requisites of fuel, water and productiveness of soil for a
reservation — the permitting them to remain in their own
country would have the same effect as a treaty of peace
and the experience of the last one hundred and eighty years
has proven the worthlessness of such treaties, and what
little attention has been paid to them by these savages.

I am, General, very respectfully,

Your most obedient servant,

C. CARSON,

Colonel 1st Cavalry, N. M. Vols., Commanding.

GENERAL CARLETON REPORT

HEADQUARTERS DEPARTMENT OF NEW MEXICO,
LAS CRUCES, N. M., February 7, 1864.

GENERAL:

I have the honor herewith to enclose a copy of the report
of Colonel Christopher Carson commanding the expedition
against the Navajo Indians, of his success in marching a
command through the celebrated *Cañon de Chelly*, the great
stronghold of that tribe, and of the killing of twenty-three
of the warriors and the capture of a large number of prisoners. These prisoners are now en route to the Bosque
Redondo.

This report is accompanied by reports of Captain Asa B. Carey, United States army, and of Captain Albert H. Pfeiffer, of the 1st cavalry New Mexico volunteers, marked B and C. I also enclose a copy of a letter from Colonel Carson, written subsequent to his return to Fort Canby.

It will be seen by these papers that the operations of the troops during the severely cold weather has been of the most praiseworthy character, and been crowned with unparalleled success.

This is the first time any troops, whether when the country belonged to Mexico or since we acquired it, have been able to pass through the Cañon de Chelly, which, for its great depth, its length, its perpendicular walls, and its labyrinthine character, has been regarded by eminent geologists as the most remarkable of any " fissure " (for such it is held to be) upon the face of the globe. It has been the great fortress of the tribe since time out of mind. To this point they fled when pressed by our troops. Colonel Washington, Colonel Sumner, and many other commanders have made an attempt to go through it, but had to retrace their steps. It was reserved for Colonel Carson to be the first to succeed; and I respectfully request the government will favorably notice that officer, and give him a substantial reward for this crowning act in a long life spent in various capacities in the service of his country in fighting the savages among the fastnesses of the Rocky mountains.

Captain Asa B. Carey, of the United States 13th infantry, the chief quartermaster of the expedition against the Navajoes, volunteered for this march, and, as usual with this gallant and energetic officer, was particularly distinguished. I hope the government will reward him with the compliment of a brevet. He is entitled to a brevet for his gallantry in assisting the intrepid Captain William H. Lewis, United States 5th infantry, who burnt the Texan train in Apache cañon on the 28th of March, 1862, and richly deserves that and also a brevet for his distinguished services in the operations against the Navajoes. I am sure the government will not be unmindful of the labors of these officers and the brave soldiers who followed them, even though the field of their operations is far removed from the more important and brilliant events of the great war.

Sergeant Andreas Herrera, of company C, 1st cavalry New Mexico volunteers, it will be seen, has again distinguished himself, and it affords me great pleasure to call attention to his name.

I believe this will be the last Navajo war.* The persistent efforts which have been and will continue to be made can hardly fail to bring in the whole tribe before the year ends. I beg respectfully to call the serious attention of the government to the destitute condition of the captives, and beg for authority to provide clothing for the women and children. Every preparation will be made to plant large crops for their subsistence at the Bosque Redondo the coming spring. Whether the Indian department will do anything for these Indians or not you will know. But whatever is to be done should be done at once. At all events, as I before wrote you, " *we can feed them cheaper than we can fight them.*"

I am, general, very respectfully, your obedient servant,

JAMES H. CARLETON,
Brigadier General, Commanding.

BRIGADIER GENERAL LORENZO THOMAS
Adjutant General U. S. A., Washington, D. C.
Official: ERASTUS W. WOOD,
Captain 1st Vet. Inf. C. V., A. A. A. General.

---

* General Carleton and Kit Carson were correct in this opinion. The subjugation of the Navajos was so complete that they never again have given the government any trouble. In 1868 they were returned to their cañon country, and there have prospered as an independent pastoral people. — E. L. S.

VI

THE KIOWA-COMANCHE EXPEDITION: Carson's Official
Report on the Battle of Adobe Walls.

HEADQUARTERS KIOWA AND COMANCHE EXPEDITION,
CAMP ON RITO BLANCO, 100 MILES EAST OF FORT BAS-
COM, Dec. 4, 1864.
CAPTAIN:
I have the honor to submit for the information of the
general commanding the following report of my operations
against the Kiowa and Comanche Indians:
I arrived at Fort Bascom, N. M., on the 10th ultimo,
with seventy-five Ute and Apache Indians.   At this place I
found all the companies composing the expedition in read-
iness to move at any moment.   I left Fort Bascom on the
12th ultimo with the following force, viz, Captain Fritz's
Company (B, First Cavalry, California Volunteers), 30
men; Lieutenant Heath with a detachment of Company K,
First Cavalry, California Volunteers, 38 men; Captain
Deus' company (M, First Cavalry, New Mexico Volun-
teers), Lieutenant Bishop and 69 men; Captain Berney's
company (D, First New Mexico Volunteers), 39 men;
Lieutenant Edmiston, with 58 men of Company A,
First Veteran Infantry, California Volunteers, and Lieu-
tenant Pettis, with 27 men of Company K, First Infantry,
California Volunteers, and two mountain howitzers.
The Infantry force was commanded by Lieut. Col. F.
P. Abreu, First Infantry, New Mexico Volunteers, and the
Cavalry by Maj. William McCleave, First Cavalry, California Volunteers.   This force was accompanied by
seventy-five Ute and Apache Indians, in charge of Lieut.
Charles Haberkorn, First Cavalry, New Mexico Volunteers,
whom I took with me for that purpose.   Lieut. J. C. Edgar
accompanied me as act'g assistant adjutant-general of the

expedition. Lieut. B. Taylor, First U. S. Infantry, as acting assistant quartermaster, and acting commissary of subsistence, and Asst. Surg. George S. Courtright, U. S. Volunteers, as surgeon to my command. Total, 14 officers, and 321 enlisted men, and 75 Indians. [Carson seems to have omitted the Captain Witham company, named in general orders, which, counting sixty men, would bring his total to the 321 :-E. L. S.] This force was subsisted to include December 31, 1864. I deemed it proper to take wagons as transportation as far as a point known as the Adobe Fort, about 200 miles east of Fort Bascom, on the Canadian River, at which point I intended to form a depot and operate with pack mules. I considered that the number of pack saddles at my disposal (100) was insufficient to transport the necessary supply of subsistence to take me to the place where I expected to find an Indian encampment. Traveled by easy stages on a practicable wagon road along the north bank of the Canadian River, having to lay over for one day on two occasions on account of snowstorms. On the 24th ultimo, while encamped on a creek known as the Arroya de la Mula, about thirty miles west of the Adobe Fort, I dispatched two Indian spies with instructions to proceed a short distance down the Canadian, and return the same evening if they saw any fresh signs of Indians. They returned about one hour after sundown, and gave me information from which I concluded that there was a camp of hostile Kiowa and Comanche Indians in my vicinity. I immediately gave orders to have all the wagons loaded and left in charge of Lieutenant Colonel Abreu with the infantry and dismounted cavalry force, and I moved forward with my entire mounted force and Lieutenant Pettis' howitzers. I marched about fifteen miles that night, and again encamped and sent my spies ahead. They returned about two hours before daybreak, when I immediately took the saddle and continued my march down the river.

About one hour after daybreak on the 25th ultimo I discovered a party of Indians on the opposite bank of the river who were calling to me to come over. I ordered Major McCleave with Captain Deus' company to cross over and pursue them, and I continued my march along the river. Soon after I discovered an Indian encampment about five miles in advance. I immediately directed Captain Fritz to advance with his company and act in conjunction with Major McCleave, who was on the opposite bank of the river with Captain Deus' company. On hearing the report of firearms in front, I concluded that a fight had commenced and I directed Lieutenant Heath, with his detachment, to advance, and I followed as fast as possible with the artillery and Captains Witham's and Berney's companies. The Indians abandoned their camp of about 150 lodges, but hotly contested the ground between there and the Adobe Fort, a distance of about four miles. At this point they took a position and made a stand. They made several severe charges on Major McCleave's command before my arrival with the artillery and the other companies, but were gallantly repulsed. On my arrival on the ground I ordered the artillery to take a position, and the engagement ceased for a short time. Finding it impossible, on account of the broken down condition of my cavalry horses, to capture any more of the stock which the Indians had in their possession, I gave orders to unsaddle, and the men to have breakfast, it being my intention to return and destroy the Indian village through which I had passed. On looking through my glass I discovered a large force of Indians advancing from another village about three miles east of Adobe Fort. In this village there were at least 350 lodges. I immediately ordered the command to saddle and the companies to take position. In a short time I found myself surrounded by at least 1,000 Indian warriors mounted on first-class horses. They repeatedly charged my command from different points, but were invariably repulsed with great loss. The two mountain howitzers, under Lieutenant Pettis, did good service, and finally drove the Indians out of range. The Indians still remained in my vicinity and I conjectured that it was their intention to keep me in my position at the Adobe Fort if possible until night, that they might have an opportunity to carry off their lodges and provisions from their village, also some stock they had left behind them in their retreat. I therefore determined to return to the village and destroy it. I now gave orders for Captain Fritz to protect my right flank with his company, dismounted and deployed as skirmishers: Captain Witham's and a part of Captain Deus' company on the left flank, and Captain Berney's and Lieutenant Heath's detachment, and a part of Captain Deus' company in the same manner to protect the rear. In this manner I commenced my march on the village. The Indians, seeing my object, again advanced, with the evident intention of saving their village and property, if possible. The Indians charged so repeatedly and with such desperation that for some time I had serious doubts for the safety of my rear, but the coolness with which they were received by Captain Berney's command, and the steady and constant fire poured into them, caused them to retire on every occasion with great slaughter.

The Indians now finding it impossible to impede my march by their repeated charges, set fire to the valley in my rear, which was composed of long grass and weeds, and the wind being favorable it burned with great fury and caused my rear to close up at double quick. I immediately saw their object and had the valley fired in my front to facilitate my march. I then retired to a piece of elevated ground on my right flank upon which the grass was short, and upon which I knew I was out of danger from the fire. Here the Indians again advanced under cover of the fire and smoke which raged with great fury, but my artillery being in position they were again repulsed with great slaughter. The fighting was constantly kept up in rear until I arrived within 500 yards of the Indian village, when the Indians made a charge forward for the purpose of rescuing a part of their property. However, a few shells from my howitzers, which were immediately put in position, drove them yelling from the ground, and the entire village and stores were in my possession. I then proceeded to destroy the village and stores, amounting to about 150 lodges of the best manufacture, a large amount of dried meat, berries, buffalo robes, powder, cooking utensils, etc., also a buggy and spring wagon, the property of Sierrito, or Little Mountain, the Kiowa chief of the Indians which I engaged. The principal number were Kiowas with a small number of Comanches, Apaches and Arapahoes, all of which were armed with rifles, and I must say they acted with more daring and bravery than I have ever before witnessed. The engagement commenced about 8:30 a. m., and lasted I may say without intermission until sunset, during which time I had 2 soldiers killed and 10 wounded, and 1 Indian killed and 5 wounded, and a large number of horses wounded (see the inclosed list). It is impossible for me to form a correct estimate of the enemy's loss, but from the number which I saw fall from their horses during the engagement I cannot call it less than 60 in killed and wounded. I flatter myself that I have taught these Indians a severe lesson, and hereafter they will be more cautious about how they engage a force of civilized troops. The officers and men engaged acted with the utmost coolness during the fight and my entire command showed a promptitude in carrying out my orders on all occasions.

I take pleasure in bringing to your notice the names of the following officers, whose conduct during the fight deserves the highest praise: they are Major McCleave, Captain Fritz, and Lieut. S. Heath, First Cavalry, California Volunteers; Captains Deus and Berney, First Cavalry, New Mexico Volunteers. Lieutenant Pettis' howitzers were well served and did remarkably good service. Lieut. J. C. Edgar, First Cavalry, New Mexico Volunteers, acting assistant adjutant-general of expedition, was remarkable for his coolness and bravery during the engagement. I am endebted to Assistant Surgeon Courtright, U. S. Volunteers, for his prompt attention to the wounded of my command. The Ute and Apache Indians acted bravely during the day.

The Indians seeing their village in flames fled to the hills and gave me no further annoyance. I regret very much that the poor condition of my horses did not permit me to follow them and secure a large amount of stock which they had in their possession, also another large village which I could observe through my glass farther down the river. The company commanders now reported to me their ammunition was nearly expended. I deemed it prudent to return and join my wagons, which I directed to follow me slowly.

About 8:30 p. m. I came upon Colonel Abreu's command encamped with the entire train on a creek about ten miles west of the Adobe Fort. Here I also encamped for the night. In the morning I moved my entire command about 500 yards for the purpose of procuring better grass for my animals. I now decided that owing to the broken-down condition of my cavalry horses and transportation and the Indians having fled in all directions with their stock that it was impossible for me to chastise them further at present. Therefore, on the morning of the 27th ultimo, I broke camp and commenced my return trip. I have traveled by easy marches in order that I may take all my animals to the fort if possible, and I have arrived at this point without any incident worthy of note. I shall continue to travel slowly to Fort Bascom, where I expect to arrive about the 10th instant, and I will await there for further instructions from the general commanding.

I am, captain, very respectfully, your obedient servant,
C. Carson,
Colonel First Cavalry, New Mexico Vols., Comd'g.
Captain Benjamin C. Cutler,
Asst. Adjt. Gen., Dept of New Mexico, Santa Fe, N. Mex.

VII

Kit Carson on the Indian: In Response to a Circular of Questions, Sent by the Congressional Joint Commission to Various Authorities.

Fort Lyon, Colorado Territory, August 19, 1865.

Captain:

I have the honor to report, for the information of the department commander, that on leaving Taos for Fort Union, New Mexico, I mislaid a letter from him, containing certain interrogatories propounded by the Hon. J. R. Doolittle, U. S. Senate (chairman of congressional committee now making inquiries into Indian affairs), and requesting answers to the same. On arriving at Fort Union, my time was necessarily occupied in making preparations for special service on the plains, which it was important should not be delayed; no time was therefore left me to answer them from that post.

I now take the earliest opportunity to reply in a general manner to those points impressed upon my memory as the most important, from a careful perusal of the letter in question.

From a long-continued residence among, or in the immediate vicinity of Indians, and from a personal observation of their manners, habits, and customs, acquired both in private life and the transaction of official business as an agent of the federal government, I have been long convinced that the only rule that can be successfully applied for their governance is one firm, yet just, consistent and unchangeable; for the Indian, judging only by the effect of that which appeals to his senses, as brought directly before his observation, regards with contempt a weak and indecisive policy as the result of hesitation, fear, and cowardice, whilst a changeable and capricious one excites his apprehension and distrust. Both of these courses should be cautiously avoided.

The rule for the government of Indians should be strong enough to inspire their respect and fear, yet protecting them from both internal dissension and external aggression. This can only be effected by a military rule, and I am therefore of opinion that the sole control of the Indians should be vested with the War Department. As at present managed, jealousies among the employés of the different departments naturally exist, and they are too often actuated by feelings of prejudice, which result in a want of that harmonious co-operation of action in the execution of official duties, so necessary to effect successful results. Indian agents, appointed solely by political influence, are often swayed by feelings of personal gain in the transaction of their business, making the government appear to act in bad faith towards the savages; then making promises, impossible to fulfill, to shield themselves from attack, they excite feelings of hostility that can only be quenched in blood. To this cause, and that of repeated acts of aggression on the part of the numerous reckless frontiersmen that swarm upon the borders of the Indian territory, may be attributed many, if not most, of our recent Indian wars, massacres, and murders, extending from Minnesota to California.

The peculiarity of the Indians' position now calls for prompt, decisive, and energetic action. The old idea of forcing them westward is exploded by the discovery of the California gold-fields and rich mines of mineral on the eastern slope of the Sierra Nevada, alluring thither in constantly increasing numbers swarms of hardy adventurers. Instead of forcing them backwards before its steady advance, civilization now encircles them with its chain of progress, and each year, as it passes away, sees the chain drawing rapidly closer around the hunting grounds of the red men of the prairie. A short-sighted policy might infer from, and leave to, this cause their extermination. That it would be accomplished is certain, but humanity shudders at the picture of the extermination of thousands of human beings until every means is tried and found useless for their redemption, whilst high motives of right impel us, out of respect to ourselves and duty to the Indians, to protect our citizens, assist in the settlement of the almost unknown interior of our country, and relieve and assist whilst controlling the red men of the west, as their hunting grounds vanish before the sturdy energy of the pioneer and backwoodsman.

If placed on reservations, with wise rules enforced by military power, the settlers will be protected from their predatory raids, and they themselves be safe against the reckless injustice of those outlaws of society thronging upon the border, whose criminality has too often been the means of rousing the Indians to thoughts of vengeance, and carrying fire and desolation to many a homestead in the west.

Allow me to suggest the necessity of extreme caution and circumspection in locating Indians, to prevent internal dissensions, upon reservations. Different tribes, besides being of different degrees of advancement in civilization, have feuds of long standing to excite them, ambition of chiefs to satisfy, and long-cherished traditions of delayed revenge to gratify.

There is nothing inimical in the bold, courageous, marauding Comanche — the wild, treacherous, nomadic Apache — the hardy, industrious, agricultural Navajo, or the lazy, degraded, almost brutalized Digger. These tribes are types of the different North American Indians, and from these, or a more extensive list carefully prepared, classifications should be made to govern officers intrusted with their removal, for it is not probable that reservations can be set apart for each tribe; and where several are located together, the nearer their characters assimilate the greater will be the success, whilst the danger will decrease in the same proportion, for one wild tribe looks down on another with a contemptuous pride — strange to us, but perfectly natural to their untutored minds, as they possess a less degree of skill in the barbaric virtues of murder, violence, and theft.

The cause to which may be attributed the present rapid decrease of the Indians are continued cruel wars among themselves, prevalence of venereal diseases, and the inordinate use of intoxicating liquors. The first of these can alone be stopped by force, and, in order to pave the way for the success of any Indian policy, should be so stopped at once. The latter of these causes being due in a great measure to their intercourse with the white men, humanity and justice demand that prompt measures be taken to arrest their fatal progress.

The beneficial results derived from placing the Navajoes upon a reservation is a successful vindication of the policy, an example of the propriety of military rule, and appears to be actuated by feelings of humanity, charity, and sound political economy. A consideration of the latter question might seem more the province of the statesman than the soldier; but in deciding a policy that has at heart the welfare of hundreds of thousands of human beings, that seeks to convert them from fierce and reckless murderers to peaceful tillers of the soil, from a source of continued expense to one of actual benefit — to remove far from the white settler, and inspire confidence and respect in the savage, I am satisfied the teachings of experience will not be overlooked or even lightly regarded. Time must elapse ere really practical results can be derived from any Indian policy; but if the one so favorably commenced in New Mexico be carried into effect with other tribes, I am indulging in no chimerical or utopian idea in believing that in the next generation civilization can advance undisturbed into the vast interior of our country, whilst from the reservations the hum of busy, productive industry will resound, and the prayers of Christianity be heard from every tribe, and America stand proudly foremost among nations as the exemplar of mercy, humanity, and philanthropy, as she now does of civilization and progress.

Commanding officers of posts on Indian reservations should be *de facto* Indian agents; then representing the power of the government, by inflicting punishment for misdeeds, and being also dispenser of its benefits, they will be looked up to with increased respect and fear, whilst the benefit in a point of economy is undoubted. This system would seem to afford greater checks to the accomplishment of frauds, and greater facilities for their detection when perpetrated.

I am, captain, very respectfully, your obedient servant,

C. CARSON,

Col. 1st N. M. Cavalry.

CAPTAIN B. C. CUTLER,

Ass't Adj't Gen'l Dep't of N. M., Santa Fe, N. M.

VIII

MAJOR (BREVET LIEUTENANT-COLONEL) ALBERT H. PFEIFFER: His Famous Adventure, from Official Records and Personal Narrative.

(From Summary of Operations, Year 1863)

June 20. — Captain A. H. Pfeiffer, wife, and two servant girls, with escort of six men of the 1st New Mexico volunteers, were attacked by a party of Apache Indians, numbering 15 or 20, at a hot spring near Fort McRae. The captain was bathing at the time, when the Indians made a rush upon the party, killing two men, Privates Nestor Quintana and Mestas. Captain Pfeiffer was wounded in his side by an arrow, and Private Dolores received two shots in his right arm and hand. A citizen named Betts, who was with Captain Pfeiffer, was also wounded. The remainder of party, except the women, succeeded in reaching Fort McRae unharmed, and reported facts to Major Morrison, commanding post. He immediately started in pursuit, with 20 mounted men, but did not succeed in overtaking the Indians. Mrs. Pfeiffer and the servant girls were found in the trail, badly wounded. Mrs. Pfeiffer and one of the servants have since died; the other doing well. Loss in this affair, two privates killed; two women mortally wounded; one officer, one private, one woman, and a citizen wounded; seven horses and two mules taken by the Indians. Indian loss unknown.

———

(Personal Narrative; Overland Monthly, date ——)

The routine of army life and the monotonous march through the wilderness does not prevent a soldier making an interesting acquaintance now and then with prominent characters. Thus the writer was so fortunate as to fall in with two well-known frontiersmen, who happened to meet at Maxwell's while we were all enjoying that gentleman's hospitality. One of them was the famous Indian fighter Kit Carson, who had come down from his mountain home on a flying visit. His personal appearance differed very widely from the type usual among men of his kind and surroundings. His voice was quite mild and whoever looked at his smooth-shaven face and his hair combed down to his head would have taken him for a minister of the gospel, rather than for a man who had for many years been the terror of the Indians all over the western country, and on whom they looked even then, about two years before his death, with fear and awe.

The other man was Lieutenant-Colonel Pfeiffer, who had served in the regiment of which Kit Carson was colonel, and the two old soldiers hugely enjoyed meeting again on this occasion. Since the Indians were constantly on the warpath at that time, it was only natural that our conversation should turn on that topic. Colonel Pfeiffer was persuaded to relate an adventure, which he was rather averse to talk about, because it awakened the reminiscence of his wife's death. There was a military post by the name of Fort McRae, now abandoned, on the banks of the Rio Grande. It is a wild looking spot and a very dangerous one, because the Indians used it a great deal for driving their stolen cattle across the river, which is comparatively shallow and free from quick sand just at that point. The river describes a semi-circle about forty miles in diameter and on account of its banks being bordered by rocks, thick bushes, and ravines, the teams cannot follow its course in that neighborhood, but have to go across what is called the " Jornado del Muerte " (the Journey of Death). The road takes its name because so many horses and cattle and even men have perished there for want of water. The military and their trains used to take large transportable water tanks for the men along with them and travel at night, so as not to be affected by the heat. The animals however had to be unhitched while the soldiers were in camp and driven fourteen miles to the vicinity of Fort McRae and back again, merely in order to get a drink of water at the Rio Grande and thus be saved, if possible, from a miserable death.

There are hot spring within ten miles of Fort McRae and thither Colonel Pfeiffer went one day, with his wife and an escort of about twelve men. While he was bathing, his men were on the lookout for Indians, at the top of a rock about ten yards from the springs, but the Indians out-witted them and captured the lady, while he had just time to seize his rifle and wade across the river without a stitch of clothing on. Knowing the Indian character, he calculated that they would not kill his wife immediately, but take her to their hiding-places and make her do menial work. He therefore made for the Fort to give the alarm and send reinforcements. He was followed by the Indians, who sent arrows after him, one of which entered his back, with the end coming out in front. In this condition, and with the arrow in his body, he ran until he reached an enclosure of rocks, where he made a halt and defended himself for several hours, while the burning sun shone on his bare body, causing him intense pain. He was known by the Indians as an excellent marks-man and when they found that they could not get him out of his stronghold without losing several of their number, they gave up the siege. They had no sooner left than he ran for dear life to the Post, nine miles away, and at last reached it, more dead than alive. When the surgeons extracted the arrow the entire skin pealed off from his body, from the effects of the scalding sun, and he was at the point of death for nearly two months. His escort, meantime, went in pursuit of the Indians, who had captured his wife, and were almost within reach of them, when the savages, finding that the lady would be an encumbrance to them, killed her on the spot and took to the bushes.

IX

CARSON PERSONAL LETTER: To His Comrade Pfeiffer.
SANTA FE, NEW MEXICO, May 8, 1863.
DEAR PFEIFFER:

I received all of your letters, but have been so busy and have been knocking about so that I really had not an opportunity of answering them. I have made out, signed, sealed and delivered to Cap't Mink, the deed of the land made over to your boy, and I trust and believe that before he arrives at man's estate that it will be a fortune to him.* Should this news of the advance of the Texans be untrue, as I hope it is, we will all go to the Navajo country about the 1st of June. If it is true, I can't say what will be done with us. We are sure, in any case, to see active service soon, so try all you can to get your horses in condition to take the field. I leave here on Monday for Ft. Garland to see that Eaton has all he is accountable for, as he has been dismissed by the President. This I don't want you to tell any person until the order is published. I will stop a couple of days at Taos going and coming and this I am very glad of, as my family are not as well as I could hope. I hope, however, they will be well shortly. I have been making inquiries of every person who has seen you and they all tell me that your face is not yet well, and that you are again drinking. When will you have sense? Can't you try and quit whisky for a little while, at least until you get your face cured? If your face ain't well when I next see you, you had better look out. There is no news of interest from the States. But next mail we expect to hear of a big fight on the Potomac. Remember me kindly to Mrs. Pfeiffer, and remember also what I say about your drinking.

Yours truly,

C. CARSON,
Col. N. M. Vols.

---

* This was a generous, spontaneous act on the part of Carson. The son was still living (1912) on the Pfeiffer ranch in Colorado. However, the Kit Carson gift was hypothecated, after being made over, by the old major (then weakened in his mind), and long was the basis of an unsuccessful suit by the heirs, to recover. — E. L. S.

X

Merchant Beuthner to Camp Nichols.
Fernando De Taos, N. M., May 27, 1865.
Major A. H. Pfeiffer,
Cold Springs or Cedar Bluffs.
Dear Major:
Your very kind favor dated Fort Union, the 19th inst,
came duly to hand, and I was glad to learn of your safe
arrival at Union, and that everything was in readiness for
the Expedition. Since your departure from here there has
been no news of importance. No papers received by Denver
mail, and none by last mail, from States. I have just received a letter from Captain Bergman dated the 20th in
which he mentions Major Morrison having returned by
Bascom, having lost all and with a narrow escape of his
life, and thinks that the Indians will take the Fort before
many days. But Bergman says they have not yet taken
the Fort. I hear many reports about the Indians, also of
the Texans, who report says are about to pay us a visit, and
should they come, united with the Indians of the Plains, perhaps my friend Kit and yourself may find hot work and
may in all possibility with so small a force be obliged to take
the back track. It would be useless for you to contend
with a large force, such as rumor says are coming, but I
am confident that Gen. James H. Carleton is fully apprized
of all facts and has prepared himself for all emergencies,
and will no doubt send you reinforcements in ample time.
And I hope, should you meet with an engagement, that you
may come out victorious, and teach the Indians that they,
when fighting you and Kit, are not fighting with Colorado
Troops, or with troops that are afraid to give them fight.
Much is anticipated, by the friends of yourself and Kit, on
this campaign, in hopes that the result of the expedition will
be permanent peace with the hostile tribes of the plains.

My earnest wishes are that success may attend you everywhere, and that he who rules our destiny, may guide you safe and unharmed through the campaign, and be spared to return once more to the pleasant City of Fernando, where you will ever meet a welcome reception by your many friends and well wishers.

Camp life on the plains, may be considered very pleasant but I can assure you that I do not in the least envy your situation. Exposed to the burning hot sun, dust, hardships and fatigues on the road, and to wind up with an empty canteen is nearly discouraging, but so it goes sometimes. But I hope you were able to get a little of the real good stuff out of the Commissary before you left Union, as it is considered a speedy remedy in cases of Snake bites, and a few drops taken before breakfast is said to be healthy for the Stomach. Captain Joe Berney and Mr. Shelby arrived from the Ojo Caliente, they remained here several days, the Captain looks bad but says he is feeling better, they have gone to the Las Vegas Springs were [where] they can have better accommodations. Captain and Mr. Shelby both wish to be remembered to you and the Colonel. You must not forget to send me your recommendation so that I can attend to having it properly endorsed, etc., also do not forget to inform me if you have done anything with Mr. Labadie as regards the house, in case I get the appointment, etc., and if he will remain at Union as I expected to be there very soon. Please answer very soon and give me the particulars of the March, a description of your Camp and things in general. By next mail I will send later papers, etc.; I will also write to the Col. by this mail. With my very many regards to Col. Kit, and hoping that you are having a pleasant time and enjoying the best of health, I remain,

Truly yours, SOLOMON BEUTHNER.

NOTE. — Your family all well, and *comesta muncho.*

S. B.

XI

THE CARSON WILL: Probated October 6, 1868.
FORT LYON, PUEBLO COUNTY,
Colorado Territory, May 15, 1868.

I, Christopher Carson, a resident of Pueblo County, Colorado Territory, knowing the uncertainty of life, and being of sound mind, do make this, my last Will and Testament To wit:

First. It is my will that of my cattle, numbering from one hundred to two hundred head, such only shall be sold from time to time, as may be necessary for the support of my children, the balance to be retained, with the increase for the benefit of my children.

Secondly. It is my will, that my seven yoke of steers, and two ox wagons shall be kept by my administrator, for the use and support of my children.

Thirdly. It is my will, that my four horses and one carriage, shall be kept by my administrator for the use and benefit of my children.

Fourthly. It is my will that my house and lot, with all the improvements, in Taos, N. M., be sold by my administrator for a sum, not less than one thousand dollars, the proceeds to be used for the benefit of my children. If the property above mentioned will not bring the sum of one thousand dollars, it is my will that it be rented annually and the amount so received, used for the benefit of my children.

Fifthly. It is my will that my furniture in my house in *Taos*, N. M., be sold by my administrator and the proceeds used by him for the benefit of my children.

Sixthly. It is my will, that some two or three pieces of land, lying in the Valley of Taos, N. M., the titles to which are in my wife's name, be rented from year to year, to the highest bidder, and the sums so received be used by my administrator for the benefit of my children.

Seventhly. It is my will, that the accruing interest, at the rate of ten per cent per annum, on a promissory note for the sum of three thousand dollars drawn in my favor and signed by L. B. Maxwell of Cimaron, N. M., be paid to my administrator, the amount so received to be used by him for the burial expenses of myself and wife.

Eighthly. It is my will, that my administrator get security for the promissory note of three thousand dollars, drawn in my favor, and signed by L. B. Maxwell of Cimaron, N. M., and failing in that to collect the note, and loan the money on good security and at the highest rate of interest obtainable, the annual interest to be used by him for the support of my children.

Ninthly. It is my will, that any moneys which may be due me from Mr. Myer of Costilla, C. T., and Mr. Rudolph, the sutler of Fort Garland, C. T., be paid over to my administrator to be used by him for the support of my children.

Tenthly. It is my will, that any moneys that may be due from L. B. Maxwell for cattle sold to Mr. Frank Pape, be paid to my administrator, the amount so receivable to be used by him for the support of my children.

Lastly. I hereby appoint Mr. Thomas O. Boggs of Pueblo County, Colorado Territory, my administrator, to carry out the provisions of this my last will and testament.

C. CARSON.

Signed this 15th day of May One thousand eight hundred and sixty-eight in the presence of J. A. Fitzgerald, H. R. Tilton.

Recorded by M. G. Bradford, Probate Judge of Pueblo County, C. T., Oct. 6, 1868.

NOTES

CHAPTER II

1, p. 9. Williams' adventures, real and alleged, form the basis for the entertaining narrative of Coyner's *Lost Trappers*. A Carson appears to have been with Williams.

CHAPTER III

2, p. 16. Thomas J. Farnham's *Travels in the Great Western Prairies* (1839).

3, p. 17. Colonel Philip St. George Cooke's *Scenes and Adventures in the United States Army* (1859). As a subaltern, Colonel Cooke was upon the Trail, with the Colonel Henry Dodge expedition, in the summer of 1834.

4, p. 18. Farnham's *Great Western Prairies*.

5, p. 18. This anecdote has origin with Surgeon and Brevet Major Dewitt C. Peters, who was Carson's Boswell.

6, p. 20. The tale appears to be a fabric woven by Colonel Henry Inman for his *Santa Fe Trail*.

CHAPTER IV

7, p. 26. Capt. George F. Ruxton's *Adventures in Mexico and the Rocky Mountains* (London, 1847).

8, p. 30. Lieut. G. Douglas Brewerton's *A Ride with Kit Carson*.

CHAPTER V

9, p. 31. The Robidoux trading post was located, probably before 1830, just below the juncture of the Uncompahgre and Gunnison rivers, in Delta County of western Colorado. The town and stream of Robideaux commemorate the old trader. The ruins of the post, or of some Robidoux post, were seen by the Captain Gunnison party in 1853, on a point of land "between the Grand and Uncompahgra rivers." Dr. Marcus Whitman, in his sensational journey from Oregon to Washington, winter of 1842-43, seems to have gone from Fort Uintah (Winte), the northern Robidoux post of later origin, down to a Fort "Uncumpagra," where he procured a new guide, for Taos. The three Robidoux brothers — Antoine, Joseph, and Louis — form a trio of traders and trappers closely identified with the history of the beaver West. Antoine was more prominent in New Mexico and Colorado, Louis in California, where at the time of the American conquest he was *jues de pas* in San Bernardino (a mountain here today bears the name), and Joseph on the Missouri. A brief sketch of the family is given in Chapter XII, this book.

10, p. 33. General James F. Rusling's *Across America, or: The Great West and the Pacific Coast* (New York, 1874). Upon a tour of inspection of army posts General Rusling spent some time, fall of 1866, at old Fort Garland, where Kit Carson was in command.

CHAPTER VI

11, p. 43. The journal account of the Pattie wanderings was compiled (1833) by that pioneer Western biographer Timothy Flint into a volume, *The Personal Narrative of James O. Pattie of Kentucky,* which leads in *Americana* of the trap trail.

12, p. 43. Gen. J. H. Simpson's *Reconnoisances in New Mexico and Texas* (Philadelphia, 1852).

CHAPTER VII

13, p. 44. The rumor of a "white race" inhabiting the interior of the Southwest persisted long after its conception by the first Spanish explorers. Occasional fair skins and blue eyes are to be found among the Navajos, Zuni, and other Southwest peoples, but the swarthy skin and black eyes and hair predominate.

14, p. 46. Extract from the journal of Antoine Leroux, of Taos, who was a guide for Lieutenant A. W. Whipple, through the country, upon one of the Pacific Railroad explorations (Vol. 3, *Pacific Railroad Surveys.* Washington, 1856). Upon modern maps the San Francisco River is entitled the Verde.

15, p. 49. Lieutenant J. C. Ives' *Exploration of the Colorado River of the West* (Washington, 1861).

16, p. 50. *Exploration of the Colorado River of the West.*

17, p. 52. A sketch of this Jedediah Smith is given in Chapter XII, and in the appendix.

18, p. 53. Farnham's *Travels in California and Oregon.*

CHAPTER VIII

19, p. 54. These statistics, for the year 1829, are to be found in Chaplain Walter Colton's *Three Years in California* (New York, 1850). It is probable that they are accurate enough for the present purpose.

20, p. 57. The Cooper reference is found in H. H. Bancroft's volumes upon California, in the series, *History of the Pacific States.* Captain John R. Cooper, a Boston merchant skipper, sailed around to the California coast in 1823, and entered into trade relations there.

21, p. 57. The mission of San Rafael, instead of that of San Jose, is mentioned by some chronicles. The mission of San Rafael, north from San Francisco, would naturally be the one if the trappers' camp were upon the Sacramento.

22, p. 64. The Kit Carson biographer is here confronted by an anomaly hard to solve. The historian H. H. Bancroft, in his account (somewhat meager) of the Ewing Young visit to California, cites letters by Young and by *presidio* officials which bear the date 1830, and place the trouble at Los Angeles as occurring October, 1830, and not 1829. This would make the party spend two summers, instead of one, in California, and would bring them back to Taos in the spring of 1831. On the other hand, Carson consistently refers to 1829 as the date of his first visit to California; his subsequent adventures, if figured from his return to New Mexico in 1830, accord much better with actual events.

CHAPTER IX

23, p. 72. The original biography, claimed by Surgeon Peters to have been written from data dictated by Carson himself, makes him say that his initial trip into the mountains was under Thomas Fitzpatrick, the noted partisan or trapper leader. However, there is no record of Fitzpatrick, at this time one of the managers of the

Rocky Mountain Fur Company, having been at Taos in the summer or fall of 1830. Chronicles of the times indicate that he spent this summer and fall in the mountains. It may well be that the Carson party was recruited in Taos to join some detachment of the Rocky Mountain Fur Company over which Fitzpatrick had especial charge. The report also is persistent that young Carson's second trapping trip was directed into Colorado rather than into the Northwest. Says the biographical sketch in *General Scott and His Staff* (Philadelphia, 1848): "When seventeen years old he made his first expedition as a trapper. The party proceeded to the Rio Colorado (California), met with numerous hardships and adventures, and had several battles with the Indians. It returned, however, safely to Taos, New Mexico; and soon after 'Kit' joined another party, to visit the headwaters of the Arkansas." This, one of the earliest sketches of Carson, must be treated with consideration; and very likely the headwaters of the Arkansas may have been the first objective point. The term, in 1830, was indefinite.

24, p. 75. *Travels and Adventures of Dr. E. White and Lady, West of the Rocky Mountains,* compiled by Miss A. J. Allen.

25, p. 76. Colonel Philip St. George Cooke's *Scenes and Adventures in the United States Army: or, Romance of Military Life* (1856). Father DeSmet styles this rock "the Great Record of the Desert," and in 1841 engraved into it his name and the symbol "I. H. S." In 1842 Fremont, upon his first expedition, chiseled into it a cross, emulating (as he says) the act of the English voyager, Weymouth, on the coast of Maine, 1605.

26, p. 77. Dr. White *Travels and Adventures.*

27, p. 78. *What I Saw in California: Being the Journal of a Tour, by the Emigrant Route and South Pass of the Rocky Mountains, Across the Continent of North America, the Great Desert Basin, and Through California, in the Years 1846, 1847,* by Edwin Bryant, Late Alcalde of St. Francisco (New York, 1848).

28, p. 79. This was Hudson Bay Company territory; and the invasion by the party in question (if such invasion occurred) should be accounted a notable undertaking.

CHAPTER X

29, p. 81. There is no record of any party of Americans spending the winter of 1830-31 in the Nez Percé country. The Fitzpatrick-Bridger-Sublette brigade of the Rocky Mountain Fur Company, as claimed by Joe Meek, wintered on the Powder River in Wyoming. Kit Carson may have been mistaken in his recollection — especially as in the annals of the Rocky Mountain company the spring march did swing over to the Snake, thence south to the Bear, and the Green, and four men were killed, in the fall or winter, by Blackfeet.

CHAPTER XI

30, p. 95. A Mr. Thompson, surveyor in employ of the Hudson Bay Company, who thus communicated to Professor James Renwick, of Columbia College. See appendix of Irving's *Astoria*.

31, p. 98. This, and following references, are from Farnham's *Travels in the Great Prairies and in Oregon Territory*.

32, p. 101. I find this report in the *National Intelligencer* (Washington) for April 21, 1829; and it probably is incorporated among American State Papers or in the regular compiled proceedings of Congress.

33, p. 102. Letter to General Atkinson, quoted in Chittenden's *History of the American Fur Trade of the West* (New York, 1901).

34, p. 103. Letter to General Ashley, in Congress; quoted in Chittenden's *History of the American Fur Trade*.

35, p. 107. *Wild Scenes in the Rocky Mountains and the Grand Prairies*, by Rufus Sage (1846).

36, p. 108. Bonner's *Life and Adventures of James P. Beckwourth* (New York, 1856).

37, p. 109. Sage's *Wild Scenes, etc.*

CHAPTER XII

38, p. 111. That Jedediah S. Smith was a very real personage is evidenced by the relics which survived him. A niece has one of the dragoon pistols carried by him in his last fight, and recovered from the Comanches; another niece has a volume of a commentary on the Bible, from his library maintained at St. Louis. The journals of his California expeditions are extant. As he was one of fourteen children, he has numerous relatives living. When young Warner met him, just in by wagon train from the Yellowstone, at St. Louis, in November, 1830, "instead of finding a leather stocking I met a well-bred, intelligent and Christian gentleman, who repressed my youthful ardor and fancied pleasures for the life of a trapper and mountaineer by informing me that if I went into the Rocky Mountains the chances were much greater in favor of meeting death than of finding restoration to health, and that if I escaped the former and secured the latter, the probabilities were that I would be ruined for anything else in life than such things as would be agreeable to the passions of a semi-savage. He said that he had spent about eight years in the mountains and should not return to them." Nor did he return. The Warner account of his death states that after the caravan for Santa Fe had suffered great thirst, Smith the adventurous and fearless rode ahead, to search for what no trail, path nor guide supplied. " He did not return." But after the arrival, July 4, of the caravan in Santa Fe, Mexican traders brought in the rifle and pistols of Smith, which they had obtained from Indians near the Cimarron River. The Indians (Comanches) said that they had been in hiding by the pools of the Cimarron, waiting for buffalo; that a white man had ridden down, had watered his horse and had drank; and that while he was standing by his horse, about to remount, one of the Indians thrust him with a lance. Whereupon, ere falling, with a pistol the white man had shot one assailant dead. The pistols and rifle being percussion cap arms, the Indians could not use them. With the caravan were two of Smith's brothers; one of whom, Peter, described to his wife the tragedy, and the wife, when a widow, before her death wrote it out as she remembered. This narrative comes down to W. R. Bacon, Esq., of Los Angeles, whose wife was a daughter of Peter Smith and niece of Jedediah. Peter differs in his narrative from the narrative of Warner, in that he says Jedediah was thrust through the right arm by the lance, and killed with pistols and rifle three of the Indians, including the chief. And Peter further alleges that a party from the train went out and recovered the captain's body, which was buried at Santa Fe. (Article by J. M. Guinn, Esq., in *Southern California Historical Society Publications*, Vol. III, Part 4.) Much data compiled by Jedediah Smith, who was an educated man, were burned, as appears, by a storehouse fire just preceding his departure for Santa Fe. For fuller appreciation of his remarkable character the reader is referred to the appendix.

39, p. 112. William Waldo, Santa Fe trader and fur hunter of the twenties, refers to Milton Sublette as " the Thunderbolt of the Rocky Mountains," and states that in the summer of 1828, on the Santa Fe Trail, only the "skill and long experience of Milton

Sublette in Indian warfare" saved a little party of traders from certain death. "The life and adventures of Milton Sublette alone would fill a large volume. William L., Milton, Saul (i. e., Solomon), and Andrew Sublette were all early and noted mountaineers. William L. was a prudent, economical man, and died rich. The other three brothers were equally reckless of life and money."— (*Missouri Historical Society Publications,* II and III.)

40, p. 118. This biography of Meek (*The River of the West,* by Mrs. Francis Fuller Victor) has been frequently quoted in my pages. It is an excellent history of Oregon, and as a personal narrative presents a vivid picture of trapper days. But knowing Meek's waggish character and his great versatility, I have taken the liberty to query his "Umentucken Tukutey Undenwatsy" (alleged to be the name of his beautiful Crow wife, the "Mountain Lamb") and his "Shiam Shaspusia" ("Big Liar," name for himself). A reply from the Superintendent of the Crow Agency, Montana, evokes a smile — in which, I am sure, somewhere Mr. Meek joins. The reply: "I beg to say that I have submitted the linguistic curiosities contained in your letter to several Indians who would be good authority. There is no Crow word on the list. 'Shaspu-sia' means 'Cheyenne.' 'Shi-am' is Cheyenne for '*pounded meat,*' or *pemmican.* U-men-tuk-en is not recognized by Crows, Cheyennes or Sioux to whom I have put it. 'Tuk-u-tey' is Sioux for 'What is it?' 'Un-den-wat-sy' is not recognized by any of the three tribes mentioned."

41, p. 119. The *Folsom* (Calif.) *Telegraph* of October 28, 1871, states that Williams was killed in 1850. However, Ruxton's *Life in the Far West,* published in 1849, narrates of his death; and this would seem definitely to establish the date, inasmuch as he was with Fremont in November, 1848.

42, p. 120. See Ruxton's *Adventures in Mexico and the Rocky Mountains.* Ruxton passed through northern New Mexico a few months after the tragedies occurred.

43, p. 121. This name has given chroniclers much trouble. It comes out Robidoux, Roubideau, Roubideaux, etc. While it would seem that "Roubideau" conforms the closest to the French, as "Robidoux" is employed by H. H. Bancroft in his histories of the West, and by the Government in the granting of the pension to Antoine, that appears as the simplest and authoritative spelling.

44, p. 122. Artist Stanley's sketches of Western scenery are to be found in many Government exploration reports, from 1840 on;

and particularly in those compilations upon the surveys for the Pacific Railroad. As draughtsman he also accompanied the Kearny column to California in 1846. He appears to have left no stone unturned in an effort to become thoroughly acquainted with the far West in all its phases. Meeting him in California, in 1846, Edwin Bryant (*What I Saw in California*) says: "Mr. Stanley, the artist of the expedition [i. e., the Kearny column], completed his sketches in oil, at San Francisco; and a more truthful, interesting, and valuable series of paintings, delineating mountain scenery, the floral exhibitions on the route, the savage tribes between Santa Fe and California — combined with camp life and marches through the desert and wilderness — has never been and probably never will be exhibited. Mr. Stanley informed me that he was preparing a work on the savage tribes of North America, and of the islands of the Pacific, which, when completed on his plan, will be the most comprehensive and descriptive of the subject, of any that has been published." Such a work would have ranked with Schoolcraft and Catlin — but evidently it never was completed.

CHAPTER XIII

45, p. 127. DeWitt C. Peters' *Kit Carson's Life and Adventures*. This, the original biography of Carson (and the basis of all succeeding biographies) is followed for events, but must frequently be revised in the sequence of the same.

46, p. 128. Peters' *Kit Carson*.

47, p. 136. Irving B. Richman's *California Under Spain and Mexico* (Boston, 1911). Figueroa died at Monterey in 1835.

48, p. 136. For this sketch of Hall Kelly, and his association with Ewing Young, the author has depended upon the conscientious S. A. Clarke's *Pioneer Days of Oregon History* (Portland, 1905).

CHAPTER XIV

49, p. 139. J. Q. Thornton's *Oregon and California* (N. Y. 1849).

50, p. 143. Rev. Gustavus Hines' *History of Oregon* (N. Y. 1889).

51, p. 144. From *History of the Missions of the Methodist Episcopal Church*, by the Reverend Enoch Mudge, in *History of American Missions to the Heathen, from Their Commencement to the Present Time* (Worcester, 1840).

52, p. 149. The American editions of this book ran into 16,000, and an English edition also was published. It still retains its leadership as an authority in that field.

53, p. 151. These extracts are from *An Evening With an Old Missionary*, in the Chicago *Advance* of December 1, 1870, and reprinted in *Exec Doc. 37*, 41st Cong., 3rd Sess.: Letter from the Secretary of the Interior, communicating *Early Labors of Missionaries in Oregon*.

54, p. 151. Dr. Whitman and Mrs. Whitman were murdered in their home by the Cayuses, November 28, 1847, eleven years almost . to a day after they had arrived at Vancouver. Mrs. Spalding was protected by the Nez Percés, among whom she and husband were much esteemed — speaking, as they did, the language. Mr. Spalding escaped by being absent; but from the anxiety of the succeeding twenty-four hours, and a terrible journey to seek his wife and child, he never fully recovered. Mr. Gray eventually became an Oregon rancher. He wrote a history of Oregon.

55, p. 153. I am following the Spalding story as told in the *Advance*, 1870. The best accounts of the journey are to be found in the Reverend Myron Eells' *Marcus Whitman: Pathfinder and Patriot* (New York, 1912), among the latest Whitman biographies. As he was the son of the Reverend Cushing Eells, Oregon missionary of 1838, who brought his young wife over the mountains, the author enhances his history with much enthusiasm and many new facts. In it are comprised reminiscences by Mr. Spalding, extracts from the journal kept by Mrs. Spalding and from that kept by Mrs. Whitman. The Gray *History of Oregon* is of course vivid upon this journey. See also *How Marcus Whitman Saved Oregon*, by O. W. Nixon.

56, p. 154. From *Proceedings of the Oregon Presbytery*, June, 1859, in *Exec. Doc. 37*, 3rd Sess., 41st Cong., 1871.

57, p. 154. *Early Labors of Missionaries in Oregon*. *Exec. Doc. 37*, 3rd Sess., 41st Cong.

CHAPTER XV

58, p. 161. *Life of Kit Carson: the Great Western Hunter and Guide*, by Charles Burdett (Philadelphia, 1869). Mr. Burdett's narrative is such a compound of Carson (via Peters) and Burdett that one finds it difficult to know where fact ends and fancy begins.

59, p. 164. Colonel James F. Meline's *Two Thousand Miles on Horseback* (New York, 1867). Carson told this story to Colonel Meline at Santa Fe in August, 1866.

60, p. 165. *Journal of an Exploring Tour Beyond the Rocky Mountains*.

61, p. 166. As Captain Simpson understood, the girl was the Arapaho belle whom, as his wife, Carson brought out to Bent's Fort with him in 1838. Carson also declared, "the Frenchman was the only man he was glad he had killed"; thus indicating that Shunan, to merit such animosity from Carson in his mild after days, must have been decidedly an "undesirable" character.

CHAPTER XVI

62, p. 169. Peters' *Kit Carson*.
63, p. 169. Peters' *Kit Carson*.
64, p. 171. Victor's *The River of the West* (Hartford, 1869).
65, p. 173. Victor's *The River of the West*.
66, p. 177. This is the trappers' and Flatheads' side of the affair. The missionaries' defense states it was only after three hours' resistance, and after all the friendly Indians had been killed fighting, that the missionary yielded to the advice of an interpreter, and surrendered. Among the missionaries Mr. Gray was reckoned as a bold, decisive man, who would not readily be intimidated.

CHAPTER XVII

67, p. 180. The post of Bent's Fort was three or four years in the building; being completed in 1832. That Carson was an inmate here, on many occasions before 1838, we may not doubt. The statement that he became official hunter in 1834 must have foundation; other statements place him here in 1832; and George Bent, son of William Bent of the post partnership, relates an incident of Carson at the fort in 1831. Carson (then scarce twenty-two) was helping to cut timber below the site, and a party of Crows stole all the party's horses, save two possessed by a couple of Cheyenne friendlies.

68, p. 181. According to General Chittenden's *History of the* this year, to slight the Hudson Bay Company, was held not in the Valley of the Green, but north one hundred and fifty miles, in the Wind River country. This change in the program almost cut the missionaries short in their journey; for when Agent Ermatinger, of the Hudson Bay Company, arrived at the customary rendezvous, expecting to convey the party on to Oregon, he found neither them nor any rendezvous. But friendly hand of passing trapper had written in charcoal upon the store-house door, here: " Come to Popoazua (i. e., Popo Agie) on Wind River and you will find plenty trade, whiskey, and white women." Thither hastened Agent Ermatinger, with the missionaries Lee and Edwards, eastbound, and arrived just as the American Fur Company caravan was to return to the States, leaving the Gray party stranded or else under necessity of going to California with a band of trappers headed there. (Reverend Myron Eells' *Father Eells*, 1894.) Concise and presumably accurate biographies of the members of the party are to be found in the appendix to the Eells' *Marcus Whitman*.

71, p. 184. Victor's *The River of the West*.

CHAPTER XVIII

72, p. 189. The Bent family were an innovation in the Western Indian and fur trade, being thorough Yankees, and not of French or Canadian extraction. The grandfather, Captain Silas Bent, commanded the Boston tea party of December 16, 1773; from his son, Silas Bent, Jr., first Judge of Common Pleas and Quarter Sessions of the District of St. Louis, descended the Bents of Bent's Fort. In all, the children numbered seven sons and four daughters. The two St. Vrains were sons of Don Jacques Marcellin (Marcelin) Ceran de Hault de Lassus de St. Vrain and Marie Felicité Chauvet Debreuil, his wife, of Spanish Lake, St. Louis County, Missouri. The Lassus-St. Vrain families were of the old French Flanders nobility — blood the proudest in Europe. Reference is made in Delassus vs. United States, 9 Peters Reports, U. S. Supreme Court, to the family history. Don Carlos de Hault de Lassus was the last Spanish governor of Upper Louisiana. There were other brothers.

73, p. 189. The precise site of the old post is across the river from the town of Robinson, and upon the large ranch of A. E. Reynolds. The outlines, indicated by mounds of adobe, may still be seen. There seems to have been a second and smaller gateway, opposite the main entrance, and opening into the corral. The descriptions in the text are taken from Colonel Henry Dodge, 1835; Thomas Farnham, 1839; Lieutenant Frederick Ruxton, 1844; Colonel Philip St. George Cooke, 1845 and 1846; Lieutenant J. W. Abert, 1845; Lewis Garrard, 1846 and 1847; Francis Parkman, 1846; an article by Mrs. John Campbell in the *Trail Magazine* (Denver), 1909; a published letter from George Bent, son of William Bent, in the *Rocky Mountain News,* and an article by him in the *Southwest Magazine;* the confirmations by Oliver Wiggins, etc.

74, p. 190. The journal of this very interesting expedition is found in Vol. 4, Exec. Docs., 1st Sess., 24th Cong., Doc. 181.

75, p. 193. *History of the Arkansas Valley.* There are many other authorities.

76, p. 193. Heap's journal of *Central Route to the Pacific* (Philadelphia, 1854).

77, p. 194. William Bent received the title of colonel by services as guide for the American column into New Mexico, 1846, and as purveyor of supplies to this Army of the West. As an Indian trader he was a marked success, and further showed his business abilities by anticipating the Government at the Big Timbers. In 1859, while operating his post at the Big Timbers, he was agent over the Cheyennes and Arapahoes, reporting, however, from St. Louis. He resigned to pursue the more profitable business of government freighting, and he also carried on a trading business with the emigrants pouring through along the Arkansas, for the new "Pike's Peak gold fields." He was very influential among the Cheyennes, the Arapahos, and other plains tribes, and served at important talks and treaties. The Kiowas called him "Hook-nose-man" or "Roman-nose." In 1864 he was located on the Arkansas "eighteen miles above Fort Lyon (Wise)." His business on the trail took him much to Missouri, where near Westport the Bent family had a large farm, with the "Bent mansion" upon it. Here at Westport he in 1867 married, having previously had two Cheyenne wives (both dead), Adalina Harvey, young daughter of Alexander Harvey (of the Upper Missouri fur-trade firm of Harvey, Primeau & Co.) and his Blackfoot wife. This year, 1867, Bent and family at the house of his son-in-law, Judge R. M. Moore, on the ranch land, adjacent to the present town of Las Animas, above the Purgatoire. His ailment developed into pneumonia, and he died May 19. He was buried on the ranch.

CHAPTER XIX

78, p. 197. Reference has frequently been made, in this narrative, to Mr. Wiggins, who as, perhaps, the only living person with memory dating back to Taos and Kit Carson before the conquest of New Mexico, has been a mine of valuable information upon these days as upon old trapper customs as well. Oliver Perry Wiggins (his name itself a reminiscence) was born July 22, 1823, on Grand Island in the Niagara River, where during the War of 1812 his father, Sergeant Samuel Wiggins, a Hudson Bay employe, occupied the island in behalf of the United States. The sergeant served also at Lundy Lane, Saratoga, and in other battles. At St. Louis his brother operated the celebrated old Wiggins Ferry; and thither bent, in September of 1837, at the age of fourteen, as a runaway wended little Oliver to be a Rocky Mountain trapper and Indian slayer. Receiving him, his uncle made arrangements to return him to his father; but that fall of 1838 Oliver crawled out of bed over the snoring Irishman put in to guard him, embarked on the waiting steamer *Anne*, for Independence Landing, and aided and abetted by crew and all, joined the Santa Fe caravan. No one knowing his name, he was nicknamed "Blue" (on account of his faded suit); and as "Blue" he was identified through several years. Carson virtually adopted him, such generosity being a characteristic of the great frontiersman. As member of a separate Carson command he accompanied the Fremont first expedition, and the second expedition as far as Fort Hall, where he was among those who turned back. He made one trip clear to Canada, sought and claimed the sweetheart of his boyhood (thirteen when he had left her), married her and established her with her brother (a Wardell) at St. Joseph, and visited her between trapper seasons. Once he was kept away from her two years by the Indians. He and Ike Chamberlain were the only Carson men with "white" wives. In the spring of 1846 he was one of six (Sol Silver, Gleeson, son of a Mormon elder, one Hall, Bragg, and a cook being the others) secretly sent forward by Brigham Young to report back upon the Salt Lake country. In 1847 he enlisted at Bent's Fort for the war. In the spring of 1849 he and Silver, the only men available to answer a call made upon Kit Carson for experienced guides, took out from Independence one of the first wagon-trains through to California. In the fifties Wiggins trapped for himself, mostly in Northwestern Colorado. In the early sixties he was much at the new settlement of Denver. In 1865, recommended by Carson, under General Herman H. Heath, he was stationed as chief-of-scouts, with rank of major, in charge of fifty Omahas and Winnebagoes, at Alkali station, Southwestern Nebraska, on the Overland Trail, his territory being Nebraska and Colorado. In 1868, the Kiowas and Arapahos having been quieted, he was transferred to Hays, Kansas, against the Sioux and Cheyennes, and served three years more. He was a trader and storekeeper south of Denver. He became patrolman in Denver, and United States marshal. After retiring from active work, he was appointed bailiff to the Federal Court, a position which he filled until at last failing eyesight relegated him to a well-earned fire-side and the company of his great-grandchildren. His body bore the marks of three grievous wounds: by Mexican brass bullet, in the thigh; by Comanche lance, in the calf — a lance that pinned him to the saddle; and by Digger arrow, in the arm. When I first talked with him he was eighty-seven, and almost blind; but his other senses were remarkably acute, and of his fine memory, as well as of his kindly disposition, I would here tender the highest appreciation. He died near the close of 1913.

79, p. 197. " Silver " may be a corruption of " Silva," the name of a New Mexican family of early date. Jesus Silva was the first settler east of the Taos range, in the Rayado country, where Carson himself later, at the opening of the fifties, tried ranching; and some Silvas lived at Taos in the forties. The fact that Sol Silver was characterized by his bushy black beard might further indicate that he was Spanish or Mexican.

80, p. 204. The Hobbs memory evidently cannot be entirely relied upon, or else Kit Carson had more than the one Indian wife. As Jim Beckwourth, the mulatto mountaineer, married a Crow heroine, " Pine Leaf," and lived in California, this may have been a daughter of his — although we have no record upon the subject.

CHAPTER XX

81, p. 207. Thus narrates Albert D. Richardson, remarking upon his ride with Carson in 1859 (*Beyond the Mississippi*. New York, 1862). General James F. Rusling, transcribing a speech by Carson at Fort Garland in 1866 (*Across the Continent*) indicates a certain illiteracy of word and accent only to be expected.

82, p. 208. *Memoirs of My Life,* by John Charles Fremont. This work, which includes a biographical sketch of Senator Benton, by Mrs. Fremont, was begun with the intention of compiling a narrative of the full five exploration trips. However, only the one volume, the first, was issued (Chicago, 1887).

83, p. 214. The Fremont Report, in Senate Documents, Vol. XI, of 2nd Session, Twenty-first Congress, also published in connection with House Reports, and as a separate bulletin for public distribution.

84, p. 217. As is to be noted, in the Spanish the name Robinson, of Kit Carson's mother, becomes " Rovenson " on the register. Rumor would assert that the Roman Catholicism in home and family bothered Kit Carson, at first; and that, amidst his perplexities, he sought relief in the expedition with Fremont. But everything indicates that he early became reconciled to the requirements of the religion in his family relations; and it is a well-substantiated fact that his wife and he were devotedly attached, one to the other. As said, he did not long survive her.

85, p. 217. From Louis H. Garrard's *Wah-to-yah, and the Taos Trail* (Cincinnati, 1850). Mrs. Carson was forty when, in April, 1868, she died. This would make her fifteen when she married.

CHAPTER XXI

86, p. 220. Unless otherwise indicated, the various quotations in this chapter are to be referred to the official report (*Sen. Doc. 174,* 28th Cong., 2nd Sess. Washington, 1845) or to the Fremont *Memoirs* (Chicago, 1887). While reproducing the Report, the *Memoirs* also interpolate, thus now and then furnishing additional information.

87, p. 222. Oliver Wiggins in *Garden of the Gods* magazine, 1902; and confirmed by conversations.

88, p. 224. Captain Howard Stansbury's *An Expedition to the Valley of the Great Salt Lake* (Philadelphia, 1855).

89, p. 226. Benton's *Thirty Years' View* (New York, 1854).

90, p. 227. The little basin of Klamath Lake was crossed. But the " Mary's Lake," which evidently was the Sink of the Humboldt, was not approached within striking distance.

91, p. 229. *A Tour of Duty in California; Including a Descrip-*

tion of the Gold Region: and an Account of the Voyage around Cape Horn; with Notices of Lower California, the Gulf and Pacific Coasts, and the principal Events Attending the Conquest of the Californias, by Joseph Warren Revere; New York and Boston, 1849.

92, p. 232. Benton's *Thirty Years' View.*

93, p. 232. From the New York *Times* of June 2, 1877; quoted in Fremont's *Memoirs.*

CHAPTER XXII

94, p. 241. Fremont's *Memoirs.*

95, p. 243. Letter to Mrs. Fremont, in the *Memoirs.*

96, p. 243. That another visit to California had been projected from the very start is shown by the fact that Lieutenant Gillespie's Washington instructions directed him to look for Fremont upon the Sacramento. Almost all this survey was in Mexican territory, and now from Monterey Fremont proceeds to open an emigrant trail to Oregon on the California or Mexican side of the Sierras. Such government operations seem today rather high-handed, for Mexico's permission to grant the passage of an armed force or of emigrants had not been asked.

97, p. 245. So far as I know, the Fremont *Memoirs* supply the only details of this the third expedition, from start to the west of the Sierras. The sole official report, I believe, is that entitled *Geographical Memoir upon Upper California, in illustration of his Map of Oregon and California,* by John Charles Fremont, addressed to the Senate of the United States (Sen. *Misc. Doc. No. 148,* 30th Cong., 1st Sess.). It was published in 1848 — having been deferred by intervening events. It relates largely to the scientific aspects of the Great Basin and the Pacific side of the Sierras, and its brevity and restraint are in marked contrast with the breezy narratives which had preceded — for the court-martial had left Fremont a somewhat disappointed, though not a defeated, man. He offers to prepare for public circulation a full journal of this third expedition, if Congress will provide therefor; but his offer was not accepted, and as he was "no longer in the public service" he reserves his extra data for future compilation.

CHAPTER XXIII

98, p. 246. By thus diverging, in a loop, Fremont was seeking, he claims, a pass below, over into the San Joaquin valley again; and he indicates that he also was making a reconnaissance on his own behalf, in search of a tract by the sea whereon he might some day settle.

99, p. 247. *Memoirs.*

100, p. 249. *Memoirs.*

101, p. 250. *Memoirs.*

102, p. 252. *Memoirs.*

103, p. 254. From an interview with Carson, in the Washington *Union* of June 16, 1847. Carson was then in Washington with dispatches.

104, p. 256. *Memoirs.*

105, p. 260. Colton's *Deck and Port.* The celebrated Bear flag was about five feet long and three wide, and was the design of William L. Todd, a settler from Illinois. The material was cotton, with a lower border of red flannel. The brown bear was painted on, facing a large star of red flannel. Below was the legend: "California Republic." This flag, long preserved by the pioneer association of San Francisco, was burned in the big fire of 1906.

106, p. 262. Irving B. Richman's *California Under Spain and Mexico.*

107, p. 263. *Memoirs.*

108, p. 264. *What I saw in California.*

109, p. 265. General Philip St. George Cooke's *The Conquest of New Mexico and California; an Historical and Personal Narrative* (New York, 1878).

110, p. 266. From the Price letter in Fremont's *Memoirs.*

111, p. 267. This exuberant declamation by Lieutenant Revere of the *Portsmouth* is found in his lively *A Tour of Duty in California.*

CHAPTER XXIV

112, p. 268. Colton's *Deck and Port.*

113, p. 269. Letter by Purser Rodman M. Price, of the *Cyane,* in Fremont's *Memoirs.*

114, p. 273. *Journal of Captain A. R. Johnston, First Dragoons,* as issued with the Reports of Lieutenant Emory.

115, p. 273. Testimony of Kit Carson, to Senator Benton, Washington, 1847.

116, p. 275. The march of the dragoons is found detailed in *Notes of a Military Reconnoissance, from Fort Leavenworth, in Missouri, to San Diego, in California, Including Part of the Arkan-*

sas, Del Norte, and Gila Rivers. By Lieut. Col. W. H. Emory. Made in 1846-7, with the Advanced Guard of the "Army of the West" (Washington, 1848).

117, p. 275. Emory's *Report.*
118, p. 275. Emory's *Report.*
119, p. 276. Emory's *Report.*

CHAPTER XXV

120, p. 280. Conclusion of the journal of Captain A. R. Johnston.
121, p. 280. *Notes* of Lieutenant Emory.
122, p. 281. Emory's *Notes.* It is stated, but without quoted authority, that Kit Carson advised the avoidance of a conflict, in the present poor condition of the column, and a march for San Diego by a "secret" trail. I do not believe this. The Californians could not possibly be evaded, in their own country; and when at the Snooks ranch the column left the main road for the hills we see what happened to them. Moreover, it is doubtful if Carson would have varied from the mountain man tactics against Indians — tactics which favored the straight, hard fight, without circumvention. The Kearny course has been criticized, but it appears to have been the most practical, and the best military course, under the circumstances.

123, p. 282. In the distances quoted I have followed the figures used by Lieutenant Emory, in his government report. By the regular trail from the mouth of the Gila to San Diego, the distances seem to have been different. Warner's Ranch is the same — about seventy-five miles — from San Diego; but Santa Isabel is placed at ten instead of fifteen miles from Warner's (therefore sixty-five from San Diego), and San Pasqual is placed at thirty-nine miles from San Diego, instead of twenty-nine, as in the Emory journal. See itinerary of the Yuma-San Diego trail in Captain Marcy's *The Prairie Traveler* (New York, 1859).

124, p. 288. Speech by Senator Benton.

125, p. 290. Peters' *Life of Kit Carson.* Here Carson is the leader and Lieutenant Beale merely a follower. Carson was somewhat at a disadvantage in relation to this his "official" biography. As he said to A. D. Richardson, in 1859, "he had looked into the book here and there but had never read it" ! The confession was candid, inasmuch as he was not able to read. Colonel Peters compiled the book from Carson's recollections, narrated not written;

and thus both parties were at a disadvantage. In after years Carson grew somewhat familiar with the book, from having the pages read to him; and General Asa B. Cary, who was with Carson in the Navajo and other Southwest campaigns of the sixties, had a copy with the Carson corrections noted in it. Unfortunately, the copy was lost; it would be most interesting, today.

126, p. 294. In 1852 the brave Beale resigned from the navy. In 1853 he was appointed to the Superintendency of the Indian tribes of California, and en route with Gwinn Harris Heap, his companion, made the initial exploration and report for a central railroad to the Pacific. His superintendency of California lasted only a short time; he engaged in further American desert expeditions, and gave his enthusiastic endorsement of the camels imported by Secretary of War Jefferson Davis for work in the Southwest. The camels later proved unsatisfactory for American pack service. Mr. Beale was brigadier general in the Civil War; became a large rancher in California; and in 1876 was appointed by President Grant minister to Vienna. He died in California, April, 1893. In 1912 his ranch lands, over 276,000 acres in the San Joaquin Valley, at last were being divided for sale.

⏤ CHAPTER XXVI

127, p. 295. *History of Oregon and California, and the Other Territories on the Northwest Coast of North America* (Boston, 1844), by Robert Greenhow; and *The Oregon Territory* (London, 1846), by the Rev. C. G. Nicolay. Both works have maps and exhaustive data upon all phases of the new country.

128, p. 296. Flores' proclamation of revolt, dated at Los Angeles, October 1, 1846.

129, p. 296. Thus claimed Fremont, in his defense at the court-martial in Washington. Carson's name is not mentioned in the official reports, or in the Emory *Notes*.

CHAPTER XXVII

130, p. 301. Cooke's *Conquest of New Mexico and California*.

131, p. 302. Peters' *Life and Adventures of Kit Carson*. The sentiment here is Carson's, although the language evidently is Peters'.

132, p. 303. Mrs. Teresina Scheurich of Taos, who as the five-year-old daughter of Governor Bent was present in the rooms when the attack was committed.

133, p. 306. There are numerous accounts of the murder: accounts by Chief Justice L. Bradford Prince, in his *History of New Mexico* (1883), by Helen Haines, in her *History of New Mexico* (1891), by Ralph E. Twitchell in his *The Military Occupation of New Mexico* (1909), by Louis Garrard in his *Wah-to-yah and the Taos Trail* (1850); and by other writers early and late. I have preferred, of course, the narrative as told to me in quiet tones by Mrs. Scheurich, upon whom, even as a child, the horrid scenes were indelibly impressed, and who grew up with her own memory and the memory of other survivors. She still has the poker with which, aided by the spoon, the hole in the wall was dug. So I have relied upon her story, supplemented by a few details from the narrative of Garrard, who was in Taos about ten weeks after the murders occurred. The Bent house still stands, in Taos; but it has been altered somewhat, and the marks of bullet and arrow, in the rooms, have faded. The headless remains of Governor Bent rest today under a handsome monument in Santa Fe cemetery.

134, p. 308. Accounts of this march by the Colonel Sterling Price command, and particularly of the battle at the pueblo, are found in the narratives cited in Note 133, in Brackett's *History of the United States Cavalry* (1865), in J. P. Dunn's *Massacres of the Mountains* (1886) and in the report by Colonel Price to the War Department, and are contained, with other details, in Cooke's *Conquest of New Mexico and California*. The affair at the pueblo was by all stories the most spectacular and the strangest siege ever laid by American troops. The enormous *casas grandes* are formidable today, although doors and windows have been cut and the wall encircling has disintegrated. But under the conditions of 1847 they were much more formidable. Save for the cannon, the tactics were medieval; and medieval must have been the scene. According to Fitzgerald, private in the Burgwin company, "the first two Americans who entered through the breach fell dead, the third was unhurt, the fourth killed," and he himself was the fifth. Garrard says that it was Jesus de Tafoya who was shot by St. Vrain; but according to the Price report Tafoya was slain at La Cañada, and Chavis was the one killed at the pueblo. The Delaware "Big Nigger," who had married a Taos squaw, asserted that assisted by his wife who loaded his rifle he killed the majority of the Americans; Garrard understood that he himself was killed behind the altar — "riddled by thirty balls"; but good authority, among them Ruxton, states that he escaped to the mountains of the upper Arkansas, where in company with three other Delawares he defied capture. The American loss was seven killed, forty-five wounded, many fatally. The ruins of the old church stand today, and from amidst the débris cannon-balls may occasionally be picked. In the desolate but sacred yard the Pueblos still bury their dead.

135, p. 311. Peters' *Life and Adventures of Kit Carson.* It must have been while now in Washington that Carson was entrusted by Mrs. Fremont with a miniature of herself (painted in 1845, during her husband's absence), to be taken across continent and placed in Colonel Fremont's hands. I find the charming miniature reproduced in Elizabeth Benton Fremont's *Recollections* (New York, 1912). Inasmuch as when Carson reached California, Colonel Fremont was en route by the Oregon Trail for Washington, to face court-martial, I do not know when or where the miniature was delivered to him.

CHAPTER XXVIII

136, p. 316. Extract from Sherman's *Home Letters* (New York, 1909).

137, p. 316. The 7th Regiment, New York Volunteers, Colonel Jonathan D. Stevenson, after a voyage around the Horn arrived at San Francisco March 7 (1847). Lieutenant Brewerton doubtless was on a furlough, pending discharge, when in May, 1848, he left for the States with Kit Carson. His narrative, *A Ride with Kit Carson,* I find in abridged state in Van Tramp's *Prairie and Rocky Mountain Adventures* (Columbus, 1857) — a volume of separate chapters largely rehash, but not without value. Where and in what shape *A Ride with Kit Carson* originally appeared, I do not know; possibly in a New York paper.

138, p. 325. By cession from the Mexican Government, treaty of 1848, the United States acquired for $15,000,000 this vast territory comprising Upper California, Nevada, Utah, Western Colorado, Western New Mexico, and Arizona down to the Gila — the remainder of that present state being taken in by the Gadsden Purchase of 1853.

139, p. 325. Little Salt Lake formerly was found near the Spanish Trail, northeast of Parowan, southwestern Utah. It has long been practically dry. The Spanish Trail continued much north of this spot, ere turning for the east and the southeast.

Where the Carson company crossed the Utah ranges I do not know. Lieutenant Brewerton's narrative, as found in Van Camp's compendium, is vague as to localities. The company may have followed a special Carson trail east out of Utah. Lieutenant Brewerton speaks of first swimming the Grand, and next, in two days' travel, the Green; but of the two rivers, the Green would be struck first by anybody approaching from the west. The lieutenant, it will be noted, lost his memoranda of the trip, and doubtless confuses rivers.

140, p. 333. As second lieutenant, Carson would receive pay of $33.33 a month, rations with a commutation value of $24 a month, forage for two horses, with commutation value of $16 a month, and one servant with commutation or cash value of $16.50 a month: total monthly pay, $89.83.

141, p. 334. Possibly without the Benton advocacy Carson might have been granted his lieutenancy; but it would have been a doubtful boon, for his utter lack of the ordinary rudiments of education would have embarrassed him much. Even as Indian Agent he was unable to make out his own reports, and while in this office, and in garrison duty later, to furnish figures that would meet the requirements of the government disbursing departments was a serious matter with him.

142, p. 337. From the Meek biography — Victor's *The River of the West.*

CHAPTER XXIX

143, p. 344. "Three square leagues" are assigned as the original nucleus of the Beaubien and Miranda Grant. To be exact, according to the Surveyor-General's report, the full extent was 1,714,764 acres. The tract is better known as "the Maxwell Grant;" for Maxwell was the actual proprietor, and after the death, in February, 1864, of Judge Beaubien, he bought out the other heirs. Eventually he erected a large "manor-house," of adobe, with encircling veranda and a central court; a portion of it still stands, in the town of Cimarron. He farmed about 5,000 acres, and accumulated a host of retainers, Mexican and Indian; a thousand horses and mules, 10,000 cattle, 50,000 sheep. Thus he lived, hospitable and carelessly wealthy, and his manor became famous through all the Southwest. As for Lucien Maxwell himself, he was born in the romantic settlement of Kaskaskia, Illinois, in 1818. His mother was Odelle Ménard, of a family which is frequently encountered in the annals of the West. The Maxwell home, built at Kaskaskia in 1808, was reproduced at the Chicago World's Fair. In 1842, at Taos, Maxwell married the Señorita Luz Beaubien. He died, in 1875, aged 57, at Fort Sumner. He is buried at the town, and there live two of his daughters. By all accounts he was a man open-handed, honest, able, and universally liked.

144, p. 346. I take this account from W. W. H. Davis' *El Gringo; or, New Mexico and Her People* (New York, 1856). Mr. Davis was first United States Attorney for the organized territory.

145, p. 347. Peters' *Life of Kit Carson.*

146, p. 348. Meline's *Two Thousand Miles on Horseback.*

147, p. 349. Sen. Docs., 31st Con., 2nd Sess.

148, p. 349. *Two Thousand Miles on Horseback.*

149, p. 350. General Philip St. George Cooke's *Recollections* in General Theodore F. Rodenbough's *From Everglade to Canon with the Second Dragoons* (New York, 1875).

150, p. 355. I find this statement, that Carson was appointed purchasing agent, in a letter from Captain Smith H. Simpson of Taos. As Captain Simpson was associated with Carson in the fifties, at Taos, he should be an authority.

151, p. 357. After recuperating at the Carson home in Taos, Fremont had proceeded to California, by the Gila Trail, and to his Mariposa tract of seventy square miles. The claim to the tract was in litigation for half a dozen years, the government asserting that title to it was incomplete. However, the United States Supreme court finally confirmed it. In 1850 Fremont was elected senator from California and drew the short term, which expired March 4, 1851; but his actual service ran only from September 9 to September 30, 1850, ill health preventing him from filling out the regular short term.

152, p. 357. From an article, *Kit Carson, Last of the Trail Makers,* by Charles M. Harvey, in the *Century Magazine.*

CHAPTER XXX

153, p. 359. Report, 1852, of D. D. Mitchell, Superintendent of Indian Affairs for the Upper Platte. *(Indian Affairs.)*

154, p. 361. United States Indian Commissioner George W. Manypenny, in Indian Affairs Reports, 1854.

155, p. 362. From Edward Everett Hale's *Kansas and Ne-*

braska: The History, Geographical and Physical Characteristics, and Political Position of Those Territories; and an Account of the Emigrant Companies, and Directions to Emigrants (Boston, 1854).

156, p. 366. The house, long a focus of interest to modern visitors in Taos, is being restored to good condition by the local lodge of Masons, and preserved as a Carson museum.

157, p. 367. Mrs. Carson could not write in English. Her language of course was Spanish.

158, p. 367. To bridge him over a difficulty Carson did find it necessary to employ just this kind of an "interpreter." That he should require any other kind creates a smile when we consider that he was an interpreter, in Indian and Spanish, himself. He gravely embodies in his report of August, 1858: "I have in the employ of the Indian department John Mostin, as interpreter, a native of Clinton County, State of New York, aged 29 years, at a salary of $500 per annum. He was appointed June 1, 1857, at this agency." Captain Smith Simpson writes in a letter to me: "This was a man who did Kit's writing for him after I went to old Mexico in 1857, for a year." Mostin, or Mostyn, unfortunately mixed the accounts, and for a brief space the honest Kit was in serious trouble, and, it is claimed, was suspended for investigation. He told Captain Simpson that it cost him $600 to make up the deficit.

159, p. 367. When I met him, Captain Smith Henry Simpson, dean of the American residents of old Taos, had a record of almost sixty years straight service as soldier and frontiersman in the border Southwest. After his arrival from the East, in Santa Fe, September, 1853, he was engaged in the Ceran St. Vrain company for the campaign (chapter XXXI) of 1855 against the Utes and Apaches. From 1855 onward he had made Taos his headquarters. In the Civil War he was three years Captain of Volunteers, in the field against the Apaches in Arizona and keeping the post of Fort Goodwin, on the Gila, there. He was military express rider on that most dangerous route between Santa Fe and Trinidad, Colorado. Out of long and very intimate experience, his knowledge of the old Southwest and of the mature Kit Carson is to be surpassed by that of no person alive.

160, p. 368. These tintypes, as reproduced among the illustrations in this narrative, were enclosed in ornate gilt frames fashionable to the period. Whether this is the first Carson photo-

graph I do not know. Another, of Carson and little Charley
Boggs, appears, and seems to date about at the same time. Carson here has a moustache. Captain Simpson's memory is to the
effect that the Taos picture is the first experience of Carson before
a camera. By the age of the boy Charley Boggs, Mr. John S.
Hough, to whom was given the other tintype in question, esti-
mates its date as about 1859. The two pictures must have been
taken within a year or year and a half of one another. The
moustache makes comparison difficult.

161, p. 370. Ex-Commissioner Francis E. Leupp's *The Indian
and His Problem.*

162, p. 371. *Indian Affairs,* 1858 (Washington, 1859). The
shrewdness of Carson in holding the Utes from Mormon influence may have prevented the "bloodless Mormon War" from
taking on a deeper tinge. In his annual report of 1859 Superintendent Collins refers to the Tabuaches as being "the same
band of Utahs that the Mormons attempted to seduce into an
alliance with them in 1857." Had the Utes actually been incited
against the soldier column of General Johnston, in the winter
of 1857-58, and thereafter, history might read different. "If
they [i. e., the Government] dare to force the issue, I shall not
hold the Indian by the wrist any longer for white men to shoot
it," had proclaimed Brigham Young; "they shall go ahead and
do as they please,"

163, p. 372. *Indian Affairs,* 1859. (Washington, 1860).

164, p. 373. *Indian Affairs,* 1860 (Washington, 1861). The
Carson reports, as published, are included in the appendix to
this narrative. Their wording—the employment of "depreda-
tion," "concomitant," "imparted," "degradation," "depravity,"
"in their manhood they will not depart therefrom," "practicable," etc—must have caused a smile among those persons who
knew the alleged author.

CHAPTER XXXI

165, p. 378. Merriwether report, 1854. *(Indian Affairs.)*
166, p. 378. Merriwether report, 1854. *(Indian Affairs.)*
167, p. 379. This battle is referred to by Peters as that of
"Ceneguilla," and by Superintendent Merriwether, in his report
of September 1, 1854, as occurring near the "village of Cone-
quilla." The former Pueblo village of Cieneguilla is located about
twenty miles southwest from Santa Fe, and is not in the Embudo

Mountains. Upon the atlas it is indicated that a Battle of Cieneguilla occurred below Santa Fe. But that this really desperate fight of March, 1854, took place in the Embudo Mountains some twenty miles (Captain Smith Simpson says about sixteen) southwest of Taos, therefore sixty or more miles north of Santa Fe, is vouched for by surviving chroniclers. The Meline reference is from his *Two Thousand Miles on Horseback*.

168, p. 379. Mr. William G. Chambers, in *Outlook* Magazine, October, 1911.

169, p. 380. General Cooke's *Recollections* in Rodenbough's *From Everglade to Cañon with the Second Dragoons;* being *History of the Second Dragoons, 1836-1875.*

170, p. 386. From a chapter upon Chaves, in *The Military Occupation of New Mexico, 1846-1851*, by Colonel Ralph Emerson Twitchell (1909).

171, p. 386. Of this remarkable Indian campaign, so little known, there were, in 1912, at least two survivors: Major Rafael Chacon, of Trinidad, Colorado, who was sergeant with B Company, volunteers; and Captain Simpson of Taos, who was commissary and quartermaster sergeant with C Company.

CHAPTER XXXII

172, p. 394. "Kit Carson was one of the original eight who raised the flag in the Taos plaza," Captain Smith H. Simpson writes to me November, 1911. "I am the only one left, but the flag is still here."

173, p. 395. It is a fact, that during the Civil War the Southern Utes and the Jicarilla Apaches remained friendly to the whites, even while the Southern Apaches and the Navajos sought the warpath.

174, p. 396. Patrick Hamilton's *The Resources of Arizona* (Santa Fe, 1884).

175, p. 396. The First Regiment, New Mexico Infantry, was organized at Fort Union and Santa Fe from July 1 to August 31, 1861, to serve three years. Officers and enlisted men not selected for retention were mustered out May 31, 1862, and the remainder of the regiment was consolidated with like remnants of the Second, Fourth and Fifth Regiments, to serve as a new regiment designated First New Mexican Cavalry. Officers and men represented many names of veterans of the Indian campaign of 1855. The varied roll stands as follows:

Colonel, Christopher Carson (vice Ceran St. Vrain resigned).
Lieutenant-Colonel, J. Francisco Chaves.
Major, Arthur Morrison.
Captains, Francisco P. Abreú, Julian Espinoza, Albert H.
Pfeiffer, Jesus María Sena y Baca, Louis Feisenthal, Charles
Deüs, Rafael Chacon, Francisco Gonzales, José Gutierrez, Ed-
ward H. Bergman.
First Lieutenants, Enriques P. Martin, Louis Dickens, John
B. Fennett, L. G. Murphy, Eben Everett (Adj.), Pantaleon Archi-
leta, William H. Brooks, B. Machowicz, Augustin P. D'Amours,
Trinidad Lopez, Nicholas Quintana.
Second Lieutenants, Donaciano Montoya, Andrés Tapia, An-
tonio Abeyta, Antonio Gallegos, Julian Soliz, John Murphy,
Henry M. Holmes, William H. Lent.
Resigned, Colonel Ceran St. Vrain; Captains José M. Valdez,
Santiago Valdez; First Lieutenant John B. Atkins; Second Lieu-
tenant José M. Martinez.
Discharged, Second Lieutenants Edmund D' Amours, Juan
Gallegos; Surgeon J. M. Whitlock.
"The First Regiment was recruited as infantry composed of
ten companies," writes to me Major Rafael Chacon, of Trinidad,
Colorado — who supplied me with the above roll, also. "My
company and that of Captain Deüs were mounted; the remainder
of the regiment, although later designated as cavalry, were not
provided with horses, and they served on foot. Colonel Ceran
St. Vrain resigned, September 30, and during the various reor-
ganizations of the regiment Kit Carson continued to be its
colonel." Major Chacon was captain at Valverde, was stationed
at old Fort Wingate (some of the time in command there) during the Navajo campaign, and is mentioned frequently in dispatches. Transferred to Arizona, he served at Fort Whipple and
helped to establish the present city of Prescott; and in May,
1864, was brevetted major and placed in command at Fort Stanton, New Mexico. He resigned in September, 1864.

176, p. 397. Reports of Colonel Canby, in *Records of the War
of the Rebellion*, Series 1, Vol. IV.

177, p. 397. Helen Haines' *History of New Mexico*.

178, p. 402. The official reports (*Records of the War of the
Rebellion*, Series I, Vol. IX) form the basis of this chapter.

179, p. 404. Report of Colonel Christopher Carson, dated
"Hdqrs. Third Column Troops in the Field. Near Fort Craig,
N. Mex., February 26, 1862," to Colonel Canby.

180, p. 405. From the account furnished to General Roden-bought *(From Everglade to Cañon with the Second Dragoons)* by Colonel Joseph McC. Bell, who was a lieutenant with the battery.

181, p. 406. Colonel Bell here says that the Carson regiment was a portion of the support, and that it was Carson who helped serve the battery. This is an error. Carson and his men were in action on the right.

182, p. 406. Colonel Bell's account.

183, p. 407. Canby's report.

184, p. 408. Bell.

CHAPTER XXXIII

185, p. 412. Says Captain Pettis, in his pamphlet upon " The California Column ": " A few of the old-timers still alive in the Territory remember him kindly and speak of him very highly as a gallant and successful Indian fighter. His army record is one of the best among the officers of the ' old army' before the war." He and Kit Carson were brother members of Montezuma Lodge No. 1 of Masons, at Santa Fe — which of course strength-ened the bonds of friendship between them. General Carleton commanded in New Mexico until the end of April, 1866; he died in San Antonio, January 7, 1873.

CHAPTER XXXIV

186, p. 418. Report of Commissioner N. G. Taylor in *Indian Affairs* volumes for 1868.

187, p. 419. This and foregoing facts may be found in the annual report of Superintendent Collins, September, 1858. *(Indian Affairs, 1858.)*

188, p. 420. Letter by Kit Carson, Taos, May, 1864. See appendix.

189, p. 425. This was the first Fort Wingate, located near the present station of Grant, and therefore about sixty miles eastward from Fort Wingate of today.

190, p. 426. This anecdote is contained in a private letter to the author from the late Captain George H. Pettis, of Rhode Island, who was first lieutenant and commanded K company (Los Pinos station) in the Navajo campaign.

191, p. 426. See *Records of the Rebellion*. For complete letter see appendix, as well as for the letter regarding leave of absence.

192, p. 427. From a letter (1909) to the author by General Asa B. Carey, who was chief quartermaster and chief of staff under Colonel Carson, and who commanded the column which penetrated the Cañon de Chelly from the West.

193, p. 427. The Carleton reply to this proposition is found in the letter of August 18, 1863, in the appendix. Accustomed to the ways of the Indians and New Mexicans, Carson evidently considered that the retention of captured women and children was a very proper solution. Sometimes the Utes or Apaches held such captives to service, and sometimes they disposed of them to the New Mexicans. In this way tribal cohesion was invaded. The idea of bondage was of course abhorrent to the Government and to General Carleton as a government officer.

194, p. 427. These extracts are from reports of operations of 1863, Department of New Mexico. Found in official volumes before cited. Few other details of the scouts have come down to us. Mr. Oscar H. Lipps, of the Indian service, in his valuable brochure *A Little History of the Navajos* relates that the Navajos still delight in telling of the time when they surrounded Kit on top of a large black rock near Fort Defiance and held him a prisoner there for three days, when he finally effected his escape.

195, p. 432. Testimony by Carson, 1865, before the *Congressional Joint Commission upon Condition of the Indian Tribes*.

196, p. 433. Report of Agent Baker, September 1, 1859 (*Indian Affairs*, 1859).

197, p. 435. The comment comes from the late Captain Pettis, who as lieutenant was in the Pfeiffer company for a short time, and who knew him well during and after the war. Albert Henry Pfeiffer was long a noted frontiersman in the New Mexico country. His father was a Lutheran minister in Prussian Germany; his mother was of noble Scotch descent. It was the tragic death of his wife at the hands of the Apaches which spurred him on to especial repute as an Indian fighter. This dramatic attack upon his party, while he was bathing in the hot springs near Fort McRae, June, 1863, is told in the appendix (No. VIII). He was a Master Mason (1859) of Montezuma Lodge, of Santa Fe — the lodge of Kit Carson and General Carleton. He and Carson were close friends, almost brothers; and as will be seen by the Carson letter (No. IX) Carson, in 1863, as god-father made over to little Albert Pfeiffer, Jr., a tract of land.

198, p. 436. The Captain Pfeiffer report is to be found in the appendix. Here are to be found also the Carson and the Carey reports. These, contained in the Records of the Rebellion, have not to my knowledge been before proffered in narratives of the Cañon de Chelly expedition; nor, so far as I know, have any of the official reports of the campaign been printed for popular perusal. It is interesting to note that Major W. T. Littebrant, Fifteenth Cavalry, had the remnants of the "Order and Correspondent Book" of the "Navajo Expedition," kept by Colonel Carson through his adjutant. Extracts from this relic were published in the Journal of the United States Cavalry Association (January, 1910); and, of course, are reproduced also in the Records of the Rebellion, Series 1, Vol. 26, Pt. 1 and Vol. 34, Pt. 1.

199, p. 436. Carson report of January 23, 1864, upon the expedition to the cañon.

CHAPTER XXXV

200, p. 446. *Records of the Rebellion.* Ka-ni-at-ze (Kaniatse) was the principal Ute chief. Colonel Meline *(Two Thousand Miles on Horseback)* makes mention of him, summer of 1866; and he was Carson's favorite in the Navajo campaign.

201, p. 450. The Pettis narrative, much quoted in this chapter, has been published as No. 5 in a series *Personal Narratives of the Battles of the Rebellion* (Providence, R. I., 1878), and reprinted (1908) as No. 12 of the publications of the Historical Society of New Mexico. Captain Pettis died in 1909, at Providence, R. I., having for eight years been State Sealer of Weights, Measures, and Balances.

202, p. 457. The bugler is alleged to have been Set-t'ainte, who possessed a French brass horn which he was accustomed to blow as signal for meals and other assemblies!

203, p. 457. From *Calendar History of the Kiowa* (17th Report, Bureau of American Ethnology; Part 1).

CHAPTER XXXVI

204, p. 467. Early in the morning of November 29, 1865, 750 Colorado Volunteers under the fighting parson, Colonel John M. Chivington, attacked an Indian village of 128 lodges, mostly Cheyenne, on Sand Creek in southeastern Colorado. The Indians were decimated, despite their display of the American flag and the white flag preceding the attack. This affair, called the "Sand Creek massacre," and the "Battle of Sand Creek" (the title depending upon the sympathy of the user), brought on Congressional investigation, and long, bitter discussion. Colorado people, whose kith and kin and property had been so viciously maltreated by treacherous Cheyenne and Arapaho, generally stood by Chivington. Had not women and children been killed, in the heat of the conflict, by the soldiery, he would have been far less criticized.

205, p. 471. *Two Thousand Miles on Horseback*, by Colonel James F. Meline.

206, p. 472. The testimony taken by this joint committee was published as appendix to the report, January 26, 1867. This appendix, of some 430 pages following the ten pages of report, and referred to as *Condition of the Indian Tribes*, has been largely drawn upon by me, and forms one of the best compilations illustrative of Civil War days in the Southwest beyond the frontier. All departmental orders issued by General Carleton, regarding Indian operations, are included in it. There likewise is a mass of testimony upon the tribes of Northwest, Southwest, and Coast.

207, p. 474. So asserts Colonel James H. Ford, in command at Fort Larned. The joint committee had power of staying military operations; and exercised this power in order to have the Comanche campaign countermanded.

208, p. 474. *Two Thousand Miles on Horseback*.

209, p. 476. If Carson signed other treaties, at this time, I have missed his name. Besides these Arkansas River treaties, a successful treaty with the Sioux also is accredited to him, by his biographer Peters and others. But that he was emissary to the Sioux does not appear in the records of the Indian department, or of the War department, within my knowledge.

210, p. 479. A courtly, intelligent German gentleman, his time in New Mexico dating back to 1857, Mr. Meyer in 1912 was still living at Costilla, New Mexican village south of the old post, and just below the Colorado line. His memories of Kit Carson and of events at the post during Carson's command were very distinct.

211, p. 482. From *Across America*, by James F. Rusling, Late Brevet Brigadier-General, U. S. V. (New York, 1874). By letter, date of June, 1884, published in the Ellis *Life of Kit Carson* (1889), General Rusling gives a few other details, from memory. He says that Carson's hair "was already well-silvered." He had "a well-knit frame and full, deep chest," a noticeably broad and open brow, a quick blue eye, usually kindly, but one "that could blaze with anger when aroused"; and a "full, square jaw and chin, that evidently could shut as tight as Sherman's or Grant's when necessary." There was about him "nothing * * * of the border ruffian or the cowboy." "Like everybody else on the border, he smoked freely, and at one time drank considerably; but he had quit drinking years before, and said he owed his excellent health and pre-eminence, if he had any, to his habits of almost total abstinence. In conversation he was slow and hesitating at first, approaching almost to bashfulness, often seemingly at a loss for words; but, as he warmed up, this disappeared, and you soon found him talking glibly, and with his hands and fingers as well — rapidly gesticulating — Indian fashion. He was very conscientious, and in all our talks would frequently say: 'Now, stop, gentlemen! Is this *right?*' '*Ought* we to do this?' '*Can* we do that?' 'Is this like human nature?,' or words to this effect, as if it was the habit of his mind to test everything by the moral law. I think that was the predominating feature of his character — his perfect honesty and truthfulness — quite as much as his matchless coolness and courage." No reference is made, by General Rusling or other printed authorities, to Carson's spectacles, but he had now been wearing, for several years, bowed glasses for near work.

212, p. 483. Sherman letter, date of June, 1884, in the Ellis *Life of Kit Carson* (1889).

213, p. 484. Bancroft's *History of Nevada, Colorado and Wyoming;* footnote to page 471. Chief Ouray performed many other services to the white settlers of Colorado. In his latter years he owned a ranch and lived in a good house, upon it, amidst his herds and crops and his Mexican employes. He died in 1880. In 1911 his widow Chipeta was still active.

CHAPTER XXXVII

214, p. 485. Thus Mrs. Scheurich stated to me. However, by letter, dated October 10, 1867, at Fort Garland, would it seem that the resignation had not yet been acted upon. Some time would be required; and I am inclined to the belief that Carson was induced to remain at his post until the final mustering out of the Volunteers, that fall. That he was proffered a commission in the regular Army, should he decide to stay in the service, is denied by friends of his at the time. His lack of education made such a commission impossible.

215, p. 487. In 1913 Mr. Hough was still a prominent citizen of Lake City, Colorado. This quotation is from a letter to me.

216, p. 487. Tilton letter in the Abbott *Kit Carson*, edition of 1874.

217, p. 490. The details and anecdotes of this Washington trip, spring of 1868, were given to me by Mr. Bennet, who as Judge H. P. Bennet was numbered as a much-respected citizen of Denver. In 1912 he was, I believe, the only member of the party alive.

218, p. 492. This stop-over in Denver by Carson was recalled for me by Mrs. D. C. Oakes, of Denver, whose husband was a member of the treaty-making company.

CHAPTER XXXVIII

219, p. 493. Letter from Dr. Tilton, January 7, 1874, in the Abbott *Kit Carson* (1874).

220, p. 494. Mrs. Teresina Bent Scheurich has frequently been quoted in these pages. She was almost constantly in the Carson household, until the removal to Boggsville. It is evident that she and her mother arrived at Boggsville, in response to the General's summons, almost upon the very day when he had been taken to Fort Lyon. That is, if Dr. Tilton's date of May 14 is accurate. In the messenger " Betts " may be the settler " Ritz," of Boggsville, or he may have been the " citizen Betts " who in 1863 was wounded, along with Major Pfeiffer, at the hot springs near Fort McRae on the lower Rio Grande.

221, p. 495. Tilton letter in Abbott's *Kit Carson*.

222, p. 496. The description of the post, and roll of officers, has been supplied me by Lieutenant-Colonel (retired) John W. Hannay, who in 1867-1868 was second lieutenant there — having joined, in 1867, with his bride, from the East. When Carson's death occurred, Lieutenant Hannay was absent from the post, on detail as paymaster's escort to Fort Union. As lieutenant-colonel, retired for disability, he recalled with much distinctness the Carson associations at the fort: advice given upon scouting topics, and the statement that of all the western wild beasts, the mountain lion was most to be feared.

223, p. 496. Tilton letter in *Abbott*.

224, p. 497. These details were told to me by Mr. (Aloys)

Scheurich himself, in a visit with him at his Taos home, in the summer of 1907. Mr. Scheurich was an active, erect man of fine Western type, and one of the very last of the oldtime freighters over the Santa Fe Trail. He died in the summer of 1908.

225, p. 497. Tilton letter in *Abbott*.

226, p. 498. Letter from Mr. Cahill, June of 1911. Mr. Cahill, who proudly bears the title " Sergeant," in memory of army days on the plains, was then coroner of Bent County, Colorado.

227, p. 500. Thus not only is early indicated the claim of Colorado, rivaling that of New Mexico, to Kit Carson, but also the trend of politics. The *Rocky Mountain News* (Denver) of June, 1868, objects to these resolutions. It asks the Pueblo Club to explain by what token they make of Kit Carson a Democrat and "dwarf to party politics a western hunter, Indian fighter, and pioneer, who belongs to the whole country." "Did he ever take part in party politics? ever attend a party club meeting? ever consent that his name should be used in that connection? If he was a democrat, was it not of the old Hickory stamp — a race of democrats now all but extinct?" In truth, there is no record of Kit Carson's political inclinations. He was for the Union, and he probably voted, if he voted, as straight as he fought. In religion he was a Roman Catholic — but more by affiliation than by protestation. As far as I have been able to ascertain, he made no submission to any especial creed, either while living or while dying. He of course had been married by the Catholic priest at Taos.

228, p. 502. Sherman letter in the Ellis *Life of Kit Carson*.

229, p. 502. William Carson eventually applied, from Boggs' ranch, for agency of the Ute Indians, but was too late. He settled at Fort Garland, and married a daughter of Thomas Tobin, mountain man and associate of Carson's at Taos and elsewhere. In 1889 William died from a revolver shot, accidentally self-inflicted, while he was unharnessing his team at the town. His family live at Alamosa (Colorado) about thirty-five miles west from Garland. Of the other children three, Teresina (Mrs. D. Allen), Kit, Jr., and Charles, were at last accounts (1912), living and residents of Colorado. There are several grandchildren, so that the Kit Carson blood is not extinct.

INDEX

Eve